THE
REINTERPRETATION
OF AMERICAN
ECONOMIC
HISTORY

THE REINTERPRETATION OF AMERICAN ECONOMIC HISTORY

EDITED BY

Robert William Fogel
University of Chicago
and University of Rochester

AND

Stanley L. Engerman
University of Rochester

HARPER & ROW, PUBLISHERS
New York, Evanston, San Francisco, London

CONTENTS

VIII. IMMIGRATION, URBANIZATION, AND THE WESTWARD MOVEMENT

IX. THE EFFECTS OF MONETARY AND FISCAL POLICY

ENLARGING THE HISTORIAN'S VOCABULARY

Daniel J. Boorstin

This volume offers historians a solid representative sample of recent scholarly efforts to use quantitative techniques to enlarge our understanding of the American past. The volume is especially needed because many of the articles originally appeared in journals which American historians do not regularly consult. And it brings together work on a wide range of topics so that the reader can judge for himself what he can learn from these ways of exploring history. Of course, a growing number of American historians are becoming literate in economics, mathematics, computer technology, and quantitative techniques. But the conventional attitudes of many of the most respected and productive members of the profession have been shaped by their casual encounter with the offprint of an article on one particular topic, or by theoretical and largely *a priori* debate over whether the people who write these articles are *really* writing history.

Within the historical profession there has been a great deal of resistance to a sympathetic incorporation of articles of the kind found in this volume into the literature of American history. The usual question is whether this kind of study conforms to the traditional canons of the historical profession. The objections, explicit or implied, have been fourfold: (1) The vocabulary is difficult, unfamiliar, or unintelligible to most historians, (2) many of the questions asked do not fit into the familiar categories of historical enquiry, (3) many of the answers given to familiar questions are not conclusive, and (4) some of the conclusions suggested are shocking, and might shatter some of the most respectable generalizations of past historians. All these objections seem to me beside the point. For if the historian is not merely the custodian of traditional techniques and accumulated learning but an adventuring searcher after the facts of life, then these objections are not "indictments" at all. Rather, they explain why the historian should cheer on all those who would help him explore the past—and especially those who offer unfamiliar techniques.

If quantitative techniques are promising but their vocabulary is unfamiliar, then it is the duty of the historian to learn that vocabulary. If the questions these scholars pose to historians are unfamiliar, then (if the questions are fruitful) the definitions of history must be revised to include them. If the answers given by these scholars are not conclusive, then they are only doing no worse than other historians. And if the conclusions may shatter some basic clichés, this is only another way of saying that we cannot now do without the quantitative techniques—along with others still undiscovered.

The historian, a student of change, should of all scholars be the most alert and receptive to new ways of exploring and interpreting the past. If man's experience and institutions are in flux, how can the historian pretend to stand still? It is hard to imagine that Gibbon or Ranke or Parkman or Henry Adams would not have welcomed, for their subjects, the sort of imaginative, exploratory scholarship offered in this volume.

In this century, and especially in recent decades, the study of history in the United States has been professionalized on a large scale and with elaborate organizational apparatus. The meetings of professional organizations have provided a forum for discussing scholarly topics, they have become a marketplace for jobs, and at least until the late 1960s they were doing much to develop a professional morale. The organizations have provided a historian's lobby not inferior to the lobby of many other professions. And, of course, they have marshalled the scholarship of the whole profession to support vast editing enterprises (such as the projected 50-odd volume *Papers of Thomas Jefferson*, the projected 40-odd volume *Papers of James Madison*, and many others), and have helped set standards for the collecting, preserving, and cataloguing of archival material.

But this professionalization has not been without its price. Historians seeking the approval of their professional colleagues have naturally encouraged one another to be preoccupied with a small number of familiar questions. And, for the most part, these have been examined with familiar tools. The rise of the profession has produced a small list of "classic controversies." These controversies—the subjects most debated in the annual national and regional meetings—have included the place of economic motivation in the framing of the federal constitution, the nature of the frontier and the westward movement, the motivations and social structure of the "Age of Jackson" and the "Age of Reform," and a few others. The learned meetings have been spiced from time to time with sessions on subjects of special contemporary interest, such as the New Deal, the causes and consequences of World War II, the place of violence, and the role of the Negro in American life. The profession has sharpened the focus of American historians, but it has also tended to narrow it.

The consolidation of professional morale has tended also to consolidate the historians' resistance to efforts to broaden their subject matter and to redefine their techniques. About twenty years ago, a scholar offering a paper at a learned society of historians could be sure of raising a chuckle with a snide reference to "sociology." More recently similar expressions of provincial self-congratulation have been stirred by reference to quantitative techniques. Isolationist tenden-cies have been accentuated because the new tools of quantitative enquiry seem complicated and require a special knowledge which venerable and respected productive historians have never acquired. This has produced in the profession a conservative isolationism.

The recent strenuous attempts to politicize the study of history and the historical profession, to make it the tool of current political, reformist, or revolutionary movements, have had very much the same effect. For if one studies the past only to find support for contemporary polemics, he will be understandably wary of new techniques, especially if they require laborious study and if their conclusions are unpredictable. I have heard opposition expressed to the pursuit of quantitative techniques because mathematics "turns off" the young people, who cannot be bothered with so exacting a vocabulary. This has, then, tended to produce a radical isolationism. And this isolationism of the radicals is no more sympathetic than that of the venerables to acquiring difficult new skills or risking the failure of "history" to support the writer's preconceived purpose.

None of these professionally isolationist objections is a solid reason for not welcoming into the fellowship of historians the scholars whose work is illustrated in this volume. While practitioners of quantitative techniques now are warned off by signs which read "No Trespassing," we should take these signs down and lay out the Welcome mat. For the study and writing of history are an experimental enterprise.

Still, some of those who have expressed misgivings about the application of quantitative techniques to the study of the past do have reasons which are better founded. These historians object that the frame of mind revealed by the works of quantitative history is somehow anti-humanistic. They ask whether quantitative techniques do not tend to narrow the area of historical enquiry and thus to stultify efforts to grasp the whole past of man. This is a reasonable, even an important, question. If it is well-founded, we should really be alarmed at the rise of quantitative techniques, and should warn our students and colleagues against them. Toward the answering of this important question, the present volume is relevant and helpful. And I would like to try to explain how.

The argument that the use of quantitative methods in history is anti-humanistic and stultifying is generally based on two assumptions. First, that the practitioners of the method inevitably give undue importance to those aspects of the past which can be measured. And, second, that the practitioners will neglect or overlook those aspects of the past which cannot be measured. These assumptions express the suspicion that scholars using quantitative methods will be narrowly mono-causational, restricting their historical vision to only one kind of factor.

Any technique, of course, is capable of misuse. Every scholar has his own bent, and while some prefer the language of mathematics or of images others prefer the language of literature. There are narrow-minded scholars among "cliometricians" just as there are among those historians who travel boastfully under the banner of belles lettres. But a fair-minded perusal of this volume will show that the best among the scholars who use quantitative methods can broaden our historical vision and loosen up our imagination. Whatever else they are, they are not mono-causational. In fact what often tends to make their statements hard to grasp is their ruthless effort to include in their calculations every conceivable fact or force—and even to offer symbols for those items that they may have left out. Whatever else their limitations, they are neither narrow-minded nor simpleminded. There is hardly a chapter in this book that will not awaken the historian to new, or incalculable, elements in the story.

It may surprise the reader who has not till now been familiar with the work of these scholars that one of their recurrent themes is a caution against the historian's traditional temptation to give cataclysmic or monistic significance to certain simple, measurable aspects of the historical story. For example, they warn us against the easy temptation to date the onset of rapid growth in particular industries from the first appearance of the major inventions. The increase in the productivity of ocean shipping between 1600 and 1850, Douglass C. North warns us (essay 12), cannot be adequately accounted for by specific technological innovations. Instead, he suggests, most of this increase must be explained by the decline of piracy and by the improvement in economic organization. In other words, changes which the textbooks are inclined to explain by a simplistic emphasis on technology must be understood in the full context of institutions. North's quest for measurement leads him to remind us of the dominant significance of forces which elude measurement.

Similarly, the chapters on the diffusion of new technologies (Part IV) remind us of the oversimplifying danger of mistaking invention for innovation. These studies of the rate of diffusion of hybrid corn, of the mechanical reaper, of the by-product coke oven, and of the steam engine—all bolstered by statistical evidence of the growth-rate in the affected industries—will give the historian pause. Essays 15, 16, and 17 will send the historian searching for the unique features in each of these inventions and will make him see in a new light the multiplex character of innovation, as well as its dependence on elusive institutional forces.

Many of these chapters then are really essays on the hitherto unexplored complexity of specific historical changes. They point in many directions toward the importance of non-economic, non-measurable forces.

Other chapters give a new meaning and suggest new nuances in the intellectual historian's familiar abstractions. "Social Justice," "Equality," and "Education"— some of the largest and vaguest abstractions with which the historian must deal—are here given both a wider and a more specific context than we usually find them in. What was the significance of the fact that unions and farmers' organizations understandably emphasized the division of the national product rather than its size? What conclusions must historians draw from the special difficulties (explored in Part II) in reconstructing the distribution of income and of wealth? Higher rates of growth in the national per capita product, as Eugene Smolensky points out, "will lead to a more rapid rise in the definition of poverty, but only when that definition rises rapidly can poverty be reduced." By his effort to trace the variability of the definition of poverty, and by relating these to the available statistics, Smolensky helps us see dimensions in the concept of Equality which may have eluded the intellectual historian.

By taking the tantalizing abstraction "Education" and treating it as a mode of human-capital formation, Theodore W. Schultz enlarges the vision of the social and intellectual historian (essay 19). He points to new connections between the ideal of a universally educated citizenry and ways of explaining increases in national income. In this way he enriches the history of American education.

This volume, then, opens out many paths from the delusively simple specific historical event (e.g., the date of an invention) to the whole of American life and also traces paths from large elusive abstractions (e.g., equality) into the dense thicket of facts. To historians who enjoy the subtlety and manifoldness of their subject as much as its concreteness, this volume will bring solace. Scrupulous historians will be charmed by the disarming reticence of these scholars, so earnest that they should not seem to prove too much. If some historians feel slightly discomfited by these unfamiliar explorations with unfamiliar tools, it is not because these chapters aim to prove a point. Rather because they offer evidence that many historical questions for which historians have glib answers are far more complex than they had imagined—and may even be unanswerable. This volume is not a special plea for one approach to history as against others. Rather it opens windows into dangerous territory, which, these scholars now show us, has been only half-explored, but which for that very reason is all the more inviting.

PREFACE

This book is designed to serve three functions:

First, to help teachers of undergraduate courses in American history introduce students to the quantitative revolution in historiography and the far-reaching substantive revisions produced by the new methodology. Not only are the scope and consequences of this revolution well illustrated in the field of economic history, but the new findings of econometric historians have important implications for the interpretation of political, social, and intellectual history.

Second, to help teachers of undergraduate economics courses demonstrate the relevancy of the principles of economics to the basic issues of American life. Tying the exposition of elementary models to major events in American history simultaneously stimulates the students' interest in economic principles and deepens their understanding of these principles.

Third, to provide teachers of economic history with a vehicle which permits the approaches and findings of the new economic history to be made a central feature of their courses.

Nine of the thirty-six essays presented below were commissioned especially for this volume.* The remainder were selected from previously published articles and books. Previously published essays were revised in varying degrees by the authors, or by the editors with the permission and cooperation of the authors, to make them more suitable for the objectives of the volume.

---

* These are essays 2, 10, 12, 13, 18, 22, 24, 27, and 34.

The essays included in the volume were chosen either because they represented important new departures in the interpretation of American history or because they show the power of simple economic theory and mathematics in illuminating the problems of American life. Of course, many of the essays satisfied both criteria.

It should be stressed that the economic theory employed in nearly all of the essays is that covered in undergraduate courses. Indeed, most of the theory is usually presented in the first-year courses of elementary principles based on such texts as those by Paul Samuelson, Leland Bach, Robert McConnell, or Richard Lipsey and Peter Steiner. This book shows that courses in economic principles are not merely the first step in learning the more complex mathematical models of economics, but that the elementary principles taught in such courses are of direct relevance to the understanding of a remarkably wide range of issues.

The mathematical techniques used in this book are also quite simple. In 80 per cent of the essays the mathematics is merely arithmetic or high-school algebra. None of the essays uses mathematics beyond the level of basic calculus. With respect to quantification, the central message of this volume is that the artful use of very simple mathematics is a powerful instrument in explaining the course of history.

A few of the essays may appear to involve more complex economic theory or mathematics than we have suggested. This is because of the elliptical writing style employed by authors who were originally addressing themselves to audiences familiar with the models of economics. In these cases the editors have provided extensive introductions which reconstruct the argument step by step from the beginning.

A book aimed at three different fields will not be used in the same way in each of them. While this volume may be the main text in courses on American economic history, for general history survey courses and for courses devoted to the principles of economics or intermediate economic theory the volume would be more appropriate as supplementary reading. Guides to the use of the book as a supplementary reader are presented below.

The title of this book may appear to be misleading. Titles such as " The Reinterpretation of American Economic History " are frequently used to suggest a central theme which can encompass the whole course of American development. In such instances, the promise is not of new evidence but of a new synthesis of previously accepted evidence.

The objective of the new economic history is both more modest and more ambitious. It is the reconstruction of American economic history on a sound quantitative basis. Fulfillment of this objective requires the systematic reexamination of all of the basic propositions that represent the corpus of the discipline. That reexamination has now been underway for more than a decade and will continue well into the future. As this volume indicates, many of the old propositions have been drastically revised. The "reinterpretation" is not merely a new view of an old house, and it is not just the adding of a new wing or the relocation of some of the walls. Even the bricks are different.

Robert William Fogel
Stanley L. Engerman

Chicago and Rochester
January, 1971

GUIDE TO USE OF THE VOLUME AS A SUPPLEMENTARY READER IN PRINCIPLES AND UNDERGRADUATE THEORY COURSES

The essays in this volume supplement principles and undergraduate theory texts in three ways. Some essays provide background material. Discussions of banks and money markets, for example, will be made more meaningful by Davis' description (Essay 22) of the way in which the fragmented, regional money markets of the 1830s were transformed into a national market over the succeeding century.

Some essays show how rigorously defined economic concepts are actually applied. Those by Kuznets, Gallman and Howle, and Easterlin (Essays 2, 3, and 4) not only describe the problems encountered in computing national income statistics but also show how these statistics may be used to evaluate the performance of an economy over time or to compare the relative achievements of different sectors of the economy.

Many of the essays illustrate the usefulness of the simple models of micro and macro theory in analyzing the pressing issues of the past and the present. Thus the chapter dealing with Andrew Jackson's war against the Second Bank of the United States (Essay 33) shows how the equation for the quantity of money can be used to trace the effect of monetary policy on the cycle of boom and bust. The chapters on the economics of slavery (Essays 24, 25, and 26) demonstrate how capital and rent theory illuminate the problem of economic exploitation. Supply and demand analysis is made relevant in chapters which show how these tools help to explain why cotton textiles emerged as the first large-scale manufacturing industry in the United States (Essay 10) and to measure the effect of the tariff on the growth of the iron industry (Essay 11). The chapter which evaluates the effectiveness of the fiscal policies of the New Deal (Essay 36) illustrates the relevance of the simple Keynesian model of income determination.

The following listing relates the essays in the volume to the standard topics of principles and undergraduate theory courses.

THEORY OF SUPPLY AND DEMAND

GUIDE TO USE OF THE VOLUME AS A SUPPLEMENTARY READER IN HISTORY COURSES

Roughly half the essays in this volume are iconoclastic in the sense that they are designed to replace some long-standing view of American economic development by its antithesis. Among the most controversial of the revisionist positions argued in this book are the following:

It was developments in Mexico and Great Britain, rather than Andrew Jackson's war with the Second Bank of the United States, which explain the boom and bust of the 1830's and the early 1840's. (Essay 33)

Slavery did not cause the economy of the antebellum South to stagnate. Quite the contrary. Between 1840 and 1860 per capita income in the South grew more rapidly than in the rest of the nation. (Essay 24)

There is no evidence to support the contention that the Civil War accelerated the rate of industrialization or of economic growth. (Essay 27)

Railroads had a relatively small impact on the settlement of the West. At least 95 per cent of the land in agriculture in 1890 would have been in production even if there had been no railroads. (Essay 14)

Fiscal policy under the New Deal was neither a success nor a failure. Despite appearances to the contrary, it was never really tried. (Essay 36)

The contribution of the remaining essays rests either in the presentation of new evidence on long-debated issues or in the exploration of some previously neglected aspect of American economic development. As Daniel Boorstin points out in his foreword, the new explorations frequently yield novel concepts which are of value not only to economic historians but to social, political, and intellectual historians. Among these are the distinction between invention and innovation, the notion of investment in human capital formation, the proposition that poverty is a relative concept, and the idea of cost-benefit analysis.

Much of the new evidence presented below is the consequence of the application of mathematical methods. These methods range from simple arithmetic operations to relatively sophisticated applications of regression analysis. Many of the writers devote considerable attention to the problems and pitfalls which must be overcome in the attempt to apply quantitative methods to history. The limitations of the historical conclusions that can be drawn from quantitative analysis are discussed at length.

To assist teachers in keying the volume to their lectures, we have classified the essays into seven broad time periods. Some essays deal with issues which cover more than one of these spans. In such instances the instructor may wish to confine the assignment of an essay to only one of these periods; repeat the assignment of the entire essay in one or more periods; or break the essay into parts, each one of which may be assigned to a given period. For example, Essay 7 by Stanley Lebergott describes the extent and character of unemployment in every recession from 1800 to 1960. If an instructor's most extensive discussion of the business cycle occurs in his lectures on the Hoover and Roosevelt administrations, he might assign Lebergott's essay at that point, using it as background material to put the great depression into a long-term perspective. Alternatively the essay may conveniently be broken into a series of shorter assignments: 1800 to 1865, 1865–1920, 1920–1960; or "unemployment before the rise of the factory, 1800 to 1820," "unemployment during the Jacksonian era," "unemployment in the period of sectional conflict," "unemployment during an era of falling prices, 1865 to 1896," etc.

TO 1865

THE
REINTERPRETATION
OF AMERICAN
ECONOMIC
HISTORY

I THE NEW ECONOMIC HISTORY : ITS FINDINGS AND METHODS

Robert William Fogel

The "new economic history," sometimes called econometric history or cliometrics, is not often practiced in Europe. However, it is fair to say that efforts to apply statistical and mathematical models currently occupy the center of the stage in American economic history. The influence of this type of research in the United States is illustrated by the proceedings of the twenty-fifth annual meeting of the Economic History Association, published in the December, 1965, number of *The Journal of Economic History*. Of the ten

Reprinted with permission from *The Economic History Review, 19* (December, 1966), 642–656. This paper was originally commissioned by The Economic History Society and was presented to their annual meeting on April 1, 1966. It was also presented to the Institut de Science Economique Appliquée on March 26, 1966.

major papers included in the issue, three practice the new economic history and a fourth is devoted to a discussion of it. Moreover, if the dissertations presented to the annual meeting are an index of the intellectual direction of the youngest generation of economic historians, then it is worth noting that six of these seven studies are cast in the new mode and the seventh is a computer analysis (of a large sample of commercial papers) aimed at revealing the motivation for the colonization of the Americas.

Econometric history gained its present eminence with extraordinary rapidity. Perhaps the first definitely formulated expression of the new approach is contained in a pair of essays written by Alfred H. Conrad and John R. Meyer in 1957, less than a decade ago [2, 23]. It was not until three years later that work in cliometrics had gone far enough to warrant a conference devoted to it. In December of 1960 Purdue University sponsored a Seminar on Quantitative Methods in Economic History. Although the organizers of the meeting had difficulty in finding a score of scholars interested enough to attend, the Purdue Seminar did much to stimulate further research in the application of the mathematical and statistical models of economics to the study of history. So successful was the first meeting that the Purdue Seminar has become an annual event. The sixth meeting was held last January. This time the problem was not where to find attendees, but how to choose thirty participants from a list, several times that number, of scholars who wanted to attend.

Even more impressive is the fact that many of the principal American centers of postgraduate work in economic history are now devoted to, or encourage, training and research in econometric history. Among the most well known of these centers are Alexander Gerschenkron's Economic History Workshop at Harvard University, Douglass North's Economic History Seminar at the University of Washington, the graduate program in economic history of Purdue University, the graduate program in economic history of the University of Wisconsin, the interdisciplinary program for economic history at the University of Pennsylvania, the joint Berkeley-Stanford Economic History Colloquium, William Parker's seminar in economic history at Yale, and the Workshop in Economic History at the University of Chicago.

I do not want to give the impression that the new economic history is universally acclaimed in the United States. The growing debate on the methodological implications of the new work reflects the existence of a significant division of opinion. Fritz Redlich is one of the most severe critics. He argues that much of econometric history is based on hypothetical models which can never be verified, and that certain of its methods are "anti-empiricistic," and "anti-positivistic." Hence, Professor Redlich concludes that the new work often produces not history but "quasi-history" [31]. Interestingly enough, those features of which Professor Redlich is most critical are, according to George G. S. Murphy, the main virtue of the new approach. Professor Murphy contends that by rigorously developing hypothetico-deductive models cliometricians are providing economic history with "a really defensible set of techniques" and "coming close to what a modern empiricist might demand of it" [24].[1]

To say that opinions are divided does not imply that the American wing of our discipline is torn by internecine warfare. While the debate is vigorous, it is also amicable. Moreover, even its severest critics believe that the new economic history has made a positive and lasting contribution to historical research. Despite his strong reservations, Fritz Redlich writes that the new approaches "are here to stay," and predicts an increasing interdependence between the new and the old work [31, pp. 491–495].

THE FINDINGS

The considerable impact of the new economic history on research in the United States is due primarily to the novelty of its substantive findings. If cliometrics merely reproduced the conclusions of previous scholarship, its methods would be of trivial consequence. However, the studies of the new economic historians have substantially altered some of the most well-established propositions of traditional historiography. They have also yielded knowledge that was hitherto considered unobtainable concerning institutions and processes central to the explanation of

---

[1] Other contributions to the discussion on the methods of the new economic history include [3, chaps. 1, 2; 5; 10; 25; 14; 15; 1, pp. 3–8, 13–26; 13, pp. 237–249; 26; 18; 28].

American economic development. I cannot within the compass of this paper do justice to the many studies produced by the new economic historians during the past decade. But I will attempt to briefly summarize some typical examples of their work.[2]

The Economics of Southern Slavery

One of the first, and one of the most influential reinterpretations of the new economic history concerns the effect of slavery on the course of economic development in the South prior to the Civil War. Until recently most history books portrayed the ante-bellum South as an economically backward agricultural region that stagnated under the burden of the plantation system. By the eve of the war, it was held, slavery had become unprofitable and hence the system was moribund. Slavery was kept temporarily in existence by the transitory resolve of a class long accustomed to its peculiar social institutions [39, 8].

This view was sharply challenged in a paper by Alfred H. Conrad and John R. Meyer [2]. They rejected as inadequate the evidence usually presented to support the proposition that the profits of slaveowners were declining. The contention that slavery was unprofitable rested largely on the fact that the prices of slaves had risen more rapidly than the prices of the commodities that slaves produced. Conrad and Meyer pointed out that this divergency did not necessarily imply declining profits, for the productivity of slaves might have risen by an amount sufficient to maintain the original level of profits. They further argued that from an economic point of view slaves were a capital good and hence that one could compute the rate of return on an investment in them by solving the standard equation for the capitalization of an income stream; that is, by finding the rate of return which equated the price of slaves to the discounted value of the stream of annual earnings derived from their employment.

Conrad and Meyer divided the slave economy into two sectors. The first was described by a production function that related the male slaves to the output of such staples as cotton, sugar, and corn. The second

was a capital-goods sector in which female slaves were used to produce new slaves. Conrad and Meyer then went on to estimate separate rates of return on slaves of each sex. The computation of the return on male slaves was the simpler case. They first derived the average capital cost per slave including not only the price of a slave, but also the average value of the land, animals, and equipment used by a slave. Estimates of gross annual earnings were then built up from data on the price of cotton and the physical productivity of slaves. The net figure was obtained by subtracting the maintenance and supervisory costs for slaves from gross earnings. The average length of the stream of net earnings was determined from mortality tables. With these estimates Conrad and Meyer computed rates of return on male slaves and found that for the majority of ante-bellum plantations the return varied between 5 and 8 per cent, depending on the physical yield per hand and the prevailing farm price of cotton. On the farms in poor upland pine country or in the exhausted lands of the Eastern seaboard the range of rates was merely 2 to 5 per cent. However, in the "best lands of the new Southwest, the Mississippi alluvium and the better South Carolina and Alabama plantations" rates ran as high as 10 to 13 per cent.[3]

The computation of the rate of return on female slaves was somewhat more complicated. Conrad and Meyer had to take account not only of the productivity of a female in the field, but of such additional matters as the productivity of her offspring between their birth and the time of their sale; maternity, nursery, and rearing costs; and the average number of offspring. Noting that very few females produced less than five or more than ten children that survived to be sold, Conrad and Meyer computed lower and upper limits on the rate of return. These turned out to be

---

[2] For a representative selection of essays in the new economic history besides those included in this volume see [1]. For a more popular, more interpretative survey see [27].

[3] An alternate approach to the estimation of the return on male slaves is contained in [9]. As with other capital goods, there was a market for the rental of slaves. Evans argued that the average annual hire price represented a good estimate of the annual net earnings on the investment in a male slave. He reduced the annual hire price for slaves of a given age by the proportion of the cohort that died during the course of the year. In so doing, Evans avoided the assumption that all slaves lived the average length of life. The result of his computation was a return of over 10 per cent during most of the years from 1830 through 1860.

7.1 and 8.1 per cent respectively. Thus, planters in the exhausted lands of the upper South who earned only 4 to 5 per cent on male slaves still were able to achieve a return on their total operation equal to alternative opportunities. They did so by selling the off-spring of females to planters in the West, thus earning rates of 7 to 8 per cent on the other half of their slave force. Proof of such a trade was found not only in the descriptions of contemporaries, but also in the age struc-ture of the slave population. The selling states had a significantly larger proportion of per-sons under 15 and over 50 while the buying states predominated in slaves of the prime working ages.

Of the many studies in the economics of slavery stimulated by the pioneering work of Conrad and Meyer, the most important was the one by Yasukichi Yasuba [40].[4] Yasuba pointed out that in order to evaluate the viability of the slave system as a whole, rather than merely the viability of slavery in a given region or occupation, one had to equate the stream of net income from slaves not with their market price, but with their cost of production—that is, with the net cost of rearing slaves. A discrepancy between the price and the cost of producing capital goods in a given industry ordinarily will not last very long.[5] The existence of an unusually high profit—of economic rent—will induce new capital-producing firms to enter or old firms to expand production until the rent is eliminated, until the market price of the capital goods falls to its cost of production.

In the case of slaves, however, the demand curve for them shifted outward more quickly than the supply curve. The lag in supply was due partly to the ban against the importation of slaves after 1808 and partly to the fact that the domestic expansion of supply was limited by biological and cultural factors. As a consequence of these restrictions, the rent on slaves increased over time. Yasuba esti-mates that during the quinquennium of 1821–1825, the average capitalized rent amounted to $428 out of an average slave price of $736, the balance representing the net cost of rear-ing the slave to maturity. In other words, during 1821–1825 capitalized rent represented

58 per cent of the market price of slaves. By 1841–1845 the capitalized rent was 72 per cent of the price of slaves, and by 1851–1855 it was nearly 85 per cent.

By showing the existence of a large and rising capitalized rent in the price of slaves over the 40 years leading up to the Civil War, Yasuba effectively demonstrated the economic viability of the slave system. More-over, the fact that Conrad and Meyer com-puted a return based on the market price rather than on the cost of producing slaves means that they underestimated the return to slavery as a system. Indeed, their computa-tion showed only that slave prices adjusted so that investors who wanted to buy into the slave system could, on the average, expect to earn merely the market rate of return.

Although slavery was a viable economic system, it could nevertheless have thwarted economic growth in the South by reducing the saving rate or by stifling entrepreneurship. Historians have long held that because of slavery, planters acquired extravagant tastes, which led them to squander their income on high living. Slavery is also supposed to have bred an irrational attachment to agriculture. As a consequence, it is said, planters shunned opportunities for profit in manufacturing.

The alleged stagnation of the ante-bellum South has been thrown into doubt by recent findings. The work of Conrad, Meyer, Yasuba, and others strongly suggests that the Southern decision to slight manufacturing was not an absurd eccentricity. It now appears to have been a rational response to profits in planta-tion agriculture that were considerably above alternative opportunities. Moreover, estimates of regional income constructed by Richard Easterlin indicate that per capita income grew as rapidly in the ante-bellum South as in the rest of the nation, averaging about 1.5 per cent per annum [6, 8].

The retarded development of the South during the last third of the nineteenth century and the first half of the twentieth was prob-ably due not to stagnation during the slave era, but to the devastation caused by the Civil War. As Stanley Engerman points out, if ante-bellum growth rates had continued through the war decade, Southern per capita income would have been twice the level that actually prevailed in 1870. So disruptive was the war that it took the South some 30 years to regain the per capita income of 1860 and another 60 years to reach the same relative position in national per capita income that

---

[4] Richard Sutch independently arrived at a position similar to Yasuba's in [33]. See also the discussion by North in [27, chap. 7] and [8].

[5] The cost of production includes the normal rate of profit.

it enjoyed at the close of the ante-bellum era [7]. The case for the abolition of slavery thus appears to turn on issues of morality and equity rather than on the inability of a slave system to yield a high rate of economic growth.

Technology and Productivity

While the issue of slavery looms large in the interpretation of American economic history, it is of limited relevance outside of that context. Of wider interest to European scholars is the new work on technology and productivity. From the time of Arnold Toynbee through that of Paul Mantoux and down to the present day, economic historians have made technological change embodied in specific machines and processes the *sine qua non* of economic advance. As a result of their work every schoolboy has been taught that it was such inventions as the spinning jenny, the power loom, the reverberatory furnace, the rolling mill, the steam engine, and the railroad that brought about the industrial revolutions of England, France, Germany, and the United States. Yet despite a considerable literature which illuminates the history of machines and their employment, we still have much to learn about the precise effects of particular innovations on productivity and about the process by which a given innovation spreads throughout an industry.

It is to the solution of these and related questions that much of the research of the new economic historians has been directed. This work falls into four main categories. The first is the attempt to "explain" observed increases in productivity—that is, to distribute the responsibility for the increase in productivity among various factors. Typical of this approach is William Parker and Judith Klein's analysis of grain production [30]. He finds that between 1840 and 1910 labor productivity in wheat grew by more than threefold. Of this increase he attributes the lion's share, 60 per cent, to mechanization; 17 per cent to the change in the regional locus of production; 16 per cent to the interaction of mechanization and regional relocation; and the remaining 7 per cent to other factors. Improvements in machines had their greatest impact on harvesting and post-harvesting operations. Professor Parker estimates that the reaper and thresher alone accounted for 70 per cent of the gain from mechanization, or over 40 per cent of the increase in over-all productivity.

It would be wrong to infer from Parker's study that the new work gives warrant to the preoccupation with technological change embodied in equipment that characterizes so much of the past literature of economic history. Parker's study aims not at extolling machines, but at identifying all the important factors that explain productivity advance in agriculture. It so happens that for the given period and crop the development of two machines dominates the explanation. Other studies have produced quite different results. Thus, new equipment plays virtually no role in Douglass North's explanation of the 50 per cent fall in the cost of ocean transportation that he finds for the 250-year period between 1600 and the middle of the nineteenth century. Almost all of the decline is explained by two other factors: the elimination of piracy and the increase in the size of the market. The elimination of piracy substantially reduced manning requirements, since military personnel were no longer needed. The increase in the size of the market lowered shipping costs by encouraging the concentration of surpluses in central markets. This development considerably reduced the amount of time ships spent in port acquiring a cargo [29].

The second category consists of studies aimed at explaining the growth of particular industries. One of the examples of this type of work is Robert Brooke Zevin's analysis of the growth of the American cotton textile industry prior to 1860 [41]. As Zevin points out, the 17 years from 1816 through 1833 are the most interesting period in the early history of the industry. During this span the output of cotton cloth expanded from 18,000,000 to 231,000,000 yards, an increase of over 11 times. Abstracting from cyclical considerations, Zevin puts the average annual rate of growth in production at 15.4 per cent. He finds that one half of this expansion was due to an increase in demand stimulated mainly by the growth of the urban and Western populations. The other half was due to a downward shift in the supply curve. Zevin explains the change in supply by improvements in textile machinery, the fall in the price of raw cotton, and the growth of skilled technicians. However, the improvement of machinery was less important than is usually presumed. It accounted for only one third of the expansion of cloth production.

Zevin's study, taken in conjunction with others, points to the inadequacy of new machinery and other forms of equipment as the sole, or even the primary, explanation of growth in the main manufacturing industries of Europe and America during the last two centuries. The preoccupation with machines has led to an underestimation of the role of demand in the promotion of industrial growth. It has also resulted in the slighting of such determinants of supply as the quality of labor, the stock of skills, the efficiency of industrial organization, and economies of scale [27, pp. 6–10].

Analyses of the diffusion of technological innovations fall into the third category. The diffusion problem promises to be one of the most popular topics of the new economic history. Peter Temin's explanation of the spread of anthracite and coke blast furnaces has already become well known [34, chap. 3; 35]. A more recent contribution is a paper on reapers by Paul David [4]. Although the reaper was invented in the 1830s, its diffusion proceeded at a very slow pace for two decades. The "first major wave of popular acceptance" of the innovation "was concentrated in the mid-1850s." The literature is ambiguous regarding the cause of this upsurge. Various writers have stressed the rise in wheat prices and the scarcity of farm labor as factors. However, these accounts do not indicate the process by which the rise in wheat prices led to an increased demand for reapers.

David points out that if, on the industry level, the supply curve of labor is less elastic than the supply of reapers, a rise in the price of wheat will raise the price of farm labor relative to the price of reapers. He also notes that reapers had to be purchased rather than rented. Thus, even though the annual cost of a reaper to a farmer was independent of farm size, his average reaper cost per acre harvested fell as the number of acres in small grains increased, until the cutting capacity of a single machine was reached. By contrast, the cost per acre of reaping by the old method was constant because, to the farmer, the supply of labor was perfectly elastic and there were no economies of scale in the old method.

The foregoing considerations suggest the existence of a threshold function that relates the farm size at which it just paid to introduce the reaper, to the ratio between the price of a reaper and the wage of farm labor. David estimates the parameters of this function and finds that at the beginning of the fifties, the relationship of reaper and labor prices was such that it became profitable to introduce the reaper only on farms with 46 or more acres in small grains. At that time, however, the average number of acres in such grains per farm was about 25. By the mid-fifties the cost of reapers had fallen relative to the price of labor. The decline reduced the threshold size to just 35 acres. At the same time the average acreage in small grains rose to 30. Thus, within a period of about five years, the gap between the threshold farm size and the average actual farm size was reduced by over 75 per cent. It is the precipitous closing of this gap that explains the accelerated diffusion of reapers during the mid-fifties.

The final category of studies on technology and productivity consists of works which attempt to evaluate the net social benefit of particular innovations. My book, *Railroads and American Economic Growth*, belongs to this category [13]. Estimation of the net benefit of railroads involves a comparison between the actual level of national income and the level that would have prevailed in the absence of railroads. The amount of national income in the absence of railroads cannot be computed directly. It is necessary to construct a hypothetico-deductive model on the basis of which one can infer, from those conditions that were actually observed, a set of conditions that never occurred.

In my book I attempted to construct such a model for the year 1890. The conceptual foundation of the model is the "social saving" of railroads. The social saving in any given year is defined as the difference between the actual cost of shipping goods in that year and the alternative cost of shipping exactly the same goods between exactly the same points without railroads. This cost differential is in fact larger than the "true" social saving. Forcing the pattern of shipments in a nonrail situation to conform to the pattern that actually existed is equivalent to the imposition of a restraint on society's freedom to adjust to an alternative technological situation. If society had had to ship by water and wagon without the railroad it could have altered the geographical locus of production in a manner that would have economized on transport services. Further, the sets of primary and secondary markets through which commodities were distributed were surely influenced by conditions peculiar to rail transportation; in the absence of railroads some different cities would have entered these sets, and the relative importance of those remaining would have changed. Adjustments of this sort would have reduced the loss of national income occasioned by the absence of the railroad.

The computation of the social saving required both estimates of the direct payments that would have been made for boat and wagon transportation services and estimates of such indirect costs as cargo losses in transit, the expense resulting from the time lost when using a slow medium of transportation, and the expense of being unable to use waterways during the winter months. Regression analysis was used to derive the cost functions of boats. The water rates that would have obtained in the absence of railroads were computed from these functions. The economic losses caused by slow service and by the vagaries of the weather were quantified by estimating the cost of expanding inventories to a size that would have permitted businesses to maintain their normal temporal pattern of distribution. The expected cargo loss was derived from insurance rates.

Because of the large amounts of data that had to be processed, my study was restricted to the social saving attributable to the transportation of agricultural commodities. The amount of this saving was estimated under three different assumptions regarding the possibility of technological adaptation to the absence of railroads. The first was that society would have relied on only the canals and roads that actually existed in 1890. The second was that at least 5000 miles of feasible and, in the absence of railroads, highly profitable canals would have been built. The third was that common roads would have been improved. Under the first of these assumptions the agricultural social saving of railroads was $373,000,000 or 3.1 per cent of gross national product (GNP) in 1890. The extension of canals and improvements of roads would have reduced the social saving to 1.8 per cent of GNP. It is interesting to note that the two main benefits achieved by the railroad were the reduction in inventories and the reduction in wagon transportation. Together these accounted for about 80 per cent of the social saving.

Albert Fishlow's penetrating, many-sided study of railroads during the ante-bellum era contains an estimate of the social saving for 1859 [11, chap. 2]. His computation covers not merely agricultural commodities, but all other freight and all passenger traffic. Fishlow finds that the social saving of railroads was about $175,000,000 or 4 per cent of GNP. Of this total, agricultural commodities account for roughly one quarter, other freight for another third, and passenger service for the balance. In comparing Fishlow's result with mine, it is important to keep in mind that Fishlow's calculation is for the case in which there would have been no technological adaptation to the absence of railroads. Given that assumption, the correspondence between our findings is extremely close. A computation of the 1859 social saving for the case of limited technological adaptation to the absence of railroads is still to be performed.

I should like to conclude this section of my paper in the way that I began it—by stressing the inadequacy of my survey of the work of the new economic historians. Among the important contributions that I have slighted are studies by Robert Gallman on Southern agriculture, Jeffrey Williamson on the determinants of urbanization before the Civil War, Stanley Lebergott on the role of labor in nineteenth-century economic growth, John Bowman on the agricultural depression of the Gilded Age, and Lance Davis on the evolution of capital markets.

THE METHODS

The methodological hallmarks of the new economic history are its emphasis on measurement and its recognition of the intimate relationship between measurement and theory. Economic history has always had a quantitative orientation. But much of the past numerical work was limited to the location and simple classification of data contained in business and government records. With the exception of the excellent work on the construction of price indexes, relatively little was done to transform this information in ways that would shed light on "rigorously defined concepts of economic analysis" until the development of national income accounting techniques [21]. The pioneers of the massive statistical reconstructions embodied in national income accounts were not economic historians, but empirical economists, such as Simon Kuznets in the United States, J. R. N. Stone and Phyllis Deane in Great Britain, and Francois Perroux and Jean Marczewski in France. While economic historians made considerable use of national income measures, they did not immediately attempt to extend the process of statistical reconstruction to the vast array of issues in their domain. Most discussions of economic historians remained primarily qualitative, with numerical information used largely as illustration.

The new economic historians are trying to end this long existing void in measurement. They have set out to reconstruct American economic history on a sound quantitative basis. This objective is extremely ambitious and the obstacles to its fulfillment are numerous. The most frustrating problem is the paucity of data. Information bearing on many vital institutions and processes in the past was either never collected or has been lost. In still other cases the data are extant but are so numerous or held in such a form that their retrieval, without the aid of modern statistical methods, would be prohibitively expensive.

As a consequence statistics and mathematics are widely employed by the new economic historians. Regression analysis is perhaps the most frequently used tool. It is the principal device on which Albert Fishlow relied in his reconstruction of the investment of railroads during the ante-bellum era [*11*, chap. 3, app. B]. Jeffrey Williamson makes heavy use of it in his study of urbanization [*37*, *38*]. And Paul MacAvoy employs a lagged form of the regression model in order to determine the relationship between grain prices and transportation rates [*22*]. Examples of the usefulness of other mathematical methods include William Whitney's employment of input-output analysis to measure the effect of the tariffs on the rise of manufacturing, and James K. Kindahl's application of the hypergeometric distribution to estimate, from two incomplete lists, the total number of state banks that were in operation immediately after the close of the Civil War [*36*, *20*].

Some historians have held that there is no point in applying powerful statistical methods to economic history because the available data are too poor. In actual practice, the correlation often runs the other way. When the data are very good, simple statistical procedures will usually suffice. The poorer the data, the more powerful are the methods which have to be employed. Nevertheless, it is often true that the volume of data available is frequently below the minimum required for standard statistical procedures. In such instances the crucial determinant of success is the ability of the investigator to devise methods that are exceedingly efficient in the utilization of data—that is, to find a method that will permit one to achieve a solution with the limited data that are available.

The way in which economic theory can be employed to circumvent the data problem is illustrated by Paul David's study of mechanical reapers. Utilization of regression analysis to compute a threshold function for reapers would have required county data on the employment of reapers by farm size, on the delivered price of reapers, and on the average wage of labor. Unfortunately, such information was not available for counties. To surmount the problem, David turned to the theory of production. He first noted that a farmer would be indifferent to the choice between mechanized and hand reaping when the cost of cutting grain on a specified acreage was the same by both methods. He also noted the absence of economies and diseconomies of scale in the employment of hand labor. These specifications together with two linear approximations yielded a threshold function with only three parameters. The parameters were the rate of depreciation, the rate of interest, and the rate of substitution between reapers and man-days of labor. The data required to estimate these parameters were available [*4*, pp. 28–39].

The union between measurement and theory is most clearly evident when one attempts to establish the net effect of innovations, institutions, or processes on the course of economic development. The net effect of such things on development involves a comparison between what actually happened and what would have happened in the absence of the specified circumstance. However, since the counterfactual condition never occurred, it could not have been observed, and hence is not recorded in historical documents. In order to determine what would have happened in the absence of a given circumstance, the economic historian needs a set of general statements (that is, a set of theories or a model) that will enable him to deduce a counterfactual situation from institutions and relationships that actually existed.

This is precisely the problem encountered when one attempts to evaluate the frequent claim that railroads greatly extended the area of commercial agriculture in the United States. It is, of course, true that the area of commercial agriculture and the construction of railroads expanded more or less simultaneously. However, it does not follow that railroads were a necessary condition for the commercial exploitation of the new lands. To settle the issue one must find a method of determining how much of the land actually settled after the advent of railroads would have been settled in their absence.

Without railroads the high cost of wagon transportation would have limited commercial agricultural production to areas of land lying within some unknown distance of navigable waterways. It is possible to use the theory of rent to establish these boundaries of feasible commercial agriculture in a nonrail society. Rent is a measure of the amount by which the return to labor and capital on a given portion of land exceeds the return the same factors could earn if they were employed at the intensive or extensive margins. Therefore, any plot of land capable of commanding a rent will be kept in productive activity. It follows that, even in the face of increased transportation costs, a given area of farm land will remain in use as long as the increased costs incurred during a given time period do not exceed the original rental value of that land.

Given information on the quantity of goods shipped between farms and their markets, the distances from farms to rail and water shipping points, the distance from such shipping points to markets, and the wagon, rail, and water rates, it is possible to compute the additional transportation costs that would have been incurred if farmers attempted to duplicate their actual shipping pattern without railroads. In such a situation shipping costs would have risen not because boat rates exceeded rail rates, but because it usually required more wagon transportation to reach a boat than a rail shipping point. In other words farms immediately adjacent to navigable waterways would have been least affected by the absence of rail service. The further a farm was from a navigable waterway the greater the amount of wagon transportation it would have required. At some distance from waterways the additional wagon haul would have increased the cost of shipping from a farm by an amount exactly equal to the original rental value of the land. Such a farm would represent a point on the boundary of feasible commercial agriculture. Consequently the full boundary can be established by finding all those points from which the increased cost of shipping by alternative means the quantities that were actually carried by railroads is equal to the original rental value of the land.

This approach, it should be noted, leads to an overstatement of the land falling beyond the "true" feasible boundary. A computation based on the actual mix of products shipped does not allow for adjustments to a nonrail technology. In the absence of railroads the mix of agricultural products would have changed in response to the altered structure of transportation rates. Such a response would have lowered shipping costs and hence extended the boundary. The computation also ignores the consequence of a cessation in agricultural production in areas beyond the feasible region on the level of prices. Given the relative inelasticity of the demand for agricultural products, the prices of such commodities would have risen in the absence of railroads. The rise in prices would have led to a more intensive exploitation of agriculture within the feasible region, thus raising land values. The rise in land values would have increased the burden of additional transportation costs that could have been borne and shifted the boundary of feasible commercial agriculture further away from water shipping points.[6]

The method outlined above is the one I used to establish the boundary of feasible commercial agriculture for 1890. It turns out that given only the active waterways of that year, at least 76 per cent of the land actually employed in agriculture would have remained employed in the absence of railroads. Moreover, a 5000 mile extension of the canal system would have increased the land in commercial agriculture to 93 per cent of that actually cultivated. The theory of rent also enables one to infer which canals would have been socially profitable. It can be shown that a new canal would have been profitable if the land it brought into the feasible region had an 1890 value which exceeded the canal's construction cost by the present value of any additional wagon transportation that would have been incurred by the absence of railroads [13, pp. 79–84, 92–107].

According to Fritz Redlich, these attempts to answer counterfactual questions by the use of hypothetico-deductive models are the most novel and the most dubious methodological aspect of the new economic history. Professor Redlich argues that counterfactual propositions are fundamentally alien to economic history. He also believes that they are untestable and hence calls essays involving such propositions "quasi-history" [31, pp. 486–487].

----

[6] For a more detailed discussion of the theoretical issues see [13, chap. 3].

However, if we are to exclude from history those studies which are based on counterfactual propositions, we will have to expurgate not only the new work, but much of the old work as well. The difference between the old and new economic history is not the frequency with which one encounters counterfactual propositions, but the extent to which such propositions are made explicit. The old economic history abounds in disguised counterfactual assertions. They are present in discussions which either affirm or deny that tariffs accelerated the growth of manufacturing; in essays which argue that slavery retarded the development of the South; in debates over whether the Homestead Act made the distribution of land more equitable; in the contention that railroads expanded interregional trade; and in virtually every other discussion which makes a legal, social, technological, administrative, or political innovation the cause of a change in economic activity. All of these arguments involve implicit comparisons between the actual state of the nation and the state that would have prevailed in the absence of the specified circumstance.

Indeed, the new economic historians have not been primarily engaged in launching new counterfactual propositions, but in making explicit and testing the ones they find in traditional history. One should not underestimate the task involved in demonstrating that comparisons which appear to be between events that actually occurred are in reality counterfactual propositions. Consider, for example, the arithmetic index of productivity popularized by John Kendrick. This measure of total factor productivity, now more than a decade old, is usually described as the ratio of an output index to a weighted index of inputs, where the weights are the shares of the factors in value added. However, it has been shown that what appears to be purely a comparison of recorded circumstances is really a disguised comparison between the actual price of the output and the price that would have obtained in the absence of technological change [*32*, pp. 34–35; *17*, pp. 387–388; *12*, pp. 642–644; *19*, pp. 3–4].

Since counterfactual propositions are merely inferences from hypothetico-deductive models, it follows that such propositions can be verified in at least two ways. The first involves the determination of whether the proposition asserted follows logically from its premises. The second requires a determination of whether the assumptions of the model are empirically valid.[7] Most of the revisions of the new economic history follow from a demonstration that one or both of these conditions for valid inferences have been violated. As noted earlier, Conrad and Meyer overthrew Phillips' proposition that slavery was moribund by showing that his conclusion rested on the false assumption that a divergence between the rates of growth of slave and cotton prices implied a decrease in profits. On the other hand, as I attempted to demonstrate in another paper, one cannot rest the case for the indispensability of railroads to the total economy on evidence which shows that railroads had the power to crush particular firms or regions. This argument involves the fallacy of composition and hence gives rise to a non-sequitur [*16*, pp. 232–234].

The foregoing suggests that the fundamental methodological feature of the new economic history is its attempt to cast all explanations of past economic development in the form of valid hypothetico-deductive models. This is another way of saying that the new generation seeks to continue an effort that was under way long before it appeared on the scene: namely the construction of economic history on the basis of scientific methods. If the new economic historians are able to advance that objective it will be partly because of what they have inherited from their predecessors and partly because they are the beneficiaries of a series of important developments in economic theory, in statistics, and in applied mathematics.

REFERENCES

1. Ralph Andreano, *New Views on American Economic Development,* Cambridge, Schenkman, 1965.
2. Alfred H. Conrad and John R. Meyer, "The Economics of Slavery in the Ante-Bellum South," *The Journal of Political Economy,* 66 (April, 1958), 95–130. (Reprinted in [*3*], chap 3.) [Reprinted below as essay 25.]
3. Alfred H. Conrad and John R. Meyer, *The Economics of Slavery and Other Studies in Econometric History*, Chicago, Aldine, 1964.
4. Paul David, "The Mechanization of Reaping in the Ante-Bellum Midwest," in Henry Rosovsky, ed., *Industrialization in Two*

---

[7] A third level of verification, the test of the predictive power of a model, may often be possible in historical analysis. Cf. [*13*, pp. 176–189].

Systems: Essays in Honor of Alexander Gerschenkron, New York, Wiley, 1966, pp. 3–39. [Reprinted below as essay 16.]

5. Lance E. Davis, Jonathan R. T. Hughes, and Stanley Reiter, "Aspects of Quantitative Research in Economic History," *The Journal of Economic History, 20* (December, 1960), 539–547.

6. Richard A. Easterlin "Regional Income Trends, 1840–1950," in Seymour Harris, ed., *American Economic History,* New York, McGraw-Hill, 1961, pp. 525–547. [Reprinted below as essay 4.]

7. Stanley L. Engerman, "The Economic Impact of the Civil War," *Explorations in Entrepreneurial History,* Second Series, *3* (Spring/Summer, 1966), 176–199. [Reprinted below as essay 27.]

8. Stanley L. Engerman, "The Effects of Slavery Upon the Southern Economy: A Review of the Recent Debate," *Explorations in Entrepreneurial History,* Second Series, *4* (Winter, 1967), 71–97.

9. Robert Evans, Jr., "The Economics of American Negro Slavery," *Aspects of Labor Economics,* A Conference of the Universities–National Bureau Committee for Economic Research, Princeton, Princeton University Press, 1962, pp. 185–243.

10. Franklin M. Fisher, "On The Analysis of History and the Interdependence of the Social Sciences," *Philosophy of Science, 27* (April, 1960), 147–158.

11. Albert Fishlow, *American Railroads and the Transformation of the Ante-Bellum Economy,* Cambridge, Harvard University Press, 1965. [Chapter IV reprinted below as essay 30.]

12. Albert Fishlow, "Productivity and Technological Change in the Railroad Sector, 1840–1910," Conference on Research in Income and Wealth, *Output, Employment, and Productivity in the United States After 1800* (Studies in Income and Wealth, vol. 30), New York, Columbia University Press, 1966, pp. 583–646.

13. Robert William Fogel, *Railroads and American Economic Growth: Essays in Econometric History,* Baltimore, Johns Hopkins Press, 1964. [Chapter VI reprinted below as essay 14.]

14. Robert W. Fogel, "A Provisional View of the 'New Economic History,' " *The American Economic Review, 54* (May, 1964), 377–389.

15. Robert W. Fogel, "The Reunification of Economic History with Economic Theory," *The American Economic Review, 55* (May, 1965), 92–98.

16. Robert W. Fogel, "Railroads and the Axiom of Indispensability," in [*1*], pp. 225–241.

17. Zvi Griliches, "Notes on the Measurement of Price and Quality Changes," Conference on Research in Income and Wealth, *Models of Income Determination* (Studies in Income and Wealth, vol. 28), Princeton, Princeton University Press, 1964, pp. 381–404.

18. Jonathan R. T. Hughes, "Fact and Theory in Economic History," *Explorations in Entrepreneurial History,* Second Series, *3* (Winter, 1966), 75–100.

19. Dale W. Jorgenson, "The Embodiment Hypothesis," *The Journal of Political Economy 74* (February, 1966), 1–17.

20. James K. Kindahl, "The Economics of Resumption: The United States, 1865–1879," (unpublished doctoral dissertation, University of Chicago, 1958); published without statistical appendices as "Economic Factors in Specie Resumption: The United States, 1865–79," *The Journal of Political Economy, 69* (February, 1961), 30–48. [The latter reprinted below as essay 35.]

21. Simon Kuznets, "Summary of Discussion and Postscript," *The Journal of Economic History, 17* (December, 1957), 545–553.

22. Paul W. MacAvoy, *The Economic Effects of Regulation: The Trunk-Line Railroad Cartels and the Interstate Commerce Commission Before 1900,* Cambridge, M.I.T. Press, 1965.

23. John R. Meyer and Alfred H. Conrad, "Economic Theory, Statistical Inference and Economic History," *The Journal of Economic History, 17* (December, 1957), 524–544. (Reprinted in [*3*], chap. 1.)

24. George G. S. Murphy, "The 'New' History," *Explorations in Entrepreneurial History,* Second Series, *2* (Winter, 1965), 132–146.

25. Douglass C. North, "Quantitative Research in American Economic History," *The American Economic Review, 53* (March, 1963), 128–130.

26. Douglass C. North, "The State of Economic History," *The American Economic Review, 55,* (May, 1965), 86–91.

27. Douglass C. North, *Growth and Welfare in the American Past: A New Economic History,* Englewood Cliffs, Prentice-Hall, 1966.

28. Douglass C. North, "Economic History," David L. Sills, ed., *International Encyclopedia of The Social Sciences,* New York, Macmillan, 1968, vol. 6, pp. 468–474.

29. Douglass C. North, "Sources of Productivity Change in Ocean Shipping, 1600–1850," *The Journal of Political Economy, 76* (Sept./Oct., 1968), 953–970. [Reprinted below as essay 12.]

30. William N. Parker and Judith L. V. Klein, "Productivity Growth in Grain Production in

the United States, 1840–60 and 1900–10,"
Conference on Research in Income and
Wealth, *Output, Employment, and Productivity
in the United States After 1800* (Studies in
Income and Wealth, vol. 30), New York,
Columbia University Press, 1966, pp. 523–
580. [An essay by Parker drawing on this piece
is printed below as essay 13.]

31. Fritz Redlich, "'New' and Traditional
Approaches to Economic History and Their
Interdependence," *The Journal of Economic
History*, 25 (December, 1965), 480–495.

32. Irving H. Siegal, "On the Design of Consistent
Output and Input Indexes for Productivity
Measurement," Conference on Research in
Income and Wealth, *Output, Employment, and
Productivity Measurement* (Studies in Income
and Wealth, vol. 25), Princeton, Princeton
University Press, 1961, pp. 23–41.

33. Richard Sutch, "The Profitability of Ante-
Bellum Slavery—Revisited," *The Southern
Economic Journal*, 31 (April, 1963), 365–377.

34. Peter Temin, *Iron and Steel in Nineteenth-
Century America,* Cambridge, M.I.T. Press,
1964.

35. Peter Temin, "A New Look at Hunter's
Hypothesis about the Ante-Bellum Iron
Industry," *The American Economic Review, 54*

(May, 1964), 344–351. [Reprinted below as
essay 9.]

36. William Whitney, "The Structure of the
American Economy in the late Nineteenth
Century" (unpublished doctoral dissertation,
Harvard University, 1968).

37. Jeffrey G. Williamson, "Antebellum Urbanization in the American Northwest," *The
Journal of Economic History*, 25 (December,
1965), 592–608. [Reprinted below as essay
32.]

38. Jeffrey G. Williamson and Joseph A. Swanson,
"The Growth of Cities in the American
Northwest, 1820–1870," *Explorations in Entrepreneurial History,* Second Series, *4* (Fall,
1966), Supplement.

39. Harold D. Woodman, "The Profitability of
Slavery: A Historical Perennial," *The Journal
of Southern History*, *29* (August, 1963), 302–
325.

40. Yasukichi Yasuba, "The Profitability and
Viability of Plantation Slavery in the United
States," *The Economic Studies Quarterly*, *12*
(September, 1961), 60–67. [Reprinted below
as essay 26.]

41. Robert Brooke Zevin, "The Growth of Cotton Textile Production after 1815" (printed
below as essay 10).

I THE PATTERN OF ECONOMIC GROWTH

National income accounting techniques were perfected during the 1930s and early 1940s. The central figure in the development of such accounts was Simon Kuznets. In 1946 he published *National Product Since 1869* [5]. The volume provided measures of gross and net national product for the economy in both current and constant dollars. It also provided measures of the contribution of each of the main industrial sectors to total output. Robert E. Gallman later extended these estimates of national product and its components back to 1834 [4]. Richard A. Easterlin, in a 1960 paper [1], constructed income accounts for each of the principal geographic regions of the nation.

It is difficult to exaggerate the contribution of national income accounts to the description and interpretation of American economic history. Before the construction of these measures, historians attempting to evaluate the performance of the economy during particular decades, and in particular regions, were forced to conjecture about the totality of economic activity from the isolated scraps of evidence they had uncovered. For example, the evidence of unemployment among industrial workers, falling prices, financial panics, and the extensive protest movements of farmers led historians to the conclusion that the years 1870–1880 were a depression era—a period during which the economy stagnated. How surprising then was Kuznets' finding that total and per capita income grew more rapidly during that decade than during any other decade between the Civil War and World War II. For although the recession of 1873–1878 was protracted, the recovery which followed it was unusually robust. Thus the dozen years following 1869 were not an era of stagnation but one of sharp contrasts; a protracted recession, which took the form of an interruption rather than a reversal in the rate of growth, was sandwiched between two periods of vigorous growth, 1870–1873 and 1878–1882 [2, pp. 127–128; 3, pp. 273–282; 6, pp. 34–38].

Gallman's extension of the national accounts into the ante-bellum era also produced several surprises. Perhaps the most startling was the discovery that far from accelerating, the rate of growth of manufacturing declined during the Civil War decade. This fact has stimulated a far reaching reexamination of the Beard-Hacker thesis that the Civil War gave an unprecedented impetus to the industrialization of the nation.[1] Easterlin's disaggregation of the national accounts to a state level produced still another unanticipated finding. His figures showed that during the twenty years leading up to the Civil War, per capita income grew nearly as rapidly in the South as in the rest of the country. Subsequent work on these accounts has shown that the South was probably growing more rapidly than the North.[2]

These are only a few examples of how the national income accounts have changed our perception of the pattern of American economic development. More than correcting the particular misimpressions of earlier eras, national income accounts give a succinct characterization of the course of total economic activity and of the changing structure of production both by industries and by geographic regions. This information forms the basis for calibration, provides a scale against which the importance of such developments as urbanization, technological change, and the impact of various government policies may be judged.

The central task of national income accounting is the combination of the qualitatively different types of goods and services produced in a given year into a single measure of total economic activity. Because apples and automobiles are qualitatively different items, they can be added together only along some common dimension. An obvious solution is to multiply each item by its price, thus putting each item into the comparable dimension of value. Consequently one can obtain a measure of total economic activity by multiplying the physical amount of the *final* output of each type of good or service by its price and then aggregating these values into a single number which represents national income or product.

The word *final* was italicized in order to stress that in getting a measure of national product it is necessary to follow a procedure which avoids double counting. If all firms were fully integrated there would be no problem of double counting, for then the value of the nation's output would be the sum of the value of the products that were sold by all firms. However, very few firms carry out all activities from the production of raw materials

---

[1] This reexamination is discussed in essay 27, below.

[2] See essay 24, below.

to the delivery of the finished product to consumers.

The problem can be illustrated by considering the measurement of final product in production of an automobile under two different sets of circumstances. In the first case the firm is fully integrated. It not only produces all of its raw materials but also fabricates the raw materials into parts, assembles the parts, and finally sells the finished car directly to consumers. The cost of the raw materials (including depreciation and normal profit on the capital used to obtain the raw materials) is $500. It costs an additional $1000 to fabricate the raw materials into parts. The cost of assembling the car is $1500. Finally, there is a cost of $600 in shipping the car to a showroom and in selling it to its eventual owner. Hence the selling price of the car will be equal to the cost of producing and delivering it: $500 + $1000 + $1500 + $600 = $3600

Now let us consider a case where a different firm is involved in each operation. Firm A produces raw materials and sells them to firm B for $500. Firm B fabricates the raw material into parts at a cost to itself of $1000. Since it paid $500 for raw materials, it sells the parts to firm C at $1500. The cost of assembly is $1500, so that firm C sells the assembled car at the cost of the parts ($1500) plus the cost of assembly ($1500), which totals $3000. It cost firm D $600 to sell the finished car. Hence the consumer pays firm D $3600.

Table 1 gives the selling price (column 1) and the value added by each firm (column 2). It will immediately be seen that if we add together the selling price of each firm, we will obtain a figure ($8600) which is greatly in excess of the value of the car. For such addition involves counting various operations several times (materials costs are counted four

times, fabrication costs three times, and assembly costs twice). The correct figure would be obtained if we counted only the selling price of the final product (the product of firm D) and omitted the selling prices of intermediate products (the products of firms A, B, and C). Alternatively we would obtain the correct figure by adding together the value added by each firm to the final price (see column 2).

Consequently, we can measure national product either by finding the value of all final goods and services or by finding value which each firm adds to the value of the final products of the economy. In practice both procedures are used. Moreover, the value of final goods and services can be obtained in two main ways. One is the *expenditure method*. Here, the economy is divided into four sectors: consumers, government, business, and the rest-of-the-world. National product is then measured as the sum of all expenditures on goods and services by consumers and government plus the investment expenditures by business (only the purchases of businesses for investment are final product—all other business purchases are intermediate products) plus net foreign investment (which equals our sales to the rest of the world minus our purchases from the rest of the world). The value of all final goods can also be measured by the *factor payment method*, since the value of all final goods must be equal to payments to labor, rental and interest payments, profits, depreciation allowances, and indirect taxes on business.

In current government terminology, the value of national product measured in any of these ways is called gross national product (GNP). Table 2 presents the national income and product account for 1956. The left-hand column gives gross national product as obtained by the payments method; the right-hand column gives GNP as obtained by the expenditure method. Since the estimating procedures are not perfect, the two methods do not usually produce exactly the same results. The accounts are thus made to balance by including on the left an item called *statistical discrepancy*. In the case of unincorporated enterprises it is not possible to obtain accurate breakdowns between payments to labor, interest, profit, and rent. Business transfer payments (charitable contributions, etc.) come out of business profit and hence must be added to the payments account. While government-owned firms do

Table 1. An Example of How to Measure the Value of the Final Product of an Industry

FIRM	SELLING PRICE (1)	VALUE ADDED (2)
A	$ 500	$ 500
B	1500	1000
C	3000	1500
D	3600	600
Total	$ 8600	$ 3600

Table 2. National Income and Product Account, 1956 (Billions of Dollars)

Compensation of employees	$241.4	Personal consumption expenditures	$267.2
Income of unincorporated enterprises	39.6	Gross private domestic investment	65.9
Rental income of persons	10.3	Net foreign investment	1.4
Corporate profits	40.4	Government purchases of goods and	
Net interest	11.9	services	80.2
Indirect business taxes	35.0		
Business transfer payments	1.3		
Statistical discrepancy	1.6		
Plus: Current surplus of government			
enterprises minus subsidies	−1.1		
Capital consumption allowances	34.3		
Charges against GNP	$414.7	GNP	$414.7

not pay taxes, the balance of surplus minus subsidies is equivalent to a tax and hence is also included on the left-hand side of the ledger.

Although GNP is the most common way of measuring national output, alternative measures may be more useful in particular instances. Hence gross national product minus capital consumption allowances is called net national product (NNP). Net national product minus indirect business taxes, business transfer payments, statistical discrepancy, and surplus net of subsidies for government enterprises, yields National Income (NI).[3] In other words National Income is the sum of payments to the owners of productive factors (land, labor, and capital).

The measure of national product used by Kuznets in essay 2 is GNP. In essay 3 Gallman and Howle use sectoral measures of value added to calculate the contribution of various industries or groups of industries to national product. In essay 4 Easterlin uses a concept called personal income, which is similar to the concept of National Income as defined above.

---

[3] The term "national income" (without capitals) is synonymous with the term national product. When used in this way it does not necessarily imply the measure defined as National Income (NI). Thus GNP, NNP, and NI are all measures of national income or national product.

REFERENCES

1. Richard A. Easterlin, "Interregional Differences in Per Capita Income, Population, and Total Income, 1840–1950," Conference on Research in Income and Wealth, *Trends in the American Economy in the Nineteenth Century* (Studies in Income and Wealth, vol. 24), Princeton, Princeton University Press, 1960, pp. 73–140.

2. Edwin Frickey, *Production in the United States, 1860–1914*, Cambridge, Harvard University Press, 1947.

3. Milton Friedman, "Monetary Data and National Income Estimates," *Economic Development and Cultural Change*, 9 (April, 1961), 267–286.

4. Robert E. Gallman, "Gross National Product in the United States, 1834–1909," Conference on Research in Income and Wealth, *Output, Employment, and Productivity in the United States After 1800* (Studies in Income and Wealth, vol. 30), New York, Columbia University Press, 1966, pp. 3–76.

5. Simon Kuznets, *National Product Since 1869*, New York, National Bureau of Economic Research, 1946.

6. Simon Kuznets, "Long-Term Changes in the National Income of the United States of America Since 1870," International Association for Research in Income and Wealth, *Income and Wealth of the United States*, Baltimore, Johns Hopkins Press, 1952, pp. 29–241.

2 NOTES ON THE PATTERN OF U.S. ECONOMIC GROWTH

Simon Kuznets

A COMPARISON OF LONG-TERM GROWTH RATES

Crude as the estimates are, we can approximate the rates of growth of the gross national product, population, and labor force in this country back to 1840, the year that may be accepted as dating the entry of this country into the period of modern industrialization. Over the one hundred and twenty years from 1840 to 1960, population grew at an average rate of about 2 per cent per year; labor force, at a slightly higher rate of 2.2 per cent per year; gross national product, at 3.6 per cent per year; per capita product at 1.6 per cent per year; and product per worker, at 1.4 per cent per year (Table 1). These rates mean that in 1960 population was about 10.5 times as large

Reprinted with omissions from Edgar O. Edwards, ed., *The Nation's Economic Objectives*, Rice University Semicentennial Publications, Chicago, University of Chicago Press, 1964, pp. 15–35.

Table 1. Rates of Growth Per Year, Gross National Product, Population, and Labor Force in the United States in Successive and Overlapping Decades and Longer Periods, 1840–1960 (Per Cent)

	PRODUCT (1)	POPULATION (2)	LABOR FORCE (3)	PRODUCT PER CAPITA (4)	PRODUCT PER WORKER (5)
Successive decades					
1. 1839–49	4.24	3.11	3.57	1.10	0.64
2. 1849–59	4.95	3.09	3.18	1.80	1.71
3. 1859–69	1.99	2.39	2.07	−0.39	−0.08
4. 1869–79	4.95	2.33	3.01	2.56	1.88
Overlapping decades					
5. 1878–82–1888–92	3.73	2.26	2.70	1.44	1.00
6. 1883–87–1893–97	3.10	2.02	2.50	1.05	0.58
7. 1888–92–1898–1902	4.04	1.80	2.50	2.20	1.50
8. 1893–97–1903–07	5.03	1.78	2.60	3.19	2.36
9. 1898–1902–1908–12	3.71	1.95	2.67	1.73	1.01
10. 1903–07–1913–17	2.60	1.87	1.95	0.72	0.63
11. 1908–12–1918–22	2.60	1.50	1.05	1.08	1.53
12. 1913–17–1923–27	3.62	1.40	1.14	2.19	2.45
13. 1918–22–1929	3.99	1.47	1.35	2.49	2.61
14. 1923–27–1933–37	−0.35	0.98	1.16	−1.33	−1.49
15. 1929–1939–41	1.37	0.74	1.21	0.62	0.15
16. 1933–37–1943–47	7.02	0.96	1.84	6.00	5.09
17. 1939–41–1948–52	4.27	1.39	1.40	2.84	2.83
18. 1943–47–1953–57	2.47	1.67	0.80	0.78	1.65
19. 1948–52–1959–61	3.24	1.71	1.19	1.50	2.03
Longer periods					
20. 1840–80	4.03	2.73	2.96	1.26	1.04
21. 1880–1920	3.52	1.88	2.23	1.61	1.26
22. 1920–60	3.15	1.31	1.28	1.81	1.84
23. 1840–1960	3.56	1.97	2.15	1.56	1.38
Absolute values[a]					
24. 1959–61	509.0	179.9	69.9	2,829	7,282
25. 1959–61 as multiple of 1840	66.7	10.4	12.9	6.4	5.2
26. 1840	7.63	17.1	5.42	446	1,408

[a] Product is listed in billions of 1961 dollars; population and labor force, in millions; and product per capita and per worker, in 1961 dollars.

as in 1840; labor force, almost 13 times; per capita product and, presumably, per capita real income, over 6 times; and product per worker, over 5 times.

How does this record compare with the long-term growth of other countries? The countries of most interest to us here are those that we now consider developed: those that have managed to take advantage of the wide potentials of modern economic growth and those that are (or were) fairly large, so that their growth conditions and problems have not been too different from those of the United States.

If then we look at the long-term records of

the United Kingdom, France, Germany, Russia (and the USSR), and Japan, allow for changes in boundaries, and observe long periods (ranging from 79 years for Japan to 117 years for the United Kingdom), the results of the comparison may be stated simply (Table 2). First, the annual rate of growth of population in the United States was much higher than in these other large, developed countries: compared with 2 per cent in this country, the rates in the other countries ranged from 1.2 per cent for Japan to 0.2 for France and, except for Japan, were half or less than half of the rate of growth of U.S. population. Second, the annual rates of growth of per capita

Table 2. Rates of Growth Per Year, Product, Population, and Per Capita Product for Selected Countries over Long Periods (Per Cent)

	DURATION OF PERIOD[a] (1)	PRODUCT (2)	POPULATION (3)	PRODUCT PER CAPITA (4)
Great Britain and United Kingdom				
Great Britain				
1. 1841–81	40	2.54	1.19	1.33
2. 1881–1921	40	1.77	0.91	0.86
United Kingdom				
3. 1921–1957–59	37	1.88	0.43	1.44
4. Total, 1841–1957–59	117	2.07	0.86	1.20
France				
5. 1841–50–1861–70	20	2.23	0.39	1.84
6. 1871–80–1901–10	30	2.00	0.22	1.77
7. 1901–10–1920–28	18.5	1.46	−0.13	1.60
8. 1920–28–1958–60	35	1.55	0.37	1.18
9. Total, 1841–50–1958–60	103.5	1.80	0.24	1.55
Germany				
1913 boundaries				
10. 1851–55–1871–75	20	1.63	0.74	0.89
11. 1871–75–1913	40	3.09	1.20	1.87
Interwar boundaries				
12. 1913–1935–37	23	0.57	0.53	0.04
Federal Republic				
13. 1936–1958–60	23	3.97	1.40	2.53
14. Total, 1913–1958–60	46	2.25	0.97	1.28
15. Total, 1851–55–1958–60	106	2.45	1.01	1.43
Sweden				
16. 1861–65–1881–85	20	2.88	0.72	2.15
17. 1881–85–1921–25	40	2.69	0.66	2.01
18. 1921–25–1958–60	36	3.77	0.59	3.16
19. Total, 1861–65–1958–60	96	3.13	0.64	2.47
European Russia and USSR				
European Russia				
20. 1860–1913	53	2.67	1.30	1.35
USSR				
21. 1913–28	15	0.54	0.54	0
22. 1928–58	30	4.40	0.67	3.71
23. Total, 1913–58	45	3.10	0.63	2.45
24. Total, 1860–1958	98	2.87	0.99	1.86
Japan				
25. 1878–82–1918–22	40	4.14	1.05	3.05
26. 1918–22–1958–60	39	3.97	1.36	2.57
27. Total, 1878–82–1958–60	79	4.05	1.21	2.81

[a] For series with initial or terminal periods longer than one year, duration is calculated between midyears.

product for the United States and for the large European countries were within a fairly narrow range: from 1.9 per cent for Russia (for a period reaching back to 1860) to 1.2 per cent for the United Kingdom (for a period reaching back to 1841), with 1.5 to 1.6 per cent for this country. We cannot place much stress on such differences, and for practical purposes, we can assume that the U.S. rate of growth in per capita product was about the same as in the large, developed European countries. The Japanese rate, estimated for 1880–1960 at 2.8 per cent, was distinctly higher. Third, the much higher rate of growth of population in the United States, combined with the same or roughly the same rate of growth of per capita product, means that there was a correspondingly higher rate of growth in aggregate product here than in the European countries. Thus, the rate of rise in gross national product in the United States was from a fifth to almost twice as high as that in the large, developed European countries.

It need hardly be mentioned that these averages are for long periods, covering subperiods that differ markedly in the rates of growth of product and population. Furthermore, for several countries, particularly Japan, the period is significantly shorter than that for the United States; and extension of the period to 1840, the initial date for this country, would only lower the averages for both the European countries and for Japan. Yet the comparison is valid and indicates the exceptional performance in the United States: high rates of growth of population and of total product, if not of per capita product, have existed over the long period 1840–1960.

The conclusions just noted would be modified only slightly if we were to extend the comparison to the smaller, developed European countries like Denmark, Norway, Sweden, and the Netherlands—to list the four for which we have long-term records. In general, the rate of growth of population in the United States was much higher, whereas the rate of growth of per capita product was either about the same or slightly higher or lower, except in comparison with Sweden, which combined a high rate of growth of per capita product, 2.5 per cent, with a low rate of population growth, 0.64 per cent (see Table 2). Indeed, the rapidity of population growth in this country is matched over the long period only in other overseas offshoots of Europe, such as Canada, Australia, and

Argentina. As a result of this rapid population growth, the United States forged ahead to a position of dominance. In 1840 the population of the United States was about 17 million; that of Great Britain was 18.6 million, significantly larger; those of France and Germany (1913 boundaries) were well over 30 million each, or almost double; and that of Russia was over 50 million, or almost three times as large. In 1960 the population of the United States, 180 million, was over three times as large as that of the United Kingdom, almost four times as large as that of France, two and a half times the total of East and West Germany, and only about a seventh below that of the USSR, despite the recent expansion in the latter's territory.

One further implication of the conclusions should be noted. We know that at present the per capita product of the United States is the highest in the world and appreciably higher than that in the developed European countries. Such comparisons are treacherous, but this statement is undeniable even if we do not accept at face value the United Nations estimates that indicate that in 1952–1954 per capita income of the United States was more than double those of the United Kingdom and France and over three times that of Germany. Nor is it easy to ascribe meaning to a calculation that shows that per capita product in the United States was almost three times that of the USSR in 1958. But let us assume moderately that the advantage in recent years is, say, one and one half to one. Then, if the rate of growth in per capita income in the United States is about the same as for these European countries, the implication is that in 1840 the per capita income of the United States was also at least one and one half times as high, and relatively higher if the rates of growth of per capita income in the large European countries were greater than that of the United States. A crude but suggestive calculation indicates that from the beginning of our period the per capita income of the United States— even before its industrialization—was close to that in the most developed country, the United Kingdom, and appreciably higher than in most European countries, let alone the rest of the world (with the exception of a country like Australia in its very early period of growth). In other words, the very high per capita income of the United States compared with those of other developed countries observed today is due largely to the fact that at the beginning of its industrialization its per capita income was already relatively high, and during the 120 years following, it managed to sustain rates of growth in per capita income that were not much lower than those of the developed countries which initially had much lower per capita incomes.

THE CHARACTERISTICS OF
LONG-TERM U.S. GROWTH

The high rate of population growth in the United States, higher than in other large, developed countries, was due primarily to the power of this country to attract immigrants. From 1840 to 1930, through three quarters of the long period covered here, the population of native stock grew from 14.2 to 82.7 million, less than six times the initial number; the population of foreign stock (foreign-born and native-born of foreign or mixed parentage) grew from somewhat less than 3 million to over 40 million, or over thirteen times the original number. In 1930 about a third of the country's total population was of foreign stock. Also, the rate of natural increase (the excess of births over deaths) may have been slightly higher here than in the older, developed countries, with the birth rates higher (particularly in the early nineteenth century) and the death rates somewhat lower. But the major source of the difference in the rate of growth of population and still more in that of the labor force was immigration—in ever-increasing streams and from diverse sources in Europe, although not from other continents. The importance of this stream for the economic growth of the United States is still not fully understood or completely analyzed, much of the past literature having concentrated on difficulties of adjustment and assimilation and having been biased by reformers concerned with short-term problems rather than with long-term gains. Nor have we paid sufficient attention to the effect of the decline in this source of growth in population and labor force—initiated in World War I, furthered by restrictive legislation in the 1920s, and sharply accentuated in the depression of the 1930s, never to be relaxed significantly—on the economic growth and adjustment problems of this country in recent years.

That the rate of growth in per capita product in the United States was no higher than in the large European countries (except moderately, compared with England) and in Japan, despite freedom from destructive impacts of the major wars which affected the latter countries and which are included in the averages cited above, is somewhat of a surprise. As to the comparison with Russia— where the average rate of growth of per capita product was raised largely during the costly three decades under authoritarian rule from 1928 to 1958 and where relative disregard of the more difficult problems of fitting economic growth to the needs and wishes of the population may account in good part for its high rate of measured increase—it is subject to grave doubts, but the results are hardly a puzzle. This is perhaps also true of the comparison with Japan, a country that started from initially very low levels and much later in time, and in which a long-lived hierarchical social system was harnessed to the cause of rapid industrialization, while many traditional industries in the fields of consumer goods and housing were preserved. To repeat, the puzzling finding is a rate of growth of per capita product in the United States that was not significantly higher than in France and Germany, only slightly higher than in the United Kingdom, and significantly lower than in Sweden.

Could the very rapid rate of growth of population and labor force in this country have restricted the rates of growth in per capita and per worker product? If so, what is the connection? Surely one cannot assume that the supply of natural resources had any limiting effects, insofar as most of the period of growth in the United States is concerned, compared with the conditions in the European countries. Could the limitation stem from difficulties in supplying adequate capital per worker, engendered by a rapidly growing labor force, despite the high long-term capital formation proportions in the United States, compared with the other developed countries? Or did the problems of adjustment and assimilation faced by immigrants lower average productivity, despite the fact that most immigrants were in the prime labor ages and presumably endowed with strong economic incentives? Or, finally, did the very high level of per capita income induce a lower rate of growth by permitting the exchange of work for leisure, since there was no great pressure to "catch up"?

These and other questions come easily to mind. But unless the hypotheses underlying them concerning the connection between the high rate of population growth and the less than record rate of growth in per capita or per worker product, or between the latter and the high per capita product, can be formulated so as to reveal links that can be studied by means of empirical data, the conjectures are not very helpful. Answers to such questions require much additional analysis of a variety of long-term data that will permit a detailed comparison of the United States' rates of growth with those in other countries. This cannot be done here and I am compelled to set the questions aside and turn to other aspects of the long-term rates of growth of product, population, and labor force in the United States. In any case, our observation of these rates should not be limited to averages over as long a period as 120 years. How have they changed *during* that period?

First, has there been a long-term acceleration or retardation in the rates of growth? For population and labor force, the answer is clear: the rate of growth has declined markedly. Thus over the first 40 years, from 1840 to 1880, despite the fact that the period includes the Civil War years, the population grew 2.7 per cent per year; during the next 40 years, the rate dropped to 1.9 per cent; in the last 40 years, from 1920 to 1960, it was only 1.3 per cent per year. Likewise, the rates of growth in the labor force, through the successive 40-year periods, declined from 3.0 to 2.2 to 1.3 per cent per year. To be sure, population growth has recovered since World War II; the rate of increase over the last decade (1950 to 1960) was 1.7 per cent per year, but it still was lower than the rate for 1880 to 1920; and the rate of growth of the labor force in the last decade was among the lowest, less than 1.2 per cent per year (reflecting the low birth rate of the 1930s), but it may recover to higher levels in the 1960s.

The retardation in the rate of growth of population and labor force was accompanied by a decline in the rate of growth of aggregate gross national product. It was slightly over 4 per cent per year from 1840 to 1880, 3.5 per cent per year from 1880 to 1920, and 3.1 per cent per year from 1920 to 1960 (over the last decade, it was 3.2 per cent per year). It should be noted that except for the earliest period all product rates are calculated from either five- or three-year averages at terminal points, to reduce the effects of short, cyclical disturbances.

But while the rates of growth of population and labor force declined to less than half of the early levels, the retardation in the rate of growth of gross national product was much

less marked—about a quarter. This means, of course, that the rate of growth of per capita or per worker product showed a significant acceleration. The rate of growth of per capita product from 1840 to 1880 was 1.3 per cent per year; from 1880 to 1920 it was 1.6 per cent per year; from 1920 to 1960 it was 1.8 per cent per year; and even in the last decade (1950s) it was only slightly below 1.6 per cent per year. The per worker product rate was slightly above 1 per cent per year from 1840 to 1880; 1.3 per cent per year from 1880 to 1920; and over 1.8 per cent per year from 1920 to 1960. Over the last decade, from 1950 to 1960, the rate of growth of gross national product per worker was 2.0 per cent per year, among the highest in the long-term record.

Two important recent monographs, one for the period since the 1880s and the other for the period since 1909, show acceleration in the rate of growth of product per worker. At the danger of overburdening this paper with statistical detail, I shall give the major conclusions of these studies in a brief listing. The conclusions of the Kendrick study are: (1) Between 1879–1919 and 1919–1953, the rate of growth of national product per unit of labor input (man-hours weighted by hourly wage rates in the base year) rose from 1.4 to 1.9 per cent per year; the rate of growth of product per unit of capital input rose from 0.4 to 1.2 per cent per year; and that of product per unit of combined factor input rose from 1.1 to 1.7 per cent per year. (2) The measured acceleration in the rate of growth of productivity was kept down by the inclusion of the government sector and the finance and services sector, for both of which measures of productivity are quite tenuous. When these are excluded, the rise in product per unit of labor input accelerates from 0.8 per cent per year in 1879–1919 to 2.4 per cent in 1919–1953. (3) Within the private domestic economy, excluding finance and services, the acceleration in the rate of growth of product per unit of labor input was observed in all sectors except contract construction. (4) Findings for individual sectors and for branches of manufacturing suggest that the divisions of the productive system in which the greatest acceleration in the rate of growth of product per unit of labor (or total factor) input occurred were either those in which such growth was quite low in the past (such as agriculture and woodworking manufactures) or those in which technological changes were particularly conspicuous (such as chemicals, petroleum, and electrical machinery, among manufactures) [2].

The Denison study also shows a rise in the rate of growth of national product per unit of factor input: from 1.2 per cent per year for 1909–1929 to 2 per cent per year for 1929–1957 (per man-hour of labor, from 1.9 to 2.5). From the analysis that attempts to allocate productivity to the various components, we can gather that of the increase in the rate of growth of productivity of some 0.8 per cent per year (from 1.2 to 2), greater education of the labor force accounts for 0.32 points while the major portion of the remainder is likely to be accounted for by an increased weight credited to the advance of knowledge [1].

Despite the difficulties of establishing long-term trends in records for the European countries and Japan, affected far more by wars and revolutions than this country, it is clear that no common pattern of marked retardation in the rate of growth of population and total product and of acceleration in the rate of per capita product exists. To be sure, for Great Britain-United Kingdom, the rate of population growth dropped from 1.2 per cent per year in 1841–1881 to 0.4 per cent in 1921–1958, and in Russia, wars and revolution reduced the rate of population growth from 1.3 per cent per year for 1860–1913 to 0.6 per cent in 1913–1958. But in France, Germany, Sweden, and Japan, there was no marked trend in the rate of population growth for the long periods under consideration. And one can infer reasonably that if the rate of population growth did not decline, it is unlikely that the rate of growth of the labor force did. Nor is there much indication of a long-term upward trend, like that observed for the United States, in the rate of growth of per capita product in the European countries and in Japan—except for the effects of the revolutionary break in Russia. England, France, Germany (except for the initial acceleration after 1870), and Japan show no increase in the rate of growth of per capita product and that of Sweden emerges only in the last period, largely since the 1940s.

THE VARIABILITY OF THE U.S. GROWTH RATE

Although it is tempting to speculate on the implications of a combination of retardation in the rates of growth of the population and

the labor force with acceleration in the rate of growth of product per capita and per worker, a distinctive feature of long-term growth in this country, we must turn now to a third aspect of our experience—the variability of growth. The rates of growth for each decade —calculated wherever possible from five-year averages centered on the initial and terminal years and thus largely eliminating the effects of business cycles of three to nine years in duration—fluctuate widely. (Table 1). Even from the 1870s to World War I, a period unaffected by a major war, the rate of growth in per capita product varied between a low of about 1.1 per cent per year (from 1883–1887 to 1893–1897) to a high of 3.2 per cent per year (from 1893–1897 to 1903–1907). Swings of approximately twenty years in the growth rates of aggregate product, population, labor force, and product per capita and per worker are observable even after we cancel out as best we can the short-term business cycles.

These long swings in the rate of growth have been the subject of increasing attention in recent years in this country, and the literature dealing with them has grown markedly. Their relevance to the interpretation of recent short-term changes is being examined afresh. Consideration of the technical details of the procedures for the isolation and description of these long swings and of the controversial hypotheses advanced in attempts to account for them would be out of place here. A few general comments may, however, point up the significance of these swings for the present discussion.

First, regardless of the procedure employed to eliminate the short-term business cycles or to distinguish the sustained, unidirectional long-term trends, if we limit the cancellation to cycles that are completed within a decade at most and if we stipulate that the underlying trends make no more than one turn in a period of at least 40 to 50 years, the resulting smoothed indexes of product, population, and labor force, as well as of per capita and per worker product, would show significant variations around the underlying long-term trend. And if we describe these variations effectively, their amplitude is found to be significantly wide in relation to the average rate of growth in the underlying trend—to the point where, at the peak of a swing, the decadal rate of growth may be over twice a high as in the underlying trend, and at the trough, less than half as high. It is hardly surprising that even if we disregard periods affected by wars and revolutions and cancel out the short-term cycles, the course of economic performance is not a simple curve that can be adequately and fully described by a second-degree equation over a period of five to fifteen decades. The capacity to attain such a smooth and sustained performance would in itself be more surprising than the observed variability and would require as much explanation as the latter.

Second, granted that the long swings in product may be due in part to prolonged underutilization of economic capacity, we must not overlook the long swings in the rates of growth of population and labor force. So long as the latter are present, even the full utilization of labor and capital will not eliminate the long swings in the rate of growth of aggregate product; and if the swings in population and labor differ in timing, as they well may if they originate in processes of natural increase, there will be long swings also in the rate of growth of output per capita, even under full employment. Thus in the United States the rate of population growth reached a low of 0.8 per cent per year in the 1930s, and while this was due to the depression following the contraction phase of a long swing, it produced a low rate of growth in labor force in the 1950s, about twenty years later. A low growth rate in the labor force leads to a low rate of aggregate growth, even under full employment, unless there is an opposite swing in the rate of growth of product per worker.

Finally, as we would expect, long swings can be found in the rates of growth of other developed economies, particularly of those for which we have long records of growth. Even in Sweden, a country for which we have tolerably good continuous estimates for a full century, from 1861 to 1960, and one that sustained a high rate of growth in product per capita, the decadal rates of growth in the latter varied from 0.9 and 1.3 per cent per year to 3.7 and over 4 per cent per year, while the rate of growth in total gross domestic product varied from 1.5 to over 5.5 per cent per year. More than two long swings can be discerned within the one hundred years. And the rates of growth in the Communist countries would probably show the same variability, if there were a long enough record undisturbed by wars or revolutions. The "echo" effects of downward swings in the rates of growth of population and labor force, even if occasioned by wars, are just as marked for the Communist countries; and in addition, the errors in planning and the struggles for political succession and their associated policy choices cannot help but affect rates of growth for periods long enough to constitute phases of long swings.

REFERENCES

1. Edward Denison, *The Sources of Economic Growth in the United States and the Alternatives Before Us,* Supplementary Paper 13, New York, Committee for Economic Development, 1962.
2. John W. Kendrick, *Productivity Trends in the United States,* Princeton, Princeton University Press, 1961.

3 TRENDS IN THE STRUCTURE OF THE AMERICAN ECONOMY SINCE 1840

Robert E. Gallman and
Edward S. Howle

I

The pace at which American national product has grown since 1840 has no equal in recorded history. Between 1840 and 1960 real national product increased nearly seventyfold. At the same time a vast territory was peopled and the standard of life of its occupants was persistently and dramatically raised.

As the economy grew the distribution of economic activity between cities and rural areas, among regions, among industries, and among types of final product changed, and these changes were part and parcel of the process of growth. This brief paper describes a few of the chief compositional changes undergone by the American economy and suggests some connections between them. It ignores spatial redistribution of activity and focuses on industrial sectors and final product flows. It is concerned chiefly with the national product and exclusively with long-term changes, as distinct from business cycles and long swings.

II

At the heart of American growth during the last century and a quarter lies the process of industrialization, and it is the unfolding of this process that accounts for the chief structural changes in the American economy. We begin, therefore, with measurements intended to show, in the most striking form, the direct and immediate consequences of industrialization. These measurements are gathered in Table 1. They show the changing shares of the two chief commodity-producing sectors, agriculture and industry, in the income generated by the two sectors.

The data underlying the table are gross value added data. Gross value added is the value of output less the value of materials consumed in production. The term "gross" means that the measure is gross of capital consumption and, therefore, involves duplication over time. In other respects the measure is net, so that value added by agriculture and industry can be summed to produce an aggregate unduplicated *except* over time.

The chief findings to be drawn from lines 1 and 2 are very clear. The share of agriculture in value added by commodity production falls while the share of industry rises. These movements are pronounced and persistent.

Industry's share goes from almost 30 per cent in 1839 to over 60 per cent by the end of the century to almost 80 per cent by 1949. Across eight of the eleven intervals in the table the share of industry rises and the share of agriculture falls.[1]

The time period contained in the table encompasses most, but not all, of the American experience with this phenomenon. The experience has continued since 1949 and probably began before 1839. Some scholars have traced the origins of modern industrialization to the 1820s and even earlier. However, the share of industry in income is so small in 1839 that one is justified in thinking that the process of structural change in the preceding decades could not have been of great quantitative significance.

The trends described in lines 1 and 2 can be decomposed into trends in constant price magnitudes and relative prices. We may ask, for example, how far the decline in the share of agriculture in value added was due to (or retarded by) price trends unfavorable to agriculture (favorable to agriculture). The question has point since so much of the discussion of agriculture's changing position in the economy has focused on the terms of trade between agriculture and industry.

The data underlying lines 3 and 4 are expressed in constant prices and, therefore, purport to show the evolving positions of the

---

[1] The precise results depend, of course, on the definitions of "agriculture" and "industry" one uses, as well as the comprehensiveness of one's conception of economic activity. Appendix I to this paper contains several alternative measures of the relative importance of agriculture and industry. The trends described by them are roughly similar.

Table 1. Shares of Agriculture and Industry in Value Added by Agriculture and Industry, 1839–1947, Current and Constant Prices (Per Cent)

	1839	1849	1859	1869	1879	1889	1899	1909	1919	1929	1939	1949
Current Prices												
Agriculture	71	61	62	57	53	39	37	38	35	24	23[a]	23[b]
Industry	29	39	38	43	47	61	63	62	65	76	77[a]	77[b]
Constant Prices												
Agriculture	78	64	61	57	53	41	35	26	22	17	19	16
Industry	22	36	39	43	47	59	65	74	78	83	81	84

[a] 1937   [b] 1947

two sectors once price changes are taken out. In broad terms, the findings to be drawn from lines 3 and 4 are the same as those we have taken from lines 1 and 2. But the structural changes shown in lines 3 and 4 are the more pronounced. The conclusion one reaches is that, on the whole, relative prices have moved in such a way as to *moderate* the decline of agriculture. The agricultural sector does not appear to have been consistently the victim of unfavorable relative price movements. Agricultural discontent and federal preoccupation with farm problems have their sources elsewhere.

III

We now widen our view and ask about the place of the commodity-producing sectors, as a group, in the economy; and we now require a new concept. As indicated above, the measures of value added by the commodity-producing sectors can be combined into an unduplicated aggregate. However, if we want to fit the commodity-producing sectors into the context of national income we must turn to a measure, net income originating, which can be derived from value added in the following way. First of all we must deduct from value added the cost of services purchased from other sectors and consumed in production (including tax payments, which can be regarded as payments for government services). According to convention we must add to the income of agriculture the rental value of the homes owned and occupied by farm operators. We must correct for changes in the value of inventories and, since national income is unduplicated over time, we must deduct capital consumption. The measure we arrive at is the sum of the earnings of the factors of production committed to the sector. It is generally a more difficult measure to produce but is clearly superior to value added as a measure of the contribution of the sector to the economy.

Unfortunately, we do not have income originating series for the nineteenth century, and we do not have a reliable national income series. We are forced to produce the latter by extrapolation from the twentieth century on gross national product, a relatively safe procedure since we are interested only in trends. We produce the sector net income originating estimates in the same way, by extrapolation on gross value added.

Here we are on shakier ground. We are assuming that the ratio of income originating to gross value added for each sector has remained unchanged since 1839. But the growing complexity of the economy has increased the density of the web of interrelations between the commodity and noncommodity sectors and may have produced a *downward* drift in each ratio. The twentieth-century evidence suggests no movement of this kind, and the stability of the nineteenth-century ratio of value added to value of output in the manufacturing sector (a ratio presumably subject to the same kinds of forces) provides us with a limited basis for projecting a constant ratio into the nineteenth century [2, pp. 38–42]. But we cannot ignore the possibility of error in this procedure, in particular in the deflated variant.

Table 2 contains estimates of the shares of national income originating in the commodity-producing and "all other" sectors. The commodity-producing sectors are now expanded to include construction, a relatively minor change, and the constant price series is restricted to the nineteenth century. Interestingly enough, the evidence suggests that the

Table 2. Shares of National Income Originating in Commodity Production and All Other Sectors, 1839–1955, Current and Constant Prices (Per Cent)[a]

	CURRENT PRICES		CONSTANT PRICES	
	Commodity Production (1)	All Other (2)	Commodity Production (3)	All Other (4)
1839	44.7	55.3	42.7	57.3
1849	41.2	58.8	44.2	55.8
1859	42.1	57.9	42.8	57.2
1869	45.6	54.4	42.7	57.3
1879	41.0	59.0	41.2	58.8
1889	44.6	55.4	47.2	52.8
1899	43.0	57.0	45.8	54.2
1909				
1919	46.8	53.2		
1929a	37.7	62.3		
1929b	40.3	59.7		
1938a	31.7	68.3		
1940b	39.2	60.8		
1950	44.0	56.0		
1955	42.8	57.2		

[a] The entries for 1929 and 1938 identified by the letter *a* are comparable to the entries for earlier dates; the entries identified by *b* are comparable to entries for later dates. The concepts underlying the *a* and *b* entries are slightly different. See Appendix II.

trend in the share of the commodity-producing sectors in the national product has been
zero. It is true that the current price figures
for 1929 and 1939 indicate that the commodity production share was substantially
below any recorded for the nineteenth century. But in 1950 and 1955 we again find
ratios approximating those of 1849, 1859,
and 1879.

Professor Kuznets' work has to some
extent prepared one for such findings [*9*, pp.
50–52, 56]. Nonetheless, it is best not to take
them at face value in the present instance. As
indicated above, the procedure used to derive
net income originating in the commodity-
producing sectors during the nineteenth
century may produce biased estimates. If so,
it is more likely that the bias is in the direction
of *understatement* of income originating in
commodity production, becoming progressively more serious as we go backward in
time, rather than the reverse. In addition, the
national income estimates are built up from
components of unequal reliability. The most
reliable are the commodity-flow components,
derived from essentially the same data underlying the estimates of income originating in
commodity production. The least reliable are
the service-flow series. There is some reason
for believing that these estimates are too high
in the early years [*4*, pp. 56–62, esp. 62].
Consequently, the data may contain two sets
of errors, both working in the direction of
understating the fraction of national income
originating in commodity production, the
error becoming more serious as we move
backward in time.

We have experimented with fairly large
adjustments to the underlying estimates and
have discovered that the findings are not very
sensitive to them. Specifically, we have worked
with 1849, the earliest year in which the share
of the commodity sectors in national income
is clearly at a twentieth-century level. We have
reduced the least reliable service component
of the national income estimate ("services
flowing to consumers, less the rental value of
residences") in 1849 by 50 per cent and have
raised the estimates of income originating in
commodity production by 20 per cent. These
adjustments raise the share of the commodity
sectors in national income from 41 per cent to
something under 50 per cent, a fairly large
change, but one that leaves intact the impression that there has been little or no trend in
the share of the commodity sectors in national
income since the middle of the last century.

Table 3. Distribution of the Labor Force and Relative
Levels of Income Per Worker, Commodity Production and All Other Sectors, 1840–1960[a]

| | PER CENT OF LABOR FORCE | | RELATIVE LEVELS OF INCOME PER WORKER | |
	Commodity Production (1)	All Other (2)	Commodity Production (3)	All Other (4)
1840	78.0	22.0	.57	2.5
1850	75.9	24.1	.54	2.4
1860	73.4	26.6	.57	2.2
1870	79.2	20.8	.58	2.6
1880	77.2	22.8	.53	2.6
1890	70.1	29.9	.64	1.9
1900	68.6	31.4	.63	1.8
1910	61.8	38.2	—	—
1920	58.8	41.2	.80	1.3
1930*a*	44.1	55.9	.85	1.1
1930*b*			.91	1.1
1940	42.2	57.8	.93	1.1
1950	42.0	58.0	1.05	.97
1960	37.2	62.8	1.15	.91

[a] The entries in columns 3 and 4 express income per
worker in the relevant sectors as ratios of income per
worker for the entire economy.

Table 3 distributes the labor force between
commodity production and all other sectors.
Two points of interest emerge immediately.
The share of the commodity-producing
sectors in the labor force is greater than the
share of these sectors in national income in all
of the years recorded until 1950. Additionally,
the fraction of the labor force attached to
these sectors remains roughly constant to
1880 and then declines, whereas the income
originating data in Table 2 suggest no trend
in the share of these sectors in national
income. Of course, for the remaining sectors
the share in labor force is low relative to the
share in income, and the former drifts upward
after 1880, while the latter remains roughly
constant.

These results imply that (1) income per
worker in commodity production was low
relative to income per worker in the rest of the
economy, but that (2) the ratio of the former
to the latter drifted upward after 1880. The
implications are made explicit in the last two
columns of Table 3, which express income per
worker in each of the groups of sectors as a
ratio of average income per worker for the
entire economy. For example, the table shows
that in 1840 income per worker in commodity
production was less than 60 per cent of the

national average, while in all other sectors it ran two and one half times the national average. Thus the relationship between the two sectors was roughly as one is to four or five. By 1900 it was as one is to three and by 1950 income per worker in each sector approximated the national average.

Are these findings reasonable or do they constitute a new basis for questioning the nineteenth-century income data? The Kuznets studies, covering a wide range of experience, also typically show convergence during growth from an initial position in which income per worker in the commodity sectors lies below income per worker in the rest of the economy. Our results, then, are not unusual.

The figures in the first two columns of Table 3 are derived from data relating to only one input, labor, while the income estimates include returns to property, as well as to labor. The sectoral differences with respect to income per worker may reflect sectoral differences in factor proportions. Table 4 is the fruit of an effort to see how far, if at all, the findings for the nineteenth century can be accounted for in this way. The table contains estimates of the distribution of labor income between commodity production and all other sectors and relative levels of *labor* income per worker. The data are imperfect since it was necessary to compute labor income as a residual and to assume a uniform rate of return on all property used in economic activity, to estimate the residual. Nonetheless, the results are worth some study.

The sectoral distributions of income (columns 1 and 2) are much less stable than those obtained in Table 2. However, this aspect of the results deserves very little attention, since it may very well be produced by the estimating procedure.

Of much greater interest is the fact that sectoral differentials in income per worker remain wide even after account is taken of sectoral differences in the use of property (columns 3 and 4). In fact Table 4 shows *wider* differentials in the early years than does Table 3. Sectoral differences in labor productivity are not accounted for by differences in the extent to which property is used in economic activity.[2]

Finally, Table 4 also shows that sectoral levels of income per worker converged. The time period over which the convergence occurred appears to be slightly longer in Table 4 than in Table 3 and the extent of convergence somewhat greater. There is a marked tendency for levels of sectoral labor productivity to draw together. Since we know that labor productivity was on the rise during the nineteenth century this means that labor productivity was increasing faster in the commodity sectors than in the "all other" sectors. In a broad sense this is the result one might have expected, since the commodity sectors were presumably the more directly, generally, and widely affected by the processes of technical change associated with industrialization. Clearly there is much more to be said on this matter, which a brief review of this type must necessarily leave unsaid. Instead, we take up the impact of structural change on productivity.

Table 4. Distribution of Labor Income and Relative Levels of Labor Income Per Worker, Commodity Production and All Other Sectors, 1840–1900

| | PER CENT OF LABOR INCOME | | RELATIVE LEVELS OF LABOR INCOME PER WORKER | |
	Commodity Production (1)	All Other (2)	Commodity Production (3)	All Other (4)
1840	34.8	65.2	.45	2.9
1850	31.8	68.2	.42	2.8
1860	30.5	69.5	.42	2.6
1870	42.9	57.1	.54	2.7
1880	37.5	62.5	.49	2.7
1890	51.7	48.3	.74	1.6
1900	49.0	51.0	.71	1.6

IV

The preceding sections have shown that during the nineteenth century labor productivity in commodity production was substantially lower than in the rest of the economy. Furthermore, the labor force attached to the commodity-producing sectors increased at a lower rate than in the remaining sectors. That is, the process of structural change of the labor force tended to increase the relative importance of the sector in which labor productivity was relatively

---

[2] At least as property is commonly defined. The differentials may be accounted for, in some measure, by labor skill differentials, resting on differences in investment in worker training.

high. Consequently, *average* labor productivity for the economy as a whole must have risen simply as a consequence of the growing weight of the high-productivity sector. It would be interesting to know what part of the growth of total productivity can be accounted for in this way.

In principle, the relative importance of the effect of structural shifts on productivity can be measured. The process is similar to that by which the change in a value of output series is partitioned into a change in prices and a change in output. In the latter case one begins by producing an appropriate price index and an appropriate output index. In the present instance, however, one begins by producing an index that measures only productivity changes *within* sectors and another that measures only changes consequent on structural shifts. The former is constructed by holding the structure of the economy constant and allowing sector productivities to change; the latter, by holding sector productivities constant and allowing the *structure* of the labor force to change. The products of the two indexes should roughly approximate an index of labor productivity drawn up directly from output and labor force data for the entire economy, just as the products of price and output indexes should approximate the appropriate value of an output index.

Table 5 contains indexes drawn up for the period 1840–1900. The output concept involved is net income originating in prices of

Table 5. Indexes of Output Per Worker, 1840–1900 (1870 = 100)[a]

	Index 1	Index 2	Index 3	Index 4
1840	76	91	69	69
1850	73	100	73	71
1860	88	103	91	89
1870	100	100	100	100
1880	121	98	119	116
1890	118	112	132	129
1900	123	115	142	146

[a] *Methods of Construction: Index 1:* Constructed by weighting income originating per worker in each sector with a constant share in workers (the arithmetic mean of the sector's share for all years).

Index 2: Constructed by weighting each sector's share in workers with a constant income originating weight (the arithmetic mean of real income originating per worker in the sector for all years).

Index 3: Product of Indexes 1 and 2.

Index 4: Derived directly from the series on real national income per worker.

1860. (We were unable to produce adequate deflated labor income series.) Three broad sectors are distinguished: agriculture, industry (manufacturing, mining, and construction) and "all other." Consequently, the impact (on productivity) of labor force shifts among all three sectors is measured. Index 1 measures changes in productivity arising *within* sectors; Index 2, changes deriving from shifts in sectoral weights. Index 3 is the product of Indexes 1 and 2, while Index 4 rests on direct measurements of national labor productivity. Indexes 3 and 4 are very similar, as they should be.

Indexes 1 and 2 record changes in productivity that sum to a total of 71 points, of which Index 1 accounts for 47 and Index 2 for 24. The suggestion is that about one third of aggregate productivity change can be accounted for by sectoral shifts.

V

We turn now to final product flows, beginning with the distribution of national product between investment and consumption and treating first the share of national product invested. Table 6 contains the relevant evidence, which displays a number of features worth noticing.

First, the share of capital formation in gross national product (GNP) rose during the nineteenth century, but has since shown no long-term tendency to change. These findings emerge from both the current and constant price series and from both the GNP I and GNP II series (the latter an unconventional and more inclusive measure than the former), although the timing, duration, and magnitude of the nineteenth-century increase varies somewhat from series to series. The GNP I concept applied in the nineteenth century is slightly less comprehensive than that used in the twentieth century, but the similarity of the current price ratios for the overlap decade of 1899–1908 suggests that the differences may not be very important.

Second, during the twentieth century the share of net capital formation in net national product has declined. The divergence between trends of the net and gross investment shares implies, of course, that the share of capital consumption in national product has increased during this century, a development arising out of the retardation of the rate of growth of capital formation and the changing

Table 6. Shares of Capital Formation in National Product, 1834-1843 to 1946-1955, Current and Constant Prices (Per Cent)[a]

	CURRENT PRICES		CONSTANT PRICES		
	GNP I	NNP	GNP I	GNP II	NNP
			1860 Prices		
1834–1843	[13]		9	16	
1838–1848	[10]		11	14	
1844–1853	[11]		13	14	
1849–1858	[15]		14	16	
1854–1863	[13]		—	—	
1869–1878	17		22	24	
1879–1888	19		22	23	
1889–1898	22		28	28	
1899–1908	21		28	28	
			1929 Prices		
1899–1908	23	14	24		15
1909–1918	22	12	23		13
1919–1928	22	12	22		11
1929–1938	16	3	15		2
1939–1948	22	7	20		7
1946–1955	24	7	20		6

[a] The figures in brackets are single-year estimates for 1839, 1844, 1849, 1854, and 1859. The Gallman estimates (1834–43 through 1899–1908) exclude changes in inventories. In other respects, GNP I is the conventional N.B.E.R. concept.

GNP II includes the value of improvements to farmlands made with farm construction materials and value added by home manufacturing.

structure of the capital stocks [*10*, pp. 173, 174]. Retardation is a phenomenon of the twentieth century; during the nineteenth century the rate of growth of capital formation displayed no pronounced tendency to fall. The structure of the capital stock did shift in such a way as to increase the relative importance of capital consumption. Nonetheless, there seems to be little doubt that this development was insufficiently strong to counter-balance the upward movement of the gross investment ratio. We can be quite sure that the ratio of net investment to net national product rose [*4*, pp. 13–15].

An increase in the net ratio, unaccompanied by an increase in the rate of growth of national product, implies a rise in the incremental capital-product ratio; a persistent, long-term increase in the ratio (constant prices) implies a rising aggregate capital-product ratio. We may ask, then, whether our finding relating to the trend of the net investment ratio in the nineteenth century is borne out by the direct evidence of the capital-product ratio.

Column 2 of Table 7 represents an effort to answer this question. It contains ratios of

the fixed reproducible capital stock to constant price gross national product (GNP I). The capital stock data exclude inventories, but since the basic investment series also exclude changes in the value of inventories there is no inconsistency here between the two lines of evidence. The capital stock data include capital domiciled in the U.S., wherever owned, whereas the investment rate series are adjusted for changes in claims against foreigners. However, the adjustment has little quantitative significance and the investment rate before this adjustment behaves almost exactly as it does after the adjustment [*4*, p. 11]. Finally, we should ideally have the ratio of capital to net national product, rather than to gross national product. But, again, the matter is unimportant.

The data show a very clear, pronounced, and persistent rise in the capital-product ratio from 1840 to 1890. Column 1 contains estimates in current prices, somewhat more reliable figures. The same general pattern, somewhat more regular, comes through here as well.

The data of columns 3–5 are designed to account for the findings of column 1, in terms

Table 7. Ratios of Fixed Reproducible Capital to Product and Income, 1840–1900, Current and Constant Prices

| | CAPITAL TO GNP | | CAPITAL TO INCOME ORIGINATING CURRENT PRICES | | |
	Current Prices (1)	Prices of 1860 (2)	Agriculture (3)	Mining and Manufacturing (4)	All Other (5)
1840	1.0	.7	1.2	.9	.9
1850	1.0	1.0	1.6	.9	1.1
1860	1.3	1.4	1.7	.9	1.6
1870	1.4	1.6	1.5	1.0	1.7
1880	1.5	1.5	1.6	1.2	1.9
1890	2.1	2.1	1.9	1.3	3.0
1900	2.1	2.1	2.1	1.5	2.9

of developments within sectors and the changing sectoral composition of the economy. The data of Tables 1 and 2 have shown that the principal sectoral change in the composition of national income had to do with the relative positions of agriculture and industry. According to the data in Table 7 the capital-income ratio in industry was persistently lower than the ratio in agriculture. Therefore, the chief sectoral change in the distribution of national income we have discussed increased the weight of a sector with a low ratio and operated in the direction of *lowering* the national capital-income ratio.

This, at least, is the direct effect. The indirect effect is quite a different matter. The rising national capital-product ratio is a consequence of increases in the sectoral ratios. But these developments cannot be understood as independent of the process of industrialization. The most dramatic sectoral change lies in the heterogeneous "all other" sector. But the data in Table 8 allow us to surmise that this movement reflects the railroad-building epic, inextricably bound to the process of industrialization.

The ratios of the other two sectors move within narrower bounds. For agriculture there may be an upward movement between 1840 and 1850, although little significance can be given to so limited a change computed from single-year estimates.[3] Then there are no significant changes for four benchmark

years, followed by a rise at the end of the century. But Tostlebe's constant price series does not record this increase and, indeed, suggests no very pronounced trend to the present [*10*, p. 205]. The industrial data show no change before the Civil War, followed by a very marked increase, an increase also appearing in the work of Creamer, Dobrovolsky, and Bornstein [*1*, p. 209].

Of course the strength of the upward movement of the "all other" ratio may be overstated. If, as we have previously suggested, the income of this sector is overstated for the earlier years then the ratio is *understated* for these years. Nonetheless, one cannot easily put aside the impression that the "all other" sector dominates the pattern of change and that, within the sector, it is the railroads that govern developments.

VI

As we have seen, the share of net capital formation in net national product rose markedly during the nineteenth century and then

[3] The denominator of the ratio is very much more sensitive to changing crop conditions, the business cycle, and other transitory phenomena than is the numerator. Therefore the ratio can change markedly from year to year and one must interpret such movements cautiously.

Table 8. Distribution of Fixed Reproducible Capital among Components of the "All Other" Sector, 1840–1900, Current Prices (Per Cent)

	Non-Farm Residences	Railroads	All Remaining
1840	51	9	40
1850	50	14	36
1860	50	20	30
1870	50	27	24
1880	46	32	22
1890	49	28	23
1900	47	26	26

Table 9. Composition of Goods Flowing to Consumers, 1839–1953, Current and Constant Prices (Per Cent)

	Perishables	Semidurables	Durables	Services
	CURRENT PRICES			
1839–1858	51	16	5	27
1869–1898	49	17	7	27
1899–1918	44	16	8	31
1919–1938	39	16	10	35
1939–1953	44	16	10	30
	1860 Prices			
1839–1858	54	14	5	27
1869–1898	51	17	10	22
	1929 Prices			
1899–1918	43	17	9	31
1919–1938	40	15	10	35
1939–1953	44	13	10	33

fell during the twentieth. Of course the share of consumption in national product followed an inverse path. We may now consider what happened to the composition of consumption. Table 9 contains the evidence we need.

The most striking feature of Table 9 is the stability displayed by the pattern of consumption. The current price estimates show that the share of durables in the totals rose strongly between the pre-Civil War period and the third and fourth decades of the present century. The share of services also increased somewhat, and it is possible that this movement was, in fact, stronger than the data in the table indicate. On the other hand, the share of perishables declined.

In constant prices the pattern displays somewhat more variability over time, but no new strong trends emerge. In fact, the increase in the relative importance of durables appears now to be compressed into a shorter time span, although one cannot be certain of this since the price bases for the two centuries are different. In constant prices the share of semidurables rises in the nineteenth century and falls in the twentieth, although neither movement is very pronounced. The curious behavior of the share of services during the nineteenth century may reflect no more than the inadequacies of the underlying estimates.

On the whole the changes are in the direction one might have expected, reasoning from the Engel curve. It is the magnitude of the changes that is a little surprising. The period

we are dealing with is one of pronounced growth, during which the pattern of life changed in important ways. We have seen, for example, that agriculture declined and industry advanced prominently in relative importance. Why are not these developments reflected in some way in the pattern of consumption?

Two related explanations may be advanced. First, the table deals only with broad aggregates. The details of these aggregates surely changed in important ways. (One need only imagine the elements composing the durables group, for example, in the pre-Civil War period and compare them with modern durables to accept this view.) On the other hand, analysis in terms of broad aggregates is a reasonable process. The pre-Civil War durables may have differed from those in use today, but they did perform essentially the same kinds of functions. Table 9 should be viewed in this context. More detailed statements should be cast in a functional framework.

Second, and perhaps more important, the histories of production of individual consumption goods are quite different at different points in time. For example, a large fraction of the food consumed in the United States before the Civil War was acquired by the consumer in raw or slightly processed form, often from local sources. Indeed, many consumers supplied themselves with food from their own farms. The process of growth since then has dramatically reduced the fraction of the population having access to such food sources. City-dwellers and those in the suburbs are supplied from a distance and acquire foods heavily processed by the manufacturing sectors. Even individual farmers depend very much less on their own production than formerly. These developments help to account for the fact that, while the share of agriculture in the national product has declined precipitously over time (Tables 1 and 2), the share of perishables in consumption has dropped very little. A consumer buying foodstuffs today buys not only goods produced by farmers, but processing supplied by manufacturers, transportation, and the services of wholesalers, retailers, and financiers. The relative stability of the share of perishables in consumption reflects the altered character of the production process.

VII

The preceding sections have described in quantitative terms the chaginng composition of the American economy since early in the nineteenth century, a period of rapid growth dominated by the process of industrialization. They contain an account of trends in the relative importance of industrial sectors of the economy, measured in terms of income generated by these sectors, and trends in the relationships among inputs and income. The theme connecting these sections has been the theme of industrialization. All of the structural changes emerged from the process of industrialization and are related, one to the other, through this process.

APPENDIX I

The purpose of this appendix is to show how far the results of the paper would have been affected had we employed somewhat different concepts and data series.

Table A1 allows the reader to compare the series in text Table 1 (shown here in lines 1–4) with alternative series. Lines 5 and 6 show the distribution of income originating in

Table A1. Shares of Agriculture and Industry in Value Added by and Income Originating in Agriculture and Industry, 1839–1949, Current and Constant Prices (Per Cent)

	1839	1849	1859	1869	1879	1889	1899	1909	1919	1929	1939	1949
I. Variant I												
Shares in value added:												
Current prices												
Agriculture	71	61	62	57	53	39	37	38	35	24	23[a]	23[b]
Industry	29	39	38	43	47	61	63	62	65	76	77[a]	77[b]
Constant prices												
Agriculture	78	64	61	57	53	41	35	26	22	17	19	16
Industry	22	36	39	43	47	59	65	74	78	83	81	84
Shares in income originating:												
Current prices												
Agriculture									37	27	26[a]	
Industry									63	73	74[a]	
II. Variant II												
Shares in value added:												
Current prices												
Agriculture	66	57	58	50	49	35	34					
Industry	34	43	42	50	51	65	66					
III. Variant III												
Shares in value added:												
Current prices												
Agriculture	70				51		35					
Industry	30				49		65					
IV. Variant IV												
Shares in value added:												
Current prices												
Agriculture	72				52		35					
Industry	28				48		65					

[a] 1937
[b] 1947

commodity production between agriculture and industry. The value added concept underlies the measurements of Variants II, III, and IV (lines 7–12). However, each variant refers to a more comprehensive conception of economic activity than does the one preceding it. In Variant II, "industry" includes construction, as well as mining and manufacturing, the two industries included in the Variant I industry sector. Variant III is identical with Variant II, except that a rough set of estimates of income earned by the agricultural sector from firewood production have been added to the Variant III agricultural sector. In Variant IV the value of farm improvements (land clearing, fencing, shed construction, etc.) carried out by farm labor is also added to the agricultural sector.

All of the series show roughly the same levels and trends. We may conclude, then, that the findings discussed in the text are not very sensitive to the concept selected and are, therefore, quite secure.

APPENDIX II (Table and Source Notes)

TABLE 1

Current prices, 1839–1899: Derived from [*3*, pp. 46–48, 54, 56]. The value of forest products, improvements to farmland made by farm labor, and home manufactures are omitted from value added by agriculture. Industry consists of manufacturing and mining. The 1839 estimate for manufacturing of the source volume ($240 million) has been revised upward (to $250 million) in the light of work underlying [*4*]. See [*4*, p. 47].

Constant prices, 1839–1899: Same source. The prices are prices of 1879. The 1839 estimate for manufacturing is $198 million. (See the preceding note.)

Current prices, 1909–1949: Derived from extrapolation of the data underlying the 1899 estimates. The extrapolating series were taken from [*12*, p. 24; *13*, pp. 283 (series K-125), 409 (series P-8); *1*, p. 315]. The extrapolating series for agriculture is gross income, for mining, the value of output. No allowance is made for twentieth-century changes in the share of value added in gross income (agriculture) or value of output (mining). The mining figure for 1947, in fact, refers to 1948. The various components of the extrapolating

series are not fully comparable. See the cited sources.

Constant prices, 1909–1949: Derived from data underlying [*3*, p. 19].

TABLE 2

1839–1899: National income was obtained by extrapolation on gross national product, the latter taken from worksheets underlying [*4*, p. 26]. The extrapolating ratio (.8884) was derived by dividing average net national product, 1899–1908, by average gross national product for the same decade [*4*, p. 26]. The net national product estimate is from [*10*, p. 520 (Variant I)]. The concepts involved are National Bureau of Economic Research concepts; hence the aggregate, net national product, is equivalent to national income. Deflation was accomplished by use of the implicit price index underlying the GNP estimates in [*4*].

Income originating in industry was extrapolated on value added by industry. (See the notes to Table 1.) The extrapolating ratio (.6556) was computed from manufacturing data for the years 1923, 1925, 1927, and 1929, taken from [*13*, p. 409, (Series P-8) and *7*, pp. 310, 311]. Additional available data for the years 1919, 1921, 1931, 1933, 1935, and 1937 were not used because the ratios in these years were affected by conditions which did not exist in the nineteenth-century years to which the extrapolation was to be carried (reconversion from war, 1919; unusually deep or prolonged depression, 1921, 1931, 1933) or because the value added data were not entirely comparable with the nineteenth century value added data. (1935, 1937. See the source.) Had we used these data, however, the extrapolating ratio would not have been much different (roughly, .622).

Manufacturing data alone were used since adequate mining and construction data were not available. We did compute a mining ratio for 1919 (.7215) and it was very close to the manufacturing ratio for that year (.7165), suggesting that the extrapolating ratio used may be adequately representative.

Income originating in agriculture was extrapolated on value added by agriculture (see the notes to Table 1). The extrapolating ratio (.6525) was derived from data in [*7*, pp. 310, 311, and *12*, p. 24] for the years 1920 through 1929, years in which the ratio varied little. We did not use available data for 1919 and

1930 through 1937, for essentially the reasons given above, in the notes relating to industry. However, had we used these years the ratio would have been only very slightly different (.6540).

Deflation of the agricultural, mining, and manufacturing series was accomplished by use of the value added price indexes in [3, p. 43], shifted to the base 1859 without re-weighting. Deflation of the construction series was accomplished by use of the implicit "gross new construction" price index underlying [4].

1919, 1929a, 1938a: Derived from [7, pp. 310, 311].

1929b, 1940b, 1950, 1955: [8, p. 5].

TABLE 3

Columns 1 and 2: [11, p. 119].

Column 3: Column 1, Table 2 divided by column 1, Table 3.

Column 4: Column 2, Table 2 divided by column 2, Table 3.

The 1960 entry in columns 3 and 4 relates the 1955 shares in income to the 1960 shares in labor force.

TABLE 4

Columns 1 and 2: Computed from data underlying columns 1 and 2 of Table 2, less estimated property income. Property income was estimated at 8 per cent of all land, improvements, equipment, and inventories used in production. The data on property are from worksheets underlying [6, p. 330]. We assumed that half the inventories of manufactured goods were held by manufacturing firms and half by firms in distribution. The income data relate to census years 1839, 1849, etc., as in Table 2.

Column 3: Column 1, Table 4 divided by column 1, Table 3.

Column 4: Column 2, Table 4 divided by column 2, Table 3.

TABLE 6

[4, pp. 11, 26, 34 and 10, pp. 92, 95 (including military)]. See also the notes to Table 2.

TABLE 7

See the notes to Tables 2 and 4. The product and income estimates relate to census years 1839, 1849, etc.; the capital stock figures, to June 1, 1840, 1850, etc. See [5].

TABLE 8

See the notes to Table 7.

TABLE 9

1839–1899: Derived from [4, p. 18].

1899–1953: Derived from [10, p. 522].

The current price estimates for 1839–1858 are unweighted averages of estimates for 1839, 1844, 1849, 1854, and 1859. All the remaining figures are unweighted averages of estimates relating to decade averages; 1869–1878, 1879–1888, etc. However, the figures for 1939–1953 were computed from overlapping decade averages and, therefore, the overlap years (1944 through 1948) receive double weight in this calculation.

TABLE A1

Variant I: Shares in value added, see the notes to Table 1. Shares in income originating derived from [7, pp. 310, 311].

Variant II: Variant I, with the addition of construction to industry. Value added by construction has been computed by subtracting the value of materials consumed in construction [3, p. 63] from the value of gross new construction [4, p. 38]. Since the value of gross new construction is less than the total value of output of construction, the procedure understates value added by construction. (See the second source cited above.)

Variant III: Variant II, with the addition of firewood to the sources of value added by agriculture. The value of firewood consumed by ultimate consumers was attributed to agriculture [4, pp. 31–33, 56]. Certainly the estimates overstate the value of final product supplied by agriculture. But there are offsets to these overestimates, since we were unable to take into account firewood supplied by agriculture and consumed as intermediate product.

Variant IV: Variant III, with the addition of the value of improvements to farmland made by farm labor to the sources of value added by agriculture. The estimates of value of improvements are decade averages (1834–1843; 1874–1883; 1894–1903) in constant prices [4, p. 35, (Variant I)] inflated by an agricultural index [*3*, p. 43]. They probably overstate the significance of this source of agricultural income. See [*4*, pp. 35, 71–76].

REFERENCES

1. Daniel Creamer, Sergei P. Dobrovolsky, and Israel Bornstein, *Capital in Manufacturing and Mining*, Princeton, Princeton University Press, 1960.
2. Robert E. Gallman, *Value-Added by Agriculture, Mining and Manufacturing in the United States, 1840–1880* (unpublished Ph.D. dissertation, University of Pennsylvania, 1956).
3. Robert E. Gallman, "Commodity Output, 1839–1899," Conference on Research in Income and Wealth, *Trends in the American Economy in the Nineteenth Century* (Studies in Income and Wealth, vol. 24), Princeton, Princeton University Press, 1960, pp. 13–71.
4. Robert E. Gallman, "Gross National Product in the United States, 1834–1909," Conference on Research in Income and Wealth, *Output, Employment, and Productivity in the United States After 1800* (Studies in Income and Wealth, vol. 30), New York, Columbia University Press, 1966, pp. 3–76.
5. Robert E. Gallman, "The Social Distribution of Wealth in the United States of America," *Third International Conference of Economic History*, Paris, Mouton, 1968, pp. 313–334.
6. Robert E. Gallman and Edward S. Howle, *Fixed Reproducible Capital in the United States, 1840–1900* (unpublished paper presented to the Purdue University Seminar on the Application of Economic Theory and Quantitative Techniques to Problems of Economic History, February, 1965).
7. Simon Kuznets, *National Income and Its Composition, 1919–1938*, New York, National Bureau of Economic Research, 1954.
8. Simon Kuznets, "Quantitative Aspects of the Economic Growth of Nations: Industrial Distribution of Income and Labor Force by States, United States, 1919–21 to 1955," *Economic Development and Cultural Change*, 6 (July, 1958), Part II.
9. Simon Kuznets, *Six Lectures on Economic Growth*, Glencoe, Free Press, 1959.
10. Simon Kuznets, *Capital in the American Economy*, Princeton, Princeton University Press, 1961.
11. Stanley Lebergott, "Labor Force and Employment, 1800–1960," Conference on Research in Income and Wealth, *Output, Employment, and Productivity in the United States After 1800* (Studies in Income and Wealth, vol. 30), New York, Columbia University Press, 1966, pp. 117–204.
12. Frederick Strauss and Louis H. Bean, *Gross Farm Income and Indices of Farm Production and Prices in the United States 1869–1937*, Technical Bulletin No. 703, Washington, D.C., Department of Agriculture, 1940.
13. United States Bureau of the Census, *Historical Statistics of the United States, Colonial Times to 1957*, Washington, D.C., 1960.

4 REGIONAL INCOME TRENDS, 1840-1950

Richard A. Easterlin

Any social change affects some groups in the population more than others, and economic development is no exception. At a point in time the opportunities that constitute the avenues of economic growth take quite specific forms, and certain groups in the population are more favorably situated for realizing these opportunities than others.

In the present chapter we examine the differential impact of economic growth on the population when subdivided by region. We wish to know whether economic growth proceeded fairly uniformly in all parts of the country or whether some areas led and others lagged, implying that the participation of different regions in the fruits of economic progress was unequal. If there were "leaders" and "laggards," were there any significant

Reprinted with omissions by permission from Seymour Harris, ed., *American Economic History*, New York, McGraw-Hill, 1961, pp. 525–547.

Figure 1. Regions and geographical divisions of the continental United States as defined by the Bureau of the Census. The groups of states in the present study are the same as those of the census, except that Delaware and Maryland are included with the Middle Atlantic division, and the District of Columbia is excluded.

changes in the identity of the regions which assumed this role? Finally, we wish to consider the processes that give rise to regional differentials in the rate of growth and to see if we can identify these at work in United States' development.

The regional classification is indicated in Figure 1. Inevitably, grouping states into larger regional aggregates leads to some distortion of reality, since there are individual cases which depart significantly from the typical regional pattern. We would find this to be so, for example, if we considered Florida separately from the rest of the South Atlantic region, or Utah or New Mexico separately from the Mountain region. But in order to bring our discussion within manageable bounds, aggregation into regions is essential.

Our time span reaches back over a century to 1840, when the level of development in the United States was much lower than today —indeed, less than one sixth, according to a comparison of the average income of the population then and today. We consider first the historical record of regional growth differentials and then turn to the question of interpretation. (See also [1].)

I

THE RECORD

The Situation in 1840

To provide a base for consideration of subsequent trends, it is necessary first to establish the nature of regional differences in economic development in 1840. Of the many possible indicators of the degree of development of an area, per capita income, because of its comprehensiveness, is perhaps the best. Since we are interested in comparison, we work with *relative* rather than absolute per capita income. Thus each entry in Table 1 was obtained by dividing the regional per capita income figure by the national average for the indicated date. For example, the table shows that in 1840 per capita income in New England was 132 per cent of the national average; in the Middle Atlantic division, 136 per cent of the average; and so on.

The 1840 pattern is readily summarized. The principal high-income region was the Northeast, where average incomes were as much as a third or more above the average. In the other two principal sections, the vast agricultural areas of the South and of the

Table 1. Personal Income Per Capita in Each Region as Percentage of United States' Average, 1840–1950

Regions[a]	1840	1860	1880	1900	1920[b]	1930[b]	1940[b]	1950[b]
United States	100	100	100	100	100	100	100	100
Northeast	**135**	**139**	**141**	**137**	**132**	**138**	**124**	**115**
New England	132	143	141	134	124	129	121	109
Middle Atlantic	136	137	141	139	134	140	124	116
North Central	**68**	**68**	**98**	**103**	**100**	**101**	**103**	**106**
East North Central	67	69	102	106	108	111	112	112
West North Central	75	66	90	97	87	82	84	94
South	**76**	**72**	**51**	**51**	**62**	**55**	**65**	**73**
South Atlantic	70	65	45	45	59	56	69	74
East South Central	73	68	51	49	52	48	55	62
West South Central	144	115	60	61	72	61	70	80
West			**190**	**163**	**122**	**115**	**125**	**114**
Mountain			168	139	100	83	92	96
Pacific			204	163	135	130	138	121

[a] At each date, states included in regions are the same as those shown in Figure 1, except as follows:
Middle Atlantic:
   All dates: Delaware and Maryland included.
West North Central:
   1840: Minnesota, North and South Dakota, Nebraska, and Kansas excluded.
   1860: North and South Dakota excluded.
South Atlantic:
   All dates: Delaware, Maryland, and the District of Columbia excluded.
West South Central:
   1840: Oklahoma and Texas excluded

1860: Oklahoma excluded. Texas excluded from Table 1 only.
   1880: Oklahoma excluded
Mountain:
   1860: Montana, Idaho, Wyoming, and Arizona excluded.
[b] For the last four dates the personal income figure used in computing per capita income was an average over the period of a business cycle, as follows:
   1920: average of 1919–1921
   1930: average of 1927–1932
   1940: average of 1937–1944
   1950: average of 1948–1953

North Central region (remember, the frontier had only recently been pushed across the Mississippi), income per capita was typically substantially below the average, by from a quarter to a third. A surprising exception occurs in the case of the West South Central area, which had the highest income level of any division. This apparent anomaly is explained by the fact that the regional figure reflects very largely the situation in Louisiana (which accounted for over 75 per cent of the division's population in 1840), where both commerce and agriculture were thriving as a result of the growing flow of trade down the Mississippi and a highly prosperous sugarcane production based on slavery.

The income averages for the Southern division include, of course, the slave population. If the slaves and their income (estimated at subsistence) are eliminated, one finds that the income of the white population in the South exceeded the national average and compared favorably with that in the Northeast [*1*, p. 92]. For the white population alone, then, it was only in the North Central region

that average income was below the national level.

Trends in Relative Per Capita Income, 1840-1950

A special advantage of relative per capita income figures is that they show at a glance whether income in a particular region was growing more or less rapidly than in the country as a whole. If the regional rate of growth exceeded the national rate, relative per capita income rose; if the regional rate was less than the national rate, relative per capita income fell. Figure 2 brings out this type of comparison even more. In this chart the divisional relative per capita income figures of Table 1 have been plotted. A line that slopes upward, indicating a rise in relative income, denotes a rate of growth faster than the average; a line that slopes downward, a rate of growth below the average. Of course the chart also enables one quickly to determine the high- and low-income regions at each date.

Let us study Table 1 and Figure 2 to see

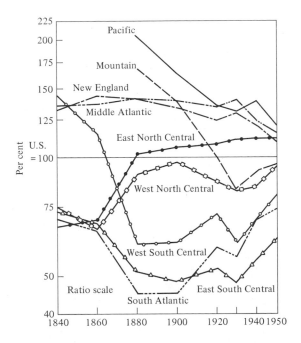

Figure 2. Personal income per capita in each region as percentage of United States' average, 1840-1950.

what we can discover about regional differences in the rate of economic growth. Consider the pre-Civil War period from 1840 to 1860 first. This was the period when industrialization was taking firm hold in the Northeast, agricultural settlement and expansion were in progress in the North Central area, and cotton production in the South's slave economy was continuing to soar in response to the seemingly ever-expanding demands of factories in Europe and the Northeast. How did these and the many other forces that were at work affect the relative growth of per capita income in the various regions?

The first point of note is that the changes in relative per capita income between 1840 and 1860 were rather small by comparison with later movements. Yet the changes that occurred are of interest. Perhaps the most significant is the difference in relative rate of growth between the Northeast and South. The two Northeastern divisions show a rising level of relative per capita income; the three Southern divisions, a declining level. As a result, the income gap between Northeast and South was greater in 1860 than in 1840. This conclusion implies a relative deterioration in the income position not only of the total Southern population but of the favored white population as well. Moreover, as we shall discuss later (see pp. 43–44), it is likely that

the figures understate the widening of the relative income gap. It should be emphasized, however, that our comparison deals only with *relative* income. In absolute terms, per capita income in the South probably rose between 1840 and 1860, and perhaps substantially. So far as they go, then, these figures do not provide much support for the view that slavery was so inimical to continued growth in the South that the institution was doomed to early extinction merely on economic grounds.[1]

The trend for the North Central region during this period was mixed. The East North Central division, which quantitatively was the more important of the two, had a rate of income growth slightly above the national average, while the West North Central section had a rate somewhat lower. It is possible that the lower rate for the West North Central section reflects the inclusion in the 1860 estimate for the region of the new frontier states of Kansas, Nebraska, and Minnesota, and if the rate of growth had been computed only for the states of 1840, Missouri and Iowa, it might compare more favorably with the national trend. But in any event, for the significantly more populous region, the East North Central, there is a clear indication that some improvement was registered by comparison with the national average, although not to the extent attained by New England, the region with the highest rate of growth.

When we move on to 1880, the date for which we have our next observation on regional income levels, some startling changes appear. The exceedingly sharp decline in relative income level in the South is outstanding. Indeed, while the underlying absolute figures are not too reliable, they suggest that not only the relative but the absolute level of per capita income in this area declined between 1860 and 1880 and that the 1880 average may have been little better than that prevailing four decades earlier. This is certainly an impressive memorial of the economic cost to the South of the Civil War and its aftermath.

---

[1] The statements in this paragraph are based on estimates for the three Southern geographic divisions comprising the states specified in Figure 1, except that the West South Central division excludes Oklahoma and Texas (Table 1, note *a*). If these two states were included, the estimates for the West South Central division and total South would be altered, but not those for the South Atlantic and East South Central divisions.

Perhaps equally striking is the addition to the regional comparison of the two new Western divisions, the Mountain and Pacific, at per capita income levels much higher than anywhere else. On the face of it, this comes as a surprise. One might have expected that these new frontier regions of the West would enter with relative income levels substantially below the average, as did the older frontier sections in the North Central region. But as one looks into the underlying situation, some good reasons appear for the much different pattern. For one thing, unlike the older frontier areas, the labor force in these regions was preponderantly engaged in nonagricultural activities, centering in large part around mining, rather than in agriculture. Indeed, in 1880 the percentage of the labor force in nonagricultural industry in the two Western divisions was not much below that in the Northeastern (see Table 7 below). Since average income from nonagricultural activities is typically much higher than in agriculture, this in itself would contribute to a higher income level, even if there were no income differences between the West and North Central regions within agriculture or within nonagricultural industry. A second important difference was the much higher ratio of workers to dependents in the West than in the North Central (or any other) region. In the West in 1880 this ratio was over 40 per cent above the national average. This difference in large part stems from the preceding one, for where mining is the major attraction instead of agriculture, migration tends to be predominantly male, rather than including whole families. This difference in the ratio of workers to dependents would clearly raise income per capita in the West relative to other regions, even if income per worker were the same everywhere, since a worker's income would have to be divided among fewer dependents. These two facts—the high proportion of the labor force in nonagricultural industry and the high ratio of workers to dependents—in themselves would have made for very high income levels in the West. But this tendency was even further reinforced by higher than average income levels in this region in both agriculture and nonagricultural industry.

Finally, in noting the more significant changes in regional income differences between 1860 and 1880, we should mention the marked improvement in relative income level in the North Central area. Both subdivisions show a very high rate of growth between 1860 and 1880 compared with the national average, and by the latter date the level in the East North Central section had actually risen slightly above the nationwide average. These trends reflect, among other things, the progressive passing of this area from the frontier stage of agriculture to highly productive commercial exploitation—in a sense, a realization of the promise that lured so many to the area. And they reflect to some extent the beginning of major nonagricultural development, chiefly in the East North Central division.

Despite the improvement in relative income levels in the North Central section, this area was still far short of the Northeastern region, where the rate of growth between 1860 and 1880, while less than in the North Central, was still about equal to the national rate. But because of the addition of the exceptionally high income regions of the West to the ranking, the Northeastern divisions were no longer the leaders. Thus the broad outline of regional income differentials that had been established by 1880 was, from high to low, West, Northeast, North Central, South.

It is this ranking which prevailed in most major respects down to the present. Perhaps the only really important difference that the 1950 figures reveal is the noticeable deterioration in relative income standing of the Mountain region. Rather than being one of the leaders as in 1880, this region had fallen below the two Northeastern divisions and even below one of the North Central divisions. But generally speaking, over the past seventy years, and in marked contrast to the preceding forty, the rankings of the various regions by per capita income level were remarkably stable.

This is not to say, however, that regional rates of growth of per capita income were the same during this period. On the contrary, instead of showing a horizontal trend, the lines in Figure 2 show a pronounced tendency to converge over time. This means that, on an average, the high-income areas experienced a rate of growth less than the national rate, while the low-income areas had a higher rate of growth. However, this tendency was not a smooth one from one period to the next. For example, an upward movement in the South did not get noticeably under way until 1900, and between 1920 and 1930 in most regions there was quite clearly a significant break in the trend. But the basic tendency toward convergence is unmistakable. As a result, while the order of regions by per capita income level in 1950 was much the same as 1880, the magnitude of the regional differences was much less. Indeed, if we were to look back into the underlying figures for individual states, we would find that regional income differences today are less than for any date in the past 110 years for which we have data.

Before leaving the trends since 1880, some interesting disparities in patterns within the major regions deserve mention. In the Northeast, the decline in relative income level set in earlier and was more pronounced in New England than in the Middle Atlantic division. In the North Central region, the East North Central division had a stronger and more persistent pattern of relative income growth than the West North Central. Finally, in the South, the South Atlantic division, which had the highest average rate of growth, rather than lying below the East South Central as in 1880, was noticeably higher in 1950, although still somewhat short of the West South Central.

Absolute Income per Capita

As was emphasized, the concern in the preceding discussion was with trends in *relative* income per capita, not the absolute level of income. Because of data deficiencies we can speak with much less certainty of the latter, but one thing is sure: Over the period as a whole, absolute levels of income rose in all divisions, and the increase was substantial in every case. Even in the shorter twenty-year periods typically covered by the data, the general tendency was almost always upward, the only important exception being the decline in the South between 1860 and 1880 noted earlier. This conclusion is an exceedingly important one, for it means that all areas did gain substantially over the long run from national economic development, even if the extent of gain differed considerably from one division to the other and from one period to the next.

Some Qualifications

Quantitative series are at best imperfect historical records. We have noted in passing a few of the cautions, conceptual or statistical, to be observed in interpreting the figures. It is time to mention some of the more important remaining ones.

First, the regional income figures for 1840 and 1860 were estimated from data relating only to commodity production (and, in the case of 1840, commodity distribution), although it should be noted that this type of economic activity provided the preponderant share of income in that period, accounting roughly for six tenths. An attempt was made on the basis of our knowledge of the relationships prevailing at later dates to adjust the regional income differences to allow for the omission of income from service activities, such as finance and real estate, personal and professional service, and government. But this adjustment did not allow for the growth in the relative importance of such activities between 1840 and 1860. Here, because of the important concentration of these activities in the Northeast, the probable result is that the figures understate to some extent the growth in per capita income in the Northeast relative to the rest of the nation between these two dates.

A second qualification is that the estimates at all dates do not allow for regional differences in the level or trend of the cost of living. Strictly speaking, therefore, they relate only to money-income differences rather than real-income differences. It is likely that the cost of living was generally somewhat lower in the South so that adjustment for this would improve the relative position of that region to some extent, although, according to calculations based on the very limited information available, not sufficiently to alter the major patterns discussed above. Also, the cost of living in the West in the latter part of the nineteenth century was probably somewhat above the national average, and adjustment for this would lower the income advantage shown by that region. But there is reason to believe that the principal outlines of the patterns shown would remain.

The estimates do include an allowance for certain forms of income "in kind," such as food and fuel produced and consumed on farms and the services of owner-occupied dwellings. However, certain types, such as household manufactures and farm improvements, are omitted, and this would tend to have some distorting effect on the figures for the earlier dates, although from the point of view of the questions with which we are concerned, probably not a major one.

Finally, there are the usual cautions against equating income changes wholly with changes in economic well-being. For example, the estimates do not reveal differences among regions in the level or trend of the distribution of income between rich and poor. They take no account of the growth of leisure. They are not adjusted to allow for the changing monotony, frustration, and insecurity in the income-getting process. Thus while the figures are perhaps very broad indicators of regional differences in the growth of economic welfare —so far as this depends on commodities and services—excessive reliance cannot be put upon them for this purpose.

In short, the tenor of these remarks is that the estimates are probably sufficiently good to reveal the major trends in regional differences in income levels but not so good that minor differences can be considered particularly significant.

Regional Shares in Total Income

The national income has often been likened to a pie which is divided among the various members of the nation. One way of looking at this process of distribution is to consider the regional shares, for example, whether the Northeast gets a bigger cut than the South and whether its piece increased in the course of economic development.

In part, the trend in a region's share in total income depends on the trend in relative per capita income. But it depends also on the change in the region's share of national population. Thus if a given region's share in the total population remains constant, an increase in relative per capita income will raise its share of total income. Similarly, if relative per capita income is unchanged, a rise in the regional share in population will lead to an increased share in total income.

Tables 2 and 3 provide the additional information that we need to study this problem. Table 2, which shows the regional shares in the national total of income at various dates, indicates that at the present the Northeast and North Central regions each get somewhat in excess of three tenths of the "pie," the South gets somewhat more than two tenths, and the West the remainder. This is in sharp contrast to the situation in 1840, when the Northeast accounted for nearly six tenths of the total by itself, the South for almost another three tenths, the North Central section for a little more than a tenth, and the undeveloped West for virtually nothing.

The general pattern of income redistribution—the rise in the shares of the North Central and Western regions at the expense of the Northeast and South—reflects in large part the redistribution of population, as Table 3 shows. But in particular instances the trend in relative per capita income played a significant part. Thus, even if its 1840 population share had remained constant, the income share of New England would have declined from 17 to 11 per cent by 1950, while if the 1840 population share of the North Central region had not changed, its income share would still have risen from around 13 to 22 per cent.

The trend in the income share of the South deserves special mention since, unlike the pattern for most other regions, it shows a significant reversal. In the first part of our period, to the latter part of the nineteenth century, the income share of the South drops sharply, indeed by almost one half. But in the twentieth century, and particularly since

Table 2. Per Cent Distribution of Personal Income by Region, 1840–1950

Region	1840	1860	1880	1900	1920	1930	1940	1950
United States	100	100	100	100	100	100	100	100
Northeast	**58**	**50**	**44**	**41**	**39**	**41**	**36**	**32**
New England	17	14	11	10	9	9	8	7
Middle Atlantic	41	36	33	31	30	32	28	25
North Central	**13**	**20**	**34**	**36**	**32**	**32**	**31**	**32**
East North Central	12	15	23	22	22	23	23	23
West North Central	2	4	11	13	10	9	8	9
South	**29**	**26**	**15**	**15**	**18**	**16**	**20**	**21**
South Atlantic	14	9	6	5	7	6	8	9
East South Central	11	9	6	5	4	4	4	5
West South Central	4	8	4	5	7	6	7	8
West		**4**	**7**	**8**	**10**	**11**	**14**	**15**
Mountain			2	3	3	3	3	3
Pacific			4	5	7	9	11	12

Table 3. Per Cent Distribution of Population by Region, 1840–1950

Region	1840	1860	1880	1900	1920	1930	1940	1950
United States	100	100	100	100	100	100	100	100
Northeast	**43**	**36**	**31**	**30**	**30**	**30**	**29**	**28**
New England	13	10	8	7	7	7	6	6
Middle Atlantic	30	26	23	22	22	23	22	22
North Central	**20**	**29**	**35**	**35**	**32**	**32**	**30**	**30**
East North Central	17	22	22	21	21	21	20	20
West North Central	2	7	12	14	12	11	10	9
South	**37**	**33**	**31**	**30**	**29**	**29**	**30**	**29**
South Atlantic	20	14	13	12	11	11	12	12
East South Central	15	13	11	10	8	8	8	8
West South Central	3	6	7	9	10	10	10	10
West		**2**	**4**	**5**	**9**	**10**	**11**	**13**
Mountain			1	2	3	3	3	3
Pacific			2	3	5	7	8	10

1930, a marked recovery is apparent, despite a virtually constant proportion of the national population. Only one other area, the West North Central, shows a reversal in trend— in this case a peak in 1900 followed by subsequent decline.

II

THE UNDERLYING FACTORS

A Theoretical Framework

In seeking to explain the course of per capita income differences among regions, it is convenient to distinguish between static and dynamic processes. The former may be illustrated by considering the long-run tendencies that would prevail in a stationary economy, one in which product demands were unchanging, factor supplies fixed, and technology constant. In such an economy any initial differences among regions in per capita income would tend to be eliminated by movements of productive factors and goods. Labor would tend to move to higher-wage areas until wage levels were equalized. Even in the absence of labor mobility, capital flows would enhance the redistribution of industry arising from differences in factor prices and thus strengthen the tendency toward elimination of such differences. Finally, whether resource flows were possible or not, free trade among regions would work in the same direction, since product prices would tend to be equalized and through this factor prices, too. This is not to suggest that regional income levels would necessarily become equal. Certain

areas might hold a monopoly on particular productive factors, or the amount of property owned per capita might be exceptionally high. Moreover, in the short run, the resource or product movements might be accompanied by changes that would temporarily widen income differences. Thus the opening of trade might affect adversely certain industries in a particular area, and out-migration might cause a decline in the proportion of workers to dependents in the population. But the essential point is that given sufficient time for adjustment, the basic tendency of the static processes would be toward convergence of income levels.

When one adds dynamic considerations to the picture, however, the conclusion becomes less certain. For the basic characteristic of a developing economy is that product demands, factor supplies, and technology are not fixed. Rather, new goods and new techniques are constantly being developed, consumption patterns are shifting, certain natural resources are being used up while others are discovered or developed, the structure of transfer costs is being modified, rates of natural population increase are changing, and so on. All these tend to alter the geographic structure of costs and prices and thus the investment opportunities in different parts of the economy. In consequence, relative factor demands and supplies in the various areas and, as a result, relative income levels, are constantly changing. But free economic forces are not the only factors at work. As we shall see, war has exerted a significant effect. Then, of course, there is the possible influence of government, which may intervene to affect the relative cost structure or, more directly, actually to bring about a redistribution of income from one area to another.

Thus the actual course of regional income levels is the outcome of a complex of factors, exerting differing influences at various times, and it is not surprising that the historical record shows no smooth and unvarying trends. A satisfactory explanation calls for unraveling the relative weight of each of the factors over time, a task beyond the scope of our present discussion. However, it may be possible for us to form a preliminary notion of some of the forces that were particularly important.

1840-1880

Let us break our period into two phases: one of diverging income levels, 1840 to 1880, and one of converging levels, 1880 to 1950. With regard to the former, it is clear that whatever the net influence of economic forces may have been, it was dwarfed by the impact of the Civil War and its aftermath. As shown in Table 1 and Figure 2, the divergence of income levels between 1840 and 1880 is a reflection of the striking deterioration in relative standing of the three Southern divisions, a deterioration very largely concentrated in the interval including the Civil War.

Agriculture was the sector of the Southern economy most severely hit by the war. Between 1840 and 1880 income per worker in agriculture dropped from 91 to 63 per cent of the national level, while in nonagricultural industry the decline was only from 94 to 84 per cent. Table 4, which indicates the per capita level of various inputs and outputs in Southern agriculture in 1870 and 1880 expressed as a percentage of the 1860 value, provides further details and also permits more precise timing of the South's sharp decline. According to the table, in 1880 the per capita level of land and certain livestock inputs in the South was only 85 per cent or less of the 1860 level, and for a number of crop and livestock outputs the level was considerably below 75 per cent. Outside the South, however, the 1880 value for most of these items (leaving aside, of course, those largely or wholly peculiar to the South) was typically above, and often substantially above, the 1860 level. Table 4 also makes clear that most, if not all, of the deterioration was concentrated in the Civil War decade; in only two instances is the 1880 value below

Table 4. Selected Inputs and Outputs Per Capita in Southern Agriculture, 1870 and 1880 as Per Cent of 1860

Inputs and Outputs	1860	1870	1880
Inputs:			
Total land in farms, acres per capita	100	77	70
Improved land in farms, acres per capita	100	82	85
Number of horses on farms per capita	100	78	82
Number of mules and asses on farms per capita	100	72	85
Crops:			
Wheat, bushels per capita	100	70	75
Corn, bushels per capita	100	62	69
Sweet potatoes, bushels per capita	100	43	50
Cotton, bales per capita	100	51	72
Tobacco, pounds per capita	100	52	67
Livestock:			
Number of swine per capita	100	57	61
Milch cows per capita	100	73	74
Meat cattle other than milch cows and working oxen per capita	100	76	73

that of 1870. Typically, agricultural performance improved between 1870 and 1880, but it was far from recovering to the prewar level.

Not all the deterioration, of course, is to be attributed to the destruction of physical capital during the war, although this was undoubtedly important. There was also the problem of disorganization arising from abolition of the slave system and the consequent need to work out new arrangements that would assure a stable and continuous labor supply. Eventually a solution was reached, chiefly in the form of the sharecropping system, but this was a time-consuming process, and in the interim productive operations were severely handicapped.

It is tempting to speculate on the probable course of income in the South had the war been averted. It seems unlikely that much striking deterioration would have occurred, for physical destruction of capital could have been avoided. On the other hand, there was some decline in the South's relative position even prior to the Civil War. Clearly, much would depend on one's assessment of the possibility of a reasonably smooth transition from the slave system to a successor.

1880-1950

The period from 1880 to 1950 provides a somewhat better opportunity to observe the play of economic forces on relative income levels in a developing economy. But even here we should not forget the influence of war (such as the effect of the two World Wars in creating an exceptional labor demand and consequently breaking down some of the social barriers to nonwhite mobility) or governmental action, as in the case of the agricultural price-support program. In the present discussion, however, we concentrate on the major long-term economic changes taking place.

Tables 5 and 6 summarize the pattern of resource mobility during the period. Table 5 is designed to bring out the direction and impact of labor mobility; Table 6, that of capital mobility. The divisions are ranked in terms of the average level of relative per capita income during the period. It can be seen from column 2 of Table 5 that the high-income divisions were typically areas of net in-migration of labor, and the low income, areas of net out-migration. Column 3 of Table 5 shows the rate of natural growth of the male population of working age, that is, of young persons reaching working age less deductions due to mortality and older persons passing beyond working age. Clearly the rate of growth was relatively high in the low-

income regions. In the absence of migration, this would have caused a relatively high rate of growth of labor supply in the low-income regions and made for divergence of income levels, other things being equal. However, when the influence of migration on labor-supply growth is considered (column 4), one finds this tendency eliminated and, if anything, somewhat reversed. For example, as a result of migration, the rate of growth of the male population of working age in the highest-income division, the Pacific, shifts from lowest to highest in the country, while in the lowest-income division, the East South Central, an opposite shift from next to highest to lowest takes place. Moreover, averaging over such a long period tends to obscure the basic relationships, and a study of the data for individual subperiods serves on the whole further to strengthen this conclusion. It appears, then, that the influence of labor mobility was not only in the direction that economic analysis would suggest, but that its magnitude was such as actually to produce some tendency toward convergence of regional income levels.

Table 6 provides similar information on capital mobility. The underlying estimates are less reliable than those for labor, are based on nonagricultural industry only, and are for only the four major regions for the period 1880 to 1920. Because of the limitation to four regions the interregional flow of capital

Table 5. Average Value of Relative Per Capita Income and Average Decade Rate of Net In-Migration, Natural Increase, and Total Increase of Males, Ages 15–64, by Region, 1880–1950

Division	Personal Income Per Capita Per Cent of United States Average (1)	MALES, AGES 15–64, PER CENT PER DECADE		
		Rate of Net In-Migration (2)	Rate of Natural Increase (3)	Rate of Total Increase (4)
Pacific	153	30	2	33
Middle Atlantic	134	7	9	16
New England	128	6	6	12
Mountain	119	15	9	24
East North Central	108	4	11	15
West North Central	90	−1	12	12
West South Central	66	4	19	22
South Atlantic	56	−4	21	17
East South Central	52	−7	19	12
Average:				
Highest four	134	15	7	21
Lowest four	66	−2	18	16

Table 6. Average Decade Rate of Net Capital Imports for Nonagricultural Industry and of Hypothetical and Actual Increase in Nonagricultural Capital Stock, by Region, 1880–1920

Region	Rate of Net Capital Imports (1)	RATE OF INCREASE IN CAPITAL STOCK, PER CENT PER DECADE	
		Hypothetical[a] (2)	Actual (3)
West	5	43	48
East	−8	38	30
North Central	7	28	35
South	9	30	39

[a] Assumes domestic savings of each region are invested entirely within region.

is understated. Nevertheless, some important features are apparent. If we leave aside the West for a moment, it appears that capital flowed on balance from the high-income East to the North Central and Southern regions. Moreover, if one takes the entries in columns 2 and 3 as substantially independent, the effect of the flow was to alter noticeably the relative rates of capital growth in the regions. In the absence of capital flows, capital invested in the East would have grown faster than in the South or North Central regions (column 2). But when allowance is made for the movement that occurred, the rate of growth is highest in the South and lowest in the East (column 3). It is noteworthy, however, that the West, the highest-income region of all, was a capital importer during this period and experienced the highest rate of capital investment of all. The investment opportunities of the West thus provided strong competition with those elsewhere, and the role that capital mobility could play in equalizing income levels through facilitating the redistribution of industry was reduced.

In addition to factor mobility, there is evidence also of the influence of "product mobility," that is, free trade among regions, in contributing to convergence of regional income levels. While no convenient summary measure is available, one may note as an example the shift of resources to labor-intensive textile and furniture production in the South and the countermovement in the Northeast. In parts of the high-labor-cost West, the shift of production toward certain types of land-intensive agriculture is to some extent another case in point. Shifts such as

these arise from the opportunity that free trade provides for entrepreneurs to capitalize on regional differentials in relative factor costs and have the effect of raising the relative demand for labor in the low-income region while lowering it in the high.

Thus the adjustment processes—via shifts of resources between regions or from one line of production to another within regions —which economic analysis suggests would be set in motion by an initial disparity in regional incomes, appear to have operated during the period with which we are concerned. But as noted earlier, in a developing economy such processes are only a part of the story. For dynamic changes in demands, technology, and resource supplies are at work as well. Did these factors tend to benefit the low-income regions more than the high and thus reinforce the tendency toward convergence arising from static processes? Unfortunately, we have no ready answer to this, for little work has been done to analyze systematically the regional impact of dynamic factors. We can, however, consider a few illustrative cases and perhaps in this way derive some idea of the manner in which these forces work. We take examples of differing demand elasticities, changes in technology, resource exhaustion and discovery, and transport developments.

Table 7. Percentage of Labor Force in Nonagricultural Industry in Each Region, 1880 and 1950

Division	1880	1950
Pacific	69	93
Middle Atlantic	75	97
New England	78	97
Mountain	73	83
East North Central	49	92
West North Central	39	76
West South Central	25	82
South Atlantic	26	82
East South Central	23	74

As incomes grow, the demand for nonfood products typically rises faster than that for food, and this creates a pressure for a redistribution of resources from agricultural to nonagricultural industries. This redistribution of resources is a source of income growth in a particular area, since earnings in non-agricultural industry typically exceed those in agriculture; indeed, it is this income differential that induces the redistribution of resources.

In 1880 the proportion of labor force in nonagricultural industry was much greater in the high-income areas than in the low (Table 7). In the ensuing decades, this gap was closed considerably, and this convergence among regions in the proportion of the labor force outside agriculture contributed to convergence of regional incomes. It must be remembered, of course, that a wide variety of factors were at work influencing the industrial structure of various regions and that the categories "agriculture" and "nonagricultural industry" are not homogeneous from one region to another. Nevertheless, it would seem that the differing income elasticity of demand for food and nonfood products, through its tendency to make for convergence of regional industrial structures as income grows, should be counted as one of the factors responsible for the convergence of regional incomes.

An illustration of the impact of technological change on regional development is provided by the changes in technology of iron and steel production during the nineteenth century. Initially the location of coal deposits played a dominant part in the location of iron production. However, as technological advances decreased the importance of coal input relative to iron ore, the location of the industry tended to shift more toward the ore deposits. This was an important factor in the more rapid growth of iron and steel and associated fabricating industries in the East North Central region than Middle Atlantic after 1880.

Possibly even more spectacular than technological change in the production of existing products has been the development of entirely new products. Outstanding examples are the introduction of the automobile, which especially benefited the East North Central division; the airplane, which was of particular advantage to the Pacific; the development of electrical manufactures, which was especially favorable to the Northeast and East North Central areas; and synthetic textiles and petrochemicals, which particularly benefited the South.

An example of resource exhaustion is provided by the forests of the Northeast and East North Central areas. By the end of the nineteenth century, these were relatively depleted, and as a result production shifted to the South and West. On the side of additions to resources there are developments such as the discovery of oil in the Southwest and West and copper in the Mountain region.

From the point of view of regional development, perhaps the most important change in the transportation system after 1880 was the further extension of the railway network. From 1880 to 1920, when the peak was reached, railway mileage in the United States as a whole increased by almost 175 per cent. Regional differences were marked. For the South the growth exceeded 300 per cent, and for the West, 400 per cent, while in the North Central and Northeast, it was less than 125 per cent. Such differences obviously spelled important differences in the development possibilities of the regions.

These are only a few of the dynamic changes that influenced regional income levels in the period since 1880, and any conclusion as to their net effect would obviously be premature. However, it should be noted that in the cases that we have discussed the changes often benefited high-income regions as frequently, if not more frequently, than low. So far as this small sample goes, therefore, there is little indication that dynamic factors systematically made for convergence of regional income levels. An exception, possibly an important one, is the difference in the income elasticity of demand for agricultural versus nonagricultural products.

REFERENCES

1. Richard A. Easterlin, "Interregional Differences in Per Capita Income, Population, and Total Income, 1840–1950." Conference on Research in Income and Wealth, *Trends in the American Economy in the Nineteenth Century* (Studies in Income and Wealth, vol. 24), Princeton, Princeton University Press, 1960, pp. 73–140.

II THE DIVISION OF THE BENEFITS OF GROWTH

Most of the great popular conflicts over economic policy, especially those of the nineteenth century, were focused primarily on issues of equity rather than those of growth. The demand for free silver, for free land, for the regulation of railroad rates, for limiting the concentration of banks, for the ten-hour day, all had as their aim the redistribution of income or wealth away from the "plutocrats of wealth" and to the working man or the small farmer. It is not necessary to resolve here the wisdom of the unions and the farmers' organizations in placing their main emphasis on the division of the national product rather than on its size. The point is that issues of equity were of central concern to common men and continue to be of concern to the historians who have been their biographers. Consequently, an adequate description of the development of the economy requires not merely a knowledge of the level and rate of growth of national income, or national income per capita, but also the determination of the changing share of various classes and groups in the annual product.

It is far more difficult to reconstruct the distribution of income or wealth than to estimate the total amount. Determination of such distributions requires detailed information on the recipients of income, detailed information which is not generally contained in the published census materials from which the national income accounts have been constructed. Consequently, while it has been possible to estimate the level and rate of growth of total and per capita income in agriculture between 1840 and 1900, we do not yet know how income was divided between large and small farms, between landlords and renters, between the self-employed and the hired hands. Similarly, while we have a fairly firm picture of the rate of growth of total and average income in manufacturing during the nineteenth century, the division of this income between labor and capital, and the manner in which the division changed, is still shrouded in mystery.

Recent work on three sources of data suggests that it may be possible to make substantial progress toward the analysis of distributional issues during the next decade. These sources are the manuscript schedules of the censuses of population and agriculture, probate records, and local tax rolls. The manuscript schedules for agriculture are available for the census years of 1840–1880. By combining data on production by farms with available price data, it is possible to obtain estimates of gross income by farms. Such information would permit the construction of distributions of income by farm size, age of household head, nationality, and race. The data in the population schedules provide a basis for constructing similar distributions for total wealth. The probate records contain information on the values of the estates of decedents. Since the dead of any given age group may be considered to be a random sample of the age group, one can use available demographic data to produce from the probate records, unbiased estimates of the distribution of total wealth.[1] Nor is the availability of such data limited to recent times. Alice H. Jones has recently used probate records to reconstruct the stock, composition, and distribution of wealth in the middle colonies in 1774 [1]. The third recently exploited source of data, tax rolls, can be utilized for the colonial era as well as for more recent times.

Two of the four essays in Part II exploit archival data in their analysis of equity issues. In essay 5 James Henretta uses the Boston tax rolls of 1687 and 1771 to measure the change in the distribution of wealth in that city over an interval of 84 years. In essay 6 Allan and Margaret Bogue are concerned with the debate over the extent of the profit of land speculators. In this connection they employed data obtained from land-entry books, county records, and business papers to estimate the rates of return on land transactions earned over a 45-year period by five Illinois speculators and over a 27-year period by two New Yorkers with large holdings in Nebraska. Stanley Lebergott sets forth his estimates of the extent of unemployment during each business recession from 1800 to 1960 in essay 7. This permits him to assess the Marxian contention that there has been an upward secular trend in unemployment rates. In essay 8 Eugene Smolensky examines the socioeconomic characteristics

---

[1] See [1] for a discussion of these techniques.

of the American poor since the beginning of the twentieth century. After considering the complexities involved in establishing a "poverty line," he estimates the proportion of the population which has fallen below this line at different points in time.

REFERENCES

1. Alice Hanson Jones, "Wealth Estimates for the American Middle Colonies, 1774," *Economic Development and Cultural Change*, *18* (July, 1970), Part 2.

5 ECONOMIC DEVELOPMENT AND SOCIAL STRUCTURE IN COLONIAL BOSTON

James A. Henretta

A distinctly urban social structure developed in Boston in the 150 years between the settlement of the town and the American Revolution. The expansion of trade and industry after 1650 unleashed powerful economic forces which first distorted, then destroyed, the social homogeneity and cohesiveness of the early village community. All aspects of town life were affected by Boston's involvement in the dynamic, competitive world of Atlantic commerce. The disruptive pressure of rapid economic growth, sustained for over a century, made the social appearance of the town more diverse, more complex, more modern—increasingly different from that of the

Reprinted with revisions by permission from *The William and Mary Quarterly*, Third Series, *22* (January, 1965), 75–92.

rest of New England. The magnitude of the change in Boston's social composition and structure may be deduced from an analysis and comparison of the tax lists for 1687 and 1771. Containing a wealth of information on property ownership in the community, these lists make it possible to block out, in quantitative terms, variations in the size and influence of economic groups and to trace the change in the distribution of the resources of the community among them.

The transformation of Boston from a land-based society to a maritime center was neither sudden nor uniform. In the last decade of the seventeenth century, a large part of the land of its broad peninsula was still cultivated by small farmers. Only a small fraction was laid out in regular streets and even less was densely settled. The north end alone showed considerable change from the middle of the century, when almost every house had a large lot and garden. Here, the later-comers—the mariners, craftsmen, and traders who had raised the population to six thousand by 1690—were crowded together along the waterfront. Here, too, in the series of docks and shipyards which jutted out from the shore line, were tangible manifestations of the commercial activity which had made the small town the largest owner of shipping and the principal port of the English colonies. Over 40 per cent of the carrying capacity of all colonial-owned shipping was in Boston hands.

This dependence on mercantile endeavor rather than agricultural enterprise had greatly affected the extent of property ownership. Boston no longer had the universal ownership of real estate characteristic of rural Massachusetts to the end of the colonial period. The tax list for 1687 contained the names of 188 polls, 14 per cent of the adult male population, who were neither owners of taxable property of any kind nor "dependents" in a household assessed for the property tax. Holding no real estate, owning no merchandise or investments which would yield an income, these men constituted the "propertyless" segment of the community and were liable only for the head tax, which fell equally upon all men above the age of sixteen. Many in this group were young men, laborers and seamen, attracted by the commercial prosperity of the town and hoping to save enough from their wages to buy or rent a shop, to invest in the tools of an artisan, or to find a start in trade. John Erving, a poor Scotch sailor whose grandson in 1771 was one of the

richest merchants in Boston, was only one of the many propertyless men who rose quickly to positions of wealth and influence.

But many of these 188 men did not acquire either taxable property or an established place in the social order of Boston. Only sixty-four, or 35 per cent, were inhabitants of the town eight years later. By way of contrast 45 per cent of the polls assessed from two to seven pounds on the tax list, 65 per cent of those with property valued from eight to twenty pounds, and 73 per cent of those with estates in excess of twenty pounds were present in 1695. There was a direct relation between permanence of residence and economic condition. Even in an expanding and diversifying economic environment, the best opportunities for advancement rested with those who could draw upon long-standing connections, upon the credit facilities of friends and neighbors, and upon political influence. It was precisely these personal contacts which were denied to the propertyless.

A second distinct element in the lower part of the social order consisted of the dependents of property owners. Though propertyless themselves, these dependents—grown sons living at home, apprentices, and indentured servants—were linked more closely to the town as members of a tax-paying household unit than were the 188 "unattached" men without taxable estates. Two hundred and twelve men, nearly one sixth of the adult male population of Boston, were classified as dependents in 1687. The pervasiveness of the dependency relationship attested not only to the cohesiveness of the family unit but also to the continuing vitality of the apprenticeship and indenture system at the close of the seventeenth century.

Yet even the dependency relationship, traditionally an effective means of alleviating unemployment and preventing the appearance of unattached propertyless laborers, was subjected to severe pressure by the expansion of the economy. An urgent demand for labor, itself the cause of short indentures, prompted servants to strike out on their own as soon as possible. They became the laborers or semi-skilled craftsmen of the town, while the sons of the family eventually assumed control of their father's business and a share of the economic resources of the community.

The propertied section of the population in 1687 was composed of 1036 individuals who were taxed on their real estate or their income from trade. The less-skilled craftsmen, 521

Table 1. Distribution of Assessed Taxable Wealth in Boston in 1687

Total Value of Taxable Wealth	Number of Taxpayers in Each Wealth Bracket	Total Wealth in Each Wealth Bracket	Cumulative Total of Wealth	Cumulative Total of Taxpayers	Cumulative Percentage of Taxpayers	Cumulative Percentage of Wealth
£ 1	0	£ 0	£ 0	0	0.0%	0.0%
2	152	304	304	152	14.6	1.8
3	51	153	457	203	19.5	2.7
4	169	676	1,133	372	35.9	6.8
5	33	165	1,298	405	39.0	7.8
6	97	582	1,880	502	48.5	11.3
7	19	133	2,013	521	50.2	12.1
8	43	344	2,357	564	54.4	14.2
9	22	198	2,555	586	56.6	15.4
10	45	450	3,005	631	60.9	18.1
11	17	187	3,192	648	62.5	19.2
12	30	360	3,552	678	65.4	21.4
13	13	169	3,721	691	66.6	22.4
14	12	168	3,889	703	67.9	23.4
15	22	330	4,219	725	69.9	25.4
16	21	336	4,555	746	72.0	27.5
17	1	17	4,572	747	72.0	27.6
18	18	324	4,896	765	73.8	29.5
19	1	19	4,915	766	73.9	29.6
20	30	600	5,515	796	76.8	33.2
21–25	41	972	6,487	837	80.7	39.0
26–30	48	1,367	7,854	885	85.4	47.3
31–35	29	971	8,825	814	88.2	53.1
36–40	21	819	9,644	935	90.2	58.1
41–45	19	828	10,472	954	92.1	63.1
46–50	16	781	11,253	970	93.6	67.8
51–60	16	897	12,150	986	95.1	73.2
61–70	19	1,245	13,395	1,005	97.0	80.7
71–80	7	509	13,904	1,012	97.8	83.8
81–90	3	253	14,157	1,015	97.9	85.3
91–100	7	670	14,827	1,022	98.6	89.3
100–	14	1,764	16,591	1,036	100.0	100.0

men engaged in the rougher trades of a waterfront society, formed the bottom stratum of the taxable population in this pre-industrial age. These carpenters, shipwrights, blacksmiths, and shopkeepers owned only 12 per cent of the taxable wealth of the town.[1] Few of these artisans and laborers had investments in shipping or in merchandise. A small store

or house, or a small farm in the south end of Boston, accounted for their assessment of two to seven pounds on the tax list (Table 1).

Between these craftsmen and shopkeepers and the traders and merchants who constituted the economic elite of the town was a middle group of 275 property owners with taxable assets valued from eight to twenty pounds.

[1] The lower 50 per cent of the property owners is treated as a whole because Tables 1 and 2 and Chart 1, below, indicate that the proportion of wealth held by this lower half of the propertied population was approximately the same in 1687 and 1771. Neither "propertyless men" nor "dependents" are repre-

sented in any of the tables. The increase in numbers of the former and the corresponding decrease of the latter constitutes a phenomenon which must be distinguished from the growing inequality of the distribution of taxable property, although both trends proceed from the same economic transformation.

Affluent artisans employing two or three workers, ambitious shopkeepers with investments in commerce, and entrepreneurial-minded sea masters with various maritime interests, bulked large in this center portion of the economic order. Of the 275 (in this middle group), 180 owned real estate assessed at seven pounds or less and were boosted into the third quarter of the distribution of wealth by their holdings of merchandise and shares in shipping (Table 3). The remaining 95 possessed real estate rated at eight pounds or more and held various investments in trade. Making up about 25 per cent of the propertied population, this middle group controlled 22 per cent of the taxable wealth in Boston in 1687. Half as numerous as the lowest group of property owners, these men possessed almost double the amount of taxable assets (Table 1).

Merchants with large investments in English and West Indian trade and individuals engaged in the ancillary industries of shipbuilding and distilling made up the top quarter of the taxable population in 1687. With taxable estates ranging from 20 to 170 pounds, this commercial group controlled 66 per cent of the town's wealth. But economic development had been too rapid, too uneven and incomplete, to allow the emergence of a well-defined merchant class endowed with a common outlook and clearly distinguished from the rest of the society. Only 85 of these men, one third of the wealthiest segment of the community, owned dwellings valued at as much as twenty pounds. The majority held landed property valued at ten pounds, only a few pounds greater than that of the middle group of property holders (Table 3). The merchants had not shared equally in the accumulated fund of capital and experience which had accrued after 50 years of maritime activity. Profits had flowed to those whose daring initiative and initial resources had begun the exploitation of the lucrative colonial market. By 1687 the upper 15 per cent of the property owners held 52 per cent of the taxable assets of the town, while the 50 individuals who composed the highest 5 per cent of the taxable population accounted for more than 25 per cent of the wealth (Table 1).

By the end of the seventeenth century, widespread involvement in commerce had effected a shift in the locus of social and political respectability in Boston and distinguished it from the surrounding communities. Five of the nine Selectmen chosen by the town in 1687 were sea captains. This was more than deference to those accustomed to command. With total estates of 83 pounds, 29 pounds, 33 pounds, 33 pounds, and 24 pounds, Captains Elisha Hutchinson, John Fairweather, Theophilus Frary, Timothy Prout, and Daniel Turell were among the wealthiest 20 per cent of the population. Still, achievement in trade was not the only index of respectability. Henry Eames, George Cable, Isaac Goose, and Elnathan Lyon, the men appointed by the town to inspect the condition of the streets and roads, had the greater part of their wealth, 105 pounds of 130 pounds, invested in land and livestock. And the presence of Deacon Henry Allen among the Selectmen provided a tangible indication of the continuing influence of the church.

These legacies of an isolated religious society and a stable agricultural economy disappeared in the wake of the rapid growth which continued unabated until the middle of the eighteenth century. In the fifty years after 1690, the population of the town increased from 6,000 to 16,000. The farms of the south end vanished and the central business district became crowded. In the populous north end, buildings which had once housed seven people suddenly began to hold nine or ten. Accompanying this physical expansion of Boston was a diversification of economic endeavor. By 1742 the town led all the colonial cities in the production of export furniture and shoes, although most industry was still carried on by master craftsmen on a small scale geared to local needs. Prosperity and expansion continued to be rooted, not in the productive capacity or geographic position of the town, but in the ability of the Boston merchants to compete successfully in the highly competitive mercantile world.

After 1750, the economic health of the Massachusetts seaport was jeopardized as New York and Philadelphia merchants, exploiting the rich productive lands at their backs and capitalizing upon their prime geographic position in the West Indian and Southern coasting trade, diverted a significant portion of European trade from the New England traders. Without increasing returns from the lucrative "carrying" trade, Boston merchants could no longer subsidize the work of the shopkeepers, craftsmen, and laborers who supplied and maintained the commercial fleet. By 1760 the population of Boston had dropped to 15,000 persons, a level it did not exceed until after the Revolution.

The essential continuity of maritime enterprise in Boston from the late-seventeenth to the mid-eighteenth century concealed the emergence of a new type of social system. After a certain point increases in the scale and extent of commercial endeavor produced a new, and more fluid, social order. The development of the economic system subjected the family, the basic social unit, to severe pressure. The fundamental link between one generation and another, the ability of the father to train his offspring for their life's work, was endangered by a process of change which rendered obsolete many of the skills and assumptions of the older, land-oriented generation and opened the prospect of success in new fields and new places. The well-known departure of Benjamin Franklin from his indenture to his brother was but one bright piece in the shifting mosaic of colonial life.

The traditional family unit had lost much of its cohesiveness by the third quarter of the eighteenth century. The Boston tax lists for 1771 indicate that dependents of property owners accounted for only 10 per cent of the adult male population as opposed to 16 per cent 85 years earlier. Increasingly children left their homes at an earlier age to seek their own way in the world.

A second factor in the trend away from dependency status was the decline in the availability of indentured servants during the eighteenth century. Fewer than 250 of 2380 persons entering Boston from 1764 to 1768 were classified as indentured servants. These were scarcely enough to replace those whose indentures expired. More and more, the labor force had to be recruited from the ranks of "unattached" workers who bartered their services for wages in a market economy.[2]

This laboring force consisted of the non-dependent, propertyless workers of the community, now twice as numerous relative to the rest of the population as they had been a century before. In 1687, 14 per cent of the total number of adult males were without taxable property; by the eve of the Revolution, the propertyless accounted for 29 per cent. The social consequences of this increase were manifold. For every wage earner who competed in the economy as an autonomous entity at the end of the seventeenth century, there were four times as many in 1771; for every man who slept in the back of a shop, in a tavern, or in a rented room in 1687, there were four in the later period. The population of Boston had doubled, but the number of propertyless men had increased fourfold.

The adult males without property, however, did not form a single unified class, a monolithic body of landless proletarians. Rather, the bottom of society consisted of a congeries of social and occupational groups with a highly transient maritime element at one end of the spectrum and a more stable and respected artisan segment at the other. Although they held no taxable property, hard-working and reputable craftsmen who had established a permanent residence in Boston participated in the town meeting and were elected to unpaid minor offices. In March, 1771, for instance, John Dyer was selected by the people of the town as "Fence Viewer" for the following year. Yet according to the tax and valuation lists compiled less than six months later, Dyer was without taxable property. At the same town meeting, four carpenters, Joseph Ballard, Joseph Edmunds, Benjamin Page, and Joseph Butler, none of whom was listed as an owner of taxable property on the valuation lists, were chosen as "Measurers of Boards." That propertyless men should be selected for public office indicates that the concept of a "stake in society," which provided the theoretical underpinning for membership in the community of colonial Boston, was interpreted in the widest possible sense. Yet it was this very conception of the social order which was becoming anachronistic under the pressure of economic development. For how could the growing number of propertyless men be integrated into a social order based in the first instance on the principle that only those having a tangible interest in the town or a definite family link to the society would be truly interested in the welfare of the community?[3]

[2] For most of the 18th century, Negro slaves compensated for the lack of white servants. From 150 in 1690, the number of Negroes rose to 1,100 in a population of 13,000 in 1730. In that year they made up 8.4 per cent of the population; in 1742, 8.4 per cent; in 1752, 9.7 per cent; but only 5.5 per cent in 1765. The 1771 tax list indicates that only 17 of 318 Negro "servants for life" were held by persons whose property holdings placed them in the lower 50 per cent of the distribution of taxable wealth; 70 by individuals in the third quarter of the economic scale; and 231, or 72.6 per cent, by the wealthiest 25 per cent of the population. A somewhat different picture is presented in Brown's *Middle-Class Democracy* [3, p. 19].

[3] For a different view, see Brown's *Middle-Class Democracy* [3, pp. 28–30, 79–95].

Changes no less significant had taken place within the ranks of the propertied groups. By the third quarter of the eighteenth century, lines of economic division and marks of social status were crystallizing as Boston approached economic maturity. Present to some degree in all aspects of town life, these distinctions were very apparent in dwelling arrangements. In 1687, 85 per cent of Boston real-estate holdings had been assessed within a narrow range of two to ten pounds; by the seventh decade of the eighteenth century, the same spectrum ran from twelve to two hundred pounds (Table 3). Gradations in housing were finer in 1771 and had social connotations which were hardly conceivable in the more primitive and more egalitarian society of the seventeenth century. This sense of distinctiveness was reinforced by geographic distribution. Affluent members of the community who had not transferred their residence to Roxbury, Cambridge, or Milton built in the spacious environs of the south and west ends. A strict segregation of the social groups was lacking; yet the milieu of the previous century, the interaction of merchant, trader, artisan, and laborer in a waterfront community, had all but disappeared.

Table 2. Distribution of Assessed Taxable Wealth in Boston in 1771

Total Value of Taxable Wealth	Number of Taxpayers in Each Wealth Bracket	Total Wealth in Each Wealth Bracket	Cumulative Total of Wealth	Cumulative Total of Taxpayers	Cumulative Percentage of Taxpayers	Cumulative Percentage of Wealth
£3–30	78	£1,562	£1,562	78	5.0%	0.3%
31–40	86	2,996	4,558	164	10.6	0.9
41–50	112	5,378	9,936	276	17.9	2.2
51–60	74	4,398	14,334	350	22.6	3.5
61–70	33	3,122	17,456	383	24.7	3.8
71–80	165	12,864	30,320	548	35.4	6.5
81–90	24	2,048	32,368	572	36.9	7.0
91–100	142	13,684	46,052	714	46.1	10.0
101–110	14	494	46,546	728	47.1	10.1
111 120	149	17,844	64,390	877	56.7	13.9
121–130	20	2,570	66,960	897	58.0	14.5
131–140	26	4,600	71,560	923	59.7	15.5
141–150	20	2,698	74,258	943	60.9	16.1
151–160	88	14,048	88,306	1,031	66.6	19.1
161–170	11	1,846	90,152	1,042	67.4	19.6
171–180	18	3,128	93,280	1,060	68.6	20.3
181–190	10	1,888	95,168	1,070	69.2	20.7
191–200	47	9,368	104,536	1,117	72.2	22.7
201–300	126	31,097	135,633	1,243	80.4	29.4
301–400	60	21,799	157,432	1,303	84.2	34.1
401–500	58	24,947	182,379	1,361	88.0	39.6
501–600	14	7,841	190,220	1,375	88.9	41.3
601–700	24	15,531	205,751	1,399	90.4	44.6
701–800	26	19,518	225,269	1,425	92.2	48.9
801–900	20	17,020	242,289	1,445	93.4	52.6
901–1,000	16	15,328	257,617	1,461	95.4	55.9
1,001– 1,500	41	48,364	305,963	1,502	97.1	66.4
1,501– 5,000	37	85,326	391,289	1,539	99.5	84.9
5,001–	7	69,204	460,493	1,546	100.0	100.0

The increasing difference between the social and economic groups within the New England seaport stemmed in part from the fact that the craftsmen, laborers, and small shopkeepers had failed to maintain their relative position in the economic order. In the 85 years from 1687 to 1771, the share of the taxable wealth of the community controlled by the lower half of the propertied population declined from 12 to 10 per cent (Table 2). If these men lived better at the end of the century than at the beginning, it was not because the economic development of Boston had affected a redistribution of wealth in favor of the laboring classes but because the long period of commercial prosperity had raised the purchasing power of every social group.

The decline in the economic distinctiveness of the middle group of property holders, the third quarter of the taxable population in the distribution of wealth, was even more significant. In 1771 these well-to-do artisans, shopkeepers, and traders (rising land values had eliminated the farmers and economic maturity the versatile merchant-sea captain) owned only 12.5 per cent of the taxable wealth, a very substantial decrease from the 21 per cent held in 1687. These men too lived considerably better than their counterparts in the seventeenth century; many owned homes and possessed furnishings rarely matched by the most elegant dwellings of the earlier period. But in relation to the other parts of the social order, their economic position had deteriorated drastically. This smaller middle group had been assessed for taxable estates twice as large as the bottom 50 per cent in 1687; by 1771 the assets of the two groups were equal.

On the other hand the wealthiest 25 per cent of the taxable population by 1771 controlled 78 per cent of the assessed wealth of Boston. This represented a gain of 12 per cent from the end of the seventeenth century. An equally important shift had taken place within this elite portion of the population. In 1687, the richest 15 per cent of the taxpayers held 52 per cent of the taxable property, while the top 5 per cent owned 26.8 per cent. Eighty-five years later, the percentages were 65.9 and 44.1 (Tables 1 and 2 and Chart 1).

Certain long-term economic developments accounted for the disappearance of a distinct middle group of property owners and the accumulation of wealth among a limited portion of the population. The scarcity of capital in a relatively underdeveloped econom-

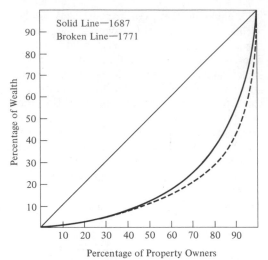

Chart 1. Lorenz curves showing the distribution of wealth in Boston in 1687 and 1771.

ic system, one in which barter transactions were often necessary because of the lack of currency, required that the savings of all members of the society be tapped in the interest of economic expansion. The prospect of rapid commercial success and the high return on capital invested in mercantile activity attracted the small investor. During the first decade of the eighteenth century, nearly one of every three adult males in Boston was involved directly in trade, owning at least part of a vessel. In 1698 alone, 261 people held shares in a seagoing vessel [2, pp. 56, 79, and Table 2]. Trade had become "not so much a way of life as a way of making money; not a social condition but an economic activity" [1, p. 194]. This widespread ownership of mercantile wealth resulted in the creation of a distinct economic "middle class" by the last decades of the seventeenth century.

A reflection of a discrete stage of economic growth, the involvement of disparate occupational and social groups in commerce was fleeting and transitory. It lasted only as long as the economy of the New England seaport remained underdeveloped, without large amounts of available capital. The increase in the wealth and resources of the town during the first half of the eighteenth century prompted a growing specialization of economic function; it was no longer necessary to rely on the investments of the less affluent members of the community for an expansion of commerce. This change was slow, almost imperceptible; but by 1771 the result was obvious. In that year less than 5 per cent of the

Table 3. Real Estate Ownership in Boston in 1687 and 1771[a]

1687			1771		
Assessed Total Value of Real Estate	Number of Owners	Cumulative Total of Owners	Assessed Annual Worth of Real Estate	Number of Owners	Cumulative Total of Owners
£ 1	0	0	£ 1	0	0
2	168	169	2	1	1
3	75	243	3	9	10
4	203	446	4	49	59
5	85	531	5	22	81
6	167	698	6	79	160
7	3	701	7	0	160
8	54	755	8	115	275
9	2	757	9	3	278
10	107	864	10	91	369
11	0	864	11	4	373
12	24	888	12	43	416
13	0	888	13	163	579
14	3	891	14	10	589
15	25	916	15	3	592
16	8	924	16	148	740
17	0	924	17	6	746
18	7	930	18	7	753
19	1	931	19	5	758
20	46	932	20	236	994
21–30	24	1,003	21–25	41	1,035
31–40	11	1,014	26–30	163	1,198
41–50	2	1,016	31–35	93	1,291
			36–40	92	1,383
			41–45	5	1,388
			46–50	42	1,430
			51–60	32	1,462
			61–70	10	1,472
			71–80	9	1,481
			81–90	3	1,484
			91–100	3	1,487

[a] The assessed annual worth of real estate in the 1771 valuation must be multiplied by six to give the total property value.

taxable population of Boston held shares in shipping of 10 tons or more, even though the tonnage owned by the town was almost double that of 1698. Few men had investments of less than 50 tons; the average owner held 112 tons. By way of contrast, the average holding at the end of the seventeenth century had been about 25 tons. Moreover, on the eve of the Revolution ownership of shipping was concentrated among the wealthiest men of the community. Ninety per cent of the tonnage of Boston in 1771 was in the hands of those whose other assets placed them in the top quarter of the population.[4] With the increase in the wealth of the town had come a great increase in the number of propertyless men

---

[4] Only 2.3 per cent of the 8898 tons of shipping for which the owners are known was held by individuals in the bottom half of the distribution of wealth (estates of 100 pounds or less in Table 2); 5.9 per cent more by those with estates valued from 100 to 200 pounds; and an additional 19 per cent by persons with wealth of 200 to 500 pounds. The wealthiest 12 per cent of the propertied population, those with estates in excess of 500 pounds, held 73 per cent of Boston's shipping.

and a bifurcation of the property owners into (1) a large amorphous body of shopkeepers, artisans, and laborers with holdings primarily in real estate and (2) a smaller, somewhat more closely defined segment of the population with extensive commercial investments as well as elegant residences and personal possessions.

A similar trend was evident in other phases of town life. In the transitional decades of the late seventeenth and early eighteenth century, the fluidity inherent in the primitive commercial system had produced a certain vagueness in the connotations of social and economic status. Over 10 per cent of the adult males in Boston designated themselves as "merchants" on the shipping registers of the period from 1698 to 1714, indicating not only the decline in the distinctiveness of a title traditionally limited to a carefully defined part of the community but also the feeling that any man could easily ascend the mercantile ladder. Economic opportunity was so evident, so promising, that the social demarcations of the more stable maritime communities of England seemed incongruous. By the sixth decade of the eighteenth century, however, rank and order were supplanting the earlier chaos as successful families tightened their control of trade. The founding in 1763 of a "Merchants Club" with 146 members was a dramatic indication that occupations and titles were regaining some of their traditional distinctiveness and meaning.

An economic profile of the 146 men who composed this self-constituted elite is revealing. Of those whose names appeared on the tax and valuation lists of 1771, only five had estates which placed them in the bottom three quarters of the distribution of wealth. Twenty-one were assessed for taxable property in excess of 1500 pounds and were thus in the top 1 per cent of the economic scale. The taxable assets of the rest averaged 650 pounds, an amount which put them among the wealthiest 15 per cent of the population.

That 146 men, 6.5 per cent of the adult male population, were considered eligible for membership in a formal society of merchants suggests, however, that mercantile activity was not dominated by a narrow oligarchy. The range of wealth among the members of the top quarter of the propertied population was so great and the difference of social background so large as to preclude the creation of a monolithic class or guild with shared interests and beliefs.

Yet the influence of this segment of society was pervasive. By the third quarter of the eighteenth century, an integrated economic and political hierarchy based on mercantile wealth had emerged in Boston to replace the lack of social stratification of the early part of the century and the archaic distinctions of power and prestige of the religious community of the seventeenth century. All of the important offices of the town government, those with functions vital to the existence and prosperity of the town, were lodged firmly in the hands of a broad elite, entry into which was conditioned by commercial achievement and family background. The representatives to the General Court and the Selectmen were the leaders of the town in economic endeavor as well as in political acumen. John Hancock's taxable wealth totaled 18,000 pounds; James Otis was assessed at 2,040 pounds, while Colonel Joseph Jackson had property valued at 1,288 pounds. Other levels of the administrative system were reserved for those whose business skills or reputation provided the necessary qualifications. Samuel Abbot, John Barrett, Benjamin Dolbeare, John Gore, William Phillips, William White, and William Whitewell, Overseers of the Poor in 1771, had taxable estates of 815 pounds, 5,520 pounds, 850 pounds, 1,747 pounds, 5,771 pounds, 1,953 pounds, and 1,502 pounds respectively. All were among the wealthiest 7 per cent of the property owners; and Barrett and Phillips were two of the most respected merchants of the town. John Scollay, a distiller with an estate of 320 pounds, and Captain Benjamin Waldo, a shipmaster assessed at 500 pounds, who were among those chosen as "Firewards" in 1771, might in an earlier period have been dominant in town affairs; by the seventh decade of the century, in a mature economic environment, the merchant prince had replaced the man of action at the apex of the social order.

Gradations continued to the bottom of the scale. Different social and occupational levels of the population were tapped as the dignity and responsibility of the position demanded. It was not by accident that the estates of the town assessors, Jonathan Brown, Moses Deshon, and John Kneeland, were 208 pounds, 200 pounds, and 342 pounds. Or that those of the "Cullers of Staves," Henry Lucas, Thomas Knox, and Caleb Hayden, totaled 120 pounds, 144 pounds, and 156 pounds. The assumption of a graded social, economic, and political scale neatly calibrated so as to indicate the relation of each individual to the whole was the basic principle upon which the functioning of town-meeting "democracy" depended. William Crafts, with a taxable estate of 80 pounds, was elected "Fence Viewer." Half this amount qualified William Barrett to be "Measurer of Coal Baskets," while Henry Allen and John Bulfinch, "Measurers of Boards," were assessed at 80 pounds and 48 pounds. The design was nearly perfect, the correlation between town office and social and economic position almost exact.

As in 1687, the distribution of political power and influence in Boston conformed to the standards and gradations of a wider, more inclusive hierarchy of status, one which purported to include the entire social order within the bounds of its authority. But the lines of force which had emerged on the eve of the American Revolution radiated from different economic and social groups than those of 85 years before, and now failed to encompass a significant portion of the population. The weakening of the "extended" family unit and the appearance of a large body of autonomous wage-earners, "proletarians" in condition if not in consciousness, had introduced elements of mobility and diversity into the bottom part of society. Equally significant had been the growing inequality of the distribution of wealth among the propertied segment of the community, notably the greater exclusiveness and predominance of a mercantile "elite." Society had become more stratified and unequal. Influential groups, increasingly different from the small property owners who constituted the center portion of the community, had arisen at either end of the spectrum. Creations of the century-long development of a maritime economy in an urban setting, these "merchant princes" and "proletarians" stood out as the salient characteristics of a new social order.

REFERENCES

1. Bernard Bailyn, *The New England Merchants in the Seventeenth Century*, Cambridge, Harvard University Press, 1955.
2. Bernard and Lotte Bailyn, *Massachusetts Shipping, 1697–1714, A Statistical Study*, Cambridge, Harvard University Press, 1959.
3. Robert E. Brown, *Middle-Class Democracy and the Revolution in Massachusetts, 1691–1780*, Ithaca, Cornell University Press, 1955.

6 "PROFITS" AND THE FRONTIER LAND SPECULATOR

Allan G. and
Margaret Beattie Bogue

From the days of the confederation through the nineteenth century, the frontier land speculator was a familiar figure in the United States.[1] Perambulating foreigners recorded the activities of this gentleman, and land speculation was discussed in both Congress and in the editorial columns of Western newspapers. Many twentieth-century students of America's political and economic development have dealt in one way or another with frontier land speculation. They have depicted the land speculator at times as a sinister figure,

Reprinted with omissions by permission from *The Journal of Economic History, 17* (March, 1957), 1–24.

corroding the morals of national or state legislators as the lawmakers endeavored to formulate land policy. Writers have sketched the antagonism between speculator and "actual settler." Nor have they ignored the effect which the speculator had upon the social and economic development of the region in which he operated. Such commentators have contributed to a literature that has its share of colorful characters and even displays the occasional symbol: star-crossed Robert Morris entering debtors' prison; the desperate debtors of the Holland Land Company advancing upon the Batavia land office; the little spade that William Scully lashed to his saddle as he set out to transplant Irish tenancy to the Illinois prairies.

There are, however, a number of overlapping and interdependent questions concerning frontier land speculation to which the answers are as yet far from complete. How and to what extent, for example, did land speculators affect the economic development of the United States? To what degree did Western land speculation contribute to the concentration of capital in America during the nineteenth century?[2] How, if at all, did this alternative avenue of investment affect the policy decisions of the American businessman? Did the land speculator actually get something for nothing, as some writers seem to suggest?[3] What rate of return did speculators in the raw lands of the frontier actually derive from their capital? The answers to the first four questions obviously are closely related to the one given to the fifth; this article will be primarily concerned with the answer to the last question.

Because the evidence bearing upon the

---

[1] Exact definition of the word "speculator" is difficult. Later in this article the word is used as it was in the newspapers of the Midwest during the mid- and late nineteenth century, where generally it denoted an individual who purchased large acreages of unimproved land, intending to sell after land values had risen sufficiently to make their sale remunerative and who was not interested in working the land as a personal enterprise or in building up a long-term tenant estate. Motivation becomes crucial, therefore, in identifying the speculator. But the student cannot always discover this. He is reduced to classifying as speculators those land-holders whose motives he can discover to have been speculative and those who in all or part of their land operations behaved in the same way as the members of the first group. Thus William Scully and Matthew Scott sold part of their original purchases in an unimproved condition; a portion is still owned by their descendants and farmed in tenancy. As far as we are concerned, the land which was sold represented speculation. The Davenports revealed in their correspondence that their intentions in Nebraska were purely speculative; yet they were willing to rent land as a means of defraying the cost of taxes and a way of enhancing the value of the land through the breaking which the tenants performed. The fact that they rented land for a time prior to its sale made them no less speculators. Local use of the term "speculator" during the nineteenth century was colored somewhat by whether or not the large landholder was resident in the community where his land lay. Historians have pointed out that the settler who held but a quarter section or less might be just as speculative in intent as the large holder; on the other hand, some would classify the land grant railroads as land speculators. Both the settler speculators and the railroads are excluded from consideration by this definition. It will be obvious from the text of the article that the speculator is considered to be a type of investor.

[2] A clue to the importance of land speculation in contributing to the concentration of capital in America during the nineteenth century is found in the list of 4047 Americans, who were "reputed to be worth a million or more," published by the New York *Tribune* in 1892. Of this group, 271 allegedly owed their fortunes to investment in some type of real estate and another 1100 had derived their wealth in part from the same source; 34 per cent in all.

[3] The negative quality of the land speculator's role is so often stressed that it is well to remember that he did make a positive contribution at times. After Congress struck the credit provisions from the land laws in the revision act of 1820, the impecunious settler could still purchase land on time from the speculator. Although they often carried it with poor grace, the speculators in the Midwest bore a substantial share of the tax burden as new communities developed. Particularly was this the case within the limits of those railroad land grants in which the alternate sections were settled by homesteaders enjoying immunity from taxation until they fulfilled the residence requirements of the homestead laws. When the speculator purchased from the land grant railroads he sometimes helped these corporations to realize a return from their grants more quickly than otherwise would have been the case, thereby assisting in the construction of transportation facilities. The returns obtained by the land speculator may be regarded to an extent, therefore, as a reward for services rendered. An incidental dividend from speculation may well have stemmed from the fact that actual settlers frequently could not afford to purchase farms large enough to make economic units in the commercial agriculture of the nineteenth century. Where speculators held land nearby such farmers could build up their holdings without squeezing neighbors off the land. Specific instances to the contrary, of course, can be presented in contradiction to these generalizations.

profits from frontier land speculation is inadequate at this point, we have ventured to work up and present relevant material which we accumulated in the course of other research. We have calculated the returns obtained by land speculators from the purchase and sale of some three townships of agricultural land in the Midwest between 1835 and 1904. Stated differently, these figures picture the returns obtained from 77,529 acres of land divided into 946 tracts which were held for periods of time varying from but a few months to some 35 years.

These data can be summarized most easily by presenting them in two parts; one section is devoted to five speculative ventures in the Grand Prairie of Illinois and a second describes the operations of the Davenport brothers of Bath, New York, in eastern Nebraska. Both groups obtained and sold greater acreages than are treated here. In order to be certain, however, that the calculations involved only land which had not been improved at the owner's expense prior to resale, considerable acreage was discarded. In the case of the Davenports another major criterion of selection was applied as well; since it was wished to have one portion of the study stand as a clear-cut illustration of the speculative opportunities presented by Federal land policy, land which the brothers purchased from grantors other than the Federal government, the state government, or the land grant railroads was discarded. The cost, sale, and tax figures for the Illinois lands were derived from the Federal land entry books, county records, and a collection of business papers belonging to one of the speculators. The land account book and business correspondence of the Davenports provided the basic data for the Nebraska study. In neither case, as shall be pointed out in greater detail later, were the sources completely free from defects.

The method of calculating returns on the investments of the speculators was not complicated. For each parcel of land that was sold as a unit, a schedule was prepared showing the initial investment and yearly taxes. Some of the Davenport schedules were more complicated than others because the brothers paid for some of their land in installments, and revenue was obtained prior to sale from rents and abortive sales. For each tract of land the rate of interest was found which, when compounded against the original investment and subsequent costs, gave a total investment at the date of sale equal to the sale price. This was called the rate of return on invested

capital. When rents or the occasional down payment from a canceled sale were obtained from a tract of land, such income was subtracted from the total investment in the tract at the date when it was received. This procedure, of course, raised the rate of return. The various rates of return on tracts sold in the same year were combined into weighted means, showing the average rate of return per dollar invested. Second, the total investment and the average rate of return per dollar invested at five-year intervals for both the Illinois and the Nebraska lands have been shown. It has been assumed in this last calculation that each tract returned year by year the rate which its ultimate sale price revealed. Knowledge of these rates was, of course, denied to the speculators themselves, prior to the sale of any given tract.

The Illinois lands totaled 34,300 acres, located in the Grand Prairie region of east-central Illinois. Scattered through Champaign, Iroquois, McLean, Piatt, Livingston, and Vermilion counties, these tracts were predominantly prairie. This acreage included portions of the holdings of Matthew T. Scott and Associates, Robert B. M. Wilson, James McReynolds, Ramsey McHenry, and Arnold Naudain and Associates.

The son of a well-to-do banker of Lexington, Kentucky, Matthew T. Scott completed his college education in 1846 and spent a year or two managing family farm lands in Ohio. Becoming interested in the possibilities for investment in the unsettled prairies of east-central Illinois, he induced a number of friends and relatives to join him in entering thousands of acres of Federal land at Danville and Vandalia land offices. Between 1848 and 1859 they purchased 45,070 acres, scattered over the two land districts. Their cash investment amounted to some $51,220. Almost 41,000 acres of the total were entered with land warrants, purchased at an average cost of $1.10 per acre. Cash purchases made up the balance.

The second investor in the Illinois group, Robert B. M. Wilson, like Scott, was more than a "speculator" in the usual sense of the word, for he, too, developed portions of his real estate. Wilson, an Irishman by birth, established a medical practice in Washington, Illinois, in 1848. Ten years later he was mixing in local politics and by the 1860s was buying real estate. With borrowed funds he acquired 27,000 acres of unimproved Iroquois County land in 1864 and 1867, at an average cost of

$2.45 per acre. These holdings were originally part of the county's swamp-land grant. Wilson quickly sold much of the land and turned several thousand acres into tenant-operated grain and livestock farms.

The careers of the remaining three investors are much more obscure. None of them developed any prairie real estate. All acquired their land much earlier than Scott and Wilson, during the great land boom of the 1830s. James McReynolds has been described as "an influential citizen of Kaskaskia," although he probably lived in Macon County during the 1830s. There he and a business associate plotted an addition to Decatur in 1837. His venture in wild, unimproved Federal land totaled 1,360 acres, located principally in Champaign County and purchased for $1.25 per acre. Little has been discovered about Ramsey McHenry other than the fact that in 1836, when he purchased 15,000 acres of Federal land in the Danville, Illinois, and Crawfordsville, Indiana, districts for $1.25 per acre, he was a resident of Baltimore. Arnold Naudain, the principal figure in a series of investments made in 1836 and 1837 in partnership with Edward Tatnall, Merrit Canby, and John Macoboy, was a Delaware politician. This group of investors purchased 28,000 acres of Federal land in the Danville and Crawfordsville districts at the cash minimum price.

The following statistics that show the rate of return per dollar invested in land at the year of sale and at five-year intervals represent combined returns from the unimproved holdings of the five speculators lying in the six counties mentioned above. We may be reasonably certain that they were not rented prior to sale. Of the total, 13,607 acres were Scott's lands; 13,905 acres belonged to Wilson; 1,109 to James McReynolds; 3,988 acres to McHenry; and 1,526 to Naudain and Associates. The calculations were based upon purchase and sale prices compiled from Federal land entry books and county deed records and upon the outlay which the owners made for taxes. In addition to taxes these five investors undoubtedly paid agent fees; some of them had to pay interest on the money borrowed to make land purchases; and some became involved in minor litigation over their holdings. No allowance has been made for such costs in calculating rates of return.

The first set of figures showing the combined average returns from the real estate at the time

Table 1. Average Returns on the Illinois Lands Studied by Year of Sale, 1840–1885.

Year Sold	Acreage	Sale Price	Per Cent Return
1840	80	$ 123	4.0
1844	80	292	11.0
1845	109	431	14.3
1846	40	116	7.0
1848	160	480	7.0
1850	195	580	6.0
1851	193	666	6.4
1852	120	698	9.1
1853	2,720	6,886	10.3
1854	2,340	10,183	7.1
1855	220	1,077	7.4
1856	440	1,800	17.5
1859	40	440	46.0
1860	160	1,110	17.1
1861	440	2,090	15.0
1862	80	840	30.6
1863	1,784	16,478	19.2
1864	2,522	23,392	16.7
1865	1,152	10,671	18.1
1866	3,634	41,686	20.5
1867	1,292	14,850	21.5
1868	4,656	35,820	125.3
1869	1,598	14,694	41.5
1870	1,093	10,300	19.1
1871	3,493	32,340	24.1
1872	1,600	14,480	17.9
1873	160	2,600	12.0
1874	1,540	9,697	12.1
1875	333	3,334	14.0
1877	640	3,000	4.0
1882	800	8,000	8.0
1883	700	6,900	7.4
1885	160	800	− .4

of sale (Table 1) illustrates how varied the earnings from investments with different histories could be. The figures for the years 1840 through 1855 represent the earnings of lands owned by two investors of the 1830s, Ramsey McHenry and James McReynolds. In comparison with the percentages that follow for 1856 through 1872, the earlier figures are low, for both men purchased their lands when the Grand Prairie was yet very sparsely settled, and held the real estate for many years before appreciable increase in land values occurred. The 14 per cent return from 109 acres sold by McReynolds in 1845 is the highest received by any of the investors on land purchased during the 1830s. The returns from the Naudain lands, also purchased in the 1830s, are obscured in this set of figures, for these lands were sold in the 1860s during the same years that Scott and Wilson were disposing of their lands. Naudain and Associates realized a rate of return from their holdings very similar to that obtained by McHenry and McReynolds.

The higher figures for the years 1856 through 1872 reflect the good fortune of Matthew T. Scott and Robert B. M. Wilson. Scott purchased and sold his unimproved real estate, almost exclusively prairie land, at a much more advantageous time than had the investors of the 1830s. During the early 1860s the wartime need for agricultural produce, the demand by settlers for farm lands, and the successful use of improved farm machinery combined to boost land values rapidly. For the remainder of the century they continued to climb. Scott's 13,600 acres, purchased almost entirely between 1851 and 1855 at an average cost of about $1.14 per acre, brought on the average $9.50 per acre after being held for an average of thirteen years. While his tax burden was greater than that of the investors of the 1830s, the rapid rise in land values brought him earnings twice as great as theirs. The Wilson investments are primarily responsible for an average return on the lands sold in 1868 of 125 per cent. Wilson's land business was even more successful than was that of Scott, for Wilson did not have to wait a full year in many cases for the real estate which he had purchased at a few dollars per acre to attract buyers at $4.00 to $10.00 per acre. He retained his 13,900 acres for an average of only four years and sold them at an average of slightly more than $8.00 per acre. Returns from scattered Scott and Wilson sales between 1877 and 1885 were much less satisfactory. There was, for instance, no return from the investment in a quarter section of Wilson land purchased in 1867 at $2.94 per acre and sold in 1885 for $5.00 per acre, rather .4 per cent per annum loss.

Turning to Table 2, which shows the total investment in these Illinois lands and the rate of return per dollar invested at five-year intervals, we note that the rate falls from 8.5 per cent in 1835 to 6.4 per cent five years later; climbs to 18.9 per cent in 1870; declines in 1875 to 6.4 per cent, and swings up to 9.4

Table 2. Per Cent Return on the Illinois Land Studied, at Five-Year Intervals, 1835–1880

Year	Investment on December 31	Per Cent Return
1835	$ 910	8.5
1840	11,179	6.4
1845	14,824	6.4
1850	19,186	6.8
1855	29,589	13.8
1860	58,983	16.1
1865	75,599	17.9
1870	63,347	18.9
1875	11,591	6.4
1880	13,799	9.4

per cent in 1880. The 1835 figures reflect the returns obtained by James McReynolds from 670 acres of land. Of the three who purchased land during the 1830s, McReynolds held his real estate the shortest length of time and, perhaps because a good portion of it was timber land, found buyers at prices yielding a higher return than those received by either McHenry or Naudain and Associates. He held his lands for an average of 15.5 years and sold them at an average price of about $5.00 per acre. The 1840, 1845, and 1850 figures are somewhat below the level of 1835, for they represent the combined earnings of the Naudain, McHenry, and McReynolds lands. The McHenry and Naudain holdings were predominantly prairie. McHenry held his real estate 17 years after purchase, on the average, and sold it for approximately $3.50 per acre. The Naudain group realized slightly more than $8.50 per acre, but held its land much longer than did the other two investors—for 27 years on the average. The higher averages of 1855 and subsequent years stem from the Scott and Wilson investments. Wilson lands were primarily responsible for the returns of 17.9 and 18.9 per cent in 1865 and 1870. The 1875 and 1880 figures decline markedly from the 1870 level, for they represent the investments of Scott and Wilson in lands held over a considerable period of years and sold in less prosperous times than were their other holdings.

Considerable mention has been made in the preceding discussion of variations in the returns obtained by the five investors. Perhaps it would be well to summarize briefly the experience of the speculators individually after considering them in the composite. As might be expected, the three holdings acquired during the 1830s made the poorest showing. The McReynolds' investment brought a return of 8 per cent; the McHenry lands, 6 per cent; the Naudain holdings, 7 per cent. The Scott and Wilson lands brought average returns to these speculators of 16 and 22 per cent.

In closing the discussion of the Illinois group attention might be called to those factors which were apparently most important in determining the rates of return which the members obtained. The time of purchase in relation to the phase of the business cycle was important, as were the business conditions at the date of sale. The speed with which settlers entered an area was largely controlled by business conditions, and the rapidity of settlement, of course, strongly influenced the frontier land market. These elements, plus the preconceptions of the speculators concerning the value of their holdings, undoubtedly governed the length of time which land was held to a considerable extent. Apparently the longer land was held, the less likely was the speculator to make a spectacular killing. Differences in the type and quality of the land—timber or prairie, wet land or dry land—made for variations in return. Although evidence on these points is scanty, undoubtedly the adequacy of transportation facilities and the success of local farmers in adapting to the peculiarities of their district also were important in explaining variations in returns.

John and Ira Davenport of Bath, New York, were able to weigh the merits of a number of types of investment during the last 35 years of the nineteenth century. In the years after 1815 their father, Ira Davenport, Sr., accumulated capital in the mercantile business of central New York and soon turned his attention as well to the possibilities for investment that lay in the West. By the 1850s he was lending money to farmers in Michigan and Illinois, speculating in Midwest lands, and also dabbling in the tax title business. At the date of his death in 1868 Ira Davenport, Sr., was a millionaire. In his will he named John and Ira as his executors and divided most of his fortune among four living children and the minor heirs of a deceased daughter. The two sons, therefore, had the task not only of managing their own shares of the estate, but also, for almost twenty years they supervised the investment of trust funds destined for their young relatives.

John and Ira Davenport kept the trust funds invested in Western farm mortgages which were negotiated on lands in Michigan, Illinois, Iowa, Kansas, and Nebraska, while handling a portion of their own funds similarly. All told, the brothers channeled some $5,500,000 into farm mortgages between 1868 and 1904. But in managing their personal investments the brothers were attracted by the possibilities in land speculation. Although some of the land was inherited or acquired in the loan business, they held at one time or another title to more than 75,000 acres of agricultural land in Nebraska, Iowa, Illinois, and Kansas, as well as timber land holdings in Michigan. A Western agent might warn them of the "develtree there," but the offerings of Wall Street were not neglected either, and Ira, particularly, invested in railroads, public utilities, and state bonds, although this part of the Davenports' financial history is unfortunately much less clear than is the story of their Western business. Trained in the idiosyncrasies of frontier investments by their astute father, while at the same time living within convenient distance of the financial capital of the country, the Davenport brothers were in a position both by training and location to turn the funds under their control into a wide range of investments. Significantly they invested heavily in the raw lands of the frontier.

Chosen for study here are some 43,229 acres of raw land which John and Ira Davenport acquired in six counties, located in the rolling prairie of eastern Nebraska, during the years 1870, 1871, and 1880 and sold during their lifetimes. The brothers purchased this acreage in part directly from the Federal government and in part obtained it from major land-distribution agencies which had acquired the land from the Federal government. Neither speculator nor hopeful farmer had intervened in the chain of title prior to the Davenports. Nor did the brothers endeavor to enhance the value of this land in any way by adding improvements at their own expense.

Of this acreage, the New Yorkers purchased 16,521 acres in Dodge County from the Union Pacific Railroad Company during 1870 and 1871, at prices ranging from $4.00 to $7.00 per acre. In making this purchase the brothers took advantage of the five-year credit plan offered by the railroad and cut their outlay by tendering in payment the company's land grant bonds which they could buy at a considerable discount during the early 1870s. Both of these circumstances have been taken into consideration in calculating the return of the Dodge County lands. In 1880 John and Ira Davenport acquired another 4817 acres of railroad lands in the Nebraska grant of the Burlington line. These holdings lay in Madison County and cost on the average $2.40 per acre.

From those lands given by the Federal government to finance the construction of a state penitentiary in Nebraska, the New Yorkers purchased 5285 acres in Lancaster and Seward counties during 1871. The price of individual tracts in this purchase varied from $3.50 to $5.00 per acre. During the same year the Davenport brothers located 16,606 acres of government land by private entry in Wayne and Pierce counties using military bounty warrants which they had acquired at a cost of approximately $1.15 per acre through brokers in New York and Chicago. Land-office fees, purchase of settler locations, and the services of an agent at Omaha combined to raise the initial cost of these lands to an estimated $1.25 per acre.

L. D. Richards of the firm of Richards, Keene and Company, located at Fremont, Nebraska, supervised the administration and sale of all the Davenport land in the six counties, although he selected local representatives in several counties with whom he split commissions. These amounted to approximately 3.5 per cent of the sale price. Consistently the Davenports urged that their lands be sold to actual farmers on adjacent lands, and that the sale price be fully equal to the actual use value of the land so that speculators would not be attracted. The Davenports began to offer their Dodge County land in 1877, and over the next ten years also opened the lands in the other five counties to sale. Between 1878 and the death of the surviving brother, Ira, in 1904, the brothers sold land from their Nebraska holdings every year.

When the average returns on these Nebraska lands by year of sale are considered, it is found that they ranged from 9 to 12 per cent over the first four years of sales. Then followed a number of years in which the rate of return did not fall below 11 per cent per annum and in one year stood slightly above 19 per cent. With 1887 the returns dropped back to nearly the level of the first years, holding fairly steady between 10 and 12 per cent. The year 1893 marked a sharp break and thereafter returns held between 6.9 and 9 per cent until 1901, when 2803 acres of land

yielded an average return of 5.7 per cent on the investment. In the following three years the returns held at 6 and 7 per cent, with the exception of one 40-acre tract in Dodge County which had been rented since the early 1880s and on which rental payments raised the rate of return up to 12 per cent.

When the calculation of the total investment of the Davenports in their Nebraska land at five-year intervals along with the average return per dollar invested was made, the results appeared less striking than the year-by-year analysis. Returns on the investment fund dropped steadily from just under 11 per cent on the $267,974 invested in 1880 down to 6.5 per cent on the $93,946 invested in the year 1900.

Table 3. Average Returns on the Nebraska Lands Studied by Year of Sale, 1877–1904

Year Sold	Acreage	Sale Price[a]	Per Cent Return
1877	40	$ 386	12.0
1878	1,521	15,643	11.0
1879	359	4,130	8.9
1880	4,592	52,014	9.2
1881	430	6,481	16.0
1882	7,050	74,778	19.2
1883	4,308	73,964	11.9
1884	1,432	22,742	14.0
1885	727	14,465	11.3
1886	160	2,007	16.0
1887	80	926	13.0
1888	320	4,632	16.0
1889	800	12,313	11.9
1890	1,880	27,205	9.6
1891	2,684	52,025	10.2
1892	640	9,187	12.2
1893	1,982	35,126	8.3
1894	200	4,574	7.3
1895	160	4,178	7.2
1896	200	6,118	7.7
1897	84	1,563	6.9
1898	640	14,919	8.6
1899	2,720	52,932	8.0
1900	5,326	108,312	7.1
1901	2,803	55,529	5.7
1902	859	23,063	6.9
1903	473	8,499	6.0
1904	40	2,895	12.0

[a] Sale commission has been deducted. Income from rent is not included in this column.

Some of the variations in return become more understandable when the county averages that underlie the aggregate averages are discussed. The relatively high returns of the early 1880s (Table 3) reflect a real-estate killing which John and Ira Davenport made on the lands purchased from the Burlington Railroad in Madison County. The brothers bought these lands in 1880 and sold them in short order on a rising land market. Although the return on individual tracts ran still higher, of course, some 4000 acres of these lands averaged 39.5 per cent on the investment when sold in 1882. By 1885 the stimulating affect of the Madison lands had disappeared from the averages. In general through the 1880s the yearly rate of return on the Union Pacific land and on the acreage obtained by locating land warrants held between 10 and 12 per cent, but the returns on penitentiary land pulled the over-all average downward. When Western real-estate prices fell generally in 1893, and returns on the Davenport lands fell across the board, the penitentiary lands still stood as the least remunerative among these investments. On 800 acres of Lancaster land that were sold in 1901, the Davenport brothers realized but 3 per cent on the funds invested.

Contrary to the case in Illinois, the survey reports describing Nebraska soils are sufficiently detailed that discussion of the relation between speculator returns and soil productivity is possible. We must remember, however, that most of the Davenport lands were located and sold before the characteristics of eastern Nebraska soils were known in more than a general way. Nor were the pioneer farmers fully aware of the variations in rainfall which, along with topography, are important in determining the productivity of agricultural land in eastern Nebraska. The Davenport lands comprised a percentage of the choicer soil types that equaled or was greater than the equivalent county percentage, with the exception only of the holdings in Lancaster County. There soil types now considered unsuitable for cropping made up 32 per cent of the Davenport lands, while the county as a whole contained but 6 per cent of the same soils. Taking soils, rainfall, and topography into consideration, the most desirable Davenport lands lay in Dodge, Wayne, and Madison counties, and it is significant that the brothers realized their highest returns in those counties. Despite the fact, however, that the farmer works under more favorable conditions in Dodge and Wayne counties, the lands in Madison County produced the highest rate of return to the speculator. Obviously productivity was not the only factor affecting proceeds.

In conclusion, it is reasonable to say that a well-informed resident of east-central Illinois could have purchased unimproved land in his neighborhood with his own funds, given the land his personal supervision, and earned something from his investment. If he bought during the mid-1830s and sold the land 20 to 30 years later, the money might have earned 6 to 8 per cent. Had he purchased land from the United States for about $1.10 per acre in the early 1850s, he might have realized 16 per cent upon his investment if he sold the land during the 1860s and 1870s. Or real estate bought during the mid-1860s at low figures and sold rapidly between 1867 and 1870 might have returned very large earnings.

Were residents of Illinois well advised to divert their funds into land speculation in preference to other uses? If the earnings from every alternative opportunity were known, a more meaningful answer could be given. The rates of return obtained by our Illinois speculators can be compared with the rate realized by moneylenders on real-estate mortgages in the same region. The usual rate on such loans down to the mid-1870s was at least 10 per cent. Those who put their money into unimproved land in the 1830s might have done better, therefore, had they financed the land purchases of others. Having lent their money, however, they quite possibly would have found themselves owners of unimproved land by foreclosure. Those who paid cash for tracts of raw prairie in the 1850s and 1860s and later sold them perhaps fared better than the moneylender. Each alternative presented elements of risk. Yet none could predict the future with complete accuracy,

Table 4. Per Cent Return on the Nebraska Land Studied at Five-Year Intervals, 1875–1900

Year	Investment on December 31	Per Cent Return
1875	$193,962	9.4
1880	267,974	10.9
1885	194,360	8.1
1890	239,442	7.9
1895	207,050	6.9
1900	93,946	6.5

and the optimism of boom times in the 1830s and 1850s tinged the judgment of the most clairvoyant.

From their Nebraska lands the Davenport brothers received handsome returns on a sizable investment. As it happened, they were also lending funds on the security of farm real estate in the same region. Although the mortgage rate stood at more than 12 per cent during the early 1870s, it had dropped by the end of the decade to the vicinity of 8 per cent, while the average rate of return per dollar invested in the Nebraska lands at the close of 1880 stood at 10.9 per cent. Although the gap had been closed considerably by 1890, the rate of return on real estate stayed above the mortgage rate until the death of Ira Davenport. Had the brothers turned their funds during the early 1870s into railroad bonds, or had they enjoyed the "average experience" of those investing in common stocks between 1871 and 1904, they would have done less well than they did by turning to the trans-Missouri prairies.

7 CHANGES IN UNEMPLOYMENT 1800-1960

Stanley Lebergott

Whether capitalism contained within itself the seeds of its destruction has been a question of lively interest since its earliest days. To some historians who saw "under the aspect of eternity," the more or less inevitable decline of any social order, any economic system, was to be expected. To the Marxists, of course, the doom of this particular order was guaranteed in a secular holy writ. To less committed economists as well, business cycle changes in the Western world have been a subject of keen concern both for the economic problems they pose and for the humanitarian issues they evoke. Now any long-term variation in the effectiveness with which an economy uses its resources must be intimately linked with variations in its ability to use its major perishable resource—manpower. Hence the American unemployment record will reflect any trend toward higher levels of unemployed resources.

Reprinted with omissions by permission from *Manpower in Economic Growth: The American Record Since 1800*, New York, McGraw-Hill, 1964, pp. 164–190.

It may also cast a distant light on a substratum of attitudes that, however confused and outdated, in fact underlies the ideologies of labor and management in today's labor-market negotiations.

MEANING OF LONG-PERIOD UNEMPLOYMENT COMPARISONS

Unemployment appears to have arrived in America with the white man. Want and misery had stalked among the Indians, of course, but unemployment was another matter. In 1850, for example, when the Gold Rush was tapering off, men walked the streets of San Francisco looking for work. But the nearby Digger Indians were fully employed, as had been their ancestors, gathering a dietary of grasshoppers and roots. In the Indian society, as in any composed of the self-employed (or serfs, slaves, or labor-camp inmates), no unemployment need exist. And even a society of wage earners can correctly boast that it has no unemployed if government policy forces disemployed workers into jobs regardless of their customary skills or earnings levels. But in a free nation, with a standard of living and social standards that permit an unemployed worker to remain without work while seeking a job he considers satisfactory, unemployment is to be expected. The social problem in such a society will concern how to reduce unemployment and how to shorten its duration, rather than how to abolish unemployment.

The first factor that affects long-period comparisons stems from this aspect of American society. As real incomes have risen over the decades so has the ability of the unemployed to refuse the first job available (if it is below standard), to delay until he finds "suitable" work. And as social institutions have changed (in particular, as unemployment compensation has been introduced, supplemental benefits pioneered, health services extended), this effect has been intensified.

A second factor in historical comparisons is that of changing social attitude. Not wholly independent of the first factor noted has been the growing willingness of society to consider that unemployment does not automatically imply character deterioration. "Everybody knows that the unemployed are the victims of their own idle, irregular courses," Arthur Young could write years ago. "Some folks won't work" was the characteristic phrase even in the 1920s. But after the extended experience of the Great Depression it became difficult to consider unemployment as something between personal fault and venial sin. After unemployment compensation to veterans in 1945-1946 helped create the phrase "the 52–20 club," after national policy of working toward maximum production and employment was first defined in 1946, the final steps were taken to demonstrate that unemployment today is considered as a social problem, requiring social as well as individual action. Out of such experience may come better reporting of actual unemployment today than, say, in 1900. Housewives may now be less ashamed to admit to a Census Bureau enumerator that the family head is without work.

A contrary force that has become particularly important since the turn of the twentieth century is the driving tendency to put women into jobs once considered the province of adult males. In 1900, 18 per cent of our labor was female. By 1960 the proportion was nearly twice as great. This difference gives an unprecedented flexibility to the labor force. For while previously one could assume that a given employment decline brought an almost precisely commensurate unemployment rise, this is no longer true. The most spectacular example, of course, was the transition in 1945–1946, when for the first time in our history, a massive decline in employment took place without bringing an almost equally massive rise in unemployment. Another recent demonstration that when women become disemployed they tend to move directly out of the labor force, rather than enter the ranks of the unemployed, is afforded by the recession change from December, 1948, to 1949. Millions of men and women lost their jobs, but while half the men became unemployed only 18 per cent of the women did.

A fourth force—the long-term improvement in morbidity and medical care—may have brought a slight reduction in unemployment rates at equivalent levels in the business cycle. We know from contemporary literature that malaria, "the agues," and "the shakes" were commonplace during the first half of the nineteenth century, whether in the Louisiana swamps or the Illinois lowlands. However, the decline in lost time since the turn of the twentieth century appears to have been less significant. Data for nonfarm male workers are available for several dates. In

1900 an average of a week was lost each year in illness; in 1915–1917, about the same; and nationwide surveys in February, 1949, and September, 1950, again report a similar figure.

Since our present (Current Population Survey) series includes among the unemployed not all persons who are ill but only those who were seeking work when they became temporarily ill, we must conclude that the improvements in public health have had some measured effect in reducing unemployment, but only a minimal one.

Finally, the extensive development of paid vacations since the 1940s has tended to reduce the level of noncyclical unemployment compared to previous decades. Summer declines in demand, seasonal shutdowns, changes in models, brought unemployment in earlier years. They do so today as well; but the growth in paid vacations has begun to neutralize this result. A forced vacation is one thing; going fishing while on the payroll is another. Some four million persons with jobs reported themselves on vacation in July, 1951, three million of them being on paid vacations, while millions vacationed in other months.

We assume that only a fortunate few enjoyed paid vacations at any point in the nineteenth century, while a crude estimate suggests that paid vacations even as recently as 1900 were only one tenth as common as in 1960.

Although we shall consider below other factors that have changed the levels of unemployment since 1800, several of the foregoing social changes have affected the very meaning of comparisons of unemployment over the years. We may contend that their effects have not been great. We may even contend that they produce fewer incomparabilities than are involved in long-period deflation of dollar aggregates in a period of changing tastes and preferences. But such contentions do not contravene the limitations that afflict long-period comparisons. We are involved here in the familiar index-number problem. We must meet it, as is usual, by "looking the difficulty boldly in the face and then passing on."

OPPOSING FORCES

1. The free American labor market prior to 1860 was largely one of pure competition, but not one of perfect competition. The extent of worker and employer ignorance about short-term changes in market opportunities and requirements beyond their immediate area is hard to imagine in these days of high communication, daily newspapers, and Employment Service reports. Wages during the 1819–1820 crisis could plummet in Philadelphia, while rates in Lexington, Kentucky, were hardly affected. This could hardly occur in a perfect market.

As late as 1900 Jacob Riis could describe how, in a Long Island suburb, "work goes often begging in my sight, while men and women starve for it in the tenement-house city."

In part these imperfections reflect ignorance as to alternatives. In part they also reflect high costs of transport. No intercity bus lines, not even the cheap jalopies of the 1930s, existed to facilitate migration. A horse cost the equivalent of three months' pay for the average worker in the 1830s. Even shoe leather had to be conserved, a pair of shoes costing a farm laborer more than a fourth of the money he received each month in addition to his board. With ignorance, cost, and resistance to mobility combining to create market imperfections, the fairly prompt meshing of job openings and available workers that was usual in the 1950s was atypical a century ago. The result was a tendency toward a higher level of unemployment during the many years of prosperity and business advance.

2. Another factor that tended to push unemployment levels in the nineteenth century above those in the twentieth was the industrial composition of the labor force. Our major employer was the farm—but farming employment is notoriously affected by the weather. In the nineteenth century the weather's effect in shortening job duration, forcing the search for new work, was pronounced. Farming could provide only seven or eight months' steady work even to those employees who were considered regular workers. "A year in some farming states, such as Pennsylvania, is only eight months' duration, four months being lost to the laborer, who is turned away as a useless animal," according to a traveler perhaps overly impressed by the 1818–1820 recession.

A writer in the 1860s urged young men to work as farmhands if they would accumulate a downpayment on a farm. Such work, he admitted, would be available only for the "seven or eight months of the busy season," but they might "teach school through the winter, or find some kind of job work."

And somewhat later Horace Greeley, telling the expectant world what he knew about farming, found that "the dearth of employment in winter for farm laborers is a great and growing evil... in its present magnitude it is a very modern evil.... Within my recollection there was timber to cut and haul to the saw mill, wood to cut... forest land to be cleared and fitted for future cultivation, even in New England."

The best over-all judgment may well be that of the serious soul who warned the potential emigrant that "unless you can obtain an engagement for six or twelve months, which you will probably be able to do if you are a steady and useful servant, you may very frequently be exposed to lost time in changing of places and looking about." What with the sharp contrasts between Old and New World practices and the normal difference of opinion between master and employee as to what constitutes "a steady and useful servant," a succession of short-term engagements must have been relatively common in this leading American industry.

Perhaps second to farming as an employer of adult men prior to 1860 was ocean transportation—the classical home of casual employment, short-term jobs. Most employees in ocean transportation were engaged in the coasting trade. Ignoring the really short trips, providing employment for a mere month or two, what about the traditional long coasting run from New England to the West Indies? A typical round trip in 1790 took five months and nine days; a typical trip in 1839 took nearly five months; and during the years of the Napoleonic Wars turnaround was reduced even further. In later years the job durations were, if anything, somewhat shortened. The next largest group in ocean transport consisted of those on trips to Liverpool, Lübeck, Kronstadt, or Le Havre. The average round-trip voyage in the 1812 period ran from six to eight months, while in later years no great change in duration took place.

Men were on the beach at the end of every such voyage until they could find another berth. Even in the palmiest days of the crimps this meant a period of unemployment. (Long-duration employment was, of course, available in whaling, but the brilliance of writers on maritime topics has shadowed the fact that only 1 or 2 per cent of the labor force was in whaling.) By the twentieth century the typical transport employer was the railroad or the street railway, the stability of whose employment was notoriously greater than shipping.

3. Still another factor was the greater extent to which the nonfarm industry was subject to the weather. For the vagaries of the weather, as well as the long winter months, augmented the irregularity of employment. All outdoor operatives, in some trades, wrote George Nettle in 1850, are "suspended during the four or five winter months." Many "go into the South for employment in the winter."

The largest manufacturing industry in the nation in the nineteenth century was constituted by country grist and oil mills. In the North and West the mills were at the mercy of the weather, and millers would be hired "only for this coming fall or so long as the Mill can run before freezing up."

When iron manufacturing was becoming a major industry in the 1830s, it was common for ironworks to shut down for several months of frost and snow.

The hand trades that preceded full-scale manufacturers offered similarly broken periods of employment. The typical example was the Haverhill farmer or the Marblehead fisherman who turned shoemaker for part of the year. And even an idealized description of the early metalworking industry referred to "Seth Steady, the blacksmith. ... [whose] hammer is heard at the dawn of day, and the fire blazes in his shop during the evenings from the 20th of September till the 20th of March."

In these many occupations that complemented farming, breaks in continuity of employment, particularly for employees, were to be expected in the shift from one to the other.

Construction, of course, provided irregular employment. Severe winter weather kept house carpenters and masons "from working for several months [out of the year]. The case is the same with the day laborer in agriculture."

Transportation was even more affected. When mud ruts constituted the only links between the states, transportation employment was notably irregular. And when the great internal roadsteads—the Erie, the Pennsylvania, the Ohio, and the other canals—were opened to navigation, they had to be closed an average of four months every year for cold weather.

4. Opposed to such influences which tended

to create a level of unemployment in the nineteenth above that in the twentieth century was the fundamental difference in the class-of-worker groups in the labor force. Slaves were not unemployed. Farmers were not unemployed. Self-employed carpenters, saddlers, weavers, and fishermen were not unemployed. Taken as a whole, such categories accounted for nearly the entire labor force in 1800. By 1950 they accounted for under 10 per cent. The decline in farming, the end of slavery, the growth of factories, transformed the labor force from one made up of slaves and husbandmen into one of wage earners:

Date	PER CENT OF TOTAL LABOR FORCE	
	Farmers	Slaves
1800	61	28
1850	46	24
1900	20	0
1950	7	0

The gains in the wage-earner groups, of necessity, meant a rise in the proportion exposed to unemployment. The normal vicissitudes of a round-about process of production, changing patterns of consumer tastes, freedom of workers to seek better jobs, freedom of employers to seek other employees than their present ones—all these meant that a rising unemployment level would tend to be associated with the new dominance of wage earners in the labor-force total. While a slave may be unproductive, and an itinerant organ grinder may earn under a dollar a week, they are not "seeking work" and do not therefore belong with the unemployed. Hence both voluntary and involuntary additions to the unemployed tend to be larger when the employee proportion of the labor force grows.

5. The steady advance of technology has brought technological unemployment in every decade since Tubal-cain (the first worker of brass and iron). Whether the proportion of employees displaced in earlier decades of this nation was greater or less than in recent decades cannot be determined without more material than is now available. Surmise, favored with little evidence, suggests no tendency toward a decrease in unemployment from this source.

UNEMPLOYMENT IN CRISIS YEARS SINCE 1807

It was a wearily perceptive and resigned former President (if John Adams could ever have rightly been called resigned) who wrote: "I am old enough to remember the war of 1745 and its end, the war of 1755 and its termination, the war of 1812 and its pacification. Every one of those wars has been followed by a general distress, embarrassments of commerce, destruction of manufactures, fall of the price of produce and lands." Let us consider some major periods of "general distress."

1807. Three days before Christmas, 1807, President Jefferson initiated the embargo. By February 500 ships in the Port of New York had been decommissioned; not a crossing was made from New York or Boston to Liverpool in 1808, and thousands of seamen entered the British service. Maritime employment, the largest nonfarm industry of the day, fell sharply, declining about 50 per cent in New York, Boston, and Norfolk. (However, shipping out of more southerly ports was not so affected, actually rising 50 per cent in the major port of Charleston.) There is little evidence that employment levels changed much in the largest industry, farming.

1812. Again in 1812 employment in shipping was slashed (by the war) as the data on tonnage entered indicate:

Year	Tonnage
1810	909
1811	948
1812	668
1813	238
1814	60
1815	701
1816	877

The cut imposed its gravest consequence on the large cities in the North. Unemployed seamen either made their way to Canada to ship in British boats, or remained on the town. But with only 60,000 seamen out of a labor force of 2.2 million, an unemployment problem of national dimensions did not develop.

1819. The first primarily commercial crisis that shook the new nation in the nineteenth century was that of 1818 to 1820. To the contagion from Europe's distress were added the effects of heavy importation of

English goods as the United Kingdom attempted to wrest its former markets from the new American factories. The effect of the crisis on employment is suggested by a report of the National Institution. Seeking to secure higher tariffs to prevent the inflow of British-manufactured goods after the end of the Napoleonic Wars, this group developed the infant industry argument, later to be attributed to Friedrich List and continental writers, and also collected a spate of numbers of employment changes in the new manufacturing centers. We can summarize its findings as follows:

while contemporary reports suggest price declines for farm products, they do not suggest any change in the extent of farm hiring. Many persons engaged in the hand trades, those premanufacturing industries where saddles, horseshoes, flour, etc., were made. But most such persons were self-employed, and contemporary reports again give no hint of significant changes in the number of employees in these firms outside the manufacturing centers. Navigation employment was affected but little, judging from port clearance reports. The declines must have been fairly well restricted to manufacturing indus-

HANDS EMPLOYED IN MANUFACTURING, 1816–1819

Location	Date	Cotton Goods	Woolens	Iron
Philadelphia	1816	2,325	1,226	1,152
	1819	149	260	52
Pittsburgh	1815	42	63	163
	1819	0	16	40
Rhode Island	1816	15,253		
	1819	3,916		

We may combine these data for the main factory centers with some for the remaining centers of any significance, to conclude that employment in cotton factories fell by about 75 per cent from pre- to post-panic level.

On the other hand, the declines were less catastrophic for industries not directly exposed to British dumping and to excessive demand fluctuation. (Factory cottons, after all, were still something of a luxury in a nation where spinning wheels were a common article of household use, rather than an antique.) Thus the reports show bricklaying employment in Philadelphia declining by only 50 per cent, brewery employment in Pittsburgh falling by only a third. We therefore take the 78 per cent fall in employment as shown in the National Institution report for the wide range of Philadelphia industries and the 68 per cent decline for a similarly wide list in Pittsburgh, to deduce that manufacturing employment in the nation generally might have fallen about two thirds. While the National Institution report undoubtedly concentrated on the areas hardest hit, these in fact had a major share of what was then factory employment.

But after all, few people were engaged in manufacturing. Most were in farming. And

tries. Since these composed less than 5 per cent of the labor force, a two thirds fall in such employment would have brought a rise of, say, 3 per cent in the national unemployment percentage. Given our estimate that less than 10 per cent of the labor force was composed of wage earners in 1800, and allowing for some increased unemployment in the hand trades and construction, it would be hard to come to a figure much higher than 4 per cent unemployment in 1819. With a labor force of 3 million, this implies a maximum unemployment figure of 120,000.

What do contemporary sources estimate? In 1822 Matthew Carey found "reason to believe that from 90,000 to 100,000 workmen were actually thrown idle and driven to labor in the country—and vast numbers on the highways" that were then being built. In other publications Carey used the lower estimate of 65,000. Carey's 1822 estimate leads to the same result as the present procedure, while the difference from his other estimates is surely *de minimis*.

1838. One guide to the amount of unemployment in the depression which began in 1837 is given by the relief data for New York, which doubled from 1837 to 1838. dropping back to pre-crisis levels by 1839.

Such a rise is considerably greater than what the Massachusetts relief data indicate for the well-known recessions of 1857 and 1873. But because of the inherent limitations of such data (not to mention the noncomparable elements of relief criteria and procedures between New York and Massachusetts), we must also look at more indirect numerical indications. Imports of pig iron—that master material of modern industry, whose consumption rate is intimately linked with cyclical variations in employment—fell by 14 per cent. Such a decline was about as great as the 1856–1857 fall. However, in 1838 imports of pig iron constituted a major source of the metal, whereas by 1857 they were much less important than domestic production. The implications we can draw for general employment levels therefore suggest that the 1838 unemployment level was worse than the 1857 level. The conclusion is reinforced by what the price data report. Metals prices fell 10 per cent from 1837 to 1838, but only 1 per cent from 1856 to 1857. Textile prices fell by 6 per cent in the earlier period and actually rose in the later. Considering the relief data, pig-iron imports, and the two price series, therefore, we conclude that the 1837–1838 recession was of greater severity than that of 1856–1857.

1858. "Not one out of five skilled workmen in the country was steadily employed" in the 1857–1861 period, according to Representative Kelley. Another contemporary view of the 1857 recession stated that "the seaboard cities and the manufacturing districts of the interior probably at this time contain not less than 100,000 unemployed adult persons."

For the major manufacturing state of Rhode Island, we have contemporary estimates of a 68 per cent fall in cotton textile jobs, 78 per cent in jewelry, 43 per cent in ironworks employment. Such declines indicate an equally great weakness in the Rhode Island labor market. The significantly milder decline in ironworks employment than in the two other industries suggests a crisis reaction, rather than a broadly spread downturn of employment. If we were to surmise, say, a 50 per cent decline in manufacturing employment but 10 per cent in other nonfarm industries, we should arrive at a 10 per cent unemployment figure.

The national extent of the decline, however, is overemphasized by these data for the Northeast. Thus while common-labor wage rates fell by about 7 per cent in New England from 1857 to 1858, the national rate fell not at all. The wage-rate data, therefore, do not confirm a decline of such severity. And the wholesale-price data, also affected by interactions in a national market, show textile prices actually rising, and metals prices falling only 1 per cent. Finally, the 30 per cent rise in relief in Massachusetts and the 16 per cent decline in pig-iron imports suggest a level of unemployment that was serious, but by no means as serious as Representative Kelley's ominous, but retrospective, words imply. We take the serious declines in employment in Rhode Island and presumably the Philadelphia area, the significant rise in Massachusetts relief, the less substantial fall in pig-iron imports, and the inconsequential price response and common-labor wage-rate response to imply a recession of intermediate severity, conceivably at the level of the 1875 and 1885 percentages. While similar data were used for making a crude surmise as to 1819 levels, the procedure is less satisfactory by 1857, since industry by then had become a much greater proportion of the labor force and had spread so widely through the land that we could not safely take data for the Northeast and Middle Atlantic states as suggesting national trends in nonfarm employment. We therefore do not estimate an 1858 level. He who cannot quiet his soul without such an estimate may use 6 to 8 per cent.

1874. The great crisis of 1873 brought in its wake distress throughout the country. Outdoor relief in Massachusetts shot up in 1873, continued to rise till 1876, and only declined significantly beginning in 1879. In central Kansas, John Ise reminisced years later, half the people in one county were on charity, with men going 200 miles to eastern Kansas to husk corn or cut wood or work for cash wages. Frickey's estimate of manufacturing production in the nation shows the same pattern, with a total decline of 19 per cent by 1876, and no significant turnaround until 1879.

As of November, 1874, according to the American Iron and Steel Institute, there were "at least a million" unemployed workers. The Institute felt that there were 100,000 in New York and Philadelphia alone. Since the labor force then totaled about 15 million workers (interpolating between the 1870 and 1880 totals), their figure implies a 6.7 per cent unemployment rate. Given the trend in production and relief, and allowing for new entrants into the labor force, the 1875 average would have ranged from, say, 6 per cent (if their estimate had been primarily a pessimistic judgment and therefore to be discounted somewhat) to 8 per cent (if they had actually been relying on reliable reports from members).

The continued decline in production and the general tendency of unemployment to accumulate after the turnaround in production suggest a higher level at the bottom point, 1876. The Silver Commission, speaking with no doubt at least the accent of politics, found that three million were unemployed about this time. If we accept the manufacturers' figure of one million for 1874, then take into account Frickey's estimate of about a 20 per cent decline from 1873 to 1876 in manufactures (as well as the Massachusetts relief data), a three-million figure is not out of the question for the end of the most prolonged depression in American history. We surmise that a figure of two million—or 13 per cent of the labor force in that year—would be a reasonable figure in the light of these partial indications.

1885. A contemporary estimate by the Commissioner of Labor, on the basis of field visits to factories and other checks, found that "about 5 per cent" of the nation's factories, mines, etc., "were absolutely idle during the year ending July 1, 1885, and . . . perhaps 5 per cent were idle a part of the time; or for a just estimate 7.5 per cent." (This level is about the same as the 8 per cent for 1875 computed from the Institute figures.) Frickey's production index shows a fall of about 16 per cent from 1883 to 1885, or about the same as his 1873 to 1875 decline. However, the Massachusetts relief figures show only a mild gain from 1883 to 1884 and then decline. Frickey's data therefore appear to confirm the 1875 to 1885 similarity, while the Massachusetts relief data do not.

As another check on the Commissioner's estimate, we may refer to the report of the Industrial Commission in 1901. "It is disputed whether unemployment has increased on the whole, say within 20 or 30 years, but no witness supposes that it has decreased." Given the language of political controversy, we may assume that no more conclusive arguments were offered for an increase than for a decrease. If the level which prevailed during the Commission's deliberations (5 per cent in 1900) more or less characterized the 1870–1890 period, we would have to increase

this 5 per cent by at least one point to give, say, a 6 per cent figure for the depression year of 1885. Under the circumstances, the Commissioner's estimate—7.5 per cent—does not appear unreasonable. Even if fancy argued for reducing it somewhat, reason offers no basis at this remove (and with such materials in evidence) for doing so.

1890–1899. The depression of the nineties has long been recognized as severe. To supplement the very limited systematic evidence on its depth, and duration, we have derived annual estimates of unemployment. These appear in Table 1.[1] They indicate a sharp rise

Table 1. Unemployment, 1890–1900

Year	Per Cent of Labor Force Unemployed
1890	4.0
1891	5.4
1892	3.0
1893	11.7
1894	18.4
1895	13.7
1896	14.4
1897	14.5
1898	12.4
1899	6.5
1900	5.0

to 1893 at the onset of the depression, italicized in most history books by the wage cuts, strife, and railroad strikes of that year. The unemployment level reached in a single bound was not reduced for six long years. In this respect the depression of the nineties was paralleled only by that of the seventies and the (somewhat longer) Great Depression. With almost equal suddenness the unemployment rate was cut in half in 1899 to usher in the twentieth century with conditions widely defined as "prosperity" and "the full dinner pail."

Since 1900. For the years 1900 to 1960 a more comprehensive summary is possible. We show below the number of years in which the unemployed portion of the labor force was less than 2 per cent, from 2 to 2.9 per

[1] [For the details of these new estimates see the book from which this selection is taken, pp. 180–184. Table 1 is taken from Table A-15, p. 522 of that book. —Editors' note.]

Per Cent	Number of years
Under 2	7
2–2.9	5
3–3.9	10
4–4.9	9
5–5.9	10
6–7.9	4
8–9.9	4
10–11.9	1
12–13.9	0
14–15.9	2
16 and over	8

cent, and so on. The median year falls in the 4 to 4.9 per cent unemployment group.

These estimates for the years prior to 1940 are intended to measure the number of persons who are totally unemployed, having no work at all. For the 1930s this concept, however, does include one large group of persons who had both work and income from work—those on emergency work. In the United States we are concerned with measuring lack of regular work and do not minimize the total by excluding persons with made work or emergency jobs. This contrasts sharply, for example, with the German practice during the 1930s when persons in the labor-force camps were classed as employed, and Soviet practice which includes employment in labor camps, if it includes it at all, as employment.

While total unemployment constitutes a useful measure of the extent to which our manpower is not fully utilized, it is not a complete measure and should not be used as such. Perhaps the most important element that is excluded is partial unemployment— the involuntary idleness during split weeks or short workdays. Various predepression surveys showed from 10 to 15 per cent of urban wage earners working part time—most of them presumably desirous of full-time work. With the onset of the depression of the 1930s, however, the percentage increased abruptly. The immediate increase appeared to be greater than that in 1921. As one example, unemployment in Detroit about doubled from the census in the spring of 1930 to the January, 1931, special unemployment census, but part-time employment increased more than 400 per cent. By March, 1932 (according to a comprehensive survey of more than 6000 companies with over three million employees, sponsored by the President's Organization on Unemployment Relief), 63 per cent of all employed manufacturing workers were on part-time work. No matter how this enormous percentage must be qualified, it is clear that it indicated a substantial quantity of underemployment among those with jobs. As the depression began to lift, the proportion on part time declined. In November, 1937, the proportion in manufacturing on part-time employment was about 20 per cent—or substantially down from the 63 per cent in early 1932. By the postwar period the proportion was further reduced. The proportion of all persons in the labor force working part time in early 1948 was about 8 per cent—and only rose to 12 per cent near the peak of the 1949 recession.

In summary, therefore, partial unemployment may have run to something like 10 per cent for most years, while during the depth of the depression something like half of all factory workers with jobs were on part-time work.

Employment is only one dimension of economic welfare. A second is the number of hours worked, or partial employment. Other dimensions of this problem are the amount of income received and the skills utilized. The general problem of underemployment, however, is still more complex, and it has received separate discussion elsewhere. It will therefore be sufficient here to emphasize that estimates of total unemployment do not include any direct allowance for this factor. The tremendous drop in the number of farms and retail storekeepers from 1940 to 1943 is one indication of the possible magnitude of such underemployment—even after allowing for the postwar return to higher levels in trade.

With this basic qualification in mind, it may be appropriate to indicate how close we came to achieving full employment over the past half century. Defining full employment is something like defining small business, low income, monopoly profit, or the just price. Definitions tend to be either imprecise or void of empirical reference. But if we think of the policy uses of the data, we can define full employment in the light of what we have achieved in the past. Let us arbitrarily define "workable full employment"—to adapt an admirable phrase of J. M. Clark's—as the level achieved at least one year in four during the past sixty years. If we do so the percentage of the civilian labor force totally unemployed at full employment would be less than 4 per cent. (The percentage would have to be

Table 2. Unemployment in Years of Economic Crisis Since 1800

Per Cent of Labor Force Unemployed	1800–1819	1820–1839	1840–1859	1860–1879	1880–1899	1900–1919	1920–1939	1940–1959
3–5	1819						1927	1949 1954 1958
6–8		1838	1858		1885	1908	1924	
9–11						1915		
12–14				1876			1921	
15–and over					1894		1930– 1940	

raised if our reference period were shorter, for it was achieved more frequently in the 1900–1929 period than in 1926–1959.) It has been asserted, however, that "full employment at high wages in a private enterprise economy is undesirable and self-destroying." We may therefore wish to set a figure based on the assumption that full employment is less common. If we set the goal at that which prevailed in 10 per cent of the years, the ratio would run to 2 per cent or less. But we may take a less pessimistic approach. High-level employment has characterized the performance of the American economy in the past half century. While even a level of 5 per cent unemployed would hardly be considered to present a major economic policy problem, such a level has been achieved in more than half this period.

UNEMPLOYMENT LEVELS SINCE 1800

The preceding discussion of unemployment trends has had two purposes. One is to see how far some attempt at estimation might go in replacing the wonderfully graphic contemporary descriptions of panic and crisis (for our judgment on whether one or another period bred more unemployment and distress tends to turn upon the relative prose styles of those who lived at various dates). A reference to numbers, highly speculative as they may be, tends to neutralize this effect. Secondly, we have attempted estimates because of the considerable interest in early discussions of "a reserve army of the unemployed," and the putative tendency for depressions in the West to grow worse and worse.

In Table 2 we have put together our best inference from the above data on unemployment in selected crisis years since 1800. From these measures the most we can conclude is that the extent of unemployment in the worst crisis years increased somewhat in the first half of the nineteenth century but has shown no trend since then. In Table 3 we have attempted speculative averages for entire decades since 1800—most speculatively for 1870–1880–1890. These figures, although based on less specific data than those for crisis years, are probably preferable guides to the main course of unemployment. The reason is simply that reported unemployment

Table 3. Unemployment: 1800–1960 Decade Averages for Per Cent of Labor Force Unemployed

Date	Decade Averages
1800–1809	
1810–1819	1–3
1820–1829	
1830–1839	
1840–1849	
1850–1859	3–6
1860–1869	
1870–1879	10 (?)
1880–1889	4 (?)
1890–1899	10
1900–1909	4
1910–1919	5
1920–1929	5
1930–1939	18
1940–1949	5
1950–1960	5

in the farm population, as census counts since 1890 have shown, is very small. And during most of the nineteenth century, from half to three fourths of the labor force was in agriculture. Hence, the percentage unemployed was necessarily limited on the rise, while it could not go below zero on the decline. Even wide variances in the estimates for crisis years therefore are lost in the decade averages when we allow for the infrequency of crises and the great role of the farm labor force. For the period since the Civil War no trend appears, particularly if we give credence to the 1870–1880–1890 figures. The more reliable data since 1900 emphasize the tremendous impact of the 1930s but report no discernible trend for 1900 to 1960.

Direct government intervention to reduce unemployment, once a crisis had occurred, began more than a century back. In early decades there was a clear response by states and municipalities, starting or speeding up public works such as turnpikes. And it is, of course, impossible to ignore the extent of active government intervention in recent decades. But for at least two of these recessions we may seriously question whether government actions to reduce unemployment taken after the beginning of the crisis had any significant effect whatever on unemployment levels. (Inadvertent tax cuts do not qualify as shrewd anticyclical policy.) The problem is really part of a deeper one, reflecting the fact that government has long been enmeshed in American economic life. Its action to put a tariff on indigo and cotton under Washington, its refusal to limit immigration in the 1880s, its action to make land available under the Homestead Act, its decision to close off immigration in 1920—these and a hundred other steps shaped the structure of the economy, affected its labor market, and thereby affected the level of unemployment that developed in response to cyclical shocks.

If we look simply to the trend in unemployment averages since 1800 (Chart 1), the evidence, such as it is, suggests a slight long-run increase in decade unemployment averages. The change from a labor force of slaves and farmers to one of wage earners, plus the shift to an economy where most goods were marketed, overshadowed the many opposing forces to create this rise. This composition

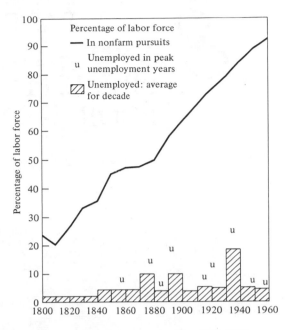

Chart 1. Unemployment trends, 1800–1960.

effect is measurable for a recent period. Thus the percentage of nonfarm employees who were unemployed declined from 1900 to 1960 (from 12.6 to 7.1). The percentage of the total labor force that was unemployed, however, actually rose because the share of self-employed fell heavily.

Yet if our concern is with the productive use of the economy's resources or with the welfare implications of unemployment, we cannot conclude that a deterioration occurred. Present definitions of unemployment fail to include time lost because of bad weather. Moreover, we are unable to measure disguised unemployment (either of wage earners in low-skill occupations or farmers on low-productivity farms). Suppose we could allow for the increased extent to which production is carried on regularly despite bad weather. Suppose further that we could allow for the extent to which an improvement in the labor market from 1800 to 1960, plus the widening system of public education, now enables adult employees to work closer to their intellectual capacity and skill limits. We might then find that no real rise had occurred in the proportion of unemployed resources, so far as either productivity or welfare implications were concerned.

8 THE PAST AND PRESENT POOR

Eugene Smolensky

SUMMARY

There are few surprises in this paper: the record on poverty in this country is too well known and conforms too well to common sense expectations for that. The most important aspects of the past record, highlighted in the subsequent pages, are the following.

1. Poverty has a meaning that varies over time and this is reflected in the way poverty is measured. Two kinds of measures are in general use. One is based, implicitly, on humanitarian precepts and measures the proportion of *families* living below some "minimum-decency" level, where "minimum-decency" is periodically given a new and higher real value. The other measures are based, implicitly, on egalitarian precepts and state the

Reprinted with revisions by permission from *The Concept of Poverty* (First Report of the Task Force on Economic Growth and Opportunity), Washington, Chamber of Commerce of the United States, pp. 35–67.

proportion of *income* going to the lowest income groups. Periodic upward revisions of the "minimum-decency" level implies an egalitarian component amidst humanitarian objectives.

2. Despite the periodic upward revisions in the definition of poverty, it is possible to make meaningful statements concerning the success of the nation in meeting poverty. There are reasonably long periods of time during which the national consensus on the definition of poverty remains unchanged. In such periods, if they are recent enough (e.g., 1947–1960), a clear and unambiguous measure of the extent to which the incidence of poverty has changed is possible. It may also be possible to derive some notion of just how variable the national consensus on the definition of poverty has been, from the definitions of poverty that have been used in the past. An attempt to do that is made in this paper, and a variable definition of poverty is derived. Using these definitions, poverty is shown to have declined by more than 35 per cent toward complete elimination in this century. All of that decline occurred since the Great Depression, for it is only in the very recent past that the rate of growth of income of some part of the poor has outpaced the rise in the egalitarian component of the minimum-decency measures.

The rate of growth of income among the lowest fifth of families has not met the demands implied by the purely egalitarian measures, however. The share of the lowest quintile in income has probably not increased in the twentieth century.

3. Except for the drastic decline in the influence of the foreign-born on the proportion of the population in poverty, there has probably not been a substantial change in the socioeconomic characteristics of the poor in this century. Certain trends with important implications are discernible however. The aged, households in which only the female parent is present, and recently, the unemployed, are a rapidly growing proportion of the population and an even more rapidly growing proportion of the poor. Growth in unemployment and underemployment of the young may foreshadow a significant increase in income inequality in the next two decades.

The failure of the proportion of the poor who are farmers to decline, despite the rapid fall in the proportion of farm families in the population as a whole, suggests that there is a hard core of farm poor that will be difficult to reach. The failure of nonwhites to decline as a proportion of the poor, despite the relatively rapid rise of nonwhite income on the average, is also suggestive of a hard core of poor.

4. This country probably does not wish to use the marketplace to solve the problems of some of the poor. For example, this nation is probably opposed to raising the levels of living of the aged by drawing them back into the labor force. Such groups must be aided by political and social change, although economic policies will also affect their level of well-being.

For the rest the long-run solution to poverty lies in achieving and maintaining full-employment for a sustained period. There are many routes to full employment and there is a role for ameliorative measures in the package of actions taken to achieve full-employment, but the recent historical record makes it perfectly clear that sustained full-employment is the *sine qua non* of poverty reduction. That this is an obvious truth makes it no less important.

5. The faster the economy grows the faster will the income level delimiting poverty grow; but, in practice, the faster the definition of poverty ascends, the more likely is the proportion in poverty to fall. That is the import of the historical record on poverty in the United States in the twentieth century.

THE MEASUREMENT PROBLEM

Choosing a Measure

There are two classes of measures relevant to a study of poverty. One aims to determine the number or the proportion of the population living at, or below, some insufficient welfare level. (Such measures will be called "minimum-decency estimates.") The second class of measures is concerned, not so much with levels of welfare, as with the way in which the total available supply of goods and services is distributed between rich and poor. (Such measures will be called "distribution estimates.") Neither of these two classes of measures is satisfactory for all of the uses to which a poverty measure is put. They are more satisfactory when used jointly. Unfortunately, neither class of measures is available in the long, continuous, and strictly comparable series needed for historical study. Yet a consideration of the strengths and weaknesses of each of these classes of measures will highlight several of the most important questions to be answered by a history of poverty in the United States. Once these questions have been posed, both kinds of measures can be jointly used to answer them. At least those that pertain to the most recent past can be answered, for a fairly complete record of the course of poverty since the 1930s can be derived. The discussion of this most recent period will also make possible some informed guesses on the course of poverty earlier, and in the foreseeable future.

Minimum-Decency Estimates

At the heart of a minimum-decency estimate is a basket of goods thought to constitute the material and psychological requisites of some specified level of welfare. When this basket of goods is priced in the marketplace, this money sum becomes a handy, one-number summary statement of the income level which separates the population into two classes—those living better than and those living worse than the specified welfare level—whatever the level happens to be.

In the United States the specified welfare level is not ever defined as biological subsistence, but rather (to quote from several studies) a "minimum-comfort" or "decent standard" of living. Nutritionists, sociologists, industry specialists, etc., specify the calorie content, floor-space requirement, clothing ration, etc., conforming, in their opinion, to a quite imprecisely specified welfare level for a very precisely specified representative family (e.g., an urban family of five, headed by a male manual worker, of age 42, having a 39-year-old wife, two sons, aged 15 and 6, and a girl, aged 12). To convert the general calorie, floor-space, and clothing requirements into a specific list of commodities, either expert advice or the actual expenditures of a sample of families having the requisite characteristics is examined. The result is an annual requirement for beef and soap, overcoats and underclothes, bus rides and sea-sick pills, which can be priced in the marketplace. The sum of annual expenditures that would result if all commodities specified were purchased is that disposable personal income *per family* which can buy the specified welfare level. For example, such a study resulted in a disposable income of $876.43 in New York City in 1914. In a more sophisticated study by the Labor Department in 1948, a disposable income of $922 for a single person was established, but the disposable income level was made to depend on the size of the family and rose to $2572 for a family of six.

Once one or a set of disposable income points describing the welfare level is established, the per cent of families earning less than that disposable income per year can be estimated, at least in recent years, either from income data obtained from a sample, or from adjusted income tax or old age survivor's insurance data. It is that group which is now called the poverty-stricken.

Having established a dollar value for the upper limit to poverty in some year, a new estimate of the proportion in poverty can then be calculated for subsequent or preceding years. Changes in the price level of the specified market basket are adjusted for, so that, for example, a 10 per cent rise in the price level raises the poverty level of disposable income by the same 10 per cent. Once an upper limit to the disposable income which defines poverty in a number of years has been established, the proportion in poverty in each of these years can then be determined.

It is not necessary for historical purposes to dwell upon the technical weaknesses of this procedure or the inappropriate uses to which the resulting minimum income level may be put. It is important for us to note two things. The first is that the resulting poverty level is pertinent to a particular time and place and that, therefore, the market basket must be reconstructed periodically. The second characteristic to be noted is that the resulting percentages of poverty-stricken should behave in a reasonably predictable way over time in an advancing economy (i.e., they should decline), and furthermore that those who remain in poverty should have predictable socioeconomic characteristics (i.e., be outside the labor force). The data, therefore, can be approached with some predetermined expectations.

The Consequences of Updating the Market Basket

From the description of the method of arriving at a market basket of goods which defines the minimum-decent cost-of-living, it is clear that this basket must be reconstituted from time to time, since many of the factors upon which it depends vary with time. The representative family changes in size and age composition over time; tastes change; as new products are introduced, calorie, shelter, and clothing requirements are met with different (and not necessarily more, or less, expensive) items. With economic growth and concomitant mechanization the energy input of the household head declines, thereby reducing his calorie requirements. The regional distribution of the population changes, with consequent changes in food, fuel, transportation, and other requirements to be met by the minimal budget. For all these reasons the market basket must be reconstituted from time to time.

In addition the price deflator for disposable income is likely to become increasingly irrelevant for yet another reason. For purposes of deriving a disposable personal-income figure in constant dollars as a minimal level of living, almost all price indices will have the disadvantage of never having been based on the same market basket which was used to derive the minimum-income estimate in the first place. Over time, therefore, the relevant market baskets may depart markedly from each other, as well as become outmoded in their own right. That is to say, a rise in the consumer price index of 10 per cent may not imply that the cost of buying the market basket of the poor has risen by 10 per cent, for the market basket underlying the consumer price index contained many items not in the market basket of the very poor in the first place, and in addition, consumption patterns have changed so that neither market basket actually is being purchased.

A new market basket with a new collection of goods that maintained the same standard of "minimum-decency" would be an absolute or fixed measure of poverty—but there is every indication that each new minimum-decency market basket will, in fact, turn out to represent a new and more expensive (though not necessarily more satisfying) standard. First of all as the output of an economy expands there are attendant changes which compel changes in the structure of the market basket. Many commodities are added to the market basket which raise the cost but not necessarily the standard of living. To the extent that economic growth implies industrialization, for example, and industrialization implies urbanization, a marked change in the composition of the market basket of the poor is also implied. A poor farmer does not buy restaurant meals, clothes fit to be seen in public, nor transportation with anything like the frequency that the poor urban dweller does. Over time the expenditures of the poor

family on education and education-related items must also expand. Finally, there is the inherently vague and relative character of any term such as "minimum-decency." Minimum-decency is a call for comparisons close at hand, and with rising income levels in the nation as a whole this is bound to be a rising standard of decency. Once having departed from biological requirements no absolute measure is possible. A group of experts looking down from an ever-rising standard of life (always called "middle-class" even when they live better than the Bourbons) will envision deprivation at some distance not too far below their own. To the extent that the experts take their budget items from consumption data, the whole process may become entirely circular. If, for example, the calorie intake of families with incomes of $3000–$5000 just meets the independently determined calorie requirement, the level of poverty will, to a large extent, be set when the expert chooses to use the food items contained in market baskets of families at any point along that $2000 range. That is, if he chooses the basket of the $5000 families, he will have gone a long way toward defining poverty at some high-income level and the opposite would result from choosing market baskets of lower-income families. Using a "typical worker's" budget will lead to setting poverty at the median income of all workers. Over time, poverty will then rise with average income, etc.

An example of the tendency for budget makers to raise the definition of poverty over time is contained in Table 1, where budgets that have been prepared at various times and by various agencies for New York City

Table 1. Selected New York City Budgets and Real Gross National Product, 1903–1959 (1959 Dollars)

Year	Real Minimum-Comfort Per Capita (1)	Real GNP Per Capita (2)	Col. (1) ÷ by Col. (2) (3)
1903–1905	$ 555	$1096	.51
1914	740	1217	.61
1918	618	1315	.47
1935	705	1383	.51
1947	984	2213	.44
1951	1021	2493	.41
1954	1011	2520	.40
1959	1082	2721	.40

workers are listed. Each budget (for goods and services) has been restated in 1959 dollars (using the consumer price index extrapolated back via the food price index) and put on a per capita basis. Except for very low budgets in 1918 and 1954 (which were not prepared by the Bureau of Labor Statistics), the real cost of the budget rises continuously. The 1959 budget is more than twice the 1903–1905 budget. As column 3 indicates, the minimum-comfort budgets per capita have generally been about one half of real gross national product per capita. Since these budgets are for a single city, many (but not all) of the factors which would necessitate increasing money expenditures to maintain the same real standard are not relevant, so that there can be no doubt that the rising money amounts, in dollars of constant purchasing power, reflect rising real standards as well.

In summary, having abandoned as irrelevant a biological definition of subsistence as the criteria by which individuals would be classified as poverty-stricken, a long historical study requires a poverty measure based on a series of different market baskets. These market baskets are very likely to represent a rising level of economic welfare. That poverty is, to some extent, a relative matter is inherent in the rejection of biological subsistence as the definition of poverty. To the extent that statistical measures based on need show a decline in poverty, that decline will have been achieved in the teeth of a rising definition. This being the case, it is foolish to expect (although not to attempt) the complete elimination (but not a reduction) of poverty. People may no longer die of malnutrition or pellagra, and debilitating illnesses from unsanitary plumbing conditions and overcrowding may someday be terminated, but poverty and social concern over it will remain.

Distribution Estimates

Minimum-budget measures of poverty are essential, though they may be relative and therefore ambiguous. However, certain aspects of this ambiguity are remediable. The remediable ambiguity is highlighted by the following question. To what extent are the changing socioeconomic characteristics of the poor revealed by the data due to the peeling off of layers of the poor population, and to what extent do they represent the working out of economic, social, and political processes? This ambiguity pervades both the absolute and relative minimum-budget measures. No extensive study of the variations in the market basket defining poverty over time has been made, so it is not possible to separate out these differing influences directly in the relative measures where variations are liable to be most serious. An alternative class of measures exists, however, which can shed light on this problem, both in the long and shorter periods. This alternative class of measures is intended to quantify the economic distance between the rich and the poor, or the poor and the average, where poor is defined in terms of the incomes of others and without any explicit reference to need. All take as their standard the degree of departure of the distribution of income from perfect equality. For example, the measure may ask: "To what extent is the share of the bottom 20 per cent approaching or departing further from 20 per cent of total income?" or, "How close is the average income of the lowest 20 per cent of the population to the national average?" And so on.

Now, a historical study of the lowest 20 per cent of income receivers in a society, when these are the poor by definition, baldly asserts that the poor are permanently with us. All pretense of eliminating poverty is abandoned. So straightforward a statement is a clear advance over the implicit hypocrisy of the relative poverty measures resulting from continual upward revision of the market basket defining poverty. Also these distribution measures add two elements of constancy not present in a relative measure based on a changing market basket. The first, of course, is that a constant proportion of the population is always being examined. This greatly simplifies any component analysis, so that when one says, for example, that the proportion of the poor who are over 65 has risen from 26 per cent to 31 per cent, the 26 and 31 per cent multiply a constant *proportion* of the total population. Secondly, some degree of stability is introduced. If the minimum market basket estimate puts 35 per cent in poverty in one year and 24 per cent in some later year, then not only is a statement that the aged rose from 26 to 31 per cent in the proportion of the poor difficult to evaluate, but the change may simply be the outcome of the changing proportion in poverty. It may well be that the aged are a larger proportion of the income group in the bottom quarter than in the bottom third of the income distribution in every year. In this case the measure chosen would suggest a change in the economic status of the aged, when there had, in fact, been no change.

Though the income distribution measures help to simplify the analysis, by themselves they add an element of uncertainty. Just how badly off are the bottom 20 per cent at different time periods? While an absolute definition of poverty will eventually become meaningless, so must it be that a purely relative measure could be misleading. Suppose, for example, that if Mr. Shriver were to ask for an additional $10 million for the Peace Corps, the Budget Bureau would insist on taking it from the War on Poverty. Surely the wisdom of such a trade-off turns, in part, on the extent of need among the differing groups to be helped—and some absolute standard of comparison is required. It would appear to be prudent therefore to use the distribution measures to complement the minimum-budget measures, thereby making the analysis more precise. The two classes of measure therefore are complementary in the study of poverty.

To the extent that the continuous upward revision in the definition of poverty reflects egalitarian sentiment, the share of income accruing to the lowest-income group is an independent measure of poverty. That is, the real issue may not be "What has happened to the proportion in poverty?" but rather, "How have the lowest-income groups fared relative to the rest of the nation?" It is perfectly plausible for the proportion in poverty (defined as some fixed or variable market basket) to decline while the lowest-income group gets a declining share of the whole pie. If the income of the lowest-income groups grew at the national average, or even more slowly, then each year some proportion of the population would, nevertheless, pass out of the poverty zone. To ask for a rising share of total income to go to the lowest-income groups when an economy is expanding is to request more than a decline in the proportion in poverty. The most severe critics of the performance of the American economy, those who allege that it has failed to disburse fairly the fruits of economic progress, generally apply this more stringent, but not necessarily inappropriate, criterion [1].

THE COURSE OF POVERTY SINCE THE SECOND WORLD WAR

The current discussion of poverty, by and large, takes as its upper limit $3000 in 1962

Table 2. Per Cent of Consumer Units With Less Than $3000 Income (in 1954 Dollars) in Selected Years

Year	Per Cent	Year	Per Cent
1929	59.2	1951	31.4
1935–1936	62.6	1952	30.1
1941	47.1	1953	29.0
1944	31.6	1954	30.2
—	—	1955	27.3
1946	32.3	1956	25.6
1947	34.9	1957	26.0
—	—	1958	26.7
—	—	1959	25.9
—	—	1960	25.4
—	—	1961	25.3
1950	34.5	1962	23.9

prices, before taxes.[1] This is the sum used by the Council of Economic Advisers in their economic report to the President for 1962 and recurs repeatedly in the House hearings on the Economic Opportunity Act. Its basis is a market basket defined by the Social Security Administration. In the discussion that follows we will use a definition of poverty that is somewhat higher because the data are most easily and reliably obtainable on that basis. The measure of poverty to be used is $3000 before income tax in 1954 dollars. (This measure raises the definition of poverty about 12 per cent above that of the Council of Economic Advisers, but leaves the trend unaffected.)

Table 2 lists the proportion of consumer units in poverty (by this definition) for each of the years 1947 and 1950 through 1962. Table 2 reveals that the growth in real income was widely distributed over this period. Using this absolute measure of poverty, the proportion of all families in poverty falls from 35 to 24 per cent, or 31 per cent of the way toward the elimination of poverty, in 15 years. Although the decline in the proportion in poverty is almost continuous over the period, very pronounced declines occur in the years 1951 and 1955. More than half of the total

---

[1] Of course no single money value can be an accurate guide to the proportions in poverty. As already indicated, age, sex composition, available assets, region, and year-to-year variability in income must be taken into account. More refined measures do not result in greatly different proportions in poverty, however, because of compensating defects in the gross measures. In any event the trend in the proportions in poverty is not likely to be highly sensitive to refinements in the measures.

decline in the proportion of those in poverty occurs in those two years. The data also seem to show a slow-down in the rate of decline in the proportion in poverty after 1956. The decline in the proportion in poverty is interrupted only twice: in 1954 and in 1957–1958.

POVERTY IN DEPRESSION AND WAR

An unbelievable 59 per cent of all consumer units were in poverty in 1929, if the measure of poverty used is 3000 (1954) dollars. This percentage rises to 63 per cent in the revival —but still deeply depressed—years of 1935–1936, falls to 47 per cent by 1941, and to 32 per cent by the end of the war. By this measure, through 1960 poverty had declined almost three fifths of the way to oblivion in about 35 years, with the decline accelerating to peak speed during the Second World War and abating thereafter.

The time path of change—increase in poverty during the early depression years, decline, thereafter, rapidly accelerating in the war years and then slowing down—is not in doubt, but the magnitude of change is most uncertain. It is possible, but highly unlikely, that 63 per cent is a reasonable estimate of the proportion in poverty in 1935–1936, but it is absurd to believe that 59 per cent of consumer units were in poverty in 1929. (That these numbers generate such an intuitive response is reason enough for insisting on a measure of poverty that changes over time.) Any more reasonable estimate of the extent of poverty during the depression and before will have the effect of reducing the rate at which poverty declines over the period, so that a 60 per cent reduction in poverty represents an upper limit to the rate of decline in poverty since 1929.

This is precisely the kind of result to be expected if some absolute measure of poverty is used over a very long period, but surprisingly, a relative measure of poverty derived by using a market basket specifically designed to describe levels of living in the 1930s does not significantly alter the proportions in poverty. The Works Progress Administration (WPA) established a set of commodities designed to provide an adequate standard of living at the lowest economic level for a family of four. In 1935 that market basket cost $1261 (on the average in the 59 largest cities), and adjusting only for price changes

that same basket would have cost about $2600 in 1954. The measure most consistently used in this paper, 3000 (1954) dollars, is a rise in the definition of poverty of about 15 per cent; but the WPA budget is very close to 3000 (1962) dollars, which is the measure in most common use. This 15 per cent rise in the definition of poverty, however, does not materially alter the proportion in poverty in any year. Utilizing the WPA budget puts the proportion of consumer units in poverty at about 50 per cent in 1929 and 54 per cent in 1935–1936. Combining the two measures of poverty by using the WPA budget only for the year 1929 reduces the rate of reduction in poverty from 60 to 50 per cent over the period 1929 to 1960.

The National Resources Committee study of consumer expenditures, upon which the 1935–1936 estimates are largely based, divides the population into thirds for comparative analysis. The bottom third of nonrelief families earned less than 750 current dollars. If that figure is taken as a measure of poverty in 1935–1936, then when revalued in 1954 dollars, the poverty level in 1954 comes to $1580, so that the definition of poverty in primary use in this paper is about a 90 per cent increase in the real content of the poverty budget. Using 750 (1935) dollars as an absolute measure of poverty results in a less spectacular but still substantial decline in poverty—40 per cent of the way toward complete elimination since 1935–1936. A relative measure of poverty, that is, 750 (1935) dollars in 1935 and 3000 (1954) dollars in 1960, results in an even more modest decline in the proportion of poverty —25 per cent of the way toward complete elimination in 25 years.

The Distribution Estimates

The distribution estimates point to a quite modest rise in the *relative* well-being of the poor since the mid-thirties. In 1935–1936 the lowest 20 per cent of consumer units received 4.1 per cent of all family personal income. Between 1935–1936 and 1947 the share of this group rose to 5.0 per cent of income— a 22 per cent rise in the share of the lowest quintile. Since 1947 the share of the lowest-income group has drifted downward to 4.6 per cent. The over-all rise of one half of one per cent in the share of total income going to the lowest quintile of the population since 1935–1936 is a movement of only 3 per cent toward perfect equality since the mid-depression. Unfortunately, data are not directly obtainable on the share of the lowest quintile in 1929.

Socioeconomic Characteristics

The broad surveys of income distribution in the prewar periods are not rich in socioeconomic data. The National Resources Committee did comment on the disproportionate number of poor living on farms, in rural communities but not on farms, in the South, and among nonwhites. Age and sex of the household head were not commented upon, but Miller [3], using the census data, did take note of these characteristics. Reviewing the changes that occurred in the socioeconomic characteristics of low-income families between 1939 and 1947, Miller found a significant change [3, p. 218]. In the earlier year the poor tended to be "normal" families hit by unemployment or underemployment, but by 1947 broken families and households headed by the aged had become prominent. In earlier periods the foreign-born would have had a prominent place among the poor.

In general, then, the socioeconomic characteristics of the poor would appear to be the obvious ones suggested by common-sense, but their proportions change over time. There is certainly, however, a pronounced tendency for groups outside the normal economic processes to rise in relative importance.

THE PRE-DEPRESSION PERIOD

The data on the extent of poverty and on the distribution of income in the pre-1929 period is extremely sketchy. There are some surveys of the Bureau of Labor Statistics which are confined to small segments of the urban working population. There are a few studies by pioneer researchers which are difficult to evaluate. And there are tax data which cover only the very highest income recipients until the Second World War. One very careful attempt to utilize all these data to get some reliable impression of changes in the income distribution as a whole since 1890 has been made, and for some time to come the results of that study will be the best guide to the historical record. The conclusions of that study follow.

By concentrating on the grosser changes in our indexes of inequality . . . we may surmise that the period between 1890 and 1955 was characterized first by a phase of narrowing inequality extending roughly from 1890 to 1920, next by a decade of somewhat increasing inequality, then by a second phase of substantial diminution in inequality from about 1930 to 1945; and finally a decade of relative stability [2, p. 214].

Deducing the course of poverty from the record on the distribution of income is treacherous. On the one hand, in the period for which data are most readily available it can be shown that declining income inequality has largely been achieved by a more rapid growth in income of the middle-income group relative to the very highest-income recipients, with the lowest group raising their relative position hardly at all. On the other hand, we know that based on even a relative and rising measure of need, the proportion in poverty has declined when there has been little change in the share of income going to the lowest-income group. That is, the income of the lowest-income group has grown at about the national average which reduced the proportion of families and individuals in poverty, even when the share of the lowest quintile was slowly falling.

Between 1935 and 1947, for example, the share of the top 5 per cent of income recipients in family personal income fell from 26.5 to 20.9 per cent, while the share of the lowest quintile went from 4.1 to 5.0 per cent, and this is the period in which the lowest quintile fared best relative to all other quintiles and the top 5 per cent. From 1935–1936 to 1960, the share of the top 5 per cent fell from 26.5 to 19.6 per cent of all family income, but the share of the lowest quintile rose from 4.1 per cent to a mere 4.6 per cent. Put another way, over the period 1935–1936 to 1960, the share of the top 5 per cent moved 32 per cent of the way toward perfect equality, while the share of the lowest 20 per cent moved only 3 per cent of the way toward perfect equality. In general, the lowest income band has benefited least from the massive relative redistribution of income away from the highest income group that has taken place since 1929, and therefore one expects that the same is true for earlier periods.

On the other hand, in the period 1947–1960, in which the share of the lowest quintile was falling as a proportion of total income from 5.0 to 4.6 per cent, the proportion in poverty based on some constant market basket fell from 35 per cent to 25 per cent.

CONCLUSION ON THE COURSE OF POVERTY

Even by the high standards for ambiguity characteristic of economists, the preceding pages are indecently of the "it's all in how you look at it" variety. Something more than that can be deduced from the record, however. That the proportion in poverty in the U.S. (whether defined in terms of a fixed or growing market basket) has declined is not in doubt. The growing American economy has distributed its additional product broadly over its population. Nor can it be doubted, however, that despite the rapid rate at which America's middle class moved to catch the highest-income group in the society, the lowest-income groups have made no appreciable headway in this direction. In general, the growth of income of the lowest fifth has been just about at the national average.

Magnitudes, if not directions, of change are in doubt, and the failure of the minimum-budget estimates and the distribution estimates to yield the same *qualitative* results, clouds the interpretation of the results. With a fixed definition of poverty, in real terms, poverty declined three tenths of the way toward total elimination between 1947 and 1962, and six tenths of the way toward total elimination between 1929 and 1962. An absolute measure of poverty puts an absurd number in poverty in 1929, however, and therefore grossly overstates the rate of decline in poverty. Revising the market basket does not alter the results significantly. For the pre-1929 period, reliance must be placed on the distribution estimates—and all that can be said is that the proportion of families in poverty most certainly declined by any absolute definition of poverty in the early decades of this century, despite heavy immigration. Constant references to one third of the nation in poverty in the 1890s and later imply, however, that on a relative definition poverty remained unchanged during the period 1890–1935. This constancy has been traced by Brady at least to 1890.

In 1890 Charles Booth, in his monumental *Life and Labour of the People* found 30 per cent of the population of London living "below the line of poverty." During the depression decade a similar ratio was dramatized in the well-known expression, "one third of the Nation." Recent statistics for American cities lead to the conclusion that approximately 30 per cent of the population have incomes insufficient to maintain a decent level of living. The attempts of investiga-

tions for more than half a century have apparently led to about the same answer to the question. "What proportion of the population does not have a minimum standard of living?" [cited in *4*, p. 2].

It may be possible to establish a two-part goal which takes into account both need and egalitarian principle, thereby simplifying the interpretation of the historical record, although it is also possible to become mired in paradox in the process.

Assume, for example, that the minimum-comfort budgets reported in Table 1 for New York City accurately reflect the *relative* rise in welfare levels demanded by some national consensus. Taking 3000 (1959) dollars as the contemporary definition of poverty, a poverty measure for each of the years 1935 and 1947 can be constructed on the assumption that the ratio of the 1935 and 1947 poverty limits for the nation as a whole should be the same as the ratio of these years to 1959, evidenced in the New York City budgets. This method, could it be relied upon, would reduce the concern with the share of the lowest quintile, for presumably full allowance for prevailing egalitarian sentiment would have been allowed for in the definition of poverty. The result is a decline in poverty from one third to one fifth of the nation between the mid-depression and 1959—about the same result obtained between the war's end and 1959, when an absolute measure of poverty is used. Staying put on a moving track requires hard running, which may in fact be the true and just nature of the poverty problem.

| | DEFINITION OF POVERTY | |
Year	Definition of Poverty (1959 Dollars)	Per Cent in Poverty
1959	$3000	23
1947	2730	27
1935	1956	37

Without some assurance that the rising poverty definition fully reflects egalitarian and humanitarian sentiment, the failure of the bottom quintile to raise its share in total income poses an important problem of interpretation, for the share in income of the lowest quintile measures how fast the income of the lowest-income group is rising relative to the national average, while the rising minimum-comfort budget also asserts that poverty has to be measured with reference to a rising national average income. In general, the minimum-comfort budgets have risen less than gross national product per capita, so that falling income shares and falling poverty levels have not been inconsistent. Also, the fourth quintile has been able to raise its mean income more rapidly than the fifth, and since the minimum-budget estimates are generally above the cut-off for the lowest quintile, the proportion in poverty falls through time. Since the bottom quintile's share in income does not rise as over-all income rises, as the fixed budget converges toward the upper-income limit of the bottom quintile, the poverty problem appears to become increasingly intransigent. Paradoxically, then, the periodic upward shift in the minimum-comfort budgets also periodically makes the poverty issue seem easier to handle.

To sum up, since the share of the lowest quintile income is in the same spirit but a more stringent relative measure of poverty than the minimum-comfort budget, choosing the minimum-comfort budget makes for a decline in poverty that some criticize as illusory, for no such decline appears when the more stringent measure is employed. The truth of the charge is not a technical matter, but rather a matter of personal evaluation. If the periodic rises in the minimum-comfort budget fully meet the need for a relative measure of poverty, then poverty has probably declined in this century in the United States.

A second result of this brief historical survey of poverty and income distribution in the United States in the twentieth century turns on the socioeconomic characteristics of the poor. It must be recognized that the ultimate cause of poverty remains undetermined. The especially identifying socioeconomic characteristics of the poor are, however, well known, and they are relatively unchanged over time. The poor are now, and have been throughout our history, disproportionately aged, or young, or disabled, widowed, divorced or abandoned, and nonwhite. The proportion in poverty at any time, therefore, will depend in part on the proportions of the population with each of these characteristics, and that proportion is largely, although not altogether, independent of the success of the economy in raising levels of well-being. The proportion of the population with each of these characteristics has been growing throughout the twentieth century. A reduction in the proportion of the population in poverty, there-

fore, must take place even though the demographic and social characteristics of the population are working in the opposite direction (although in this country the cessation of immigration in the 1920s is a demographic fact that made the reduction in poverty considerably simpler than would have been the case in the preceding forty years).

It is crucial in the determination of policy to divide into two groups those who are poor because they suffer from some debilitating socioeconomic characteristic. One group would be those who are outside of the normal economic process—the aged and women heading households might be two examples. This group is outside the market process because it is quite clear that this nation does not want their problems to be solved by drawing them back into the labor force. If this is so, the means to keep these individuals out of the labor force ought to be reconsidered. The power of the state or group mores can be used to involuntarily exclude these individuals from the labor force, or the analogue to the traditional market-place technique of sufficiently large transfer payments to remove the temptation to labor can be utilized. It is not clear that the former method, the one in primary use today, is more consistent with the free-enterprise ethic than is the latter.

That second group, those who are poor even though they are in the labor force, poses an entirely different set of issues. The nonwhites, the farmers and other rural dwellers, women who are willing and anxious to work, youths just now entering the labor force, the involuntarily unemployed of all kinds, and that 40 per cent of the poor who have no socioeconomic characteristics which would appear to be obviously debilitating, what is to be done about the market failures that keep these individuals in poverty? The historical record gives some indication of an answer.

It can be no accident that the sharp declines in income inequality occurred in the period 1880 to 1910 and 1940 to 1945. These were years of extraordinary economic growth in the society as a whole. Per capita income on the other hand rose very slowly in the 1920s. Careful examination of the record during the Second World War suggests that a long sustained period of full-employment is an extraordinary stimulus towards reducing income inequality. A long and sustained full-employment breaks down the barriers to mobility that help to maintain poverty. During the Second World War, for example, the shift out of agriculture came in extraordinary numbers, even though agricultural income per worker during this period was rising relative to nonagricultural income per worker. Nonwhites left the farms in greater proportions than whites. At the same time there was a flow of labor from low-income regions to high-income regions. Within other occupations income differences between the highest- and lowest-income groups narrowed. In short, in the scramble for workers in a period of high employment, especially one in which prices and wages are not highly flexible upward, people are moved geographically and occupationally. They move because there is some place to go: jobs are redefined and reassigned and traditional social barriers of race and sex fall. Sustained full-employment creates a condition in the labor market which makes it cheaper for firms to rethink the tasks assigned to labor, to reorganize them, and to make them available to individuals not skilled enough to take those jobs as traditionally designed. Labor moves from low- to high-income occupations, industries, and regions. Furthermore, given the opportunity, it would appear that an income differential between what is being earned in the low-income, low-skilled occupations and what could be earned in a higher-skilled occupation can narrow and yet, at least for some time, employees will move to the higher-income occupation in increasing numbers. Of course there are many routes to full-employment and rapid growth, and choices among those routes should be made with the socioeconomic characteristics of the poor in mind.

EXPLAINING THE COURSE OF POVERTY

Standard Western economic theory makes no prediction about the course of income inequality over time, although it generates the expectation that gains in output will be widely distributed. Pareto, a national socialist, believed that market economies generate an unchanging distribution of income. Marx, of course, believed that a capitalist economy would generate growing income inequality. The most eminent contemporary student of income distribution, Simon Kuznets, believes that income inequality increases in the early stages of industrialization and decreases in later stages. Whether or not Kuznets is right about the early stages of development, he is certainly right about the latter—the spread of industrialization and declining economic inequality have come together in the twentieth century in the United States. It is primarily for this reason that the old socialist tradition in the discussion of income distribution is dying out. Rather than discussing the distribution as a whole with its implications for deep-seated and widespread social change, the discussion now is on the amelioration of the conditions of the poor. Because property income contributes only modestly to the income inequality in the distribution of wages in making the whole of the income distribution unequal, the discussion has left expropriation of property far behind, and in its place is the press for limited social reform that takes cognizance of the socioeconomic characteristics of the poor.

There is no shortage of explanations of the decline in income inequality, at least in the United States in this century, and especially of the period since 1929. There are diminishing skill differentials in the labor force because the widespread rise in education levels and the decline in immigration have made the labor force more homogeneous, while mechanization has hit the highly skilled and the unskilled more severely than the semiskilled. Unions have in some periods tended to bargain in ways that reduce major differentials. And the high-income occupations have grown more rapidly than the low.

The government through its progressive tax structure and its even more progressive system of transfer payments and direct provisions of services is said to play a part.

Then, too, the labor force has grown more slowly than the supply of capital, raising the returns of labor relative to capital so rapidly that interest and dividend income have fallen drastically as a proportion of personal income. Since wages are more equally distributed than property income, the net result is a decline in income inequality.

All in all, the variety of explanations constitutes an embarrassment of riches. The author's studies of the income distribution since 1920, however, point to two factors of primary quantitative significance. Both have already been mentioned. One is the decline in the share of personal income that takes the form of property income. The other is the geographic spread of industrialization throughout the United States [6].

The changes that have been noted in the distribution of income among persons have also been noted among the states of the United States. When the low-income regions are gaining on the high, so are low-income persons in the distribution for the nation as a whole. Conversely, when the poor regions are losing ground relative to the rich regions, income inequality increases in the distribution of all families in the nation. What is responsible for these parallel changes in the two income distributions?

The enormous and persistent differences in income per worker which have existed between farmers and others in the labor force is at the heart of the matter. The factors that simultaneously produced the observed changes in the size and spatial distributions of income have been the shift of labor from the agricultural to the nonagricultural sector and the sometimes concomitant and sometimes diverse movements of earnings per worker in the two sectors.

Of all the ways in which an individual can raise his income there has been one which was (and is) open almost exclusively to the lowest-income groups and which was taken advantage of in such large numbers and with such dramatic effect as to produce, simultaneously, sizeable reductions in income inequality in the size and spatial distributions. This was the shift of labor out of agriculture.

The same lack of interdependence that has allowed large differences in income per worker to persist for so long has also made possible diverse movements in mean income per worker in the two sectors and in dispersion in the two sectors. As a consequence, movements in average earnings have sometimes tended to reinforce the effects of the labor force shift and sometimes have been a strong enough counterforce to swamp the movement towards equality implicit in the relative and absolute declines in the agricultural labor force [5, p. 68].

At least since 1850 in the United States declining income inequality and rising growth were proximately attributable to the same factor—the withering away of the agrarian sector. Generally this was reinforced by a tendency for agricultural income per worker to rise relative to nonagricultural income per worker, but the post-Civil War collapse of Southern agriculture, and the agricultural depression of the 1920s upset the pattern. In those two periods the fall in agricultural income per worker relative to nonagricultural income per worker was sufficient to reverse the decline in inequality.

But agriculture is no longer the repository of an overwhelmingly large group of the poor. What does this past history tell us about the future of the Negroes, women, and the middle-aged, unskilled white workers in the slowly growing industries caught in the backwash of economic growth? More, I think, than is often assumed.

In general it is correct to say that the jobs made newly available to the low-income disadvantaged population are, like the industries transferred to the low-income regions, those being abandoned by the higher-income workers and regions. Nevertheless, the relative increase in earnings is greater for the low-income groups than the high, and income inequality declines in the process. So, for example, New England workers are moved from the woolen mills to the electronics plants, thereby raising their incomes. The mills move South, raising Southern income and generating a rapid growth in the service sector. The rural population of the South moving into the urban service industries find their wages higher by a considerably larger percentage than was the rise in the New England workers' wages. Income inequality declines!

Rapid growth, therefore, raises the levels of living of the population as a whole and reduces physical deprivation. The income of the fourth quintile of income recipients rises faster than the national average, at least in some periods, and certainly the long-term trend is up, relatively for the fourth, third, and second quintiles. Their rise was so rapid during the Second World War that it is fair to speak perhaps for the first time in the century, of a decline in poverty, even if in relative terms. One suspects that the change from Roosevelt's one third of a nation to Johnson's one fifth of a nation constitutes a permanent change in the proportion in poverty, a change that will not be eliminated by future upward shifts in the minimum-comfort budget.

If this is so, the poverty issue may prove difficult to deal with in the future, for the share of the lowest quintile in total income appears to be highly stable over the long run.

Indeed, the contemporary period may be one of decreasing relative shares for the lowest-income groups, and this declining trend may be accelerating. There are many sources of error due to both omission and commission in the income-distribution statistics. On balance, it is the judgment of most experts in this area that the data are biased towards over-estimating the degree of decline in income inequality. This judgment rests, by and large, on a belief that capital gains and income supplements in the form of expense accounts, automobiles, stock options, etc., are accruing to a much greater extent at the upper end of the income distribution than at the lower, and these do not find their way into the income-distribution statistics. A bias of less than one half of 1 per cent in the income share would be sufficient to wipe out all the gains made by the lowest quintiles since 1935. This, and the apparent secular increase in levels of unemployment in the last decade, point to the possibility of a serious trend towards increasing inequality during the next decade. (A potential offset is the rise in family size at the upper end of the income distribution relative to family size at the lower end of the distribution.)

Unless the minimum-comfort budgets rise considerably more slowly than gross national product per capita, poverty is likely to appear a very intransigent problem in the next decade, unless full-employment is achieved soon and with it a rapid rise in the growth rate.

There is a paradox here. Higher rates of growth will lead to a more rapid rise in the definition of poverty, but only when that definition rises rapidly can poverty be reduced. That is the lesson of this history.

REFERENCES

1. Gabriel Kolko, *Wealth and Power in America*, New York, Frederick A. Praeger, 1962.
2. Irving B. Kravis, *The Structure of Income*, Philadelphia, University of Pennsylvania Press, 1962.
3. Herman P. Miller, "Factors Related to Recent Changes in Income Distribution in the United States," *The Review of Economics and Statistics*, 33 (August, 1951), 214–218.
4. Herman P. Miller, *Trends in the Income of Families and Persons in the United States: 1947 to 1960*, Washington, D.C., 1963.
5. Eugene Smolensky, "Industrialization and Income Inequality: Recent United States Experience," *Papers and Proceedings of the Regional Science Association*, 7 (1961), 67–88.
6. Eugene Smolensky, "An Interrelationship Among Income Distributions," *The Review of Economics and Statistics, 45* (May, 1963), 197–206.

III THE EXPLANATION OF INDUSTRIAL EXPANSION

One of the most obvious lines of continuity between the new and the old economic history is their common preoccupation with the explanation for the growth of particular industries. No topic has received more attention from cliometricians than this one—a fact which is reflected in the length of Part III. Like their predecessors, the new economic historians are impressed with the contribution of technological change to industrial expansion. Thus three of the next six essays focus on this issue. Nor is there anything novel about the industries which have been singled out for special attention. Cotton textiles, iron, and steam railroads are, after all, the classic cases in the traditional treatment of the Industrial Revolution.

What is novel about the work of econometric historians in the study of industrial expansion is their attempt to pass beyond the mere identification of the factors responsible for growth to the measurement of the relative contribution of these factors in a wide array of industries. Growth-inducing factors may be grouped into two categories: those which lead to an increase in the demand for a product and those which lead to an increase in the supply. Essays 9, 10, and 11 set out to determine whether demand or supply factors were more important in promoting the growth of the iron and cotton textile industries. Essays 10 and 11 go on to attempt to measure the contribution of each of the principal growth-inducing factors on both the demand side and the supply side. These measurements are based on what, by the standards of previous work in history, are relatively elaborate models.

Essays 12, 13, and 14 measure the rate of technological change in transportation and agriculture. They also assess the factors responsible for such change. Since each of the essays attaches a different name to its measure (total factor productivity in essay 12, and labor productivity in essay 13, and the social saving in essay 14), these indexes may appear to be entirely different. In actuality they are very closely related.

In the next section of this introduction we set forth the basic proposition on which these measures of technological change rest. We then go on to demonstrate the interrelationship between the measures used in each of the last three essays of Part III. The conclud-ing section of the introduction attempts to elucidate certain of the concepts on which the supply and demand models of essays 9, 10, and 11 are based. It is intended particularly for readers who are new to the language and models of economic theory.

THE MEASUREMENT OF TECHNOLOGICAL CHANGE

The measurement of technological change rests on the assumption that in the production of goods and services there is a systematic relationship between inputs and output. Such systematic relationships are described by equations which are called *production functions*. A production function gives the maximum amount of the output of a given commodity which can be obtained from various combinations of inputs.

There are many functional forms by which inputs and outputs may be related to each other. One of the most widely used forms is given by equation 1.

$$Q = AL^{\alpha_1}R^{\alpha_2}K^{\alpha_3} \tag{1}$$

In this equation Q stands for output. L, R, and K represent three inputs, namely labor, raw materials, and capital. Of course most production processes involve many different types of labor, capital, and raw materials. However, for analytical as well as empirical reasons it is convenient to combine all of the various types of labor used in a production process into a single index which measures the total labor input. The same procedure can be followed for raw materials and capital. The three powers, α_1, α_2, and α_3, are the output elasticities of the three inputs. The concept of elasticities is discussed in more detail below. Briefly, an elasticity is a coefficient which measures the percentage change in one variable that will be brought about by a 1 per cent change in another variable. Thus α_1 is the percentage change in output that would be brought about by a 1 per cent change in the labor input, when the level of the other inputs is held constant.

The A in equation 1 is an index of productive efficiency. It is called the index of *total factor productivity* and is frequently used to measure technological change. The nature of A is more clearly revealed if equation 1 is rewritten to make A the dependent variable, as in equation 2.

$$A = \frac{Q}{L^{\alpha_1} R^{\alpha_2} K^{\alpha_3}} \qquad (2)$$

From this formulation it is clear that when the powers of the inputs sum to one, A is the ratio of an index of output to a geometric average of the inputs.[1] Consequently A will rise whenever output increases more rapidly than the average increase in the inputs. Among the factors which most frequently cause increases in productive efficiency are new machinery and equipment, improved organization, and improvements in the quality of labor and raw materials.

In essay 11 it is shown that the index of productive efficiency defined by equation 1 is identical with

$$A = \frac{n w^{\alpha_1} r^{\alpha_2} i^{\alpha_3}}{P} \qquad (3)$$

where w, r, and i are the cost of a unit of labor, of raw materials, and of capital respectively; P is the price of the product; and n is a factor of proportionality. This identity is frequently useful in practical work, since often it is easier to find the price data needed to compute A from equation 3 than the data on physical inputs and outputs needed to compute A from equation 2. Indeed, Douglass North makes use of this duality in measuring the rate of growth of efficiency in ocean shipping.

Equations 2 and 3 are methods of measuring the *level* of efficiency in a given industry. However, often one is concerned not with the level but with the way in which efficiency (as measured by A) changes over time. It is a simple matter of calculus to transform equations 2 and 3 into equations which measure the rate of change in efficiency. The

exact mathematical operations need not detain us, since only the results of these manipulations are pertinent here. The rate-of-growth transformations desired are

$$\overset{*}{A} = \overset{*}{Q} - (\alpha_1 \overset{*}{L} + \alpha_2 \overset{*}{R} + \alpha_3 \overset{*}{K}) \qquad (4)$$

and

$$\overset{*}{A} = \alpha_1 \overset{*}{w} + \alpha_2 \overset{*}{r} + \alpha_3 \overset{*}{i} - \overset{*}{P} \qquad (5)$$

In this notation variables capped by asterisks stand for the rates of growth of the variables represented by the uncapped letters. Thus $\overset{*}{A}$ is the percentage rate of growth of A. Equation 4 states that the rate of growth of the efficiency index is equal to the rate of growth of output minus an arithmetic average of the rates of growth of the inputs. Equation 5 states that the rate of growth of efficiency may also be measured by the difference between an arithmetic average of the rates of change in input prices and the rate of change in the price of output. In this last formulation, efficiency increases whenever input prices grow more rapidly on the average than the price of output (or when input prices on the average fall less rapidly than the price of output).

Ocean Shipping (Essay 12)

Equation 5 is the one which Douglass C. North employs to measure the rate of growth of efficiency in ocean shipping. North also sets out to determine how much of the value of $\overset{*}{A}$ which he computes was due to better organization and how much to new equipment. To answer this question, he derives an equation (equation 11 in his paper) which relates the increase in efficiency to such factors as the cargo capacity of ships, the rate of capacity utilization, ship speed, and the time spent in port.

North finds that over the period from 1600 to 1784, the improvement in efficiency was a moderate 0.5 per cent per year and that most of this gain is explained by two developments: a reduction in the average size of the crew and a reduction of the time that ships were required to be in port. For the period 1814–1860, the rate of growth of efficiency is a substantial 3.3 per cent a year. Singled out as the main explanatory factors are the increase in the capacity of ships and the greater utilization of capacity.

---

[1] Students are more familiar with arithmetic than with geometric averages. Both methods of averaging usually give quite similar results. For example, the arithmetic average of three grades (90, 86, and 70) is

$$\frac{90 + 86 + 70}{3} = 82$$

The geometric average of the same grades is the cube root of their product; i.e., it is

$$\sqrt[3]{90 \times 86 \times 70} = (90)^{1/3} (86)^{1/3} (70)^{1/3} = 81.5$$

North argues that most of these changes were due to improved organization rather than new equipment. He attributes the reduction in port time to the system of selling tobacco through commission brokers (called factors), and the transfer of inventories, previously held on scattered plantations, to central depositories. Both developments made it easier for ships to obtain cargoes. The increase in the rate of utilization of capacity came about largely because of an increased flow of immigrants to the United States. Immigrants thus provided a return cargo to ships whose main business was the transportation of bulky raw materials from the U.S. to Europe. The reduction in the average size of a ship's crew was due to another institutional change: the decline in piracy. As long as piracy was a substantial threat, each ship was armed and carried a complement of military personnel for the protection of the ship. As the threat of attack diminished, military complements became superfluous. It was the elimination of military complements which caused the average crew size to decline.

By far the most substantial factor accounting for the increase in efficiency was the increase in the average capacity of ships. The increase in capacity was important because the transportation cost per ton of cargo on ships of large size (500 to 1000 tons) was substantially below that of smaller ships (25 to 100 tons). It might therefore seem that innovation in ship design was the main factor accounting for the rise in efficiency. North argues against such an inference. He holds that no new technological knowledge was required for the switch from fleets of predominantly small ships to fleets of predominantly large ones. Throughout the period highly efficient large ships coexisted with small, less efficient ones.

In this view the shipping industry may be divided into two sectors, each with its own production function; these are a small-ship sector and a large-ship sector. Moreover, the efficiency index of the large-ship sector was greater than that of the small-ship sector. The efficiency index of the entire industry is a weighted average of the sector indexes. The weights are the shares of each sector in total shipping services. It follows that even if the efficiency of each sector remained constant, the over-all industry efficiency index would rise over time as long as the share of large ships in the total fleet increased.

What then explains the dominance of the small over the large ship in the seventeenth and eighteenth centuries and then the rapid shift toward large ships between 1800 and 1860? North again finds the answer not in new technological knowledge, but in institutional change. He argues that the elimination of piracy made it feasible to build large, light vessels for the exclusive purpose of carrying cargoes.[2]

Steam Railroads (Essay 14)

In his study of American railroads Robert W. Fogel investigates the effect of the improvement in transportation technology on the growth of national product. The question he asks is: "By how much did the substitution of railroads for water and wagon transportation increase the economy's productive capacity?" Recognizing that there were many avenues through which railroads might have affected the growth of the economy, Fogel divides these lines of influence into two categories, primary effect and derived effects. The *primary effect* of railroads was their impact on the cost of transportation. The *derived effects* included such things as the impact of railroads on the spatial distribution of economic activity, on the demand for manufactured goods, on human psychology, on political power, and on social organization. Clearly, the railroads could have increased the productive capacity of the economy through either their primary or derived effects or through both.

The central device employed by Fogel in measuring the primary benefit of the railroads is the *social saving*. The social saving in any given year is defined as the difference between the actual cost of shipping goods in that year and the alternative cost of shipping exactly the same bundle of goods between exactly the same set of points without railroads. Unfortunately the social saving is not a precise measure of the increase in the productive capacity of the economy, or of full-employment national income, made possible by

---

[2] Of course, if the elimination of piracy involved an increase in the productive resources employed by navies, some part of the rise in North's index of total factor productivity will be due to the fact that certain inputs were not properly measured. These inputs were counted in the beginning of the period when they were provided by the industry but not at the end of the period when they were provided by governments.

railroads. Rather it is a measure of the upper limit of the primary effect of railroads.

Fogel's measure will be more clearly understood if one divides the economy into two sectors. One sector produces all things but transportation. The activities of the second sector, which produces transportation, can be carried on under either of two production functions. The railroad production function is more efficient than the nonrailroad production function. Since the quantity of transportation service to be produced is fixed, the substitution of the railroad for the nonrailroad production function makes it possible to produce the fixed amount of transportation service with less inputs than was true previously. The social saving, then, is the amount of additional output of all other things that can be produced by the productive factors which have been released from the transportation sector.

For those who prefer the language of mathematics, the argument of the preceding paragraph can be restated as follows.[3] Let

$$Q_o = f(L_o, K_o) \tag{6}$$

$$Q_T = g(L_w, K_w) \tag{7}$$

$$Q_T = h(L_r, K_r) \tag{8}$$

where

Q = output
L = labor
K = capital
o = a subscript denoting the sector producing all other things
T = a subscript denoting the transportation sector

The h process (the production of transportation service with railroads) is superior to the g (the production of transportation service without railroads), so that Q_T can be produced under h with less labor and capital than under g. In other words

$$L_w = L_r + \Delta L \tag{9}$$

$$K_w = K_r + \Delta K \tag{10}$$

National income under the g function is $Q_o + Q_T$. Substitution of the h for the g function, keeping Q_T constant, will release

---

[3] Those who do not prefer the language of mathematics should skip to the next paragraph.

ΔL and ΔK for employment in the production of all other things. National income (Y) will then be

$$Y = Q_o' + Q_T \tag{11}$$

where

$$Q_o' = f(L_o + \Delta L, K_o + \Delta K) \tag{12}$$

Consequently, the social saving, which is the increase in national income permitted by the superior transportation technology (or the loss in going from the superior to the inferior technology), is given by

$$Q_o' + Q_T - (Q_o + Q_T) = Q_o' - Q_o \tag{13}$$

or

$$Q_o' + Q_T - (Q_o + Q_T)$$
$$= \frac{\partial Q_o}{\partial L} \Delta L + \frac{\partial Q_o}{\partial K} \Delta K \tag{14}$$

which may be expressed in value terms as

$$\left(\frac{\partial Q_o}{\partial L} \Delta L + \frac{\partial Q_o}{\partial K} \Delta K\right) P_o = (Q_o' - Q_o) P_o \tag{15}$$

where P_o is the price of all other things.

Fogel does not compute the social saving on the transportation of all things, but only on agricultural commodities. This restriction was necessitated by the large amounts of data that had to be processed in the computation. The agricultural social saving is estimated under three different assumptions regarding the possibility of technological adaptation to the absence of railroads. The first was that society would have relied on only the canals and roads that actually existed in 1890. The second was that at least 5000 miles of feasible and, in the absence of railroads, highly profitable canals would have been built. The third was that common roads would have been improved. Under the first of these assumptions the agricultural social saving of railroads was $373 million or 3.1 per cent of gross national product in 1890. The extension of canals and improvements of roads would have reduced the social saving to 1.8 per cent of GNP. It is interesting to note that the two main benefits achieved by the railroad were the reduction in inventories and the reduction in wagon transportation. Together these accounted for about 80 per cent of the social saving. While Fogel does not compute the social saving on nonagricultural commodities for 1890, he conjectures that it was less than 3 per cent of GNP.[4]

Although a total social saving of 3 to 5 per cent of GNP is quite large, it is not large enough to warrant the frequent contention that railroads were indispensable to the development of the American economy during the nineteenth century. Readers should not, however, leap from Fogel's attack on the "axiom of indispensability" to the conclusion that railroads were unimportant to the economy of the nineteenth century. Few innovations are capable of adding as much as 1 or 2 per cent to the productive capacity of a nation. Compared to other advances in technology, the railroad certainly stands out as one of the most important. Yet not even the railroad can be made a necessary condition for the advance of a process as many-sided as economic growth.

How is the social saving related to the efficiency index defined by equation 2, and to its rate-of-change transformation—equation 4? Albert Fishlow has shown elsewhere [4, pp. 643–644] that the social saving divided by the actual cost of railroad transportation is a measure of the change in technical efficiency with respect to those goods carried by railroads.[5] Indeed, it can be shown that this ratio multiplied by the share of railroads in the output of the transportation sector is in fact equal to the change in the total factor productivity index of the transportation industry which was induced by the substitution of railroads for alternative conveyances. Consequently one may use the social saving to compute the contribution of railroads to $\overset{*}{A}$ in the transportation sector.

Although he did not do so in essay 14, Fogel has elsewhere suggested that the ratio of the social saving on all transportation services to the net revenue of railroads in 1890 was about 0.60.[6] Since the efficiency of rail-

roads in 1890 was due to improvements spread over the previous 60 years, a ratio of 0.60 implies that the substitution of railroads for water and wagon transportation caused efficiency with respect to railroad-transported goods to increase at an annual rate of 0.79 per cent. Available data suggest that the railroad share of transportation in 1890 was approximately 0.90 per cent.[7] Thus the substitution of railroads caused the total factor productivity of transportation to rise at 0.71 per cent per annum (0.9×0.79). The contribution of railroads to the growth of total factor productivity in the economy as a whole is obtained by multiplying 0.71 by the share of the transportation sector in national income.[8] The computation yields a figure of 0.08 per cent (0.11×0.71). In other words the substitution of railroads for alternative conveyances probably accounted for about 10 per cent of the average annual rate of increase in the over-all efficiency of the economy between 1830 and 1890.[9]

Agriculture (Essay 13)

William N. Parker measures the growth of labor productivity in grain farming between 1840 and 1910. In the notation of this introduction, Parker's index of labor productivity (M) is given by

$$M = \frac{Q}{L} \qquad (16)$$

and the rate-of-growth transformation of equation 16 is

$$\overset{*}{M} = \overset{*}{Q} - \overset{*}{L} \qquad (17)$$

The relationship between Parker's index and the index of total factor productivity defined

---

[4] In a subsequent essay Fogel crudely estimated the social saving on nonagricultural commodities at $189 million or 1.6 per cent of GNP [5, p. 40].

[5] Fishlow's proof is for the case of an arithmetic index of total factor productivity. However, arithmetic and geometric indexes usually give quite similar results.

[6] Fogel has crudely estimated that the social saving on all freight was $329 million in 1890. To this he adds Fishlow's estimate of an 1890 passenger social saving of $300 million [5, p. 40]. The sum of these figures divided by the total operating revenue of railroads in 1890 [9, p. 434] yields a figure of 0.59.

[7] The estimate is based on Barger's data [2, pp. 184, 254]. Railroad passenger-miles were converted into railroad ton-miles according to the ratio (2.31) of revenue per passenger-mile to revenue per ton-mile. Waterway ton-miles were given one fifth of the weight of railroad ton-miles. Thus, there were 115.0 billion equivalent railroad ton-miles, of which railroads produced 103.9 billion and waterways 11.1 billion.

[8] The share of transportation in national income in 1890 was about 0.11 [7, p. 89].

[9] The annual rate of growth of total factor productivity over the period from 1850–1889 has been estimated at 0.75 per cent. This is a revised estimate of the figures presented in [1], privately communicated.

by equations 2 and 4 will be more evident if these equations are rewritten in a form that is slightly different from that in which they were originally presented, namely

$$A = \left(\frac{Q}{L}\right)\left(\frac{L}{R}\right)^{\alpha_2}\left(\frac{L}{K}\right)^{\alpha_3} \qquad (2.1)$$

and

$$\overset{*}{A} = (\overset{*}{Q} - \overset{*}{L}) + \alpha_2(\overset{*}{L} - \overset{*}{R}) + \alpha_3(\overset{*}{L} - \overset{*}{K}) \quad (4.1)$$

By substituting equation 16 in 2.1 and equation 17 into 4.1 we obtain

$$A = M\left(\frac{L}{R}\right)^{\alpha_2}\left(\frac{L}{K}\right)^{\alpha_3} \qquad (2.2)$$

and

$$\overset{*}{A} = \overset{*}{M} + \alpha_2(\overset{*}{L} - \overset{*}{R}) + \alpha_3(\overset{*}{L} - \overset{*}{K}) \quad (4.2)$$

If we focus on the rate-of-change version of the index of total factor productivity presented in equation 4.2, it will be seen that $\overset{*}{A}$ will equal $\overset{*}{M}$ when either (or both) of two conditions is met:

$$\alpha_2 = \alpha_3 = 0$$

or

$$(\overset{*}{L} - \overset{*}{R}) = (\overset{*}{L} - \overset{*}{K}) = 0$$

Now α_2 and α_3 would be close to zero if raw materials and capital (including land) were a small part of the value of all inputs. On this basis it is reasonable to assume that $\alpha_2 \cong 0$. But the same assumption cannot be made for α_3, since capital may have represented as much as 40 per cent of the value of inputs. Consequently the closeness of Parker's measure of the rate of change in labor productivity to the rate of change in total factor productivity turns on the relationship between the rates of growth of the capital and labor inputs. If $\overset{*}{K}$ was approximately equal to $\overset{*}{L}$, then $\overset{*}{M}$ would be a good approximation of $\overset{*}{A}$.

Parker estimates the growth of labor productivity for three grains. His findings indicate that over the 70 years from 1840 to 1910, labor productivity grew at annual percentage rates of 2.0, 1.9, and 1.9 for wheat, oats, and corn respectively. Parker goes on to explain these rates. The equation which lies behind his explanation is quite complex. However equation 18 is an approximation which captures the main features of Parker's procedure.[10]

$$\overset{*}{M} = \phi_1(\overset{*}{y_1} - \overset{*}{x_1} - \overset{*}{v_1}) + \phi_2(\overset{*}{y_2} - \overset{*}{x_2} - \overset{*}{v_2})$$
$$+ \phi_3(\overset{*}{y_3} - \overset{*}{x_3} - \overset{*}{v_3}) \quad (18)$$

where

$x =$ labor per acre (designated as *abc* in essay 13)

$v =$ the share of national output of a crop that is produced in a given region

$y =$ output per acre

$\phi =$ the share of the national labor input for a crop that is employed in a given region

$1,2,3 =$ subscripts denoting the three regions into which Parker divides agriculture—the Northeast, the South, and the West

For each grain Parker partitions the value of $\overset{*}{M}$ among his three variables ($\overset{*}{v}$, $\overset{*}{x}$, and $\overset{*}{y}$) by determining what the value $\overset{*}{M}$ would have been if one or two of these variables had had zero values. The cases he considers may be presented in tabular form as follows:

Value of $\overset{*}{M}$	Given the Following Values of		
	$\overset{*}{v}$	$\overset{*}{y}$	$\overset{*}{x}$
$\overset{*}{M_1}$	0	$\overset{*}{y}$	0
$\overset{*}{M_2}$	0	0	$\overset{*}{x}$
$\overset{*}{M_3}$	$\overset{*}{v}$	0	0
$\overset{*}{M_4}$	0	$\overset{*}{y}$	$\overset{*}{x}$
$\overset{*}{M_5}$	$\overset{*}{v}$	0	$\overset{*}{x}$
$\overset{*}{M_6}$	$\overset{*}{v}$	$\overset{*}{y}$	0

Parker finds that changes in regional shares ($\overset{*}{v}$) and in yields per acre ($\overset{*}{y}$) each accounts for only a small part of the change in labor

---

[10] Equation 18 is a differential approximation to Parker's basic equation. As such it fails to capture the interaction effects. These omissions are relatively small.

productivity ($\overset{*}{M}$) for each of the three grains. By far the greatest part of the value of $\overset{*}{M}$ is due to the value of $\overset{*}{x}$ (the change in labor per acre).

Parker relates these measures to the conceptual categories usually employed by historians. Thus he suggests that the share of $\overset{*}{M}$ attributable to $\overset{*}{v}$ may be taken as a measure of the impact on labor productivity of the "Westward movement" and that the share of $\overset{*}{M}$ due to $\overset{*}{x}$ measures the effect of mechanization on labor productivity. The great importance which Parker attaches to the role of mechanization leads him to consider the factors which determined the rate of diffusion of new machinery among various regions, among farms of different sizes, and with respect to different operations.

A CONCEPTUAL FRAMEWORK FOR THE EXPLANATION OF INDUSTRIAL EXPANSION

Essay 11 presents a model which permits one to measure the influence of all of the factors on both the demand and supply side which contribute to the growth of the output of an industry. In that model, for example, the index of total factor productivity appears as one of the variables in the supply equation. It thus becomes possible not only to measure the rate of change in productive efficiency but also to state by how much the observed change in efficiency increased the output of the industry in question.

In this part of the introduction we aim to explain certain of the concepts that are presumed in essay 11. We will then attempt to demonstrate how that model can also be applied to Robert Zevin's explanation of the growth of the cotton textile industry in essay 10.[11]

The Determination of Industrial Output[12]

In a competitive system the price and output of an industry's product are determined by the supply of and the demand for that prod-

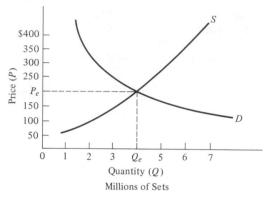

Figure 1

uct. This proposition is illustrated in Figure 1. Here the demand for (say) television sets in the United States is shown by curve D, while the supply of television sets is shown by curve S.[13] The intersection of these two curves gives the equilibrium price (P_e) and the equilibrium output (Q_e).

The demand curve of Figure 1 is the mathematical expression of the fact that there is a systematic relationship between the quantity of television sets which consumers want to buy and the price of such sets. The curve has a negative slope (slopes downward from left to right) because consumers will purchase more sets, all other things being equal, at lower prices that at higher ones. The demand curve is merely one of several ways by which information on consumers' willingness to purchase sets may be described. The same information can be given in tabular form (see Table 1). It can also be given by an algebraic equation:

$$Q = 10{,}375\ P^{-1.5} \qquad (19)$$

Table 1. The Demand for Television Sets

Price (In Dollars) (1)	Quantity Demanded (In Millions of Sets) (2)
50	29.3
100	10.4
150	5.6
200	3.7
250	2.6
300	2.0
350	1.6
400	1.3

---

[11] Zevin's paper, which is published here for the first time, was originally presented to the Workshop in Economic History of the University of Chicago on April 16, 1965. The model developed by Fogel and Engerman was stimulated, in part, by their attempt to interpret Zevin's argument.

[12] Readers versed in economic theory should skip to p. 112.

---

[13] The demand and supply curves of Figure 1 are not empirically derived. They are hypothetical illustrations designed to facilitate the exposition.

In this equation P is the price of television sets and Q is the quantity of sets that consumers want to purchase. Thus, the demand curve of the diagram is merely a graph of the equation and the table. If the various values in column 1 of Table 1 are substituted for the P of equation 19, the equation will yield the values of Q given in column 2 of the table.

Similarly, the supply curve of Figure 1 is the mathematical representation of the fact that there is a systematic relationship between the quantities that producers are willing to sell and the price of the commodity. Since the S curve is positively sloped (slopes upward from left to right) it states that the lower the price of the product, the fewer the number of units that will be supplied.

Empirical studies of the markets for a wide variety of products almost always disclose that demand curves have negative slopes. In the case of supply, empirical studies often yield curves with positive slopes, thus indicating that as output expands, it costs more to produce each additional unit of product. However, in some industries additional units of output can be produced at the same price as the earlier ones. Then the supply is portrayed by a horizontal curve as is shown by S in panel a of Figure 2. If the cost of producing a unit of output declines as output expands, the supply curve (S) will have a negative slope as shown in panel b in Figure 2.

The adjective "equilibrium" is attached to the price and quantity given by the intersection of the demand and supply curves, because no other price or quantity can persist in the market described by these curves. Suppose, for example, producers in the industry underestimate demand and produce only Q_1 of output instead of Q_e because they mistakenly believed that the market price for their product was going to be P'_e. Figure 3, panel a, shows that with only Q_1 units of

output on the market, consumers will be willing to pay as much as P_1 for each unit. Indeed, consumers' competition for the limited quantity will tend to drive the price to that level. But with a price of P_1, producers will want to produce an output of Q_2. Consequently, in the next production period they will expand output, moving in the direction of the equilibrium price and quantity. Similarly, as is shown in panel b of Figure 3, an output (Q_3) in excess of the equilibrium quantity will lead to a price below P_e. Consumers would purchase Q_3 of output in a given production period only at a price of P_3. That price will cause producers to contract output, thus moving in the direction of the equilibrium quantity. Only when Q_e is produced will the industry be in equilibrium. For then the market price will be P_e and entrepreneurs will have no incentive either to expand or to contract their operations.

A change in the equilibrium output of the industry requires a change (a shift) in the demand curve or in the supply curve or in both curves. Figure 4, panel a, shows a case in which the demand curve shifts from the position shown by D to that shown by D'. This shift represents an increase in demand, since at any given price (look along any line perpendicular to the price axis) consumers will want to consume a greater quantity than they previously did. As a result of the increase in demand (shift of the demand curve to the right), equilibrium output increases from Q_1 to Q_2 and equilibrium price rises from P_1 to P_2. The case of an increase in supply is shown in Figure 4, panel b, where the supply shifts from S to S'. As a result the equilibrium output rises from Q_1 to Q_3, while the price falls from P_1 to P_3. In Figure 4, panel c, both demand and supply increase, leading to a rise in output from Q_1 to Q_4. At the same time

Figure 2

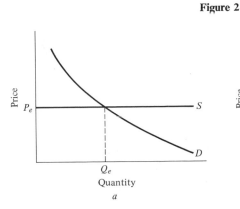

Q_e

Quantity

a

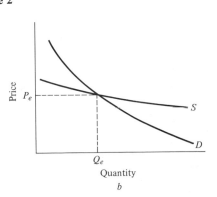

Q_e

Quantity

b

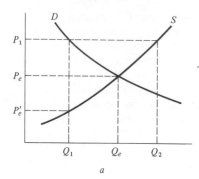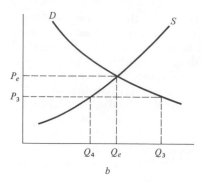

Figure 3

the price falls slightly from P_1 to P_4 as the downward influence on price due to the increase on supply exceeds the upward influence on price due to the increase in demand.

From the foregoing it follows that the explanation of the growth of the output of an industry involves the distribution of the observed increase among factors responsible for the shifts in supply and demand. To understand how such an allocation can be made it is necessary to consider the nature of demand and supply functions in more detail.

The Demand Function

The demand function given in equation 19 (and graphed in Figure 1) is a special case of a more general demand function for television sets. Equation 19 shows how the quantity of television sets purchased would change as the price of these sets changed when the other factors which influence the sales of television sets (such as average income, population, and the price of substitutes such as hi-fi outfits) remain fixed at predetermined levels. The more general demand function from which equation 19 was derived is given by equation 20.

$$Q = [Y^{\varepsilon_y}\, N^{\varepsilon_n}\, P_s^{\varepsilon_s}]\, P^{-\varepsilon} \qquad (20)$$

where

$Q =$ the quantity sold, measured in millions of sets

$Y =$ per capita income, measured in dollars

$N =$ the population, measured in millions of persons

$P_s =$ the average price of hi-fi sets, measured in dollars

$P =$ the average price of TV sets, measured in dollars

$\varepsilon_y, \varepsilon_n, \varepsilon_s, -\varepsilon =$ the powers to which Y, N, P_s, and P are raised. As will be shown later, these powers have a very important interpretation.

In deriving equation 19 from equation 20, it was assumed that the powers of Y, N, P_s, and P were 0.9, 0.8, 0.4, and 1.5, respectively. When these values are substituted into equation 20 we obtain

$$Q = [Y^{0.9} N^{0.8} P_s^{0.4}] P^{-1.5} \qquad (20.1)$$

The final step of the derivation of equation 19 required the specification of the values of Y,

Figure 4

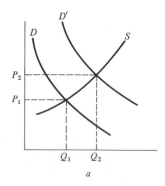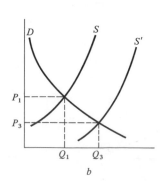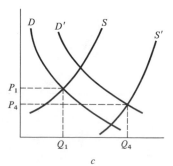

N, and P_s. These were assumed to be \$2000, 180, and \$400, respectively. If the reader performs the indicated computation he will find that the value of the bracketed variables is 10,375, the constant of equation 19. Consequently, the bracketed variables in equation 20 and 20.1 determine the constant of demand equation 19.

Given the powers of the bracketed variables, the value of the constant of the demand equation will change as Y, N, or P_s change. Suppose, for example, that the size of the population and the price of hi-fi sets remain constant but that average per capita income rises from \$2000 to \$3000. Now if we substitute into equation 20.1 we get a new value for the bracketed variable and equation 20.1 reduces to

$$Q = 14{,}945\ P^{-1.5} \qquad (19.1)$$

Both this equation and equation 19 are plotted in Figure 5. Equation 19 is represented by curve D and equation 19.1 by curve D'. Consequently, this diagram shows that a shift in the demand curve to the right (increase in demand) is due to an increase in the value of one of the variables (other than the price of television sets) on which the number of sets sold depends. It might be noted that if per capita income had declined, the curve D' would have been on the left of D. Such a leftward shift in the demand curve would have indicated a decline in the demand for television sets.

In our example the shift in the demand curve was shown to be due to a change in per capita income. Quite clearly a change in one of the other variables (population or the price of hi-fi sets) could have shifted the

Figure 5

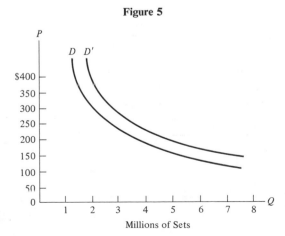

Millions of Sets

demand curve. Thus changes in demand are due to changes in the value of one or more of the variables (other than the price of television sets) which determine the number of television sets which consumers desire to purchase.[14] These variables, which are bracketed in equations 20 and 20.1, will be referred to collectively as the shift term or shift variables of the demand function.

The concept of elasticity. One of the most important properties of a demand curve is the *coefficient of price elasticity*. It will be designated by the symbol ε. The coefficient of price elasticity is defined as the ratio of the percentage change in output to the associated percentage change in price, when all of the other independent variables of the demand function are held constant. Expressed symbolically, the definition is

$$\varepsilon = - \frac{\overset{*}{Q}}{\overset{*}{P}} = - \frac{\Delta Q/Q}{\Delta P/P} \qquad (21)$$

where

$\overset{*}{Q} = $ the percentage change in output

$\overset{*}{P} = $ the percentage change in price

$\Delta P, \Delta Q = $ the change in P and Q respectively

While it will not be proved here, it can be shown that in demand functions such as those given by equations 19, 20, and 20.1 the coefficient of price elasticity is the absolute value of the power to which P, the price, is raised. Thus in equation 19 the coefficient of elasticity is 1.5. From our definition of elasticity it follows that if there is a 10 per cent decline in price (all other variables on the right-hand side of the demand function remaining constant), the output will rise by 15 per cent. That is, since by definition $\varepsilon = -\overset{*}{Q}/\overset{*}{P}$, then if $\varepsilon = 1.5$ and $\overset{*}{P} = -10$, we have $1.5 = -\overset{*}{Q}/-10$ or $\overset{*}{Q} = 1.5 \times 10 = 15$.

The value of the coefficient of elasticity (ε) can vary from ∞ to $+\infty$, if we include demand curves with positive slopes. However, if we limit consideration only to negatively-sloped demand functions, then the limits are ∞ and 0. Figure 6 shows demand functions with $\varepsilon = \infty$, 0, and 1. A demand function with

[14] Changes in several of the variables may be offsetting. In equation 20.1, for example, a 2 per cent rise in population would offset a 4 per cent decline in the price of hi-fi sets so that there would be no shift in the demand curve.

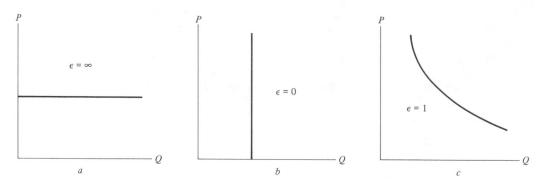

Figure 6

an elasticity of 1 at all points, such as is shown in panel *c* of Figure 6, has the property that any change in price will be exactly offset by a change in quantity in the opposite direction, so that total revenue remains unchanged. Thus curves with unitary elasticity at all points have the property that total revenue remains unchanged, regardless of movements in price. If the elasticity of demand has any value between 1 and ∞ (but not including 1), the percentage change in quantity will exceed the percentage change in price. Such demand curves are said to be *elastic*. If the value of ε lies between 1 and 0, but does not include 1, the percentage change in quantity will be less than the percentage change in price. Such curvse are said to be *inelastic*.

It follows from the definition of elasticity that with a given change in supply, the increase in the output of an industry will be greater, the greater is the absolute value of the demand elasticity. This point is illustrated in Figure 7. Thus in an industry in which supply is shifting down due to technological advance or other factors which have lowered the cost of production, the greater the value of ε, the greater will be the increase in output.

It is also possible to define elasticity coefficients which relate percentage changes in output to percentage change in independent variables in the demand function other than price. Thus the per capita income elasticity of output (ε_y) is the ratio of the percentage change in output to the percentage change in average income. Expressed symbolically the definition is

$$\varepsilon_y = \frac{\overset{*}{Q}}{\overset{*}{Y}} = \frac{\Delta Q/Q}{\Delta Y/Y} \tag{22}$$

where

$\overset{*}{Q}$ = the percentage change in output

$\overset{*}{Y}$ = the percentage change in per capita income

Similarly, one can define an elasticity which relates the percentage change in output to the percentage change in the average price of substitutes for television sets. The elasticity is designated by the symbol ε_s and is called the *cross elasticity of substitution*. Symbolically

$$\varepsilon_s = \frac{\overset{*}{Q}}{\overset{*}{P}_s} = \frac{\Delta Q/Q}{\Delta P_s/P_s} \tag{23}$$

Figure 7

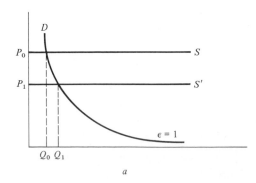

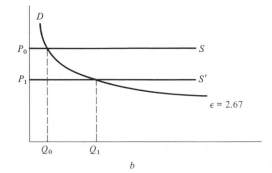

where

$\overset{*}{Q}$ = the percentage change in output

$\overset{*}{P}_s$ = the percentage change in the average price of substitutes for television sets

It is possible to demonstrate that in a demand function of the algebraic form of equations 20 and 20.1 the powers of the independent variables give the relevant coefficients of elasticities. Thus in 20.1 the values of the per capita income elasticity, the population elasticity, and the cross elasticity of substitution are 0.9, 0.8, and 0.4 respectively.

The Supply Function

In essay 11 it is shown that the nature of the supply function of an industry depends on the nature of that industry's production function. For the ability of an industry to expand its output depends on the ease with which it can vary its inputs and on the technical relationship between inputs and outputs, which is described by the production function. Not all inputs can be varied at the same speed. In most industries the inputs of labor and raw materials can be varied more quickly than the input of capital. Capital usually takes the form of plant and equipment. These can be varied only if the time period is long enough to permit their reproduction. Economists call such a time period the *long run*. The time period during which the inputs of labor and raw materials can be varied, even though the available plant and equipment are fixed, is called the *short run*. Under these definitions the *short run* lasts until enough time has elapsed to change the quantity of physical capital that is employed in the production process. Clearly then, the duration of the short run will vary from industry to industry, depending on the nature of the capital equipment and plant. In general, the more expensive and more specialized the capital equipment, the longer will be the duration of the short run.

It follows that two supply functions are needed to describe the way in which an industry expands its output. One supply function gives the prices at which the industry will expand to a given level of output in the short run. The second function describes the way in which output expands in the long run.

Fogel and Engerman show that if an industry has the type of production function

given by equation 1, its long-run supply function will be

$$P = [nA^{-1}w^{a_1}r^{a_2}i^{a_3}] \qquad (24)$$

and its short-run supply function will be

$$Q = [mA^{1/a_3}w^{-a_1/a_3}r^{-a_2/a_3}K]\,P^{(a_1+a_2)/a_3} \quad (25)$$

where

P = the price of output
Q = output
A = the index of total factor productivity
w = the price of a unit of labor service
r = the price of a unit of raw material
i = the price of a unit of capital service
K = the input of capital
m, n = proportionality factors
$\alpha_1, \alpha_2, \alpha_3$ = the output elasticities of the inputs in the production function

The two supply curves are shown in Figure 8.

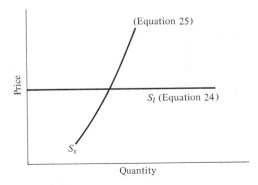

Figure 8

Several characteristics of these supply curves should be noted. One is that in the long run the price at which output is supplied is independent of the level of output. This is expressed in equation 24 by the fact that output (Q) does not enter into the equation. The same point is expressed in Figure 8 by the long-run supply curve which is perpendicular to the price axis (horizontal to the output axis), indicating that increases in output, in the long run, do not affect the price at which the product will be supplied. Equation 24 also states that in the long run the price of output will change only if the prices of the inputs (w, r, and i) change or if there is a change in the efficiency of production (A). If, for example, there is a decline in the price of raw materials (r), the long-run supply curve shown in Figure 8 will shift downward. A rise in the price of raw materials would shift the same curve upward.

In the short run, the price of output will increase as output increases, since in equation 25 price is positively related to the quantity of output (Q). The upward sloping supply curve follows from the fact that in the short run entrepreneurs cannot increase their input of capital. Consequently if they increase output by increasing the inputs of the variable factors—labor and raw materials—they will be putting a greater and greater burden on the capital required to produce their product. The more intensively the capital equipment is used, the more will be the cost of producing an additional unit of output. Or to put the same point in other words, the more intensively capital is used, the smaller the increase in output that will be brought about by a given increase in labor or raw materials. The last formulation is sometimes called *the law of diminishing returns*.

The bracketed symbols in equations 24 and 25 represent the variables that may cause these supply curves to shift. They will be referred to individually as the shift variables of their supply curves. Collectively the bracketed variables of each equation will be referred to as the shift term of their respective supply curves. It will be noted that as in the long-run supply curve, changes in the prices of inputs or in the index of the productivity of the inputs (A), can cause the short-run supply curve to shift. However, the short-run supply curve has a shift variable not included in the long-run curve—capital (K). The presence of K indicates that given enough time, the industry will be able to increase its capital, and the industry will then be in a new short-run period. If there are no changes in input prices or in the productivity index (A), then the new short-run curve will be exactly the same as the old one, except that K will be larger. Thus changes in the quantity of capital available to the industry shift the short-run supply curve, thus putting the industry in a new short-run position.

The interrelationship between the short- and long-run supply curves are illustrated by Figure 9. Initially the industry is in both long-run and short-run equilibrium, with the original demand curve (D) intersecting both the short- and long-run supply curves at an

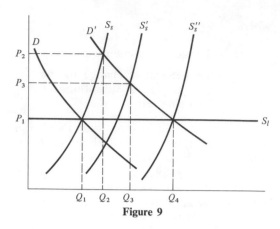

Figure 9

output of Q_1 and a price of P_1. Let there be an increase in the demand which causes that curve to shift to the position shown by D'. In the short run the industry will be able to increase output only by varying the inputs of labor and raw materials. Hence, its ability to meet the increased demand will be governed by the original short-run supply function, S_s. Hence there will be a new short-run equilibrium at an output of Q_2 and a price of P_2. However, P_2 is greater than the long-run supply price of the industry. Thus the firms of the industry will be earning high profits. These high profits will induce new firms to enter the industry, and/or induce old firms to expand their plant, thus increasing the quantity of capital used by the industry. After some time, plant and equipment will have expanded enough to shift the short-run supply of the industry to the position shown by curve S' Now the short-run equilibrium output has changed to Q_3 and the short-run equilibrium price has fallen from P_2 to P_3. Since P_3 is still above the long-run equilibrium supply price, and since profits are still above normal, additional capital formation will take place. Given a further passage of time, the quantity of the capital available to the industry will eventually expand to a point such that the short-run supply will be given by curve S_s'', at which time the industry will again be in both short- and long-run equilibrium. The price will have fallen back to P_1 and output will have expanded to Q_4.

In this example, the shift in the short-run supply curve was brought about by increases in capital. A more complicated example can be devised. Consider the case where there is an increase in demand followed shortly afterward by a reduction in the price of raw materials. Then the shifts in the various curves that would take place in moving from one long-run equilibrium to the other are

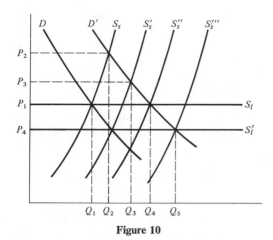

Figure 10

given by Figure 10. Here again the industry is initially in long- and short-run equilibrium at P_1 and Q_1, where curves D, S_s, and S_l all intersect. The increase of demand to D' brings about a new short-run equilibrium at a price of P_2 and an output of Q_2. At this point, before the industry has had the time to increase its stock of capital, there is a fall in the price of raw materials (r). The decline in r simultaneously shifts the long-run supply to the position of S'_l and the short-run supply curve to S'_s. As a consequence there is a new short-run equilibrium given by P_3 and Q_3. Since profits are above normal, new capital will be attracted into the industry. After a while the stock of capital will increase to a point that the short-run supply curve will be given by S''_s. It will be noted that while the price has fallen to the old long-run equilibrium of P_1, firms are still earning excess profit because the decline in the price of raw materials reduced the long-run supply price to P_4. Hence capital will continue to accumulate in the industry until capital expands to the point that the short-run supply is at S'''_s. Then the industry will be in long- and short-run equilibrium at a price of P_4 and an output of Q_5.

As long as the short-run equilibrium price is above the long-run equilibrium, firms will be earning a greater-than-normal profit. This excess profit is referred to as a *quasi-rent* and is a transitory return to the owners of capital that will disappear when the capital stock becomes large enough to bring the industry into long-run equilibrium.

The Rate of Growth of Output

The preceding discussion has revealed that the *level* of output of an industry is determined by the intersection of the demand and supply curves for the product of the industry. *Changes in the level* of output are due to shifts in either the demand and supply curves or in both. The shifts in the demand and supply curves are due to changes in the shift terms of these functions. In the case of demand, the shift terms include such variables as per capita income, population, and the prices of substitutes. In the case of supply the shift variables are the index of productive efficiency, the prices of inputs, and (in the short run) the stock of capital.

In the early stages of industrial development, the characteristic feature is the rapid rate at which the new industries expand their output. In studying such industries it is of interest not only to measure this rate of growth but also to explain it. To "explain," in this context, means to state how much of the observed rate of growth may be attributed to the growth of each of the variables in the shift terms of the demand and supply functions. This requires the derivation of a single equation which relates the rate of growth of output to the shift variables of both the demand and supply curves.

Fogel and Engerman show that the equation needed to explain the growth in the output of an industry between two short-run equilibriums can be derived by solving equations 20 and 25 for Q to first obtain

$$Q = (Y^{\varepsilon_y} N^{\varepsilon_n} P_s^{\varepsilon_s})^{\gamma/(\gamma + \varepsilon)}$$
$$\cdot (m A^{1/a_3} w^{-a_1/a_3} r^{-a_2/a_3} K)^{\varepsilon/(\gamma + \varepsilon)} \quad (26)$$

and then its rate-of-growth transformation

$$\overset{*}{Q} = \frac{\gamma}{\gamma + \varepsilon} \left(\varepsilon_y \overset{*}{Y} + \varepsilon_n \overset{*}{N} + \varepsilon_s \overset{*}{P_s} \right)$$
$$+ \frac{\varepsilon}{\gamma + \varepsilon} \left(\frac{1}{\alpha_3} \overset{*}{A} - \frac{\alpha_1}{\alpha_3} \overset{*}{w} - \frac{\alpha_2}{\alpha_3} \overset{*}{r} + \overset{*}{K} \right)$$
$$(27)$$

To explain the growth of an industry between two long-run equilibriums, it is necessary to substitute equation 24 into equation 20 to first obtain

$$Q = Y^{\varepsilon_y} N^{\varepsilon_n} P_s^{\varepsilon_s} (A^{-1} w^{a_1} r^{a_2} i^{a_3})^{-\varepsilon} \quad (28)$$

and then its rate-of-growth transformation which is

$$\overset{*}{Q} = \varepsilon_y \overset{*}{Y} + \varepsilon_n \overset{*}{N} + \varepsilon_s \overset{*}{P_s}$$
$$- \varepsilon(-\overset{*}{A} + \alpha_1 \overset{*}{w} + \alpha_2 \overset{*}{r} + \alpha_3 \overset{*}{i}) \quad (29)$$

Cotton Textiles (Essay 10)

Robert Zevin attempts to explain the growth of the American cotton textile industry between 1815 and 1833. During these 18 years the industry surged toward modernity and became the American prototype of the factory system. The annual domestic production of cotton cloth, which rose at an average rate of 15.4 per cent per year, went from a mere 18 million yards in 1815 to over 231 million yards in 1833. At the same time, the small spinning mills of previous years gave way to relatively large-scale integrated firms such as the Boston Manufacturing Company and the Merrimack Manufacturing Company.

The traditional explanation for this phenomenal expansion turns primarily on the introduction of the power loom and, to a lesser extent, on the tariff. The power loom was first employed in America by Francis Lowell at the end of 1814. Prior to that time cotton mills were "almost exclusively yarn mills, with weaving 'put out' to women in the neighborhood to be done on hand looms at home" [6, p. 197]. With such a technology few manufacturers found it advantageous to move the weaving process from the home to the factory. The advent of the power loom drastically altered prevailing arrangements. Cotton mills established after 1815 were integrated enterprises which used machinery not merely to transform raw cotton into yarn, but also to turn yarn into finished cloth. At the same time, the cost of cloth fell markedly. As a consequence, it has been usual to attribute the expansion of the industry to a downward shift in the cloth supply curve brought about by the mechanization of weaving. The increase in the tariff following 1816 is supposed to have assisted the emergence of the new technology by protecting mill owners from the ravages of British competition.

Zevin does not deny that the power loom was an important force in transforming the technology of the American textile industry. However, he eschews preoccupation with a single innovation. Zevin points out that technological advance in the manufacturing process is not the only factor which might explain the downward shift in the cloth supply curve. Moreover, Zevin contends that the increase in the demand for cloth was at least as important as the supply change for the explanation of the extraordinary growth of output. He also contends that the change in the tariff had only a trivial effect on the long-run expansion of demand.

With a few modifications, the model presented in this introduction can be used to analyze the development of the textile industry. Since Zevin holds that the period of his analysis greatly exceeds the time required for the reproduction of capital, the industry supply situation is appropriately described by the long-run function designated above as equation 24. The demand function given above as equation 20 must, however, be modified to be suitable to the present problem. As in the case of television sets, Zevin believes that per capita income (Y), and population (N) were important variables in determining the quantity of cloth which consumers desired to purchase. Zevin's formulation differs from equation 20 in two respects. First, Zevin suggests that the demand for domestic cotton cloth was affected by the price of not one, but two close substitutes. These were the price of wool cloth (P_w) and the American price of British cotton cloth. The latter may be considered to be equal to the price of British cloth in U.S. warehouses before the tariff was levied on it (P_b), multiplied by Φ where Φ is equal to one plus the tariff rate. Second, Zevin recognizes a difference between the price of cloth at the mill (P) and the price of the cloth in ultimate markets. That difference was due to the cost of transportation (T) incurred in delivering cloth from the mill to its markets.[15] Taking these modifications into account, the demand function appropriate to Zevin's problem is

$$Q = Y^{\varepsilon_y} N^{\varepsilon_n} (P_b \Phi)^{\varepsilon_b} P_w{}^{\varepsilon_w} (P + T)^{-\varepsilon} \quad (30)$$

All but two of the demand elasticities were previously defined: ε_b is the cross elasticity of the demand for American cotton cloth with respect to the American (post-tariff) price of British cloth, ε_w is the cross elasticity of the demand for American cotton cloth with respect to the price of wool cloth.

Proceeding in the manner described above, we can solve equations 24 and 30 for the equilibrium quantity of output. The solution will be expressed in the form of a new equation which has the rate-of-growth transformation given by equation 31.

$$\overset{*}{Q} = [\varepsilon_y \overset{*}{Y} + \varepsilon_n \overset{*}{N} + \varepsilon_b \overset{*}{P_b} + \varepsilon_b \overset{*}{\Phi} + \varepsilon_w \overset{*}{P_w} - \varepsilon \Omega \overset{*}{T}]$$
$$- \varepsilon(1 - \Omega)[-\overset{*}{A} + \alpha_1 \overset{*}{w} + \alpha_2 \overset{*}{r} + \alpha_3 \overset{*}{i}] \quad (31)$$

---

[15] Hence $P + T$ is the wholesale price of the cloth in the market to which it is consigned.

All of the symbols in this equation have been defined previously except Ω, which is the share of transport costs in the delivered price of domestic cloth. Hence $(1 - \Omega)$ is the share of the mill price in the delivered price. The terms grouped in the first set of square brackets give the rate of shift of the demand curve, while those grouped in the second set of square brackets give the rate of shift of supply.

The bulk of Zevin's paper is devoted to the scrutiny of the available data and the estimation from them of the probable values of the variables, elasticities, and weights of equation 31.[16] The difficulty of the task that Zevin set for himself is revealed by his discussion of the data. It is in the determination of the various demand elasticities that the data deficiencies become most acute. In principle these parameters could be estimated by use of regression analysis. While continued search may provide the data needed for such a procedure, they were not available to him. Hence, Zevin was forced to assign values to the demand elasticities based on his knowledge of these parameters for recent times and comparable products. Given the sensitivity of his division of the growth of output to the value of these elasticities, certain of Zevin's conclusions have the character of informed guesses rather than empirically confirmed findings.

Nevertheless, Zevin's essay represents a substantial advance over previous attempts to explain the growth of the cotton textile industry. He has, for the first time, attempted to deal simultaneously with all of the issues which bear on the expansion of cloth production and with their interrelationship. Moreover, while some of the measures he presents are quite sensitive to error, others are not. In this connection, it does not seem likely that future research will upset his principal finding that the changes in demand accounted for half of the growth of output.

---

[16] Zevin does not present estimates of the national values of Ω and $\overset{*}{T}$. Rather he divides the national market into three regions and estimates the values of these variables for each region. However, since Zevin gives the weight of each region in the total market, the national values of Ω and $\overset{*}{T}$ are obviously implicit in his calculation.

Similarly, while Zevin does not give the output elasticities of the production function, he does give the shares of each of the factors in the value of output. In an industry with a production function like that given by equation 1 the factor shares will, in both short- and long-run equilibrium, be equal to the corresponding output elasticities.

Finally, while those estimates which are guesses are debatable, the debate cannot be resolved without uncovering new bodies of data.

Iron (Essay 11)

The wide fluctuations in the production of American iron between 1842 and 1858 have been under debate for more than 100 years. According to protectionists, the sharp rise in production from 1842 through 1847 was due to the high protective tariff of 1842. And the slump which began in 1848 was caused by the repeal of the tariff. This view has been challenged by such eminent economists as David Wells and F. W. Taussig. Taussig argued that while the tariff stimulated the output of the backward (charcoal) sector of the American iron industry, it had little effect on the growth of output in the modern (anthracite) sector. In his view, the main factor affecting the growth in the output of American anthracite iron between 1842 and 1858 was not the tariff, but technological change.

Fogel and Engerman attempt to resolve this debate by applying a slightly modified version of the supply and demand model described in this introduction. They hold that observed prices and output levels in the American iron industry represented short-run rather than long-run equilibriums. Consequently they take equation 25 as the appropriate description of the industry's supply curve. They modify the demand curve given as equation 20 by the substitution of Gross National Domestic Investment (I) for per capita income (Y) and population (N). Since pig iron was primarily an investment good, they hold that I is a better measure of the market size than Y and N. Imported iron is designated as the principal substitute for domestic iron and its prices are represented by the symbol P_i. Thus the basic equation employed to explain the growth of output is

$$\overset{*}{Q} = \frac{\gamma}{\gamma + \varepsilon} \left(\Psi \overset{*}{I} + \varepsilon_i \overset{*}{P_i} \right)$$
$$+ \frac{\varepsilon}{\gamma + \varepsilon} \left(\frac{1}{\alpha_3} \overset{*}{A} - \frac{\alpha_1}{\alpha_3} \overset{*}{w} - \frac{\alpha_2}{\alpha_3} \overset{*}{r} + \overset{*}{K} \right)$$
$$(32)$$

where Ψ is the elasticity of the demand for output with respect to I and ε_i is the cross elasticity of demand with respect to the price of imported iron.

Much of essay 11 is devoted to the problem of obtaining estimates of the parameters of this equation, given the paucity of available data. Fogel and Engerman point out that it is possible to overcome the data shortage if there is some way of establishing the value of γ by making use of prior information. Two alternative methods are considered, both of which yield essentially the same estimates of the parameters.[17]

The conclusions which follow from these estimates contradict the view that the principal effect of the tariff was on the backward charcoal sector of the industry. Fogel and Engerman find that the tariff did much more to accelerate the growth of the anthracite sector than the charcoal sector. In this connection, they hold that while the advance of technology accounted for less than a quarter of the growth of output in the anthracite sector between 1842 and 1858, the rise in demand accounted for nearly half of this growth. Moreover, if the tariff had been maintained at the 1842 level, the rate of growth of anthracite iron would have been increased by 19 per cent and demand would have accounted for more than half of the growth of the augmented output. In the charcoal case it was the reduction in demand, not the stagnation of technology, which accounted for the decline of that sector. Indeed, Fogel and Engerman suggest that total factor productivity probably increased more rapidly between 1842 and 1858 in the "backward" charcoal sector than in the "modern" anthracite sector.

Iron (Essay 9)

Peter Temin addresses himself to one of the issues that has most agitated historians of the American iron industry: the explanation for the rapid rise of the coke process of pig iron production, beginning just before the onset of the Civil War, after several decades of the relative neglect of this process.

Since the late 1920's, the reigning solution to this problem has been the one put forth by Louis C. Hunter. Hunter noted that there were two fuels used to produce pig iron in the West during the 1840s and 1850s, coke which was made from bituminous coal, and charcoal which was produced from wood. He also noted that two fuels were used to make pig iron in the East; namely, anthracite coal and charcoal. Since transportation costs were high and since the deposits of bituminous coal were located in the West, while the deposits of anthracite were located in the East, each kind of coal could be employed profitably by blast furnaces only in the region in which it was located. Charcoal was used in the blast furnaces of both regions.

Beginning in the late 1830s, after the development of the hot blast, anthracite rapidly replaced charcoal as the main fuel in Eastern blast furnaces. By 1850 most of the pig iron produced in the anthracite region used that fuel. The substitution of coal for charcoal proceeded far more slowly in the West. Although the use of coke in blast furnaces considerably antedated the use of anthracite, the capacity of coke blast furnaces in 1850 was only 29 per cent that of anthracite furnaces. Moreover, within the bituminous region, charcoal blast furnaces still dominated production, accounting for over 90 per cent of the region's output in 1849. Between 1850 and 1858 the capacity of coke blast furnaces tripled. In so doing they became the dominant form of pig iron production in the bituminous region [3]. This trend continued through and beyond the Civil War era. By 1875 bituminous pig iron became the primary form of crude iron, not only in its region but on a national level as well [8, p. 266].

Hunter contended that both the initial lag and the later surge in the production of coke iron were due to demand factors. He said that since the region which produced bituminous pig iron was located in western Pennsylvania and Maryland, its market in 1840 was largely rural. But the rural demand for iron was mainly for agricultural implements and other artifacts requiring a highly refined form of wrought iron of the type produced by charcoal furnaces. On the other hand, bituminous furnaces produced a cheaper but inferior quality of iron suitable for castings and for the poorer grades of rolled iron such as that used in the manufacture of rails. With the passage of time, the demand for low-grade iron increased more rapidly than that for high grade. Thus by the eve of the Civil War, the output of low-grade bituminous iron had leap-frogged that of the more refined iron. Hunter attributed this rapid growth in the demand for coke iron largely to the burgeoning demand for rails.

Temin suggests an alternative explanation

---

[17] A critique of their estimating procedures is contained in [10].

for the pattern in which the Western iron industry developed. He argues that the surge in the consumption of coke iron was due to supply rather than to demand factors. He accepts Hunter's point that in 1840 coke and charcoal furnaces produced two different qualities of iron. However, he contends that while charcoal pig was a very highly refined iron both before and after the war, coke pig improved from a low-grade to a medium-grade iron without a rise in price. Temin goes on to suggest that available data make it possible to choose between these alternative hypotheses. In this connection he asserts that the movement in the price of anthracite iron relative to both the prices of charcoal iron and coke iron demonstrates that his explanation is the correct one.

REFERENCES

1. Moses Abramovitz and Paul A. David, *Economic Growth in the United States* (Mimeographed, Stanford Research Center in Economic Growth), 1965.

2. Harold Barger, *The Transportation Industries, 1889 to 1946*, New York, National Bureau of Economic Research, 1951.

3. Stanley L. Engerman and Robert W. Fogel, *The Growth of the American Iron Industry, 1810-1860: A Statistical Reconstruction* (in progress).

4. Albert Fishlow, "Productivity and Technological Change in the Railroad Sector, 1840–1910," Conference on Research in Income and Wealth, *Output, Employment, and Productivity in the United States After 1800* (Studies in Income and Wealth, vol. 30), New York, Columbia University Press, 1966, pp. 583–646.

5. Robert W. Fogel, "Railroads as an Analogy to the Space Effort: Some Economic Aspects," *The Economic Journal*, 76 (March, 1966), 16–43.

6. Constance McLaughlin Green, "Light Manufactures and the Beginnings of Precision Manufacture," Harold F. Williamson, ed., *The Growth of the American Economy*, Englewood Cliffs, N.J., Prentice-Hall, 1951, pp. 190–210.

7. Simon Kuznets, "Long-Term Changes in the National Income of the United States of America Since 1870," International Association for Research in Income and Wealth, *Income and Wealth of the United States*, Baltimore, Johns Hopkins Press, 1952, pp. 29–241.

8. Peter Temin, *Iron and Steel in Nineteenth Century America: An Economic Inquiry*, Cambridge, M.I.T. Press, 1964.

9. United States Bureau of the Census, *Historical Statistics of the United States, Colonial Times to 1957*, Washington, D.C., 1960.

10. Gavin Wright, "Studies in Econometric History," Michael D. Intriligator, ed. *Frontiers of Quantitative Economics*, Amsterdam, North–Holland Publishing Co. (forthcoming).

9 A NEW LOOK AT HUNTER'S HYPOTHESIS ABOUT THE ANTE-BELLUM IRON INDUSTRY

Peter Temin

The process whereby innovations diffuse throughout an economy or throughout the world has interested many people at many times. One of the more intriguing examples of this process is the spread of the use of coke to make pig iron, which has interested investigators because of two seemingly incompatible properties. The use of coke in the blast furnace was one of the enabling innovations of the Industrial Revolution in Britain, and it played a similarly important role in the industrialization of many, if not all, other industrializing countries in the nineteenth century. Despite this importance, however, the spread of coke was not rapid; there was often a delay of as

Reprinted by permission from *The American Economic Review, 54* (May, 1964), 344–351.

much as a half a century in the spread of this innovation from Britain to other countries. Coke was the fuel for well over 90 per cent of the blast furnaces in Great Britain before 1810. But half a century later, at the start of the Civil War, the proportion of pig iron smelted with this fuel in the United States had barely attained the level of 10 per cent of the total.

The example of America is particularly intriguing. The contrast between the long delay in adopting the new process and the subsequent rapid expansion of its use is striking. In addition, the delay has been made to appear even more problematical by the recent book of Habakkuk, which has emphasized the extent to which the United States led Britain technologically in certain areas before the Civil War [3]. The problem before us is the reconciliation of the evidences of continuous progress in the United States with the neglect of this important innovation.

Many reasons have been given to explain the half-century delay in the adoption of coke in America. The strongest reasons given in the nineteenth century were that charcoal was much more plentiful in this country than in England and that American ironmasters were opposed to the use of coke due to ignorance, irrationality, or both. Louis C. Hunter, in a classic article published in 1929, showed conclusively that these reasons were false and propounded a new hypothesis to explain the delay [4]. This paper will build upon Hunter's masterful analysis and suggest some alterations in his hypothesis about the ante-bellum iron industry.

Hunter pointed out that the cost of charcoal was almost entirely the cost of labor incurred in preparing it, the cost of the original wood accounting for little or nothing in the price. The availability of wood in the United States consequently had little influence on this price, and charcoal—here as in England—was a more expensive fuel than coke. As for ignorance and irrationality, Hunter showed that the pig iron made with coke was inferior to the iron made with charcoal, which implies that the reluctance of the ironmasters to accept a new fuel in place of the old was an accurate, rational reaction to quality differences in the iron produced. These two observations by Hunter form the cornerstone of any modern discussion of the diffusion of coke smelting in America.

Hunter did not spell out the mechanism by which the low quality of pig iron made with coke restricted its production, but the obvious inference is that the low quality implied a low price, which destroyed the profitability of the new process. Pig iron made with coke sold for a 20 per cent discount from the price of charcoal pig iron during the 1850s, a difference of six dollars. The cost of charcoal to make a ton of pig iron was approximately nine dollars, and I have endeavored to show elsewhere that the reduction in the price of fuel attendant upon the use of coke was not sufficient to compensate for the reduced price of the product [5, chap. 3]. The ante-bellum ironmaster was offered no inducement in the form of higher profits to use coke—a fact which is borne out in the not completely pleasant experiences of those ironmasters who tried. There were good reasons in other words, why the technical progress in the ante-bellum era noted by Habakkuk for light manufacturing did not extend to all areas of the economy.

By the advent of the Civil War, however, a change was beginning to be evident, and the amount of pig iron made with coke began to rise faster than the total production of pig iron in America. The second part of Hunter's hypothesis endeavors to explain this development. It states that the character of the demand for iron was changing at the time of the Civil War, from a price-inelastic demand that was sensitive to changes in quality to one that was more price-elastic and less sensitive to changes in quality. The former pattern was characteristic of an agricultural demand in which small lots of iron were bought for use under a wide variety of conditions; the latter was the result of an industrial demand in which larger amounts of iron—relative to the total purchases of a firm or farm—were purchased for a specific purpose. The most important specific purpose was for the production of rails—a product that did not benefit from the use of high quality iron.

Two factors urge the reconsideration of this part of Hunter's hypothesis. As with the earlier part of the argument, Hunter did not outline a mechanism by which the change in demand caused a change in the method of production. Such a mechanism is considerably harder to specify than the one which translated a low quality of product into low profits because it involves a shift in demand curves, and even a shift in the elasticity of demand curves—always a difficult event to identify. In addition, recent work on the proportion of pig iron used for the production of rails has raised the possibility that the shift in demand noticed by Hunter was not large enough to effect the change in productive techniques under discussion [2, chap. v].[1]

I would like to suggest an alternative to this part of Hunter's hypothesis. In the course of discriminating between my suggestion and the theory proposed by Hunter, both the mechanism involved and the relation of this mechanism to other work will be shown.

The increasing use of coke for a blast furnace fuel at the time of the Civil War may be seen as a reaction to changes in the cost and price structure of the American iron industry. Hunter's hypothesis is that the changes were in the demand for iron, that the demand for low-quality, low-cost iron rose relative to the demand for high-cost and quality iron. An alternative explanation is that the cost of making coke pig iron fell or that its quality improved; i.e., that the changes were on the supply side. The cost of making pig iron with coke does not seem to have changed with respect to the cost of using charcoal before the 1870s and the introduction of "hard driving," and this explanation may be dismissed. Discrimination between the two remaining alternatives—Hunter's hypothesis of changing demand and my suggestion of quality improvement in coke pig iron—is a harder task.

This task is facilitated by the existence of a third fuel—different from both charcoal and coke—suitable for use in the blast furnace, and a third type of iron. The fuel was anthracite, found in eastern Pennsylvania and parts of Wales. Coke was used before anthracite in Britain, as the technical knowledge necessary for the ignition of the somewhat recalcitrant anthracite was not discovered until the late 1830s, but anthracite became the variety of mineral fuel used initially in America. Its production rose rapidly in the 1840s, and it accounted for over half of American pig iron production in 1860.

There are two possible reasons why anthracite was adopted before the Civil War and coke was not, corresponding to the two reasons proposed to explain why coke was adopted later. Anthracite is found east of the Alleghenies, while bituminous coal lies to the west. Demand may have differed in the two regions in such a fashion as to induce the production of a type of pig iron in the East that could not have been profitably produced in

the West. Alternatively, the quality of the pig iron made with anthracite may have differed from that of coke pig iron, while the character of demand was unimportant. (The costs of making pig iron with the two different mineral fuels were approximately equal at this time. If there was a difference between them, it was that it was cheaper to produce pig iron with coke than with anthracite).

As long as the commerce in heavy products such as pig iron was separated by the Allegheny Mountains into two markets, there was little evidence generated that would enable the modern observer to discriminate between these hypotheses. In 1852 the Pennyslvania Railroad completed its through line from Philadelphia to Pittsburgh, and the cost of transportation across the mountains was reduced. Pig iron made in eastern Pennsylvania with anthracite began to be sold in Pittsburgh in competition with the locally produced pig iron made with coke. If the character of demand was different in the two regions, we would expect pig iron made with anthracite to sell in Pittsburgh at approximately the price of pig iron made with coke; i.e., at a substantial discount from the price of pig iron made with charcoal. If, on the other hand, it was the nature of the varieties of pig iron that made a difference, we would expect to find an equally clear price differential existing between pig iron made with anthracite and with coke.

As it turns out, pig iron made with anthracite sold in Pittsburgh at the same price as charcoal pig iron. Consumers in the West were willing to pay substantially more for pig iron made with anthracite than for pig iron made with coke in the ante-bellum era, and we conclude that pig iron made with anthracite differed significantly in its quality from pig iron made with coke. The reasons for this are clear. The main debilitating element in the coking coal available in the 1840s and 1850s was sulphur, and the anthracite deposits of eastern Pennsylvania were relatively free of this impurity.

The delay in the use of coke in the United States may now be placed in perspective. Ironmasters in the United States were adopting the new technology based on mineral fuel. Because of a difference in resources, however, they adopted it in a different form than that used originally in Britain. And because the innovations permitting use of the American resources, i.e., anthracite coal, were not introduced until the 1830s, they adopted it after a delay. The deposits of anthracite in

---

[1] [A summary of this work is reprinted below, as essay 14.—Editors' note.]

the United States are very highly concentrated in a few counties of northeastern Pennsylvania, and the high cost of transport to the far reaches of the large American economy prevented the use of this fuel from completely eclipsing pig iron production with charcoal. Consequently pig iron made with charcoal still accounted for about a third of the total at the start of the Civil War.

By this time the cost of transportation had declined enough to permit pig iron made with anthracite to compete with pig iron made with charcoal in places other than the Eastern Seaboard. But as Hunter noted, more changes were in progress at the close of the ante-bellum years than those in the cost of transport. In a closely related development, the demand for iron was beginning to shift. The plentiful use of castings typical of the 1840s had begun to wane; the demand for rails had begun to rise. The economy was also expanding geographically, and this led in turn to the discovery of new resources. We seek to know which of these developments made the use of coke in Western blast furnaces more attractive than the importation of pig iron made with anthracite from eastern Pennsylvania

Price comparisons again carry the key. The price of pig iron made with coke had to rise relative to the price of other types of pig iron if coke rather than one of the other fuels was to be used. If this price rise occurred because of a change in demand, as Hunter asserted, a price differential should have been maintained between pig iron made with anthracite and pig iron made with coke. The former class of iron was of higher quality than the latter before the Civil War, and there is no evidence that its quality deteriorated after that time. Only if the quality of pig iron made with coke improved until it was equal to that of pig iron made with anthracite could their prices become equal.

Yet this is precisely what happened. The extant price data for the Civil War years are obscure due to the paucity of comparable sources and the rapid changes in prices in these years. When prices do become available on a comparable and sustained basis, in the early 1870s, they show that pig iron made with coke and pig iron made with anthracite sold for the same price. In fact the popular method of quoting prices was to refer to pig iron by grade, including iron made with anthracite and with coke in a single classification. The quality of pig iron made with coke had improved to the point where this type of iron was interchangeable with pig iron made with

anthracite. There had been a change in the supply curve of pig iron made with coke, in other words, a change that enabled producers of pig iron with this fuel to supply more value to consumers with the same expenditure.

To what can we attribute this change in supply? The exploitation of high-quality coking coal is the obvious candidate. The modern observer of the ante-bellum iron industry cannot help but be struck by the absence of one of the most famous names of the American iron industry. I refer to Connellsville, the home of the metallurgical coke known by its name and famous for both its hardy physical structure and its relative chemical purity. This variety of coking coal was used in the expansion of coke pig iron production after the Civil War; its freedom from sulphur may be taken as the cause of the improvement in the quality of pig iron made with coke. The Connellsville coal region was initially discovered in the 1840s, but its exploitation is usually dated from 1859—the date of the construction of the first blast furnace in Pittsburgh designed specifically to use this coal. This deposit was newly discovered in the boom of the 1840s and did not become known in the few years of the boom. The following decade did not witness a rise of pig iron production above its previous peak, and the inducement to use new resources was not strong. Only when the production of pig iron began to rise again at the end of the ante-bellum era was the new source of coke exploited.

While this provides an explanation for the improvement in the quality of pig iron made with coke, it is not clear that the discovery of new coal fields can be made a simple function of the expansion of the economy. This was certainly a potent factor, but it is also possible that ironmasters increased their search for new coal on the basis of increasing technical knowledge. Quite possibly, Western ironmasters only came to realize that poor coal was the source of their difficulties in the course of the 1850s, their lack of exploration previously being determined as much by ignorance of what to look for as ignorance of where to look. We find an awareness of the difficulties of using sulphurous coal in these years, but we also find early writers criticized by later ones for their overoptimism on the usefulness of many coal deposits. The process by which Connellsville coke was brought into use, therefore, retains some of its mystery even now.

The changing supply curve for pig iron made with coke thus explains the increased use of coke in this country. When a supply of bituminous coal became available that would produce an iron equal in quality to that made with anthracite, the relative price of coke pig iron rose and its production was encouraged. The growth of the transportation network, therefore, encouraged the universal use of mineral fuel in the United States iron industry through promoting geographical exploration and the exploitation of new resources, rather than by improving the competitive position of anthracite pig iron, as might have been anticipated in 1850. In addition, technical developments after the Civil War reduced the cost of using coke relative to the cost of using anthracite, and coke came to be the universal fuel for American blast furnaces.

But what about the change in demand noticed by Hunter? If the preceding argument is correct, the switch to coke would have taken place whether or not there was a change in the character of the demand for pig iron around 1860. Such a change, however, could have helped the transition, and we may ask whether or not it did.

The most important component of demand from this point of view is the demand for rails, as the quality of iron used was not a major concern in this area. Robert Fogel has estimated that the proportion of pig iron used for the production of rails in the antebellum era was less than 10 per cent [2, pp. 130–135]. This low figure, coupled with the absence of a rising trend near 1860, suggests that the effects of changing demand may be neglected. Albert Fishlow has revised Fogel's estimates, and his data show that the proportion of pig iron used for rails was rising in the 1850s, reaching a level of about 20 per cent by the end of the decade [1, pp. 132–149]. This estimate gives greater scope to the influence of demand, but even it does not say anything about the actual effect.[2]

The problem is that even if the production of rails did use an increasing proportion of the pig iron produced in the late 1850s, this could have been the effect of an increased supply of low-cost pig iron—made with coke—as easily as it could have been the cause of the increased production of pig iron with coke. The resolution of this problem requires the specification of the relevant demand and supply functions. Among the demand functions that need to be specified is the demand for rails, including the demand for rails to be used to replace worn-out rails, and the nature of this demand (together with the reciprocal supply of scrap coming from the worn-out rails themselves) is precisely the point on which Fogel and Fishlow differ. The problem does not appear to be easily soluble, and at this point we cannot assess the extent to which changes in the composition of demand helped the transition from charcoal to coke in the blast furnaces of the American iron industry. What the preceding argument has shown is that this help was not needed to effect the transition observed.

Can we conclude, then, that the railroad was not important for the American iron industry? The answer is no. This discussion has been concerned with changes in the production of pig iron and has discussed that part of the iron industry that made this material. Rails, however, were made from wrought iron, and the effects of rail production were to be found in the branch of the industry that made wrought iron (and later steel) from pig iron rather than in the branch that made pig iron from ore. The proportion of wrought iron produced used for rails was much higher than the proportion of pig iron so used, and the production of rails had a direct impact on the activities of rolling mills —in contrast to the indirect effect that has been claimed for blast furnaces. The production of rails led to the growth of integrated iron works and the use of the three-high mill in the ante-bellum era and to the exploitation of the Bessemer process in the years following the Civil War. The use of the Bessemer process was an important change for the iron industry: among its effects were several important changes in the production of pig iron after 1870 that may reasonably be attributed to the demand for rails.

---

[2] [In the final published versions of Fishlow's and Fogel's work the discrepancy between the two estimates has narrowed but not disappeared. While the revisions made by both authors have resulted in more similar trends, there is still some disagreement over levels. These differences result from different models of the market for rails, and the proper identification of the demand for rails has not yet been agreed upon. —Editors' note.]

REFERENCES

1. Albert Fishlow, *American Railroads and the Transformation of the Ante-bellum Economy*, Cambridge, Harvard University Press, 1965.

2. Robert William Fogel, *Railroads and American Economic Growth: Essays in Econometric History*, Baltimore, Johns Hopkins Press, 1964.
3. H. J. Habakkuk, *American and British Technology in the Nineteenth Century*, Cambridge, University Press, 1962.
4. Louis C. Hunter, "The Influence of the Market upon Technique in the Iron Industry in Western Pennsylvania up to 1860," *Journal of Economic and Business History*, *1* (February, 1929), 241–281.
5. Peter Temin, *Iron and Steel in Nineteenth-Century America: An Economic Inquiry*, Cambridge, M.I.T. Press, 1964.

IO THE GROWTH OF COTTON TEXTILE PRODUCTION AFTER 1815

Robert Brooke Zevin

The first great expansion of modern industrial activity in the United States took place in New England from the end of the War of 1812 to the middle of the 1830s. By the census of 1840 factories had become familiar

This paper was first drafted while the author was a member of the Economic History Workshop under the direction of Alexander Gerschenkron. It represents a portion of a larger study of New England industrialization which I hope will soon be completed and in print. The numbers in Table 1 and several of the assertions in the text are preliminary results drawn from that study. I am indebted to my colleagues in the Economic History Workshop and to the members of the economic history seminars conducted by Robert W. Fogel at Chicago and Alexander Gerschenkron at Harvard for many valuable criticisms. I would particularly like to acknowledge the efforts of Professors Fogel and Peter Temin to clarify the central argument in my own mind and I hope for the reader as well.

landmarks at hundreds of New England water-power sites; large cities such as Lowell and Holyoke had been created entirely by the advance of industrial activity, while Fall River, Pawtucket, Worcester, and the like had been greatly enlarged and transformed by the same advance. About 100,000 people were employed by large-scale manufacturing enterprises, with 20 or 30 employing up to 1500 employees each. This amounted to about one seventh of the entire New England labor force, without taking account of the large additional numbers engaged full or part time in the construction industries and in small-scale manufacturing activities like leather tanning, boots and shoes, palm leaf hats, and the work of blacksmiths. By contrast, in 1816 large-scale manufacturing enterprises employed about 5000 people or slightly more than 1 per cent of the regional labor force.[1]

This remarkable explosion of industrial activity was dominated in every sense by the

[1] The 1840 New England labor force was estimated at 715,000 or 32 per cent of the 1840 New England population. The 1816 labor force was estimated to be 470,000 or 30 per cent of an 1816 New England population linearly interpolated between the New England population figures for 1810 and 1820.

expansion of the cotton textile component of manufacturing. The cotton industry was the only major New England industry to expand steadily in the very earliest years of the period from 1816 to the early 1820s. In the late 1830s cotton textiles accounted for two thirds of the value added in all large-scale New England manufacturing. The industry's share had expanded from less than 10 per cent in 1810, so that the growth of cotton textile output accounted for a very large share of the growth of total manufacturing. Moreover the growth of many other industries—woolens, cast iron, textiles and other machinery—was importantly influenced by the growth of the cotton industry.

It is of interest, therefore, to see to what extent we can isolate the forces which explain the timing and the rate of growth of cotton textile production. Tables 1 and 2 describe the phenomena we wish to understand. The remarkable advance of 1816–1833, which is plainly apparent from the annual data in Table 1, is summarized and contrasted with the following period in Table 2. The years from 1805 to 1815 witnessed higher rates of growth of output. However the second wave of progress poses more interesting analytical problems because of its longer, sustained progress in the absence of the violent stimuli of

Table 1. New England Cotton Industry Output, 1805–1860[a]

Year	Yards of Cloth (000's)	Value Added[b] ($000's)		Annual Increase (Per Cent)	
		Cloth	Total	Cloth	Total
1805	46	2	16		
1806	62	3	22	(c)	34.6
1807	84	4	29	(c)	35.9
1808	181	10	64	(c)	121.0
1809	255	13	90	(c)	40.6
1810	648	34	228	(c)	153.0
1811	801	42	282	(c)	23.7
1812	1,055	55	372	(c)	31.9
1813	1,459	77	515	(c)	38.4
1814	1,960	103	691	(c)	34.2
1815	2,358	124	831	(c)	20.3
1816	840	44	—	−64.4	—
1817	3,883	204	—	362.0	—
1818	7,216	379	—	85.8	—
1819	9,941	522	—	37.8	—
1820	13,874	728	930	39.6	—
1821	22,292	1,170	1,394	60.7	49.9
1822	30,171	1,584	1,820	35.3	30.6
1823	41,459	2,177	2,424	37.4	33.2
1824	55,771	2,928	3,186	34.5	31.4
1825	69,677	3,658	3,928	24.9	23.3
1826	84,349	4,429	4,710	21.1	19.9

Table 1 (continued)

Year	Yards of Cloth (000's)	Value Added ($000's)		Annual Increase (Per Cent)	
		Cloth	Total	Cloth	Total
1827	95,005	4,988	5,281	12.6	12.1
1828	111,187	5,837	6,142	17.0	16.3
1829	128,779	6,761	7,078	15.8	15.2
1830	141,616	7,435	7,765	10.0	9.7
1831	161,566	8,482	8,817	14.1	13.5
1832	205,836	10,806	11,238	27.4	27.4
1833	231,486	12,153	12,639	12.5	12.5
1834	238,260	12,509	13,009	2.9	2.9
1835	250,773	13,166	13,692	5.3	5.3
1836	283,182	14,867	15,472	12.9	13.0
1837	308,079	16,174	16,858	8.8	9.0
1838	315,440	16,561	17,290	2.4	2.6
1839	317,605	16,674	17,436	.7	.8
1840	323,000	16,958	17,762	1.7	1.8
1841	353,111	18,538	19,465	9.3	9.6
1842	373,895	19,629	20,660	5.9	6.1
1843	369,565	19,402	20,469	−1.1	− .9
1844	395,762	20,778	21,969	7.1	7.3
...					
1850	596,867	31,336	33,567		
...					
1855	634,200	33,296	36,165		
...					
1860	857,225	45,004	48,464		

a Output figures are computed from a variety of sources. The primary ones are the U.S. censuses of manufacturing for 1810, 1820, 1840, 1850, and 1860, the McLane Report, and Massachusetts censuses of manufacturing dated 1837, 1845, and 1855. The census year figures through 1844 can most accurately be interpreted as giving rates of production near the end of the year indicated. Interpolations have been made on the same basis. The last three rows in the table are best interpreted as giving rates of production for the middle of the indicated years. Since interpolations were made by using a constructed series of year-end spindle capacity and productivity, they are best interpreted as giving a capacity rather than an actual output figure. I intend to adjust for capacity utilization in subsequent work. However, this omission is of little significance in the present article since output was almost certainly at capacity in the years analyzed in Table 4.

The reader who is familiar with the work of Lance E. Davis and H. Louis Stettler, III [*11*] will be aware of discrepancies between their output series and the one presented here. Considering the substantial differences in techniques of estimate, the differences in our numbers—at least after 1831—are comparatively minor. Davis and Stettler employ a different source from mine for the year 1831. They also interpret early census figures as accurate totals of the preceding year's output, while I think they more nearly represent rates of output at the end of census periods. Their interpolations are based on the output of sample firms while mine are based on aggregate statistics of new investment. I believe that variations in their sample output often reflect random influences on individual firms rather than industrywide fluctuations. Finally, Davis and Stettler are primarily interested in the years after 1831, while I am primarily interested in the years before. As a result their two methods of extrapolation from 1831 back to 1826 are somewhat crude and arbitrary by their own admission. In general their estimates for the three subsections of New England as presented in Table 4, page 221 of their article, add to an output figure more nearly equal to mine than their alternative estimate of total New England production presented in the last column. The earliest year employed in my analysis for which Davis and Stettler also have an estimate is 1828. Using either the sum of their sub-regional or their over-all regional estimates produces rates of growth from 1828 to 1833 and from 1833 to 1860 which are nearly identical with those used in the present article.

b Computed in constant 1831 prices.

c Cloth output is not computed independently of total output before 1816.

Table 2. Growth in the Cotton Industry, 1815–1860

| Period | COMPOUND ANNUAL RATE | |
	All Cotton Goods (Per Cent)	Cloth Only (Per Cent)
1815–1833	16.3	29.0
1815–1824	16.1	42.1
1824–1833	16.5	17.1
1833–1860	5.2	5.1
1833–1844	5.2	5.0
1844–1850	8.0	7.8
1850–1855	1.5	1.2
1855–1860	6.0	6.2

embargo, non-intercourse, and war, which influenced the earlier decade. We can judge how substantial the rate of progress was in these seventeen years by observing that in the year of least advance, 1830, the rate of growth still exceeded that of the cyclical recovery of 1844–1850, which was the best period of expansion experienced by the New England industry from 1833 to the present.

The production of yarn not made into factory cloth reached a peak in 1815, not to be equaled until the late 1830s. Thus the growth we wish to explain is the growth of cloth production. A complete explanation should also account for the remarkably small incidence of the ordinary business cycle on the growth rates of the industry from 1816 to 1833 when compared with the years from 1834 through 1860.

How can we explain this exceptional increase? We shall attempt to determine the relative contributions made to the total expansion by the dynamics of the demand and supply curves for cotton textiles. We shall also try to isolate the principal reasons for the behavior of each.[2] We begin with demand.

---

[2] The concept of a single demand curve or a single supply curve for cotton textiles is a highly artificial and abstract tool which will greatly facilitate the argument. Each piece of cloth can be characterized by a vector whose elements are: width; count of yarn (warp and woof); style of weave; nature of bleach, dye, or print. In practice each of these elements assumed anything from several to several hundred values. There were thus many thousands of supply and demand curves for different qualities of cloth. Our single curves are meant to summarize the weighted average in these many related markets.

THE ROLE OF CHANGES IN DEMAND

Effective real demand for the cotton textile makers' products may have changed because of a change in the share of the domestic market supplied by domestic producers; or a change in the relative prices of close substitutes (linen, woolens, leather); or a change in total population; or a change in the composition of population among classes with different propensities to consume manufactured cotton goods; or changes in the real income available to the population; or the distribution of income among different classes; or changes in the transportation and distribution networks which altered the relationship between the price prevailing in final markets and the price realized by producers.[3] We shall assess each of these factors in turn.

1. Import Substitution

In the years 1816, 1817, and 1818, British textile products virtually flooded markets in the United States and other parts of the world after being contained by the barriers of embargo and warfare for nearly ten years. Our first concern is to estimate the extent to which the growth of New England cotton cloth production subsequent to 1816 can be viewed as a substitution of domestic for foreign supply following the tariffs of 1816, 1824, and 1828. Unfortunately we have no reliable estimate of the amount or value of American textile production or of cotton textile imports for the early post-war years. The total of "general merchandise imports" for 1816, 1817, and 1818 was $226 million [29, p. 538]. If we suppose that cotton manufactures accounted for one tenth to one sixth of this total, then imports averaged between $7.5 million and $12.5 million a year.[4] These goods were priced in the American market between 20 cents and 30 cents a yard. Pairing the high and low prices and total import values yields estimates of 37.5 and 41.25 million yards per year. Pairing the highest price

---

[3] We could with equal propriety assume that textile producers sold to the final market, in which case the distribution of mill products should be considered a purchased input as part of a discussion of shifts in the supply curve.

[4] Cotton manufactures were one seventh of general merchandise imports in 1820 and one tenth in 1830 [29, pp. 538, 549]. Cf. [22, p. 474].

estimate with the lowest import value estimate and conversely yields extreme possibilities of 25 and 62.5 million yards a year.
Allowing for the fact that a large part of
imported cotton manufactures consisted of
yarn rather than cloth it seems most probable
that cotton cloth imports averaged between
25 and 30 million yards a year in the three
years after the war and almost certainly were
less than 40 million yards. In 1820 the value
of imports of manufactured cotton goods was
$8 million, indicating that imports of cloth
in that year were comparable to the years
1816–1818 [*29*, p. 549]. An attempt to estimate the net importation of cotton cloth by
the United States in subsequent years indicates an average quantity of 35 million yards
a year in the period 1821–1825, with fluctuations between 31 and 39 million yards. For
the period 1826–1830 an average importation
of 33 million yards was estimated with a
range from 22 to 46 million yards.[5]

Thus imports of cotton cloth remained
nearly constant while domestic production
soared. If we suppose that all of the New
England and foreign cloth under consideration was a perfectly homogeneous commodity, then American consumption of that
commodity increased some three and one-
half times between 1820 and 1830, from 50
to 175 million yards, while the share of that
consumption supplied by New England increased from about 30 per cent to some 80
per cent. From this point of view we could
attribute an increase of eight thirds over the
decade to the result of the tariffs and the
balance of the ninefold increase to other
causes.[6]

Although attributing less than half the
total expansion to the tariff, this estimate still
clearly overstates its effect by a wide margin.
Imports from Britain and the products of
New England mills tended to fall into quite
distinct product classifications. The imports
were largely ginghams, woven in intricate

---

[5] There are no direct records of quantities imported into the United States for these years. These
estimates rely heavily on the fact that British exports
of cotton cloth constituted the overwhelming bulk of
American imports. Figures on both the quantity and
the declared value of British exports of cotton goods
are given for the years 1823–1827 in [*11*, p. 117] and
for the overlapping period, 1827–1830 in [*22*, p. 295].
The declared values of U.S. imports of cotton cloth
are available for 1820, 1830, and 1840 in [*32*, p. 545].
For the years 1821–1825, they appear in [*19*, p. 23].

The U.S. dollar figure divided by the British sterling
figure always produces a number within 10 per cent of
the current exchange rate of $4.86 except in 1830 when
the differences in the time period covered by the U.S.
fiscal year and transport delays seem to account for the
divergence. Therefore it was assumed that British
exports accounted for all of American imports. Net
American imports were estimated by multiplying the
quantity of British exports by the ratio of the value of
U.S. imports minus re-exports to U.S. imports, all for
cotton cloth goods, for the years 1823–1830. For 1821
and 1822 the quantity of cloth to be multiplied by this
ratio was estimated by dividing the value of imports
by the average ratio of this value to the quantity of
British exports for the period 1823–1829. American
re-exports for the entire period are given in [*12*, p. 118].

---

[6] [Zevin's argument can be restated as follows. Let

C = the domestic consumption of cotton cloth in
1820
P = the domestic production of cotton cloth in
1820
S = the share of domestic production in
consumption in 1820
c = the decade rate of growth of C
p = the decade rate of growth of P
s = the decade rate of growth of S

Then by definition

$$S = \frac{P}{C} \qquad \text{(I)}$$

or

$$P = SC \qquad \text{(II)}$$

But for 1830 the relationship expressed by equation II
will become

$$P(1 + p) = S(1 + s) C(1 + c) \qquad \text{(III)}$$

Dividing equation II by equation III one obtains

$$(1 + p) = (1 + s)(1 + c) \qquad \text{(IV)}$$

Zevin's argument is that import substitution only
increased the nation's share in total consumption but
did not affect the level of total consumption. He
points out that the domestic share rose from 27.8 to
80.1 per cent (i.e., $1 + s = 80.1/27.8 = 2.88$) while
the total consumption of cloth increased from 50
million to 175 million yards (i.e., $1 + c = 175/50 =
3.50$) and the domestic production of cloth rose from
13.9 million to 141.6 million yards (i.e., $1 + p =
141.6/13.9 = 10.2$). It follows from equation IV that
if the increase in consumption (c) had been zero,
$(1 + p)$ would have been equal to 2.88 instead of
10.2. Hence the value of $(1 + p)$ attributable to
$(1 + s)$ is 2.88. One may therefore say, as Zevin does,
that less than half of the value of $(1 + p)$ is a consequence of import substitution.

Readers may note a semantic difficulty in Zevin's
exposition. He speaks as if he is explaining the increase in domestic production (which is p) when in

patterns to which the power loom had not yet been adopted. New England power looms were supplying plain weaves—sheeting, shirting, and, somewhat later, twills—usually made of lower count yarns than the British cloths. On the one hand New England had completely abandoned fancy hand-loom weaving for the American market to the British and the Pennsylvanians by the late 1820s [*33*, pp. 76–77, 93–94]. On the other hand, there were virtually no imports of low count, plain weave British or Indian goods after 1816. Although there is no disagreement about this fact, there is a substantial literature devoted to the question of whether or not the use of the power loom would have caused such a cessation of low price imports without the prohibitive tariff rates of 1816, 1824, and 1828.[7]

fact he is explaining one plus the increase $(1 + p)$. Furthermore, when s and c are relatively small, one can compute p either from equation IV or from equation V

$$p = s + c \qquad (V)$$

This result follows directly from equation IV since

$$(1 + p) = (1 + s)(1 + c) = 1 + s + c + sc$$

or

$$p = s + c + sc$$

Hence if s and c are relatively small, sc can be neglected. For example, if $s = 0.03$ and $p = 0.04$ then $p = 0.03 + 0.04 + .0012 = 0.0712$. Use of equation V would yield a figure of 0.0700. Thus the error involved in using equation V instead of equation IV, in this case, is less than 2 per cent.—Editors' note.]

[7] One source, arguing that the tariff of 1816 was a meaningful prohibition of coarse Indian cottons, calculates that the six and one quarter cent minimum rate amounted to an ad valorem rate of 83.5 per cent on these goods. This would imply that in the absence of a tariff such goods would have sold for little more than ten cents a yard after all expenses. At such a price they would surely have continued to find a substantial market regardless of inferior quality [*9*, p. 4].

Another opponent of the proposed Baldwin Tariff, writing at the same time, comes to a very different conclusion. "Now for ten years before that time [1816], our cotton goods were infinitely superior to the coarser East-India cottons, which this law prohibited; and the former were preferred by the farmers throughout the United States. Indeed, there was no competition between them; for the common East-India goods are made of the poorest Bengal cottons, the staple of which is so short, that it more resembles

Once we concede that there were not merely two relevant categories of cotton cloth—high quality and low quality—but rather a range encompassing hundreds or thousands of different quality cloths, a somewhat more complicated possibility emerges. The minimum duty on cotton cloth was increased with each tariff from 6.25 cents in 1816 to 8.75 cents after 1828. At the same time the domestic and world prices of all cotton cloths were falling at various rates, so that every year new types of cloth fell beneath the critical line required to produce any particular ad valorem rate of duty. We do not have sufficiently precise disaggregate data to quantify this progressive effect of rising minimum duties in a world of falling prices. To the discussion above we can only add the judgment of Taussig that the bulk of the effective protection enjoyed for this period was acquired in one swoop and became superfluous sometime between 1824 and 1832.[8]

In the market for plain cloths which New England mills supplied in significant quantities, New England already supplied nearly 100 per cent of market requirements in 1816. The growth of output over the following seventeen years cannot be ascribed to a continuing process of supplanting British products through technical advances, higher tariffs, or changing consumer preferences, since one or more of these factors had already

the blossom of the sycamore than it does our cotton. ... It is difficult to conceive how these goods could interfere in any important degree with our manufacturers. Such then was the actual condition of our coarse cotton manufactures in 1816, enjoying as much of our home market as they could supply." [*7*, pp. 45–46]. In this concluding remark, Cambreleng correctly recognizes the necessary delay between a market opportunity and the completion of the supply response.

Mrs. Ware concludes, "It is impossible to say whether the tariff was actually responsible for the exclusion of India cottons or whether it merely killed an already dying trade." For higher price goods where the effective duties rose from 25 per cent in 1816 to nearly 50 per cent in 1828, Mrs. Ware argues that protection was not really afforded. "The Rhode Island manufacturers, who wished to erect a high enough barrier to exclude the English calico which competed with their ginghams, failed to secure the protection they desired and were gradually forced to abandon the manufacture of these cloths." [*33*, p. 71].

[8] [*25*, pp. 29–36]. Taussig believed that the minimum system was not prohibitive when enacted in 1816, but became so for all significant types of goods after the deflation of 1819.

been sufficient to complete the task in 1816.[9] Any doubt about the long-run unimportance of the tariff as a continuing stimulus to demand for domestic cotton goods is completely dispelled if we confine our analysis to the growth of production from the peak in 1815 to the boom year 1833. Sales of New England cotton cloth increased at an extraordinarily rapid rate over this period; yet the initial year is one in which war conditions provided more complete protection for all textile products than could any tariff. Moreover 1815 marked the end of a lengthy string of years during which warfare and the events preceding the war had effectively insulated American markets from European goods. We conclude that while the tariff may have had demand augmenting effects which contributed to the cyclical recovery from the postwar depression, the tariff made no significant contribution to the secular growth of American demand for New England mill products over the period from 1815 to 1833.

2. Shifts in Population and Income

When we consider the relation between the demand for cotton goods and the markets for such substitutes as linen, woolens, and leather, we come immediately to the question of the distribution of the population between seaboard and interior, and between rural and urban locations. Before 1816, the peacetime cash market for textile products of any material was largely limited to major urban centers. The rural population supplied its own cloth needs and accounted for only occasional luxury purchases of manufactured textile products. Only the urban populations had the purchasing power to create markets for manufactured goods and only urban populations lacked the ability to satisfy their needs in any other way.

After 1816 the rapid settlement of the West created a new source of demand. Initially the population of these Western areas did not have the sheep, the flax, the spinning wheels, or the looms with which to supply its own textiles. There was at the same time a complementary emphasis on cash crops and commercial agriculture which gave the West part of the means with which to purchase textile products and other necessary manufactures. Unfortunately it is not possible to say anything definite about the actual distribution of the final consumers of New England cotton cloth. The mills in the northern region usually sold their entire output to a Boston wholesaler. These wholesalers and the mills in the southern region customarily sold to several dozen middlemen in the major ports and commercial centers. These middlemen, in turn, sold part of their purchases directly to the public and part to retailers in other places or to still another middleman.[10] There is at least some reason to suppose that the urban and/or Western markets were most important.[11]

The growth and redistribution of population cannot account for more than a small shift in the demand curve for cotton textiles when compared with the stupendous growth of production. Total United States population advanced in the 1820s and 1830s at a rate of one third each decade. In 1830 population had advanced 34 per cent over the 1820 level; by 1833 it stood 47 per cent ahead

---

[9] A completely accurate description of the role of British competition is still more complex. After 1830 Britain continued to supply roughly 20 per cent of American cotton textile consumption, basically the most expensive, high quality portion. However, over time the nature of luxury goods was changing as the Americans succeeded in turning yesterday's luxury items into today's staples. Around 1830 the British lost their American market for checks, plaids, stripes, and calicoes, as domestic manufacturers adopted the power loom to more complicated weaves, and also developed a very inexpensive substitute for the British products by manufacturing printed calicoes from plain, power-loom cloths. The British continued to supply an upper quintile of luxury goods which now consisted of shirtings and prints made from what were, by American standards, extremely high-count yarns (numbers 50 to 150). Only a handful of New England mills competed at all in this market before 1860.

[10] In this discussion the "southern region" of New England refers to Rhode Island, Connecticut, and all of Massachusetts except for metropolitan Springfield and the counties of Middlesex, Hampshire, and Franklin. The "northern region" encompasses the rest of New England. On the sales of New England mills see [31]. Also [33, pp. 161–197, 309–310]. On the distribution of household manufactures and the consequent demand for factory made textiles see [27, chaps. V and VI]. On the organization of the trade in cotton textiles see the pages cited in [33] and also [16, pp. 24–26].

[11] Most initial sales were to Boston, New York, and Philadelphia. The latter two cities were not only the largest in the United States but the two principal commercial centers and points of transshipment for the Western trade. See the sources cited above in footnote 10.

of the 1820 level; and in 1840 it had advanced 78 per cent.[12] By contrast the advances in New England cotton cloth production from 1820 to each of these dates were 921 per cent, 1568 per cent, and 2228 per cent, respectively. If we try to measure the growth of each of the two special groups of consumers discussed above, the results are still not very dramatic compared with these advances. The population residing in areas containing at least 10,000 persons was 442,000 in 1820, 771,000 in 1830, and 1,344,000 in 1840, representing advances from 1820 of 74 per cent and 200 per cent [29, p. 14]. The population residing west of the Alleghenies increased at nearly the identical rate, from 2,217,000 in 1820 to 3,672,000 in 1830 and 6,377,000 in 1840.[13] To summarize, we have found that total population was expanding at a rate of slightly less than 3 per cent a year, while the two components of the population which might have had especially high propensities to consume cotton cloth each expanded at a rate of about 5.5 per cent a year in both the 1820s and the 1830s. Hence on the most liberal estimate, the effect of population growth on demand can account for a little under one third of the growth of New England cotton cloth output, which averaged 17.1 per cent a year between 1824 and 1833, a comparison free of any important cyclical influence.[14]

Other important possibilities which might account for a dramatic outward shift in the demand curve for cotton cloth are a significant increase and/or redistribution of real income. It is not our intention to contribute another summary judgment to the substantial and still inconclusive literature debating the course of per capita national income before 1840. Rather it is hoped that the entire study of which this essay is a part will provide one of the numerous elements from which a more accurate description of the early nineteenth-century economy can be constructed.

Nevertheless, for the problem at hand we need some measure of the changes in per capita real incomes in the period from 1816 to 1840. Any estimate within the extremes postulated in the existing literature will suffice, since no one claims increases in income which are comparable in order of magnitude with the production increases we are trying to explain. We take Robert Martin's admittedly inadequate estimates, since they are the only ones specifically quantified. Deflating by both a general price index and a cost of living index, Martin shows real per capita income declining from 1819 to 1829. For the twenty years from 1819 to 1839 his two series show increases of 17 per cent and 15 per cent, respectively [21, p. 6]. If we suppose an income elasticity of demand approximately equal to unity, then we cannot account for more than a 1 per cent annual increase in per capita real national demand for cotton cloth due to increases in income.

It might be argued that the growth of consumer demand is more adequately measured by the growth of agricultural exports than by the combined effect of the population and per capita income growth. However the real value of agricultural exports advanced 45 per cent from 1821 to 1831 and 160 per cent from 1821 to 1841, or less than Western population growth in both periods.[15]

3. Transportation Improvements and the Growth of Demand

We have yet to consider the effects of transportation and distribution innovations on the demand curve faced by New England cotton mills. If it became possible over time for textiles to be shipped to a given group of consumers with greater efficiency, this would have the effect of increasing demand for textiles at the mill. Any given price quoted at the mill would be translated into a lower price at the site of final consumption and hence into a greater quantity demanded at the mill. Our question then is to estimate the extent to which the locational distribution of consumers already in existence in 1816 could be more efficiently reached in 1833. If the

---

[12] [29, p. 7]. The source gives simple linear interpolations between decennial census figures.

[13] [29, p. 13]. The population figures given are the sums of the populations for the East North Central, West North Central, East South Central, and West South Central census regions.

[14] Since we have population figures only for the census years, and since our output estimates for those years are substantially more reliable than for intervening years, we add herewith the rate of growth of cotton cloth output from 1820 to 1840, which was 17 per cent a year.

[15] The value of agricultural exports was deflated by the Warren-Pearson wholesale price index. For U.S. agricultural exports, see [24, p. 31]. The Warren-Pearson index is reproduced in [29, p. 115].

effect of transportation improvements was to change the prior spatial distribution of consumers—enabling them to concentrate where they had previously been sparse or nonexistent—then that effect has already been taken into account by considering the rate at which population grew west of the Appalachians and in urban centers.

It can be shown that the rate of growth of demand faced by the cotton textile mill which was due to transportation improvements is given by the following formula:

$$\lambda_i = e_i \, \frac{\dot{T}_i}{P + T_i} \, \theta_i \qquad (1)$$

Where λ_i is the rate of growth to be estimated, e_i is the price elasticity of demand for cotton textiles among the final consumers being reached by the transportation improvements, T_i is the unit cost of shipping textiles to the area, P is the unit price of textiles at the mill, $\dot{T}_i$ is the time rate of change of T_i caused by transportation improvements, and θ_i is the proportion of total demand accounted for by the area benefiting from the improved transportation facilities.

This formula is far simpler than the acquisition of the data necessary to make use of it. Only educated guesses can be made about the probable value range of the e_i's by making use of recent studies of consumer demand. In most cases P, T_i, and $\dot{T}_i$ are readily obtainable. The difficulties are in estimating θ_i. Empirically we can only attempt to estimate θ_i as some function of the ratio of the population in the area in question to the entire population that constituted the market. The formula for λ_i expresses an instantaneous rate of change, but we can only observe T_i and θ_i at rather widely separated intervals. This is unsatisfactory since θ_i is constantly changing over time as a result of transportation improvements as well as shifts in population. Even worse, the only accurate observations we have for population come from the census years 1810, 1820, 1830, and 1840; while the dates we might want to mark off with important transportation developments would all fall nearer to mid-decade, 1816, 1825, and the mid-1830s. Nevertheless we shall attempt to construct a reasonable estimate of λ_i for each of the major regions of the nation.

The first five or ten years of the period we are considering were marked by developments in transportation as revolutionary as those in cotton textile production. Immediately after the War of 1812 steam power was successfully applied to navigation up the Hudson, the Connecticut, the Mississippi, and its tributaries. In 1818 the Pennsylvania Turnpike reached Pittsburgh and the National Road reached Wheeling further down the Ohio. New York State completed the Champlain Canal in 1823 and the Erie Canal in 1825. Thereafter major transportation improvements affecting the movement of goods to the West came at a more moderate pace to the end of our period. The Oswego Canal was finished in 1828 and the Welland Canal in 1833, creating a route from Albany to Lake Erie alternative to the Erie Canal. The canal around the falls of the Ohio at Louisville was opened in 1830, making it possible for steamboats to progress from New Orleans to Pittsburgh. The Pennsylvania Main Line was completed to Pittsburgh in 1834.

The steamboat lowered the cost of shipping goods from New Orleans to Louisville from an average level of 5 to 6 cents a pound in 1815–1816 to about 1 cent in the years 1822–1825. By the late 1820s rates were fluctuating around an average level of 1/2 cent and they showed little trend from that point to 1840 [5, pp. 53–57]. Assuming an average of 2 1/2 yards of standard cloth to the pound, the steamboat meant reductions in unit shipping costs from 2 cents per yard in 1815 to 0.4 cents in 1824, to 0.2 cents thereafter. If transport costs up the Mississippi had fallen no more than in proportion with the Warren-Pearson wholesale price index from 1816 to 1824 they would have averaged 1.15 cents per yard instead of 0.4 cents. Adding the actual transport cost to the average price of Russian brown sheeting in New York produces a price 4.8 per cent lower than adding 1.15 cents to the same average price for the years 1816–1824. This 4.8 per cent is a maximum estimate of the percentage reduction in price to the ultimate consumer as a result of the steamboat, since the price paid by that consumer also included freight from New York to New Orleans, middlemen's profits, and other handling and insurance charges. If we take the price elasticity of demand at an arbitrary even number, like two, then the total increase in demand from the region served by the Mississippi as a result of the steamboat was 9.6 per cent, or an average of about 1 per cent a year over the nine years, from 1816 through 1824.[16] (To find the effect on the demand curve which faced the mills, this figure of 1 per cent must be multiplied by the share of the total market involved in the area served by the Mississippi steamboats.) If we arbitrarily suppose that Eastern manufactured goods reached consumers in Alabama, Arkansas, Louisiana, Mississippi, Missouri, and Tennessee by steamboat while other Western consumers were reached by different routes, we find the total population of those areas in 1820 to have been about 860,000. This was 40 per cent of the population in the West; one third of the combined populations of the West and urban areas; little more than one quarter of the previous group plus those living in western New York, western Pennsylvania, and present-day West Virginia; and less than one tenth of the population of the United States. If we use the penultimate figure and take $\theta_i = 0.25$ then with demand increasing from the region served by Mississippi steamboats at a rate of 1 per cent a year, such steamboats increased the total demand facing the New England mills at a rate of 0.25 per cent a year from 1815 to 1824.

The same calculation applied to changes from 1824 to 1833 yields negligible further effects of the steamboats. If we suppose that transport costs up the Mississippi fell from 1824 to 1833 only in proportion to the Warren-Pearson wholesale price index rather than by the observed amount, we find that the New York price of Russian brown sheeting plus transport costs would have been 10.56 cents in 1833 rather than 10.37 cents. Hence a high estimate of the price reduction to Mississippi Valley consumers is 1.8 per cent. Again assuming an elasticity of two, the total increase in demand over the nine years is 3.6 per cent, or a compound rate of 0.4 per cent a year. This last number must be still further reduced by some weight which appropriately reflects the area's share in total demand for cotton textiles. This time $\theta_i = 0.25$

would most certainly be an upper bound. The states mentioned above had about the same share in the population totals for 1830 as had been the case in 1820.[17] But by 1830 other areas had developed greater potential as markets for manufactured textiles, and improved canals and roads had eroded the area which received Eastern manufactures via New Orleans. Thus further improvements in transporting merchandise up the Mississippi in the years 1824–1833 increased the total demand facing Eastern textile mills by less than 0.1 per cent a year.

We turn now to transportation advances on the overland routes from Philadelphia and Baltimore to the West. These may have been the most important routes for Eastern manufactured goods throughout our period [17, pp. 16, 18, 21]. Once again the dramatic transportation savings are concentrated at the beginning of the period: "An extraordinary reduction in rates of wagon carriage from the Eastern seaboard to the Ohio River took place between 1816 and 1823 [6, p. 74]." In 1815 the cost of shipping goods from Philadelphia overland to Pittsburgh and then down the Ohio to Louisville was 11 cents to 12 cents a pound. In 1816 the Philadelphia to Pittsburgh part of the journey cost another 1 cent or 2 cents. Rates for shipments from Baltimore to Wheeling and then down the Ohio were lower than the Philadelphia rates. Even shipments from Baltimore to Pittsburgh were less expensive than shipments to the same point from Philadelphia. From this information we can safely estimate the average cost of shipping a pound of dry goods from Baltimore or Philadelphia to Cincinnati or Louisville at about 10 cents per pound in 1815–1816.[18]

The Pennsylvania Turnpike, the National Road, and the use of steamboats rather than flatboats for the shipments down the Ohio

---

[16] Strictly speaking the value of e estimated in Table 4 will be sensitive to the assumed e_i used in computing λ (and d). While it might be better to simultaneously determine both e_i and d, the discrepancy created by this procedure is minor. In addition, footnote 23 gives reasons why e_i and e could differ.

[17] If the populations of western New York, Pennsylvania, and Virginia are added to the 3,672,000 residing in Western states in 1830 [21, p. 11], the total population of the economic West was nearly 4,800,000 in 1830 [28, p. 67]. This population plus those living in cities of 10,000 or more gives a total of 5,500,000 of which the Mississippi Valley states already mentioned contained 1,500,000.

[18] The figures in this paragraph are from [6, pp. 73–87]. Ten cents is Berry's estimate of the average rate from Baltimore to Cincinnati for the decade 1811–1820 [6, p. 87].

were all responsible for the dramatic fall in rates which Berry mentions. By the early 1820s overland rates from Philadelphia to Pittsburgh were about 3 cents, from Baltimore to Wheeling about 2 cents, from either of those points down river to Cincinnati or Louisville from 0.18 cents (by flatboat to Cincinnati) to 0.5 cents (by steamboat to Louisville). Thus we would not be far wrong in taking 2.5 cents per pound as the average expense of shipping goods to the West by these routes in 1824. These costs showed no significant further declines to 1840.[19]

Using the same method as above—an assumed ratio of 2 1/2 yards of cloth to the pound, an assumed price elasticity of two, an assumed contribution of transportation equal to the difference between the actual decline in transport costs and the decline which would have been proportional to the movement of the Warren-Pearson wholesale price index, and an assumed price in the West equal to the New York wholesale price plus transport costs—we find that the demand for cotton cloth in the Western market served from Baltimore and Philadelphia increased by 15.6 per cent from 1815 to 1824 as a result of transportation improvements, or at a compound annual rate of 1.6 per cent a year. From 1824 to 1833 there were no demand augmenting transportation improvements on these routes. We have still to compute an appropriate θ_i with which to weight the impact of this 1.6 per cent growth on aggregate demand facing the mill owners. If we assume that the population served by these routes consisted of those consumers living in the states or future states of Illinois, Indiana, Kentucky, Michigan, Ohio, West Virginia, Wisconsin, and the western part of Pennsylvania, then the total population affected was about 1,450,000. This represented about 45 per cent of the sum of the populations of the Western states, the western portions of New York and Pennsylvania, and urban areas. Taking $\theta_i = 0.45$, we conclude that improvements in overland transportation to the West from 1815 to 1824 caused total demand for New England mill products to expand during that period at the rate of 0.7 per cent a year. From 1824 to 1833 no effect on total demand can be ascribed to further improvements.

We turn last to the Erie Canal. The reduction in transport costs from Albany to Buffalo which resulted from the canal's completion, and the additional reduction in costs on the New York to Albany leg of the journey which resulted from the use of steamships on the Hudson, were by far the most dramatic cost savings of our three cases. However, more clearly than in the previous two cases, the great bulk of Western population which the canal came to serve did not arrive in the West until after the canal had been built. Of the 581,000 people residing in Ohio in 1820, for example, less than 42,000 had more convenient access to Lake Erie than to the Ohio River and were thus in a position to receive goods through the new Western gateway at Buffalo rather than through Pittsburgh, Wheeling, and New Orleans [17, p. 8]. Thus we have already taken account of the principal demand-augmenting effects of the canal by measuring the rate of growth of Western population, which was due in a considerable degree after 1825 to the existence of the canal. One important effect of the canal which was realized before 1824 was the economic penetration of western New York itself. Traffic was moved on the canal from Albany to Rochester as early as October, 1823. The population of western New York in 1820 was some 350,000. We might assume that the average freight haul to reach this population from Albany was 140 miles (one half the distance from Albany to Rochester). Assuming further that overland freight from Albany in 1815 cost 30 cents a ton mile, while canal rates in 1824 were 6 cents a ton mile, and that rates up the Hudson River to Albany fell from 6.2 cents a ton mile in 1815 to 1 cent a ton mile in 1824, we can estimate that the total cost of shipping a ton of goods from New York City to the average consumer in western New York State fell from a little more than $50 a ton in 1815 to a little less than $10 a ton in 1824.[20] Using the same methods as above we can estimate that the price of cotton goods in western New York was 2.5 per cent lower in 1824 than it would have been without the transportation developments of the preceding eight years. Again assuming an elasticity of two, transportation induced growth of demand in this region can be estimated at 0.53 per cent per year. Using the same method as before, θ_i would be

---

[19] [6, pp. 75–87]. Two and one half cents is Berry's estimate of the average rate from Baltimore to Cincinnati in the decade 1821–1830.

[20] The freight rates are based on information contained in [1, p. 411] and [26, pp. 133, 137, 442].

slightly less than 0.11. With some extra allowance for the effects on northern New York State and Vermont resulting from the Champlain Canal, the total demand-augmenting effects of the New York State canal system can be taken at 0.07 per cent per annum from 1815 to 1824.

In summary we might estimate that transportation developments concentrated in the nine years before 1824 may have augmented the rate of growth of total demand for cotton textiles by little more than 1 per cent a year (0.25 per cent + 0.7 per cent + 0.07 per cent, the sum of effects for Mississippi steamboats, reduced overland rates, and the New York canal system, respectively). From 1824 to 1833 it appears that we can safely neglect to make any allowance for the growth of effective demand caused by transportation developments.

4. Price Elasticity and the Rate of Increase in Demand

Before making a final judgment about the proportion of increased production which was due to the growth of demand from all causes, it will be useful to begin to consider evidence which allows us to say something about the simultaneous interaction of demand and supply. The rate of growth of output can be decomposed in the following fashion:

$$1 + g = (1 + d)(1 + ep) \qquad (2)$$

Here g is the rate of growth of output, d is the rate of shift in the demand curve, e is the elasticity of the demand curve over the relevant arc, and p is the rate of change of the relative (or real) price of cotton textiles.[21] To make sense out of such a formulation we must stipulate that shifts in the demand curve are proportional—that is, after n years the quantity demanded at any price whatsoever is equal to $(1 + d)^n$ times the quantity demanded at the same relative price at the beginning of the period. Under this formulation the arc elasticity of the demand curve between any two relative prices is invariant with respect to any shifts in the demand curve. Hence our formula separates the growth of output into a component due to shifts in demand, d, and one due to the relative

behavior of supply, ep.[22] The growth rates, g, already appear or can easily be calculated from Tables 1 and 2. The rate of shift of the demand curve, d, is the number we have tried to estimate thus far. We shall calculate p, the rate of change of relative price, from the prices in Table 3, deflated by the Warren-Pearson price index. This is a crude way of getting at relative price, but our only purpose in employing this formula is to produce a crude estimate of e, the arc price elasticity of demand. The formula can be used to show the value of e implied by any d and conversely. The a priori range of reasonable values for one of these variables may help to establish a narrower range of acceptable values for the other. Also the values which seem appropriate in one time period may further limit acceptable values in another period.

Table 4 displays alternative paired values of d and e consistent with the data and our specifications of the problem.[23] Three distinct

---

[21] [See footnote 6 above.—Editors' note.]

[22] More accurately the formula decomposes growth into a component due to the shift in demand, d, and one due to the shift in price, ep. The latter term is not really a supply term since the rate of change, p, is itself a function of both d and the supply curve. In general d and p will be positively correlated; p will be less negative when d is larger. Hence a larger d term implies a smaller ep. In this sense d overstates the contribution of demand and ep understates the role of supply. The number d does give the rate at which industry output could have grown if supply responded in a passive fashion to shifts in the demand curve; while ep gives the rate at which output grew because of supply shifts, down or to the right, which expanded the market at a rate in excess of d.

[23] The three rates of change, g, d, p, are always calculated as compound rates from initial to final years bounding the periods considered. While this presents the three rates in the only natural fashion, the calculated elasticity is only one of several alternative definitions of the price elasticity of demand over the same arc. However, whenever such a calculation produces an e of an appropriate sign and magnitude, the same would have to be true for alternative calculations of e, such as one employing rates of change from the last year backwards to the first. It should also be noted that this elasticity is a property of the demand for cotton textiles which confronts the producer. Its relationship to the elasticities, e_i, which prevail in the various markets of ultimate consumers, will depend on the behavior and institutional structure of the chain of middlemen who connect producers with those markets. We follow the custom of presenting the absolute values of those calculated elasticities which have the proper sign.

Table 3. Price and Cost of Cotton Cloth, 1814–1860 (Cents Per Yard)

Year	Price of Russian Brown Sheeting N.Y.[a]	Labor Costs[b]	Total Costs[b]	Gross Return[c]	Profits[d] (Nashua Co.)
1814	30.53				
1815	28.95				
1816	24.77[a]				
1817	24.74				
1818	22.93				
1819	21.06				
1820	21.37				
1821	21.37				
1822	21.37				
1823	20.70	3.75	9.75	10.95	
1824	14.57	3.65	10.43	4.14	
1825	14.42	3.67	11.45	2.97	
1826	12.92	3.77	8.92	4.00	
1827	12.83	3.30	7.51	5.32	2.72
1828	12.25	3.07	7.67	4.58	3.42
1829	9.92	2.75	7.15	2.77	.49
1830	9.50	2.22	6.20	3.30	.97
1831	10.83	2.00	5.57	5.26	2.26
1832	9.75	2.10	5.82	3.93	2.07
1833	10.17	2.17	6.77	3.40	1.27
1834	9.33	1.83	5.40	3.93	.93
1835	10.50	1.75	5.67	4.83	1.17
1836	11.75	1.87	5.73	6.02	1.86
1837	10.08	2.35	6.17	3.91	1.64
1838	9.00	2.17	5.31	3.69	1.55
1839	9.58	2.18	5.52	4.06	2.28
1840	8.17	1.90	4.57	3.60	.37
1841	8.00	1.95	4.87	3.13	1.50
1842	6.75	1.76	4.01	2.74	.89
1843	6.17	1.51	3.63	2.54	.10
1844	7.75	1.50	3.60	4.15	1.80
1845	7.08	1.61	3.48	3.60	1.95
1846	7.58	1.64	3.64	3.94	2.40
1847	7.67	1.73	4.88	2.79	1.39
1848	6.58	1.45	3.39	3.19	.79
1849	6.00	1.36	3.86	2.14	.46
1850	6.95	1.32	5.05	1.90	.85
1851	7.00	1.24	4.20	2.80	.27
1852	6.00	1.31	3.81	2.19	.44
1853	6.33	1.28	4.13	2.20	.79
1854	7.00	—	—	—	.93
1855	7.58	—	—	—	.53
1856	8.00	2.02	4.83	3.17	.96
1857	9.00[a]	—	—	—	1.15
1858	8.00	—	—	—	.90
1859	7.25	1.55	4.47	2.78	1.30
1860	7.00[a]	1.62	4.35	2.65	1.46

[a] These prices are the average of the monthly prices given by Cole [8]. The source reports prices in cents per yard beginning in 1824 and in dollars per " piece " until the end of 1825. The average dollar price was converted to cents per yard by multiplying by .01357, the average ratio of the two figures for the 24 months of overlap. The high ratio was .01429; the low value was .01323. For 1816 the source gives no prices in February and March and we have averaged the other ten months. For 1860 the source gives no prices at all for this series. We have assumed a price of 7 cents. This price prevailed in the last seven months of 1859, when average prices for two companion cotton cloth series were the same as those which prevailed in 1860.

[b] From a manuscript in the collection of the Rhode Island Historical Society, Providence, Rhode Island, " Returns of Labor and Returns of Work Done," covering the activities of the Blackstone Manufacturing Company.

[c] The column of prices minus the column of total costs.

[d] Computed from the manuscript collection of the records of the Nashua Manufacturing Company, Baker Library, Harvard University, Cambridge, Mass., *AF-1, passim.*

Table 4. The Relation Between Annual Rates of Growth in the Demand for Cotton Cloth and Price Elasticity, 1815–1860

Period	Rates of Growth (Per Cent)		The Value of *e* if *d* Is Equal to:			The Value of *d* (Per Cent) if *e* Is Equal to:			
	Price (1)	Quantity (2)	4% (3)	6% (4)	8% (5)	1.0 (6)	1.5 (7)	2.0 (8)	2.5 (9)
1815–1824[a]	−1.5	42.1	24.4	22.7	21.0	40.0	39.0	38.0	37.0
1815–1824[b]	−1.5	13.6	6.15	4.78	3.46	11.9	11.1	10.3	9.5
1824–1828	−4.1	18.9	3.49	2.97	2.46	14.2	12.0	9.9	7.8
1828–1833	−3.2	15.8	3.55	2.89	2.26	12.2	10.5	8.8	7.2
1824–1833	−3.6	17.1	3.53	2.93	2.37	13.1	11.1	9.3	7.5
1833–1860	−1.3	5.1	.75	(c)	(c)	3.7	3.1	2.3	1.7

[a] The growth rate shown in the first row is for cloth actually manufactured in factories.
[b] The growth rate shown in the second row is for all cloth woven from factory-made yarn.
[c] These elasticities have meaningless signs.

periods are analyzed in Table 4: the years from 1815 to 1824, from 1824 to 1833, and from 1833 to 1860. The middle period is divided into two subperiods at the year 1828. All the terminal years were characterized by prosperity for the economy generally and the cotton textile industry in particular. The analysis is thus not unduly influenced by cyclical disparities in the terminal years. The three periods are distinguished by distinctly different and successively lower rates of growth in the output of cotton cloth.

Columns 3 through 5 tabulate the elasticities implied by the assumptions that demand was expanding at 4, 6, or 8 per cent a year. These assumptions bracket the estimates suggested by our previous discussion of the 1820s and 1830s. In particular, for the period 1824 to 1833, we have suggested that the populations in urban centers and west of the Appalachians—those with the greatest propensity to consume manufactured textiles— were growing at a rate of about 5.5 per cent a year. After 1824 transportation made a negligible further contribution to demand. Increasing per capita incomes may have caused demand to expand by another 1 per cent a year. Thus the most likely growth rate of demand for 1824–1833 would fall in a range from 6 per cent to 8 per cent. This implies an arc price elasticity over this period between 2 and 3, which is not an implausible result for a new product with a very rapidly declining relative price.

After the period of initial introduction, when prices had already fallen enough to induce most consumers to adopt the new product and spend a significant portion of their incomes on it, we would expect the price elasticity of demand to approach a value much nearer to unity. For the period 1833 to 1860 an elasticity of 1.5 implies that demand increased by 3.1 per cent a year, or approximately at the same rate as total United States population.

From 1824 to 1860 we can say that the direction and general order of magnitude displayed by our calculated *e*'s and *d*'s are in accord with reasonable expectations and the evidence considered thus far. This direction of movement and the stability of the estimates is confirmed by the results for the two subperiods, 1824–1828 and 1828–1833. For all that, it must be conceded that the values of *e* or *d* or both are somewhat higher than the evidence would seem to warrant for the decade before 1833 and somewhat lower for the period after 1833. Several factors which have not yet been discussed render the calculated values even more in accord with reasonable expectations.

Thus far we have only analyzed the price of cotton textiles relative to the Warren-Pearson wholesale price index. We might more realistically suppose that consumer purchases were determined in a two-stage process. The over-all level of textile purchases would naturally respond to the prices of textile products relative to general prices. The composition of these purchases among various alternative textile products would depend on the internal structure of textile prices. Because the technological advances in cotton textile production were adapted to the manufacture of woolens with a lag of ten to twenty years, the price of cotton goods fell relative to the price of woolens from 1815 to the early 1830s and rose thereafter. For this reason we should expect the demand for cotton goods to increase more rapidly than the rate indicated by the growth of per capita income and Western and urban population before 1833 and less rapidly than the same indicated rate after 1833. In addition we might expect the share of woolens in total textile consumption to increase and the share of cotton goods to decrease as a consequence of increasing per capita income, if, relative to cotton goods, woolens were a luxury good with a steeper Engel curve. In that case it is not unlikely that the price elasticity of demand for cotton cloth could have been one or less than one, while the elasticity of demand for all textiles was somewhat greater in the period 1833–1860, because of the different income effects which were components of the two elasticities.

The first row in Table 4 remains entirely unsatisfactory. If demand was growing as much as 8 per cent a year we are forced to conclude that price elasticity was an unbelievably high number. If price elasticity was a more believable 2.5 we conclude that demand was growing at a rate far in excess of our previous indications. To resolve the problem we must reconsider both g and d. The growth rate we have shown for the years 1815–1824 is the rate at which industry output of yards of cotton cloth expanded over the period. In 1815 the principal output of the New England industry was yarn and not cloth. The yarn was sold to households and woven into cloth on hand looms. Some was sold to mills which produced cloths of a mixture of woolen and cotton yarn. A fairly small portion reached ultimate consumers as thread, knitting yarn, or candle wicking. The balance was woven into cloth under the supervision of the spinning mill and hand looms which were located either in nearby homes or in the factory itself. Our estimate of yards produced in 1815 includes only those woven within the factories. The quality and price of this cloth was more or less indistinguishable from cloth produced outside of factories. The flood of inexpensive British cotton goods in 1816 closed most of the New England spinning mills. Household weaving made use of British yarns and many consumers found it advantageous to purchase manufactured British cloth. Only the American mills which

employed the power loom continued to produce substantial quantities of cloth in 1816 and thereafter.

The relevant comparison for our present purposes would therefore be between total production of hand-loom cloth in 1815 and total production of factory-made cloth in 1824. In 1809 the 510,000 pounds of yarn produced in Rhode Island, comprising 60 per cent of total New England production, was disposed of as follows. The factories and surrounding households converted 200,000 pounds directly into cloth; 124,000 pounds were sold for use as thread or knitting yarn; the balance of 186,000 pounds was sold to local families or merchants outside of the vicinity for use as candle wicking or on household looms [*13*, p. 427]. Our estimate depends on the first and some portion of the last categories. We suppose that by 1815 some three quarters of all the yarn produced in New England was woven into cotton cloth. We suppose further that on the average each pound of yarn was converted into three yards of cloth.[24] Since New England mills produced an estimated 7,860,000 pounds of yarn in 1815, these estimates would imply that that yarn was used to produce a total of 17,700,000 yards for American consumption. The second row of Table 4 is computed on the basis of the growth from 1815 to 1824 of total consumption of cloth produced from New England manufactured yarn.

Thus, comparing the first and second lines of Table 4, it is apparent that the largest portion of the explanation for the phenomenal expansion of factory cloth production in New England is due to a change in the composition of total production between home and factory. In 1815 less than one seventh of the cloth produced from New England yarn was woven in New England factories, while the corresponding figure of 1824 was 100 per cent. Even if total production

---

[24] Tench Coxe, writing in 1814, asserts that Rhode Island mill owners calculated four yards of cloth to each pound of yarn as a rule of thumb [*10*, p. 669]. The estimate appears to be biased by Coxe's desire to calculate a potentially maximum importance for the expanded textile industry he hoped for. Rhode Island mills were also already concentrating on higher-count yarns which made lighter cloths. The standard power loom product of the early 1820s weighed about three yards to the pound and the coarsest cloths suitable for the frontier weighed an average of two and one half yards to the pound.

had been unchanged over these nine years, production of factory cloth would have increased at a compound annual rate of 25.1 per cent a year merely from the conversion of existing spinning mills into integrated mills.

On the other hand, if all cloth had been produced in factories as early as 1815, total production would still have expanded at a compound annual rate of 13.6 per cent a year because of the operation of conventional supply and demand factors. The implications of this rate of growth, as indicated in the second line of Table 4, are not inconsistent with the analysis we have been making of demand.

Between 1810 and 1820 population in the Western states increased from 1,078,000 to 2,217,000, or at a compound annual rate of 7.5 per cent compared with 5.7 per cent in the 1820s and 5.5 per cent in the 1830s.[25] Furthermore it is unlikely that very much of this trans-Appalachian migration took place during the years of the Non-Intercourse Act and the war. In the nine years after the war, therefore, Western population may have expanded at a rate greater than 10 per cent per annum. This was also the period, as we have seen, of the most dramatic developments toward improved transportation to the West. Population growth and transportation improvement in the West must each have encouraged the other. Population residing in areas with 10,000 or more inhabitants increased comparatively slowly in the decade from 1810 to 1820, from 339,000 to 442,000, or at an annual rate of less than 3 per cent [29, p. 14]. If three quarters of the total market for cotton cloth in 1815 consisted of those living in the West and one quarter of those living in urban areas then the annual rate of increase of total demand over the period 1815–1824 would have been approximately 7.5 per cent because of Western population growth, another 0.5 per cent because of urban population growth, and, as estimated above, about 1 per cent because of transportation developments. Adding, we get a total rate of growth of demand of about 9 per cent a year. It is highly doubtful that per capita income levels were greater in 1824 than they had been in 1815, so that no additional effect needs to be added on that account.

_____

[25] *Supra*, footnote 13.

5. Summary

We can now summarize the entire discussion of the growth of demand for cotton cloth. During the period of most rapid expansion of output from 1815 to 1833, demand was also expanding at a rapid pace of some 8 per cent or 9 per cent a year. The principal reason for this expansion was the suitability of power loom cotton cloth for the exploding population of the West. Growing incomes, growing urban populations, improved transportation, and the relatively high price of close substitutes also played a part. Because most of these factors grew less important over the period, the rate of growth of demand was decelerating. In the first nine years it averaged 9 per cent or 10 per cent a year and in the last nine years 7 per cent or 8 per cent a year. After 1833 the influence of these forces became even less pronounced; Western and urban populations grew at slower rates; per capita income increases led to smaller increments in demand; the relative price of close substitutes declined; so that demand increased at an average rate of only 3 per cent or 4 per cent a year from 1833 to 1860. The price elasticity of demand was also high and was also declining during the first eighteen years of rapid growth, averaging perhaps slightly more than 2.5 at the beginning and a little more than 2.0 at the end. In the twenty-seven years after 1833 the average price elasticity of demand was still lower, most probably in a range from 0.75 to 1.5.

THE ROLE OF SUPPLY CHANGES

The implication of the previous discussion is that developments on the supply side of the New England cotton textile industry account for less than half of the spectacular growth of output during the eighteen years following the close of the War of 1812. While factory cloth production expanded at a compound annual rate of 29 per cent, a large part of this growth rate is the result of a shift of the weaving of cloth from home to factory. That shift took place when spinning mills which were already producing in 1815 were later converted into integrated mills which included the weaving process. If we take the effect of this conversion and spread it out over the entire eighteen year period, it is sufficient by itself to have produced an annual compound growth of factory cloth production equal to

11.8 per cent. Thus the increase in cloth production due to change in either the demand or supply schedules was equal to only 15.4 per cent a year ($1.29 \div 1.118 = 1.154$). With demand increasing by 8.5 per cent per year, shifts in the supply curve by themselves produced an annual rate of growth of 6.4 per cent ($1.154 \div 1.085 = 1.064$).[26] Since the rate of growth of total cloth production accelerated over the eighteen year period while the rate of growth of demand was decreasing, the supply-determined component of growth increases substantially in importance from at most 4.2 per cent a year before 1824 to at least 8.5 per cent a year in the succeeding nine years ($1.135 \div 1.09 = 1.042$ and $1.172 \div 1.08 = 1.085$).

These growth rates attributed to supply are the equivalent of the term *ep* in the formula underlying Table 4. Our task is now to examine the changes in the supply curve which determined *p*, or the rate of change of price, given the specifications we have determined for the shape and rate of shift of the demand curve. We cannot proceed with the analysis without making some simplifying assumptions about the shape of the supply curve and the way it changed over time. In 1815 we suppose that the American supply curve of hand-loom cotton cloth was an ordinary upward sloping function which became nearly vertical at the observed level of production, reflecting capacity constraints imposed by available supplies of yarn, looms, and weavers. Under wartime demand conditions it is probable that the cost level at which the supply curve became vertical was some considerable amount below the prevailing price level at which it intersected the demand curve. The length of that segment is a measure of prevailing industry disequilibrium or the rents per unit of output which accrued to the factors in inelastic supply that constituted a constraint on output. This belief is consistent with the very rapid rate of output expansion which is apparent in Table 1 for the war years, as well as the preceding periods of non-intercourse and embargo.

We shall argue below that as a consequence of the peace the demand curve for domestic cotton cloth contracted more rapidly than the domestic supply curve, leaving the supply curve entirely above the demand. The only exception was a very short segment representing the supply curve of the newly emerging power loom industry. To simplify the subsequent discussion we shall make the unrealistic assumption that the supply curve of American power-loom cloth can be represented for the entire period by two straight line segments; the first segment perfectly horizontal extending to the industry's capacity level of output, the second perfectly vertical. In 1816, then, the supply curve consisted of a short horizontal segment up to a quantity of 840,000 yards, then a vertical segment from the top of which extended another upward sloping segment corresponding to the old supply curve for hand-loom cloth. The demand curve for domestic cloth passed through the first vertical segment of the supply curve.

It is possible to estimate at least a crude upper bound for the magnitude of the rents which accrued to scarce factors employed in the wartime cotton textile industry. For this purpose we compare the years 1814 and 1816, since data from the intervening year reflect the transition from wartime to peacetime conditions. Total raw material costs per yard of finished cloth are estimated at 12.11 cents in 1814 and 13.45 cents in 1816.[27] Subtracting these costs from the prices in Table 3 leaves rough estimates of value added per yard at 18.42 cents in 1814 and 11.32 cents in 1816. The Warren-Pearson wholesale price index was slightly more than 20 per cent higher in 1814 than it was in 1816. If we inflate the 1816 value added estimate to 1814 prices we get 13.64 cents per yard. The difference between this figure and the actual 1814 price is 4.78 cents, or 15.7 per cent of the total price of cotton cloth in 1814. This is a maximum estimate of the rents accruing to 1814 factors for two reasons. First, it reflects whatever technical progress the domestic industry may have realized over the two years. Second, and more important, the 1816 industry had lost not only the rents and abnormal profits of

---

[26] [Using the approximation formula discussed in footnote 6, the rate of increase was 6.9 per cent.—Editors' note.]

[27] Raw material costs per yard of cloth were computed by multiplying the averages of the monthly price of Georgia upland cotton in New York City by .486. For the derivation of this factor see *infra* p. 143. The cotton prices averaged to compute costs for 1814 and 1816 were for the twelve months beginning July, 1813, and July, 1815, respectively. The quotations were taken from [*8*, pp. 163, 169, 172, 176].

the war years but some portion of its normal profits and remuneration as well. It seems safe to assert that the elimination of wartime rents made a positive but relatively small contribution to the total observed price decline from 1815 to 1833.

Henceforth we shall concern ourselves only with the supply curve for power-loom cloth. This supply curve could change over time for three sorts of reasons. Additions to capacity could extend the horizontal segment further to the right. Changes in the relative prices of inputs could raise or lower the level of the horizontal segment. Technological change could both lower the curve and extend it further to the right. The latter would be the case when a technological innovation increased the output which could be produced with a given stock of equipment, waterpower, or workers. There were significant developments in all three areas.

1. The Adoption of the Power Loom

The power loom has a commanding claim to our first attention. Its innovation corresponds exactly with the initiation of the enormous increase in production which we are trying to explain. We shall therefore consider why it was adopted and with what effect.

The first practical looms were developed by Francis Cabot Lowell with the help of Paul Moody in the winter of 1814–1815. While visiting England in 1810 Lowell became acquainted with the successful introduction of Horrocks' crank loom in Glasgow and Manchester. During his long stay, which was much occupied with other concerns and pleasures, he managed to make some casual observations of power loom weaving in Lancashire. Returning to Boston after the beginning of hostilities, Lowell hired Moody to assist him in developing a model power loom. The result of their efforts was a substantially new invention operated by a camshaft, and bearing little resemblance to the looms which had initially inspired Lowell [*34*, pp. 28–33; *2*, p. 9; *14*, pp.1–40, *passim*].

The Boston Manufacturing Company was organized in 1813 with the intention of spinning and weaving cotton by power and under one roof for the first time. Lowell persuaded his brother-in-law, Patrick Tracy Jackson, and another very wealthy Boston merchant, Nathan Appleton, to join him in providing the new venture with a generous capital of $400,000. The buildings were constructed in Waltham, Massachusetts, a short distance from Boston along the Charles River. The first small mill, with about 2000 spindles, was in nearly full operation by 1816. A larger mill of 3500 spindles was in operation by the autumn of 1818 [*14*, p. 49].

In 1818–1819, as he gained experience with the problems of economically spinning and dressing yarn for power looms, Moody developed several manufacturing processes of more lasting significance than the so-called Waltham loom.[28] The double-speeder was the first in an important sequence of American improvements of the roving process—the transformation of carded cotton into loose strands, or rovings, which are ready for the next process, yarn spinning. The inadequacies of the Waltham loom and the nature of the American market placed a premium on the ability to produce low count yarns of great strength and uniformity, and left producers increasingly uninterested in their ability to flexibly vary the count of yarn spun, or any other quality parameter. The double-speeder was well-suited to these altered values. So too, was the dead spindle. The filling frame which enabled the spinning of the woo directly upon bobbins ready for the looms, was an invention peculiarly useful in an integrated mill.

The principal problem which had plagued experiments in power weaving for decades was dressing the warp rapidly and cheaply, but still giving it sufficient strength to withstand the strains imposed by the loom. The success of Horrocks' loom had been largely due to the dressing machine which he also developed. The Waltham dresser was the most important element in the complex of machines which made up the Waltham System. All of these improvements were made before 1820.

This early narrative of the Boston Manufacturing Company has often been told. So much sympathetic and heroic history has been written by the principals, their associates, or their admirers, so many admirably complete and meticulous records have been left as a legacy for historians, and so much prestige and power has accrued to the descendants of those principals and to the public and private institutions which they established and supported, that we are likely

---

[28] The following paragraphs are based on the accounts in [*2, 14, 34*].

to form an unbalanced and misleading impression of the history of the integrated cotton industry.

Most accounts have taken their lead from the narrative written by Appleton himself.

In 1816 a new tariff was to be made. The Rhode Island manufacturers were clamorous for a very high specific duty. Mr. Lowell was at Washington, for a considerable time, during the session of Congress. His views on the tariff were much more moderate, and he finally brought Mr. Lowndes and Mr. Calhoun to support the minimum 6 1/4 cents the square yard, which was carried.

In June 1816, Mr. Lowell invited me to accompany him in making a visit to Rhode Island, with a view of seeing the actual state of the manufacture. I was very happy to accept his proposition. At this time the success of the power loom, at Waltham, was no longer a matter of speculation or opinion: it was a settled fact. We proceeded to Pawtucket. We called on Mr. Wilkinson, the maker of machinery. He took us into his establishment—a large one; all was silent, not a wheel in motion, not a man to be seen. He informed us that there was not a spindle running in Pawtucket, except a few in Slater's old mill, making yarns. All was dead and still. In reply to questions from Mr. Lowell, he stated, that during the war the profits of manufacturing were so great, that the inquiry never was made whether any improvement could be made in machinery, but how soon it could be turned out. We saw several manufacturers; they were all sad and despairing. Mr. Lowell endeavored to assure them that the introduction of the power loom would put a new face upon the manufacture. They were incredulous;—it might be so, but they were not disposed to believe it. We proceeded to Providence, and returned by way of Taunton. We saw, at the factory of Mr. Shepherd, an attempt to establish a vertical power loom, which did not promise success.

By degrees, the manufacturers woke up to the fact that the power loom was an instrument which changed the whole character of the manufacture; and that by adopting the other improvements which had been made in machinery, the tariff of 1816 was sufficiently protective [2, pp. 13–14].

No doubt the Rhode Island cotton industry was prostrate in 1816. So were almost all New England textile firms except for an occasional Slater or Waltham mill. Although the price of cotton cloth had not fallen as rapidly as some other prices, the price of raw cotton had actually increased as a result of renewed British demand from 20 cents in June, 1815, to 31 cents in June, 1816 [8, pp. 172, 176]. New England manufacturers were simply unable to deliver cloth to markets at costs which did not exceed prevailing prices. Rhode Island manufacturers must have been primarily concerned with raising one or lowering the other of these two variables. Appleton refers to what must have been their acute unhappiness at learning that he and Lowell were pleading for a system of protection which seemed primarily designed to protect the price of the Waltham product and not of Rhode Island ginghams. Lowell was also frustrated on this and other similar trips in his efforts to purchase the rights to use various technical improvements, including one developed by the same Mr. Shepherd of Taunton [2, p. 10]. However the principal frustration of this trip was plainly the refusal of the Rhode Island manufacturers to purchase Waltham System machinery or patent rights.

The reasons for this refusal are not hard to find. Certainly it was not because all of the technically experienced, economically hard-pressed, Rhode Island manufacturers were "incredulous," at the idea of weaving cloth on power looms. Not only were Rhode Islanders as well informed of British events as the Boston Associates, they had among them a recently arrived Scottish mechanic who had brought with him a far more intimate knowledge of Horrocks' loom and dressing machine than what Lowell had acquired.

From several accounts it appears that at least three major Rhode Island mills were actively interested in developing a power loom in 1815–1816 [4, p. 546; 35, p. 289; 5, pp. 70–71]. Two good reasons for these men in the southern district not to have purchased the wares proffered by Appleton and Lowell were the enormous advances over cost at which Waltham machinery was priced and their own imminent success in producing a superior loom at less expense.

It is simply not credible that a fortuitous initiative on the part of Lowell was responsible for the adoption of power looms, since numerous people began almost simultaneously to attack the problems of operating an integrated, power loom mill. The traditional view of the power loom as an American response to relatively dear or inelastically supplied labor is also not credible [15, esp. pp. 24–29, 30, 35, 137–138]. New England population was growing faster than the opportunities to employ it in the decades before 1820. The economic malaise in the half decade following the war produced large-scale emigration from New England and much comment about the necessity of employing the region's surplus population. This would hardly have been a propitious period for a widespread and ambitious effort motivated by a desire to save labor inputs.

The power loom was an important cost-saving innovation. It was in fact virtually a life-saving innovation. As late as the 1820 census, a comparison of firms which unambiguously indicated use of the power loom against the balance of firms—many of which must also have employed power looms, and many of which produced only knitting yarn, thread, or wicks—indicates that the former group was operating 81 per cent of its stated spindle capacity against 62 per cent for the remainder.[29]

The principal motive for introducing the power loom was a desire to regain competitive viability by cutting costs. The stimulus which brought this desire to the fore was the traumatic pressure which material and product price movements put on the manufacturers' gross margins. The result of adopting the power loom was to lower direct operating costs by a very substantial margin. Before 1815 Batchelder claims to have paid hand loom weavers from 3 cents to 7 cents a yard for goods whose direct expenses in power loom weaving departments aggregated 1 cent [*34*, pp. 28–33]. In the Providence area weaving rates for various fancy stripes and ginghams in 1814 ranged from 7 cents to 11 cents. By 1823 the power loom had cut these hand loom rates in half. By 1827 the same rates had declined 75 per cent [*33*, p. 307]. Apparently these large cost savings, initially about 4 cents and eventually 6 cents to 9 cents per yard of finished cloth, were sufficient to bring idle spinning mills back into profitable production when they were converted to integrated mills.

2. The Rate of Technical Progress and Changes in Factor Prices

While the fall in hand loom weaving rates provides a measure of the initial direct cost savings from power looms, continued cost saving improvements in the spinning and preparatory departments of mills could not

be reflected in weaving rates. Better measures of the total effect of technical improvements on costs after 1820 can be constructed from the changing ratio of industry value added in 1831 prices to industry employment, and total labor costs figures for individual mills such as the series presented in Table 3.

For the three years centered on 1824, average labor costs at the Blackstone mills were 3.69 cents a yard. They declined to an average level of 2.03 cents in 1832–1834 and hardly at all to the three years centered on 1840. There is reason to believe that mills, such as Blackstone, situated in the southern district, engaged in more strenuous efforts to reduce labor costs by substituting capital for labor than their northern counterparts in the 1820s. For the entire industry, constant price output per worker grew at a more modest 3.5 per cent a year from 1820 to 1831. Even with the generous estimate computed from the Blackstone records, labor cost savings account for only a little more than one third of the total decline in costs over these nine years, which is 4.54 cents (comparing centered three-year averages). The remaining decline of 2.88 cents occurred in nonlabor costs. Most of this decline was due to the fall in raw cotton prices.[30] The cost of the raw cotton accounted for nearly 40 per cent of the value of plain sheetings from the early 1820s to the early

---

[29] [*30*, pp. 28–223, 291–299.] Where the return merely indicated the possession of some kind of looms it was assumed that all mills were equipped with power looms if the ratio of spindles in use to looms in use was between 15 and 70. If the ratio exceeded 70 it was assumed that part of the reported mills had no looms and the whole was so categorized. If the ratio was below 15, it was assumed that the looms were hand looms.

[30] An attempt to independently calculate raw cotton costs per yard of cloth using lagged cotton prices, prevailing yields of yarn to cloth, assumed transportation and storage costs of 10 per cent of the value of raw cotton, and an assumed weight of one third of a pound for a finished yard of Blackstone cloth, produces estimates equal to about 97 per cent of nonlabor costs, as reported by the Blackstone mills from the late 1820s to the Civil War. For the early 1820s, however, the estimates fall short of Blackstone nonlabor costs by a little more than 1 cent per yard. These additional expenses are made up, in small part, of interest on borrowed money and, for the most part, of administrative, material, and labor costs associated with the company's rapid expansion of capacity in 1823–1825. The former costs should more appropriately be included in the gross return to capital which is considered below. The latter, amounting to about 1 cent per yard, should not have been included in operating costs at all since it really represents additional costs of plant and equipment. It is not clear to what extent the expenses incurred by Blackstone in the early 1820s were typical of the entire industry. If they were not, then 1 cent per yard should be subtracted from the decline in costs and added to the decline in gross margins in our discussion of the period 1824–1833.

1830s. The decline in raw cotton prices from roughly 25 cents a pound before 1820 to 15 cents in the early 1820s and 10 cents in the early 1830s meant declines in the price of most cloths between one third and one fourth of these changes. From 1816 to 1833, the indicated fall in raw cotton costs per yard would be between 4 cents and 5 cents.

We can isolate three principal components of the price of cotton cloth from the Blackstone figures in Table 3. Direct operating costs divided into the principal components of labor and raw cotton inputs and the residual, which is the gross return to capital per unit of output. The stability of the three elements over the period covered is remarkable. In 1823–1825, 1832–1834, and 1859–1860, labor costs average between 21 and 22 per cent of price in each period. For the same three periods nonlabor costs fluctuate in a narrow range between 40 and 41 per cent of price, while gross capital earnings lie between 36 and 38 per cent. Thus all three components of cotton textile price declined at the same rate in excess of the decline in the Warren-Pearson price index. Therefore each contributed to total price declines over the periods 1824–1833 and 1833–1860 in approximately the proportions given above. Although their rates of decline were all uniform and equal to the rates of relative price decline given in Table 4, the causes of their respective behaviors were far from uniform.

The decline in raw cotton costs per yard of cloth was essentially due to the decline in the price of raw cotton. This in turn was the result of supply developments in the American South and demand developments in Britain quite independent of the situation of the New England cotton industry. To some small extent, however, technological progress contributed to the decline in raw material costs, since the average New England mill was able to produce about .80 pounds of yarn from a pound of raw cotton in 1815, .83 pounds in the early 1820s, and .93 pounds from the mid-1830s to the Civil War.

Decreasing labor unit costs were in no sense caused by changes in the price of labor. Average annual money earnings of workers in New England cotton mills rose by 15 per cent from 1825 to 1833 and by another 4 per cent to 1860. Real earnings rose 16 per cent in the first period and 3 per cent in the second.[31] Hence the entire decline in labor

costs is due to technological change sufficient to more than offset increasing real wage payments.

If we attempt to extend these considerations back in time to the beginning of our period we must deal with substantially greater obstacles. Data on textile operations in 1815 are not nearly as comprehensive and reliable as those we have been using for the early 1820s. It is therefore even more difficult to disentangle the effects of changes in relative factor prices and changes in technology. One number which can be estimated with some certainty is the cost of raw materials per yard of finished cloth in 1815. From Table 3 we can calculate total raw material costs per yard of cloth at 4.6 cents for the Blackstone mills in 1833. This figure is overwhelmingly accounted for by the purchase of raw cotton. However it also includes the transportation and insurance of the cotton as well as the purchase and handling of other raw materials. We shall take the price of a pound of raw cotton as an index of the unit price of all these materials and services. Since the cloth is of the same quality in 1815 and 1833, a yard of it contains the same quantity of the same count of yarn. Therefore the only difference in the pounds of raw cotton required to produce a yard of finished cloth would be caused by a change in the ratio of the pounds of yarn which could be produced from a pound of raw cotton. Because of technical change and/or because of the substitution of capital for raw cotton the ratio did change from about .80 in 1815 to about .93 in 1833.

We can now calculate raw material or nonlabor costs per yard of cloth in 1815. There was a considerable lag between the purchase of raw cotton at a Northern port and the reappearance of the same cotton in the form of finished cotton cloth ready for market. Since the Blackstone and most other New England mills charged their operations with the cost of raw cotton as it was drawn out of inventory on a first-in, first-out basis, stated raw material costs reflected a lagged price of raw cotton. For this reason we take our index of raw material costs in 1833 as the average monthly price of Georgia upland cotton in New York City for the twelve months beginning July, 1832. Similarly for 1815 we have averaged the same series of monthly prices for the year beginning July, 1814.[32] The cotton cost index for 1833 is

---

[31] These changes are computed from [*18*, pp. 46–47].

[32] Cotton prices are from [*8*, pp. 169, 172, 242, 247].

exactly 11 cents. Raw material costs per yard of cloth equal 4.6 cents (.418 × 11 cents). As indicated above, the only reason why the factor (.418) should have been any different in 1815 than it was in 1833 is the changing ratio of pounds of finished yarn spun from a pound of raw cotton. Therefore in 1815 material costs per yard equal 11.34 cents [.418 × (.93/.80) × average price of cotton = .486 × 23.33 cents].

It is now possible to isolate the contribution made by the decline in the relative price of raw cotton to the decline in the relative price of cotton cloth. If there had been no technological changes from 1815 to 1833 and no substitution of capital for cotton then raw material costs per yard in 1833 would have been (.486) (11 cents) = 5.35 cents. If we use the Warren–Pearson index to restate the 1833 price of cloth and the material costs per yard just calculated in 1815 prices, we find that the deflated price of cloth fell by 10.75 cents while the constant technology raw material costs per yard fell by 1.77 cents. Hence the decline in the price of raw cotton by itself accounts for one sixth of the total deflated decline in price.

Since real wages rose from 1815 to 1833, the remaining five sixths of the decline in relative price must be due to some combination of technological change, the elimination of any disequilibrium payments earned in 1815, and any other diminution in the rate of return to capital. If we wish to estimate an upper bound on the average rents earned per yard of cloth in 1815, we can employ the same method used above on page 138. That is, the rent cannot be greater than the change in price minus raw materials costs from 1815 to 1816, adjusted for changes in the general price level. This is because there were certainly no rents earned in 1816. Using this method yields results for 1815 quite similar to those already calculated for 1814. The upper bound on the rent component in the 1815 price is 4.87 cents, or 16.8 per cent of the total price. This drop of 4.87 cents in deflated value added per yard from 1815 to 1816 "accounts" for 45 per cent of the total decline in deflated price from 1815 to 1833. Unfortunately this upper bound appears to exceed the true figure by such a wide margin as to render it nearly useless. News that the war had ended spread through the United States in the early months of 1815; the pell-mell expansion of the American textile industry came to a halt; the sharpest drop in the price of sheetings took place between May and June with the first arrival of British goods. The greatest impact of British competition was delayed until the spring of 1816, after which time most American mills were closed because of their inability even to cover variable costs. It is apparent therefore that the sharp drop in value added per yard from 1815 to 1816 is more likely to reflect the abnormal losses inherent in the 1816 price structure than any events which were still being earned in 1815. I shall assume that rents were a negligible component of the average 1815 price of cloth. It follows that over 80 per cent of the decline in the relative price of cloth from 1815 to 1833 is due to technical progress realized over the same period or to changes in the rate of return to capital.

3. The Growth of Capacity

We turn to the last component of price, the gross margin available to maintain and compensate capital. The last two columns of Table 3 present alternative, conceptually different indices of this component, one for a Rhode Island and one for a New Hampshire mill. Although year-to-year movements are erratic, both series indicate a pronounced secular decline. The averages for the gross returns calculated from the Blackstone records are, 1823–1828: 5.31 cents; 1829–1833: 3.73 cents; 1834–1843: 3.84 cents; 1844–1853: 2.89 cents; 1859–1860: 2.83 cents.

It is logical to ask what happened to the quantities and prices of the factors which had to be paid out of these gross margins. An examination of the capital required at current market prices to produce one yard of cloth in a typical mill of the southern or northern New England region indicates that the two series of returns to capital show no secular trend when divided by the respective series of capital requirements. This is not surprising if the market price of capital equipment simply capitalized the available margins at the going rate of interest and if interest rates themselves showed no secular trend.

Such was apparently the case. The system of integrated manufacturing produced a substantial, discontinuous drop in direct costs from the outset. Direct costs of production which had been above the prevailing demand curve for most of the industry were suddenly below for those who possessed the new equipment and the ability to operate and maintain it. There was a vertical gap between the supply curve and the demand curve at capacity output. This gap, indicative of

Table 5. Dividend Payout Rates of Northern New England Cotton Mills, 1817–1860

Year	Rate[a] (Per Cent)	Sample Size[b]	Weighted Average Rate[c]	Sample Size
1817	17.0	1		
1818	12.5	1		
1819	12.5	1		
1820	15.0	1		
1821	20.0	1		
1822	27.5	1		
1823	25.0	1		
1824	25.0	1		
1825	16.3	2		
1826	8.0	2		
1827	8.8	2.5		
1828	8.2	5		
1829	5.0	5.5		
1830	6.3	6		
1831	13.8	6.5		
1832	13.1	7		
1833	11.1	8.5		
1834	11.0	12		
1835	11.9	14	12.7	12
1836	11.8	14	10.6	12
1837	6.5	14	4.5	12
1838	10.7	15	9.4	13
1839	10.8	18	11.8	13
1840	4.3	19	3.7	13
1841	8.3	20	8.2	14
1842	2.6	22	4.0	16
1843	6.4	22.5	6.8	16
1844	13.6	23	13.8	16
1845	16.0	23	16.9	17
1846	15.3	25.5	17.6	17
1847	9.6	26	12.4	18
1848	5.1	25	5.7	17
1849	7.9	26	11.4	18
1850	6.0	27	6.5	19
1851	3.2	27	4.5	19
1852	5.3	28	6.0	19
1853	7.7	29.5	8.2	20
1854	7.4	30.5	8.0	21
1855	4.9	31	6.1	22
1856	6.5	30	6.6	23
1857	4.8	30	5.5	23
1858	2.3	30	2.9	23
1859	7.2	30	7.0	23
1860	9.7	30	9.7	25

[a] The arithmetic average of dividend payments as a per cent of par value by all cotton mills listed [20, pp. 90–92]. Stock dividends were included. New companies were not added to the sample until their first dividend payment. Companies which interrupted payments were kept in the sample. Payments averaged are those actually made during the year shown.

There follows a list of the companies added to the sample for all or part of each year. In every case but two these companies remained in the sample through 1860

industry disequilibrium, was available as a rent to those factors in relatively inelastic supply which effectively constrained the rate of growth of capacity. Those factors were the closely related abilities to build, install, operate, and maintain the new machinery. The rents were earned by those individuals with a thorough understanding of the technical processes of manufacturing cotton textiles. Sometimes, when those individuals were also suppliers of capital, their less talented associates shared part of these rents as an unearned windfall.

As evidence for this interpretation we offer the following. The prices of textile machinery fell much more rapidly than their production costs in the two decades after 1816. In the years immediately before and after 1820 the Boston Manufacturing Company sold machinery at average prices 50 per cent above direct costs. By 1830 the successor, Locks and Canals Company, contracted to make machinery for a 30 to 35 per cent advance above costs. By the late 1830s, it contracted to build the Massachusetts Cotton Mills for a profit of 5 to 10 per cent on direct costs. Average dividend rates of the Locks and Canals Company and the successor, Lowell Machine

once they had been added: 1817: Boston Manufacturing Co.; 1825: Merrimack Manufacturing Co.; 1827: Chicoppee; 1828: Hamilton Cotton, Nashua; 1829: Appleton; 1831: Lowell; 1833: Suffolk, Tremont; 1834: Amoskeag, Lawrence, Palmer, York; 1835: Great Falls; 1838: Boott Cotton Mills, Perkins; 1839: Coheco, Thorndike; 1840: Bartlet; 1841: Stark Mills; 1842: Dwight, Massachusetts Cotton Mills; 1843: Otis; 1846: Columbian, James Steam Mills, Laconia; 1849: Naumkeag; 1850: Bay State Mills; 1852: Atlantic Mills, Pepperell; 1853: Bates; 1854: Lyman. The Lowell Manufacturing Company was dropped from the sample after 1847 and the Bay State Mills after their failure in 1858.

[b] If a firm made its first dividend payment on the second semiannual payment date in a given year, this observation was given only half the weight of the sum of payments by a firm which made two regular semiannual dividends. The number which appears in this column is thus actually equal to half the number of semiannual dividend payments which were averaged in the given year and is frequently less than the total number of firms observed.

[c] These payout rates are from Tsung-yuen Shen [23, p. 199]. Shen's computations are based on the same source as mine. His figure represents the dollar sum of all dividend payments divided by the dollar sum of stated capital for all of the paying firms. Because of the more stringent requirements which this method imposes on the data, Shen's sample is a restricted subset of mine. The figures are reproduced to demonstrate that little is changed by this method. For the twenty-six overlapping years, the rank difference correlation coefficient for the two series is .956.

Shop, were 1827–1836: 17.8 per cent; 1837–1846: 11.9 per cent; 1847–1856: 9.0 per cent; 1857–1860: 2.0 per cent [*14*, pp. 40–42, 71–76, 101; *20*, pp. 91–93].

Table 5 presents average annual dividends for most of the cotton mills which were listed on the Boston Stock Exchange. These mills, especially in the earliest years, owned and operated their own machine shops, or were closely interlocked with a machine shop. Their very high rates of return in the early years must reflect abnormal profits on machine building and related skills. Almost none of the firms which simply purchased machinery from others managed to survive. Mere money was no guarantee of profits in the earliest phase of postwar expansion. The failure of the first owners of the Saco Manufacturing Company and the Great Falls Manufacturing Company illustrate this. The Saco mill was begun in the late 1820s by a group of Boston merchants attracted by the high profits in the industry but without any technically competent members. In the 1830s a successful mill was managed on the same site by Samuel Batchelder. The Great Falls Manufacturing Company was the unsuccessful enterprise of otherwise successful New Hampshire merchants until it was brought under the control of Patrick Tracy Jackson and the Boston Associates in the late 1830s. Jackson's annual treasurer's reports in the collection of Harvard University's Baker Library contrast strongly with those of his predecessors by virtue of their detailed discussion of the technology of production.

The most important beneficiaries of the industry's growth in the years before 1833 were always men of considerable technical skill such as Jackson, Francis C. Lowell, and Moses Brown, all of whom augmented their fortunes; or Samuel Slater, Paul Moody, Kirk Boott, and Batchelder, who built fortunes out of their technical skills. A letter from Moses Brown to Samuel Slater from an earlier period when knowledge of the Arkwright spinning process was the binding constraint on the industry is indicative, I believe, of the position occupied later by those with a similar knowledge of power loom technology:

I . . . want the assistance of a person skilled in the frame or water-spinning. An experiment has been made which has failed, no person being acquainted with the business, and the frames imperfect. . . . We hardly know what to say to thee; but, if thou thought thou could'st perfect and conduct them to profit, if thou wilt come and do it, thou shalt have all the profits made them, over and above the interest of the money they cost and the wear and tear of them. We will find stock and be repaid in yarn . . .[33]

One could hardly ask for a less ambiguous definition or offer of the economic rent created by a scarce skill.

We conclude that the decline in margins as we have calculated them was in large part the result of a process of adjustment to the industry disequilibrium which prevailed after the end of the War of 1812 and the introduction of the power loom. The power loom lowered the supply curve for cotton cloth in one discontinuous jump. The industry's problem then became to produce as much power loom cloth as could be sold with normal profits. Continued technical progress after 1815, falling raw cotton prices, and increasing demand all tended to prolong the length of time required to close the gap. In the absence of these other forces increasing capacity (by means of increasing the stock of skilled personnel) would lead to steadily declining prices until the demand curve intersected the horizontal portion of the supply curve and the gap was eliminated. The entire decline in unit prices would be borne by the portion used to pay rents to skilled personnel. The returns to capital estimated in Table 3 are indices of that rent because it is one of their major components. The decline in those margins is thus a delayed realization of the cost savings which were made available in a continuous fashion by the introduction of the power loom but could not be realized until supply had "caught up" with demand. In addition a small component of the price decline observed in 1816 represents the elimination of quasi-rents and abnormal profits which were earned under the disequilibrium conditions that prevailed in the wartime cotton industry.

CONCLUSION

We have seen that the period of spectacular expansion of the New England cotton textile industry was characterized by exceptionally favorable developments on both the demand and supply sides of the industry. The growth of factory cloth production appears particularly

---

[33] Moses Brown to Samuel Slater, December 10, 1789, Quoted in [*3*, pp. 38–39].

spectacular because of the contribution made in the early years by the transfer of the weaving function from homes to factories. After adjusting for this influence, we have found that the growth of demand made a somewhat greater contribution to the remaining growth of output—still a healthy 15.4 per cent a year—than did supply developments. The relative importance of expanding demand declined from more than twice that of supply effects in the first nine years to somewhat less than that of supply effects in the last nine years. On the supply side, roughly one sixth of the price reduction which the industry was able to make over this period was the result of falling raw cotton prices. The balance reflects real technological progress. Most of this progress was realized through one group of innovations at the beginning of the period. The entire period can probably be characterized as one of adjustment to industry disequilibrium. The reestablishment of equilibrium in the early 1830s would then account for the well-defined end to the spurt in production. As further evidence for this view we can argue that so long as the gap between supply and demand exists, the industry should not respond with output variations to changes in general business conditions. That is, if we view the business cycle as causing the demand curve for cotton cloth to swing alternately closer and farther from the origin in a pattern superimposed on its secular expansion, those swings would not affect industry output so long as they did not proceed far enough to eliminate the vertical gap. The greater the gap, moreover, the greater the degree of insulation from the business cycle. The increasing incidence of cyclical troughs on industry output in 1830, 1834, and 1839 gives some support to the view that the disequilibrium—as a secular rather than a cyclical phenomenon—was eliminated during the 1830s.

Interestingly, technical progress made a very modest contribution to the growth of total cotton cloth production from 1815 to 1833. Shifts in the demand curve alone would have caused production to expand at some 8 per cent or 9 per cent a year compared to a total growth rate of 15.4 per cent a year. This implies a supply induced growth of 6 per cent or 7 per cent a year. Approximately five sixths of this, in turn, can be attributed to technological developments. Hence during the eighteen years of the most revolutionary changes in the technology of cotton textile production, those changes, by themselves, could only have caused cloth production to expand at the fairly evolutionary pace of 5 per cent to 6 per cent a year. It is also of interest to note that the effects of this technical progress are distinct in time from the causes. The years 1815 to 1824 certainly encompassed the major share of great technological innovations for the period: yet, the following nine years saw the greatest impact on prices and production. It is no accident that the absolute contributions of demand and supply moved in opposite directions while the total rate of growth remained nearly the same over this period. The total rate of growth was constrained to the rate at which the supply of technically skilled personnel could be increased. Hence any reduction in the rate of growth of demand allowed supply to play a more important role as the industry's constant rate of growth took it more rapidly toward equilibrium, forcing it to pass on to consumers a greater portion of the previously realized gains in technology and reduced factor prices.

REFERENCES

1. Robert Greenhaigh Albion, *The Rise of New York Port*, New York, Charles Scribner's Sons, 1939.
2. Nathan Appleton, *Introduction of the Power Loom and Origin of Lowell*, Lowell, B. H. Penhallow, 1858.
3. William R. Bagnall, *Samuel Slater and the Early Development of the Cotton Manufacture in the United States*, Middletown, J. S. Stewart, 1890.
4. William R. Bagnall, *The Textile Industries of the United States, 1639–1810*, Cambridge, Riverside Press, 1893.
5. Samuel S. Batchelder, *Introduction and Early Progress of the Cotton Manufacture in the United States*, Boston, Little, Brown and Co., 1863.
6. Thomas Senior Berry, *Western Prices Before 1861: A Study of the Cincinnati Market*, Cambridge, Harvard University Press, 1943.
7. [Churchill C. Cambreleng], *An Examination of the New York Tariff Proposed by the Hon. Henry Baldwin*, New York, Gould and Banks, 1821.
8. Arthur H. Cole, *Wholesale Commodity Prices in the United States, 1700–1861: Statistical Supplement: Actual Wholesale Prices of*

Various Commodities, Cambridge, Harvard University Press, 1938.

9. Committee of Merchants and Others, of Boston, *Report on the Tariff*, Boston, Wells and Lilly, 1820.

10. Tench Coxe, "Digest of Manufactures," *American State Papers, Finance, II* (13th Congress, 2nd Session, Document No. 407), Washington, D.C., Gales and Seaton, 1832.

11. Lance E. Davis and H. Louis Stettler III, "The New England Textile Industry, 1825–60: Trends and Fluctuations," Conference on Research in Income and Wealth, *Output, Employment, and Productivity in the United States After 1800* (Studies in Income and Wealth, vol. 30), New York, Columbia University Press, 1966, pp. 213–242.

12. Friends of Domestic Industry, *General Convention of the Friends of Domestic Industry, Reports of Committees*, Baltimore, 1832.

13. Albert Gallatin, "Report on Manufactures," *American States Papers, Finance, II* (11th Congress, 2nd Session, Document No. 325), Washington, D.C., Gales and Seaton, 1832.

14. George S. Gibb, *The Saco-Lowell Shops: Textile Machinery Building in New England, 1813–1949*, Cambridge, Harvard University Press, 1950.

15. H. J. Habakkuk, *American and British Technology in the Nineteenth Century*, Cambridge, University Press, 1962.

16. Fred Mitchell Jones, *Middlemen in the Domestic Trade of the United States: 1800–1860* (Illinois Studies in the Social Sciences, vol. XXI, No. 3), Urbana, University of Illinois, 1937.

17. A. L. Kohlmeier, *The Old Northwest as the Keystone of the Arch of American Federal Union*, Bloomington, Principia Press, 1938.

18. Robert G. Layer, *Earnings of Cotton Mill Operatives, 1825–1914*, Cambridge, Committee on Research in Economic History, 1955.

19. [Henry Lee], *Report of a Committee of the Citizens of Boston and Vicinity, Opposed to a Further Increase of Duties on Importations*, Boston, Nathan Hale, 1827.

20. J. G. Martin, *Martin's Boston Stock Market: Eighty-Eight Years*, Boston, Joseph G. Martin, 1886.

21. Robert F. Martin, *National Income in the United States: 1799–1938*, New York, National Industrial Conference Board, 1939.

22. Timothy Pitkin, *A Statistical View of the Commerce of the United States of America*, New Haven, Durrie and Peck, 1835.

23. Tsung-yuen Shen, "A Quantitative Study of Production in the American Textile Industry, 1840–1940," (Unpublished doctoral dissertation), Yale University, 1956.

24. Walter Buckingham Smith, *Economic Aspects of the Second Bank of the United States*, Cambridge, Harvard University Press, 1953.

25. F. W. Taussig, *The Tariff History of the United States*, 4th ed. rev., New York, G. P. Putnam's Sons, 1898.

26. George Rogers Taylor, *The Transportation Revolution*, New York, Holt, Rinehart & Winston, 1962.

27. Rolla Milton Tryon, *Household Manufactures in the United States: 1640–1860*, Chicago, University of Chicago Press, 1917.

28. Frederick Jackson Turner, *Rise of the New West*, New York, Crowell-Collier, 1962.

29. United States Bureau of the Census, *Historical Statistics of United States, Colonial Times to 1957*, Washington, D.C., 1960.

30. United States Congress, "Census of Manufactures for 1820" *American State Papers, Finance, IV* (17th Congress, 2nd Session, Document No. 662), Washington, D.C., Gales and Seaton, 1858.

31. United States Congress, House, *Documents Relative to the Manufactures in the United States* (22nd Congress, 1st Session), Washington, D.C., 1833.

32. United States Department of Commerce, *Statistical Abstract of the United States, 1924*, Washington, D.C., 1925.

33. Caroline F. Ware, *The Early New England Cotton Manufacture*, Boston, Houghton Mifflin Company, 1931.

34. Samuel Webber, *Historical Sketch of the Commencement and Progress of the Cotton Manufacture in the United States up to 1876*, New York, D. Appleton and Company, 1879.

35. George S. White, *Memoir of Samuel Slater . . . with a History of the Rise and Progress of Cotton Manufacture*, Philadelphia, 1836.

II A MODEL FOR THE EXPLANATION OF INDUSTRIAL EXPANSION DURING THE NINETEENTH CENTURY: WITH AN APPLICATION TO THE AMERICAN IRON INDUSTRY

Robert William Fogel and
Stanley L. Engerman

If any single objective may be called the desideratum of economic historians, it is the explanation of industrial expansion. From the very beginning of the discipline its scholars have enshrined this aspect of their subject matter. They have given the eulogistic name of Industrial Revolution to the surges in the growth of manufacturing industries which began in the late eighteenth century in England and in the nineteenth century in the United States and elsewhere.

Reprinted with revisions by permission from *The Journal of Political Economy*, 77, (May/June, 1969), 306–328.

Over the years it has been easier to describe the phenomenon for which an explanation was sought than to provide the desired explanation. Until recently the thrust of research was toward the description of the main categories of factors on which an explanation would turn. Chief among these categories was the introduction of new machines and equipment. Thus every schoolboy has been taught about the mechanical inventions of the Industrial Revolution. The flying shuttle, the spinning jenny, the mule, and the power loom are presented as the revolutionary forces of the textile industry. The equipment which occupies the same position in the iron industry includes the puddling furnace, the rolling mill, and the coke or anthracite blast furnace. To many scholars the most revolutionary of all the mechanical innovations was the steam railroad. It has been singled out as a necessary condition for the advance not merely of a single industry but of regional specialization and over-all economic growth.

Compared with the emphasis placed on new machinery and equipment, all other factors in the growth of industry have been slighted. Some historians have, however, stressed the importance of increases in demand. W. W. Rostow, for example, argued that the rapid expansion of the demand for rails was the main factor in the growth of the iron industry during the two decades preceding the Civil War. Others have provided evidence which suggests that the primary impetus to the growth of at least some industries was neither the increase in the demand for their products nor changes in their productive techniques. Rather it may have been drastic reductions in the cost of the raw materials or other inputs which these industries purchased. Still other historians have investigated the economies of large-scale enterprise, which reduced the cost of both production and distribution.

Two factors have made such research fall short of an explanation of the growth of either particular enterprises or whole industrial sectors. The first has been the absence of a theory regarding the way in which the various explanatory factors are related to each other. Such a theory is a necessary condition for measuring the relative importance of these factors. The second has been the paucity of the data needed to estimate the parameters of an explanatory model. As it turns out, the theory required for the desired measurements follows rather directly from the economists' traditional analytic tools of supply and demand. This discovery has led to a number of recent studies which have for the first time attempted to assess the relative effect of increases in population, rises in income, the introduction of new machinery, and the reduction in the cost of inputs on the expansion of American industries during the nineteenth century.[1]

However, the paucity of data has been as formidable an obstacle to the new work as it was to the old. Much of the recent research has been based not on the measurement of the relevant parameters but on informed guesses as to their probable magnitudes. The central challenge of econometric history thus increasingly becomes the formulation of models which not only have considerable explanatory force but which are also consistent with the severe data constraints of historical research.

In the next section of this paper we set forth a model that attempts to meet these twin requirements. The model is applicable to competitive industries characterized by constant returns to scale. In its simplest form the model is valid for industries which are too small to have an appreciable effect on the market price of the labor, capital, or raw materials which they consume. However it can be altered to deal with industries whose expansion leads to an increase in the prices of inputs. Hence the assumptions of the model are probably appropriate to many American and European manufacturing industries during the nineteenth century. Moreover the number of parameters which have to be estimated are relatively small, the estimating procedures are quite simple, and the data required are relatively abundant. Finally, the model drops the assumption, often made in econometric analysis, that observed prices

---

[1] Temin's study of the American iron and steel industry [9, esp. pp. 29–34, 214–230] represents a point of departure for the new work. Using a somewhat more elaborate model, Zevin [13] provides an explanation of the remarkable growth in the production of cotton cloth between 1815 and 1833. Temin [10], Fogel and Engerman [3], and Wright [12] have attempted to measure the factors responsible for the growth in the production of raw cotton during the ante-bellum era. Sylla [6] is concerned with the estimation of cross-elasticity of demand between government bonds and private securities.

and output levels represent positions of long-run equilibrium. Instead it is assumed that what is observed is merely a succession of short-run equilibriums.

In the final section of the paper we use the model to explain the growth of American pig iron production between 1842 and 1858, and we discuss the problem of estimating the parameters of the model under the stringent data constraints usual to historical investigations.

THE MODEL

Everyone who has had a course in the principles of economics knows that in a competitive system the price and output of an industry's product are determined by supply and demand. A change in the equilibrium output (or price) requires a shift in the demand curve (see Fig. 1a), the supply curve (see Fig. 1b), or both (see Fig. 1c). In order to turn this type of analysis from a pedagogic device into an instrument of measurement, it is necessary to give an algebraic interpretation to the geometric concept of the shifting intersection of two curves. For simplicity of discussion, let D stand for the shift variables of the demand equation and S for the shift variables of the supply equation. (See Table 1 for complete definition of symbols.) These equations can be written as:

$$Q = DP^{-\varepsilon} \tag{1}$$

and

$$Q = SP^{\gamma} \tag{2}$$

where Q is output, P is price, ε is the

Table 1. Definition of Symbols

Q	Output
P	Price
D	Shift term of demand function
S	Shift term of supply function
ε	Elasticity of demand
γ	Elasticity of supply
A	Index of productive efficiency
L	Input of labor
R	Input of raw materials
K	Input of capital
α_j	Output elasticities of the inputs; $j = 1, 2, 3$
w	Wages
r	Cost of a unit of raw materials
i	Rental rate of a unit of capital
λ	Lagrange multiplier
π	Profit
Y	Gross national product
I	Gross domestic investment
P_i	Price of imported iron
P_w	Wholesale price index
ψ	Investment elasticity of demand
ε_i	Cross-elasticity of demand with respect to P_i
ε_w	Cross-elasticity of demand with respect to P_w
δ_j	Elasticity of factor prices with respect to Y; $j = 1, 2$
σ_j	Coefficient of time in the equations for factor prices; $j = 1, 2$
β_j	Elasticity of factor prices with respect to Q; $j = 1, 2$
ϕ	Defined by equation (26)
β	Defined by equation (28)
w_1	Part of w that is independent of Q
r_1	Part of r that is independent of Q
u, v	Uncorrelated random variables
b, m, n, z_1, z_2	Constants

elasticity of demand, and γ is the elasticity of supply. From this simple system of simultaneous equations we obtain the following

Figure 1

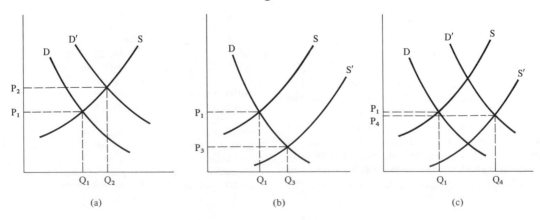

(a)   (b)   (c)

solutions for equilibrium price and output:

$$Q = D^{\gamma/(\gamma + \varepsilon)} S^{\varepsilon/(\gamma + \varepsilon)} \qquad (3)$$

and

$$P = \left(\frac{D}{S}\right)^{1/(\gamma + \varepsilon)} \qquad (4)$$

Since we are concerned primarily with explaining the rate of growth of output (rather than the rate of change in price), we focus on equation 3 and its rate-of-growth transformation, equation 5:

$$\overset{*}{Q} = \frac{\gamma}{\gamma + \varepsilon} \overset{*}{D} + \frac{\varepsilon}{\gamma + \varepsilon} \overset{*}{S} \qquad (5)$$

The letters capped with asterisks stand for the rates of growth of variables represented by the uncapped letters. Throughout the remaining discussion the same convention will be followed, that is, the capped letters will represent the rate of change in variables designated by uncapped letters.

It will be noted from equation 5 that if the rate of shift of demand ($\overset{*}{D}$) exceeds the rate of shift of supply ($\overset{*}{S}$), then the rate of growth of output ($\overset{*}{Q}$) will be greater the more that γ exceeds ε. However if $\overset{*}{S}$ exceeds $\overset{*}{D}$, then $\overset{*}{Q}$ will be greater, the greater the amount by which ε exceeds γ.

Further, if demand is completely inelastic ($\varepsilon = 0$), then the rate of growth of output will be equal to the rate of shift in demand alone. But if supply is completely inelastic ($\gamma = 0$), the rate of growth in output will be equal to the rate of shift in supply alone.

In the case in which supply is infinitely elastic (the supply curve is a horizontal line), equation 5 does not hold.[2] Then the rate of growth of output is given by

$$\overset{*}{Q} = \overset{*}{D} - \varepsilon \overset{*}{P} \qquad (6)$$

However, if it is demand that is perfectly elastic, the rate of growth of output is given by[3]

$$\overset{*}{Q} = \overset{*}{S} + \gamma \overset{*}{P} \qquad (7)$$

The Supply Function

Estimation of the values of $\overset{*}{S}$ and $\overset{*}{D}$ requires a more explicit specification of the industry's supply and demand functions. In a competitive industry the supply function is determined by three general considerations: (1) the technical relationship between inputs and outputs (the production function), (2) the period of production, and (3) the prices of the inputs.

We assume that the production function is Cobb-Douglas in form, with constant returns to scale, as shown by

$$Q = AL^{\alpha_1} R^{\alpha_2} K^{\alpha_3}; \qquad \alpha_1 + \alpha_2 + \alpha_3 = 1 \qquad (8)$$

The symbols Q, L, R, and K stand for output, labor, raw materials, and capital, respectively. The three powers, α_1, α_2, and α_3 are the output elasticities of the three inputs.

The A in the production function is an index of productive efficiency, and as such is frequently referred to as a measure of technological change. The nature of A is more clearly revealed if equation 8 is rewritten to make A the dependent variable:

$$A = \frac{Q}{L^{\alpha_1} R^{\alpha_2} K^{\alpha_3}} \qquad (9)$$

From this formulation it is clear that when the powers of the inputs sum to one, A is the ratio of an index of output to a geometric average of the inputs. It will be shown below that there is not one, as is usually presumed, but two price duals for equation 9.

The supply function of an industry is derived from the production function and the accounting equation for profit. Both the equation for profit and the production constraint can be incorporated into the following single equation by means of the Lagrange multiplier:

$$\pi = PQ - wL - rR - iK \\ - \lambda(Q - AL^{\alpha_1} R^{\alpha_2} K^{\alpha_3}) \qquad (10)$$

---

[2] Because then the simultaneous system represented by equations 1 and 2 reduces to just equation 1.

[3] Equations 6 and 7 hold in any case. Equation 5 follows obviously from these two equations. When the demand or supply curve is infinitely elastic, the elimination of $\overset{*}{P}$ cannot be carried out.

The new symbols in this equation are:

$\pi = $ profit
$P = $ the price of output
$w = $ the wage rate
$i = $ the rental rate per unit of capital
$r = $ the average price of a unit of raw materials
$\lambda = $ the Lagrange multiplier

Differentiation of equation 10 with respect to each of its variables yields the first-order conditions under which profit will be a maximum. The supply function is derived from the solution of the first-order conditions. However it should be noted here that the procedure yields two supply functions—one for the long run and a second for the short run—because in the long run capital is variable, while in the short run it is not. The long-run supply function is given by equation 11 and the short-run supply function by equation 12. Both equations are plotted in Figure 2.

$$P = [nA^{-1}w^{\alpha_1}r^{\alpha_2}i^{\alpha_3}] \qquad (11)$$

and

$$P = [m^{-\alpha_3/(\alpha_1 + \alpha_2)}A^{-1/(\alpha_1 + \alpha_2)}w^{\alpha_1/(\alpha_1 + \alpha_2)}$$
$$r^{\alpha_2/(\alpha_1 + \alpha_2)}K^{-\alpha_3/(\alpha_1 + \alpha_2)}]Q^{\alpha_3/(\alpha_1 + \alpha_2)} \qquad (12)$$

The new symbols in this equation are n and m, which are constants with values determined by the output elasticities of the production function.[4]

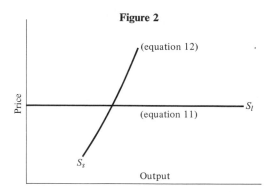

Figure 2

(equation 12)

(equation 11)

S_l

S_s

Price

Output

The equation for the short-run supply curve can also be rewritten with Q as the dependent variable:

$$Q = [mA^{1/\alpha_3}w^{-\alpha_1/\alpha_3}r^{-\alpha_2/\alpha_3}K]P^{(\alpha_1 + \alpha_2)/\alpha_3} \qquad (13)$$

In the long run the price at which output is supplied is independent of the level of output. This is expressed in equation 11 by the fact that output (Q) does not enter into the equation. In the short run the supply price is affected by the level of output, since entrepreneurs cannot increase their input of capital. Hence in equation 12, P is an increasing function of Q.

The shift variables are shown in brackets. The bracketed symbols of equation 13 are equal to S in equation 2; the power of P in equation 13 is equal to the power of P in equation 2—that is, $\gamma = (\alpha_1 + \alpha_2)/\alpha_3$. Moreover when supply is infinitely elastic, the P of equation 1 is equal to the bracketed symbols of equation 11. It is also worth noting that changes in the efficiency index (A) or in the prices of the variable inputs will bring about changes in both the long- and short-run supply curves. However the short-run supply curve has a shift variable not included in the long-run curve—capital (K). The presence of K indicates that given enough time, the industry will be able to increase its capital and will then be in a new short-run period. If there are no changes in input prices or in the productivity index (A), then the new short-run curve will be exactly the same as the old one, except that K will be larger.

If equations 11 and 13 are solved for A, we obtain, respectively,

$$A = \frac{nw^{\alpha_1}r^{\alpha_2}i^{\alpha_3}}{P} = n\left(\frac{w}{P}\right)^{\alpha_1}\left(\frac{r}{P}\right)^{\alpha_2}\left(\frac{i}{P}\right)^{\alpha_3} \qquad (14)$$

and

$$A = m^{-\alpha_3}\left(\frac{w}{P}\right)^{\alpha_1}\left(\frac{r}{P}\right)^{\alpha_2}\left(\frac{Q}{K}\right)^{\alpha_3} \qquad (15)$$

These equations are duals to equation 9.[5] They are useful in practical work, since often it is easier to find the price data needed to compute A from equations 14 or 15 than to find the data on physical inputs needed to compute A from equation 9.[6] During periods when only short-run equilibrium prevails, equation 15 is the appropriate one.

---

[4] Since n and m are factors of proportionality which disappear when the variables of equations 11, 12, and 13 are expressed in index number form, they will be ignored in the subsequent discussion.

[5] Cf. footnote 4.

[6] The solution of equations 11 and 13 for one of the factor prices yields the factor-price frontier. In the short run the factor-price frontier of an industry includes the utilization rate (Q/K) as an argument.

The Demand Function

No attempt will be made to derive the demand curve from a utility function. We merely assume that the demand function may be represented adequately by an equation of the form

$$Q = [bI^\psi P_i^{\varepsilon_i}] \, P^{-\varepsilon}, \qquad (16)$$

where:

> I = an index of gross domestic investment
> P_i = the price of imported iron
> ψ = the investment elasticity of demand
> ε_i = the cross elasticity of demand with respect to the price of imported iron
> b = a constant

Our warrant for this assumption is the observation that equations such as that given by 16 usually fit the data quite well. When applied to the iron industry, the assumption that the demand function is linear in the logs yields a regression in which the correlation coefficient is equal to 0.98.

The variables shown in brackets represent the shift term of the demand function. We do not mean to imply that I and P_i are necessarily the only variables which should enter into the shift term. Depending on the problem at hand, one may want to introduce the prices of more than one substitute or other variables such as income, population, or transportation costs. However, I and P_i are the most appropriate variables for the problem at hand, since pig iron was used to make investment goods and imported iron was the main substitute for domestically produced iron.

With this understanding we return to equations 1–4. Substituting the shift terms of equations 13 and 16 for S and D in equations 1–4, we obtain:

$$Q = (bI^\psi P_i^{\varepsilon_i})P^{-\varepsilon} \qquad (17)$$

$$Q = (mA^{1/\alpha_3}w^{-\alpha_1/\alpha_3}r^{-\alpha_2/\alpha_3}K)P^\gamma \qquad (18)$$

$$Q = (bI^\psi P_i^{\varepsilon_i})^{\gamma/(\gamma + \varepsilon)}$$
$$\cdot (mA^{1/\alpha_3}w^{-\alpha_1/\alpha_3}r^{-\alpha_2/\alpha_3}K)^{\varepsilon/(\gamma + \varepsilon)} \qquad (19)$$

$$P = \left(\frac{bI^\psi P_i^{\varepsilon_i}}{mA^{1/a_3}w^{-a_1/a_3}r^{-a_2/a_3}K}\right)^{1/(\gamma + \varepsilon)} \qquad (20)$$

So far we have assumed that the prices of inputs are independent of the level of the output of the industry. We now drop that assumption and suppose wages and raw material to be related to industry output by[7]

$$w = z_1 e^{\sigma_1 t} Y^{\delta_1} Q^{\beta_1} \qquad (21)$$

and

$$r = z_2 e^{\sigma_2 t} Y^{\delta_2} Q^{\beta_2} \qquad (22)$$

In these equations z_1 and z_2 are constants, Y is gross domestic product, and t is time. Together they measure influences on w and r which are independent of conditions specific to the iron industry. Hence equations 21 and 22 will yield positive values of β_1 and β_2 only if factor prices and Q are significantly correlated after account has been taken of general conditions in the factor markets.

Substituting for w and r in equations 18, 19, and 20, we obtain

$$Q = (mA^{\phi/\alpha_3}w_1^{-(\alpha_1/\alpha_3)\phi}r_1^{-(\alpha_2/\alpha_3)\phi}K^\phi)$$
$$\cdot P^{[(\alpha_1 + \alpha_2)\phi/\alpha_3]} \qquad (23)$$

$$Q = (bI^\psi P_i^{\varepsilon_i})^{\phi\gamma/(\phi\gamma + \varepsilon)}$$
$$\cdot (mA^{\phi/\alpha_3}w_1^{-(\alpha_1/\alpha_3)\phi}r_1^{-(\alpha_2/\alpha_3)\phi}K^\phi)^{\varepsilon/(\phi\gamma + \varepsilon)} \qquad (24)$$

$$P = \left(\frac{bI^\psi P_i^{\varepsilon_i}}{mA^{\phi/\alpha_3}w_1^{-(\alpha_1/\alpha_3)\phi}r_1^{-(\alpha_2/\alpha_3)\phi}K^\phi}\right)^{1/(\phi\gamma + \varepsilon)} \qquad (25)$$

where

$$\phi = \left(1 + \frac{\alpha_1}{\alpha_3}\beta_1 + \frac{\alpha_2}{\alpha_3}\beta_2\right)^{-1} \qquad (26)$$

or

$$\phi = (1 + \gamma\beta)^{-1} \qquad (27)$$

and

$$\beta = \frac{\alpha_1}{\alpha_1 + \alpha_2}\beta_1 + \frac{\alpha_2}{\alpha_1 + \alpha_2}\beta_2 \qquad (28)$$

In these equations

w_1 = the part of w that is independent of Q, and
r_1 = the part of r that is independent of Q.

---

[7] In these equations wages and raw material prices are assumed to be given to the firm but to vary with the output of the industry.

The value of ϕ can vary between zero and one. When $\phi = 1$, $w_1 = w$, $r_1 = r$, and equations 24 and 25 reduce to equations 19 and 20, respectively. In that case the rate of growth transformations of equations 24 and 25 are

$$\overset{*}{Q} = \frac{\gamma}{\gamma + \varepsilon} (\psi \overset{*}{I} + \varepsilon_i \overset{*}{P_i})$$
$$+ \frac{\varepsilon}{\gamma + \varepsilon} \left(\frac{1}{\alpha_3} \overset{*}{A} - \frac{\alpha_1}{\alpha_3} \overset{*}{w} - \frac{\alpha_2}{\alpha_3} \overset{*}{r} + \overset{*}{K} \right) \quad (29)$$

and

$$\overset{*}{P} = \frac{1}{\gamma + \varepsilon} (\psi \overset{*}{I} + \varepsilon_i \overset{*}{P_i})$$
$$- \frac{1}{\gamma + \varepsilon} \left(\frac{1}{\alpha_3} \overset{*}{A} - \frac{\alpha_1}{\alpha_3} \overset{*}{w} - \frac{\alpha_2}{\alpha_3} \overset{*}{r} + \overset{*}{K} \right) \quad (30)$$

Finally, taking the rate-of-growth transformation of equation 11 and substituting for the value of $\overset{*}{D}$ and $\overset{*}{P}$ in equation 6 we obtain

$$\overset{*}{Q} = \psi \overset{*}{I} + \varepsilon_i \overset{*}{P_i} - \varepsilon(- \overset{*}{A} + \alpha_1 \overset{*}{w} + \alpha_2 \overset{*}{r} + \alpha_3 \overset{*}{i})$$
$$(31)$$

Thus when $\phi = 1$, equation 29 is the extended equation explaining the growth of the output of a competitive industry with constant returns to scale between short-run equilibriums. Equation 31 is the extended equation explaining the growth of output for the same type of industry between long-run equilibriums.

THE GROWTH
OF PIG IRON PRODUCTION, 1842–1858[8]

The growth of pig iron production during the 1840s and 1850s has received a considerable amount of attention. Several factors combined to make these last two ante-bellum decades of special interest. First, they were an era of rapid change in the technology of blast furnaces. In 1840 virtually all furnaces

used charcoal as the fuel in the process which transformed ore into pig iron. By 1855 more than half the capacity of blast furnaces was based on a technology which employed mineral fuels (raw anthracite or bituminous coal, coked bituminous coal, or some combination of these three types).[9] Second, the 1840s and 1850s were an era of sharp contrasts in the business fortunes of furnace operators. The years from 1842 through 1847 appear to have been a period of unprecedented expansion in the production of pig iron. Output increased from 230,000 gross tons in 1842 to 765,000 in 1847 (see col. 4 of Table 2), an annual rate of growth of 27 per cent. But ten years later production was still at the 1847

Table 2. Estimates of Pig Iron Production 1840–1860 (in Thousands of Gross Tons)

Year (1)	A.I.S.A. and Carey (2)	Grosvenor (3)	Revised A.I.S.A. (4)
1840	287	347	347
1841	—	360	278
1842	215	376	230
1843	—	386	358
1844	—	427	486
1845	—	486	574
1846	765	551	687
1847	800	598	765
1848	800	570	696
1849	650	543	627
1850	564	564	481
1851	—	—	413
1852	500	—	541
1853	—	—	723
1854	657	—	657
1855	700	—	700
1856	789	—	789
1857	713	—	713
1858	630	—	630
1859	751	—	751
1860	821	—	821

SOURCES: The data for cols. 2 and 3 are from Temin [9, pp. 264–266]. The revised A.I.S.A. series is from Fogel [2, pp. 151–166] and is the series used in the regressions discussed below.

---

[8] The data presented in this section of the paper are preliminary and subject to revision. Unless otherwise identified, the source of the various series referred to below is Fogel and Engerman, *The Growth of the American Iron Industry, 1810–1860* (in prep.). This study will describe the manner in which the series were constructed.

[9] In 1833 charcoal furnaces represented 100 per cent of capacity. In 1840 they still accounted for 86 per cent of capacity. Over the next decade the charcoal share declined to 58 per cent. It declined further during the next eight years, reaching 44 per cent in 1858. Capacity is defined as the maximum observed output per week, multiplied by the maximum observed number of weeks operated per year. The observations were for the period 1854–1857.

level. Over the same decade the average real price of pig iron declined at a rate of 3.5 per cent a year. Third, there was a substantial increase in the abandonment rate of furnaces during the last half of the 1840s. From 1846 through 1857 some 186 furnaces with a capacity of 163,000 tons—nearly half the capacity in existence in 1840—were abandoned. Nevertheless the total capacity of blast furnaces increased at an average annual rate of 6.25 per cent. Hence between 1840 and 1858 total capacity increased from 379,000 to 1,188,000 gross tons.

What were the factors which produced such sharp contrasts? This question has commanded the attention of a number of distinguished economists, historians, and public figures, including Wells [11], Carey [1], Taussig [8], Hunter [5], and Hewitt. To Carey, Hewitt, and other protectionists the answer was to be found in tariff policy. The iron industry was pulled out of a depression by the high duties imposed on imported iron under the tariff of 1842. The protection provided by this enactment nurtured the boom of the middle forties. And it was the subsequent elimination of the high duties under the tariff of 1846 which, according to this view, explains the decade of stagnation that followed. On the other hand, Grosvenor [4], an ardent publicist for free trade, and Wells challenged not only the role assigned to the tariff but even the pattern of production depicted by Carey and the reports of the American Iron and Steel Association (A.I.S.A.).[10] Wells held that since 1840 "no matter what has been the character of the legislation, whether the tariff was low or high, whether the condition of the country was one of war or peace, the increase of the production has been at an average of about 8 per cent per annum, or more than double the ratio of the increase of population" [11, pp. 8–9].

Taussig [7, 8] assumed a position intermediate between these extremes. He agreed with the protectionists that the high duties through 1846 helped support the growth of pig iron production. He noted that imports of iron showed a distinct decrease during the four years (1843–1846) when the tariff of 1842 was in effect and that following the reduction of duties under the act of 1846 there was a distinct increase in iron imports. Taussig nevertheless held that the most basic factor affecting the growth of the American iron

industry was technological innovation. In particular, he argued, the introduction of the anthracite process in the manufacture of pig iron reduced the cost of producing that commodity by an amount sufficient to make American furnaces competitive with British furnaces, regardless of the level of the tariff. Consequently he held that the main effect of the tariff was on the less efficient charcoal sector of the industry. Under the impact of the high duties of 1843–1846, a number of new charcoal furnaces were built that would not otherwise have been profitable. While the subsequent lowering of duties retarded the growth of charcoal iron, it "did not prevent a steady growth in the making of anthracite iron." There was no doubt, Taussig continued, "that, had there been no duty at all, there would yet have been a large production of anthracite pig" [7].

Which of the various arguments set forth to explain the course of pig iron production are correct? The question can be answered by applying the model set forth in the previous section of this paper to available data on output, inputs, and prices for the ante-bellum iron industry.

Problems of Estimation

In the introduction we stated that the meager data requirements of the model and the ease with which its parameters can be estimated make it particularly suitable for historical work. When considered statistically, several features of the demand and supply functions —that is, of equations 17 and 18—may appear to contradict this claim. First, both of these equations are overidentified. Second, the efficiency index (A), which is one of the arguments of the supply function, cannot be computed unless the parameters of the supply function are known. Third, it is difficult to measure the size of the capital stock.

These difficulties can be circumvented by substituting equation 2 for equation 18. The structure then becomes

$$Q = [bI^\psi P_i^{\varepsilon i}]P^{-\varepsilon}e^u \qquad (17.1)$$

and

$$Q = SP^\gamma e^v \qquad (2.1)$$

where u and v are uncorrelated random variables. Solving for the reduced-form equations, we obtain

$$Q = (bI^\psi P_i^{\varepsilon i}e^u)^{\gamma/(\gamma + \varepsilon)}(Se^v)^{\varepsilon/(\gamma + \varepsilon)} \qquad (32)$$

---

[10] Compare cols. 2 and 3 of Table 2.

and

$$P = \left(\frac{bI^{\psi}P_i^{\varepsilon}e^{u}}{Se^{v}}\right)^{1/(\gamma + \varepsilon)} \quad (33)$$

In the reformulated structure, equation 17.1 is just identified. Equation 2.1 is also just identified, since it involves the constraint that the power of S is one. Moreover, rewriting equation 2.1 as

$$Se^{v} = \frac{Q}{P^{\gamma}} \quad (2.2)$$

it is clear that given γ, one can compute the value of the shift term directly from the available data on output and price.

Our problem can now be reformulated as follows: Since equation 2.1 is linear in the logs, the position of the supply curve is given by a point (log P, log Q) and the slope (γ). Determination of the supply curve resolves the identification problem, leaving only the coefficients of the demand curve to be estimated from equations 32 and 33. It can easily be seen that if the supply curve is known (γ is given), the remaining parameters can be identified from either equation 32 or 33. Of course each value of γ will produce a different set of estimates for the demand parameters. Our problem thus reduces to the conditions under which the available data justifies the selection of one value of γ from the array of all possible values. If the industry production function is Cobb-Douglas with constant returns to scale and if $\phi = 1$, the value of γ may be estimated from the data on factor shares. Furthermore, as will be shown below, by imposing an a priori restriction dictated by theory, one can estimate γ without any knowledge of the underlying production function. Under that restraint the assumption of a Cobb-Douglas production function is unnecessary. However if the available evidence warrants the Cobb-Douglas assumption, then it, together with the a priori restriction, yields estimates of ϕ and β. Consequently we propose to overcome the acute shortage of data which prevents direct estimation of the supply curve by making use of certain prior information.

Unfortunately the data needed for the direct estimation of the aggregate production function of American blast furnaces are not yet available. Nevertheless it is possible to construct a prima facie case for the proposition that the production function is of the type given by equation 8. First, available evidence suggests that it is reasonable to assume constant returns to scale for the blast furnace sector. The largest furnaces were those using anthracite fuel. Their average capacity[11] in 1856 was only 4200 tons per annum—less than 0.5 per cent of aggregate capacity. More compelling is the relative constancy of the average size. It increased by only 4 per cent between 1842 and 1858. While it is true that the average capacity of charcoal furnaces increased more rapidly—from 1050 to 1300 tons per annum, or by 24 per cent over the same seventeen-year-period—there is no evidence that, within given regions, larger furnaces of a given type were more likely to survive than smaller ones. Of the 229 charcoal furnaces in Pennsylvania in 1849, 52.5 per cent were smaller than the average of their regional types.[12] Of the 103 firms that failed during the 1840s, 56.2 per cent were smaller than the average of their regional type. The difference in these ratios is small and is not statistically significant.[13] Second, available evidence suggests relative constancy in the factor shares of the blast furnace sector prior to the Bessemer era. The published census does not give factor shares before 1860. However, factor shares for 1870, a year in which Bessemer production was still minimal, were 0.18, 0.65, and 0.17 for labor, raw materials, and capital, respectively. These shares are not significantly different from the 1860 shares.

Casual examination of available evidence also suggests that factor prices were independent of the level of production. The assumption that $\phi = 1$ formed the basis of Temin's analysis of the ante-bellum iron industry. He justified this assumption by arguing that

---

[11] See footnote 9 for the definition of capacity.

[12] There were two regions, East and West. Each region contained two types of blast furnaces, hot blast and cold blast.

[13] The χ^2 value of a test of association between the failure rate and furnace size was 1.12 and is not significant at either the 1 or 5 per cent levels. A regression of maximum observed output on various characteristics revealed that regional location was the main factor explaining variations in the capacity of charcoal furnaces.

The growth in average size appears to have been due to a shift in the regional locus of the demand for charcoal iron. There was a decline in the demand for this metal in the East and South, where charcoal furnaces tended to be smaller than the national average, and a rise in demand for charcoal iron in the West, where furnaces tended to be larger than the national average.

raw materials were "locally available" and abundant and that the labor employed in the iron industry utilized "skills that were widely known" [9, p. 32].

Hence as a first approximation, γ was estimated from the 1860 census data on the factor shares. The logarithmic transformation of equations 32 and 33 were then fitted to time-series data for the period 1842–1858. The resulting regressions were:[14]

$$\log Q = 1.292 + 0.441 \log I$$
$$(2.94)$$
$$+ 1.212 \log P_i + 0.273 (\log S + v) \quad (32.1)$$
$$(4.82) \qquad\qquad (2.61)$$
$$R^2 = 0.79$$
$$DW = 1.09$$

and

$$\log P = 0.309 + 0.106 \log I$$
$$(2.94)$$
$$+ 0.290 \log P_i - 0.174 (\log S + v) \quad (33.1)$$
$$(4.82) \qquad\qquad (-6.95)$$
$$R^2 = 0.96$$
$$DW = 1.09$$

The elasticities derived from these equations are shown in Table 3.

An alternative approach to the estimation γ involves the Hicks-Slutsky condition that the sum of the elasticities of substitutes must be equal and opposite in sign to the price (own) elasticity. If for the moment we assume that the only substitute for domestic pig iron was imported pig iron, this condition implies that $-\varepsilon_i = \varepsilon$, or that[15]

$$\left| \frac{\varepsilon}{\varepsilon_i} \right| = 1$$

---

[14] There are twelve degrees of freedom since there are no observations for 1843. The Durbin-Watson coefficients are in the indeterminate range. The numbers in parenthesis are the "t" values of the coefficients. The t values of the coefficients of $\log I$ and $\log P_i$ in equations 32.1 and 33.1 are identical, since these coefficients of 32.1 are equal to those of 33.1 multiplied by a constant (γ).

[15] The preceding argument may be restated as follows: Demand curves defined in money terms must be homogeneous of degree zero. Consequently if I is measured in real terms, and if ε_i is the only non-zero cross-elasticity, the homogeneity condition implies that

$$\left| \frac{\varepsilon}{\varepsilon_i} \right| = 1$$

Table 3. Values of the Parameters of Equations 19 and 20 for $\gamma_{4.2}$ and $\gamma_{3.5}$

Parameter	$\gamma = \dfrac{a_1 + a_2}{a_3} = 4.2$	$\gamma = 3.5$
ε	1.57	1.77
γ	4.18	3.50
ψ	0.61	0.60
ε_i	1.67	1.77
$\varepsilon/(\gamma + \varepsilon)$	0.27	0.34
$\gamma/(\gamma + \varepsilon)$	0.73	0.66
$1/(\gamma + \varepsilon)$	0.17	0.19

It can be shown that in a system such as that given by equations 32 and 33, there is a functional relationship between the least-square estimate of

$$\left| \frac{\varepsilon}{\varepsilon_i} \right|$$

and the assumed value of the supply elasticity. Over the range $0 \le \gamma \le \infty$, moreover, this function is single-valued and has the form shown by Figure 3. Consequently there is a unique value of γ that satisfies the Hicks-Slutsky condition.

As it turns out,

$$\left| \frac{\varepsilon}{\varepsilon_i} \right| = 1$$

when $\gamma = 3.5$. When equations 32 and 33 are regressed with that value of γ, one obtains:

$$\log Q = 1.502 + 0.396 \log I$$
$$(2.69)$$
$$+ 1.177 \log P_i + 0.336 (\log S + v) \quad (32.2)$$
$$(5.19) \qquad\qquad (2.99)$$
$$R^2 = 0.809$$
$$DW = 1.08$$

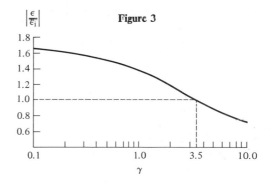

Figure 3

and

$$\log P = 0.429 + 0.113 \; \log I$$
$$(2.69)$$

$$+ \; 0.336 \log P_i - 0.190 \, (\log S + v),$$
$$(5.19) \qquad (-5.93)$$

$$\quad (33.2)$$

$$R^2 = 0.946$$
$$DW = 1.08$$

While the difference between $\gamma_{3.5}$ and $\gamma_{4.2}$ is statistically significant, this difference has no effect on the resolution of the historical problem which is at issue. As shown by Table 3, the values of ψ, ε_i, and ε derived from the new regressions are very close to those obtained from the old ones. Both sets of values imply essentially the same explanation for the growth of pig iron production.

Use of the Hicks-Slutsky condition yields a unique value of γ without requiring a particular assumption about the form of the underlying production function. However if, as we have argued, it is warranted to assume that the underlying production function is Cobb-Douglas (with $\sum \alpha_j = 1$), then the result obtained from the Hicks-Slutsky condition also implies estimates of ϕ and β (the average elasticity of factor prices with respect to the level of industry output). If we designate the true values of ϕ and γ as ϕ_0 and γ_0 and let $\gamma_1 = (\alpha_1 + \alpha_2)/\alpha_3$, it follows that $\phi_0 = \gamma_0/\gamma_1$. Thus our estimate of ϕ_0 is 3.5/4.2 or 0.83. The estimate of β may now be derived by substituting into equation 27 to obtain

$$\frac{3.5}{4.2} = \frac{1}{1 + 4.2 \, \beta}$$

or

$$\beta = 0.048$$

This value of β implies that Temin was correct in his judgment that changes in the level of pig iron production had little effect on the level of factor prices. The average year-to-year fluctuation in the output of pig iron was 6.8 per cent, and the maximum year-to-year fluctuation was 55 per cent. Hence, $\beta = 0.048$ implies that changes in output induced average annual changes in factor prices of less than 0.4 per cent. It also implies that during the period in question,

changes in output never induced annual changes in average factor prices in excess of 3 per cent.

As already noted, $\gamma_{3.5}$ will equal γ_0 only if the sum of the elasticities of the omitted prices in equation 17 is equal to zero. If the sum is positive, $\gamma_{3.5}$ is not a lower bound but another upper bound. One obtains a lower bound only if the sum of the omitted elasticities is negative—that is, if the omitted commodities are net complements to iron.

It might be argued that lumber is a close substitute which has been omitted. However within the range of price variation actually observed between 1840 and 1860, iron and lumber were not substitutes but complements. The major uses of iron were for rails, nails, stoves, boiler plate, and edge tools. One did not substitute wooden pegs for nails when the price of lumber fell relative to the price of iron. Nor was lumber substituted for iron in the manufacture of boilers, stoves, rails, or cutlery. Quite the contrary, a decline in the price of lumber would increase the construction of houses, fences, wagons, and such, and hence increase the demand for nails and other products of iron. The thrust of this argument, then, is that the cross-elasticity of the demand for iron with respect to the price of lumber was negative.

But what was the sign of the elasticity of the large number of substitutes and complements that were only weakly related to iron? These weakly related commodities are represented by the wholesale price index. That index was implicitly included in the regressions run on equations 32.2 and 33.2, since the prices of both domestic and imported pig iron were deflated by an index of wholesale prices. Such deflation is equivalent to the assumption that the elasticity of the index ε_w was equal to zero ($\varepsilon_w = \varepsilon_i - \varepsilon = 0$). The assumption can be tested by rerunning equation 33.2 without imposing a constraint on the elasticity of the wholesale price index (P_w). The result is:

$$\log P = 1.426 + 0.195 \; \log I + 0.376 \; \log P_i$$
$$(3.36) \qquad\qquad (6.05)$$

$$- \; 0.348 \log P_w - 0.191 \, (\log S + v)$$
$$(-1.70) \qquad\quad (-6.56) \qquad (33.2a)$$

$$R^2 = 0.95$$
$$DW = 1.6$$

It will be noted that the coefficient of log P_w (which equals $\varepsilon_w/[\gamma + \varepsilon]$) has a negative sign but is not statistically significant at the .95 level. Hence the available evidence suggests that the net elasticity of the omitted prices is negative. Since the price indexes employed in equation 33.2a depart from those dictated by theory, this conclusion is not beyond challenge. However pending the construction of better price indexes, it seems appropriate to treat $\gamma_{3.5}$ as a lower bound of γ_0, $\phi_{0.83}$ as a lower bound of ϕ, and $\beta_{0.048}$ as an upper bound of β.

The Explanation of the Growth of Output

With the elasticities derived from equations 32.1 and 33.1 and the rates of growth of the variables (see Table 4), it is possible to explain the growth of pig iron production between 1842 and 1858. On the average, the output of this metal grew at a rate of 3.62 per cent per annum over the seventeen-year period. Shifts in the supply curve account for all of this increase. Indeed, the contribution of demand was negative. It declined at 0.25 per cent per

Table 4. Average Annual Rates of Growth of Variables, 1842–1858, and Values of Elasticities

Variable	Rate of Growth (%)
Q	3.62
P	−2.46
D	−0.25
S	13.92
I	8.93
P_i	−3.40

Elasticity	Value
ε	1.57
γ	4.18
ψ	0.61
ε_i	1.67
$\varepsilon/(\gamma + \varepsilon)$	0.27
$\gamma/(\gamma + \varepsilon)$	0.73
$1/(\gamma + \varepsilon)$	0.17

SOURCES: The rates of growth of Q, P, and D were estimated from equations 29 and 30. The other rates of growth were obtained by regressing the logs of the variables on time.

year. The fall in demand was not due to a lack of growth of the internal market. In the absence of countervailing influences, the increase of gross domestic investment would have caused demand to expand by 5.42 per cent per annum. However this stimulus was offset by the fall in the price of imports. The decline in the price of imported iron reduced the demand for domestic pig iron by 5.67 per cent per annum.

Much of the fall in the price of imported iron is explained by the reduction in tariff duties. If the duties of the act of 1842 had been kept in force throughout the period, the price of British iron would have declined at an annual rate of only 1.67 per cent. Hence about 50 per cent of the drop in demand induced by the fall of import prices is attributable to the lowering of tariff duties;[16] the other 50 per cent was due to conditions in the British market and reductions in transportation costs. If the tariff had remained at the level prescribed by the act of 1842, the output of pig iron in 1858 would have been nearly 885,000 tons instead of the 630,000 actually produced. A higher tariff would also have reduced the rate of decline in the real price of pig iron from 2.46 to 1.96 per cent per annum. This would have made the real price of pig iron in 1858 about 10.8 per cent greater than the price actually observed.

As already noted, increases in supply accounted for all of the observed increase in pig iron production. Even with the higher level of duties advocated by the protectionists, about two thirds of the increase in output would have been attributable to shifts in the supply curve. Despite appearances this finding does not support Taussig's contention that technological change was the principal factor responsible for the growth of output. Taussig's correction of the Wells-Grosvenor argument did not go far enough. He underestimated the importance of demand factors in explaining the growth of the production of anthracite iron. He also erred in assuming that the decline of charcoal production was due primarily to the inability of this sector to keep pace with the technological progress of the anthracite furnaces. These conclusions emerge from a

---

[16] Here and in the rest of the discussion we consider only first-round effects of the tariff. In particular, we assume that investment, factor prices, and technological change are independent of the level of the tariff on iron.

consideration of Tables 5 and 6. The elasticities shown in these tables were derived by fitting equation 33 to the data on anthracite and charcoal furnaces. The results of the regressions were:[17]

$$\log P = 3.40 + 0.252 \log I$$
$$(4.7)$$

$$+ 0.312 \log P_i - 0.141 (\log S + v)$$
$$(4.1) \qquad (-5.7)$$
$$(33.3)$$

$$R^2 = 0.928$$
$$DW = 1.03$$

and

$$\log P = 4.93 + 0.0118 \log I$$
$$(0.41)$$

$$+ 0.208 \log P_i - 0.138 (\log S + v)$$
$$(3.3) \qquad (-6.8)$$
$$(33.4)$$

$$R^2 = 0.962$$
$$DW = 0.862;$$

where equation 33.3 describes the anthracite sector, and 33.4 describes the charcoal sector.

Two features of Tables 5 and 6 are particularly striking. One is that the demand for anthracite iron was more sensitive to the price of imports than the demand for charcoal iron. This result is not surprising. Imports were more nearly like anthracite iron, both having been used widely for rails and other relatively low-grade forms of iron. Nor is it surprising to discover that investments had a bigger impact on the demand for anthracite iron than on the demand for charcoal iron. The cruder metal was employed extensively in those forms of investment that were growing most rapidly, while the more refined charcoal iron was used for such relatively slow-growing items as malleable castings, wagon axles, hand tools, and firearms.

What is surprising is that in the case of anthracite, the greater value of ψ swamps the effect of the greater value of ε_i. As a consequence the increase in the demand for anthracite iron alone increased the output of that

[17] The value of γ was estimated from data on factor incomes for appropriate furnaces in Pennsylvania in 1860. Given γ, all of the other elasticities can be computed from equations 33.3 and 33.4.

Table 5. Average Annual Rates of Growth of Variables, 1842–1858, and Values of Elasticities for Anthracite Pig Iron

Variable	Rate of Growth (%)
Q	13.19
P	−1.89
D	8.47
S	21.95
I	8.93
P_i	−3.40

Elasticity	Value
ε	2.48
γ	4.61
ψ	1.79
ε_i	2.21
$\varepsilon/(\gamma + \varepsilon)$	0.35
$\gamma/(\gamma + \varepsilon)$	0.65
$1/(\gamma + \varepsilon)$	0.14

SOURCES: See note to Table 4.

Table 6. Average Annual Rates of Growth of Variables, 1842–1858, and Values of Elasticities for Charcoal Pig Iron

Variable	Rate of Growth (%)
Q	−1.44
P	−2.59
D	−4.41
S	14.12
I	8.93
P_i	−3.40

Elasticity	Value
ε	1.18
γ	6.07
ψ	0.085
ε_i	1.52
$\varepsilon/(\gamma + \varepsilon)$	0.16
$\gamma/(\gamma + \varepsilon)$	0.84
$1/(\gamma + \varepsilon)$	0.14

SOURCES: See note to Table 4.

product at an annual rate of 5.5 per cent. This is about 42 per cent of the observed increase in the output of anthracite pig. If demand had remained unchanged between 1844 and 1859, the product of anthracite furnaces would have been just 220,000 tons, about half the actual product of that year. Moreover if the tariff had been maintained at its 1842 level, the rate of growth of output would have been 15.7 per cent, with more than half of this rate due to increases in demand. Thus the supply effect appears to dominate the expansion of the anthracite sector only if one neglects the effect of the reduction in the tariff on the course of the industry. Furthermore the growth in supply was not explained exclusively by the growth in efficiency. Quite the contrary, it is probable that most of the rise in the supply of anthracite was due to the growth of capital.[18]

The last point is particularly important, since the growth of the capital stock is not independent of shifts in demand. Even if the long-run supply curve remained constant, increases in demand would cause the short-run supply curve to shift outward. For as increases in demand raised the short-run equilibrium price relative to the long-run price, new capital would be invested in the industry. Thus while $\overset{*}{K}$ appears in the supply term of equation 29, part of its value may be attributable to changes in demand. In principle one can decompose $\overset{*}{K}$ into demand and supply components. Unfortunately the data required for such a partition are not yet available. However this correction could only strengthen the case already made for the predominance of demand considerations in explaining the growth of the anthracite sector.[19]

Another surprising discovery is the rapid rate—14.1 per cent per annum—at which the supply curve for charcoal iron shifted outward. If demand had remained constant, the output of charcoal iron would have risen at an annual rate of about 2.3 per cent. Since the prices of inputs were probably increasing, and since the rate of capital formation in this sector of the industry was only a little over 2 per cent per annum, most of the increase in supply must have been due to technological advance. In other words, the decline in the production of charcoal iron is attributable exclusively to the sag in the demand for this metal, a sag which was sufficient to offset a substantial increase in technological efficiency.

Maintenance of the tariff at the level of 1842 could have reversed the absolute but not the relative decline in the output of charcoal iron. With the higher tariff the decline in demand would have slowed to 1.67 per cent per annum. This would have made the positive effect of supply greater than the negative effect of demand. The net result would have been a positive rate of growth in output of not quite 1 per cent per annum (0.84[−1.67]+0.16· [14.12] = 0.86). Still, even under the more favorable tariff rate, the charcoal sector would have declined relative to the rest of the iron industry, to manufacturing output, to GNP, and to population. For unlike the anthracite sector of the industry, the market for charcoal iron increased very slowly as the economy grew. The elasticity of the demand for charcoal iron with respect to gross domestic investment (ψ) was only 0.085.

It thus appears that the factors explaining the progress of the iron industry during the 1840s and 1850s were more complex than either side of the tariff controversy was willing to grant. In retrospect the fervent support given by the ironmasters to tariff legislation is easy to understand. The duties they advocated would have given a considerable fillip to demand. Yet a continuation of the high tariffs of 1842 could not have prevented the relative decline of the charcoal sector. The static market for highly refined iron and the increased competition of foreign and domestic substitutes presented charcoal ironmasters

---

[18] Work is proceeding on the collection of the data, needed to compute $\overset{*}{A}$. Using the measure of the capital stock given in footnote 9, $\overset{*}{K}$ was 16.25 per cent per annum, or 75 per cent of the value of $\overset{*}{S}$. Since factor prices probably did not rise very much, it is unlikely that changes in $\overset{*}{A}$ directly accounted for as much as half of the estimated supply shift.

[19] A higher tariff would have increased the short-run equilibrium price relative to the long-run equilibrium price. Consequently, if the tariff of 1842 had been maintained, $\overset{*}{K}$ would have been larger than it

actually was, and $\overset{*}{S}$ would have increased by an amount equal to the increase in $\overset{*}{K}$. Since $\overset{*}{w}$, $\overset{*}{r}$, and $\overset{*}{A}$ are assumed to be independent of $\overset{*}{K}$, it follows that $\overset{*}{A}/\overset{*}{S}$ would have had a lower value than that suggested by the discussion in footnote 18 and the accompanying text.

with an enormous challenge. Between 1840 and 1858 over 200 charcoal-iron firms collapsed under this competitive pressure. An increase in tariff rates would have stimulated the production of anthracite iron more than that of charcoal iron. But as Taussig pointed out, anthracite furnaces did not need a tariff to survive. Although the fillip provided to this sector by technological advance was less than he thought, the demand for anthracite iron induced by the growth of the economy more than offset the increased competition of foreign producers.

REFERENCES

1. Henry C. Carey, "Review of the Report of Hon. D. A. Wells," *Miscellaneous Works*, Philadelphia, Baird, 1872.
2. Robert W. Fogel, *Railroads and American Economic Growth: Essays in Econometric History*, Baltimore, Johns Hopkins Press, 1964.
3. Robert W. Fogel and Stanley L. Engerman, "The Economics of Slavery," (printed below as essay 24).
4. W. M. Grosvenor, *Does Protection Protect?*, New York, Appleton, 1871.
5. Louis C. Hunter, "The Influence of the Market upon Technique in the Iron Industry in Western Pennsylvania up to 1860," *Journal of Economic and Business History, 1* (February, 1929), 241–281.
6. Richard E. Sylla, "Finance and Capital in the United States, 1850–1900." Unpublished paper presented to the Workshop in Economic History, University of Chicago, November 3, 1967.
7. F. W. Taussig, "The Tariff, 1830–1860," *The Quarterly Journal of Economics, 2* (April, 1887–1888), 314–346.
8. F. W. Taussig, *The Tariff History of the United States*, 5th ed., New York, Putnam, 1910.
9. Peter Temin, *Iron and Steel in Nineteenth Century America: An Economic Inquiry*, Cambridge, M.I.T. Press, 1964.
10. Peter Temin, "The Causes of Cotton-Price Fluctuations in the 1830's," *The Review of Economics and Statistics, 49* (November, 1967), 463–470.
11. U.S. Congress, House of Representatives. *Report of the Special Commissioner of Revenue for the Year 1868*. (Series No. 1372, 40th Congress, 3d session: Executive Document 16) Washington, D.C., 1868.
12. Gavin Wright, "An Econometric Study of Cotton Production and Trade Before 1860," Unpublished paper presented to the Workshop in Economic History, University of Chicago, October 20, 1967.
13. Robert Brooke Zevin, "The Growth of Cotton Textile Production After 1815," (printed above as essay 10).

12 SOURCES OF PRODUCTIVITY CHANGE IN OCEAN SHIPPING, 1600-1850

Douglass C. North

Among economic historians technological change has always held the pre-eminent position as a source of economic growth. Clearly, in the sense that man's productive capacity is always limited by the "state of the art," this imposes at least an upper limit on output. Yet in a world where technological information is at least nominally free, differences in ability to make efficient use of the state of knowledge must account for the widely disparate experience of national economies.

While the relative importance of the other factors making possible the efficient use of technology is extremely difficult to isolate on a macro-economic level, it may be more amenable to measurement on a micro-economic level. This essay presents evidence on sources of productivity

Reprinted with revisions by permission from *The Journal of Political Economy*, 76 (September/October, 1968), 953–970.

change in ocean shipping from 1600 to 1850, its objective being to identify as precisely as possible those sources of productivity usually lumped into the general category of technological change. The conclusion which emerges from this study is that a decline in piracy and an improvement in economic organization account for most of the productivity change observed.

I

Although the available data are scanty, it is possible to approximate a measure of the growth of total factor productivity in ocean shipping for the period from 1600 to 1770. The reciprocal of a freight rate index provides such a proxy, because the major input costs of seamen's wages and shipbuilding costs remain almost constant throughout this whole period.[1] After the American Revolutionary War, however, costs of shipbuilding clearly

rose because of higher costs of ship timber and some increase in seamen's wages, at least on the American routes. Accordingly for the period from the end of the War of 1812 onward, the movement of input prices is given by a weighted average of shipbuilding costs, seamen's wages, and the Warren-Pearson index as a proxy for other costs (victualing, maintenance, and insurance costs are the major items). When this index of input prices is divided by an index of U.S. export freight rates, we obtain the desired measure of total factor productivity.[2]

The data provide clear indication of a substantial productivity improvement in shipping over this period. On a half-dozen commodity routes and covering the period

---

[1] Davis [5, p. 137] indicates stability of seamen's wages in England between approximately 1700 and the American Revolution. Additional data by Walton [12] also indicate that seamen's wages on American

colonial routes did not change. Shipbuilding costs appear to have been steady throughout the period until the Revolution, although both Davis [5, pp. 92–93] and Albion [1] suggest that there may have been some slight rise in shipbuilding costs over this period. However the data collected for the larger study in progress give no indication of any trend in shipbuilding costs, which appear to have been approximately steady throughout the prewar period.

[2] For a discussion of this method of obtaining total factor productivity, see [7].

Figure 1. Total Productivity Index.

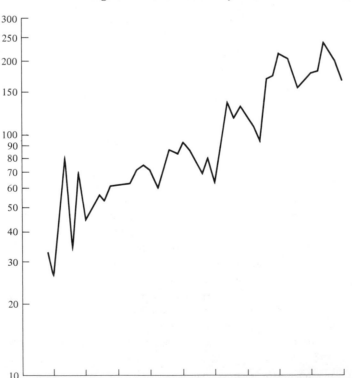

from the mid-seventeenth century to the American Revolution, freight rates fell by half, with the average for all routes being slightly less than 1/2 of 1 per cent per year.[3] From the late eighteenth century until the end of the War of 1812, the freight rate data are so influenced by recurrent wars that it has not been possible to construct an American series. While substantial productivity improvement presumably took place, no clear evidence of the timing can be precisely observed. However from 1814 onward the index plotted in Figure 1 rises at an average of 3.5 per cent— a rate not equaled in any other period in shipping history covered by the larger study.[4]

One can confidently conclude, therefore, that productivity was improving in ocean shipping from 1600 on. Although the evidence for the first half of the century is tenuous, it is apparent that from the mid-seventeenth century onward productivity rose at a significant rate, which accelerated still more during the first half of the nineteenth century. It is probable that the period of acceleration began in the years immediately following the close of the Revolution.

II

To assess those changing cost characteristics of the industry which determined the properties of the supply of ocean shipping over time, it is necessary to break down the cost determinants and to examine each in turn.[5] Equation 1 shows one way in which the cost of a voyage may be analyzed:

$$C_v = P_s S + P_t T \tag{1}$$

where P_s = cost per day at sea, P_t = cost per day in port, and S and T denote number of days per voyage at sea and in port. The P_s can in turn be divided into (1) the cost per day at sea for labor, P_{sL}; (2) daily amortization of the capital cost of the ship, P_{so} (where o refers to the cost of the ship); and (3) other costs per day at sea, P_{sj} (particularly insurance costs). Thus we have the identity:

$$P_s = P_{sL} + P_{so} + P_{sj} \tag{2}$$

The corresponding identity for P_t is

$$P_t = P_{tL} + P_{to} + P_{tj} \tag{3}$$

To convert cost per voyage, C_v, to a cost per payload ton, c, we need to divide by K, capacity, and λ, the load factor (the ratio of the actual cargo to the maximum cargo). Thus cost per payload ton is:

$$c = \left(\frac{C_v}{K\lambda}\right) \tag{4}$$

Since ocean shipping during 1600–1850 was a highly competitive industry and on the industry level exhibited those features characteristic of constant costs, the average freight rate would have tended to equal the cost per payload ton.[6] Consequently the index of total factor productivity can be written as

$$A = \frac{P_i}{c} \tag{5}$$

where A is total factor productivity, P_i is an index of input prices, and c is the freight rate index.

Equations 1–5 can be transformed from a system which relates absolute values to a system which relates the percentage changes of the corresponding variables. The transformed system is given by equations 6–10:

$$C_v^* = \alpha(P_s^* + S^*) + (1 - \alpha)(P_t^* + T^*) \tag{6}$$

$$P_s^* = \beta_1 P_{sL}^* + \beta_2 P_{so}^* + \beta_3 P_{sj}^* \tag{7}$$

$$P_t^* = \sigma_1 P_{tL}^* + \sigma_2 P_{to}^* + \sigma_3 P_{tj}^* \tag{8}$$

$$C^* = C_v^* - K^* - \lambda^* \tag{9}$$

$$A^* = P_i^* - C^* \tag{10}$$

---

[3] These commodity routes are: wine, Cadiz to London, 1640–1783; oil, Boston to London, 1700–1774; sugar, Barbados to London, 1678–1717; sugar, Jamaica to London, 1678–1717; tobacco, Chesapeake to London, 1630–1775; bullion, New York to London, 1699–1789; flour, New York to Jamaica, 1699–1768. They will be presented in detail in the larger study and are available in [12].

[4] It is interesting to note that even the fall in real costs of shipping that occurred in the last half of the nineteenth century primarily because of the shift from sail to steam does not equal in magnitude the fall in the real cost of shipping in the first half of the nineteenth century.

[5] The breakdown and analysis presented here make use of the study done by Oi [10, chap. 1].

[6] In the period from the Revolutionary War to the Civil War, rising ship construction costs reflected some increase in real costs of ship timber.

The interpretation of these is illustrated by equation 6. The asterisk means that each variable so denoted is expressed as a percentage rate of change: C_v^* is the percentage rate of change in cost per voyage and P_s^* in the cost per day at sea. Hence equation 6 states that the percentage increase in the cost per voyage is a weighted average of two sums—the sum of the percentage changes in cost per day at sea and the number of days at sea per voyage and the sum of the percentage changes in the cost per day at shore and the number of days at shore per voyage. The weights are α and $(1 - \alpha)$, with α equal to the base-period share of the cost of a voyage incurred at sea, so that $(1 - \alpha)$ becomes the share incurred in port. Similarly equation 7 says that the rate of change in cost per day at sea is a weighted average of the indicated rates of change, the weights (β_i) representing base-period shares in the daily cost of a ship at sea.[7]

Substituting equations 6 through 9 into

---

[7] The method of deriving equations 6–10 from equations 1–5 will be shown for the first two cases. The same procedure was followed in the derivation of the other equations. The derivation of 6 from 1 is as follows:

$$C_v = P_s S + P_t T \qquad (1.0)$$

Differentiating with respect to time, we obtain

$$\frac{dC_v}{dt} = \frac{dP_s}{dt}S + \frac{dS}{dt}P_s + \frac{dP_t}{dt}T + \frac{dT}{dt}P_t \quad (1.1)$$

which can also be written as

$$\frac{dC_v}{dt}\frac{C_v}{C_v} = \frac{dP_s}{dt}\frac{SP_s}{P_s} + \frac{dS}{dt}\frac{P_s S}{S} + \frac{dP_t}{dt}\frac{TP_t}{P_t} + \frac{dT}{dt}\frac{P_t T}{T} \quad (1.8)$$

Dividing through by C_v and collecting terms gives

$$C_v^* = (P_s S/C_v)(P_s^* + S^*) + (P_t T/C_v)(P_t^* + T^*) \quad (1.3)$$

where $C_v^* = (dC_v/C_v)/dt$, and the other starred variables are of a corresponding form. Setting $\alpha = P_s S/C_v$ transforms equation 1.3 into equation 6, for then $P_t T/C_v = (1 - \alpha)$.

The derivation of equation 7 from 2 is similar:

$$P_s = P_{sL} + P_{so} + P_{sJ} \qquad (2.0)$$

hence

$$\frac{dP_s}{dt}\frac{P_s}{P_s} = \frac{dP_{sL}}{dt}\frac{P_{sL}}{P_{sL}} + \frac{dP_{so}}{dt}\frac{P_{so}}{P_{so}} + \frac{dP_{sJ}}{dt}\frac{P_{sJ}}{P_{sJ}} \quad (2.1)$$

or

$$P_s^* = P_{sL}^* \frac{P_{sL}}{P_s} + P_{so}^* \frac{P_{so}}{P_s} + P_{sJ}^* \frac{P_{sJ}}{P_s} \quad (2.2)$$

Substituting the β_i for the coefficients of the starred terms on the right-hand side of 2.2 transforms that equation into equation 7.

---

10 yields the basic equation for the explanation of total factor productivity.

$$\overset{*}{A} = P_i^* + \overset{*}{K} + \overset{*}{\lambda} - \alpha(\beta_1 P_{sL}^* + \beta_2 P_{so}^* + \beta_3 P_{sj}^*) - (1 - \alpha)(\sigma_1 P_{tL}^* + \sigma_2 P_{to}^* + \sigma_3 P_{tj}^*) - \alpha\overset{*}{S} - (1 - \alpha)\overset{*}{T} \quad (11)$$

In the computations equation 11 was calculated in its logarithmic form; that is, all the starred terms were defined as logs of the compound rates of change. The rate of change in productivity is then obtained by taking antilogs, subtracting 1 from the result, and multiplying by 100.

To explain the growth of productivity in ocean shipping is to describe how and why the variables on the right-hand side of equation 11 changed. While the data required for a precise explanation of the movement of $\overset{*}{A}$ are not yet available, we do have enough information to establish roughly the values of the variables set out in equation 11 and the proximate determinants of these rates.

Available evidence on ship size suggests that shipping capacity increased very slowly per unit until about 1800, and thereafter the size per unit increased rapidly.[8] Table 1 from a study by Usher [11] suggests the general contours of this growth. Usher's data are reinforced by information on the North American and West Indian trades presented in Davis [5, chap. IV], which shows that the tonnage per ship increased rapidly after the Revolution. From less than 150 tons in the Atlantic trade before the Revolution, tonnage had risen by 1820 to approximately 250 [2, p. 79; 6, pp. 289–290].[9] Although packet boats averaged substantially higher tonnages than regular freighters, some indication of what was happening is nevertheless shown by

---

[8] Davis [5, chap. IV] indicates that the average size of ships engaged in the Virginia, Maryland, and Carolina trade changed little in the period from 1686 to 1776, ranging from 116 to 176 tons and showing no appreciable trend toward increased size. These data are supported by a large sample of ship sizes from both the tobacco trade with England and the West Indian trade from Colonial America, in which Walton [12] indicates no discernible trend in ship size as a result of sampling 6338 ships over the period.

[9] This is substantially above the average size of all sailing ships in ocean trade. The figure of 120 tons used for 1814 more accurately mirrors average over-all ship size at that time.

Table 1. Percentage of Vessels in Each Size Class

Year	Under 40 Tons	40–99 Tons	100–419 Tons	420–1199 Tons	1200–1999 Tons	2000–3999 Tons	Over 3999 Tons	Total
England:								
1572	33.0	45.6	21.4	—	—	—	—	100
1582	27.4	35.4	35.4	1.8	—	—	—	100
1788	5.6	18.4	67.3	8.7	—	—	—	100
	Under 100 Tons							
United Kingdom:								
1788	31.1		62.1	6.8	—	—	—	100
1830	25.2		62.4	12.4	—	—	—	100
1869	9.6		27.4	45.9	15.6	1.2	.3	100

the fact that average size of packets in 1820 was 400 tons; in 1830, 600 tons; in 1840, 800 tons; in 1850, 1200 tons; in 1855, 1500 tons [6, p. 289]. Another, and perhaps better, index of the growing size of ships is provided in Table 2, which gives the average tonnage of full-rigged ships built at Kennebunkport and Portsmouth between 1825 and 1859.

Labor costs, P_{sL}, depend in large measure on manning characteristics of ships, the latter customarily defined by a tons-per-man ratio. This ratio changes because of two distinct factors influencing manning characteristics: (1) for a given ship size, the crew size falls over time, resulting in a higher tons-per-man ratio; (2) observable at any moment of time throughout this study is the fact that larger ships, as compared with smaller ships, will produce a higher tons-per-

man ratio (as shown for 1776 in Figure 2).[10] It is noteworthy that in the pre-Revolutionary period, despite the obvious economies to be garnered from larger ships, no change took

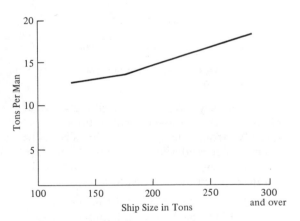

Figure 2. Tons Per Man by Ship Size in 1776, North Atlantic Route.

place in ship size.[11] Therefore all improvements in manning efficiency during that period came from a decline in crew requirements per constant average ship size.

In contrast, in the period following the

---

[10] However available evidence suggests that, if anything, somewhat higher costs per ton prevailed for larger ships.

[11] This apparent enigma will be discussed in a dissertation by Richard Yates [15].

Table 2. Size of Full-Rigged Ships Built at Kennebunkport and Portsmouth

Years	KENNEBUNKPORT No.	Average Size (Tons)	PORTSMOUTH No.	Average Size (Tons)
1825–1829	3	300	19	361
1830–1834	5	324	16	458
1835–1839	7	372	24	572
1840–1844	4	452	12	655
1845–1849	22	575	23	833
1850–1854	28	890	43	1063
1855–1859	21	905	31	1087

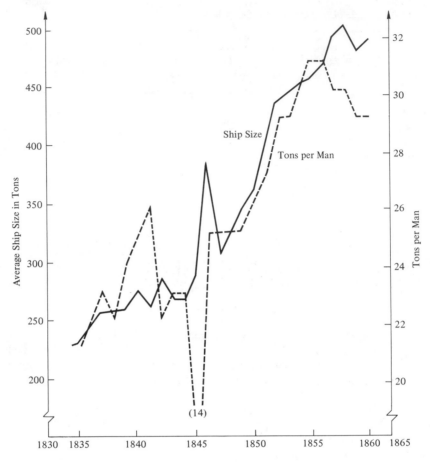

Figure 3. Average Ship Size and Tons Per Man, All Ships Entering New York Port, 1834–1860.

Revolutionary War, the strikingly great change in the tons-per-man ratio stemmed directly from changes in ship size. The average size and tons per man of all ships entering New York in selected years in the eighteenth century were as follows:

1715–1719   49.5 tons   4.4 tons per man
1735–1739   58.2 tons   6.1 tons per man
1763–1764   57.9 tons   6.9 tons per man

Compare these figures with Figure 3, which shows the average size and tons per man of all ships entering New York annually from 1835 to 1860.

It was the decline in piracy and privateering, permitting ships to reduce both manpower and armament, which contributed most to the fall in P_{sL} prior to 1800. The tons per man of a given size ship were consistently lower on routes still infested with pirates (East Indies, Mediterranean, West Indies) than on routes free of pirates (Baltic, North Europe, North Atlantic). The fall in size of crew for a given size ship between 1640 and 1775 is shown in Figure 4. Figures on the fall in number of guns per ship run counter to figures on rising tons per man, indicating that armament costs declined during this

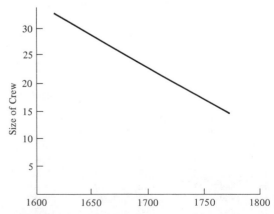

Figure 4. Size of Crew for a 250-ton Ship on North Atlantic Route, 1640–1775.

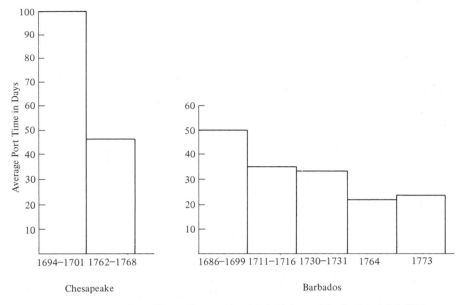

Figure 5. Average Port Time, Chesapeake, 1694–1768, and Barbados, 1686–1773.

period.[12] The substantial improvement in tons-per-man prior to the Revolutionary War was, therefore, basically a function of the growing security of shipping.

An additional result of the decline in piracy was a lowering of insurance costs, which by 1770 had fallen to approximately two thirds of the 1635 rate and which continued to drop throughout the first half of the nineteenth century.

Labor costs in port, P_{tL}, also reflected reduced manning requirements. To the extent that crews could be laid off in the home port and sometimes even in foreign ports and a new crew hired when the ship was ready to go to sea, labor costs in port could be lower than those at sea.

The changing ratio of port time to sea time was an important aspect of shipping development throughout this period. Essentially, the over-all change reflected a declining proportion of time spent idle in port as compared with time spent carrying goods at sea. This pattern is shown for Colonial and West Indian ports in Figure 5.

On the North Atlantic trade, tobacco ships in the seventeenth century made only one round trip per year, and average port time in Virginia or Maryland was approximately 100 days. Between 1690 and 1692 in Maryland,

out of 213 ships 42 per cent stayed in port longer than 105 days and only 18 per cent cleared in less than 44 days [*14*, p. 355]. Beginning in the middle of the eighteenth century, by a speedup particularly due to the employment of Scottish factors and the inventorying of tobacco in the New World, some ships began to make two round trips a year and significantly cut their time in American ports. By the time the first packet boats were in service, three round trips to England a year became the established pattern for these ships, resulting in a dramatic shift in the proportion of time spent at sea.

To what extent did speed of sailing account for this increase in number of voyages per year? Throughout the whole Colonial period up to the Revolutionary War no trend is apparent. Walton's study indicates that ship speed from the Caribbean to New York and New England ranged trendlessly between 1.3 and 1.6 knots and, on the reverse route, between 1.7 and 1.8 knots, during 1686–1775. It is clear, however, that ship speed did increase in the nineteenth century. The average passage time of east-bound packets (New York to Liverpool) between 1818 and 1827 was 24 days; westbound, it was 38 days. Although these ships were faster then freighters and therefore not wholly representative, their records are indicative of increased speed, since such passage times are between one half and two thirds of the pre-Revolutionary averages.

---

[12] For evidence of the decline in crew size and armament in the West Indian trade between 1675 and 1775 as a result of declining piracy, see [*13*, pp. 67–68].

Finally we consider load factor, for which the information is far more fragmentary. Traditionally most of the world's commodity routes had been only semiproductive, with bulk goods carried one way and the ship predominantly in ballast for the return. (An exception was the West Indian route, where two-way commodity trade prevailed.) In the Atlantic routes the situation improved somewhat as a growing colonial population required more and more imports; although their demand was for manufactured goods, far less bulky than the raw materials they exported, some increase did occur in the load factor on the return trip.

The striking increase, however, took place in the 1840s and 1850s due to the flood of immigration. There can be little doubt that the dramatic fall in freight rates in that period was significantly influenced by the very substantial resultant increase in the load factor.

The foregoing discussion of the determinants of the growing efficiency of ocean shipping is summarized in Table 3, which not only contrasts the rate of productivity improvement between the two periods but also brings out the divergent sources of improving efficiency. In the first period, falling labor costs and declining port time account for the growing productivity; in the second period, increasing ship size and (to a lesser degree) improved load factor account for the changes.

One can ask at this point, however, the extent to which technical changes in shipping and in ship construction account for the changes in manning requirements and, indeed, in observed ship speed. There is no doubt that the ship of the nineteenth century was in striking contrast to the ship of the early seventeenth century. Except for one crucial point it could be argued that smaller crews were made feasible precisely by technological improvements in sail and rigging. The obstacle to this argument is that by 1600 the Dutch had developed a ship, the flute, which cost less to contruct than existing ships, had a tons-per-man ratio similar to that of nineteenth-century ships on the Atlantic route, was at least as fast as existing ships, and could be (and was) constructed of 500–600 tons

Table 3. Determinants of the Rate of Growth of Total Factor Productivity

1600–1784	1814–1860
Percentages	
$\overset{*}{A}$ = 0.45	$\overset{*}{A}$ = 3.30
P_i^* = 0.00	P_i^* = 0.53
$\overset{*}{K}$ = 0.00	$\overset{*}{K}$ = 3.15
$\overset{*}{\lambda}$ = 0.00	$\overset{*}{\lambda}$ = 0.95
P_{sL}^{*} = −0.37	P_{sL}^{*} = 1.72
P_{so}^* = 0.00	P_{so}^* = 3.85
P_{sj}^* = −0.20	P_{sj}^* = −1.54
P_{tL}^* = −0.15	P_{tL}^* = 1.59
P_{to}^* = −0.37	P_{to}^* = 3.85
P_{tj}^* = −0.18	P_{tj}^* = −1.54
$\overset{*}{S}$ = 0.00	$\overset{*}{S}$ = 0.00
$\overset{*}{T}$ = −0.37	$\overset{*}{T}$ = 0.00
Fractions	
a = 0.408	a = 0.593
$1-a$ = 0.592	$1-a$ = 0.407
β_1 = 0.550	β_1 = 0.344
β_2 = 0.065	β_2 = 0.121
β_3 = 0.385	β_3 = 0.535
σ_1 = 0.498	σ_1 = 0.245
σ_2 = 0.104	σ_2 = 0.246
σ_3 = 0.398	σ_3 = 0.509

Table 3—*continued*

Sources and Assumptions for Table 3

Variable or Parameter	1600–1784	1814–1860
$\overset{*}{A}$	1. Factor prices held steady. 2. Freight rate series given in [*12*].	1. Rate of change of index A (see Figure 1). Productivity index of 3.5% results from $A = P_i/C$, against 3.3% resulting from equation 11; difference is due to rounding errors.
P_i^*	1. No change.	1. The change in the Warren-Pearson index offsets rise in seamen's wages and ship construction costs.
$\overset{*}{K}$	1. No change.	1. Ship size increased from 120 tons to 500 tons (see Figure 3).
$\overset{*}{\lambda}$	1. No change.	1. Load factor increased from 50% to 80%.
P_{sL}^*	1. Seatime per voyage—no change. 2. Crew size fell by half. 3. Wage held constant.	1. Sea time per voyage—no change. 2. Crew size increased, 8 to 18. 3. Wages increased $12/mo. to $15/mo.
P_{so}^*	1. No change.	1. Ship size increased (from 120 to 500 tons). 2. Shipbuilding costs rose (see index).
P_{sj}^*	1. Victualing costs fell by half. 2. Remainder of costs held steady. 3. Sea time stayed the same.	1. Rate of change per annum for other costs, 1814–1860 (see weights).
P_{tL}^*	1. Port time per voyage fell by half. 2. Crew size fell by half. 3. Wages constant. 4. Captain not discharged in home port. 5. Sea time = 110 days. 6. Foreign port time = 100 days. 7. Home port time = 155 days.	1. Three trips per year, or 4 months per round-trip voyage. 2. 70 days at sea, 20 in foreign port, and 30 in home port (crew paid for 10 of these). 3. Crew increased from 8 to 18 (including 1 captain and 1 first mate). 4. Wages increased $12/mo. to $15/mo. 5. Captain's pay = $30/mo. First mate = $20/mo. 6. Crew paid 30 days, first mate 30 days, captain 50 days.
P_{to}^*	1. Port time fell by half per voyage. 2. Ship size and construction costs held steady.	1. Port time held steady. 2. Ship size increased. 3. Shipbuilding costs rose (see weights or index).
P_{rj}^*	1. Port time fell (from 100 to 50 days) 2. Crew size (victualing) fell by half. 3. Remainder of costs held steady.	1. See explanation of P_{sj}^*.
$\overset{*}{S}$	1. No change (per voyage; speed constant).	1. No change.
$\overset{*}{T}$	1. Port time fell by half (both home and foreign).	1. No change.

Table 3—*continued*

Base Year for Weights Below	1600–1625	1814
α	Fraction of the total costs per voyage, TC/v, incurred at sea	$= P_s/C_v$
$1 - \alpha$	Fraction of TC/v incurred in port	$= P_t/C_v$
β_1	Fraction of total cost at sea per voyage, TCS/v, attributed to labor costs	$= P_{sL}/P_s$
β_2	Fraction of TCS/v attributed to capital costs	$= P_{so}/P_s$
β_3	Fraction of TCS/v attributed to all other costs	$= P_{sj}/P_s$
σ_1	Fraction of total cost in port per voyage, TCP/v, attributed to labor costs	$= P_{tL}/P_t$
σ_2	Fraction of TCP/v attributed to capital costs	$= P_{to}/Pt$
σ_3	Fraction of TCP/v attributed to all other costs	$= P_{tj}/P_t$

burden.[13] While the design was copied and modified over the next two centuries, the essential economic characteristics were not basically altered. The enigma to be explained, therefore, is why the flute (or ships of similar design) took so long to spread to all the commodity routes in the world, once it had entered the Baltic route and the English coal trade in the first half of the seventeenth century. The answer lies in the very nature of the flute and its great advantages in that it was lightly built, frequently carried no armament, was easy to sail, and had simple rigging. These characteristics had all come about because the Dutch enjoyed a large-volume bulk trade in the Baltic, where piracy had already been eliminated. Only as privateering was driven from other seas and as improvements took place in market organization was it possible to put into general service ships designed exclusively for the carrying trade.[14]

The one place where new technological development may have had important influence is in ship speed; but even here the answer is not altogether clear. Ships constructed in the seventeenth and early eighteenth centuries were capable of speeds equal to those achieved by nineteenth-century sailing ships. West Indian packets in the early eighteenth century averaged speeds equal to the Atlantic packets of 1820–1860, and many Atlantic crossings in the seventeenth century were made in from twenty to thirty days (as compared with the packets' average of twenty-four). Even the *Mayflower* made the return voyage to England in thirty days. The privateering needs of Americans in the Revolutionary War and in the War of 1812 tended to encourage the building of faster ships, and this trend continued after the war. It is interesting to note, however, that this improvement had already occurred by 1820, and the small increase in average speed achieved by packet boats between 1820 and 1860 was not a result of new knowledge in ship design. Therefore to the degree that technological change is looked on as a shift in the production function reflecting advances in knowledge, this was not such a case.[15] Moreover the improvement in speed occurred at a period (between the Revolutionary War and the War of 1812) for which we have as yet no way to measure productivity change. The fall in real shipping costs between 1815 and 1860 was only modestly influenced by increased speed.

The conclusion one draws is that the decline of piracy and privateering and the development of markets and international trade shared honors as primary factors in the growth of shipping efficiency over this two-and-a-half-century period.

---

[13] For a description of the flute and its development, see [5 and 4].

[14] The evolution of the sailing ship is actually distorted when much emphasis is laid on the flute itself. (In the larger study, the complex and diverse patterns of naval architecture will be more comprehensively set forth.) The flute should be regarded in this brief essay as representative of a type of sailing ship which evolved, rather than as a unique phenomenon.

---

[15] The celebrated clipper ship has been purposely omitted from the discussion. It was designed for increased speed and was successful where inventory costs (either passengers or cargo) were high, since—at least in its extreme version—it traded substantially higher costs per payload ton for the increase in speed.

Appendix. Total Factor Productivity Index, 1814–1860

Year (1)	Wage Series (2)	(Shipbuilding) Capital Cost Series (3)	Warren-Pearson Series (4)	18% × Col. 2 (5)	22% × Col. 3 (6)	60% × Col. 4 (7)	$P_i =$ Σ Cols. 5, 6, and 7 (8)	c = Freight Rate Index (9)	A = (Col. 8 ÷ Col. 9) (×100 To Get A Index for Figure 1) (10)
1814	100.0	100.0	100.0	18.0	22.0	60.0	100.0	300.0	0.33
1815	100.0	103.0	93.4	18.0	22.7	56.0	96.7	363.3	0.27
1816	100.0	106.1	83.0	18.0	23.3	49.8	91.1	238.0	0.39
1817	84.6	109.2	83.0	15.2	24.0	49.8	89.0	109.2	0.82
1818	92.3	112.3	80.8	16.6	24.7	48.5	89.8	266.9	0.34
1819	92.3	115.4	68.7	16.6	25.4	41.2	83.2	122.2	0.68
1820	153.8	118.5	58.2	27.7	26.1	34.9	88.7	191.7	0.46
1821	84.6	121.6	56.0	15.2	26.8	33.6	75.6	148.3	0.51
1822	92.3	124.7	58.2	16.6	27.4	34.9	78.9	140.8	0.56
1823	92.3	127.8	56.6	16.6	28.1	34.0	78.7	147.1	0.54
1824	92.3	130.9	53.8	16.6	28.8	32.3	77.7	127.2	0.61
1825	100.0	133.9	56.6	18.0	29.5	34.0	81.5	134.1	0.63
1826	107.7	128.5	54.4	19.4	28.3	32.6	80.3	127.9	0.63
1827	107.7	123.1	53.8	19.4	27.1	32.3	78.8	125.0	0.63
1828	105.1	117.8	53.8	18.9	25.9	32.3	77.1	106.7	0.72
1829	102.5	112.4	52.7	18.5	24.7	31.6	74.8	100.1	0.75
1830	100.0	107.1	50.0	18.0	23.6	30.0	71.6	100.0	0.72
1831	107.7	110.8	51.2	19.4	24.4	30.7	74.5	124.5	0.60
1832	107.7	114.5	52.2	19.4	25.2	31.3	75.9	99.9	0.76
1833	100.0	118.2	52.2	18.0	26.0	31.3	75.3	87.8	0.86
1834	100.0	121.9	49.5	18.0	26.8	29.7	74.5	88.3	0.84
1835	107.7	125.6	54.9	19.4	27.6	32.9	79.9	87.0	0.92
1836	115.4	129.3	62.6	20.8	28.4	37.6	86.8	99.9	0.87
1837	107.7	133.0	63.2	19.4	29.3	37.9	86.6	110.8	0.78
1838	107.7	136.7	60.4	19.4	30.1	36.2	85.7	124.4	0.69
1839	107.7	140.4	61.5	19.4	30.9	36.9	87.2	109.1	0.80
1840	107.7	144.1	52.2	19.4	31.7	31.3	82.4	134.4	0.61
1841	107.7	147.8	50.5	19.4	32.5	30.3	82.2	83.2	0.98
1842	100.0	151.5	45.1	18.0	33.3	27.1	78.4	56.5	1.39
1843	100.0	155.2	41.2	18.0	34.1	24.7	76.8	66.7	1.15
1844	107.7	158.9	42.3	19.4	34.9	25.4	79.7	61.5	1.30
1845	107.7	151.8	45.6	19.4	33.4	27.4	80.2	66.7	1.20
1846	107.7	144.6	45.6	19.4	31.8	27.4	78.6	72.4	1.08
1847	115.4	137.5	49.5	20.8	30.3	29.7	80.8	85.1	0.95
1848	115.4	130.4	45.1	20.8	28.7	27.1	76.6	45.0	1.70
1849	115.4	123.2	45.1	20.8	27.1	27.1	75.0	43.5	1.72
1850	115.4	116.3	46.2	20.8	25.6	27.7	74.1	34.4	2.15
1851	115.4	117.7	45.6	20.8	25.9	27.4	74.1	35.6	2.08
1852	115.4	119.3	48.4	20.8	26.2	29.0	76.0	42.8	1.78
1853	115.4	120.9	53.3	20.8	26.6	32.0	79.4	51.1	1.55
1854	115.4	122.5	59.3	20.8	27.0	35.6	83.4	50.2	1.66
1855	115.4	124.1	60.4	20.8	27.3	36.2	84.3	47.4	1.78
1856	115.4	125.7	57.7	20.8	27.7	34.6	83.1	46.2	1.80
1857	115.4	127.3	61.0	20.8	28.1	36.6	85.5	35.6	2.40
1858	115.4	128.9	51.1	20.8	28.4	30.7	79.9	37.2	2.15
1859	115.4	130.5	52.2	20.8	28.7	31.3	80.8	40.4	2.00
1860	115.4	132.1	51.1	20.8	29.1	30.7	80.6	49.7	1.62

SOURCES: Column 2, [8, pp. 530–538]. Column 3, from data collected on shipbuilding costs 1600–1919 for larger study Column 4, Warren-Pearson index converted to 1814 base. Columns 5, 6, and 7, geometric ratio of 1814 and 1860 weights of each input. Column 9, sources for this index are presented in detail in [9, pp. 236–238].

REFERENCES

1. Robert Albion, *Forests and Sea Power: The Timber Problem of the Royal Navy*, Cambridge, Harvard University Press, 1926.
2. Robert G. Albion, *Square Riggers on Schedule: The New York Sailing Packets to England, France and the Cotton Ports*, Princeton, Princeton University Press, 1938.
3. Robert Greenhalgh Albion, *The Rise of New York Port, 1815–1860*, New York, Charles Scribner's Sons, 1939.
4. Violet Barbour, "Dutch and English Merchant Shipping in the Seventeenth Century," *The Economic History Review, 2* (January, 1930), 261–290.
5. Ralph Davis, *The Rise of the English Shipping Industry*, London, St. Martin's Press, 1962.
6. John G. B. Hutchins, *The American Maritime Industry and Public Policy, 1789 to 1914: An Economic History*, Cambridge, Harvard University Press, 1941.
7. Dale Jorgenson, "The Embodiment Hypothesis," *The Journal of Political Economy, 74* (February, 1966), 1–17.
8. Stanley Lebergott, *Manpower in Economic Growth: The American Record Since 1800*, New York, McGraw-Hill, 1964.
9. Douglass C. North, "The Role of Transportation in the Economic Development of North America," in *Les Grandes Voies Maritimes dans le Monde, XV–XIX Siècles*, Paris, SEVPEN, 1965, pp. 209–246.
10. Walter Y. Oi, "The Cost of Ocean Shipping," Allen R. Ferguson, Eugene M. Lerner, John S. McGee, Walter Y. Oi, Leonard A. Rapping, and Stephen P. Sobatka, *The Economic Value of the United States Merchant Marine*, Evanston, Northwestern University Press, 1961, pp. 107–164.
11. Abbot Payson Usher, "The Growth of English Shipping, 1572–1922," *The Quarterly Journal of Economics, 42* (May, 1928), 465–478.
12. Gary Walton, "Quantitative Study of American Colonial Shipping," Unpublished doctoral dissertation, University of Washington, 1966.
13. Gary Walton, "Sources of Productivity Change in American Colonial Shipping, 1675–1775," *The Economic History Review, 20* (April, 1967), 67–78.
14. V. J. Wyckoff, "Ships and Shipping of Seventeenth Century Maryland," *Maryland Historical Magazine, 34* (December, 1939), 349–361.
15. Richard Yates, "The Behavior of Costs in the Ocean Transportation Industry, 1658–1850," Unpublished doctoral dissertation, University of Washington, forthcoming.

13 PRODUCTIVITY GROWTH IN AMERICAN GRAIN FARMING: AN ANALYSIS OF ITS 19th-CENTURY SOURCES

William N. Parker

I

All words define life for us and color it, but some words have special power to impress upon experience their inheritance of form and shading. "Productivity" is one of these subtly dominant words. A historian opening his

A version of this paper was delivered at the meetings of the Mississippi Valley Historical Association at Omaha in May, 1963, and portions of it were given at the meeting of the Economic History Society at Reading, England, in April, 1964.

vocabulary to such a word must marry economics and embrace the crudest of its statistical relatives. Yet, as in all marriages, both parties are affected. The word "productivity" pushes a historian toward economics, but the phrase "productivity growth" pushes an economist toward history. The economist who uses it must ask himself, how over history can productivity change?

"Productivity" implies a process with outputs and inputs which can be measured and compared. In a closed system the sum of the inputs should equal the sum of the outputs. Otherwise is not the measurement of the inputs incomplete? *Ex nihilo nihil fit.* Now we know that over recent history the physical volume of output in the American economy has increased. By applying price weights to output series in physical units, or by dividing output series expressed in value terms by an index of price changes, an index of this growth is produced. The statistical and philosophical issues in such manipulations of the data are well known. When similar operations are performed on inputs of labor, capital, and land, an index rising less rapidly than the output index is observed. If the output index is divided by the input index, a rising ratio of output to inputs appears. This rising ratio is a measure of the growth in productivity of the measured inputs. But such a change implies that some elements are missing from the input index. What parts of the inputs in the circular process of production must be missing from this index to produce this result? The answer is, of course, the inputs of knowledge about how to combine materials and men in efficient production. Such improvements are revealed statistically in changes in the value of inputs relative to output, but these changes disappear in physical input indices, or in value indices deflated by a series of input prices. Improvements in technical knowledge and changes in economic organization have not been part of measured inputs—and economists are still at a loss to apply measurement to them.

The growth in productivity of the measurable inputs in American agriculture—labor, capital, and land—has been the object of several recent studies.[1] Such studies have the great merit of showing agriculture as a single industry, related to other industries within a model of an entire economy. The measurement of capital, however, poses obscure and difficult problems, and the aggregation of inputs into a single index yields a statistic far removed from the facts of markets, techniques, and producers' organizations and responses. In the present study, measurement has been made only of the inputs of labor and land, and separate estimation made of output per unit of labor and output per unit of land. The measurement has been made by crop, region, and—in the last analysis—by each of the various farm operations.[2] The periods chosen for comparison are the years around 1840 and those around 1910.[3] Between these terminal years most of the geographical extension of American farming, the mechanization by horsepower of its operations, and the development of a national distribution and marketing system, with accompanying regional specialization in production, took place. The output of the grains increased between 1840 and 1910 as follows: wheat—653 per cent, oats—690 per cent, and corn—695 per cent. For these terminal dates, data on the labor inputs by operation and by region have been assembled from contemporary sources and combined with estimates

---

"residual" labeled "technological change," but including all improvements in knowledge and organization [5, p. 944]. John W. Kendrick's calculation of "total factor productivity" shows an increase of about 35 per cent between 1870 and 1910 [4, p. 362].

[2] Appendix Table A2 gives a summary of the estimates on which the indices are based.

[3] Labor input data from 1830–1860 and 1890–1910 were used to represent conditions as of 1840 and 1910. Clearly unrepresentative cases were discarded. Output estimates were derived from the Census of 1840 and the U.S. Department of Agriculture estimates for 1907–1911. For yields and acreage in 1907–1911, USDA estimates were used. For 1840, yields by state were estimated from contemporary sources—mainly reports to the U.S. Patent Office by county reporters in the late 1840s—and by extrapolation from USDA estimates beginning in 1867. These yield estimates were then divided into the 1840 Census output data to give acreage harvested, by state. Obviously such estimates are only rough approximations, especially for the early period. Since the taking of the 1840 Census was carried out over eighteen months, we cannot even be sure that the published figures represent the crop of 1839/1840 or 1840/1841. The estimates then are useful to show the trend of output and productivity over this seventy-year period, not to specify these figures exactly for either of the terminal dates.

---

[1] Lester B. Lave, applying very restrictive assumptions to the dubious data, estimated that labor productivity increased by about 95 per cent from 1850 to 1920. This increase is attributed in about equal proportions to a growth of capital per worker and a

Table 1. Productivity Growth: Total and Separated by Source (1840 to 1910)[a]

	Total Labor Productivity (1)	INDICES SHOWING SEPARATE EFFECTS OF:			
		Regional Shift (2)	Yield Rises (3)	Regional Shift & Yield Rises Combined (4)	Mechanization (5)
Wheat	417	109	118	118	246
Oats	363	123	106	118	186
Corn	365	130	119	143	227

[a] 1840 equal to 100. The numbers in table are the 1910 level of each category divided by the 1840 level, and multiplied by 100.

NOTE: Each index given above is the result of a separate statistical operation. They may be roughly compared to show the relative order of magnitude of each of the three separate sources of the total productivity increase. However, they cannot be directly added or multiplied together to produce the total index. Full treatment of the mathematical relation among the indices is contained in [*10*].

SOURCE: Table A1.

of crop yields per acre and total acreages by region. From these data estimates of the growth in output per manhour by crop for the regions and for the United States as a whole have been prepared. The estimates show that average national labor productivity over this period rose over fourfold in wheat and just under that amount in oats and corn. The indices are given in column 1 of Table 1.

Productivity growth of this measurable sort in 19th-century American agriculture may be viewed as the combined result of responses of entrepreneurs, workers, and investors to certain opportunities offered in the economy. Two opportunities are particularly important: (1) the opportunity to employ growing supplies of productive factors, (2) the opportunity to utilize improvements in knowledge about how to combine these factors in production. This paper tries to assess the relative importance of these forms of opportunity, by a statistical partitioning of the total improvement among them. It tries also to consider the historical meaning to be given to such a statistical finding.

II

The opportunity to employ growing supplies of the factors of production is economists' jargon for what is called in historians' jargon the "Westward movement." Each bit of jargon emphasizes a different aspect of the reality. The historians' term summons up the picture of a vast and confused migration, carried out by many different kinds of people for many different motives. It invites comparisons with other great migrations, the push of the Germans to the East, of the Slavs into Asia, of Europeans across the Atlantic and into the New World. The economists' term, though more specialized in its ring, is no less evocative. It assimilates the migration of small farmers and planters onto new land in the United States into an enormous economic process going on in the Western world of the nineteenth century on many fronts— the expansion of petty capitalistic enterprise into new and risky ventures. Westward movement from this view was part of the gamblers' game by which continents were opened to trade and settlement, mineral resources tapped, and the initial uncertain investments made in railroads, steamships, steel mills, and all the complicated paraphernalia of modern industry. Some brief consideration of this process as it occurred in American agriculture is useful before we examine its effects on the productivity of American farm labor.

Both in its Westward extension and in the transformations back East, American agriculture may be looked on as a high-risk enterprise with strong elements of speculation. Speculation in land, i.e., the holding of land in the hope of a rise in its value, occurred everywhere in the West. It accounts for much of the high rates of turnover of farm operators—5 per cent to 15 per cent annually in the first five to ten years of residence—found whenever historians have compared names in the successive state or federal manuscript censuses.[4] But the sheer risks of farming in a new area and the narrow financial margin on which new farmers worked also pushed the farming frontier along. These two efforts, continuous and strenuous, to hold land for a price rise—and to farm it in the face of ignorance, weather, grasshoppers, and markets in the hope of a "killing"—were entrepreneurial activities as bold, and at times as stupidly reckless, as those which made and lost great industrial fortunes.

Now there are two limits to such activity in a market economy. One, and often the narrower and relevant one, is simply a man's managerial capacity—his ability to use other productive factors and to invent ways to organize them. The other is his financial resources relative to factor prices and factor productivity. Both of these limits are strongly influenced by technology—in particular by the economy of using a large piece of capital equipment which cannot be efficiently shared among small producers. With such a piece of capital it is easier to organize production and to convince bankers or investors of the opportunity.

In nineteenth-century agriculture there was no clear technological advantage to large-scale production. An ambitious farmer might buy more farms, but he gained no economies by consolidating them. In buying more land, he met the second limit, the financial obstacle. Its presence cannot be set down simply to the inadequate credit system on the frontier. Easier credit under such conditions would have raised still further the price of land. Enterprise was too vigorous and too widely diffused, competition for finance, land, and labor too intense to permit large concentrations of wealth in land. The large farmer suffered the disadvantages of the liberal land policy and the prevailing sentiment in favor of the settler. He also suffered as well from the imperfection of the labor market, i.e., the willingness of the small farmer to exploit

his own and his family's labor. In cotton the plantations could survive against the small farms after 1865 only by the most ingenious devices of debt peonage and social pressures to imprison a freed labor force. In wheat the "bonanza" farms in Minnesota and North Dakota appeared to have a temporary advantage in the 1870s, but this vanished when mixed grain and livestock farming appeared. It would have taken a very strong technical advantage to the large farm to overbalance the high costs of hired farm labor—and such an advantage did not exist. So capital and many ambitious entrepreneurs moved into— or remained in—manufacturing, marketing, and transportation. Here production was less risky or less competitive and some technical advantages of large-scale plants could be used to give the initial impetus to a family fortune. In every neighborhood, to be sure, some farmers were richer than others, but profits were too low, risks and land prices too high, entry into the industry too easy, and competition too keen to permit a process of wealth concentration to get much beyond the level of local significance. The very cumbersomeness of large farms, the difficulties of communication and control accentuated the usual disadvantages of the large-scale production organization.

Thus the efforts of the farmers to extend their enterprises cancelled themselves out and left individual farms small scale. The effects of this feature of the history are best considered in connection with the level of practice in the next section. These efforts, however, probably did find their outlet in the rapid extension of the frontier. It may be argued, of course, that the growth of population along the fringe of empty land would have produced an extension of settlement by small farmers, each content to till his 80, or 160, acres. But the frontier did not move in so orderly a fashion. There was a pull from the frontier—the lure to make a fortune in land and in the farming of virgin soil; men were attracted to it so fast and in such numbers that it quickly disappeared.

What effect did Westward movement at this rate have on agricultural productivity? To isolate its direct and immediate effects, we may refer back to the index of labor productivity mentioned above (see Table 1, column 1). That index was constructed from three components at the two terminal dates (1840 and 1910): (1) the average labor requirements per acre in each region, (2) the

---

[4] Malin found "persistence rates" between 30 and 40 per cent for the first five years residence up to 1880 rising to 50–65 per cent thereafter to 1930, with some exceptions, in the Kansas townships studied [6]. Bogue, using only the federal census returns, found decennial persistence between 37 per cent and 56 per cent in four Iowa townships [1, p. 196]. Other studies, cited by Bogue, for Iowa and Illinois and the study of Trempeleau County, Wisconsin, made by Curti and his group give similar results [2, pp. 65–76].

average crop yield per acre in each region, (3) the importance of each region in national output, as shown by its share of national production at each date. The formula and some details of this index and the data used are given in Appendix A below. Now it is possible to construct an alternative estimate holding labor inputs per acre and grain output per acre at their 1840 levels in each region, but weighting each region by its share of national output in 1910. This is equivalent to an assumption that Westward movement took place without technological change, or more precisely, that technological change proceeded in each region just far enough to balance a fall in yields and rise in labor inputs that would otherwise have accompanied the absolute expansion of acreage in production. The index thus derived shows that only a small part of the threefold total improvement is due to this interregional shift. The figures, given in column 2, Table 1, are: wheat—109; oats—123; corn—130.

Enough caution in the interpretation of these figures will, as usual, remove their surprising character. They do not say that the roughly sevenfold increase in production occurring between 1840 and 1910 in these crops could have occurred east of the Mississippi River without a sharp rise in costs. They do show that if Westward movement had occurred with pre-Civil War machinery, seeds, and techniques, little productivity gain would have been registered simply through the movement to new land alone.[5] Iffy statements of this sort are subject to many quali-

fications, and they are not designed to thrill those who look on history as a "seamless-web." But they afford the only numerical means at our disposal of giving a first approximation of the relative importance of the nineteenth-century expansion for the growth in productivity in these crops.

III

That portion of the rise in labor productivity not attributable to the expansion into better lands must be attributed to the use of more capital per worker or to improved techniques; i.e., better knowledge or better diffusion of knowledge. Capital per worker is a shadowy creature in quantitative economic history, and measurement of its change lies beyond the scope of our research. The improved knowledge consisted in improved farming practices, improved breeds and seeds, and improved equipment.[6] In each case the history has two parts: the development of the art and its dissemination. In both parts the organization of American farming was of consequence.

Improved Knowledge

The story of the reaper, the thresher, and the combine has been often told, and no quantifying revisionist can diminish their significance in the small grains. Mechanical threshing had already reduced labor requirements in that operation in the 1850s from about 1.4 hours per bushel (flail threshing and winnowing with a sheet) to one half to three quarters of an hour for the simple machines then used, and the operation took less than twenty minutes per bushel by 1910.[7] In the other operations, which involve work on the

---

[5] The main reason for the difference between corn and the small grains is simply that in wheat the acreage transfer was from regions of fairly high yields—the Northeast (as far south as Virginia) and the Ohio Valley—to the Plains, whereas in corn the relative importance of the South (with very low yields) was large in the 1840s and 1850s and declined thereafter. In corn, even in 1840, there is also a striking difference in labor requirements per acre between the Old Northwest and the south and Northeast, due not only to easier plowing but also to less use of the hoe in cultivation. The question then arises whether this was due to the easier physical conditions—flat land, regular fields, etc.—or to a greater willingness to adopt the horse-drawn cultivator. To the extent that the latter was the case, our index overstates the improvement due simply to the interregional shift. Or more accurately, the effects of the interregional shift should be broken down between those due to easier physical conditions in the new regions and those due to the readier acceptance of improvements in a new region.

[6] This question is considered in [9]. A bibliography, on which these impressions are based, is given in that manuscript.

[7] The figure for flail threshing is from the 13th Annual Report of the Commissioner of Labor (1898); that for the machines of the 1850s is from a sample of documents in Virginia and Maryland, and the 1910 figures are from eighty-six separate sources, mostly studies at state colleges or Agricultural Experiment Stations. See also [13]. Clarence Danhof, in a note to me, estimates the reduction between the flail and the simple machines as from 1/10 to 1/25 of the value of the crop, an indication of the differential saving in this process compared to other operations.

soil, or traveling over the field, labor hours per unit of output depend both on labor used per acre and the output per acre, i.e., the yield of the land. The latter depends upon seed quality, natural conditions of soil and climate, and practices of cultivation, while the labor hours per acre, though depending in corn partly on the amount of cultivation given to the land, depend more closely on the choice of implements and the power source.

Since the portion of the productivity increase attributable to the changed distribution of the acreage among regions is, as indicated earlier, quite small, it is desirable to apportion the large remainder between changes in yields in the regions and reductions in labor per acre due to mechanization. Here, too, the problem—at a superficial statistical level—is not difficult. In wheat, yields changed hardly at all. In oats in the West yields went down slightly as production moved into the small grains region of the Plains. Holding labor inputs per acre and the regional distribution of acreage at its 1840 regional levels and applying the 1910 yields, the indices shown in column 3, Table 1, read: wheat—118, oats —106, corn—119. Allowing *both* Westward movement and improvement in crop yields to affect the indices, but holding to 1840 labor inputs per acre, we have indices (column 4, Table 1) as follows: wheat—118, oats—118, corn—143. The rest of the improvement (i.e., from 118 to 417 in wheat, from 118 to 363 in oats, from 119 to 365 in corn) is produced in our indices by the shift from the per acre labor inputs of the earlier period to those of the later period in each region as well as by interactions with the other sources of change. The effect of mechanization, without Westward movement or rises in yields, is shown directly by the large indices due to mechanization alone (column 5, Table 1). These then are the rough measures of the impact of mechanization and its diffusion.

The effects of mechanization are not, of course, fairly considered in isolation from Westward movement since much of the machinery was specially suited to the corn and wheat belts and found its best use in that flat and open terrain. And conversely, the heavy concentration of these crops in the Midwest was partly due to the very existence of the machinery to cultivate corn and to harvest the wheat and oats. The fact that in combination, mechanization and Westward movement had a stronger effect than would

have been expected, taken separately, reflects the "interaction effect" between these two phenomena. It indicates that the interregional shift occurred into just that region in which labor requirements were being most sharply reduced by mechanization. Column 5 in Table 2 shows the index allowing for the effects of both Westward movement and mechanization. In the absence of any interaction effects, the combined index would be the simple product of the two separate indices (column 4). The difference between such a product and an index actually computed from the regional data (column 5) will usually show roughly the strength of this effect.[8] Since the mechanization in corn, largely through introduction of the cultivator, affected all regions rather evenly, the interaction effect is less for corn than for the other two grains.

In view of its importance, then, some comment on the character of nineteenth-century mechanization is in order. Although by the end of the century the farm machinery industry was an oligopoly, it was originally a local industry, like wagon-making or milling, an industry of small beginnings. The development of standard farm machines for the whole Midwest market came with the movement of wheat into the terrain on which standardized machinery could readily work. It followed several decades of local developments and the process of trial and error, in which many small makers tried and patented many different designs and discarded them. Since labor requirements per acre in these crops, using all such machinery, fell in the older regions also, the Midwest market must have stimulated development of machinery adaptable to Eastern conditions. This practice of many small-scale experiments appears also in the development of plant strains and livestock breeds. Here, too, even after large-scale effort appeared in the form of the Agricultural Experiment Stations, an enormous process of trial and error was at work. Even more than in machinery development, local adaptation was essential in view of the movement of crops continually into new geographic

---

[8] This is not exactly true since negative interaction effects in some regional shifts may cancel out positive ones. Negative effects require that the shift in production occur relatively more heavily into a region with relatively less than the average fall in labor requirements per acre. This condition does not hold in our indices.

Table 2. Productivity Growth 1840–1910

	Total Labor Productivity (1)	INDICES SHOWING INTERACTION EFFECTS			
		Separate Effects of		Col. 2 × Col. 3 (4)	Combined Index of Mechanization and Regional Shift (5)
		Mechanization (2)	Regional Shift (3)		
Wheat	417	246	109	295	377
Oats	363	186	123	228	372
Corn	365	227	130	296	330

SOURCE: Table A1.

conditions.[9] Corn, where variation is even greater and the correct adaptation even more uncertain, still awaits its historian, but there is no doubt that continual variation and improvement in seed occurred. Similarly in farm practices, crop rotation, and times of planting, the two million farms in the United States in 1860 constituted two million experiment stations in which, despite many instances of peasant-like conservatism, an interest in change and improvement was widespread.[10] We may imagine then the small-scale American farms spreading out over this vast landscape, sending out tillers and reproducing themselves as the frontier advances, connected by a commercial and communications net, and receiving through that net impulses to improvement, new ideas, seeds, stock, and machinery, generated at other points within or outside of this agricultural economy.

Given the receptive and sensitive social organization, the developments which appeared were strongly influenced by the internal logic of the technological changes themselves. The failure to mechanize the corn or the cotton harvest, one may argue, was due less to any special cheapness of labor for those crops, than to the intrinsic physical difficulties of applying standard mechanical technology to simulate the picking motions of the human hand. And if this is true within mechanical techniques themselves, it is even truer in considering the slow development

of those biological techniques which have so altered American agriculture since 1940. A process of technological change was unfolding across the Western countries in the nineteenth century, moving according to the intellectual opportunities offered in the application of a scientific attitude and its developing techniques and instruments to problems offered by nature. The secrets of nature lay deeply hidden, and time, experience, scientific theorizing, and instruments and organization of the research were all required to uncover them. Small inventions were shaped by patterns of factor proportions and product demand, but the timing of the great changes did not respond to purely economic opportunities, however wide.

Diffusion of Techniques

We must postulate, then, a high receptivity to innovation in the small units making up American nineteenth century agriculture, and an ability in the farmers themselves to invent new techniques. It is, of course, hard to apportion credit as between the farm operators and the commercial matrix in which they were set. Clarence Danhof, in an illuminating chapter of his book, shows the importance of those who dealt with the farm population—the farm journalists, transport agents, seed and machinery dealers—in spreading innovations [3, chap. 2]. It will remain an open question as to the farmers' role—how much they originated and how much they permitted themselves simply to be acted upon. Certainly the almost complete lack of oligopolistic elements within agriculture itself gave almost no premium to industrial secrecy. Where an improvement could be patented or produced commercially, there

---

[9] This is a development which Malin has documented for wheat and Moore has documented for cotton [7, pp. 96–101, 162–188; 8, pp. 27–36, 145–160].

[10] This is the burden of Danhof's Gay Prize study, based on a wide survey of the farm journal literature [3].

was of course an incentive to monopoly of it. Its producer then was no longer a farmer but a manufacturer with a strong commercial interest in its sale. But many innovations were not patentable, and even when they were, the achievement of the final successful invention was hit upon only after a long process involving considerable interchange of information among the various farmer-experimenters. These in turn had no advantage in retaining personal property in an innovation while local prestige and professional pride impelled them to boast about it. One who has examined nineteenth-century European technical journals cannot help being struck by the similarity in tone and motivation between engineers' accounts of those achievements and farmers' endless letters to the *Prairie Farmer* or the *American Farmer*, detailing feeding practices or techniques of cultivating corn. Historians have dealt with the American farmer in economic history as a businessman, a laborer, a capitalist, a politician, a mystic, and a myth. He was also an engineer and a member of a class of engineers which—unlike a woman with a treasured recipe—liked to share its secrets. The farmer long complained that it was the competitive nature of agriculture that, in an industrial economy, made cooperative enterprise necessary. But it was that very competitive character that made cooperation possible. Since farmers were too numerous to recognize mutual interdependence in their production decisions it was all the easier for them to recognize their social interdependence through which the knowledge of production techniques was spread.

Another feature of an organization is the relation between the scale of enterprise and the kinds of individuals inhabiting the niches in it. It is perfectly conceivable that a small-scale organization of agriculture might not be conducive to innovation while large farms, as in the English case, might be the instruments of agricultural change. Even in the most progressive and commercial parts of the North, one cannot suppose that farmers were all equally ready to innovate. A range existed, and in every neighborhood innovation almost certainly depended upon the fact that its leaders were men of prestige. But the competitive economic organization helped to give prestige in the local community to good farming and economic success. Indeed in the deconcentrated organization of farming, with the rapid turnover of population and short

histories on the land, there were almost no other sources of local prestige. This does not mean that the successful leaders were necessarily wiser than their neighbors. The process of successful innovation was—by virtue of the very state of knowledge—a random one, which depended like a lottery upon many participants with a few prizes. Moreover a lucky gain by a rural family might have the usual productivity-improving effects, raising hopes and incentives, enlarging funds for experiment, and for the family's education. But for the agricultural ladder to work in this way, not only competitive organization but a high level of literacy, commercial-mindedness, and imitativeness had also to be diffused among the population. In this respect, differences between organization and value systems in North and South need further investigation. The South's agricultural achievements can easily be underrated by writers somewhat less commercial-minded than the planters, but the organization and the values were quite different.

Toward the end of the nineteenth century a shift occurred toward government-sponsored research and experimentation. It is not at all certain that the Experiment Station system would have had an important effect half a century earlier. So long as farmers would experiment and diffuse rapidly the results of their experiments, and so long as scientific methods were purely inductive, there was an advantage to the system of numberless private experiments, none bearing the official seal of Organized Science. Elaborate experiments under artificial conditions had little practical use, and the early Experiment Station bulletins are full of the records of such wastes of time and money. To be fruitful, large-scale research required sophisticated statistical tests of empirical results and close attention to theoretical questions of genetics and nutrition. Once these began to be studied, the way was cleared for the great twentieth-century rises in productivity. The nineteenth-century rises were the result of fairly simple adaptations of plants and practices together with a rather full exploitation of the possibilities of horsepower in mechanical operations. Such developments depended much more upon the organization and motivation of the agricultural population than upon organized science. But by some curious social process that guides the destinies of institutions, the Experiment Stations came into full use just as fundamental knowledge developed to the point at which it could be effectively employed. Such coincidences are the best that the social scientist can do to match the historians' concept that "great occasions produce great men." Here the occasion produced the great institution; without it the leveling off of our productivity curve, observable between 1900 and 1930, would probably have continued today.

IV

Measurement and analysis of historical phenomena may sometimes tell new things. They may also correct some old impressions derived solely from literary evidence. Often they confirm prevailing views and give to them a solidity and precision which they previously lacked.

That mechanization was the central actor in our study is hardly surprising. But its presence was felt, not only in wheat and oats, but in corn production as well. Since corn harvesting remained a hand operation well beyond our period, this result might not have been anticipated. It appears mainly because the horse-drawn cultivator replaced the hoe in digging around the corn plants and between the rows. Other small gains in plowing and planting, even improvements in picking and husking, were made possible by very simple inventions. The improvements in corn production did not form the basis of great machinery industries and in some cases were not even patented. They do not make much of a splash in the puddle of literary sources. Nor were they directly uncovered by our analysis since productivity data show effects, not causes. But knowledge of an effect is needed to encourage one to search the record for evidences of the cause.

It appears a bit novel, too, to observe that the differences in labor requirements in the three major regions—and particularly as between the Northeast and the West—were as small as they seemed to be in 1840. The result of this fact was to produce in our indices a relatively small productivity gain attributable to Westward movement. This permitted us to make a more exact statement of the effect of Westward movement than might have been otherwise possible. Its effects, from the indications of our evidence, were not directly to reduce labor requirements, but rather to permit the vast expansion of acreage and production without the sharp rises in those

requirements that would certainly have occurred if production had been confined to the East. Most of the positive reduction in labor requirements came, in our period, from mechanization. In the period after 1910 it was due first to the replacement of the horse by the tractor and then to improvements in yields permitted by innovations in fertilizers and in plant strains. This evidence is not irrelevant in the search after that elusive historical phenomenon: the causes of the Westward movement. The motivating force evidently did not lie in any well-justified impression that the move West would result in a striking, immediate, and long-continued improvement in the conditions of farming above current conditions in New York, Pennsylvania, or Virginia. The pull of the West then had something more about it than an immediate release from grinding poverty.

Apart from these new impressions, work with the indices appears to have furnished a frame within which the nonquantitative evidence can be sorted out and examined. One cannot write history with numbers, but analysis of a bit of history into its components can produce chapter headings, and statistically determined weights of the components can tell a scholar how much research time each chapter is worth.

Our estimates and indices are not, of course, historical facts in the usual sense of that word. They are scientific measurements of tendencies of which the facts are an imperfect record. Their statistical basis, particularly for the early period, is not as good as that which is possible in the physical, or even the other social sciences, where laboratory experiments or sample surveys—especially designed for a purpose and often reproducible—can be employed. History remains a dark terrain, but that is no reason not to gather all the evidence and treat it with the best statistical techniques at our disposal. Our work appears, too, to deviate from another often stated canon of historical scholarship. It is essentially an exercise in "iffy" or "hypothetical" history. We cannot really say what would have happened if the expansion of output had occurred without Westward movement. To speculate on that eventuality would have required measurement of quite a different kind—a measurement of hypothetical reaches of the cost curves of the Eastern regions. Such measurement, though not conceptually impossible, is practically beyond reach. But we can state what mechanization would have done to labor requirements under the outputs and the regional distribution of the crop in 1840. And we can say what labor requirements would very probably have been if Westward movement and output expansion had occurred without mechanization.

The use of statistics, instead of "real facts" or examples, and the measurement of things which never happened, do not trouble the conscience of an economist. He sees them indeed as the usual operations in scientific thinking. His cautions are different from those of the historian. He would be troubled at the neglect in our analysis of the inputs of capital—the land clearing and improvement, the horse power, and the machinery costs that Westward movement and mechanization involved. These costs may not have fallen as rapidly per unit of output as the labor requirements, and indeed some of them— notably machinery—may have risen. To this extent our measure of the gain in labor productivity overstates the gain in the productivity of labor and capital taken together.[11] Equally important as a qualification to our work is the measurement of output in terms of bushels, rather than in dollars of farm income. The economist, like the farmer, is interested ultimately not in the physical product, but in its money value. Most of the elements controlling this value lie outside the power of the individual farmer. He can endeavor to increase his own income, in money terms, by rapid and intelligent adjustment to markets and the conditions of supply. If farmers do so as a group, agriculture functions more efficiently, and so more productively, in the economy. Did farmers in 1910 come closer to giving consumers what

they wanted, and to predicting the shifts in production opportunities occurring through the changes in techniques, market conditions, transport routes, and market demand? This question is not answerable in terms of bushels per man-hour; indeed it is not wholly answerable in terms of income per farmer.

On both these economic issues there is considerable evidence indicating on balance that our measure probably does not overstate the extent of the productivity increase. The productivity of capital may well have increased as fast as that of labor over our period, and the efficiency of the agricultural organization in anticipating and responding to change in the conditions of supply and demand was almost certainly very greatly improved. Such conclusions can, with much more research, be specified more exactly and tested. In the process of such econometric work, one learns not only about numbers and estimates, but also about the more human parts of history.

APPENDIX: DATA AND FORMULAE

The textual discussion of the indices may be stated succinctly by a formula. Define, first, the following symbols:

L = Labor (man-hours)
O = Output (bushels of threshed or shelled grain)
A = Land (acres planted)
R^1 = Northeast (New England, New York, Pennsylvania, New Jersey)
R^2 = South and border (coastal states, Delaware through Louisiana, West Virginia, Kentucky, Tennessee, Arkansas)
R^{2a} = Border (Maryland, Delaware, Virginia, West Virginia, Kentucky, North Carolina, Tennessee)
R^{2b} = Other R^2
R^3 = West (all other states)
US = United States, total or average
a = Preharvest operations (man-hours per acre)
b = Harvest operations (man-hours per acre)
c = Post-harvest operations (man-hours per bushel)
v = Regional output divided by U.S. total output
w = Regional acreage planted divided by U.S. total acreage planted
y = Output per acre planted

---

[11] Some evidence is available on the direction of movement of these costs. We know that horsepower per farm and per acre did not in fact increase much over our period. Most of the mechanization then was accomplished by using the existing work stock of a farm more efficiently, and some improvements in the breeds of work animals helped to permit this. With the decline of woodland and open grazing, the costs of feeding work animals probably went up, but the cost of grain fell because of the very mechanization in which the animals furnished the power. As for the machinery itself, it was so very productive and its price fell so sharply as the industry grew, that it cannot have produced much rise in costs per unit of output of grain. Finally the initial costs of farm-making almost certainly declined sharply with the shift from woodland to prairie cover. On this point, some calculations have been made in the papers by Primack [*11, 12*].

Then designate the 1840 and the 1910 values by the subscripts 1 and 2, respectively. Labor input per bushel in any region is $(a + b)/y + c$, and the U.S. average over all regions is

$$\sum_{R^1}^{R^3} \left(\frac{a + b}{y} + c \right) v,$$

that is, each region's input weighted by its share in national output.

The labor input per bushel in period 1 (1840) then is:

$$\sum_{R^1}^{R^3} \left(\frac{a_1 + b_1}{y_1} + c_1 \right) v_1$$

Dividing this 1840 value by the figure obtained using period 2 data in this formula and multiplying by 100, the index of bushels per unit of labor input in the second period relative to the first period is obtained.

The direct effects of mechanization can be seen by holding yields (y_1) and regional weights (v_1) constant, substituting period 2 values (a_2, b_2, c_2) for period 1 values of the labor variables in the formula, and dividing the result into the period 1 average figure already calculated. It is apparent then that a family of eight averages and indices can be generated, involving eight alternative assumptions about the values of the variables. These are shown in Table A1 below. The indices used in the text are taken from this table.

Table A2 shows the regional figures used in the calculation. The labor data are medians, derived from an extensive survey of the contemporary farm records, plantation documents, agricultural journals in the various regions, as well as reports of state and federal agricultural societies and agencies. Data on yields were derived from contemporary sources, and from projection of USDA estimates for period 1. USDA and Census figures were used for production data and for yield estimates in period 2.

The techniques of estimation and the sources are fully displayed in [*10*].

REFERENCES

1. Allan G. Bogue, *From Prairie to Corn Belt: Farming on the Illinois and Iowa Prairies in the Nineteenth Century*, Chicago, University of Chicago Press, 1963.

2. Merle Curti, *The Making of an American Community: A Study of Democracy in a Frontier County*, Stanford, Stanford University Press, 1959.

3. Clarence H. Danhof, *Change in Agriculture: The Northern United States, 1820–1870*, Cambridge, Harvard University Press, 1969.

4. John W. Kendrick, *Productivity Trends in the United States*, Princeton, Princeton University Press, 1961.

5. Lester B. Lave, "Empirical Estimates of Technological Change in United States Agriculture, 1850–1958," *Journal of Farm Economics, 44* (November, 1962), 941–952.

6. James C. Malin, "Turnover of the Farm Population in Kansas," *The Kansas Historical Quarterly, 4* (November, 1935), 339–359.

7. James C. Malin, *Winter Wheat in the Golden Belt of Kansas: A Study in Adaptation to*

Table A1. Labor Requirements (U.S. Average and Indexes) as Affected by Interregional Shifts, Regional Yields, and Regional Labor Inputs Per Acre

| Index | PERIOD FOR VALUES OF | | | LABOR REQUIREMENT $(L/O)^a$ | | | PRODUCTIVITY (O/L) INDEX $(i_1/i_n \times 100)$ | | |
	v	y	abc	Wheat (1)	Oats (2)	Corn (3)	Wheat (4)	Oats (5)	Corn (6)
i_1	1	1	1	3.17	1.45	3.50	100	100	100
i_2	1	2	1	2.68	1.37	2.94	118.3	105.8	119.0
i_3	1	1	2	1.29	0.78	1.54	245.7	185.9	227.3
i_4	2	1	1	2.90	1.18	2.70	109.3	122.9	129.6
i_5	1	2	2	1.05	0.72	1.32	302.1	201.2	265.2
i_6	2	1	2	0.84	0.39	1.06	377.3	371.7	330.2
i_7	2	2	1	2.69	1.23	2.45	117.8	117.9	142.9
i_8	2	2	2	0.76	0.40	0.96	416.7	362.6	364.6

$^a \Sigma((a + b)/y + c) v$.

SOURCE: [*10*, p. 533].

Table A2. Labor Inputs, Yields, Output and Acreage Weights, by Major Regions, 1840–1910

	L/A a		L/A b		O/A y		L/O $\dfrac{a+b}{y}$		L/O c		L/O $\dfrac{a+b}{y}+c$		v		w	
	(1)	(2)	(1)	(2)	(1)	(2)	(1)	(2)	(1)	(2)	(1)	(2)	(1)	(2)	(1)	(2)
Wheat																
R_1	19.1	11.6	15.0	3.0	14.5	17.5	2.35	0.83	0.73	0.19	3.08	1.02	.334	.046	.259	.035
R_2	11.3	10.7	12.5	3.0	8.4	12.3	2.83	1.11	0.73	0.29	3.56	1.40	.342	.075	.459	.087
R_3	12.4	4.7	15.0	2.3	13.0	14.0	2.11	0.50	0.73	0.19	2.84	0.69	.324	.879	.282	.878
US	13.6	5.5	13.9	2.4	11.3	14.0	2.43	0.56	0.73	0.20	3.16	0.76				
Oats																
R_1	14.3	9.3	12.8	3.4	28.5	29.7	0.95	0.43	0.40	0.23	1.35	0.66	.422	.087	.316	.077
R_2	8.8	9.5	11.0	4.5	13.9	17.0	1.42	0.82	0.40	0.24	1.82	1.06	.332	.044	.506	.068
R_3	8.8	3.9	12.8	2.6	29.3	26.5	0.74	0.25	0.40	0.10	1.14	0.35	.246	.869	.178	.855
US	10.5	4.7	11.9	2.8	21.3	26.1	1.05	0.29	0.40	0.12	1.45	0.41				
Corn																
R_1	98.3	46.4	13.0	13.0	33.5	36.8	3.32	1.61					.097	.026	.057	.020
R_{2a}	52.0	26.7	10.1	10.1	21.8	24.4	2.85	1.51					.344	.099	.310	.106
R_{2b}	67.3	21.3	4.3	4.3	11.8	16.1	6.07	1.59					.279	.175	.465	.285
R_3	46.2	14.2	13.0	7.6	32.7	31.0	1.81	0.70					.280	.697	.168	.589
US	60.8	18.2	8.1	7.0	19.6	26.2	3.52	0.96								

Subhumid Geographical Environment, Lawrence, University of Kansas Press, 1944.

8. John Hebron Moore, *Agriculture in Ante-Bellum Mississippi*, New York, Bookman Associates, 1958.

9. William N. Parker, "The Social Process of Agricultural Improvement: Sources, Mechanisms, and Effectiveness in the United States in the 19th Century," (Unpublished paper presented at the Third International Congress on International History, Munich, Germany, August, 1965).

10. William N. Parker and Judith L. V. Klein, "Productivity Growth in Grain Production in the United States, 1840–60 and 1900–10" Conference on Research in Income and Wealth, *Output, Employment, and Productivity in the United States After 1800* (Studies in Income and Wealth, vol. 30), New York, Columbia University Press, 1966, pp. 523–580.

11. Martin L. Primack, "Land Clearing under Nineteenth Century Techniques: Some Preliminary Calculations," *The Journal of Economic History, 22* (December, 1962), 484–497.

12. Martin L. Primack, "Farm Capital Formation as a Use of Farm Labor in the United States, 1850–1910," *The Journal of Economic History, 26* (September, 1966), 348–362.

13. Leo Rogin, *The Introduction of Farm Machinery and Its Relation to the Productivity of Labor in the Agriculture of the United States During the Nineteenth Century*, Berkeley, University of California Press, 1931.

14 RAILROADS AND AMERICAN ECONOMIC GROWTH

Robert William Fogel

To establish the proposition that railroads substantially altered the course of economic growth one must do more than provide information on the services of railroads. It must also be shown that substitutes for railroads could not (or would not) have performed essentially the same role. Writers who have held either that railroads were crucial to American economic growth or enormously accelerated this growth implicitly asserted that the economy of the nineteenth century lacked an effective alternative to the railroad and was incapable of producing one. This assertion is without empirical foundation; the range and potentiality of the supply of alternative opportunities is largely unexplored.

In the investigation of the incremental contribution of the railroad to economic growth it is useful to distinguish between the primary and the derived

Reprinted with revisions by permission from Robert William Fogel, *Railroads and American Economic Growth: Essays in Econometric History*, Baltimore, Johns Hopkins Press, 1964, pp. 207–237.

consequences of this innovation. The primary consequence of the railroad was its impact on the cost of transportation. If the cost of rail service had exceeded the cost of equivalent service by alternative forms of transportation over all routes and for all items, railroads would not have been built and all of the derived consequences would have been absent. The derived consequences or aspects of the innovation included changes in the spatial distribution of economic activity and in the mix of final products. They also included the demand for inputs, especially manufactured goods and human skills, required for railroad construction and operation as well as the effects of that construction and operation on human psychology, political power, and social organization. Those who have held that railroads were indispensable to American economic growth could have based their position either on the ground that the reduction in transportation costs attributable to railroads was large or on the ground that the derived consequences of railroads were crucial (even if the reduction in transportation costs were small) or on some combination of the two types of effects.

THE PRIMARY EFFECT OF RAILROADS

Summary of the Findings

In this study the investigation of the primary effect of railroads is limited to transportation costs connected with the distribution of agricultural products. Chapters II and III[1] discuss the increase in the production potential of the economy made possible by the availability of railroads for the transportation of such goods. The main conceptual device used in the analysis of this problem is the "social saving." The social saving in any given year is defined as the difference between the actual cost of shipping agricultural goods in that year and the alternative cost of shipping exactly the same collection of goods between exactly the same set of points without railroads.

This cost differential is in fact larger than the "true" social saving. Forcing the pattern of shipments in a nonrail situation to conform to the pattern that actually existed is equivalent to the imposition of a restraint on

society's freedom to adjust to an alternative technological situation. If society had had to ship by water and wagon without the railroad it could have altered the geographical locus of agricultural production or shifted some productive factor out of agriculture altogether. Further, the sets of primary and secondary markets through which agricultural surpluses were distributed were surely influenced by conditions peculiar to rail transportation; in the absence of railroads some different cities would have entered these sets, and the relative importance of those remaining would have changed. Adjustments of this sort would have reduced the loss of national income occasioned by the absence of the railroad.

For analytical convenience the computation of the social saving is divided into two parts. Chapter II deals with the social saving in interregional distribution. In 1890 interregional distribution began with the farm surpluses concentrated in the eleven great primary markets of the Midwest. Over 80 per cent of the agricultural products that entered into interregional trade were shipped from the farms to these markets. The surpluses were then transshipped to some ninety secondary markets located in the East and South. After arriving in the secondary markets the commodities were distributed to retailers in the immediately surrounding territory or were exported.

The interregional social saving is computed for only one year—1890. The social saving per ton-mile was greater, however, in 1890 than in previous years; the tonnage of agricultural goods carried by railroads increased more rapidly than gross national product; and the average distance of an interregional haul increased over time. Hence both the absolute interregional social saving and that social saving relative to total national product was greater in 1890 than in previous years.

Only four commodities are included in the interregional computation, but these—wheat, corn, pork, and beef—accounted for over 90 per cent of the tonnage of interregional agricultural shipments. While it is possible to include all commodities in the computation, the increase in the accuracy of the estimate would not justify the effort required to do so.

Of the various forms of transportation in use in 1890, the most relevant alternative to railroads were waterways. All of the eleven primary markets were on navigable waterways.

---

[1] [This and subsequent references are to the book from which this selection is taken.—Editors' note.]

Lakes, canals, rivers, and coastal waters directly linked the primary markets with secondary markets receiving 90 per cent of the interregional shipments. Consequently it is possible to compute a first approximation to the interregional social saving by finding the difference between payments actually made by shippers of agricultural products and the payments they would have made to water carriers if shippers had sent the same commodities between the same points without railroads.

The total quantity of corn, wheat, pork, and beef shipped interregionally in 1890 was approximately equal to the local deficits of the trading regions of the East and South, plus net exports. The local net deficits of a trading area are computed by subtracting from the consumption requirements of the area its production and its changes in inventories. The average rail and water distances of an interregional shipment are estimated from a random sample of the routes (pairs of cities) that represent the population of connections between primary and secondary markets. The water and rail rates per ton-mile for the various commodities are based on representative rates that prevailed in 1890 over distances and routes approximating the average condition. The application of observed water rates to a tonnage greatly in excess of that actually carried by waterways is justified by evidence which indicates that water transportation was a constant or declining cost industry

These estimates of tonnages shipped, rates, and distances reveal that the actual cost of the interregional transportation of corn, wheat, pork, and beef in 1890 was $87,500,000 while the cost of transporting the same goods by water would have been only $49,200,000. In other words the first approximation of the interregional social saving is negative by about $38,000,000. This odd result is the consequence of the fact that direct payments to railroads included virtually all of the cost of interregional transportation, while direct payments to water carriers did not. In calculating the cost of shipping without the railroad one must account for six additional items of cost not included in payments to water carriers. These items are cargo losses in transit, transshipment costs, wagon haulage costs from water points to secondary markets not on waterways, capital costs not reflected in water rates, the cost resulting from the time lost when using a slow medium of transportation,

and the cost of being unable to use water routes for five months out of the year.

The first four of the neglected costs can be estimated directly from available commercial data.

It is more difficult to determine the cost of the time lost in shipping by a slow medium of transportation and the cost of being unable to use water routes for about five months during each year. Such costs were not recorded in profit and loss statements, or publications of trade associations, or the decennial censuses, or any of the other normal sources of business information. Consequently they must be measured indirectly through a method that links the desired information to data which are available. The solution to the problem lies in the nexus between time and inventories. If entrepreneurs could replace goods the instant they were sold, they would, *ceteris paribus*, carry zero inventories. Inventories are necessary to bridge the gap of time required to deliver a commodity from its supply source to a given point. If, on the average, interregional shipments of agricultural commodities required a month more by water than by rail and if water routes were closed for five months out of each year, it would have been possible to compensate for the slowness of water transportation and the limited season of navigation by increasing inventories in secondary markets by an amount equal to one half of the annual receipts of these markets. Hence the cost of interruptions and time lost in water transportation is the 1890 cost of carrying such an inventory. The inventory cost comprises two elements: the foregone opportunity of investing the capital represented in the additional inventory (which is measured by the interest rate) and storage charges (which were published).

When account is taken of the neglected costs, the negative first approximation is transformed into a positive social saving of $73,000,000 (see Table 1). Since the actual

Table 1. The Social Saving in the Interregional Distribution of Agricultural Commodities

First approximation	$−38,000,000
Neglected cargo losses	6,000,000
Transshipping costs	16,000,000
Supplementary wagon haulage	23,000,000
Neglected capital costs	18,000,000
Additional inventory costs	48,000,000
Total	$ 73,000,000

1890 cost of shipping the specified commodities was approximately $88,000,000, the absence of the railroad would have almost doubled the cost of shipping agricultural commodities interregionally. It is therefore quite easy to see why the great bulk of agricultural commodities was actually sent to the East by rail, with water transportation used only over a few favorable routes.

While the interregional social saving is large compared to the actual transportation cost, it is quite small compared to annual output of the economy—just six tenths of one per cent of gross national product. Hence the computed social saving indicates that the availability of railroads for the interregional distribution of agricultural products represented only a relatively small addition to the production potential of the economy.

The estimation of the social saving is more complex in intraregional trade (movements from farms to primary markets) than in long-haul trade. Interregional transportation represented a movement between a relatively small number of points—eleven great collection centers in the Midwest and ninety secondary markets in the East and South. But intraregional transportation required the connection of an enormous number of locations. Considering each farm as a shipping point, there were not 11 but 4,565,000 interior shipping locations in 1890; the number of primary markets receiving farm commodities was well over a hundred. These points were not all connected by the railroad network, let alone by navigable waterways. The movement of commodities from farms to primary markets was never accomplished exclusively by water or by rail. Rather it involved a mixture of wagon and water or wagon and train services.

This is the crux of the intraregional problem. If the evaluation of the impact of interior railroads merely involved an analysis of the substitution of water for rail transportation, there would be no reason to expect a large social saving. Considered in isolation, boats were a relatively efficient substitute for the iron horse. However the absence of the railroad would have required greater utilization not only of water service but also of wagon service. It is the additional amount of very costly wagon transportation that would have been needed for the shipment of each ton of agricultural produce leaving the farm, which suggests that the social saving attributable to interior railroads probably exceeded the social saving of the more celebrated trunk lines.

The intraregional social saving—which covers twenty-seven commodities—is estimated in two ways. The first computation (estimate α) is a direct extension of the method used for long-distance shipments. It is the difference between the actual cost of shipping goods from farms to primary markets in 1890 and the cost of shipping in exactly the same pattern without the railroad. However in the intraregional case the assumption that pattern of shipments would have remained unchanged despite the absence of railroads implies that wagons would have carried certain agricultural commodities over distances in which wagon haulage costs greatly exceeded the market value of the produce. As a result estimate α introduces an upward bias that is too large to ignore.

It is possible to estimate the intraregional social saving by a method that reduces this upward bias. Without railroads the high cost of wagon transportation would have limited commercial agricultural production to areas of land lying within some unknown distance of navigable waterways. If the boundaries of this region of feasible commercial agriculture were known, the social saving could be broken into two parts: (1) the difference between the cost of shipping agricultural commodities from farms lying within the feasible region to primary markets with the railroad and the cost of shipping from the same region without the railroad (i.e., an α estimate for the feasible region), and (2) the loss in national product due to the decrease in the supply of agricultural land. The social saving estimated in this manner (estimate β) would be less than the previous measure since it allows for a partial adjustment to a nonrail situation. Moreover by disaggregating the social saving, estimate β provides additional information on the gestalt of the railroad's influence on the development of agriculture.

A first approximation of the α estimate can be computed on the basis of the relationship shown in equation 1:

$$\alpha = x \left[w(D_{fb} - D_{fr}) + (BD_{bp} - RD_{rp}) \right] \quad (1)$$

where

x = the tonnage of agricultural produce shipped out of counties by rail
w = the average wagon rate per ton-mile
B = the average water rate per ton-mile

R = the average rail rate per ton-mile

D_{fb} = the average distance from a farm to a water shipping point

D_{fr} = the average distance from a farm to a rail shipping point

D_{bp} = the average distance from a water shipping point to a primary market

D_{rp} = the average distance from a rail shipping point to a primary market

The first term within the square bracket $w(D_{fb}-D_{fr})$ is the social saving per ton attributable to the reduction in wagon transportation; the second term $(BD_{bp} - RD_{rp})$ is the social saving per ton on payments to water and rail carriers. One of the surprising results is that only the first term is positive. In the absence of railroads wagon transportation costs would have increased by $8.92 for each ton of agriculture produce that was shipped interregionally by rail. Payments to water carriers, however, would have been $0.76 per ton less than the payments to railroads. In other words the entire first approximation of the α estimate of the social saving —which amounts to $300,000,000—is attributable not to the fact that railroad charges were less than boat charges but to the fact that railroads reduced the amount of expensive wagon haulage that had to be combined with one of the low-cost forms of transportation.

To the $300,000,000 obtained as the first approximation of α it is necessary to add certain indirect costs. In the long-haul case it was shown that the first approximation of the social saving omitted six charges of considerable importance. In the intraregional case, however, three of these items are covered by the first approximation. Wagon haulage costs are included in equation 1. Transshipment costs would have been no greater in the nonrail case than in the rail case. In both situations bulk would have been broken when the wagons reached the rail or water shipping points and no further transshipments would have been required between these points and the primary markets. Since all government expenditures on rivers and canals financed out of taxes rather than tolls were assigned to interregional agricultural shipments, their inclusion in the intraregional case would represent double counting.

Three indirect costs do have to be added to the first approximation of α. These are cargo losses, the cost of using a slow medium

Table 2. Preliminary α Estimate (In Millions of Dollars)

First approximation	300.2
Cargo losses	1.3
Cost of slow transportation	1.7
Cost of limited season of navigation	34.0
	337.2

of transportation, and the cost of the limited season of navigation. As is shown by Table 2 these neglected items amount to only $37,000,000 which, when added to the first approximation, yields a preliminary α estimate of $337,000,000 or 2.8 per cent of gross national product.

Execution of the β estimate requires a theoretical structure that will make it possible to infer the location of the boundary of feasible commercial agriculture from observed data. The theory of rent provides such a structure. The applicability of the theory of rent can be demonstrated by considering a hypothetical example. Suppose that Congress passed a law requiring all farmers in an area of land one mile wide and a hundred miles long, running westward from the Mississippi River through the state of Missouri along the 40th parallel, to send their products to market (St. Louis) by wagon and boat. Suppose that Congress also prohibited these farmers from responding to the law by changing the kinds or the proportions of the commodities that were produced for the market. Finally assume that the rate from all rail shipping points in the strip to St. Louis were exactly the same as Mississippi River rates from the 40th parallel to St. Louis.

Under these circumstances farms lying along the Mississippi would be unaffected by the law as would all farms that were just as far from the Mississippi River as from a rail shipping point. For all other farmers the law would result in a decline in the prices they received at the farm for their various commodities. Since the output of the farms in question is very small relative to total agricultural production, no output decisions on the part of these farmers could affect prices in primary markets. The reduction in prices paid at the farm and the corresponding fall in land values would be completely explained by the increased cost of transportation. The farther a farm was from the Mississippi, the greater would be the fall in the value of that farm land. At some distance from the

Mississippi the increase in the cost of wagon transportation would be such that land values would be zero. All land lying beyond this distance would have a negative price. Hence given the value of each plot of land prior to enactment, the quantities of agricultural commodities shipped to St. Louis from each of the farms, the wagon rates, and the distance from each farm to a rail shipping point, one could determine the boundary of feasible commercial agriculture after the enactment. The boundary would be located along a set of points at which the increase in the cost of transporting the market-bound output from a farm to a shipping point was exactly equal to the pre-enactment rental value of that land.

The hypothetical example indicates the basic procedure for establishing the boundaries of feasible commercial agriculture. There are, of course, differences between the hypothetical example and the actual problem. Thus transportation costs from rail and water shipping points to primary markets will not be the same for most farms. Since water costs were in fact generally less than rail costs, the boundary of feasible production is pushed out. Moreover when the whole country is considered, one cannot ignore the effect of the cessation of agricultural production in land beyond the feasible range on the level of prices in primary markets. Given the relative inelasticity of the demand for agricultural products, the reduction in production would have tended to raise prices in primary markets. The rise in prices would have led to a more intensive exploitation of agriculture within the feasible region, thus raising land values and increasing the burden of additional transportation costs that could have been borne by various farms. Hence calculation of the feasible range on the basis of the actual 1890 land values and shipment statistics tends to understate the limits of feasible commercial agriculture, and overstates the amount of land that would have remained unused in the absence of the railroad.

The theory of rent can also be used to estimate the loss in national income brought about by the decrease in the supply of land. The 1890 rental value of the lands lying beyond the region of feasible commercial agriculture represents the amount by which the annual product of labor and capital utilized on this territory exceeded the value of the product of the same amount of labor and capital when applied at the margin. If the land in the nonfeasible region had not been available, the labor and capital employed on it would have been utilized either at the intensive or extensive margin. Hence if the quantity of displaced factors had been small, the fall in the value of the output of these factors would have been equal to the annual rental value of the land they had previously occupied. This loss in national income could be estimated by decapitalizing the land values, i.e., multiplying land values by appropriate mortgage rates of interest. The amount of labor and capital employed on nonfeasible terrain, however, was quite large so that their displacement would have led to a fall in national income which exceeded the decapitalized value of the nonfeasible lands.

Unlike the α estimate, the β estimate of the social saving has downward as well as upward biases. While the upward biases may be stronger than the downward ones, these conflicting errors tend to cancel and make β a more acceptable approximation of the true social saving than α.

Data pertaining to the North Atlantic states indicate that in this region the boundary of feasible commercial agriculture would have been located between 40 and 50 airline miles from navigable waterways. The feasible boundary would probably have been closer to waterways in the North Atlantic region than in other sections of the nation. This is indicated by the fact that farm land values relative to outshipments were probably lower in this area than in all other areas except the Mountain states. At the same time the cost of wagon transportation was higher on the average in the North Atlantic region than outside it. Nevertheless in computing the β estimate it is assumed that in all regions of the country the boundary of feasible commercial agriculture fell 40 airline miles from a navigable waterway.

Table 3 shows that 76 per cent of all agricultural land by value was within 40 miles of natural waterways and canals actually in use in 1890 as well as abandoned canals that would have been in use in the absence of railroads. Table 3 shows also that the loss in national income due to the diminished supply of land would have been $154,000,000. The loss is not equally distributed. Close to three quarters of it is concentrated in the North Central states. Indeed more than half of the decline falls in just four states: Illinois, Iowa, Nebraska, and Kansas. This finding

Table 3. Loss in National Product Due to the Decrease in the Supply of Land (By Regions) (Thousands of Dollars)

	Value of Farm Land (1)	Value of Farm Land Beyond Feasible Region (2)	Col. 2 as a Per Cent of Col. 1 (3)	Loss in National Product (4)
North Atlantic	1,092,281	5,637	0.5	331
South Atlantic	557,399	117,866	21.1	8,452
North Central	4,931,607	1,441,952	29.2	110,476
South Central	738,333	158,866	21.5	14,191
Western	800,952	218,216	27.2	19,919
United States	8,120,572	1,942,537	23.9	153,572

does not support the frequently met contention that railroads were essential to the development of commercial agriculture in the prairies. Rather, the concentration of the loss in a compact space suggests that most of the productive agricultural land that fell outside of the feasible region could have been brought into it by a relatively small extension of the canal system.

Adding an α estimate for the feasible region to the loss in national income attributable to the diminished supply of land yields a first approximation of β amounting to $221,000,000 (see Table 4). The further addition of indirect charges of $27,000,000 results in a preliminary β estimate of $248,000,000 or 2.1 per cent of gross national product.

The preliminary estimates of the intraregional social saving are based on the severe assumption that in the absence of railroads all other aspects of technology would have been unaltered. It seems quite likely, however, that in the absence of railroads much of the capital and ingenuity that went into the perfection and spread of the railroad would have been turned toward the development of other cheap forms of land transportation. Under these circumstances it is possible that

Table 4. Preliminary β Estimates (In Millions of Dollars)

First approximation		220.9
Loss due to diminished supply of land	153.6	
α estimate for feasible region	67.3	
Cargo losses		1.0
Cost of slow transportation		0.7
Cost of the limited season of navigation		25.5
Total		248.1

the internal combustion engine would have been developed years sooner than it actually was, thus permitting a reduction in transportation costs through the use of motor trucks.

While most such possibilities of a speed-up in the introduction and spread of alternative forms of transportation have not been sufficiently explored to permit meaningful quantification at the present time, there are two changes about which one can make fairly definitive statements. These are the extension of the existing systems of internal waterways and the improvement of common roads. Neither of these developments required new knowledge. They merely involved an extension of existing technology.

Figure 3.5 presents a system of canals that could have been built in the absence of railroads.[2] Although the thirty-seven canals and feeders proposed are only 5000 miles in length, their construction would have brought all but 7 per cent of agricultural land within 40 airline miles of a navigable waterway. Allowing for the projected waterways, the α estimate is reduced to $214,000,000 (1.8 per cent of gross national product) and the β estimate falls to $175,000,000 (1.5 per cent of gross national product).

Such an extension of internal water transportation is more than an historian's hallucination. The proposed canals would have been technologically, and, in the absence of railroads, economically, feasible.[3] Built across

---

[2] [This map is on p. 93 of the book from which this selection is taken.—Editors' note.]

[3] Even if the amortization period of canals is put as low as twenty-five years, the reduction in β implies a social rate of return of 45 per cent on the investment in the proposed canals. If the reduction in the α estimate is used, the implied return is 76 per cent.

the highly favorable terrain of the North Central states and Texas, the average rise and fall per mile on the proposed system would have been 29 per cent less than the average rise and fall on those canals that were successful enough to survive railroad competition through 1890. The water supply along the routes would have been abundant. Even if worked at full capacity, no canal in the system would have required more than 65 per cent of the supply of water available to it. And in no case would the agricultural tonnage carried by a canal have exceeded one third of its capacity.

According to data published by the Bureau of Public Roads, the intraregional social saving could have been further reduced by the improvement of common roads. The Bureau estimated that improvements would have reduced the cost of wagon haulage to ten cents per ton-mile. This rate implies a boundary of feasible commercial agriculture located at an average of 80 airline miles from navigable waterways. The doubling of the distance of this boundary together with the construction of the proposed canals would have brought all but 4 per cent of agricultural land within the feasible region. Under these circumstances the value of α is $141,000,000 or just 1.2 per cent of gross national product, while the value of β is $117,000,000 or slightly less than one per cent of gross national product.

It thus appears that while railroads were more important in short-haul movements of agricultural products than in long-haul movements, the differences are not as great as is usually supposed. It is very likely that even in the absence of railroads the prairies would have been settled and exploited. Cheap transportation rather than railroads was the necessary condition for the emergence of the North Central states as the granary of the nation. The railroad was undoubtedly the most efficient form of transportation available to the farmers of the nation. But the combination of wagon and water transportation could have provided a relatively good substitute for the fabled iron horse.

Extension to all Commodities

Of course the social saving has been computed only for agricultural commodities. Ultimate conclusions regarding the significance of the primary effect of railroads must await the computation of the social saving on non-agricultural items. It has been suggested that one can obtain a reasonable estimate of the social saving in the transportation of all freight by multiplying the combined inter- and intraregional figures by four. The suggestion is rationalized on the ground that agricultural products probably accounted for about one fourth of the ton-miles of transportation services provided by railroads in 1890. The procedure implies a total social saving of 7.1 per cent of gross national product if the α estimate of the intraregional saving is used, ($214,000,000 \times 4)/$12,000,000,000, or 6.3 per cent if the β estimate is used, ($190,000,000 \times 4)/ $12,000,000,000. Unfortunately this simple way of moving from the agricultural to the total social saving probably leads to so large an overestimate of the true total that the figure derived from the computation is useless for most purposes.

Data on the ton-miles of railroad service utilized in shipping nonagricultural commodities can hardly be classified as decisive information. As has been shown, comparisons of transportation costs based only on direct payments to railroad and water carriers for the ton-miles of service provided by each introduced negative components into the social saving in both the inter- and intraregional cases. The important elements in the agricultural social saving were the cost of supplementary wagon transportation, the cost of increasing inventories to compensate for interruptions in navigation, and other indirect charges. The cost of increasing inventories alone equaled 65 per cent of the interregional social saving, and supplementary wagon transportation similarly dominated the intraregional computation.

However there is no simple relationship between these all-important charges and the ton-miles of service actually provided by railroads. That is why it was not possible to estimate the intraregional social saving from the interregional one by extrapolating on the ton-miles of railroad service. Since intraregional shipments of agricultural products required only one half of the ton-miles of railroad service consumed by shipments between regions, such an extrapolation would have led to the erroneous conclusion that interior railroads were considerably less important than the trunk lines. The intraregional problem turned on the extent of the increase in supplementary wagon transportation that would have been required for each ton of freight shifted from railroads to boats. This increase could not have been derived from data on the amount of railroad service actually consumed.

Consequently no firm estimate of the social saving on nonagricultural items can be obtained without the detailed, protracted research required to determine such matters as: the geographic patterns of the production and consumption of nonagricultural goods, the extent to which the observed geographic patterns permitted the substitution of water for rail transportation, the amount of supplementary wagon transportation that would have been required in the nonrail case, the extent to which additions to the canal system would have permitted further reductions in the social saving through the substitution of water for wagon transportation, and the cost of the additional inventories of nonagricultural commodities required to compensate for the slowness and unavailability of water transportation during certain months of the year.

Such a study would probably reveal that the social saving per ton-mile of railroad service was lower for nonagricultural commodities than for agricultural commodities. This conclusion is suggested by the fact that products of mines dominated nonagricultural freight shipments in 1890. Coal alone accounted for 35 per cent of the nonagricultural tonnage. Iron and other ores brought the share to over 50 per cent.

Unlike agricultural commodities which were produced on farms occupying nearly a million square miles of land in over 2000 counties in every state of the nation, the production of coal was highly concentrated. Nine states accounted for about 90 per cent of all coal shipped from mines in 1890. And within these states production was further concentrated in a relative handful of counties. Forty-six counties shipped 76,000,000 tons —75 per cent of all the coal sent from the mines in the nine states. Moreover all of these counties were traversed by navigable rivers, canals actually constructed, or the proposed canals of Figure 3.5.[4] Consumption of coal was also geographically concentrated. Just fifteen cities—all on navigable waterways—received 43 per cent of all coal shipped from mines.

The production and consumption of iron ore were even more localized than coal. The

Report on Mineral Industries prepared for the Eleventh Census reported that 73.11 per cent of the output of iron ore in 1890 was produced in four localities embracing a territory of barely 10,000 square miles (less than one third of 1 per cent of the territorial expanse of the United States). With respect to consumption, about 80 per cent of all iron ore was received by blast furnaces located in thirty-one counties.

Consequently the transportation pattern of minerals more nearly approximated the conditions of the *inter*regional than the *intra*regional distribution of agricultural commodities. Products of mines were carried from a relatively small number of shipping locations to a similarly small number of receiving locations. Many of these shipping and receiving centers were directly linked to each other by waterways, and a limited extension of the canal system could have provided water connections for many of those points that did not already have them. It thus appears likely that only a small amount of additional wagon transportation would have been required for each ton of coal or ore shifted from railroads to waterways. Moreover the cost of increasing inventories to compensate for the slowness of and interruptions in water transportation would have been quite low. The total value of all products of mines in 1890 was well below the value of the agricultural commodities that entered intraregional trade. Hence the opportunity cost of the increased inventories of minerals would have been well below that found for agriculture. Additional storage costs, if any, would have been trivial. Minerals required neither very expensive cold storage facilities nor shelters. They were stored on open docks or fields.

Still another consideration militates against an extrapolation from the agricultural to the total social saving by use of data on the tons of goods carried by railroads or the ton-miles of service railroads provided. That is the fact that the $214,000,000 presented as the agricultural social saving already includes substantial elements of the social saving on nonagricultural items. Although all of the capital costs of the improvement of waterways were charged to agricultural commodities, most of this cost should be distributed among nonagricultural items. Similarly the wagon rates used in the computations assumed zero return hauls so that these rates cover most of the additional wagon cost that would have been incurred in shipping

---

[4] [See footnote 2.—Editors' note.]

nonagricultural commodities to farms. It is possible that as much as 35 per cent of the $214,000,000 should be assigned to the social saving induced by railroads in transporting products of mines, forests, and factories. If the "pure" agricultural social saving is about $140,000,000, then extrapolation to the total saving on the basis of ton-miles yields an α estimate of $560,000,000 or 4.7 per cent of gross national product. This result, taken together with the earlier comments on the upward bias of such an extrapolation, suggests that careful study will yield an α estimate for all commodities that is well below 5 per cent of gross national product.[5]

---

[5] For theoretical reasons previously discussed, the α concept of the social saving developed in chapter II can only provide an upper bound to the true social saving. Of course many upper bounds are possible; the task is to find the least upper bound compatible with theoretical and data limitations.

In applying the α concept of the social saving to all items carried by railroads in the year 1860, Albert Fishlow [*1*, chap. II] produced an estimate equal to about 5 per cent of gross national product. His estimate of the agricultural saving alone is about two and one-half per cent of gross national product. This result may seem to be in contradiction with the lower figures put forth here, especially since it is clear that the social saving increased over time.

The seeming contradiction is explained by the fact that in order to avoid the introduction of downward biases, Fishlow chose figures which, to quote him, made his estimate of the benefit of railroads "quite generous." Moreover, Fishlow did not take account of the reduction in water and wagon costs that could have been achieved by an extension of the canal system and improvements in common roads. Hence his computation of an α type estimate contains upward biases that put it well above a least upper bound.

Fishlow did attempt to compute an unbiased estimate of the social saving for agricultural commodities. This estimate is based on the assumption that the change in the value of agricultural land between 1850 and 1860 reflects the increase in national income attributable to railroads. If the circumstances of the situation examined by Fishlow approximated a partial equilibrium model, the assumption would be appropriate. (Cf. *2*, chap. IV) However when 10,000 miles of railroads are introduced and make supramarginal a land area equal to one third of that previously in use, conclusions derived from a partial equilibrium rent model do not apply. Under such conditions a general equilibrium model must be used. It can be shown that in a general equilibrium model the change in agricultural rent arising from a reduction in transport costs may be less than, greater than, or equal to the change in income originating in agriculture. Indeed it is entirely

Ultimate judgment of the primary effect of railroads on American economic growth must not only await the computation of the social saving on nonagricultural items; it must also await research on the likelihood that the existing scientific and technological knowledge would have allowed society to find more effective substitutes for the railroad than were examined here. The most interesting possibility is that in the absence of railroads, motor vehicles would have been introduced at an earlier date than they actually were. Another alternative is that inland navigation could have been kept open throughout the year. No less an engineer than R. H. Thurston pronounced as feasible a plan to keep the Erie Canal in operation during the winter by the application of artificially generated heat. He put the cost of such a scheme at $4800 per mile. At this rate a canal system of 10,000 miles could have been kept in operation throughout the year for less than two thirds of the inventory charges indicated for the compensation of interruptions in shipping agricultural products. The capacity of the economy to have adjusted to the absence of railroads cannot be fully ascertained without further research in the engineering and scientific literature of the nineteenth century.

THE DERIVED EFFECTS

To facilitate discussion the derived effects of railroads will be divided into two groups. The term "disembodied" will be applied to those consequences that followed from the saving in transportation costs per se and which would have been induced by any innovation that lowered transportation costs by approximately the amount attributed to railroads. The term "embodied" will be applied to those consequences that are attributable to the specific form in which railroads provided cheap transportation services.

The Relationship Between the Primary and Derived Effects

If it is assumed that the existence of railroads did not alter the stock of resources (e.g., the

---

possible that the effect of railroads per se was to reduce land rents and that the observed rise is attributable entirely to the increase in capital and labor that took place between 1850 and 1860. Without information on elasticities of substitution one cannot disentangle the effect of the introduction of railroads from the effect of changes in other endowments.

territory of the United States) then the combined inter- and intraregional (α) social saving of $214,000,000 may be interpreted as an upper limit estimate of the amount by which railroads changed the production potential of the economy through a reduction in the cost of transporting agricultural products per se. As such, the social saving subsumes all of the disembodied effects of railroads. In particular, the social saving includes all of the increase in national income attributable to regional specialization in agriculture induced by the decline in shipping costs. Based as it is on actual outputs and shipments, the social saving represents the increased cost of transportation that the nation would have incurred if, in the absence of railroads, it attempted to maintain the pattern of production and distribution that actually existed in 1890. In other words by increasing its transportation bill on agricultural commodities by the amount of the social saving, the nation could have reaped all of the benefits of regional agricultural specialization and trade in the absence of railroads that it obtained with them. Hence the nation need not have been saddled with a geographic locus of production that reduced national income by more than the social saving.[6]

Of course the social saving may exclude some disembodied effects because the stock of resources was altered by the existence of railroads. It has been suggested that without railroads the nation's income potential would have fallen not merely because the rise in transportation costs would have diverted resources from other productive activities but also because the rise in costs would have reduced the rate of growth of population. A decline of potential income by $214,000,000

with the 1890 population of 63,000,000 held constant implies a fall in per capita income of about $3.40, i.e., a decline from about $190 per capita to somewhat under $187 per capita. The contention that the absence of railroads would have reduced population, then, is based on the hypothesis that the rate of growth of the American population was a positive function of the level of per capita income.

But the empirical support for this hypothesis is slender. The population of the United States grew at a higher rate between 1800 and 1850 than between 1850 and 1900, although both the level and rates of growth of per capita income were substantially higher in the latter period than in the former one. While the crude death rate fell during the nineteenth century, the crude birth rate fell even more rapidly. The consequence was a substantial decline in the American reproduction rate. Since the same pattern was evident in the industrialized countries of Europe, one might well argue that—at least with respect to natural reproduction—a decrease in per capita income induced by the absence of railroads would have increased rather than retarded the rate of population growth.

The exact relationship between the rate of immigration and the level of per capita income in both the United States and the countries of emigration has not yet been clearly established. Nevertheless even if it is granted that immigration into the United States was strongly and positively correlated with the differential in per capita income, it by no means follows that the absence of railroads would have reduced immigration. The social saving implies a fall in the average income level of the United States relative to the rest of the world because the social saving was computed on the assumption that only the United States would have been deprived of railroads. This assumption obviously biases the estimated social saving upward. Given the highly favorable situation of the United States with respect to navigable waterways, it is possible that in a situation in which all nations were deprived of railroads, income would have fallen less in the United States than in the rest of the world. Under these conditions the suggested relationship between migration and income levels implies that the absence of railroads would have increased American immigration. Indeed at this point one cannot rule out the possibility that in a world forced to rely on water and wagon

---

[6] The normal operation of the market would have generated forces that led the economy to a geographic distribution of agriculture consistent with the production frontier implied by the social saving. Whenever the exploitation of land became so intensive that the marginal product of labor and capital in the East fell below that in the West by more than the extra cost of transporting Western goods, the opportunity to increase profits would have directed resources to the more productive territories. As Kent Healy has pointed out, the shift of population into the West did not wait for the coming of the iron horse. By 1840 "before a single railroad had penetrated that area from the coast, some 40 per cent of the nation's people lived west of New York, Pennsylvania and the coastal states of the South" [*3*, pp. 130–131].

transportation, the American advantage would have been so great that the turn in its terms of trade with the rest of the world would have more than offset the increased cost of transportation.

It may be that the decisive feature of the railroad's contribution to economic growth was not that it allowed society to produce transportaion service at a much lower cost than would otherwise have been possible but that it embodied low-cost service in a distinctive and uniquely important form. Although other mediums may also have been able to provide cheap transportation, the optimum geographic locus of activity in railroad and nonrailroad economies might have differed. In the absence of railroads the spatial distribution of population could have been altered in a manner unfavorable to economic growth. Under a changed dwelling pattern people given to extravagance might have received a larger share of the nation's income and thus retarded the accumulation of capital. Moreover changes in the climatic or physiographic environment of sections of the population could have altered the way in which they allocated their time between leisure and income-producing activities. Such embodied consequences would not be subsumed by the estimates of the social saving given above.

Leaving aside disputes regarding the role of climatic conditions in economic growth, the force of this line of argument is undermined by the findings of Chapter III. Chapter III reveals that in the absence of railroads, extensions of canals and improvements in wagon roads would have kept in use all but 4 per cent of the land actually worked in 1890. Such a limited reduction in the supply of land leaves scant scope for alterations in the geographic locus of economic activity— hardly enough scope to warrant the assumption that aggregate propensities for saving and leisure would have been significantly altered by railroad-induced changes in the physiographic or climatic environment of the population.

One could also argue that shifts in political circumstances and social institutions would have reduced the production potential of the economy beyond the level indicated by the social saving. Thus one might conjecture that railroads gave the North a crucial edge in the Civil War—that in the absence of railroads Northern generals would not have developed a strategy capable of defeating the insurrec-

tion. It might be further argued that a Southern victory would have saddled the nation with institutional arrangements—such as slavery—that inhibited the growth of productivity in agriculture and in other sectors of the economy. While the possibility of such a course of development may be worth investigating, the currently available evidence is too tenuous to make this conjecture an acceptable basis for believing that national income would have fallen by more than the social saving. In the light of current knowledge one could just as well argue that in the absence of railroads the West would have been more closely allied with the South and hence a military conflict would have been avoided. It could be further asserted that whatever the moral repugnance and inefficiencies of slavery, the consequences of its continuation would not have reduced economic growth as much as did the destruction of resources and the disruption of Southern agriculture caused by the Civil War. The axiom of indispensability cannot be resurrected on sociopolitical grounds without stronger evidence than is now available.

The "Take-Off" Thesis

Perhaps the most persuasive theory of embodied consequences is the one which holds that the inputs required for railroad construction induced the rise of industries, techniques, and skills essential to economic growth. According to Rostow [4] the growth of America's modern basic industrial sectors can be traced directly to the requirements for building and, especially, maintaining the railway system. Through their demand for coal, iron, machinery, and other manufactured goods railroads are supposed to have ushered the United States into a unique period of structural transformation that built modern growth into the economy. Rostow calls this period of radical transformation the "take-off into self-sustained growth." He holds that it occcurred between 1843 and 1860.

At first sight it might appear that available data support Rostow's contention that the eighteen years from 1843 through 1860 witnessed a unique structural transformation in the economy. According to data compiled by Robert Gallman the manufacturing share of commodity output increased from 21.1 per cent to 32.0 per cent over a period closely approximating the one singled out by Rostow

—1844 through 1859. While this shift towards manufacturing is impressive, averaging 3.6 percentage points per quinquennium, it is by no means unique. Gallman's series extends from 1839 to 1899. Of the 12 quinquennia included in the study, the manufacturing share increased by 3.0 points or more in half. However only one of these high-rate-of-change periods falls during Rostow's "take-off" years. Four belong to the epoch following the Civil War. Indeed the increase in the manufacturing share during the fifteen years from 1879 to 1894 exceeded that of 1844–1859 by 50 per cent.

Unfortunately there is no aggregate measure equivalent to Gallman's for the period prior to 1839. Available information indicates, however, that the decade of the 1820s may have witnessed a shift toward manufacturing comparable to that observed for the "take-off" years. This possibility is supported by the sharp decline in the home manufacture of consumer's goods and by the fact that urban population increased at twice the rate of the population as a whole. It is also buttressed by the rapid rise of the cotton textile and iron industries. The production of cotton cloth increased by over 500 per cent between 1820 and 1831. In the latter year the output of textiles was 40 per cent greater in America than it had been in Great Britain at the close of its "take-off." The growth of iron production outstripped that of cotton. The output of pig iron increased from 20,000 tons in 1820 to 192,000 tons in 1830, a rise of nearly 900 per cent. By 1830 iron, like textiles, was a substantial industry. In this branch of manufacture, too, American production in 1830 exceeded British production at the close of the era that Rostow designated as the British "take-off."

The development of cotton textiles and iron during the 1820s was so rapid that even if all other commodity-producing sectors grew no faster than the population, the manufacturing share of commodity output would have increased by 1.5 percentage points. And if manufacturing industries other than iron and cotton grew at three times the rate of population, the manufacturing share in commodity output would have risen by nearly 6 percentage points. Since the production of woolen textiles, carpets, paper, primary refined lead, sugar, and meat packing expanded from three to twenty-five times as rapidly as the population, the last alternative seems quite reasonable.

Available evidence thus tends to controvert the view that the period from 1843 to 1860 or any other eighteen-year period was one of unique structural change. Instead the data suggest a process of more or less continuous increase in the absolute and relative size of manufacturing extending from 1820— a good argument can be made for viewing 1807 as the starting date—through the end of the century.

The doubt attached to Rostow's dictum on the existence of very short periods of decisive structural transformation does not imply that historians must abandon the concept of "industrial revolution." One should not, however, require a revolution to have the swiftness of a coup d'etat. That manufacturing accounted for about 10 per cent of commodity production in 1820 and 48 per cent in 1889 is certainly evidence of a dramatic change in what was, by historical standards, hardly more than a moment of time. One need not arbitrarily abstract eighteen years out of a continuum to uphold the use of a venerable term.

If the growth of manufacturing during the two decades prior to the Civil War was not the crossing of the Rubicon pictured by Rostow, it was nonetheless large and impressive. The question of the relationship between this growth and the materials required for the construction and maintenance of railroads still remains.

The Iron Industry

Iron is the most frequently cited example of an industry whose rise was dominated by railroads. Hofstadter, Miller, and Aaron, for example, report that the railroad was "by far the biggest user of iron in the 1850s" and that by 1860 "more than half the iron produced annually in the United States went into rails" and associated items. Such reports, however, are not based on systematic measurements but on questionable inferences derived from isolated scraps of data. Casual procedures have led to the use of an index that grossly exaggerates the rail share, to the neglect of the rerolling process, and to a failure to consider the significance of the scrapping process.

The systematic reconstruction of the position of rails in the market for iron requires the development of a model of rail consumption that incorporates the largest number of available data fragments in an internally consistent manner. A model which meets this specification involves the following variables:

R_t = tons of rails consumed in year t

R_{dt} = tons of rails produced domestically in year t

R_{ft} = tons of rails imported in year t

R_{jt} = tons of worn rails scrapped in year t

M_t = track-miles of rails laid in year t; a track-mile of rails is defined as one half of the miles of rails in a mile of single track.

w_t = the average weight of rails in year t per track-mile of rails laid in year t; i.e., $w_t = R_t/M_t$

M_{st} = track-miles of rails used in the construction of new single track in year t

M_{et} = track-miles of rails used in the construction of new extra track in year t; extra track refers to second and third tracks on a given line, sidings, etc.

M_{rt} = track-miles of rails used in the replacement of worn out rails in year t

t = time measured in years

The model can be set forth as follows:

$$R_t = M_t w_t \tag{1}$$

$$R_{dt} = R_t - R_{ft} \tag{2}$$

$$M_t = M_{st} + M_{et} + M_{rt} \tag{3}$$

$$\frac{\sum_0^t M_{et}}{\sum_0^t M_{st}} = \alpha_t \tag{4}$$

$$M_{rt} = \beta_1 M_{t-1} + \beta_2 M_{t-2} + \ldots + \beta_n M_{t-n} \quad \sum \beta_i = 1 \tag{5}$$

$$R_{jt} = \lambda_1 R_{t-1} + \lambda_2 R_{t-2} + \ldots + \lambda_n R_{t-n} \tag{6}$$

Four of the variables in these equations, w_t, R_{ft}, M_{st}, and t, are determined exogenously.

The first three equations are definitional identities. The fourth equation states that the ratio of total extra track to total single track increased linearly with time. The fifth and sixth equations state that the amount of rails replaced in any given year and the amount of scrap generated by the replacement process were functions of the rails laid in all previous years. The parameters of the fifth and sixth equations were in turn determined by the assumption that rail life was a stochastic process that could be described by a log-normal distribution with a mean of 10.5 years and a standard deviation of 3 years. This hypothesis is strongly supported by data on rail life published in the Tenth Census. Moreover the estimates produced by the model proved to be relatively insensitive to various other assumptions, consistent with the census data, regarding the parameters and form of the distribution of rail life.

Various tests indicate a high degree of conformity between estimates produced by the model and available data fragments. Thus the model is within one percentage point in predicting the iron industry's "rule-of-thumb" for the share of the track replaced during a year, within 8 per cent of the reported ratio of rails required for new consumption to total rail consumption for 1856, and within 3 per cent in predicting the average weight of rails on main track at the end of 1869. The estimates of rail consumption generated by the model for the years 1849 through 1869 are also consistent with the consumption series published by the American Iron and Steel Association.

The model does more than conform to alternative estimates. It reveals the substantial magnitude of two previously neglected processes. The first of these is replacements. The model shows that replacements became an important part of total rail consumption early in the 1840s. In fifteen of the thirty years following 1839 replacements represented more than 40 per cent of total rail requirements; in five of these years replacements accounted for more than two thirds of requirements. Moreover the variability of rail life acted like a moving average, smoothing the peaks and troughs of new construction to produce a fairly continuous and predictable increase in the amount of rails required for replacements. Hence the use of rails gave rise to a mechanism that made the demand for the product considerably more stable than it would have been if demand depended only on new construction.

The model also reveals that the scrap metal generated in the replacement process rapidly became a significant part of the supply of crude iron. The availability of scrap in turn spurred the development of the rerolling of old rails. As early as 1849 one fourth of all domestically produced rails were rerolled from discarded ones. By 1860 rerolling accounted for nearly 60 per cent of domestic production. Thus although replacements rapidly became a substantial part of total rail consumption, replacement demand had little effect on the growth of blast furnaces. Replacements generated their own supply of crude iron. And scrapped rails that were not rerolled supplanted pig iron as an input in the production of other products. Consequently the net addition to pig iron production required for rails between 1840 and 1860 amounted to less than 5 per cent of the output of blast furnaces.

The significance of railroads appears somewhat greater if account is taken of all forms of railroad consumption of iron from all sectors of the iron industry. On this basis railroads accounted for an average of 17 per cent of total iron production during the two decades in question. While it is true that the railroad share rose to 25 per cent in the final six years of the period, what is more germane to the evaluation of the Rostow thesis is the fact that during the quinquennium ending in 1849, railroad consumption of domestic crude iron was just 10 per cent of the total. Even if there had been no production of rails or railroad equipment whatsoever, the domestic crude iron consumed by the iron industry would have reached an average of 700,000 tons in the second quinquennium. The rise over the previous quinquennium would still have been 338,000 tons—an increase of 94 per cent as opposed to the 99 per cent rise that took place with the railroads. Clearly railroad consumption of iron had little effect on the rate of growth of the industry during the crucial first decade of Rostow's "take-off" period; the new high level of production attained by the iron industry during 1845–1849 did not depend on the railroad market.

The strongest statement that can be made in support of Rostow's thesis is that the demand for railroad iron played an increasingly important role during the fifties in maintaining the *previous* level of production when the demand for other items sagged. Otherwise one could just as well argue that nails rather than rails triggered the 1845–1849 leap in iron production. Indeed in 1849 the domestic production of nails probably exceeded that of rails by over 100 per cent.

Other Industries

The position of railroads in the market for the products of other industries designated by Rostow appears equally limited. In the case of coal, direct consumption during the two decades ending in 1860 was negligible. While the pace of experimentation increased in the fifties, few coal-burning locomotives were in regular service until the last two years of the decade. Wood was the fuel that powered the land leviathan. On the second stage of demand the picture changes slightly. The iron industry was a major consumer of coal. It required 8,300,000 tons of this fuel to manufacture all of the domestic rails produced during 1840–1860 and 4,300,000 tons to manufacture the iron required for rail fastenings, locomotives, and cars. All told, railroads consumed 12,600,000 tons of coal through their purchases of rails and other products made of iron. Over the same two-decade period total coal production was 211,700,000 tons. Thus coal consumed by railroads through consumption of iron products represented less than 6 per cent of the coal produced during the "take-off."

Railroads exercised a still more modest influence on the development of the modern lumber industry—this despite the huge quantities of wood consumed as fuel and in the construction of track. The paradox is partly explained by the fact that wood burned in the fire boxes of railroad engines was not lumber. A similar consideration is involved in connection with the railroads' consumption of cross ties. Throughout the nineteenth century railroad men believed that ties hewed by axe would resist decay better than sawed ties. Consequently lumber mills supplied ties amounting to only 450,000,000 feet B. M. during the "take-off" years. This was less than one half of one per cent of all lumber production. When the lumber required for car construction is included, the figure rises by half a point to 0.96 per cent. The modest position of railroads in the market for lumber products emphasizes the scale of lumber consumption by other sectors of the economy.

The share of the output of the transportation equipment industry purchased by railroads is also surprising. From 1850 through 1860 some 26,300 miles of new track were laid. During the same time, about 3,800 locomotives, 6,400 passenger and baggage cars, and 88,600 freight cars were constructed. Yet value added in the construction of railroad equipment in 1859 was only $12,000,000 or 25.4 per cent of value added by all transportation equipment. The output of vehicles drawn by animals was still almost twice as great as the output of equipment for the celebrated iron horse.

As for other types of machinery, railroads directly consumed less than 1 per cent. Again the situation does not change appreciably if indirect purchases at more remote levels of production are considered. When the share of machinery consumed by the lumber, iron, and machine industries attributable to the railroad is added to that of transportation equipment, the railroad still only accounts for about 6 per cent of machine production in 1859.

The transportation equipment, rolling mill, blast furnace, lumber, and machinery industries were the main suppliers of the manufactured goods purchased by railroads. Using value added as a measure, railroads purchased slightly less than 11 per cent of the combined output of the group in 1859. Since these industries accounted for 26 per cent of all manufacturing in that year, railroad purchases from them amounted to a mere 2.8 per cent of the total output of the manufacturing sector. Railroad purchases from all the other manufacturing industries raise the last figure to just 3.9 per cent. This amount hardly seems large enough to attribute the rapid growth of manufacturing during the last two ante-bellum decades to the "requirements for building and, especially, for maintaining substantial railway systems."

IMPLICATIONS FOR THE THEORY OF ECONOMIC GROWTH

The most important implication of this study is that no single innovation was vital for economic growth during the nineteenth century. Certainly if any innovation had title to such distinction it was the railroad. Yet despite its dramatically rapid and massive growth over a period of a half century, despite its eventual ubiquity in inland transportation, despite its devouring appetite for capital, despite its power to determine the outcome of commercial (and sometimes political) competition, the railroad did not make an overwhelming contribution to the production potential of the economy.

Economic growth was a consequence of the knowledge acquired in the course of the scientific revolution of the seventeenth, eighteenth, and nineteenth centuries. This knowledge provided the basis for a multiplicity of innovations that were applied to a broad spectrum of economic processes. The effectiveness of the new innovations was facilitated by political, geographic, and social rearrangements. All of these developments began before the birth of the railroad and the railroad was not needed for the transformation in economic life that followed from them.

The English Industrial Revolution did not wait for the coming of the iron horse. It was virtually completed before the first railroad was built. The millions that migrated to the American West before 1840 did not do so because they anticipated the windfall gains that the incipient competitor to waterways would bring. They moved to the West because even without railroads the growth of population and capital in Europe and the eastern portions of the United States made investments in the new lands more profitable than a comparable investment in the old ones. It was the heavy demand for nails, stoves, and various forms of cast iron rather than rails that elicited the leap in the American production of pig iron during the 1840s. The acceleration in urbanization that paralleled the rapid expansion of industry and commerce also preceded the railroads. And the large market for their products that Eastern textile firms found in upstate New York before 1835, and in territories further to the West before 1840, were reached by waterways and wagons.

The railroad—like the improvement of the steam engine, the mechanization of textile production, the development of refrigeration, or the introduction of the puddling and rolling process—was a part rather than a condition for the Industrial Revolution. Along with a series of other inventions, it emerged out of a widespread effort to apply scientific and technological knowledge to the improvement of products and the reduction of costs. This search for new methods was distinguished not only by the vigor with which it was pursued but also by the fact that it frequently yielded more than one solution. Arkwright and Hargreaves separately invented different spinning machines. Bessemer and the Siemens brothers found alternative ways of producing cheap steel. Watt relied on the sun and planet while Pickard used the crank and connecting rod to transform reciprocating into rotary motion. In transportation, too, the search for cheap sources of service yielded more than one solution.

If correct, this stress on the multiplicity of solutions along a wide front of production problems clashes with the notion that economic growth can be explained by leading sector concepts. Such concepts suggest that the search for, or discovery of, new solutions was limited to narrowly selected industries and that growth in other sectors had to wait for breakthroughs in the anointed ones. It is the hero theory of history applied to things rather than persons. In the American case virtually every two-digit manufacturing industry was experiencing rapid growth during the last two decades of the ante-bellum era. The observed growth was not induced by a single technological change that linked all manufacturing enterprises to the railroad, like a string of freight cars attached to a locomotive. Rather it was induced by a multiplicity of innovations in these industries coupled with a series of cost saving developments in transportation as well as developments on the demand side that served to expand markets (accelerated population growth in Europe, rapid urbanization, etc.).

This view makes growth the consequence not of one or a few lucky discoveries but of a broad supply of opportunity created by the body of knowledge accumulated·over all preceding centuries. Luck may have determined which breakthroughs came first or which of the many possible solutions was seized by society. It may have affected the timing of particular innovations and the relative rates of growth of particular industries. Chance factors no doubt affected the precise path that growth followed. But chance operated within the set of opportunities created by the scientific revolution.

The theory of overwhelming, singular innovations has probably been fostered by the modus operandi of competitive economies. Under competition firms tend to choose the most efficient of the available methods of production. Alternatives that could perform the same functions at somewhat greater cost are discarded and escape public attention. The absence from view of slightly less efficient processes creates the illusion that no alternatives exist. This illusion is heightened by the fact that the chosen process has an optimal set of institutional arrangements, appurtenances, and personnel. Given the fact that the

operation of the economy has adjusted to the selected process, business success will frequently depend on the speed and effectiveness with which firms adopt these supplementary arrangements. Thus accessories of the innovation become *conditionally* indispensable and add to the impression of the massive and overwhelming character of the basic selection. Yet these accessories—in the case of railroads they were such things as automatic coupling devices, block signals, fast freight services, time tables, types of rails, varieties of freight cars, geographic locations—usually make no independent contribution. They are merely the conditions under which the primary innovation operates and through which it imparts its contribution to economic growth.

Emphasis on the multiplicity of opportunities does not mean that the particular nature of the solutions society selects are without significance. Cheap inland transportation was a necessary condition for economic growth. Satisfaction of this condition did not entail a specific form of transportation. The form by which the condition was in fact satisfied did effect, however, particular features of the observed growth process. It determined the names of some of the chief decision makers, it added new products to the bill of output, and it modified the location of economic activity. Changes of this sort defined a particular path of economic growth, a path distinct from that which would have been followed if society had embraced some other solution. In other words the fact that the condition of cheap transportation was satisfied by one innovation rather than another determined, not whether growth would take place, but which of many possible growth paths would be followed.

REFERENCES

1. Albert Fishlow, *American Railroads and the Transformation of the Ante-Bellum Economy*, Cambridge, Harvard University Press, 1965.

2. Robert W. Fogel, *The Union Pacific Railroad: A Case in Premature Enterprise*, Baltimore, Johns Hopkins Press, 1960. (The chapter referred to is reprinted below as essay 31.)

3. Kent T. Healy, "American Transportation Before the Civil War," Harold F. Williamson, ed., *The Growth of the American Economy*, Englewood Cliffs, N.J., Prentice-Hall, 1951, pp. 116–132.

4. Walt Whitman Rostow, *The Stages of Economic Growth*, Cambridge, University Press, 1960.

IV THE DIFFUSION OF NEW TECHNOLOGY

Historians have tended to identify the onset of rapid growth in particular industries with the dates of the major inventions associated with these industries. The essays in Part III cast doubt on this oversimplified view of industrial expansion. For in at least some industries it was changes in demand, rather than in technological efficiency, that dominated their growth. Moreover it cannot be assumed that rapid advances in technological efficiency coincided with the dates of major new inventions. In the case of ocean shipping, Douglass North (essay 12) found that a rapid and protracted increase in total factor productivity took place despite the absence of a single major new invention. According to North the rise of efficiency was due largely to the change in the proportion of large ships in the Atlantic fleet. This diffusion of large ships was set off, not by new technological knowledge, but by a change in institutional conditions.

Even when the growth of an industry is dominated by one or more inventions, it is wrong to assume that the economic impact of these inventions coincides with, or immediately follows, the date of the invention. Quite the contrary. The interval between an invention and its commercial application (i.e., between invention and innovation) is usually quite protracted. As Zvi Griliches points out in essay 15, the idea of breeding modern hybrid corn goes back at least to 1918. But it was not until nearly two decades later that farmers in any state began raising hybrid corn in commercial quantities. And in some states the interval between the invention and the innovation was three decades. Hybrid corn is not an isolated example. An investigation of 46 products and processes in a variety of industries revealed that the span between invention and innovation averaged about 14 years. However in some cases (fluorescent lamps, the cotton picker, the gyrocompass) the interval was in excess of 50 years, while in other cases (DDT, long-playing records, the spinning mule) it was under 5 years [1, pp. 305, 307].

Students of the diffusion process also have noted that there is usually a further lapse of time between the commercial application of an invention and its general adoption by the firms which make up an industry or a geographic region. This point is well illustrated by the history of the mechanical reaper. The first sale of that machine was in 1833. Yet as Paul David states in essay 16, thirteen years later accumulated sales were still substantially under 1000. The market for the reaper did not really begin to flourish until the end of the decade of the forties. Then during the eight-year period which began in 1850, a total of 69,700 machines were sold. In the case of hybrid corn, Griliches found that the elapsed interval between 20 per cent adoption and 80 per cent adoption by farmers was 3 years in Iowa and 8 years in Alabama. The pattern is by no means limited to agriculture. According to Edwin Mansfield, 15 years elapsed between the innovation of the by-product coke oven and its adoption by 50 per cent of the major producers of pig iron [2, p. 136]. In essay 17 Peter Temin examines the diffusion of the steam engine in 1838. He finds that the rate of adoption varied widely among industries.

Consequently the effect of an invention on the economic efficiency of an industry depends not merely on its cost reducing potential but also on the rapidity with which the invention is applied and diffuses through the industry. The essays of Part IV are concerned with the determinants of the rate of diffusion of three major inventions: hybrid corn, the mechanical reaper, and the steam engine.

REFERENCES

1. John L. Enos, "Invention and Innovation in the Petroleum Refining Industry," Universities —National Bureau Committee for Economic Research, *The Rate and Direction of Inventive Activity: Economic and Social Factors*, Princeton, Princeton University Press, 1962, pp. 299–321.
2. Edwin Mansfield, *Industrial Research and Technological Innovation: An Econometric Analysis*, New York, W. W. Norton, 1968.

15 HYBRID CORN AND THE ECONOMICS OF INNOVATION

Zvi Griliches

The idea that a cross between plants that are genetically unlike can produce a plant of greater vigor and yield than either of the parental lines dates back to Darwin and earlier. Serious research on hybrid corn, however, did not begin until the first years of this century, and the first application of research results on a substantial commercial scale was not begun until the early 1930s. During the last 25 years the change from open pollination to hybrid seeds has spread rapidly through the Corn Belt, and from the Corn Belt to the rest of the nation. The pattern of diffusion of hybrid corn, however, has been characterized by marked geographic differences. As shown in Fig. 1, some regions began to use hybrid corn much earlier than others, and some regions, once the shift began, made the transition much more rapidly than others. For example, Iowa farmers began planting hybrid corn earlier than did Alabama farmers, and Iowa farmers increased their acreage in hybrid

Reprinted with revisions by permission from *Science, 132* (July 29, 1960), 275–280.

corn from 10 to 90 per cent more rapidly than did Alabama farmers.

Although the explanation of area differences in the pattern of diffusion of hybrid corn constitutes the main contribution of the study reported here,[1] it is worth drawing attention first to the striking similarity in the general pattern of diffusion of hybrid seed in the various areas. Almost everywhere the development followed an S-shaped growth curve. As illustrated in Figure 1, the rate of

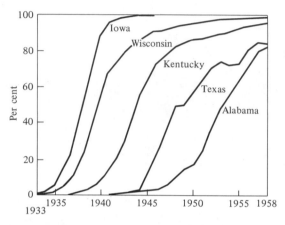

Figure 1. Percentage of All Corn Acreage Planted to Hybrid Seed.

change is slow at first, accelerating until it reaches its peak, at approximately the midpoint of development, and then slowing down again as the development approaches its final level.[2] Interestingly enough this pattern of development also applies to increases in the use of farm equipment—combines, corn pickers, pickup balers, and field forage harvesters. Similar patterns occur in the use of new drugs by doctors and in the diffusion of other new items or ideas. Thus the data on hybrid corn and other technical changes in U.S. agriculture support the general finding that the pattern of technical change is S-shaped.

Although the finding that technical change follows this pattern is not very surprising or new, it is very useful. It allows us to summarize large bodies of data on the basis of three

major characteristics (parameters) of a diffusion pattern: the date of beginning (origin), relative speed (slope), and final level (ceiling). The interesting question then is, given this general S-shape, what determines the differences among areas in the origin, slope, and ceiling? Why were some areas ahead of others in first using hybrid corn? Why did hybrid corn spread faster in some areas than in others? Why did some areas reach higher levels of equilibrium than others?

Date of Availability

Although the *idea* of breeding hybrid corn as we know it today goes back at least to 1918, to D. F. Jones and the double cross, the dates at which superior hybrids actually became available in different areas varied widely. Hybrid corn was not a once-and-for-all innovation that could be adopted everywhere, rather it was an invention of a new method of innovating, a method of developing superior strains of corn for specific localities. The actual process of developing superior hybrids had to be carried out separately for each locality. It is important to remember this fact before one blames, for example, the Southern farmers for being slow to plant hybrid corn. Although superior hybrids became available in the Corn Belt in the early 1930s, it was only in the middle of the 1940s that good hybrids began to appear in the South. Thus the date for a given area on which commercial quantities of superior hybrid seed were first produced is one of the major determinants of the development in that area.

We can take the date on which an area began planting 10 per cent of its corn acreage to hybrid corn as the date on which superior hybrids became available to farmers in commercial quantities. As shown in Fig. 2, different areas in the United States reached the 10 per cent level on different dates. For example, this level was reached in 1936 in some parts of Iowa and in northern Illinois but was not reached until after 1948 in some parts of Alabama and Georgia. The usefulness of the 10 per cent level as a measure of the commercial availability of hybrid corn seed is indicated by the very close correspondence between this and an alternative measure. From records of state yield tests and from other publications it is possible to determine in what year hybrids first outyielded open-pollinated varieties by a substantial margin in a given locality.

---

[1] A more detailed and technical account of this study can be found in [*1*].

[2] In [*1*] I show that the data fit the logistic growth curve very well. Unpublished data by small subdivision—county and crop-reporting districts—give essentially the same picture, though the development is somewhat more irregular in the marginal corn areas.

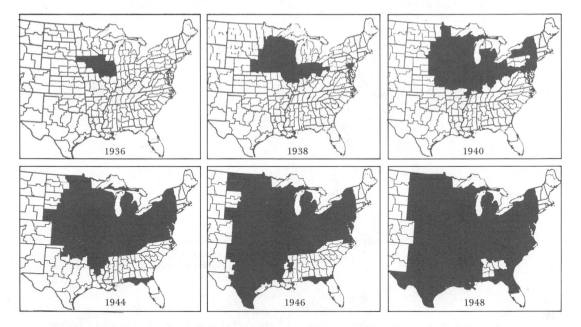

Figure 2. The Spread of Hybrid Corn: Areas that Planted 10 or More Per Cent of Their Corn Acreage to Hybrid Seed in Specified Years.

The "10 per cent" definition used in this study has a .93 Spearman rank correlation coefficient with the "technical" definition.

Area differences in date of first planting of hybrid corn can be explained in terms of differences in date of availability of hybrid corn seed. Area differences in date of availability, in turn, can be explained, in part, in terms of some simple economic factors. Innovators among the seed producers first entered those areas where the expected profits from the commercial production of hybrid corn seed were largest. They entered the "good" areas ahead of the "poor" ones. It is no accident that, though the major innovation occurred in Connecticut, commercial development began in the heart of the Corn Belt where the potential market—farmers who buy and plant corn seed—was largest. The profits that seed producers can expect to make in a given region depend upon the size of the market for corn seed in that region and the cost of entry in that region.

Market Density and Cost of Entry

The close correlation for an area between the date of availability of hybrid corn seed and the market for corn seed may be seen by comparing Fig. 2 with two reasonable measures of the market. The first measure is the density of corn acreage in 1949, shown in Fig. 3; the second measure is the density of corn pickers in use on farms, shown in Fig. 4 (the second measure is the better index of the "goodness" of a corn area and provides the best simple outline of the Corn Belt). This correlation is also demonstrated by plotting the date of entry of hybrid-seed producers into an area, as measured by the date on which farmers devoted 10 per cent of their corn acreage to hybrid corn, against the average market density of the area. As shown in Fig. 5 the lower the market density, the later the date of entry into a given area. The rank correlation is high (.7), and even higher (.9) if the Southeast is excluded from the computations. The Southeast is a special case. It was entered later because of the relative lateness of the research contributions by the region's experiment stations and the obstacles put in the way of private seed companies in that area. Moreover when one gets down to a certain low level it does not really pay to discriminate between areas on the basis of their relative market densities, and other variables become more significant.

Deviations in the correlation between the spread of hybrid corn and the distribution of the market can be explained by the cost of entry factor. Cost of entry depends, among

CORN FOR ALL PURPOSES
Acreage, 1949

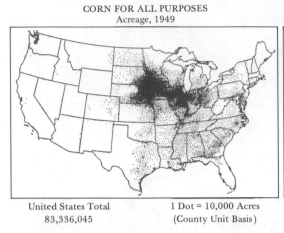

United States Total
83,336,045

1 Dot = 10,000 Acres
(County Unit Basis)

Figure 3. The Market for Hybrid Seed.

CORN PICKERS
Number of Farms Reporting, April 1, 1950

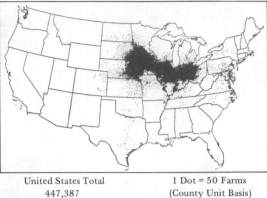

United States Total
447,387

1 Dot = 50 Farms
(County Unit Basis)

Figure 4. Corn Pickers on Farms, 1950. This is a better index than corn acreage of the "goodness" of an area with respect to corn growing and provides the best single outline of the Corn Belt.

other things, on how different the area is from those already entered, and on whether experiment stations have already developed inbred lines and whole hybrids adaptable to the area. Study of Figs. 2, 3, and 4 shows first that the spread was much faster latitudinally than it was longitudinally. The reason, in part, is that an important factor determining the range of adaptability of a particular hybrid is the length of the growing season. To a large extent this is a function of latitude, and as one moves east or west the chances that the same hybrid will be adaptable to new areas are much higher than they are if one moves north or south. Nevertheless the movement north seems to have been faster than the movement

Figure 5. Average Market Density by Date of Entry: Corn Acres as a Percentage of Land in Farms for Crop-Reporting Districts Reaching 10 Per Cent Use of Hybrid Seed Corn in a Specified Year.

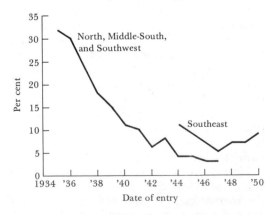

south. This is partly because of the larger markets in the North but is also a reflection of the special contributions of the Minnesota and Wisconsin agricultural experiment stations. They entered hybrid corn research very early in the game and contributed a great deal more than one would have expected from them just on the basis of the relative importance of corn in their states. Similarly, the contributions of Texas, Louisiana, and Florida stations came earlier and were relatively larger than those of the other stations in the South, which produced little of importance till the middle 1940s. This would explain to some extent why hybrid corn moved into the Southwest before it did into the Southeast. Moreover quite a few of the Corn Belt inbreds and hybrids proved adaptable in the Southwest. It was more like the Corn Belt than was the Southeast, and it did not suffer to the same extent from insect and disease problems that corn-breeders in the Southeast had to deal with.

Since cost factors in areas that are close together are likely to be similar, we may assume that entry into the neighborhood of an area makes entry into the area itself more likely, and thus we may use the earliest date of entry into any of the immediately neighboring areas as a proxy variable for the cost of entry into the given area. This variable and the measure of market density, taken together, explain to a large extent the variability in the dates on which hybrid corn was introduced in different parts of the country and support the statement that the innovators were influenced by considerations of profit, entering those areas first where the expected profits from innovation were highest.

Rates of Acceptance

The rate at which farmers in a region accepted hybrids, once hybrid corn became available, also varied from area to area. This rate was highest in Iowa and the surrounding area and lowest in some of the areas of the Southeast and the Mississippi Delta states. The differences in the rates of acceptance are largely demand phenomena, not a result of different supply conditions. After the first few years, in most of the places and most of the time, the supply of seed was not the limiting factor. The rate of acceptance is taken to be the relative speed of the diffusion process—that is, it is the slope coefficient of the S-shaped curve.[3] The measure is such that a value of 1.00 means that it takes 4 years for the acreage devoted to hybrid corn to rise from 12 to 88 per cent, while a value of 0.5 implies that it would take 8 years, or twice as long, for this same rise to occur.

The rate at which farmers accept a new technique depends, among other things, on the magnitude of the profit to be realized from the change-over. This hypothesis is based, first, on the general observation that the larger the stimulus the faster the reaction to it, and, second, on the fact that in an uncertain environment it takes a shorter time to find out that there is a difference, if that difference is large.[4] Farmers doubted that this new hybrid corn was any good, and it took them some time to become convinced of its superiority. Individual farmers followed a development pattern of their own in shifting from open-pollinated to hybrid seed in planting their corn acreage. Almost no farmer planted 100 per cent of his corn acreage to hybrid seed the first time he tried it.

Yield Per Acre and Acres Per Farm

The rate at which farmers shifted to hybrid corn depends, among other things, upon the profitability of such a shift. This in turn depends upon the absolute superiority of hybrids in corn yield in bushels per acre, and on the average number of acres per farm planted to corn.

It is widely accepted that hybrids outyielded open-pollinated varieties by approximately 15 to 20 per cent and that this *percentage* superiority did not vary much between different areas. Since similar percentage increases in yield imply different absolute increases in bushels per acre in areas where the previous yields were different, a good measure of the absolute superiority of hybrids over open-pollinated varieties is given by the long-run level of corn yields in various areas. The distribution of corn yields in the United States shows strikingly close correlation with the distribution of rates of acceptance of hybrid corn. The higher the yield, the higher the rate of acceptance.

Where the rate of acceptance fails to correlate with the yield per acre, the failure can be explained by taking into account the difference in the average number of acres of corn per farm (corn acreage per farm increasing as one moves from East to West), since what is important is not only the profitability per acre but also the profitability per farm. A large fraction of the variability between areas in the rate of acceptance of hybrid corn by farmers can be explained with the help of these two "profitability" variables.

Equilibrium Level

In an analysis of the use of hybrid corn in this country, one must consider, finally, differences in the equilibrium level reached—that is, differences in the fraction of the acreage which is ultimately devoted to hybrid seed. Different levels were found in different areas of the country. By 1959 close to 100 per cent of the corn acreage in most of the Corn Belt and in its northern and eastern fringes was planted to hybrid seed. Substantially lower percentages were found only in the western fringes of the Corn Belt and in the deep South. In the South the level is still changing, moving towards an equilibrium level of approximately 70 to 80 per cent of the corn acreage planted to hybrid seed. The western parts of Nebraska, South Dakota, and Kansas have already reached their equilibrium level of approximately 30 to 60 per cent. These are areas of very low and very variable yields, where the use of hybrid seed is unprofitable

---

[3] More exactly, the measure is the slope coefficient of the logistic growth curve as adjusted for ceiling differences. For an explanation of this measure see [*1*].

[4] This is analogous to sequential sampling. The "average sample number"—that is, the expected length of the experiment—will depend, among other things, inversely on the difference between the means of the two populations being sampled and directly on their variance.

except on the better land or on land under irrigation.

Differences in the equilibrium level are explained by differences in the *average* profit to be realized from the shift to hybrid seed. In an area of high average profit no farmer faces a loss from the shift. In areas of low average profit a substantial proportion of the farmers face the possibility of having no return or even of sustaining a loss on their investment. The ceiling, or the fraction of the corn acreage that will ultimately be planted to hybrid seed, is not unique or constant. It will change with the introduction of better hybrids, with improvements in the market for corn, and with large changes in corn acreage. Nevertheless for almost all of the areas except the very marginal ones, a constant ceiling fits the data well. Variation in these ceilings across the country can be explained in good part by the same two measures of profitability: the average absolute superiority of hybrids and the average number of acres per farm planted to corn.

Relation to Studies by Sociologists

It may prove useful to relate the results of this study to earlier work by sociologists in this area. In previous analyses of similar data it was mainly individual behavior that was investigated—that is, Who are the first and who are the last to adopt hybrid corn?—and an attempt was made to explain such behavior on the basis of differences in personality, education, economic status, and social environment. An attempt to use some of these variables (for example, level-of-living indexes) in explaining differences between states in the rate of acceptance of hybrid corn proved unsuccessful in this study.

It is my belief that in the long run, and when the country is taken as a whole, many of these variables either do not vary enough to be significant or tend to cancel themselves out, leaving the economic variables as the major determinants of the patterns of technological changes. This does not imply that the "sociological" variables are not important if one wants to know which *individual* will be first or last to adopt a particular technique, only that these factors do not vary much from area to area. Moreover the distinction between "economic" and "sociological" variables is partly semantic, and a very difficult one to make in practice. Some of the variables used in this study—for example,

yield of corn and corn acres per farm—are closely correlated with such variables as education, level-of-living, and socioeconomic status. It is very difficult to discriminate between the validity of the assertion that hybrids were accepted slowly because it was a "poor corn area" and the assertion that the slow acceptance was due to "poor people." Poor people and poor corn are very closely correlated in the United States. Nevertheless one may find a few areas where this is not so. Obviously the slow acceptance of hybrids on the western fringes of the Corn Belt—in western Kansas, Nebraska, South Dakota, and North Dakota—does not reflect low economic status of the people but is the result of "economic factors" which make this a poor corn area.

Summary and an Implication

This study has increased our understanding of a body of data. What were originally puzzling and seemingly peculiar patterns in the data have been explained. The use of hybrid seed in an area depends, in part, upon the date at which superior hybrids become available. This date, in turn, depends upon the activities of seed producers guided by their expectations of profits, and upon the contributions of the various experimental stations. Thus the South was late in getting hybrids because the market for seed was substantially poorer there than in other areas and because Southern experiment stations produced few hybrids of importance until the middle 1940s. The use of hybrid seed in an area also depends upon the rate at which hybrids are accepted by farmers. This rate, in turn, depends upon the profit farmers expect to realize from the shift to hybrids. Thus farmers in the Corn Belt accepted hybrids at a faster rate than farmers in the South because the absolute magnitude of profit was higher in the Corn Belt than in the South. Similarly the fraction of acreage ultimately planted to hybrid seed depends upon expectations of profits to be realized from the change and the distribution of these expectations around their mean.

When uncertainty and the fact that the spread of knowledge is not instantaneous are taken into account, it appears that American seed producers and American farmers have behaved, on the whole, in a fashion consistent with the idea of profit maximization. Where the evidence appears to indicate the contrary,

I predict that a closer examination of the relevant economic variables will show that the change was not as profitable as it appeared to be.[5]

This study of hybrid corn has at least one interesting implication. Hybrid corn was an innovation which was more profitable in the "good" areas than in the "poor" areas. This probably is also a characteristic of many other innovations. Obviously tractors contribute more on large than small farms, and so forth. Hence there may be a tendency for technological change to accentuate regional disparities in levels of income and rates of growth. Moreover this tendency is reinforced by the economics of the innovation process, which results in the new techniques being supplied to the "good" areas before they are supplied to the "poorer" areas, and also in the more rapid acceptance of these techniques in the "good" areas. A lag of this sort can by itself cause long-run regional differences in levels of income. The kinds of inventions we get, and the process by which they are distributed, may lead to aggravation of the already serious problem of regional differentials in levels of income and growth.

---

[5] That these findings are not restricted to hybrid corn has been confirmed by a recent study of the spread of a series of industrial innovations (diesel locomotives, continuous mining machines, and so on) within particular industries. It was found there that (1) the logistic growth curve summarized the data well, and (2) most of the variability in the rate of acceptance of different innovations can be explained on the basis of the relative profit to be realized from the innovation and the size of the required initial investment [2].

REFERENCES

1. Zvi Griliches, "Hybrid Corn: An Exploration in the Economics of Technological Change," *Econometrica, 25* (October, 1957), 501–522.
2. Edwin Mansfield, "Technical Change and the Rate of Imitation," *Econometrica, 29* (October, 1961), 741–766.

16 THE MECHANIZATION OF REAPING IN THE ANTE-BELLUM MIDWEST

Paul A. David

I

The widespread adoption of reaping machines by Midwestern farmers during the years immediately preceding the Civil War provides a striking instance of the way that the United States' nineteenth-century industrial development was bound up with *concurrent* transformations occurring in the country's agricultural sector. On the record of historical experience, as Alexander

Reprinted, with revisions and elimination of most of the extensive footnote documentation, by permission from Henry Rosovsky, ed., *Industrialization In Two Systems: Essays in Honor of Alexander Gerschenkron*, New York, John Wiley and Sons, 1966, pp. 3–39.

Gerschenkron has cogently observed, "the hope that industry in a very backward country can unfold from its agriculture is hardly realistic." Indeed even when one considers countries that are not very backward it is unusual for agricultural activities to escape an uncomplimentary evaluation of their efficacy in creating inducements for the growth and continuing proliferation of industrial pursuits. As Albert Hirschman puts it, "Agriculture certainly stands convicted on the count of its lack of direct stimulus to the setting up of new activities through linkage effects: the superiority of manufacturing in this respect is crushing."[1] But having conceded that much regarding the general state of the world, the student of economic development in nineteenth century America is compelled to stress the anomalous character of his subject, to insist that in a resource-abundant setting, highly market-oriented, vigorously expanding, and technologically innovative agriculture did provide crucial support for the process of industrialization.

Such support in the form of sufficiently large demands for manufactures and supplies of raw material suitable for industrial processing would, undoubtedly, have been less readily forthcoming from a small, or economically backward agrarian community. It is precisely in this regard that United States industrialization may be seen as having diverged most markedly from the historical experience of continental European countries, where backward agriculture militated against gradual industrial growth, and the successful pattern of modernization of the economy tended to be characterized by an initial disengagement of manufacturing from the agrarian environment.

However to treat the generation of demand for manufactures during the process of industrialization as taking place within a framework of static, pre-existing intersectoral relations, summarized by a set of input-output coefficients, does not prove to be an entirely satisfactory way of looking at the connections between the character of agriculture and the growth of industrial activities

in the United States. Adherence to such an approach leads one, *inter alia*, to gloss over the problems of accounting for alterations in the structure of intersectoral dependences, although those alterations often constitute a vital aspect of the process of industrialization. It is not wholly surprising that pursuit of a static "linkage" approach has tended to promote the misleading notion that the expansion and modernization of the agrarian sector constituted a *temporal* precondition for rapid industrial development in the United States, whereas in many crucial respects it is far more useful to regard the two processes as having gone hand in hand. As a small contribution to the study of the interrelationship between agricultural development and industrialization in the American setting, this essay ventures to inquire into the way that—with the adoption of mechanized reaping—an important element was added to the set of linkages joining these two sectors of the mid-nineteenth-century economy.

II

The spread of manufacturing from the Eastern seaboard into the transmontane region of the United States during the 1850s derived significant impetus from the rise of a new demand for farm equipment in the states of the Old Northwest Territory. That impetus was at least partially reflected by the important position which activities supplying agricultural investment goods came to occupy in the early structure of Midwestern industry. In the still predominantly agrarian American economy of the time it is not unexpected that a substantial segment of the total income generated by industrial activities was directly attributable to the manufacture of durable producers' goods specifically identified with the farmer's needs—leaving aside the lumber and related building materials flowing into construction of farm dwellings, barns, sheds, and fences. If in addition to value added in the production of agricultural implements and machinery in 1859/60, one were also to include half the value added by the manufacture of wagons and carts, saddles and harnesses, and the variety of items turned out by blacksmiths' shops, the resulting aggregate would represent over 4 per cent of the value added by the nation's entire industrial sector. That is, rather more than the proportion contributed by the manufacture of machine

[1] The now familiar concept of "linkage effects" refers to the stimuli of cost reductions and demand expansions. These are channelled through the "forward" and "backward" linkages between a sector of the economy (or an industry) and other sectors (or industries) that buy its output and supply it with inputs, respectively.

shop and foundry products, which at the date in question ranked as the country's seventh largest industry in terms of current value added. However on the eve of the Civil War the production of agricultural implements and machinery *alone* generated just as large a proportion of total industrial value added in the preponderantly agrarian Western states; in Illinois, this single branch of manufacturing accounted for fully 8 per cent of the total value added by the state's industries in 1859/60.

To appreciate the importance of the position that the agricultural implements and machinery industry assumed in the structure of Illinois' early manufacturing sector, it must be realized that at the time there was no single branch of industry which in the nation as a whole contributed so large a portion of aggregate value added in manufacturing. Cotton goods production, America's largest industry in 1859/60, accounted for only 6.6 per cent of the national aggregate.

When one looks at a rapidly developing center of industrial activity in the Midwest such as Chicago was during the 1850s, the manufacture of agricultural implements and machinery is found to have had still greater relative importance as a generator of income. The growth of agricultural commodity-processing industries, especially meat-packing in Chicago during the latter half of the century, suggests that the Garden City's meteoric rise to the status of second manufacturing center in the nation by 1890 might be taken as a demonstration of the strength of *forward* linkages from commercial agriculture. It is not an object of the present essay to assess the validity of that impression. Nevertheless it should be remarked that during Chicago's first major spurt of industrial development, a movement which saw manufacturing employment in the city rise from less than 2000 in 1850 to approximately 10,600 by 1856, the forward-linked processing industries were less significant to the industrial life of the city than was an activity based on *backward* linkage from agriculture. The branch of manufacturing in question was the farm implements and machinery industry: in 1856 it accounted for 10.8 per cent of total value added by Chicago's industrial sector, compared with 6.3 per cent contributed by the principal processing industries, meat-packing, flour- and grist-milling, and distilling, combined [2].

Among the salient characteristics of the agricultural scene in the ante-bellum Midwest, two appear as having been crucial to the emergence during the 1850s of a substantial regional manufacturing sector bound by demand-links reaching backward from commercial agriculture. First, the settlement of the region and the extension of its agricultural capacity during that decade proceeded with great rapidity, encouraged by favorable terms of trade and improvements in transportation facilities providing interior farmers with access to distant markets in the deficit foodstuff areas to the east. Between the Seventh and the Eighth Censuses of Agriculture over a quarter of a million farming units came into existence, and about 19 million acres of improved farm land were added in Illinois, Indiana, Michigan, Iowa, and Wisconsin. This represented a rate of increase in the number of farms of 7 per cent per annum, and a 9 per cent annual rate of expansion in improved acreage.

Second, agricultural practice in this region of recent settlement was not the static crystallization of long experience typical of stable agrarian societies. Far from being a closed issue, choices among alternative production techniques were rapidly being altered and Western farming was thereby being carried in the direction of greater capital-intensity and higher labor productivity. On the eve of the Civil War this burgeoning farm community was in the midst of a hectic process of transition from hand methods to machine methods of production, from the use of rudimentary implements to reliance in increasingly sophisticated machinery. Among the items of farm equipment being introduced on a large scale in the Midwest during the 1850s were steel breakers and plows, seed drills and seed boxes, reapers and mowers, threshers, and grain separators.

The importance that the newly introduced reaping and mowing machines (especially the former) had assumed among the products of the agricultural implements and machinery industry of the Midwest by the end of the 1850s provides some indication of the direct impact of the shift to more capital-intensive farming techniques upon the expansion of an agrarian market for industrial products. According to the Census of 1860, reapers and mowers accounted for 42 per cent of the gross value of output of all agricultural implements and machinery in Illinois and for 78 per cent of the gross value of output of the corresponding industrial group in Chicago. A few years earlier, in 1856, when the Midwestern boom was still in full swing, reaper and mower production in Chicago had dominated that center's farm equipment output-mix to an even greater degree.

Despite the fact that the history of commercial production of mechanical reaping machines in the United States stretched back without interruption to the early 1830s, this industry was one that only began to flourish in the 1850s. From 1833, the date of the first sale of Obed Hussey's reaping machine, to the closing year of that decade, a total of 45 such machines had been purchased by American farmers. At the end of the 1846 harvest season Cyrus H. McCormick determined to abandon his efforts of the previous six years at manufacturing his reaping machine on the family farm in Rockbridge County, Virginia, and set about transferring the center of his activities to a more promising location, Chicago. The known previous sales of all reaping machines at that time aggregated to a mere 793, but by 1850 some 3373 reapers in all had been produced and marketed in the United States since 1833. A scant eight years later it was reckoned that roughly 73,200 reapers had been sold since 1845, fully 69,700 of them since 1850. And most of that increase had resulted from the burst of production enjoyed by the industry during the five years following 1853.

The major portion of this production had taken place in the interior of the country, and it is apparent that in the absence of farmers' readiness to substitute machinery for labor during the 1850s, an equally rapid pace of agricultural expansion—had such in fact been feasible—would have provided a considerably weaker set of demand stimuli for concurrent industrial development in the region. The latter facet of the late ante-bellum agrarian scene must, therefore, be the prime focus of our interest; it cannot be taken as a given, but must be explained. That should not, however, be regarded as a dismissal of the first-mentioned aspect of Midwestern agricultural development in this period. As shall be seen when we come to grips with the problem of explaining the mechanization movement, the speed of agricultural expansion and the substitution of machines for farm labor were intimately connected developments between which causal influences flowed in both directions.

III

In view of the consequences for agricultural and industrial development that followed from the mechanization of reaping during the 1850s, it might be supposed that this episode in the modernization of American farming and the formation of backward linkages between the enterprises of field and factory would have been thoroughly explored by economic historians. To be sure, virtually all the standard accounts of the development of agriculture in the United States up to 1860 mention the introduction of the machines that Obed Hussey and Cyrus H. McCormick had invented in the 1830s. Yet the literature remains surprisingly vague about the specific technical and economic considerations touching the adoption of these devices by American farmers. We have called attention to the fact that although the twenty years prior to 1853 had witnessed a slow, limited diffusion of the new technique, the first major wave of popular acceptance of the reaper was concentrated in the mid-1850s. Thus the intriguing question to which an answer must be given is: why only at that time were large numbers of farmers suddenly led to abandon an old, labor-intensive method of cutting their grain, and to switch to the use of a machine that had been available since its invention two decades earlier?

In this inquiry the impact of the mechanization of small grain harvesting upon U.S. agriculture is not the prime subject of concern.[2] Nevertheless it would hardly be possible to account for the upsurge of demand for reaping machinery without considering the economic implications of the new harvesting technology and the specific circumstances surrounding its introduction. The traditional story of the ante-bellum adoption of mechanical reaping, a version to be found in any number of places, e.g. [1, pp. 281–294], is set out along the following lines. During the first half of the nineteenth century arable land was abundant in the United States, but the amount of small grains (especially the amount of wheat) that an individual farmer could raise was limited by the acreage that could be harvested soon after the ripening of the crop. Labor was scarce, and harvest labor notably dear as well as unreliable in supply. Compared with the method of harvesting using the grain

---

[2] See [5] for a recent quantitative study which attributes to mechanization the major part of the increase in labor productivity in U.S. small grain production during the nineteenth century. Wheat, oats, and rye are the small grain crops considered in the present paper. [See also the essay by Parker on pp. 175–186 above.—Editors' note.]

cradle—an improvement on the sickle that had come into quite general use even in the transmontane wheat regions by the middle of the century—the new mechanical reapers effected a saving in labor. When Midwestern farmers were led to increase production as a result of the rise in wheat prices during the 1850s (a rise augmented by the impact of the Crimean War upon world grain markets), the demand for reaping machines rose, and their adoption went forward at an accelerated pace. The movement thus initiated received renewed impetus from the extreme shortage of agricultural manpower occasioned by the Civil War. By saving labor, and therein relaxing the constraint on cultivated acreage imposed by hand methods of harvesting, the introduction of the reaper made possible the rapid expansion of small grain production that occurred during the latter half of the nineteenth century.

This account may vary in some details from any particular historian's version of the events in question, but it contains all the generally accepted elements of the story. It specifically follows the historiographic tradition of ascribing to the rise in wheat prices during the 1850s a causal role in bringing about the transition from cradling to mechanical reaping prior to the outbreak of the Civil War. Upon a moment's reflection, the latter is seen to be the analytically unexpected aspect of this tale of a change in technology; it is far more usual for discussions of the choice of technique to be couched, implicitly or explicitly, in terms of the relative prices of the substitutable factors of production (grain cradlers and reaping machines in this instance) and to say nothing about the price of the commodity being produced.

Yet precisely why this departure from the classical (or, properly speaking, neoclassical) treatment of the choice between labor-intensive and capital-intensive factor proportions is called for in the case of the adoption of the mechanical reaper, is not revealed by the statement. That it remains rather ambiguous about the lines of causation linking dear labor, high grain prices, expanded production acreage, and the spreading use of the reaper must, with all diffidence, be attributed to the ambiguities of the literature from which the statement itself has been constructed.

The leading contributions to American economic history can be examined without finding any clear views as to whether it became profitable for farmers to adopt the mechanical reaper only when they found it profitable to increase the acreage of wheat sown per farm, or whether it was the expansion of grain cultivation in Midwestern agriculture as a whole that led to a general substitution of machinery for labor in harvesting operations. The literature is no less ambiguous in the answers it offers to two closely related questions. Did the adoption of mechanical reapers make rapid expansion of grain cultivation in the Midwest possible by raising the scale on which it could be profitably grown (and harvested) by individual farming units? Or was it simply that the widespread substitution of the reaper for the grain cradle alleviated the scarcity of agricultural labor which otherwise would have restricted wheat production in the newly developing Western regions to appreciably lower levels?

There is no question that mechanical reaping effected a saving in harvest labor requirements; the evidence marshalled in Leo Rogin's pathbreaking work, [6], is nothing if not conclusive on that point. Yet, to the present writer's knowledge, no systematic attempt has been made to compare the magnitude of the savings in wage costs with the capital costs of a reaper to Western farmers during the first decade of the machine's widespread adoption. It is therefore not surprising that the traditional accounts fail to divulge whether (or not) the new harvesting technique proved more profitable than grain cradling under all plausible relative factor prices, or whether (or not) it was economically superior to cradling for all scales of farm operations.

These are, indeed, crucial questions. If the answers are in the affirmative, then the rate at which the reaper replaced the cradle in Western grain fields during the 1850s depended solely upon the capacity of the agricultural machinery industry; Bidwell and Falconer's assertion that "Reapers were introduced as fast as they could be manufactured" would be more than a mere figure of speech [1, p. 293]. It would be literally true and would carry the implication that the replacement of hand-harvesting methods would have occurred much earlier in American history were it not for technically unsolvable problems of designing and manufacturing a reaping machine. One would then have to find more convincing technical obstacles than are discussed in the authoritative works on the reaper to account for the lag between the first sale of Hussey's machine in 1833, the filing of the original McCormick patent in 1834, or even the first sale of McCormick's machine in 1840, and the eventual adoption of the innovation in the 1850s (*4*, chaps. 5–10; *6*, pp. 72–75, 85–91). If the mechanical reaping technique actually was superior to hand-harvesting with the cradle, regardless of relative factor prices or scale, this would also pose something of a problem for those writers, who, like H. J. Habakkuk, regard the mechanization of agriculture in the United States as an "obvious" illustration of the labor-saving bias of American technology fostered by nineteenth-century conditions of relative labor scarcity (*3*, pp. 100–102).

It is quite clear, however, that the traditional accounts of the introduction of the reaper do not entertain such notions. By placing emphasis on the effects of rising grain prices and the extension of wheat production, they imply that altered demand for agricultural products was of fundamental significance in determining the rapid rate at which the innovation supplanted hand methods of harvesting small grains in the Midwest during the 1850s. This line of explanation, taken broadly, would suggest that the sudden growth of the market for the reaper—coming nearly two decades after the machine first began to be sold—was a consequence of the specific conditions surrounding Midwestern agricultural development towards the close of the late ante-bellum era. Even had the rise of the market for farm machinery not provided significant impetus to the initial industrialization of the region, the implications of this hypothesis for our general view of the process of the diffusion of technology would make it important to try to formulate the economics of the traditional account in a fashion sufficiently precise to permit its re-examination in the light of pertinent evidence.

Suppose, for the moment, that it is justifiable to assert that the saving of labor achieved with the mechanical reaper was not so great as to render cradling an inferior technique in all relevant factor price situations. It may then be argued that mechanization of reaping spread through the agricultural sector as a result of an alteration in factor prices which accompanied the expansion of grain cultivation in the West. In other words, the standard versions can be read as saying that the "agricultural boom" set in motion by the rising grain prices of the mid-1850s added to already existing pressures

upon the available harvest labor force in the region, drove up the farm wage rate relative to the cost of harvesting machinery, and thereby created a situation in which it became profitable for farmers to substitute machinery for labor in harvesting small grain. This argument requires the not unreasonable assumption that the supply schedule of harvest labor facing the farm sector in the Midwest was less elastic than the supply schedule for agricultural machinery; otherwise, the outward shift of the demand schedules would not have resulted in the relative price of harvest labor being raised to a level at which continuing substitution of machines for cradlers would take place. Granting that assumption, the argument may be completed by noting that as the availability of the new method of harvesting rendered the demand schedule for labor more elastic than would otherwise have been the case, substitution itself tended to check the extent of the actual rise in relative wages caused by the expansion of aggregate grain production. In this manner the use of the reaper throughout the grain regions held down the total cost of production, although it could not prevent some rise in costs, and made possible a larger volume of total output at any given level of grain prices.

For this analysis, in which mechanization appears as a change "imposed" upon grain farmers by the general expansion of Midwestern agriculture, the relative inelasticity of the farm labor supply schedule is crucial. The greater the emphasis that is placed upon the role of related competitive demands for labor, such as regional railroad construction, to cite but one significant source, the less thoroughly tied to exogenous events (e.g., the Crimean War) affecting world grain prices is the explanation offered for the timing of the adoption of mechanical reaping.

In the picture just presented, *the individual farmer's* desire to increase his acreage under wheat does not appear as influencing his decision to purchase a reaper and dispense with the services of cradlers. Nor can the personalization of the collective market process described be justified with any plausibility. Since there is no reason to suppose that the labor supply schedule facing the individual farmer was less elastic than the supply curve for agricultural machinery that confronted him, why should there be any connection between *the individual farmer's* decision to sow more wheat and his choice of the new reaping technique? Yet the literature is replete with statements suggesting such a connection: "When the wheat from an acre of land would sell for more than the price of the land, it was considered a safe investment to sow more land in wheat and buy a reaper" [1, p. 293]. "Americans also had a very strong incentive to develop machines which would enable farmers to cultivate a larger area. The alternative was to leave land uncultivated" [3, p. 101]. If such statements represent something more than illustrations of the ease with which efforts to write economic history as the intended outcome of purposive individual actions, rather than their interplay in impersonal markets, can lead to what may be called "fallacies of decomposition," their authors must have in mind a set of considerations influencing the introduction of mechanical reaping which is quite distinct from the process of market-imposed adjustments already set forth.

To put it most simply, these statements may be taken to imply either that there were significant economies of scale associated with the use of the reaper, or that diseconomies of scale existed in the use of labor for cradling grain that were not encountered with the mechanized technique, given the range of farm size relevant to the ante-bellum Midwest. Both situations would arise from the presence of indivisibilities among the inputs of the microproduction function for harvesting small grains.

In the apparent absence of feasible cooperative arrangements for sharing the use of harvesting machinery among farms, at this time the reaping machine itself constituted an indivisible input for the farmer. Since he typically had to purchase it rather than rent it when it was needed, the relevant cost of using a reaper in harvesting was the average annual cost over the life of the machine. Within a particular season, however, the cost of a reaper per acre harvested would fall as the acreage was increased. It would continue falling to the point at which the cutting capacity of a single machine during the feasible harvest was reached. By contrast, given a perfectly elastic supply of labor and no diseconomies of scale in its use, the saving in wage costs obtained by substituting the mechanical reaper for cradlers would remain constant per acre harvested. It is possible, therefore, that below some level of acreage to be harvested—which we shall call the "threshold" farm size—the total capital cost

of a reaper (or of more than one reaper) exceeded the potential reduction in wage costs, making its adoption unprofitable in comparison with the method of cradling.

Exactly where the threshold point was located in the spectrum of farm acreage devoted to the small grains was determined by relative factor prices. The saving of labor achieved with the reaper being essentially technologically fixed per acre harvested, a doubling of the total yearly reaper cost relative to the money wage cost of harvesting an acre with the cradle would double the number of acres that would have to be harvested before the costs per acre would be the same with either technique.[3] While it is conceivable that so great a saving of labor was effected by the reaper that the costs per acre harvested by machine were lower for any finite total acreage, so long as both the money wage rate and the cost of a reaper were positive and finite, the existence of *significant* economies of scale associated with mechanical harvesting cannot be taken to have been a purely technical matter; relative wage rates must not have been so high that it was profitable for the farmer to adopt the new method at any level of grain production.

In principle the existence of diseconomies of scale in the use of labor for harvesting grain with cradles would operate in the same manner as economies of scale associated with the mechanical reaper. Harvest workers required a certain amount of supervision to maintain their efficiency, and the addition of hands required to cut the grain on a larger acreage presumably taxed the farmer's supervisory capacities. The harvest had to be carried out in a limited number of days lest the ripe grain be lost through shattering or spoilage. It was therefore not feasible simply to employ the optimum number of hired hands that could be supervised at any one time for as long a period as it would take to cut the grain. Assuming that the average productivity of cradlers would begin to decline when the amount of supervision they received fell below some minimum, we may say that the manpower requirements per acre

---

[3] The relationship between the relative price of labor, vis-à-vis the reaper, and the threshold size is developed formally in Appendix A. Even without that derivation it is readily seen that if the labor cost per acre harvested by cradle is constant, threshold size must vary in direct proportion to the *relative* cost of capital.

would have been greater for larger acreages. Consequently savings in labor obtained by switching to mechanical reaping would tend to rise as the acreage to be harvested increased. Even if the capital costs of a reaper were constant per acre, this could define a threshold size beyond which farmers would find it advantageous to mechanize.

There is evidence of considerable contemporary dissatisfaction about the quality of hired help on farms during the first half of the nineteenth century, and American farmers frequently commented on the necessity of supervising temporary help in order to keep them on the job and careful in their work. But it is difficult to gauge the extent to which the inferior quality of hired help failed to reflect itself in the general level of farm wages. Moreover among the complaints registered

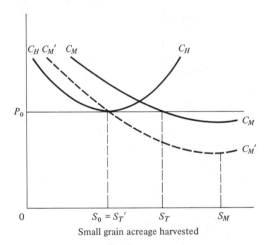

Figure 1. Hypothetical Long-Run Average Cost Curves for Harvesting.

by farmers are those specifically citing the carelessness of hired hands with machinery. If there were diseconomies of scale in the use of harvest labor, we do not know that these were restricted to the employment of cradlers rather than labor in general, and that they did not simply place a limit on the scale of farm operations in the free states. It therefore seems justifiable to restrict the discussion of scale effects to consideration of those which arose from spreading the fixed cost of harvesting machinery over large grain acreage.

Figure 1 depicts the hypothesized situation in terms of alternative long-run unit cost curves for hand methods and machine methods of grain harvesting on independent farms. The supposed existence of some fixed costs with either process causes both the

hand-method cost curve, $C_H C_H$, and the machine-method curve, $C_M C_M$, to decline over a range of total harvested acreage, but, because of the *additional* fixed cost entailed by the reaper, the curve $C_M C_M$ goes on falling after the hand method unit costs begin rising. The rise in unit costs results from the limitation on the total supervisory capacity of the farmer, a restraint which eventually also causes the $C_M C_M$ curve to turn upward at a larger scale of operations. In the situation shown, the representative farm operating with the hand method of harvesting is taken to be in equilibrium at size S_o, with the market price of grain (per acre harvested, assuming constant yield per acre) equal to minimum units costs at P_o. Beyond S_o lies S_t—the threshold size at which unit costs with the hand method are equal to those with the machine method—whose location is determined by the factors influencing the relative positions of the two curves.

The argument that the individual farmer's decision to adopt mechanical reaping was tied up with a simultaneous decision to expand his grain acreage, the latter being promoted by a rise in the relative price of grain, may now be quickly restated in terms of Figure 1. If there were no initial costs involved in increasing grain acreage under cultivation, with the market price at P_o it would clearly pay to abandon the hand method of harvesting and expand the representative farm from S_O to S_M'. However the costs of acquiring, clearing, and fencing new land, or simply of preparing land already held, were hardly insignificant even on the open prairies. If these costs, relative to the market price of grain, were sufficiently large to prevent expansion beyond S_T, they would have effectively blocked the concomitant adoption of the mechanical reaper.[4] The significance of the rise in grain prices during the 1850s in bringing about widespread introduction of the reaper was, accordingly, that higher prices induced the typical farmer to increase his grain acreage beyond the previous threshold size by lowering the relative unit costs of expansion. In so doing, the farmer would take advantage of the $C_M C_M$ cost curve.

---

[4] In terms of Figure 1 we can say that, spread over the total acreage to be harvested, the unit cost of expanding farm acreage beyond S_T was at least equal to the difference between P_o and the $C_M C_M$ cost curve at S_M.

The presence of scale considerations in the choice between hand method and machine method of harvesting grain was not explicitly recognized in setting forth our earlier argument, in which the change in technique was depicted as an adjustment imposed by the relative inelasticity of the aggregate supply schedule for farm labor. That hypothesis may, nonetheless, be quite readily stated within the framework of the microanalysis summarized by Figure 1. The contention is simply that because the threshold point moved inversely with changes in the price of labor relative to the cost of the reaper, the relative rise in farm wage rates (resulting from the collective reponse to higher grain prices in the mid-1850s) drove the threshold size downward to the point at which adoption of the reaper became profitable even on farms that had not enlarged their cultivated acreage. This is shown in Figure 1 as a downward shift in the position of the long-run machine-method cost curve relative to $C_H C_H$, lowering the threshold size (S_T) to the optimum acreage (S_o) established under the regime of the older harvesting technique.[5]

IV

On formal grounds our two versions of the switch to mechanical reaping thus turn out to be entirely compatible; they merely stress what may have been different aspects of a single story—one directing attention to forces working to push farms across the old threshold point, and the other emphasizing that an alteration in relative factor prices may have brought the threshold down to the vicinity of previously established farm size.

The empirical requirements of these two hypotheses are equally apparent. To credit either version we must at least have some evidence that at the beginning of the 1850s the threshold size for adoption of the reaper lay above the average small grain acreage on Midwestern farms, not only in the region as a whole, but in those areas especially devoted to these crops. Once that is established, further evidence of a substantial decline in the threshold size as the result of an alteration

in relative factor prices during the decade would lend credence to the view that the adjustment in technique was imposed by the inelasticity of the labor supply, whereas acceptance of the pure individual farm-size adjustment view would hinge on a finding that over the course of the 1850s average grain acreage on Midwestern farms rose to the neighborhood of the threshold size that had existed at the opening of the period.

Appendix A provides a brief discussion of the evidence required and the way it has been used in calculating the threshold acreages for adoption of mechanical reapers by grain farmers in the Western states during the period under study.[6] The computations are readily made by linearizing the cost functions for the hand and machine methods of harvesting. It is sufficient here to consider the results of those calculations in conjunction with such information as is available regarding actual small grain acreage on the average Midwestern farm. This may be done with the aid of Figure 2, which depicts the relationship we have found between threshold size and relative costs of labor and capital for the basic hand-rake reaping machine—on the assumption of linear cost functions.

Figure 2 also shows the threshold function for the self-raking type of reaper which, by mechanically delivering the cut grain to the ground beside the machine either in gavels or in swath, dispensed with the need for a man to sweep the grain from the platform of the hand-rake machine. However since self-rakers did not win popularity in the Midwest until the latter half of the 1850s, well after the initial acceptance of the basic hand-raking machines manufactured by the McCormick Co., the discussion will focus on the pioneering hand-rake model. Our conclusions, therefore, relate to the influence of alterations in market forces on the adoption of the basic reaper during the 1850s, rather than to the role played by the continuing technical refinement and elaboration of the device.

At the daily wage rate paid grain cradlers during the harvest and the average delivered price of a McCormick hand-rake reaper that prevailed in Illinois at the end of the 1840s and early in the 1850s, specifically in the period 1849–1853, the delivered purchase price of a reaper was equivalent to the hire

---

[5] Note that the downward shift in $C_M C_M$ is equivalent to a rise in the market price of grain being accompanied by an upward shift in the $C_H C_H$ cost curve which is not matched by a rise in unit costs with the machine technique.

[6] [A detailed examination of the evidence used in the calculations is provided by the Appendix to the original article, pp. 30–39.—Editors' note.]

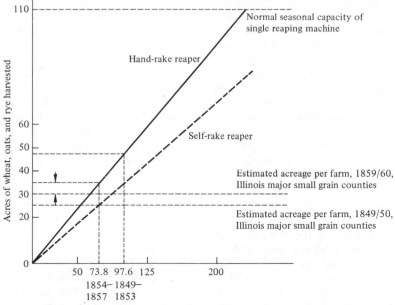

Figure 2. Threshold Functions for Adoption of the Reaper.

of 97.6 man-days labor with the cradle. From Figure 2 it is seen that these factor prices established a threshold level at 46.5 acres of grain. Where it was possible to hire cradlers on a monthly basis, instead of by the day, and therefore to pay the lower per diem wages implied in typical monthly agreements, the abandonment of cradling in favor of mechanical reaping would have reduced harvesting costs only on farms with more than 74 acres of grain to be cut. Hiring all the labor required for the harvest on a monthly basis was, however, generally not worthwhile for the farmer, so the lower threshold level is more relevant to the problem at hand.

Although there are no direct statistics for the average acreage sown with wheat, oats, and rye on Midwestern farms at the beginning of the 1850s, from the available data pertaining to average yields per acre and to the number of bushels of grain harvested per farm it is clear that a 46.5 acre threshold still lay well above typical actual acreage, even in the regions principally devoted to small grain cultivation at the mid-century mark. It is estimated that at the time of the Seventh Census (1850) the farms in Illinois averaged from 15 to 16 acres of wheat, oats, and rye. In the 16 leading grain counties (of 99 counties in Illinois), which as a group produced half of the state's principal cereal crop at that time, the average farm land under

wheat, oats, and rye ran to approximately 25 acres. Among these major small grain counties, Winnebago County in the northernmost part of the state is representative of those with the highest average small grain acreage per farm, while Cook County was one of those having the lowest average acreage. Yet on the 919 farms in Winnebago County the average worked out to 37.2 acres of small grain, still 10 acres under the threshold level, and in Cook County the 1857 farms averaged but 18.6 acres apiece.

Two closely related points thus emerge quite clearly. First, in the years immediately surrounding the initiation of reaper production in the Midwest (1847) and the establishment of the McCormick Factory at Chicago (1848), the combination of existing average farm size and prevailing factor prices militated against widespread adoption of the innovation. The admonitions appearing in Western agricultural journals during 1846 and 1847 against purchase of the new reaping machine by the farmer "who has not at least fifty acres of grain," would appear in the light of the considerations presented here to have been quite sound advice. Second, observations of the sort made by a reliable contemporary witness, Lord Robert Russell, who traveled in the prairie country in 1853, that "the cereals are nearly all cut by horsepower on the *larger farms* in the prairies," become understandable simply on the grounds of the scale considerations affecting the comparative profitability of the reaper. It is not necessary to explain them by contending that the larger farms were run by men more receptive to the new methods of scientific farming or less restrained by the limitations of their financial resources and the imperfections of the capital market, however correct such assertions might prove to be.

An initial empirical foundation for the plausibility of both our hypotheses having thus been established, we turn now to consider the evidence relating to the character of the adjustments themselves. During the mid-1850s, as the aggregate labor supply constraint hypothesis suggests, the price paid for harvest labor in Illinois did rise more rapidly than the average delivered price of a hand-rake reaper; in the period 1854–1857 a McCormick reaper cost the farmer, on average, the equivalent of only 73.8 man-days of hired cradlers' labor, compared with 97.6 man-days in the preceding period 1849–1853. In consequence, as Figure 2 shows, the threshold point dropped from over 46 to roughly 35 acres. By the middle of the decade, then, the average small grain acreage above which it paid the farmer to abandon cradling had fallen below the average acreage that had existed in the leading grain-producing area like Winnebago County, Illinois, at the beginning of the decade, and lay only 10 acres above the average on the 21,634 farms in the state's leading grain counties in 1849/50.

At the same time there is some evidence pointing to a rise in the average grain acreage harvested per farm, such as is proposed by the individual farm-size adjustment version. It is difficult, at present, to say just how large an increase in average acreage occurred during the 1850s in the specialized small grain regions of the Midwest, for the simple reason that the Census of Agriculture in 1860, unlike the previous Census, neglected to publish the statistics of the number of farms on a county-by-county basis. In Illinois, as a whole, however, the number of acres of wheat, oats, and rye harvested per farm is estimated to have been roughly 19 per cent higher in 1859/60 than it had been ten years earlier. Of course it is possible that in the transition from cereal to corn and live-stock production that was under way in the state during this decade, specialization in small grain cultivation became more concentrated, and, therefore, that the increase in

the typical farm acreage sown with those crops in the leading regions of their cultivation was considerably greater than 19 per cent. But such evidence as can be brought to bear on the matter does not point in that direction. Broadly speaking, small grain cultivation was spatially no more concentrated in Illinois at the end of the 1850s than at the beginning, and wheat production became, if anything, geographically more dispersed. It is therefore not wholly unreasonable to assume that small grain acreage per farm in the areas especially devoted to those crops increased at the same rate as it did in Illinois as a whole. On that basis one may conjecture that the number of acres under wheat, oats, and rye on a typical farm in the state's leading small grain regions increased from 25 to 30 in the course of the 1850s. The story of the adoption of the mechanical reaper in the years immediately before the Civil War should thus be told in terms of the effects of both an expansion of grain acreage sown on individual farms and the downward movement of the threshold size as a result of the rising relative cost of harvest labor. But of the two types of adjustment taking place during the 1850s, the former must properly be accorded lesser emphasis. As Figure 2 reveals, on farms in the leading grain regions of Illinois the estimated increase in average small grain acreage was responsible for less than a third of the subsequent reduction of the gap existing between threshold size and average acreage at the opening of the decade. Moreover among the Midwestern states experiencing rapid settlement during the 1850s, Illinois was singular in the magnitude of the expansion of its average farm size. Elsewhere in the Midwest the relative rise in farm wage rates is likely to have played a still greater role in bringing the basic reaping machine into general use during the decade preceding the Civil War.

V

Although the questions considered in the preceding pages are very specific, we have arrived at answers with rather broader implications. Historians of United States agriculture have maintained that during the nineteenth century the transfer of grain farming to new regions lying beyond the Appalachian barrier played a significant part in raising labor productivity in agriculture for the country as a whole. The connection between the spatial redistribution of grain production and the progress of farm mechanization figures prominently among the reasons that have been advanced to support this contention. Some writers suggest that inasmuch as heavier reliance was placed on the use of farm machinery in the states of the Old Northwest before the Civil War, and, similarly, in the Great Plains and Pacific coast states during the last quarter of the century, the geographical transfer of agriculture into these areas was tantamount to a progressive shift of grain farming towards the relatively capital-intensive region of the technological spectrum. But the mechanism of this putative interaction between spatial and technological change has not been fully clarified, and as a result important aspects of the interrelationship between the historical course of industrialization and the settlement of new regions in the United States remain only imperfectly perceived.

To make some headway in this direction it is necessary to distinguish two possible modes of interaction between spatial and technological changes in United States agriculture: One involves adjustment of production methods in response to alterations of relative prices that were associated, either causally or consequentially, with the geographical relocation of farming; the other turns on purely technological considerations through which regional location influenced choices among available alternative techniques. Now the general statement that the conditions under which farmers located in the country's interior carried on grain production especially favored the spread of mechanization is sufficiently imprecise to embrace both interaction mechanisms: the influences of market conditions as well as those of technological factors peculiar to farming in the different regions. One may well ask whether such ambiguity is justified. Without establishing the dominance of purely technical considerations it would be unwarranted to suggest that shifts of small grain farming away from the Eastern seaboard automatically, in and of themselves, accounted for increases in the extent to which that branch of United States agriculture became mechanized.

In the case of reaping operations it is certainly true that there were technical features of Midwestern farming which in contrast with those characteristic of the Eastern grain regions proved inherently more congenial to the general introduction of ante-bellum reaping machines. On the comparatively level, stone-free terrain of the Midwest the cumbersome early models of the reaper were less difficult for a team to pull, less subject to malalignment and actual breakage; because the fields were unridged and crops typically were not so heavy as those on Eastern farms, the reapers cut the grain close to the ground more satisfactorily, and the knives of the simple cutting mechanism were not so given to repeated clogging.

Yet despite the relatively favorable technical environment (and larger average small grain acreages on farms) in the Midwest, we have seen that the prevailing factor and product market conditions during the 1840s and early 1850s militated against extensive adoption of mechanical reaping equipment even in that region. Against such a background the fact that a large-scale transfer of small grain production to the Old Northwest Territory took place during the 1850s does not appear so crucial a consideration in explaining the sudden rise in the proportion of the total American wheat crop cut by horse power between 1850 and 1860. Instead it seems appropriate to emphasize that during the Midwestern development boom that marked the decade of the 1850s the price of labor—as well as the prices of small grains—rose relative to the price of reaping machines, and that the pressure on the region's labor supply reflected not only the expanded demand for farm workers, but also the demand for labor to build railroads and urban centers throughout the region—undertakings ultimately predicated on the current wave of new farm settlement and the expected growth of the Midwest's agricultural capacity. If one is to argue the case for the existence of an important causal relationship between the relocation of grain production and the widespread acceptance of mechanical reaping during the 1850s, the altered market environment, especially the new labor market conditions created directly and indirectly by the quickening growth of Midwestern agriculture, must be accorded greater recognition, and the purely technical considerations be given rather less weight than they usually receive in this connection.

There is, however, a sense in which the decline in the cost of reaping machines relative to the farm labor wage rate may be held to have reflected the interaction of the technical factors favoring adoption of the early

reapers in the Midwest with that region's
emergence as the nation's granary during the
1850s. The rising share of the United States
wheat crop being grown in the interior did
mean that, *ceteris paribus*, a larger proportion
of the national crop could be harvested by
horse power without requiring the building of
machines designed to function as well under
the terrain and crop conditions of the older
grain regions as the early reapers did on the
prairies. For the country as a whole, as well
as for the Midwest, this afforded economies
of scale in the production of a simpler, more
standardized line of reaping machines. It
thereby contributed to maintaining a situation
in which the long-run aggregate supply
schedule for harvesting machinery was more
elastic than the farm labor supply. Thus it
may be said, somewhat paradoxically, that
the movement towards regional specialization
in small grain farming directly made possible
greater efficiency in manufacturing and thereby promoted the simultaneous advance of
mechanized agriculture and industrial development in the ante-bellum Midwest.

APPENDIX A: THRESHOLD FARM SIZE

The element of fixed cost present with the
mechanical reaping process for harvesting
grain makes it necessary to take account of
the scale of harvesting operations in cost
comparisons of hand and machine methods.
One means of doing this would be to stipulate the acreage to be harvested and then
proceed to ask how the profitability of
mechanical reaping compared to cradling
was affected by the prevailing level of factor
prices. This appendix tackles essentially the
same question by posing it in a slightly
different way. The question can be put as
follows: given alternative sets of factor prices,
at what alternative scale of harvesting operations would it be a matter of indifference (on
cost grounds) to the farmer of the 1850s
whether he adopted the reaper or continued
to rely on the cradle? The answer is to be
found from a computation of that acreage,
called the threshold size, at which the total
costs of the two processes were just equal
and beyond which abandoning the cradle
would become profitable, other things remaining unchanged.

It is not, however, necessary to calculate
the total cost of harvesting an acre of grain

at different scales of operation, as depicted
by the long-run unit cost curves of Figure 1.
In the first place, as will be seen, the activities
of the harvest other than the actual cutting
of grain—raking, binding, and shocking—
may be omitted from consideration as not
significantly influencing the choice between
machine and hand reaping. Second, all that
is required is the computation of the total
saving of money wages effected by adoption
of the mechanical reaper and the *additional*
fixed capital charge that the farmer would
incur in order to have the machine at his
disposal during the harvest season. What
must be known, therefore, is:

L_s : the number of man-days of labor
dispensed with by mechanizing the
cutting operation, per acre harvested
w : the money cost to the farmer of a
man-day of harvest labor
c : the fixed annual money cost of a
reaper to the farmer

From this information the threshold size, S_T,
in acres to be harvested can be determined,
since, *ceteris paribus*, total costs of cutting
the grain are the same for both processes when

$$c = \sum_{i=1}^{S_T} L_{s_i} w \qquad (1)$$

where the index i designates the acre in the
sequence of acres ($i = 1, \ldots, S_T$) harvested.

Actually the problem can be further simplified. From the available information it
appears justifiable to assume that within the
range of normal daily cutting capacity of the
reaper there were no economies or diseconomies of scale in the use of labor in
cradling, and that the saving of labor effected
by the mechanical reaper per acre harvested
was a technically determined constant. In a
word, the cost functions for the two processes
may be taken as linear over the relevant range
of operations. Consequently, we may replace
equation 1 with the much simpler expression,

$$c = S_T L_s w \qquad (1a)$$

The average annual capital cost, or effective
rental rate on a piece of durable equipment,
may be reckoned as the sum of the annual
depreciation of the equipment and the annual
interest cost on the capital invested in it. One
can think of the latter as an opportunity cost,

since for half the year, on average, the owner's funds are tied up in the machine instead of being lodged elsewhere at interest. Alternatively the interest cost is to be thought of as the actual charge made for a loan of the purchase price of the equipment. Strictly speaking, in calculating the interest cost of a mechanical reaper, allowance should be made for the fact that funds were locked up in these machines for periods longer than a year; it is known that Midwestern farmers purchased reapers on credit during the 1850s and paid them off only over an extended period of time. Yet within the range of accuracy we can hope to attain in the present calculations, the niceties of compound interest may be foregone and the interest cost computed on a simple basis. The half-life of reapers was not, in any case, so long as to render this a serious omission.

An equivalently liberal attitude is warranted regarding the question of depreciation charges. Rather than play with formulas that attempt to take into account the actual time pattern of loss of value through wear and tear and obsolescence, straight-line depreciation over the physical life of the machine may be assumed.

As a result of the foregoing simplifications, the average annual gross money rental charge is quite straightforwardly given by

$$c = [(d + 0.5(r)]C \qquad (2)$$

where

d = the straight-line rate of depreciation
r = the annual rate of interest
C = the purchase price of a reaper

Putting this together with equation 1a, we have the relation defining the threshold size in terms of the prices of harvest labor and reapers, the rate of interest, and the "technical" coefficients L_s and d:

$$S_T = \left(\frac{d + 0.5r}{L_s}\right)\left(\frac{C}{w}\right) \qquad (3)$$

From the form of equation 3 it is apparent that, given the rate of interest the threshold

for harvesting machines of specified durability and labor-saving characteristics is directly proportional to the relative price of the reaper (C/w). Thus the threshold functions shown in Figure 2 of the text appear as positively sloped rays from the origin of a graph of acreages against the ratios of reaper prices to wage rates. The slopes of these lines are determined by inserting the relevant values of the parameters: d, the depreciation rate is found to have been .10; the annual interest rate charged by the McCormick Company on loans for the purchase of their reaper during the 1850s was .06; for the standard hand-rake reaper, we find the saving of labor (L_s) was 0.273 man-days per acre harvested. The threshold function for the self-rake reaper, also shown in Figure 2, is based on the values for d and r given above, and an estimated labor saving of 0.364 man-days per acre harvested.

REFERENCES

1. Percy W. Bidwell and John I. Falconer, *History of Agriculture in the Northern United States*, Washington, Carnegie Institution of Washington, 1925.
2. P. A. David, *Factories at the Prairies' Edge: A Study of Industrialization in Chicago 1848–1893*, (Manuscript).
3. H. J. Habakkuk, *American and British Technology in the Nineteenth Century*, Cambridge, University Press, 1962.
4. William T. Hutchinson, *Cyrus Hall McCormick, Seed-Time, 1809–1856*, New York, The Century Company, 1930.
5. William N. Parker and Judith L. V. Klein, "Productivity Growth in Grain Production in the United States, 1840–1860 and 1900–1910," Conference on Research in Income and Wealth, *Output, Employment, and Productivity in the United States After 1800*. (Studies in Income and Wealth, vol. 30), New York, Columbia University Press, 1966, pp. 523–580.
6. Leo Rogin, *The Introduction of Farm Machinery in its Relation to the Productivity of Labor in the Agriculture of the United States During the Nineteenth Century*, Berkeley, University of California Press, 1931.

17 STEAM AND WATERPOWER IN THE EARLY 19th CENTURY

Peter Temin

Waterfalls are not at our command in all places, and are liable to be obstructed by frost, drought, and many other accidents. Wind is inconstant and unsteady: animal power, expensive, tedious in the operation, and unprofitable, as well as subject to innumerable accidents. On neither of these can we rely with certainty. But steam at once presents us with a faithful servant, at command in all places, in all seasons. . . .

(Oliver Evans, 1805)

Reprinted with omissions by permission from *The Journal of Economic History, 26* (June, 1966), 187-205.

The use of steam power in manufacturing has long been recognized as an important part of the English Industrial Revolution, but in studies of the United States the role of the steam engine in manufacturing has been overshadowed by its application in railroads. This paper attempts partially to redress the balance by examining the use of stationary steam engines in America about 1840. Section I explores the characteristics of the supply of stationary engines in America, contrasting the engines used in America with those used in Britain. Section II discusses the demand for steam engines, that is, the factors underlying the choice between steam and water-power in different industries.

The examination as a whole provides a new example of the diffusion of an innovation in the American setting. It therefore provides a new chance to assess some generalizations about the nature of American technology. Both the plausibility of these generalizations and the extent to which our imperfect knowledge allows us to either confirm or refute them are in question.

I

The improvements by James Watt in the late eighteenth century for the first time permitted the steam engine to be employed for industrial purposes. The Watt engine, like the Newcomen engine that preceded it, was a "low-pressure" engine, that is, it derived its power from the pressure of the atmosphere acting against a vacuum produced by the condensation of steam. Shortly after 1800 a new type of engine, the "high-pressure" engine, was introduced. This engine used steam at higher than atmospheric pressure to push against the atmosphere in the same way that the low-pressure engine used the atmosphere to push against a vacuum. It therefore operated without a condenser; the steam was exhausted into the air at the end of the stroke and the cumbersome apparatus for condensing it and producing a vacuum was lacking.

The possibility of using high-pressure steam was known before 1800, but its use required well-made boilers and accurately machined cylinders and pistons—items which were not within the skills of machinists before the start of the nineteenth century. As a result of many improvements in the years around 1800, some possibly connected with the production of low-pressure steam engines, mechanical

skill was improved to the point where high-pressure steam could be employed. The high-pressure steam engine with cylindrical iron boilers was introduced simultaneously in Britain and America by Richard Trevithick and Oliver Evans in 1803–1804. That this development, which was an application of new mechanical skills to known mechanical principles, should have come simultaneously in both countries is an indication of a community of skill in the two lands, at least among a few adventurous machinists.

The high-pressure steam engine fared differently in the two countries, in ways that are not easily understood. One authority states that Trevithick's engine was widely adopted in Britain soon after its invention, while Evans' engine was opposed and neglected in the United States [1, pp. 95–97]. Yet thirty years later almost all stationary steam engines in Britain were low-pressure engines and almost all those in America used high pressure.[1] Since the development of the steam engine after 1838—for example, the invention of the Corliss engine—encouraged the use of high rather than low pressure, it might not be unfair to say that Americans were using the more advanced technology by that time. On the other hand the economic significance of this difference in the 1830s is not apparent.

Beyond the records of Evans' attempts to maintain his patent monopoly on the construction of high-pressure engines, the record of the early adoption of steam engines in America is very fragmentary.[2] About a dozen steam-powered plants are mentioned in the 1820 Census, the McLane *Report* of 1833 has notices of over one hundred stationary steam engines in use in 1831, and the 1838 *Report on Steam Engines* [5] records over one thousand in use as of that date. Unfortunately although over one hundred of the engines enumerated by the 1838 *Report on Steam*

---

[1] Only 65 out of 305 stationary steam engines in Birmingham were high pressure, while only 63 out of over 1200 stationary steam engines in the United States were low pressure in 1838.

[2] There were at least 10 steam engines built in America before Evans introduced his, and his engine was pirated extensively in the years before 1825. In fact the opposition to Evans was probably a reaction to his attempted patent monopoly and his litigious personality, rather than to his invention: a reflection of the demand for the high-pressure engine, not its lack. (Evans' patent expired in 1825.)

Engines were built in 1831 or before, only about a dozen engines appear in both the 1831 and 1838 surveys. The McLane *Report* is known to be incomplete, and the absence in it of the engines mentioned later may be attributed to this failing. The *Report on Steam Engines* was known by its authors to be incomplete in some areas, but has been accepted as complete for the regions in which the McLane *Report* found steam engines. If this is so, then almost all of the steam engines existing in 1831 must have worn out by 1838.

The limited life of American steam engines is also apparent in our information on the engines built by Oliver Evans and his successors. Evans died in 1819, and the firm of Rush & Muhlenberg succeeded him, Rush being Evans' son-in-law and Muhlenberg his partner. Of the engines built by Evans himself, only one—built in 1817—survived to be included in the 1838 *Report on Steam Engines*. In addition the average age of the engines built by Rush & Muhlenberg was only five years, just one stationary engine built by them before 1828 surviving till 1838. Finally, the Pittsburgh Steam Mill, established in 1809 by Evans, was by 1838 using an engine built in 1828.

English steam engines, some authors believed, never wore out, but American engines apparently did [*1*, p. 106]. American engines could have been made more carelessly than British engines; high-pressure engines could have worn out more quickly than low; or the high opinion of British engines may be unfounded. In any case, since most American engines wore out within a decade, it cannot be supposed that the *Report on Steam Engines* contains information about the use of steam power for any but a few years immediately preceding 1838.

The data in the *Report* indicate that steam-engine construction in 1838 was a small-scale business carried on for a predominantly local market. The approximately 1100 steam engines existing in 1838 whose builders are known were built by 250 different builders, the average builder making less than five steam engines. Of these builders 131 had built only one engine, including 31 engines built for the builder's own use. The ability to build steam engines clearly was widely distributed by 1838, and economies of scale were not important. On the other hand there were a few large engine builders; 25 builders had made over 10 engines apiece, and 6 had made over 30. There is no evidence, therefore, that there were either economies or diseconomies of scale in the production of steam engines.

The importance of a national market for American economic development has been stressed by many writers. The small-scale nature of steam-engine production suggests that the national market may not have been important for the diffusion of this particular innovation—an implication borne out by the data shown in Table 1 on the interregional trade in steam engines. With the exception of the South, interregional trade was clearly minimal; the only significant non-Southern exchange was the use in Connecticut of engines built in New York. The South, however, built only one third of the engines it used whose origin is known. Pittsburgh and English engines were used in Louisiana and Baltimore, and Philadelphia engines were used in Virginia. The "national" market in steam engines existed only in the sale of Northern-built engines in the South.[3]

It has also been asserted that the backward linkage from textiles to machinery production was important, being "strategic" for the development of the machinery industry—the seventh largest industry in 1860. Fully 90 per cent of the value added in the machinery sector shown by the 1860 Census, however, was accounted for by the production of steam engines. And, as Table 1 shows, the Middle Atlantic and Western regions were self-sufficient in steam engines by 1838 despite the absence of a well-developed textile industry in these regions. Whatever the link between the makers of textile machinery and of steam engines in New England, the builders of steam engines in other regions do not seem to have suffered from its absence.

With the possible exception of the South, therefore, the ability to make steam engines

---

[3] The precise numbers in Table 1 depend on the definitions of regions, but the conclusions do not. The regional breakdown used here differs from that used elsewhere primarily in its division of several states into two regions. This results from the use of the Allegheny Mountains as the division between the middle Atlantic and the Western regions and the allocation of what is now West Virginia to the West rather than to the South. As the mountains were a far greater barrier to trade than state boundaries, this division is preferable to the more usual one. (See the notes to Table 1 for the possibility that the difference between the South and other regions was exaggerated.)

Table 1. Locus of Construction of Stationary Steam Engines in Various Regions, 1838[a]

LOCATION OF BUILDER	LOCATION OF ENGINE				
	New England	Middle Atlantic	West	South	Total U.S.
	(Number of Engines)				
New England	260	2	1	2	265
Middle Atlantic	35	288	2	69	394
West	0	11	343	38	392
South	0	2	0	55	57
England	3	1	0	14	18
Unknown	6	38	30	28	102
Total number of engines observed	304	342	376	206	1228
Number of engines estimated or reported with incomplete data[b]	13	36	124	215	388
Total number of engines allocated by *Report* to different regions	317	378	500	421	1616

[a] The definition of regions is as follows: New England: Maine, N.H., Vt., Mass., Conn., R.I.; Middle Atlantic: eastern N.Y., eastern Pa., N.J., Del., Md., D.C.; West: western N.Y., western Pa., Ohio, Mich., W. Va.; South: Va. (excluding W. Va.), N.C., S.C., Ga., Fla., La.

[b] The engines listed as estimated or inadequately reported are those for which a location was given; an additional 244 engines were assumed to exist by the writers of the *Report*, but their presumed location was not given. They apparently were built in Louisville, and therefore probably were located in the South and West. If Louisville is considered part of the South, the inclusion of these engines in the table would sharply reduce the difference between the South and the other regions.

was widespread.[4] As most American steam engines were high-pressure engines, it can be inferred that the ability to make high-pressure engines was easy to acquire. The continued use of low-pressure engines in Britain then cannot be attributed to an inability to make high-pressure engines in that country. Nor can the residual use of low-pressure engines in the United States in 1838 be explained by such a hypothesis. All but two of the American builders of stationary low-pressure engines had also built high-pressure engines existing

in 1838, and five of the six largest stationary steam-engine builders also made a few low-pressure engines.

The hypothesis that American practice rested on accurate theory not known or believed in England fares no better. Oliver Evans argued for the use of the high-pressure engine on theoretical grounds, resting his case on the results of recent experiments which seemed to show that the product of pressure and volume was an *exponential* function of temperature. If the heat were raised, the pressure of steam in a constant volume, therefore, would rise more than proportionately. The use of high temperatures and pressures was by this means rendered economical. The experiments, unfortunately, were not accurate, and the form of the ideal gas law is not exponential. The product of pressure and

---

[4] The South is only a *possible* exception as it may have been more profitable to use imported steam engines in the South than to build them. The pattern of trade shown in Table 1 would then have been the result of Southern exploitation of their comparative advantage, not a reflection of their lack of knowledge.

volume is only a linear function of temperature, and the argument of Evans cannot be used to justify the use of high pressure.

If Evans was mistaken in his theory, his opponents were equally confused. One argument current in the 1830s asserted that the same quantity of water converted to steam gives the same mechanical effect whatever the pressure. This conclusion followed from the assertion that for a given weight of water the product of the pressure and volume of the resultant steam was a constant. If the pressure of steam were increased, its volume and therefore the distance through which it would act would be reduced proportionately. The amount of work obtained by boiling a given quantity of water was therefore supposed to be constant and independent of the pressure. The error in this reasoning lies in the unstated assumption that pressure is increased only by reducing the volume and never by raising the temperature. Since steam pressure can be raised by heat, there is no reason for the product of pressure and volume of steam from a given weight of water to be constant.

The theory of the steam engine was not worked out until after 1840, and all theoretical discussions of the benefits of high-pressure steam engines before then were bound to be inadequate. In addition since the efficiency of steam engines varied with the type of boiler and the extent to which steam was used expansively, and since the range of efficiency was wide in both England and America, it is hard to know whether there was a systematic difference between the efficiencies *actually attained* with the two types of engines. The only explicit comparison I have discovered showed no difference.

Further evidence for the competitiveness of high- and low-pressure steam engines at this time is provided by the continued use of high-pressure engines in steamboats on the Western rivers of the United States and of low-pressure engines in steamboats along the Atlantic coast. Western steamboats used high-pressure engines because of their light weight and flexibility; Eastern steamboats continued to use the safer—for steamboats—low-pressure engines [*4*, pp. 129–133]. Neither the advantages nor the disadvantages of high pressure in steamboat operation were present for stationary steam engines, yet the geographical difference in steamboat practice was carried over into the realm of stationary steam engines. Table 2 shows the regional

Table 2. Statistics of Low-Pressure Steam Engines by Region, 1838[a]

	New England	Middle Atlantic	West	South	Total
Total number	14	30	0	19	63
Number imported from England	0	1	0	13	14
Average age in years	2	11	—	11	9

[a] The regions are the same as those in Table 1.

distribution of low-pressure engines; the Northeastern regions built their own, and the South imported them from England. None of the low-pressure steam engines in the United States in 1838 were being used west of the Allegheny Mountains, and none had been built in the West.

This, of course, was not just a coincidence. Several important makers of steam engines made both stationary and steamboat engines; their numbers are shown in Table 3. Most important builders of steamboat engines also made stationary engines, and it is not surprising that the pattern in the marginal use of low-pressure stationary engines followed the practice in steamboat engines. However only about one third of the important builders of stationary steam engines were also important builders of steamboat engines, and the existence of the two thirds who did not make steamboat engines should be remembered when generalizing about the importance of transfers of skills between the different types of steam-engine builders. (The same

Table 3. Number of Major Steam-Engine Builders in the United States, by Type

Type of Engine	Builders Who Had Made Five or More Engines of the Specified Type or Types Existing in 1838
Stationary	56
Steamboat	20
Locomotive	11
Stationary and steamboat	17
Stationary and locomotive	1
Steamboat and locomotive	1
All three types	0

caveat applies, *a fortiori*, for transfers of skills between builders of locomotive engines and the builders of other types of steam engines.)

The difference between American and British practice thus appears more as a matter of style than of economy. The British practice may be attributed to Watt's conservatism and the American lack of fear of explosions; but there is no evidence that British practice was less efficient than American by 1840 nor that *stationary* high-pressure engines were any more dangerous than low-pressure engines. After 1840, with the introduction of the Corliss engine in the United States, it is possible that the British preference for low-pressure engines was a disadvantage, but that is a separate story.

II

We turn now to the demand for steam power for industrial uses, in particular the cost elements affecting the choice between steam and waterpower in various industries and locations. The two sources of power were competitors, but not exact substitutes. Three differences are of importance. First, since waterpower was available only at fixed locations, its use generally involved transport charges on materials and products. Second, although steam power could be generated anywhere, its location away from a source of coal or wood involved transport charges on the fuel. Third, capital costs formed a greater part of the total costs for waterpower than for steam power, and the choice between the two at any location was affected by the interest rate.

The relative costs of steam and waterpower for two groups of New England cotton mills about 1840 are shown in Table 4. Since both water and steam power were being used in cotton mills at this time, it is not surprising to find that costs were nearly equal. Had they been unequal, the capital goods used in one or both processes would have been revalued to produce equality. If large profits or large losses were then being made by the suppliers of either waterwheels or steam engines, the suppliers of one or the other type of equipment would have soon left the market. But since both types of equipment continued to be supplied, there is no apparent evidence of such a disequilibrium. The importance of the three differences between steam and water-

Table 4. A Contemporary Estimate of Power Costs for Cotton Mills, About 1840 (Annual Cost Per Horsepower in Dollars)

	Water		Steam	
Capital costs				
Water rights	$200		—	
Steam engine	—		$150	
Waterwheel, gearing, etc.	190		—	
Foundations	90		20	
Total	480		170	
6 per cent of total		$29		$10
Operating Costs				
Coal for steam engine				35
Wages to operate engine				7
Other costs dependent on power source				
Heat for factory		11		
Transportation costs		8		
		$48		$52

power therefore can be seen from the cost comparison of Table 4.

(1) The costs in Table 4 are the costs for mills located in a favorable location for each type of power. The steam mills were located at Newburyport, on the Atlantic coast, where it was not necessary to transport goods or fuel overland to the mills. The water-powered mills were located at Lowell, a desirable spot for mills using waterpower as the sum of direct power costs and transportation expenses was comparatively low. Industries using materials heavier than cotton would have had larger overland transportation costs to a waterpower site; industries using local materials—such as sawmills and flour mills—would have incurred only small charges for transport.

(2) Coal was used to fire steam engines in New England, although wood could also have been used. The cost of the coal included the cost of transporting it from Pennsylvania to Newburyport; it was consequently more expensive than it was in Pennsylvania, and cotton mills had less incentive to use coal than plants located near coal mines.

(3) The data in Table 4 show that capital costs were a far more important part of the costs of waterpower than of steam power. At a 6 per cent interest rate, 60 per cent of the

costs resulting from using waterpower were capital costs, while only 20 per cent of the costs of using steam power were in that category. If the interest rate were higher, the relative cost of waterpower would increase. The capital costs in Table 4 cannot be accepted at face value, however, as there is no allowance for depreciation. The payment for water rights was a payment to locate within the large river development of the Proprietors of Locks and Canals at Lowell. It therefore represented a share of the cost of building the dams and canals necessary to obtain power from the river. Depreciation on these structures and on the mill foundations may be assumed to be negligible. On the other hand, steam engines depreciated rapidly—as the comparison of steam engines in 1831 and 1838 showed—and waterwheels were also impermanent. Although waterwheels cost more than steam engines, they almost certainly depreciated more slowly and probably added a smaller depreciation charge to the total costs.

These three differences between water and steam power increased the incentive of Western industries to use steam. In the flat Midwest waterpower was scarce, coal was cheap, and capital was dear. On the other hand the specific locational requirements of individual industries may have been more important in determining the demand for steam power than the general influence coming from location in the West. We therefore turn to an examination of individual industries.

Data on the distribution of steam power in 1838 appear in Table 5, where industries are placed into three groups according to the ratio of the steam power used to the value added produced in the industry [see *2*, p. 474 and *3*, pp. 46–47]. We seek to explain the proportion of each industry's power derived from steam. The grouping of industries in Table 5—adopted due to the absence of data on total power utilization in 1838—is heavily influenced by the *total* need for power in the various industries, and it therefore does not necessarily correspond to a grouping based on the *proportion* of an industry's power derived from steam. Nevertheless the data in Table 5 can be used to derive estimates of the proportion of steam power used in some industries.

The ratio of steam power to value added for all manufacturing in 1838 was about .15 horsepower per $1000 of value added. According to the data in Table 5, this ratio

was the same for the textile industry as a whole. As most textile mills were cotton mills, and as the average steam-powered cotton mill of the time used approximately one horsepower for every $1000 of value added, we may infer that about 15 per cent of all value added produced in textile mills was made in mills using steam power about 1840.[5]

The costs of steam power were falling relative to the costs of waterpower at this time, and builders of the newer mills had a greater incentive than their predecessors to use steam.[6] If 15 per cent of existing mills were using steam, a higher proportion of the new mills must have been. The data are broadly consistent with the hypothesis that American manufacturers were using the newest technology at a reasonable rate; more than that cannot be said with confidence. The more interesting question concerns the differences between the cotton industry and other industries. Do the differences between the two sources of power noted above explain the differential use of steam and waterpower in different industries?

The primary metals industry—in which the iron industry occupied a position similar to the position of the cotton industry in textiles—was the other industry with a ratio of steam power to value added similar to that for all manufacturing. By a calculation similar to,

---

[5] This result was obtained by dividing the ratio of horsepower used per dollar of value added for the industry as a whole by the ratio to steam-powered cotton mills alone. The use of power in steam-powered cotton mills was derived as the product of the power used per spindle and the value added per spindle.

Woolen textiles represented a significant proportion of the textile industry, and their presence renders the above calculation even more speculative than it would be for the cotton industry alone. If woolen mills did not use any steam power, the conclusion in the text is unaffected. If they used some steam power, the figure in the text is too low (high) if the horsepower used in woolen mills per dollar of value added was lower (higher) than in cotton mills. In addition, water-powered mills used more power per spindle than steam-powered mills (due to the use of a different type of spindle), and the proportion of *power* used in the textile industry in 1838 that was generated by steam was only about 10 per cent.

[6] The average coal consumption per horsepower declined steadily in the first half of the nineteenth century, while the technology of waterpower utilization remained relatively stable up to the introduction of the water turbine after 1840. In addition, waterpower in New England was beginning to become scarce after about 1830.

Table 5. Percentage Distribution of Steam Power and of Value Added in Manufacturing by Industry Groups, 1838

	Steam Power (% of Total in all Industries)	Value Added (% of Total in all Industries)	Steam Power / Value Added (Ratio to Average in all Industries[a])
Average users of steam power			
Textile products	13	13	1.0
Primary metals	12	10	1.2
Heavy users of steam power			
Food products	33	11	3.0
Lumber and wood products	23	10	2.3
Light users of steam power			
All other industries	19	56	0.3

[a] Derived by dividing the entries in the first column by the corresponding entries in the second.

but more speculative than, the one used for the cotton industry, we may infer that about 25 per cent of the power used in the iron industry was generated by steam.[7]

[7] The ratio of value added per employee was about one third (36 per cent) more for the iron industry than for industry as a whole in 1859, and this may be projected back to 1838. Multiplying this ratio by the ratio in the last column of Table 5 gives the ratio of steam power per employee in industry as a whole. The amount of steam power used in 1838 amounted to .072 horsepower per employee for manufacturing as a whole, implying that the ratio was about .12 for the iron industry. In a steam-powered rolling mill about .85 horsepower per employee was used; in a steam-power blast furnace, about .37. I assume that the amount of power used per employee was independent of the nature of the power used. Then if the iron industry had been composed entirely of rolling mills, steam power would have been about 15 per cent of the total power used; if the industry had been only blast furnaces, about 30 per cent. As employment was probably somewhat lower in rolling mills than in blast furnaces, the ratio for the industry as a whole was near 25 per cent. Less wrought iron than pig iron was produced at this time, and output per employee was similar in the two branches of the industry.

As the amount of power used per employee varied in the cotton industry according to the type of power used, there was a divergence between the proportion of power used that was generated from steam (about 10 per cent) and the proportion of the industry's value added that was produced in steam-powered plants (about 15 per cent). The 25 per cent figure for the iron industry is the proportion of employees who worked in steam-powered plants; I have assumed this was equal to the proportion of the industry's power derived from steam.

The iron industry was located outside New England and produced a product that was heavy in relation to its value. Both factors should have encouraged the use of steam power; yet although the use of steam in ironworks in 1838 was greater than its use in the cotton industry, our very approximate data indicate that it still was limited. An explanation for the continuing preference for waterpower is not hard to find: it was the result of using charcoal for fuel. Charcoal cannot be transported easily, and ironworks using charcoal have to be located in extensive woodlands where they can make their own charcoal. As water was also needed for cooling, there was little inconvenience in locating the works at a waterpower site. And as the direct costs of waterpower were lower than the direct costs of steam power, waterpower continued to be used.

The influence of charcoal was on the wane in 1840. Rolling mills were increasingly using mineral fuel, and blast furnaces (at least in the East) were about to follow suit. Ironworks began to be located near coal mines, away from the headwaters of streams. In the years after 1840, also, the industry continued its westward migration into a region of high interest rates. The lessening of the locational constraint of charcoal, the "migration" towards coal, and the increasingly high interest rates the industry had to pay encouraged the transition from water to steam power.

The food-products industry was composed mainly of sugar mills and flour and grist mills. Of these, sugar mills used the greater amount of steam power in 1838. Located almost exclusively in Louisiana, sugar mills began using steam power in 1822 with engines imported from England. American engine builders in Tennessee and Ohio then began to supply engines (for about half the price of the British engines), and the use of steam spread. As much as three fourths of the sugarcane grown in Louisiana in 1833 may have been ground by steam.

In the iron industry technical characteristics of production discouraged the use of steam power by reducing the transportation charges incurred by using waterpower. For sugar mills the cost of transporting the sugarcane to a waterpower site to be crushed was prohibitive, and waterpower was ruled out altogether. Sugarcane was grown in southern Louisiana, where the land was too flat to provide suitable waterpower sites. Since the cane had to be crushed immediately after being cut (otherwise the juice in the stalk fermented and was ruined) it could not be transported to a distant mill to be crushed, nor could it withstand delays due to loss of power. Wind power was ruled out due to its unreliability, and the choice was between animal and steam power. While adequate cost comparisons do not seem to be available, the quotation from Oliver Evans that heads this paper indicates that there was reason for preferring steam.

Less than one third of the flour and grist mills operating in 1869 used steam power, and we may presume that the proportion in 1838 was smaller. The large steam power consumption of the food-products industry in 1838 was then a result of the preference for steam in sugar mills and the large *total* power requirements for flour and grist mills. Too little is known about the costs of flour milling before the Civil War to justify any conclusion about the source of power in this industry. It is interesting to note, however, that Oliver Evans was a millwright and that his innovations in flour-milling machinery—which amounted to the introduction of a form of automatic production—were at least as well known as his invention of the high-pressure steam engine. He opened a demonstration steam-power flour mill in Pittsburgh

in 1809 to publicize the use of his steam engine for flour milling. The mill does not seem to have been profitable nor to have encouraged others to imitate it; reissues of Evans' guide to the use of his flour-milling machinery continued to talk exclusively in terms of waterpower up to the Civil War. The causes for this sequence of events are not clear, and the question about the rationality of flour millers remains moot.

Sawmills were the largest single user of steam power in 1838. While this undoubtedly resulted in large part from the large total power needs of sawmills, it also owed something to their location at this time. Over one third of the sawmills using steam power were located in the lower Mississippi Valley where the opportunities to use waterpower were severely limited. Other sawmills were scattered in location and subject to offsetting influences. Logs were presumably floated down rivers to the mills, and there would have been little or no extra cost in locating the mill near a waterfall if one was available. On the other hand, sawmills in scattered locations must have paid high rates of interest, which would have encouraged the use of steam. Without being able to quantify the influence of these factors, it can only be said that the use of steam in sawmills indicates that innovations were not being ignored even in the industries of the backwoods.

Finally the group of light steam-power users lumped together in Table 5 is too diverse to permit much generalization. For these industries little power of any sort was needed, and steam power was used in small units when it was used.[8] The industries were largely urban in character—a characteristic notably lacking in most of the processing industries discussed so far—and their use of steam appears to have been a response to this environment.

What can we conclude from this discussion of the demand for steam power? Although steam power was used widely in manufacturing by 1840, most of its use was concentrated in a few industries and it provided the main power supply for almost none. The direct

---

[8] The average size of steam engines in this group was under 10 horsepower, compared to an average of about 20 for all manufacturing and over 100 for iron rolling mills. The industries in this group included—in order of the amount of steam power they used in 1838—foundries and machine shops, leather and tanning, paper and publishing, grinding white lead, etc.

costs of steam power were higher than the costs for waterpower, and industries used steam only when the freedom of location gained by using steam was large. In other words in the years before it became important as a supplier of land transportation, the steam engine functioned as a *substitute* for such transportation, allowing power to be brought to the raw materials when it was expensive to bring the materials to waterpower sites.

It has been asserted often that American technology was "labor-saving." Americans, in other words, are said to have used larger amounts of capital per worker than their European counterparts. The steam engine was not a labor-saving innovation in this sense, since its use involved a lower ratio of capital costs to labor costs than the use of waterpower, and the costs of producing its fuel—cutting wood and mining coal—were primarily labor costs. Yet there is no evidence that the steam engine was neglected. Indeed the relatively high interest rates west of the Allegheny Mountains presumably encouraged its adoption. If the assertion about American technology means that Americans saved labor under all circumstances, it is not supported by the evidence on the demand for steam engines. If the assertion means that the relative costs of labor and capital discouraged the use of "capital-saving" innovations, such as the steam engine, it is not supported by the data on interest rates in America, and the response of the demand for steam engines to high rates.

III

Examination of the diffusion of the steam engine shows the limitations of our knowledge of the spread of innovations in the early nineteenth century. We know only the grossest characteristics of the diffusion process and even less about the relative costs of different production methods in particular industries. To the extent that our knowledge extends, the market appears to have worked well, although the characteristics of the market for steam engines differ from those usually ascribed to the "American market." Local rather than national markets were of primary importance, and pressure to favor labor-saving over capital-saving innovations is not evident.

REFERENCES

1. H. W. Dickinson, *A Short History of The Steam Engine*, Cambridge, University Press, 1939.
2. Allen H. Fenichel, "Growth and Diffusion of Power in Manufacturing, 1838–1919," Conference on Research in Income and Wealth, *Output, Employment, and Productivity in the United States After 1800*, (Studies in Income and Wealth, vol. 30), New York, Columbia University Press, 1966, pp. 443–478.
3. Robert E. Gallman, "Gross National Product in the United States, 1834–1909," Conference on Research in Income and Wealth, *Output, Employment, and Productivity in the United States After 1800*, (Studies in Income and Wealth, vol. 30), New York, Columbia University Press, 1966, pp. 3–76.
4. Louis C. Hunter, *Steamboats on the Western Rivers*, Cambridge, Harvard University Press, 1949.
5. United States Congress, House, *Report on the Steam Engines in the States* (25th Congress, 3rd Session), Washington, D.C., 1838.

V INVESTMENT IN EDUCATION: ITS MAGNITUDE AND SIGNIFICANCE

The role of education in economic development was, until recently, badly neglected by economic historians. Even a hasty reading of the leading texts will substantiate this contention. The development of the educational system has not been afforded the lengthy treatment given to transportation, commerce, the banking system, trade unions, or manufacturing. Typically, discussions of education are limited to perfunctory references to such matters as the movement for universal free schooling before the Civil War and to the Morrill Act. This neglect does not imply that economic historians failed to recognize that there was a nexus between education and economic growth. However it was difficult to go beyond that vague generalization to a relatively precise statement of the nature and magnitude of the contribution of education to growth.

The intellectual bottleneck was recently broken when economists began to treat education as an investment which becomes embodied in those who are educated. To some the term "human capital formation" may seem to be a misnomer; and linking "human" and "capital" together may be considered a perversion of the meaning of both words. For capital is *usually* identified with inanimate objects—usually, but by no means always. As Stanley Engerman points out in essay 18, human beings were clearly recognized as a form of capital in the slave society of the antebellum South. Moreover since prices of slaves varied with age, health, and skill levels, it was clear that vocational training (many artisans were slaves) and similar types of education were forms of capital formation. The abolition of slavery did not end the ability of education to increase the income from human labor. Rather it changed the ownership of the right to enjoy the income produced by such capital formation from the slaveowner to the freedman.

Essay 19 by Theodore W. Schultz is one of the landmark papers in the development of the concept of human capital. Schultz set out to estimate the annual amount of capital formation through education over the period from 1900 to 1956. He divided the investment in education into two categories: direct expenditures and foregone earnings. He found that both direct and indirect expenditures on education have risen more rapidly than expenditures on physical capital formation. Consequently the annual investment in this form of human capital formation rose from 9 per cent of physical capital formation in 1900 to 34 per cent in 1956. In essay 20 Albert Fishlow extends the estimates of investment in education back to 1860. He also compares the direct expenditures on education in the United States with those of France, the United Kingdom, and Germany during the last half of the nineteenth century. Douglass North (essay 21) discusses the role of human capital formation in the development of the economy during the pre-Civil War era.

Given the estimate of the annual investment in education, it is possible to determine the rate of return on this investment and the contribution of education to rate of growth of the U.S. economy. Stanley Engerman surveys recent research into these issues in essay 18. The data he assembles show that the rate of return was high but that it varied from grade to grade. In general, a given dollar investment in elementary education yielded a higher return than the same investment at the college level. Engerman presents data on the contribution of education to U.S. economic growth over the period from 1909 to 1965. During these years, education accounted for between one eighth and one fourth of the growth of total output. A comparison with other countries reveals that education contributed about twice as much to the growth of the American economy as it did to the growth of most other nations for which corresponding estimates have been computed.

18

HUMAN CAPITAL, EDUCATION, AND ECONOMIC GROWTH

Stanley L. Engerman

One of the most important ideas to emerge from recent studies of economic growth has been the concept of human capital formation. While the view that capital formation is a major factor in economic growth is quite old, capital was traditionally identified with man-made goods. This emphasis on inanimate objects tended to divert attention from the fact that there were categories of expenditures which increased the future income of individuals and societies but which were embodied in people rather than in goods. Since investment represents a reduction in present consumption in exchange for future income, it is clear that conceptually appropriate definitions of capital formation and national income would include not only costs of education, health, on-the-job training, and migration, but also costs of pregnancy

The author wishes to acknowledge the helpful comments of Sherwin Rosen and Lewis Solmon.

and child-rearing.[1] Similarly, in theoretical analysis of the investment decision there is little formal difference between human capital formation and physical capital formation.[2]

The clearest visualization of human capital formation can be seen in the analysis of slave societies. In such a society it is obvious that slaves represent a form of capital to the members of the free society. Indeed it was frequently claimed that in the ante-bellum South human capital formation in the form of slaves substituted for investment in physical capital. Southerners, it was argued, spent their funds to raise and maintain slaves rather than purchasing machines and equipment.[3] Slaves were bought and sold on the open market, and their value was affected by their ability to produce future income. Prices varied with sex, age, health, and skill level. Slavery being profitable to the individual planter, the market price of a slave was equated to the discounted value of the expected excess of earnings over subsistence costs from the time of purchase. In such a society it was clear that expenditures which increased the number of slaves and their ability to produce future income raised the value of capital embodied in slaves. Thus expenditures upon child-raising, health care, training in skills, and geographic relocation were as much capital formation to their owners as were their purchases of structures and equipment.

The abolition of slavery did not affect the ability of expenditures upon health, training, migration, and child-raising to increase the income from human labor. As was noted after the Civil War, ending the slave system did not destroy the value of the human capital embodied in the former slave. Rather it meant a redistribution of the ownership rights to the value of that capital from the slave-owner to the freedman.[4] Changing the ownership rights to capital does not alter the fact that certain categories of expenditures will increase future incomes.[5] Whether made by slaveowners, governments, or the individual, these expenditures will have the same effects upon future incomes, and such costs exist in all societies, whether slave or free. The basic difference between human capital formation in slave and free societies is that in the former the costs are paid for and benefits go to the owner of the slave, while in free societies most of the benefits and some, but often not all, the costs accrue to the individual in whom the investment is embodied.[6]

The role of investment in humans in free societies has often been overlooked because most of such expenditures have either been ignored or treated as consumption within conventional national income accounting. The traditional procedures of national income accounting have restricted the concept of investment to physical commodities. The reworking of the national accounts for 1929 and 1965 by John Kendrick indicates the importance of expenditures upon human capital formation. Investment in education and

---

[1] For a reworking of the United States national income accounts to allow for these items, see [23]. See also [25, chap. 5].

[2] The major differences relate to the fact that outside of slave societies, individuals cannot transfer their property rights in their own person. There is also a distinction between ownership of one's own human capital and physical capital in that the former cannot be bequested to heirs while the latter can.

[3] For a discussion of this point see [13]. The basic error in the argument, the fact that all societies undertake human capital formation in providing for their offspring, is discussed below.

[4] Therefore freeing the slaves was probably the most massive redistribution project ever undertaken by the United States government. Strictly speaking the total value of human capital in the former slaves could have risen or fallen as a result of emancipation, the outcome depending upon individual work incentives as well as the over-all efficiency of the entrepreneurial class. Also if there were monopsonistic elements in the purchase of labor after the war, some redistribution to landowners could have occurred. Nevertheless the most important effect was the redistribution of the annual surplus of marginal product above subsistence to the freedmen.

[5] Of course the quantity of such expenditures could be effected by ownership. It has been argued that, because of capital market imperfections and other reasons, health, migration, and training expenditures made by the post-bellum freedmen were less than those made on their behalf in the ante-bellum South.

[6] In this analysis and throughout the paper the family is not considered separately from its individual members, so we consider as individual expenditures those made by parents on behalf of their children. Becker's distinction between general and specific training is useful in determining who benefits from particular investments, and therefore provides some indication as to who will pay the costs [3, chap. II]. In free societies there will still be cases where employers pay the cost and receive the benefits of human capital formation embodied in employees.

training, medical and health, mobility, and child-rearing totaled over one quarter of conventionally measured GNP in 1929 with the ratio rising to about 34 per cent in 1965.[7] In both years the total investment in human capital formation was in excess of the officially measured investment in physical capital.[8] In 1965 investment in education and training alone exceeded the officially estimated gross investment. Therefore it is clear that the excluded component has been an important part of society's provision for the future, and one that has been growing quite rapidly relative to national income.

While several categories of human capital formation can be distinguished, the largest expenditure component (and the one most frequently studied) has been formal education. For this reason most of the discussion below will be restricted to education. However the same analytical issues arise for the other types of human capital formation, and the theoretical treatment is similar. There are costs, involving either expenditures of cash or time spent in nonearning purposes, and there are benefits, in the form of an increased present value of an income stream. This increase could be due to enhanced productivity at a given length of working life, higher incomes due to movement to more productive employment, or a longer working life attributed to either less loss of time due to illness or longer life expectancy. Measures of rates of return and contributions to economic growth can therefore be calculated for each category of human capital formation.

I

In this section I shall describe problems in the estimation of the costs and benefits of education. In the next section it will be shown how this information can be used to measure the rate of return upon education, a measure necessary for the understanding of private and social decisions concerning the amount of education to be provided.

---

[7] See [23]. If we exclude costs of child-rearing and research and development, thus restricting the concept to the usual definition of human capital formation, the ratios are 17 per cent and 26 per cent of conventionally measured GNP, respectively.

[8] Officially measured investment also excludes the value of all consumer durable purchases except for residential structures.

Table 1. Educational Expenditures, 1840–1956 (Millions of Current Dollars)

	Direct Expenditures on Education	Foregone Earnings	Total Educational Expenditures
	1. Fishlow		
1840	$ 9.2	$ 6.2[a]	$ 15.4
1860	34.7	24.8	59.5
1880[b]	106.4	72.1	178.5
1900	289.6	213.9	503.5
	2. Schultz		
1900	299	105	404
1920	1437	1062	2499
1940	3861	2478	6339
1956	16295	12405	28700

[a] I have estimated foregone earnings in this year as 40 per cent of total educational expenditures, the approximate ratio for other nineteenth-century years. Based upon enrollment rates this is probably an overstatement.

[b] Solmon's estimates for 1880, prepared on a state-by-state basis, yield education expenditures about 73 per cent higher than Fishlow's [36]. Solmon's estimates of foregone earnings are two and one-half times those of Fishlow, due to Solmon's estimation of higher costs of agricultural labor foregone. The ratio of foregone earnings to total educational expenditures in Solmon's estimates is 58 per cent.

SOURCES: [*12*, pp. 423, 430; *30*, pp. 578, 580].

1. Costs

Recent estimates of the total costs of investment in education from 1840 to 1965 are presented in Table 1. The central concept in the measurement of the costs of education is the economist's notion of opportunity costs. To the economist the cost of any item is equal to the value of the opportunities foregone by the purchaser—the alternative use of his funds or his time. The cost to an individual of investment in education is equal to the current consumption (or alternative investments) foregone. Foregoing of current consumption can arise in two ways. First, expenditures could be made out of current income for tuition, books, school supplies, etc., thereby reducing current consumption from current income in the expectation of a higher future consumption.[9] Second, reduced or no current

---

[9] This expenditure component, whether paid for by the individual or by the government, is included in conventional GNP measures but not as an investment expenditure. Most international comparisons of educational capital formation are restricted to this component, excluding the value of foregone opportunities.

income could be accepted by attending school rather than undertaking employment. The value of the income foregone would depend upon the current alternatives available to the individual, which would reflect his past education. Since education raises incomes, an increase in the number of years of education received by an individual would increase the amount of earnings foregone in further schooling. Similarly a shift in the type of employment from occupations which require only seasonal labor to occupations which use labor year-round would raise the costs of education.[10] For example, Fishlow argues that the cost of income foregone attributable to education in rural areas in the nineteenth century was trivial, the school year being adjusted to provide for free-time during harvests and other periods of peak labor demand [12].[11] With the twentieth-century expansion in urban-industrial employment, and the extension of schooling into older age groups, the costs of income foregone have risen sharply. This rise has been not only in terms of total costs, but also relative to direct expenditures upon education. Fishlow has estimated the ratio between foregone earnings and total expenditures on education was constant from 1860 to 1900, the former comprising about 40 per cent of the latter. For the twentieth century, Schultz, using a different measure for foregone earnings, shows an increase of from 26 per cent of total expenditures in 1900 to 43 per cent in 1956 [30]. The major increase occurred in the decade after 1910, with the rise of high schools.

---

[10] This is true only in terms of conventional national income accounting which regards the imputed value of leisure as zero. If the choice were between leisure and schooling (as well as employment), with leisure valued at the marginal wage rate, then any increased time in school which reduces voluntary leisure is not costless. Therefore a shift such as described in the text need not directly effect the measured costs of education. The increase occurs only when leisure is given a zero valuation for accounting purposes. The measures of income foregone in rural areas made by Fishlow [12] and Solmon [36] assume this, and they may understate the welfare costs of education in agricultural areas.

[11] See Solmon for detailed state-by-state study of rural school time and its seasonal pattern in 1880 and 1890 [36]. While his estimates differ from Fishlow, his estimate of the period for which earnings are foregone are smaller in rural than in urban areas.

The estimation of income foregone presents several difficult theoretical and empirical issues. While data on direct expenditures have generally been collected by various governmental bodies, the preparation of estimates of income foregone requires frequent resort to assumptions about the values of relevant variables. It is necessary to find the approximate opportunity cost for the school-aged population, and a simple aggregation may ignore important differences relating to location and ability.[12] Moreover the age at which it is assumed productive employment can begin is a social convention, and the conventional age of school-leaving has been rising over time. Estimates using a higher age of entry into the labor force will show a lower cost attributable to school attendance for both the individual and society. This can be seen in a comparison of the overlapping 1900 estimates of Fishlow and Schultz. Fishlow, seeking consistency over the course of the nineteenth century, used age 10 as the age of potential labor force entry. Schultz, seeking consistency for the twentieth century, used age 14. Therefore Fishlow's estimated cost of income foregone by students in 1900 is based upon a larger number of potential labor force members than is Schultz's, and is correspondingly higher. Since the choice of the appropriate age to use is based upon arbitrary social conventions, there is no correct procedure. However the use of the earlier age would provide a better indication of what society is foregoing.

Beginning in the mid-nineteenth century various states have legislated on the minimum age of entry into the labor force. This could give rise to possible differences between the costs to society and the costs to the individual due to removal from the labor force of people able to work but below the legal minimum school-leaving age. There is a cost to society accepted in the passage of legislation. However if people are law-abiding, school attendance is costless to individuals. Since the legal prohibition means that productive

---

[12] E.g., by reducing Schultz's single opportunity (manufacturing) into two alternatives based upon location (agriculture and manufacturing), Fishlow cut the estimated cost of income foregone in 1900 in approximately one half. The reason for Fishlow's higher cost, the age at which people are considered to be potential labor force members, is discussed below.

employment could not be obtained, they are foregoing zero income in attending school.[13]

While the entire foregone income costs are borne by the individuals, the direct expenditures can be made either by the individual himself or by the government out of tax revenues collected. In measuring expenditures upon education for the national income accounts it is irrelevant who pays. However the question of who pays will obviously effect the quantity of education which individuals will obtain.[14] Since 1850 there has been an increase in the share of educational expenditures made by governments out of tax revenue relative to privately paid tuition and other costs, particularly at the elementary and secondary school level.[15] Since an individual's tax payments are considered to be independent of his particular schooling needs and desires, the additional cost to each individual attributable to government expenditures upon education is zero.[16] Considering the education tax bill itself as a variable to be voted upon, some discrepancy between private cost and cost to society will exist whenever there is any individual differential between taxes paid and the costs of education received. Thus government provision of education has some element of a transfer in kind to benefit people with school-aged children.[17] We would expect those receiving this subsidy to increase their amount of schooling.

The distinction between private and social costs means that the rate of return to education could be different for the individual and for society. We would expect the private rate of return to those receiving education to exceed the social rate of return, particularly at lower levels of education, where there are no costs of income foregone and the direct costs are almost entirely paid for out of tax-collected funds. This would be true if all benefits were captured by the private individuals receiving education. We should note, however, that most advocates of the public financing of education stress the existence of social benefits above those captured by individuals, raising the measured social rate of return. While the reliance on government tax collections may mean more education than would occur if each person paid for his own education, the presence of social benefits would mean that such an expansion was economically desirable.[18]

2. Benefits

The treatment of the benefits of education provides more conceptual and empirical difficulties than does that of costs. Not only is the distinction between private and social benefits more subtle, but there remain many unresolved problems of empirical determination. While the benefits of education may be in

---

[13] Stigler has argued that compulsory education laws had no long-run effect upon enrollment rates, the laws following high enrollment rates rather than vice versa [38]. This has recently been questioned by Fishlow [12]. The social costs of an increased age of labor force entry would be the same whether it resulted from private decisions or government compulsion, but the interpretation of private costs would differ depending upon the cause of the prolonged schooling.

[14] It is usually argued that a shift from private to government payment of the costs will increase total expenditures upon education and the number receiving education. However the specific outcome will depend upon the allocation of the tax burden and the expenditures which are reduced due to taxation. Once the tax is paid, though, it becomes worthwhile for all individuals to increase their education. Counterarguments to the usual assumption that public provision raises total education expenditures have been made by Friedman [14, chap. VI], based mainly upon the divisibility of such expenditures.

[15] However the share of public direct expenditures has been relatively constant at about 80 per cent of total direct expenditures from 1880 to 1956. The rise occurred in the period before 1880. In the twentieth century the share has remained constant despite the increased college attendance (where the public-private ratio is approximately one half) because of the decline in the share of private primary and secondary education. These estimates are based upon Fishlow and Schultz.

[16] This may be a poor approach to decision-making in regard to education, particularly at lower levels of government. There the individuals benefiting and those taxing are the same. Once the tax bill is treated as variable the marginal cost is not zero.

[17] Publicly owned and operated schools are not the only way to achieve this objective. See [14, chap. VI].

[18] It is possible to design programs, such as payment of students for attending school, so that even the foregone income does not result in private cost. Another argument for government support of education, more specifically loans, would be an imperfect capital market which reduces the ability of individuals to finance expenditures which yield private benefits.

the form of current consumption,[19] future consumption from given income,[20] or higher future income, it is exclusively the latter which has been measured to date. The estimates discussed below of the benefits of education are restricted to the higher incomes captured by individuals receiving education.

The basic source of the data used to measure these benefits of education has been the income-by-education-completed data collected by the Bureau of the Census since 1940. These show that a positive correlation exists at each age between the income earned by an individual and the quantity of education he had previously received. No data collected to date has shown any other pattern. Even adjusting for property income and hours worked, both of which are positively correlated with education, this relationship remains.[21]

The benefits of, e.g., the ninth year of education are measured as the difference between the average income of a person with nine years of education and one with eight. The measured benefit of a college education as opposed to high school education is the difference between the incomes of the average college graduate and that of the average high school graduate. The total benefits of education to any level would be the difference between the average income at that level and that of the uneducated—the payments to raw physical bodies. The annual benefits for each level of education must be accumulated over the lifetime of the individual and discounted at the market rate of interest to determine anticipated lifetime benefits. Since the process of education takes time, unless there were some positive correlation between working life and education received, the earning period of the educated would be less than that of those without education. Given the expectations as to years to be worked, and the age-education-income profiles we can compute the present value of the income stream for varying quantities of education received by persons of given ages. Therefore we can determine the increased present value of lifetime income attributable to completion of each level of education.

The use of observed income-education profiles to compute private benefits of education presents several difficulties, but there is no systematic bias in either direction.[22] The profiles do not allow for consumption benefits of the types described above, nor for the increased ability of the educated to perform certain services which would otherwise have to be purchased in the market.[23] On the other hand, it is argued that the benefits of education are overstated because the levels of education attained are positively correlated with other variables which would lead to higher incomes even with lesser amounts of education. If those who obtain more education are also the more natively intelligent, the more ambitious, the more able, or those with richer parents, the observed income-education profile measures more than the benefits of education per se. If those with any of the above characteristics did not attend college it would still be expected that their incomes would be higher than the average (in ability) high school graduate. For this reason Becker, in his rate of return calculations, and Denison, in his estimates of the contribution of increases in education to economic growth, have reduced the observed differentials [3, chap. IV; 8, chap. 7; 9, chap. 8].[24] However while this issue has been widely discussed, more study is required before anything conclusive can be said concerning the need to make such reductions and, if they are

---

[19] If going to school yields pleasure; this could of course be negative.

[20] If the educated can more efficiently spend future income.

[21] See [34] for data on wage rates by age and education level taken from the 1960 Census.

[22] Miller has commented that the use of a single cross-sectional profile will understate lifetime income streams because of failure to take future growth in income into account [26]. However if the income for all groups rise, it would remain possible for the benefits of additional years of education to be the same as in the earlier cross-section. The question of the benefits of additional education relates to the possibility of differential shifts in the age-education-income profiles over time, not just a general movement upward for all groups.

[23] See Weisbrod for examples, as well as a sample calculation of the value of obtaining enough education to be able to compute one's own income tax [40].

[24] For empirical justifications of such adjustments see [3, chap. IV; 8, chap. 7; and 27]. Griliches has recently questioned the need to make such an adjustment by Denison [18]. A recent study, based upon a sample of A.T. & T. employees, suggests that about one quarter of the differences in earnings between high school and college graduates were attributable to "non-schooling factors" [41].

necessary, the appropriate orders of magnitude.[25]

The question remains as to why education should provide such benefits. The relationship between education and income clearly indicates that the educated are regarded as more productive workers than are the uneducated. However for those interested in the design of educational systems, a crucial question is the exact mechanism by which education has this effect.[26] Education may be required to enable individuals to enter into specific occupations (at least under current legal arrangements). At the lowest level, literacy may be required for the performance of certain tasks at which there would otherwise be considerably lower productivity; e.g., the ability to read and understand directions might be essential to factory work. Beyond these simple cases, however, the substitutability between on-the-job training for specific skills and the acquisition of more general skills via education must be considered. If it is the performance of specific tasks which raises productivity, then it could possibly be more efficient to provide less generalized education and allow more time for specific, on-the-job training. Yet this is the opposite of the development of most educational systems, in which there has been an increase in the number of years of general education provided and where the shift has been to more generalized curricula.

Therefore it would appear that much of the anticipated benefits from education are from generalized skill levels, not specific occupational abilities. Recent work, by Ben-Porath and others, suggests that the educative process should be regarded as providing a more

flexible and adjustable labor force [4]. The more educated can presumably be more easily and inexpensively trained to new positions when there are changes in the industry-occupation output mix. The more rapid are such shifts in occupational structure and requirements, the greater is the importance of the generalized ability to be trained and the less important is training for the performance of specific skills. What education provides is the ability to avoid economic obsolescence. The more educated are considered not only more able to respond to changing geographic and occupational opportunities, but also more alert to the possibilities of introducing profitable economic changes. Schultz, and Nelson and Phelps, have argued that the educated undertake more invention and innovation, and are quicker to adopt new techiques and methods [32, 28]. Therefore both the level of and the diffusion of innovations would be expected to be more rapid, the higher is the level of education achieved by a society. The educated themselves would benefit from the more rapid adoption of profitable procedures in the form of higher entrepreneurial incomes.

What this line of argument suggests is that the relationship between education and income would vary with the rate of economic growth and the rapidity of structural change. At low levels of structural change the over-all pay-off to formal education would be less than that in societies undergoing more rapid transformation.[27] Conversely the ability of a society to respond to the stimulus of externally provided knowledge will be greatly effected by the level of education achieved.[28]

In the preceding discussion of the private benefits from education it has been assumed that all of the benefits of increased education have been captured by the individuals receiving that education in the form of higher incomes. There may, however, be cases where this is not true. It is necessary to consider

[25] A related issue is the correlation among the varieties of human capital formation. If the educated are more mobile, take better care of themselves, and receive more on-the-job training, the use of average income profiles overstates the "pure" benefits of education as such, though not perhaps in some ultimate causal sense. However, as Becker shows, the rates of return to education per se need not be mis-stated if we calculate separate rates of return to each component of human capital [3, chap. IV].

[26] It is assumed here that education raises productivity and does not serve merely as a screening device to provide higher incomes to "certified" individuals. While even an efficient screening device provides social benefits, it would imply that increased education is not itself the cause of enhanced productivity, and that perhaps alternative, less expensive, screening procedures could be devised.

[27] This ignores the problem of the relationship between education and the factors causing technological transformation. Education may not only condition the response, but also provide the knowledge which is a primary cause of structural change in the economy.

[28] Easterlin notes that in the nineteenth century the "followers" in the process of industrialization "almost uniformly had relatively high school enrollment ratios as early as 1830" [10].

various external benefits in the calculation of the social rate of return. One simple source of such a difference can be seen in the calculations by Becker and Hansen described below [*3, 20*]. In measuring the private benefits to education, they used after-tax incomes. This implies that the individual's utility is reduced to the extent of his tax payments.[29] Hansen's calculation of social benefits used before-tax incomes, arguing that the higher incomes received in the market are the measure of the increased productive ability of the educated. This treatment of taxes paid by the individual to the government is one illustration of how the benefits of education may be captured by individuals other than those receiving the education.

There may be other benefits of education not fully captured by the individual. Within the conventional economic sphere the customary cases discussed are the external benefits of research and development and their embodiment in invention and innovation. If the latter are positively correlated with education and if, due to legal or other reasons, inventors and innovators do not capture their true social product, the use of education-income profiles would understate the contribution of these people to society and, therefore, the contribution of education.[30]

A more general statement of the contribution of education to economic growth, which

suggests large uncaptured benefits, is that only through education is it possible to have the social and political framework appropriate for modern economic development. This argument states that mass education and literacy is necessary for political stability, and that through political stability economic growth becomes possible.[31] While this argument can surely be questioned, and many counter-examples presented, we see this position most clearly in the traditional treatments of the role of education in American society. While it has influenced the discussion concerning the education of the native-born, the debates concerning the amalgamation of immigrants into American society emphasized this form of social benefit to the almost complete exclusion of economic benefits. A similar point has reappeared, this time with more attention paid to individual economic benefits, in the debates concerning aid to ghetto education. While attention is paid to the education-income relationship, the use of redistributive government tax-expenditure policy for schooling is frequently justified by its contribution to social stability and the reductions anticipated in the amounts required to pay for certain governmental services, such as police protection and welfare.

II

In calculating the rate of return to education we wish to find that rate which equates the present value of the stream of benefits attributable to education to the present value of the costs of obtaining that education. Equation 1 will be used to indicate the data necessary to compute the rate of return upon the thirteenth year of education.

$$C + X_o = \sum_{i=1}^{n} \frac{Y_i - X_i}{(1 + r)^i} \qquad (1)$$

where

C = direct expenditures for the thirteenth year of education
X_i = annual earnings of those receiving twelve years of education

---

[29] This follows a long tradition which omits the benefit of government—provided goods and services from the utility value of an individual's consumption, regarding the tax as a forced draft upon the individual and not a voluntary exchange for certain government-provided consumption. The justification, in the short run, would be that for each individual the government-provided goods and services are independent of tax payments. This cannot be true in the long run, and it can be argued that Hansen should have used the before-tax income in the computation of the private benefits and included the allocated part of the tax going to education as a private cost. Then average private and social returns would be the same under this procedure, with rates varying by individuals to the extent of any net redistribution via the government budget.

[30] This could imply that all technological change should be attributed to education. Becker has used Denison's estimates of the sources of U.S. growth between 1929 and 1957 to set bounds on the social return to education. By attributing all the residual growth in knowledge to education Becker obtains a social rate of return double the private return. Becker suggests that the true social rate is probably below this maximum [*3*, chap. V].

[31] Of course this begs the questions about political organization and growth. Even then, however, it could be argued that education and literacy are required for economic development independent of the political institutions and system of control.

Y_i = annual earnings of those receiving thirteen years of education

n = the total number of years earnings will be received after the thirteenth year of education

r = the rate of return upon the thirteenth year of education

i = the observations for each year

The total cost of acquiring one more year of education is $C + X_0$—the sum of direct expenditures and earnings foregone in attending school that year. The annual benefits obtained from that year of education are the values of $Y - X$. These benefits are to be received for n years of productive life after this thirteenth year of education is completed. The rate of return, r, from this additional year of education is computed by solving equation 1.

The data necessary for this computation are: direct expenditures on education, average annual earnings of those with twelve years of education and of those with thirteen, and the length of the period over which income will be earned. To determine whether education has been a profitable investment it is then necessary to compare the calculated rate of return with the rates of return earnable on alternative investments.[32] In this example, as in the studies described below, the benefits of education are restricted to higher earnings. If we were to argue that education increased future consumption for given earnings, this would be added to the benefit stream, raising the rate of return upon education. Similarly if going to school yields positive pleasure, this could be treated as an additional benefit of education (or as a reduction in the cost of education) again yielding a higher rate of return.

Rates of return calculated in several studies of the United States are presented in Table 2. All used data were collected by the Bureau of the Census for age-education-income profiles. For a full understanding of these calculations and their implications it would be necessary to turn to the original studies. The Becker and Hansen calculations of private rates of return are based upon private

---

[32] If it is argued that the private costs of education mainly replace consumption expenditures rather than expenditures upon other investments, the appropriate comparison would be the rate of return upon education with the discount rate applied to future consumption. With perfect markets, however, that would be the same as the market rate of interest.

Table 2. Rates of Return to Education, United States

A. *Private Rates of Return, White Male High School and College Graduates (Becker)*[a,b]

	College	High School
1939	14.5%	16%
1949	13.0	20
1956	12.4	25
1958	14.8	28

B. *Private and Social Returns to Education, Males, 1949 (Hansen)*[a]

	Level	Private[b]	Social[c]
Grades	1–2	∞	8.9%
	3–6	∞	14.5
	7–8	∞	29.2
	9–10	12.3%	9.5
	11–12	17.5	13.7
	13–14	5.1	5.4
	15–16	16.7	15.6

C. *Private Rates of Return, White Males, by Regions, 1959 (Hanoch)*[a,b]

Level	North	South
5–7	—[d]	—[d]
8	21.8%	14.4%
9–11	16.3	18.2
12	16.0	18.8
13–15	7.1	9.3
16	12.2	11.0
17+	7.0	7.3

[a] These are marginal rates for each level, giving the effects of increased education over the preceding level.
[b] Benefits based on after-tax income.
[c] Benefits based on before-tax income.
[d] Extremely high (above 100%).

SOURCES: [*3*, p. 128; *20, 19*].

costs (including foregone opportunities) and after-tax incomes. Hanoch's calculations are based upon private costs and before-tax income. The social rate of return computed by Hansen is derived from before-tax incomes and all costs of education, whether paid for by individuals (directly or in the form of income foregone) or by the government.[33] Except for the Becker calculation described above, there have been no estimates of any of the broader concepts of social returns. It is usually argued that the sum of private returns and narrowly defined social returns,

---

[33] Hansen's private rates of return generally exceed the social rate of return, though the difference narrows at higher levels of education.

which do yield rates of return in excess of those upon alternative investments, are lower bound estimates of the true social rate, so that policies to expand education are justified.[34]

The logic of these calculations can be understood by placing oneself in the position of a person making a decision as to whether or not to continue schooling. Information is available as to the current costs of obtaining this education, as well as benefits to be expected. These benefits are indicated by the currently observed age-education-income profile.[35] In this sense the calculations represent *ex ante* rates of return, being based on the information available at the time at which the individual decisions are made. They do not describe the actual (*ex post*) rates of return earned by any cohort of individuals. For those individuals currently receiving income who were educated previously, it is probable that their costs of education were less than the costs of those currently being educated.[36] Therefore the actual rate of return for that cohort would be higher than the *ex ante* expectations implied by this procedure, and would be higher than that estimated for the cohort currently undergoing education. Of course the *ex post* rate of return earned by those being currently educated could be quite different from their *ex ante* calculations, being either higher or lower than anticipated. There could be windfall gains to the educated, due to shifts in the demand for certain types of labor, or for the same reason, there could be economic obsolescence of skills learned. While the education-income profiles used in these calculations reflect the outcome of past supply-demand conditions, the estimation procedure usually treats these profiles as indicative of the expectations of those making investment decisions.

It may be, however, that the form of the calculations described above do not accurately reflect the actual decision-making process of individuals. Assuming that people can and do make calculations of this form, and ignoring problems of the utility to be attached to different amounts of income, the calculations above used incomes for the entire expected productive lifetime of each individual. This implies that people have a planning horizon equal to their expected lifetime. If, however, individuals have shorter planning horizons, then their decisions would be based upon a smaller stream of benefits and the rate of return would be less than that calculated on the basis of a lifetime horizon. Schultz, e.g., has argued that the actual horizon is much shorter than the expected remaining life, because of the great uncertainty people have about future economic developments [*33*]. If so, people will tend to underestimate the rate of return to be obtained from additional education.

The three studies presented in Table 2, although referring to different groups and years and applying different adjustment procedures to the raw data, show a somewhat consistent pattern. Generally rates of return were higher for earlier levels of education, implying diminishing economic returns to increased education at each point in time. Private rates of return for lower levels of education were quite high, because most direct costs of elementary school attendance were paid for by governments and the value of foregone income was negligible. Nevertheless even the social rates of return computed by Hansen for these early years of education are high relative to the rates of return earned upon investment in physical capital.

The only one of the set of calculations which was directly concerned with making comparisons over time were those by Becker. In the years shown in Table 2 there was a sharp rise in the rate of return upon high school education, with relatively constant return to college education. Surveying some data relating to earlier twentieth-century years, Becker argues that the post-1939 situation represents a reversal of the earlier pattern. Income differentials by education level appeared smaller in 1939 than they were in the preceding period. Comparing Hansen's rates for 1949 with Hanoch's for

---

[34] Alternative rates of return depend, of course, upon what is chosen for purposes of comparison. Stigler's estimated after-tax rates of return to capital invested in manufacturing averaged 7 per cent between 1938 and 1957 [*39*; See *3*, p. 115]. It has been estimated that the rate of discount applied to the marginal tax dollar collected from consumers was 6 per cent in 1953 [*11*]. Therefore expenditures on education yielded at least the rates upon these alternatives.

[35] Becker adjusted his estimates for assumed expected changes in the distribution of income by education completed, rather than assuming an unchanged distribution. See also footnote 22.

[36] This would be true of foregone earnings if all wages rose at the same rate, so that the costs (the absolute dollar differentials) were lower in earlier periods. Correspondingly the annual benefits would be increasing over time.

1959 indicates little marked change in either direction at most levels. It would seem easier to argue for constancy in rates of return in this time period than for either pronounced increases or decreases in the pay-off to education.

There are, unfortunately, no calculations for the nineteenth-century United States. No one has yet found a body of data sufficient to systematically estimate rates of return.[37] It is possible that rates of return for contemporary underdeveloped economies may provide some clue to rates of return at lower levels of national income, though such comparisons can only be suggestive. Differences in the level of technology and the quantity of complementary factors, particularly physical capital, preclude drawing any general conclusions. There have been rate of return estimates prepared for several Latin American countries as well as for India in the late 1950s [6, 15]. The rates of return for India were roughly comparable at all education levels with those found for the United States. Latin American-United States differentials did have more variation by education level, but in general the Latin American rates of return were comparable with those found in the post-war United States. The major differences were the considerably higher rates of return to elementary schooling in Venezuela and the higher return to college graduates in the rapidly growing economies of Mexico and Venezuela.[38] At lower levels of education, however, the rates of return (private and social) were similar. There would be no presumption, therefore, of a marked change in the rate of return to primary education in the United States since the nineteenth century, but more direct study of the question is necessary before anything conclusive can be said on this issue.

III

The recent economic interest in education has developed out of the problems of explaining

past economic growth. Once it became clear that increases in physical capital could account for only a small part of the great increases in output in the United States and elsewhere, economists sought other factors which could be used to explain growth. To understand these studies and their implications for the role of education, it will be useful to first briefly summarize the production function approach to the measurement of contributions to economic growth.

The aggregate production function for each period of time expresses the relationship between output (national income) and various inputs. In the simplest production function the two inputs considered are the stock of physical capital (or its service flows) and the quantity of the labor force (measured either in number of bodies or number of man-hours). In the earlier studies which measured the contributions of increases in labor and capital to the growth in national income a large component remains unexplained.[39] This unexplained component, called the residual, became something which it was necessary to explain in order to understand the process of economic growth, and many economists have redefined the inputs into the production function for this purpose.

To understand the issues we can use the production function underlying most current studies, the Cobb-Douglas. This is:

$$Y = A \; K^{\alpha}L^{\beta} \qquad (2)$$

where Y is national income, K, capital input, L labor input, A a shift term, and α and β the respective shares of capital and labor in income (summing to one).[40] To explain the rate of growth of income, equation 3 is derived from equation 2, where · refers to the change in a particular time period.

$$\frac{\dot{Y}}{Y} = \frac{\dot{A}}{A} + \alpha \; \frac{\dot{K}}{K} + \beta \; \frac{\dot{L}}{L} \qquad (3)$$

The rate of growth of income is equal to the residual ($\dot{A}/A$), plus the rate of growth of each of the factors weighted by its share in output. Since the labor share is generally

[37] Becker has suggestive inferences drawn from data on relative wages by skill level. Although the wages of skilled workers relative to those of unskilled have declined, the absolute differences have increased so that rates of return to skill need not have fallen [3, chap. III].

[38] It should be noted that Becker suggests a higher rate of return to high school and college education in 1900 than in 1940.

[39] See, e.g., [29, 1, 37, 22]. Kendrick did make one adjustment for the changing mix of labor by industries, weighting labor input by relative industry wages in each year [22].

[40] For a description of this function and some of its properties see [5].

three times the capital share (75 per cent vs. 25 per cent), for equal percentage rates of growth of the inputs, the growth in labor explains three times as much of the growth as the increase in physical capital.

In breaking down the residual, one of the first steps was the redefinition of the labor input. The measures previously used had been of labor in physical units, implying that each body (or man-hour) should be considered as an equivalent input. This, however, is clearly not the case, since the market does not consider all bodies equally productive. Rather a worker whose average income is $10,000 is considered to represent twice as much labor input as one whose income is $5,000. The use of this market information on relative incomes permits adjustment of the number of physical units to allow for changes in the quality of labor. All that is necessary is to find an appropriate variable correlated with income.[41]

The variable most frequently used has been based upon the quantity of education received by members of the labor force. As discussed above, the education-income profiles indicate that people with more education are valued more highly in the market than people with less education. If, e.g., persons with a college education earn $10,000 and those with high school educations only $5,000, we consider those completing college as twice as much economic input as those completing only high school. If we use these relative incomes to weight the quantities of labor in each education category, we can derive an index of labor quality which changes over time with changes in the number of people in each education category.[42] Thus, E, the quality index is:

$$E_t = \sum \frac{Y_i}{\bar{Y}} \cdot \frac{N_i}{N} \qquad (4)$$

where $(Y_i/\bar{Y})$ is the relative income of the ith educational level in the base year ($\bar{Y}$ being the average income for all groups in the base year); N_i is the quantity of labor in that category in the year, t, for which the index is calculated; and N the total labor force.[43] The rate of growth of total labor input is:

$$\frac{\dot{L}}{L} = \frac{\dot{N}}{N} + \sum \frac{Y_i}{\bar{Y}} \left(\frac{\dot{N}_i}{N}\right) \qquad (5)$$

The quantity of labor input can increase due to increases in the physical number of units of labor of constant quality, increases in the quality of a constant number of physical units of labor, or some combination of the two. A doubling of the average quality of labor (E) with an unchanged number of workers (N) represents the same increase in labor input (L) as a doubling of the number of workers of constant quality. The average quality of the labor will increase as the average level of education in the labor force rises, with more people shifting upward into higher educational categories.

The effect of this redefinition of labor upon the measurement of the growth contribution of labor can be seen by looking at Denison's estimates for the period 1929–1957 [8, p. 265]. The net increase in physical units of labor input, defined as man-hours adjusted for the estimated effects of the changes in hours worked upon productivity, was 1.08 per cent per annum. This increase accounted for approximately 27 per cent of the growth of total output. Denison estimated that the average quality of the labor force grew at 0.93 per cent per annum.[44] This yields an

---

[41] The discussion follows the procedure used by Denison, though it ignores several of his refinements and adjustments. For criticisms of specific adjustments and uses of data see [2, 34, 18] among others.

[42] The relative incomes for different levels of education completed have remained roughly constant for the period in which good data exist in the U.S. Therefore no major index number problem arises from the choice of a base year.

[43] Selowsky has stressed that this measure of increased quality should not be confused with the measure of the contribution of education [35]. If there is any turnover or new entrants in the labor force, some expenditures on education are necessary to hold the average quality constant. Selowsky estimated that one tenth of the U.S. growth rate between 1950 and 1962 was attributable to this maintenance factor, while accepting Denison's estimate of 15 per cent for the contribution of quality increases attributable to education. The relative importance of the maintenance factor is much larger in less developed economies, the relative contribution of the maintenance component being 10 times as important as the increase component in India.

[44] In this measure Denison reduced differentials by education levels to 60 per cent of the observed levels, attributing the remainder to ability, intelligence, father's income, and other factors discussed above. This should reduce the rate of growth of labor quality. For a criticism of the assumptions and methods of this adjustment procedure see [18]. In his own work Griliches uses the unadjusted income differentials, arguing that it is not possible to separate out the pure effects of education.

HUMAN CAPITAL, EDUCATION,
AND ECONOMIC GROWTH *253*

Table 3. Estimates of the Growth Contribution of Increased Quality of the Labor Force to Growth of Total Output

	Rate of Growth of Output (1)	Rate of Growth of Quality (2)	Contribution of Quality Increase to Growth[a] (3)
United States:			
1909–1929[b]	2.82%	.56%	12%
1929–1957[b]	2.93	.93	23
1950–1962[c]	3.32	.62	15
1945–1965[d]	3.59	.71	14
Belgium 1950–1962[c]	3.20	.58	14
Denmark 1950–1962[c]	3.51	.18	4
France 1950–1962[c]	4.92	.37	6
Germany 1950–1962[c]	7.26	.15	2
Netherlands 1950–1962[c]	4.73	.32	5
Norway 1950–1962[c]	3.45	.33	7
United Kingdom 1950–1962[c]	2.29	.37	12
Italy 1950–1962[c]	5.96	.55	7
Mexico 1940–1964[e]	6.34	.39	3
Chile 1940–1964[e]	3.73	.53	7
India 1950–1960[e]	3.74	.03	1

[a] Rate of growth of quality (col. 2) multiplied by the labor share in output and divided by column 1.
[b] From [8, pp. 265–266].
[c] From [9, chaps. 15, 21].
[d] From [21].
[e] From [35].

increase in total labor input (before adjusting for the effects of the changing age-sex composition of the labor force) of 2.01 per cent per annum—almost double that attributable to the increased units of physical input.

Increased average quality attributable to education explains approximately 23 per cent of the growth in total output and 42 per cent of the growth of output per person employed.

Table 3 presents estimates of the measured contribution of the increase in labor force quality (attributable to increased education) to economic growth in the United States, as well as in several European and underdeveloped economies. It is clear that its measured contribution has been greater in the United States than in the other countries, as was the rate of increase of quality. Even in the postwar period the increase in labor force quality in the United States has been higher than elsewhere. The increase accelerated after 1929 with the widespread diffusion of first high school and then college education.

The previous discussion had assumed that

the output elasticity with respect to labor quality was equal to the output elasticity of the physical units of labor input. The appropriateness of this assumption has been tested by Griliches, not for the entire economy, but separately for agriculture and manufacturing [see 18]. The test used regressions of production functions in which the physical input and quality index were treated as separate inputs, and their coefficients were free to vary. These tests indicated no statistically significant differential between the two coefficients, providing some justification for the procedure used by Denison. Therefore in his sectoral estimates Griliches also used the output elasticity of labor to measure the growth contribution of changes in labor quality. However, unlike Denison, Griliches did not adjust income-differentials by education level for ability and other factors. Nevertheless his results, presented in Table 4, do not differ significantly from those of Denison's for the aggregate economy. The growth contribution in manufacturing was greater than in agriculture both because of the greater growth in the quality index in

Table 4. Estimates of the Growth Contribution of Increased Quality to Growth of Total Output, Agriculture and Manufacturing, United States

	Rate of Growth of Output	Rate of Growth of Quality	Contribution of Quality Increase to Growth
Agriculture: 1940–1960	2.47%	0.67%	12.2%[a]
Manufacturing: 1947–1960	3.22	1.00	22.6

[a] The measured contribution includes scale effects since the sum of coefficients exceeded one.

SOURCES: [*16, 17*].

the former sector and because of its greater output elasticity with respect to labor.

These calculations all suggest a positive contribution from education to economic growth in the United States. There are, however, many reasons to argue about the specifics of these calculations and to indicate under what conditions they be too low or too high. Nevertheless most economists appear to agree that results qualitatively different from those summarized above are unlikely.[45]

---

[45] For an early estimate of the contribution of education to economic growth based upon a somewhat different procedure, but which yields results similar to Denison's see [*31*]. Schwartzman, by making two key adjustments, does cut the growth contribution of education to U.S. growth between 1930 and 1960 to one third of Denison's estimate [*34*]. Since the critique is of Denison's over-all procedure it is probable that the international comparisons based on Denison in Table 3 would not be affected, the measured contribution of education in all countries being reduced. Denison, for 1930–1960, had estimated an increase in labor force quality of 32.6 per cent; 14.2 per cent attributable to additional school years and the remainder to additional days in school. Schwartzman reduces the contribution of increased days per year of school by 30 per cent, claiming that to count increases in school years and school days as equivalent as done by Denison overstates the effect of the latter. The major difference, however, is Schwartzman's use of hourly earnings in nonagriculture industries classified by age and education level, rather than Denison's income-education profile. This takes out the effects of positive correlations between education and property earnings and education and hours worked. Schwartzman estimates the quality of the labor force due to more school years to have increased by approximately 6.8 per cent, less than one half the Denison increase, and his adjustment for school-days raises the total increase to 11.9 per cent. Even then, however, the contribution of increased education to growth in national income per person employed would exceed the contribution of increased physical capital for this time period.

These conclusions, plus the data on international differences in income levels presented below form the basis for the emphasis in both developed and underdeveloped economies upon educational expansion.

In discussing causes of international differences in income levels, it is necessary to differentiate between developed and underdeveloped economies. Calculations made by Denison for those European economies listed in Table 3 show that the cross-section average quality differentials vis-à-vis the United States are quite small. With the exception of Italy, the average quality per labor force member in 1960 for each of the countries was at least 90 per cent that of the United States.[46] Average quality differentials can explain only a small part, generally less than 10 per cent, of United States-European differences in income per person employed.[47] The results of a study of Canadian-United States differentials in average quality of labor and income differentials leads to a similar conclusion concerning comparative levels of quality per person employed (Canada's is

---

[46] [*9*, chap. 8]. The average quality index in Italy was 80 per cent that of the United States. The major difference between the United States and Europe has been the greater dispersion of education levels in the United States. Most European nations have large concentrations at the legal age of school leaving, whereas the United States distribution peaks at both ages of leaving primary and secondary schools. Denison comments that the greater dispersion in the United States may aid the economy in being more flexible in matching supplies and demands for labor.

[47] The major determinant was the residual called by Denison "lags in the application of knowledge, general efficiency, and errors and omissions." This could include the effects of education on the process of industrial diffusion, with the implication that the spread between private and social returns to innovators was greater in the U.S. than elsewhere.

94.3 per cent of that of the United States) and its contribution to the differentials in income levels (19.8 per cent).[48] However a comparison of the United States with underdeveloped economies made by Anne Krueger concludes that the most important differences relate to the stock of educated capital [24]. She argues that the lower levels of education achieved in these societies are more important in explaining their backwardness relative to the United States than their absence of physical capital, though education differentials do not fully explain the income differentials. Therefore while expansions in the stock of human capital arising from education in underdeveloped economies should increase their rates of economic growth and narrow their income differentials from the developed economies it will not alone be sufficient to close the gap.

IV

The preceding sections have dealt almost exclusively with human capital formation through education. This does not mean that education is the sole, or even the most important, form of human capital formation in the explanation of economic growth. Improvements in health (particularly the decline in infant mortality), immigration, internal migration, and on-the-job training in specific skills and in problem-solving have all played major roles in development through the lifetime productivity of the population. More studies of these varieties of human capital formation can be expected which will cast light on the process of economic growth in the United States and elsewhere, as well as provide important guides to policymakers in those nations which wish to undertake measures to promote economic development.

REFERENCES

1. Moses Abramowitz, *Resource and Output Trends in the United States Since 1870*, National Bureau of Economic Research Occasional Paper 52, New York, 1956.

2. Moses Abramowitz, "Economic Growth in the United States: A Review Article," *The American Economic Review, 52* (September, 1962), 762–782.
3. Gary S. Becker, *Human Capital: A Theoretical and Empirical Analysis, with Special Reference to Education*, New York, Columbia University Press, 1964.
4. Yoram Ben-Porath, "Production of Human Capital and the Life Cycle of Earnings," *The Journal of Political Economy, 75* (August, 1967), 352–365.
5. Murray Brown, *On the Theory and Measurement of Technological Change*, Cambridge, University Press, 1966.
6. Martin Carnoy, "Rates of Return to Schooling in Latin America," *The Journal of Human Resources, 2* (Summer, 1967), 359–374.
7. D. J. Daly and D. Walters, "Factors in Canada-United States Real Income Differences," *The Review of Income and Wealth*, Series 13 (December, 1967), 285–309.
8. Edward F. Denison, *The Sources of Economic Growth in the United States and the Alternatives Before Us*, Supplementary Paper No. 13, New York, Committee for Economic Development, 1962.
9. Edward F. Denison, *Why Growth Rates Differ: Postwar Experience in Nine Western Countries*, Washington, The Brookings Institution, 1967.
10. Richard A. Easterlin, "A Note on the Evidence of History," C. Arnold Anderson and Mary Jean Bowman, eds., *Education and Economic Development*, Chicago, Aldine, 1965, pp. 422–425.
11. Otto Eckstein and John Krutilla, "The Cost of Federal Money, Hell's Canyon, and Economic Efficiency: Part I," *National Tax Journal, 11* (March, 1958), 1–20.
12. Albert Fishlow, "Levels of Nineteenth-Century American Investment in Education," *The Journal of Economic History, 26* (December, 1966), 418–436. [Reprinted below as essay 20.]
13. Robert W. Fogel and Stanley Engerman, "The Economics of Slavery," (printed below as essay 24).
14. Milton Friedman, *Capitalism and Freedom*, Chicago, University of Chicago Press, 1962.
15. A. M. Nalla Gounod, "Investment in Education in India," *The Journal of Human Resources, 2* (Summer, 1967), 347–358.
16. Zvi Griliches, "The Sources of Measured Productivity Growth: U.S. Agriculture, 1940–1960," *The Journal of Political Economy, 17* (August, 1963), 331–346.
17. Zvi Griliches, "Production Functions in

[48] [7]. The Canadian-United States income differential was less than Europe-United States differences, accounting for the greater contribution of differences in labor quality to differences in income levels in the former comparison.

Manufacturing: Some Preliminary Results," Conference on Research in Income and Wealth, *The Theory and Empirical Analysis of Production* (Studies in Income and Wealth, vol. 31), New York, Columbia University Press, 1967, pp. 275–322.

18. Zvi Griliches "Notes on the Role of Education in Production Functions and Growth Accounting," Conference on Research in Income and Wealth, *Education, Income, and Human Capital* (Studies in Income and Wealth, vol. 35), New York, Columbia University Press, 1970, pp. 71–115.

19. Giora Hanoch, "An Economic Analysis of Earnings and Schooling," *The Journal of Human Resources, 2* (Summer, 1967), 310–329.

20. W. Lee Hansen, "Total and Private Rates of Return to Investment in Schooling," *The Journal of Political Economy, 81* (April, 1963), 128–141.

21. Dale W. Jorgenson and Zvi Griliches, "The Explanation of Productivity Change," *The Review of Economic Studies, 34* (July, 1967), 249–284.

22. John W. Kendrick, *Productivity Trends in the United States*, Princeton, Princeton University Press, 1961.

23. John W. Kendrick, "Studies in the National Income Accounts," *Forty-Seventh Annual Report, National Bureau of Economic Research* (June, 1967), pp. 9–15.

24. Anne O. Krueger, "Factor Endowments and *Per Capita* Income Differences Among Countries," *The Economic Journal, 78* (September, 1968), 641–659.

25. Simon Kuznets, *Modern Economic Growth: Rate, Structure, and Spread*, New Haven, Yale University Press, 1966.

26. Herman P. Miller, "Lifetime Income and Economic Growth," *The American Economic Review, 55* (September, 1965), 834–844.

27. James Morgan and Martin H. David, "Education and Income," *The Quarterly Journal of Economics, 77* (August, 1963), 423–437.

28. Richard R. Nelson and Edmund S. Phelps, "Investment in Humans, Technological Diffusion, and Economic Growth," *The American Economic Review, 56* (May, 1966), 69–75.

29. Jacob Schmookler, "The Changing Efficiency of the American Economy: 1869–1938," *The Review of Economics and Statistics, 34* (August, 1952), 214–231.

30. Theodore W. Schultz, "Capital Formation by Education," *The Journal of Political Economy, 68* (December, 1960), 571–583. [Reprinted below as essay 19.]

31. Theodore W. Schultz, "Education and Economic Growth," N. B. Henry, ed., *Social Forces Influencing American Education*, Chicago, National Society for the Study of Education, 1961, pp. 46–88.

32. Theodore W. Schultz, *Transforming Traditional Agriculture*, New Haven, Yale University Press, 1964.

33. Theodore W. Schultz, "The Rate of Return in Allocating Investment Resources to Education," *The Journal of Human Resources, 2* (Summer, 1967), 293–309.

34. David Schwartzman, "The Contribution of Education to the Quality of Labor, 1929–1963," *The American Economic Review, 58* (June, 1968), 508–514.

35. Marcelo Selowsky, *Education and Economic Growth: Some International Comparisons*, Unpublished doctoral dissertation, University of Chicago, 1967.

36. Lewis C. Solmon, "Estimates of the Costs of Schooling in 1880 and 1890," *Explorations in Economic History, 7* (No. 4), Supplement.

37. Robert M. Solow, "Technical Change and the Aggregate Production Function," *The Review of Economics and Statistics, 39* (August, 1957), 312–320.

38. George J. Stigler, *Employment and Compensation in Education*, National Bureau of Economic Research Occasional Paper 33, New York, 1950.

39. George J. Stigler, *Capital and Rates of Return in Manufacturing Industries*, Princeton, Princeton University Press, 1963.

40. Burton A. Weisbrod, "Education and Investment in Human Capital," *The Journal of Political Economy, 70* (October, 1962, Part 2), 106–123.

41. Burton A. Weisbrod and Peter Karpoff, "Monetary Returns to College Education, Student Ability, and College Quality," *The Review of Economics and Statistics, 50* (November, 1968), 491–497.

19 CAPITAL FORMATION BY EDUCATION

Theodore W. Schultz

I propose to treat education as an investment in man and to treat its consequences as a form of capital. Since education becomes a part of the person receiving it, I shall refer to it as *human capital*. Since it becomes an integral part of a person, it cannot be bought or sold or treated as property under our institutions. Nevertheless it is a form of capital if it renders a productive service of value to the economy. The principal hypothesis underlying this treatment of education is that some important increases in national income are a consequence of additions to the stock of this form of capital.

Reprinted with omissions by permission from *The Journal of Political Economy*, 68 (December, 1960), 571–583. [The original paper contains 21 footnotes which give assumptions, additional estimates, and underlying calculations, and it also lists the sources of data appearing in each of the six tables. Anyone undertaking research in this area will undoubtedly want to study the omitted footnotes and the list of sources which are a part of the original paper. Acknowledgment of the debt of the author to colleagues and graduate students also appears as part of the original paper.—Editors' note.]

Although it will be far from easy to put this hypothesis to the test, there are many indications that some, and perhaps a substantial part, of the unexplained increases in national income in the United States are attributable to the formation of this kind of capital.

Education can be pure consumption or pure investment, or it can serve both these purposes. But whatever it is in these respects, education in the United States requires a large stream of resources. The principal task of this paper is to present a set of estimates of the value of the resources that have been entering into education. These resources consist chiefly of two components—the earnings that students forego while attending school and the resources to provide schools. Our estimates begin with 1900, cover the next five decennial years, and close with 1956. The annual factor costs are given in current prices. A major section is devoted to the earnings that students forego while they attend school, both because of their importance and because these foregone earnings have heretofore been neglected. More than half the total resources that enter into high school, college, and university education consists of the time and effort of students. The section on costs of the educational services that the schools provide introduces estimates of the value of school property used for education, along with current expenditures for salaries, wages, and materials.

Capital formation by means of education is neither small nor a neat constant in relation to the formation of nonhuman capital. It is not small even if a substantial part of the total cost of education were strictly for consumption. What our estimates will show is that the stream of resources entering into elementary education has increased less than that entering into either high school or higher education. But even so, it has been increasing at a larger rate than has the gross formation of physical capital. In 1900 the total cost of elementary education was equal to about 5 per cent of gross capital formation compared to 9 per cent in 1956. Comparable figures for high school and higher education combined are 4 per cent in 1900 and almost 25 per cent in 1956.

It is held by many to be degrading to man and morally wrong to look upon his education as a way of creating capital. To those who hold this view the very idea of human capital is repugnant, because for them education is basically cultural and not economic in its

purpose, because education serves to develop individuals to become competent and responsible citizens by giving men and women an opportunity to acquire an understanding of the values they hold and an appreciation of what they mean to life. My reply to those who believe thus is that an analysis that treats education as one of the activities that may add to the stock of human capital in no way denies the validity of their position; my approach is not designed to show that these cultural purposes should not be, or are not being, served by education. What is implied is that, in addition to achieving these cultural goals, some kinds of education may improve the capabilities of a people as they work and manage their affairs and that these improvements may increase the national income. These cultural and economic effects may thus be joint consequences of education. My treatment of education will in no way detract from, or disparage, the cultural contributions of education. It takes these contributions for granted and proceeds to the task of determining whether there are also some economic benefits from education that may appropriately be treated as capital that can be identified and estimated.

Let me now present the sources of the estimates that follow, making explicit the underlying assumptions and commenting on the data so that the reader may have a basis for determining the limitations of these estimates. The more important economic implications that emerge from this study will be left until later.

I. EARNINGS THAT STUDENTS FOREGO

It will be convenient to draw an arbitrary line between elementary and secondary schools and to assume that no earnings are foregone on the part of children who attend elementary schools.[1] Beyond the eighth grade, however, these earnings become important. The time and effort of students may usefully be approached as follows: (1) Students study, which is work, and this work, among other things, helps create human capital. Students are not enjoying leisure when they study, nor

---

[1] This assumption is plausible enough in the case of our society at the present time. But back no further than 1900, many of these children were of considerable economic value as workers, and some parents were keeping them from school for that reason.

Table 1. Estimates of Earnings Foregone by High School and College or University Students in 1949

Age	Median Income (Dollars) (1)	Weeks Worked (2)	Income Per Week (Dollars) (3)	Annual Earnings Foregone in Attending School (Dollars) (4)	In Weeks Equivalent to Average Earnings of Workers in Manufacturing (5)
14–17:					
Male	311	24	13.00	520	—
Female	301	20	15.00	600	—
18–19					
Male	721	32	22.50	900	—
Female	618	29	21.30	852	—
20–24:					
Male	1669	40	41.70	1669	—
Female	1276	36	35.40	1416	—
25–29:					
Male	2538	44	57.70	2308	—
Female	1334	33	40.40	1616	—
Per Student:					
High School	—	—	—	583	11 weeks
College or university	—	—	—	1369	25 weeks

are they engaged wholly in consumption; they are here viewed as "self-employed" producers of capital. (2) Assume, then, that if they were not in school, they would be employed producing (other) products and services of value to the economy, for which they would be "paid"; there is, then, an opportunity cost in going to school. (3) The average earnings per week of those young men and women of comparable age and sex who are not attending school or of students while they are not in school are a measure of the (alternative) value productivity of the students' time and effort. (4) The cost of living of students and nonstudents may be put aside because they go on whether young people go to school or enter the labor market and are about the same except for minor items, such as books, extra clothes, and some travel in getting to and from school.

Estimates of the earnings that students have foregone were made in the following manner: High school students were treated separately from college and university students. The year 1949 was taken as a base year in determining the "earnings" per week of young people, both males and females, for each of four age groups. Students' foregone earnings were calculated on the assumption that, on

the average, students forego 40 weeks of such earnings, and then expressed in earning-equivalent weeks of workers in manufacturing in the United States. The results appear in Table 1; they indicate that high school students forego the equivalent of about 11 weeks and college or university students about 25 weeks of such earnings. These 1949 earnings ratios were applied to particular years between 1900 and 1956; an adjustment was then made for unemployment, as set forth in Table 2.

Two sorts of limitations need to be borne in mind in interpreting and in using these estimates. The first pertains to the 11-week and 25-week estimates for the base year 1949; the other is inherent in applying the 1949 relationships to other years.

Many of the young people who did work in 1949 were employed for only a few weeks during the year. It seems plausible that their earnings per week would be below those of workers of equivalent abilities who worked most or all of the year. To this extent, our estimates are too low. Also, it could be that students rate somewhat higher per person in the particular abilities for which earnings are received than do those not in school who are earning income. To the extent that there are

Table 2. Annual Earnings Foregone by Students Adjusted and Not Adjusted for Unemployment, 1900–1956, in Current Prices

| | | ANNUAL EARNINGS FOREGONE PER STUDENT WHILE ATTENDING | | | |
| | | HIGH SCHOOL | | COLLEGE OR UNIVERSITY | |
Year	Average Weekly Earnings, All Manufacturing (Dollars) (1)	Unadjusted (Dollars) (2)	Adjusted for Unemployment (Dollars) (3)	Unadjusted (Dollars) (4)	Adjusted for Unemployment (Dollars) (5)
1900	8.37	92	84	209	192
1910	10.74	118	113	269	259
1920	26.12	287	275	653	626
1930	23.25	256	224	581	509
1940	25.20	277	236	630	537
1950	59.33	653	626	1483	1422
1956	80.13	881	855	2003	1943

such differences, other things being equal, our estimates of earnings foregone are again too low. On the other hand, some students have held jobs while they were attending school; the earnings they have received from such jobs should have been subtracted from our estimates. Then, too, young people are probably burdened with more unemployment relative to the number employed than is the labor force as a whole. Thus of the four factors just mentioned, two pull in one direction and two in the other. They may be compensating factors.

There is also the question: What would the earnings of school-age workers have been if all of them had entered the labor market? But the question is not relevant because our problem is not one that entails a large shift in the number of human agents. The elasticity of the demand, either in the short or the long run, for such workers over so wide a range is not at issue. Instead we want to know what earnings a typical student has been foregoing at the margin. Even so, our estimate of earnings foregone are substantially reduced by the effects of the large shift of students into summer employment; the earning figures that we are using, drawing on the 1950 Census, are heavily weighted by this summer employment. As pointed out above, many who did work for pay worked only a couple of months or so.

The other difficulties stem from applying the 1949 "structural" relationships to other periods, especially to earlier years. The only adjustment that has been introduced is that for movements in unemployment. It is not easy to isolate the changes resulting from legislation. Stigler suggests that "on the whole

compulsory school attendance laws have followed more than led the increase in enrollments of children over 14" [2, p. 8 and Appendix B]. Child labor laws may have done likewise. In any case these laws may be viewed as a comprehensive private and public effort to invest in education, the child labor laws having the effect of eliminating some job opportunities.

There is a presumption in favor of the view that high school students in 1949 were attending school more weeks per year than did high school students in earlier years. Such evidence as I have been able to uncover, however, suggests that for 1900, 1910, and 1920 most high school students, including those who were attending secondary preparatory schools, were being instructed so that they could win entrance into a college or university and that these students were attending school about as many weeks per year as high school students in more recent years. Between the early twenties and the mid-forties, there may have been a small dip in this variable as a consequence of the large increases in high school enrollment and the fact that high school instruction was no longer devoted primarily to the preparation of students for college.

The weekly earnings of workers who possess the capabilities of students and who are of that age group may have changed substantially since 1900 relative to the earning of those employed in manufacturing. But it is not possible even to guess whether their earnings have become more or less favorable relative to the earnings of workers in manufacturing. The age groups that appear in Table

1 represent young people who had had more years of schooling than did the same age groups in 1900. But this would also be true of workers in manufacturing. The fact that the wage ratio between skilled and unskilled workers has narrowed may imply that our estimates of earnings foregone by high school students during the earlier years are somewhat too high, or more plausible, that the estimates for college and university students are on the low side for those years.[2] It would be exceedingly difficult, however, to isolate the effects of these changes.

II. COSTS OF THE SERVICES PROVIDED BY SCHOOLS

Ideally we want a measure of the annual flow of the inputs employed for education.

_____

[2] In [*1*, p. 595], Keat estimates the wage ratio of skilled to unskilled workers to have been 201 in 1903 and 142 in 1956.

This flow consists of the services of teachers, librarians, and school administrators, of the annual factor costs of maintaining and operating the school plant, and of depreciation and interest. It should not include expenditures to operate particular auxiliary enterprises, such as providing room and board for students, operating "organized" athletics, or other noneducational activities. School expenditures for scholarships, fellowships, and other financial aids to students should also be excluded, because they are in the nature of transfer payments; the real costs involved in student time are already fully covered by the opportunity-cost estimates.

Tables 3 and 4 give these costs of schools for elementary, secondary, and higher education.

III. TOTAL COSTS OF EDUCATION

The estimates of the costs of elementary education were complete as set forth in

Table 3. Annual Resource Costs of Educational Services Rendered by Elementary and Secondary Schools in the United States, 1900–1956, in Current Prices (Millions of dollars except Column 4 in Billions)

| | PUBLIC SCHOOLS | | | | | | PRIVATE SCHOOLS | | PUBLIC AND PRIVATE SCHOOLS | | |
Year	Gross Expenditures (1)	Capital Outlay (2)	Net Expenditures (3)	Value of Property (4)	Implicit Interest and Depreciation (5)	Total Public (6)	Gross Expenditures (7)	Total Private (8)	Total (9)	Secondary (10)	Elementary (11)
1900	215	35	180	.55	44	224	27	28	252	19	233
1910	426	70	356	1.1	88	444	54	56	500	50	450
1920	1,036	154	882	2.4	192	1,074	104	108	1,182	215	967
1930	2,317	371	1,946	6.2	496	2,442	233	246	2,688	741	1,947
1940	2,344	258	2,086	7.6	608	2,694	227	261	2,955	1,145	1,810
1950	5,838	1,014	4,824	11.4	912	5,736	783	769	6,505	2,286	4,219
1956	10,955	2,387	8,568	23.9	1,912	10,480	1,468	1,404	11,884	4,031	7,853

Table 4. Annual Resource Costs of Educational Services Rendered by Colleges and Universities in the United States, 1900–1956, in Current Prices (Millions of Dollars)

Year	Gross Expenditures (1)	Auxiliary Enterprises (2)	Capital Outlay (3)	Net Expenditures (4)	Value of Physical Property (5)	Implicit Interest and Depreciation (6)	Total (7)
1900	46	9	17	20	254	20	40
1910	92	18	30	44	461	37	81
1920	216	43	48	125	741	59	184
1930	632	126	125	381	1925	154	535
1940	758	152	84	522	2754	220	742
1950	2662	539	417	1706	5273	422	2128
1956	4210	736	686	2788	8902	712	3500

Table 5. Earnings Foregone and Other Resource Costs Represented by High School Education in the United States, 1900–1956, in Current Prices

Year	Number of Students (Millions) (1)	Earnings Foregone per Student (Dollars) (2)	Total Earnings Foregone (3)	School Costs (Millions of Dollars) (4)	Additional Expenditures (Millions of Dollars) (5)	Total (6)
1900	.7	84	59	19	3	81
1910	1.1	113	124	50	6	180
1920	2.5	275	688	215	34	937
1930	4.8	224	1,075	741	54	1,870
1940	7.1	236	1,676	1,145	84	2,905
1950	6.4	626	4,006	2,286	200	6,492
1956	7.7	855	6,584	4,031	329	10,944

Column 11 of Table 3, inasmuch as no earnings were foregone in accordance with our assumption.

Table 5 summarizes the principal components entering into the costs of high school education. A comparison of columns 3 and 6 shows at once the importance of the earnings that students forego relative to total costs of this education. That such foregone earnings should have been a larger proportion of total costs of high school education during the earlier years (and a larger proportion of total costs of high school than of college and university education in all years) comes as a surprise. Earnings foregone while attending high school were well over half the total costs in each of the years; they were 73 per cent in 1900 and 60 per cent in 1956; the two low years were 1930 and 1940, when they fell to 57 and 58 per cent of total costs. During 1950 and 1956 they were 62 and 60 per cent, respectively. Other

and more general economic implications of these changes in resource costs of high school education will be considered later.

Table 6 provides similar estimates for college and university education. Here, too, earnings foregone by students are exceedingly important (see cols. 3 and 6). In 1900 and 1910 these earnings were about half of all costs, rising to 63 per cent in 1920 and then falling to 49 per cent in 1930 and 1940. With inflation and full employment, they then rose to 60 and 59 per cent in 1950 and 1956.

IV. CONCLUDING OBSERVATIONS

When costs of all levels of education are aggregated, the proportion of total costs attributable to earnings foregone has clearly risen over time. This is due to the much greater importance of secondary and higher education in more recent years, a change

Table 6. Earnings Foregone and Other Resource Costs Represented by College and University Education in the United States, 1900–1956, in Current Prices

Year	Number of Students (Thousands) (1)	Earnings Foregone Per Student (Dollars) (2)	Total Earnings Foregone (3)	School Costs (Millions of Dollars) (4)	Additional Expenditures (Millions of Dollars) (5)	Total (6)
1900	238	192	46	40	4	90
1910	355	259	92	81	9	182
1920	598	626	374	184	37	595
1930	1101	509	560	535	56	1151
1940	1494	537	802	742	80	1624
1950	2659	1422	3781	2128	378	6287
1956	2996	1943	5821	3500	582	9903

that outweighs the decline in the foregone earnings proportion of high school education alone. For all levels of education together, earnings foregone were 26 per cent of total costs in 1900 and 43 per cent in 1956. Probably the actual 1900 figure should be somewhat higher than this because of foregone earnings of children in the higher grades of elementary school (ignored here), but such an adjustment would not substantially alter the picture.

Between 1900 and 1956, the total resources committed to education in the United States rose about *three and one-half times* (1) relative to consumer income in dollars, and (2) relative to the gross formation of physical capital in dollars. Accordingly if we look upon all the resources going into education as "consumption" based on consumer behavior, our estimates would not be inconsistent with the hypothesis that the demand for education has had a high income elasticity.

If, however, we treat the resources entering into education as "investments" based on the behavior of people seeking investment opportunities, our estimates then are not inconsistent with the hypothesis that the rates of return to education were relatively attractive; that is, they were enough larger than the rate of return to investments in physical capital to have "induced" the implied larger rate of growth of this form of human capital.

Again it should be stressed that the underlying private and public motives that induced the people of the United States to increase so much the share of their resources going into education may have been cultural in ways that can hardly be thought of as "consumption," or they may have been policy-determined for purposes that seem remote from "investment." Even if this were true, it would not preclude the possibility that the rates of return on the resources allocated to education were large simply as a favorable by-product of whatever purposes motivated the large increases in resources entering into education. If so, the task becomes merely one of ascertaining these rates of return. If, however, consumer and investment behavior did play a substantial role in these private and public decisions, then, to this extent, economic theory will also be useful in explaining these two sets of behavior.

Not only have the streams of resources entering into elementary, high school, and higher education increased markedly, but they have changed relative to one another.

1. Though elementary education by this measure has increased at a slower rate than has either of the other two, it has come close to doubling its position relative to gross physical capital formation; it rose from about 5 to 9 per cent of the latter between 1900 and 1956.

The total costs of elementary education have been strongly affected by changes in enrollment and attendance. Increases in the average number of days that enrolled students have attended school played almost as large a part as did the increase in enrollment; the first of these rose 60 and the second 73 per cent between 1900 and 1956. However it should be noted that this factor of attendance has nearly spent itself: average daily attendance is now within about 10 per cent of its apparent maximum. Enrollment, on the other hand, will turn upward in response to the growth in population. Meanwhile the salaries of elementary-school teachers have been declining relative to wages generally. Altogether, however, it seems plausible that investment in elementary education will not continue to rise at the rate that it did during the period covered by our estimates.

As previously noted, some earnings were undoubtedly foregone by elementary pupils, especially by children attending the upper grades. We have come upon bits of data that suggest that these earnings may have been appreciable during the early part of this period. Farm families, particularly, at that time still placed a considerable value on the work that their children could do for them; moreover, fully a third of the population had farm residences in 1900 and 1910. Surely a poor country endeavoring to establish a comprehensive program of elementary education must reckon the cost entailed in the earnings that older children will have to forego.

2. The annual national cost of high school education has risen markedly, so much so that in 1956 it was equal in amount to nearly 13 per cent of gross physical capital formation compared to somewhat less than 2 per cent in 1900.

Enrollment in high school advanced from 0.7 to 7.7 million between 1900 and 1956. It had already reached 7.1 million in 1940. The effect of the upsurge in population that began in the early forties had started to make itself felt by 1956, the proportion of young people embarking upon a high school education being very large—indeed, it was approaching its maximum. The increases in this

Table 7. Total Costs of Elementary, High School, and College and University Education in the United States, 1900–1956, in Current Prices (Millions of Dollars)

Year	Elementary (1)	High School (2)	College and University (3)	Total (4)
1900	230	80	90	400
1910	450	180	180	810
1920	970	940	600	2,510
1930	1,950	1,870	1,150	4,970
1940	1,810	2,900	1,620	6,330
1950	4,220	6,490	6,290	17,000
1956	7,850	10,950	9,900	28,700

ratio were striking; for example in 1900 only about 11 per cent of the fourteen-to-seventeen age group was enrolled in secondary schools; by 1956 it was about 75 per cent.[3]

Let me emphasize once more the fact that earnings foregone have made up well over half the total costs of high school education. In 1956 they were three fifths of total costs, which is somewhat less than at the beginning of this period. From this experience one may infer that poor countries, even when they are no less poor than were the people of the United States in 1900, will find that most of the real costs of secondary education are a consequence of the earnings that students forego while attending school.

3. The trend of total cost of higher education has been similar to that of high school costs. It rose at a slightly smaller rate than did total high school cost in the early part of the period, and at a larger rate later. Relative to gross physical capital formation, it was about 2 per cent in 1900 and slightly less than 12 per cent in 1956.

Enrollment in higher education increased from 328,000 in 1900 to 2,996,000 in 1956.

[3] However of this fourteen-to-seventeen age group, 88 per cent was enrolled either in elementary school, high school, or college.

Of the eighteen-to-twenty-one age group, 4 per cent were in residence and enrolled as undergraduates in higher education in 1900; by 1956, 32 per cent of this age group were thus enrolled. The numbers in the college age group will increase substantially soon, as the children born with the upsurge in birth rates of the early forties reach these ages. The proportion of this age group that will begin higher education is not readily discernible. The upper limit is not near at hand, as it is for elementary and high school education; there are many indications that it will continue to increase for some time to come.

Earnings foregone by students attending colleges and universities were also about three fifths of total costs in 1956. Here, however, we appear to observe an upward trend between 1900 and 1956.

4. Altogether, total costs of education have increased much more rapidly than have the total costs of the resources entering into physical capital. Between 1900 and 1956 the total costs of the three levels of education covered by this study have risen from 9 to 34 per cent of the total entering into the formation of physical capital.

Several more steps must be taken, however, before we can gauge the increases in the stock of capital developed by education and its contribution to economic growth. These steps will entail allocating the costs of education between consumption and investment, determining the size of the stock of human capital formed by education, and ascertaining the rate of return to this education.

REFERENCES

1. Paul G. Keat, "Long-Run Changes in Occupational Wage Structure, 1900–1956," *The Journal of Political Economy, 68* (December, 1960), 584–600.

2. George J. Stigler, *Employment and Compensation in Education*, National Bureau of Economic Research Occasional Paper No. 33, New York, 1950.

20 LEVELS OF NINETEENTH-CENTURY AMERICAN INVESTMENT IN EDUCATION

Albert Fishlow

From the earliest time the United States and her predecessor colonies stood close to or at the very forefront of the world in the educational attainment of the mass of the populace. The first available literacy statistics of 1840 testify to that past impressive accomplishment: over-all, more than 90 per cent of white adults achieved this degree of minimum competence, and even in the laggard South the record was not significantly poorer. At that date only Scotland and Germany are comparable, with England and France much farther behind. What therefore seems to be the case is that popular education successfully preceded an extensive system of publicly supported and controlled schools.[1]

Reprinted with omissions by permission from *The Journal of Economic History*, *26* (December, 1966), 418–436.

[1] For a more extensive discussion of the ante-bellum period see [2].

However it became quite clear by the 1850s that public education was to be the model for the future. During that decade many of the Midwestern states established the requisite statutory and financial bases for a viable public system. Within the Southern states as well, the philosophy of the Northern common-school reformers had perceptible influence. North Carolina was the only one to emerge with a full-fledged public system, replete with superintendent; but legislation in this same direction was passed in Tennessee, Alabama, and Texas. In many of the others, the annual hortatory messages of the governors stand as evidence of increasing sentiment in favor of public education. In any event the Civil War made that previous debate solely academic. Reconstruction generally saw mandatory constitutional provision for education similar to that in the Northern states, and despite its subsequent erosion and the general Southern backwardness in education, the pattern of public schools was retained.

In this paper I seek to assess the magnitude of both public and total resources allocated to education in the United States during the last half of the nineteenth century as the system of public education gathered full strength. Such a measure permits us to evaluate the contribution of government to American educational development from two aspects: the relative importance of public compared to private outlay and the significance of educational expenditure among all governmental functions. To provide an accurate portrayal of total resource costs, moreover, the earnings foregone of students are also estimated—necessarily in an approximate fashion. The second part of the paper seeks to place these magnitudes in perspective by reference both to contemporary European expenditures and also to present-day educational efforts.

I

Table 1 sets out estimated total and public expenditures for formal education in the United States from 1840 through 1900. Although private expenditures have for the most part been derived rather than calculated, a variety of internal checks suggests that the portrayal is accurate. Two observations follow from these data. In the first instance, there is the obvious increase in public finance of educational expenditure; in the second, the continuing high level of private support throughout.

As for the former, public expenditures expanded from 47 per cent of total outlays in 1850 to 79 per cent in 1900. However dramatic, this transition to public funds was less a factor in the origin of state common schools than might appear. As Table 1 makes clear, as late as 1860 public revenues were a bare majority. The commanding position of governmental responsibility thus was attained well after the acknowledged ante-bellum triumph of the common school in enrollment. The lag reflects the continued use of private financial supplements, such as rate-bills, until rather late. New York, for example, did not attain completely free schools until 1867, and Connecticut, until 1868. Nor in the South did state sources of finance replace private until the 1870s.

Beyond this widening public support of extant common schools, one can also point to the rise of public secondary and higher education as a factor contributing to larger public participation. In 1850 there were hardly more than a hundred high schools at most, and academies many times more numerous satisfied the appetite of those who desired and could afford further education; by 1900 the number of public high school students outnumbered those in private secondary institutions. Where the pre-Civil War era saw minor public finance and that almost exclusively in the South, public institutions (including normal schools) enrolled nearly 40 per cent of college and professional students in 1900. If 1850 ratios of public provision be applied to these two categories in 1900, the corresponding aggregate public contribution would have shrunk to 68 per cent of that actually realized; of the two effects, provision

Table 1. Expenditures for Formal Education
(Million Current Dollars)

Fiscal Years	Public	Total	Ratio, Public to Total
1840	n.a.	9.2	
1850	7.6	16.2	.47
1860	19.9	34.7	.57
1870	61.7	95.4	.65
1880	81.5	106.4	.77
1890	147.4	187.3	.79
1900	229.6	289.6	.79

of public secondary schools is the more important.

Yet if public expenditures rose dramatically over the period, it is equally correct that private support of education remained considerable at its end. It did so principally at the extreme levels of elementary and of higher education. The former accounted for more than $20 million in costs in 1900, the latter for $28 million. Catholic parochial schools figured prominently in the expenditure for primary schools; Lutheran denominational schools were the next largest single group. As a consequence private enrollments in the lower grades were concentrated by century's end in the North Atlantic and North Central regions; in 1890 these two areas included almost three fourths of the pupils. By contrast, as late as 1870, 39 per cent of comparable day-school enrollment was to be found in the South; before the Civil War, the proportion may well have been larger. The aggregate thus conceals an important change in composition, one which nativist movements like the American Protective Association did not fail to detect. Despite this and other later opposition, private denominational education has continued to flourish and, the complete acceptance of the public-school idea notwithstanding, private elementary and secondary outlays continue to bulk large. In 1960 such expenditures came to 10 per cent of the corresponding public total, not greatly dissimilar to the 1900 mark of 13 per cent. The reason for this small decline, moreover, is to be found not in private enrollments—which are today proportionately larger—but in more rapidly rising quality of public schools.

If the private contribution at the elementary level has flagged slightly in recent years, it has been more than compensated by the rapid growth of private institutions of higher learning. Enrollments between 1900 and 1960 grew at an annual rate of almost 4 per cent; although public universities experienced a still more vigorous increase, private colleges and professional schools nevertheless accounted for a larger share of total educational expenditure in 1960 than in 1900. The net result of these two circumstances is a continuing high private component of education to the very present. Indeed the private share of total expenditures in 1960 is identical to the 21 per cent calculated in Table 1 for 1900.

Thus far we have limited ourselves to direct costs. Yet as the research of Schultz, Becker, and others has shown, the indirect contribution resulting from the foregone earnings of those attending school is a major part of total expense. Although it does not appear on any ledger, it is as real to society and to individuals as are teachers' salaries or tuition payments. For 1900 Schultz has estimated such opportunity cost at about two fifths of direct expenditures, a proportion that rises to almost unity in 1956, as enrollment rates in secondary and higher education greatly increased [3].

Table 2 provides estimates of income foregone in 1860, 1880, and 1900. They have been prepared on a somewhat different basis than those of Schultz, which they overlap and from which they diverge in the terminal year of 1900. What he has done is to extrapolate back upon the manufacturing wage a reasonably well-based 1949 estimate of alternative earnings of high school and college students. The deficiencies of the method are the three implicit assumptions of constancy of the effective school year,[2] of the mix of potential occupations, and of the relationship between adult and child wages. The present entries seek to avoid these difficulties by reliance as far as possible upon direct observation of child remuneration and by allowance for changing of occupational mix and increasing of length of the effective school year. The effect of these substitutions, taken by themselves, is to reduce by a fourth Schultz's 1900 estimate, principally due to the explicit allowance for agricultural labor as an alternative to school.[3] Table 2 in fact displays a larger sum; what creates this magnification beyond Schultz's $105-million total is the inclusion in these calculations not only of high school and college students but also of elementary pupils ten years of age and older. Historically the observed participation in the labor force of such children testifies to a positive, even if perhaps increasingly small, marginal product. Specifically, in the United States over the period 1870–1900 children ten to fifteen represented 6 per cent of the total labor force. Logically the imposition of

---

[2] By which I mean the average number of days actually attended per enrolled pupil.

[3] Our technique, without adjustment for labor force participation, implies foregone earnings for college and secondary students of $80 million against Schultz's $105 million. If all students were engaged in nonagricultural activities, the resulting estimate is slightly greater than Schultz's.

Table 2. Opportunity Costs of Education

	1860	1880	1900
(1) Number of students (million)			
Male	2.86	5.52	9.34
Female	2.62	5.20	9.38
(2) Number ten years and older (million)			
Male	1.86	3.67	6.35
Female	1.70	3.46	6.38
(3) Potentially engaged in nonagriculture (million)			
Male	.49	1.05	2.10
Female	.56	1.13	2.19
(4) Proportion of year foregone	.32	.38	.46
(5) Average annual nonagricultural earnings			
Male	$87	$101	$124
Female	62	74	90
(6) Potentially engaged in agriculture (million)			
Male	.53	.97	1.40
Female	.16	.32	.48
(7) Number of months foregone			.3
(8) Average monthly earnings in agriculture			
Male	$5.80	$4.96	$6.18
Female	5.46	4.67	5.82
(9) Total earnings foregone (million)[a]	$24.8	$72.1	$213.9

[a] Line 6 times line 7 times line 8, plus line 3 times line 4 times line 5.

compulsory elementary education does not alter the present social cost associated with such a deployment of resources.[4] The inclusion of younger children creates a further problem, however. It is no longer reasonable to assume, as one could with high school and college students, that the aggregate social cost of foregone earnings can be approximated by multiplying the average alternative wage by all students. Even in a regime where education was totally lacking, not all children would work. It is necessary then to make allowance for the lack of productive alternatives enjoyed by many younger pupils; Table 2 seeks to do this as well.

What it does not do is to make any allowance for a possibly declining wage associated with increased employment of children. Since the implied increment to the total labor force is of the magnitude of 20 per cent, this would seem to be not a trivial matter for the determination of *social* costs. (Individuals would continue to be concerned with the current wage in figuring their private costs.) Yet the

consequences may be more modest. If wages were determined by an aggregate production relationship of unitary elasticity—like the Cobb-Douglas form—the effect from this source could be as little as a 2 per cent reduction in opportunity costs, because the effective increase in labor input, as measured by the ratio of opportunity costs to total labor force compensation, is of only this size. This calculation assumes a constant ratio of child to adult wages, however. To the extent that absorption could not continue at this level, there is a further overstatement.

Despite the layering of conjecture inherent in the construction of these estimates, they do admit of at least two reasonably secure conclusions. The first relates to the magnitude of the private contribution to education through the medium of foregone earnings. In the three years, 1860, 1880, and 1900, such opportunity costs were about the equivalent of the total public contribution to all levels of the educational system. Since Table 2 has been consistently structured to minimize the estimates, it is doubtful such a comparison overstates their role.

This burden was a very real one, and its unequal incidence upon lower-income groups

---

[4] From the individual standpoint, of course, such legislation removes the option of alternative earnings as a factor in the decision to attend school.

reduced the egalitarianism inherent in the American system of public education. Although the Commissioner of Education in 1910 took pride in the results of a survey of the economic status of parents of high school students, asserting that they "indicate the thoroughly democratic character of our public high schools," he qualified this observation only a few lines farther on. After noting the wide social range encompassed by the enrollment, the Commissioner remarked: "It is noticeable that a much larger proportion of children from the well-to-do families than from those of more moderate circumstances or from the families of the poor are found in our high schools."[5] In no small measure it was the imperfection of the capital market, which prevented persons from borrowing to invest in themselves, that led to this discrimination. Only those who could self-finance their opportunity costs could afford education.

The prospect of foregone earnings also played a part earlier and at a less advanced level. The entire history of compulsory education and of child-labor legislation is usefully viewed as social intervention to prevent present opportunity costs from having weight in the educational decision. Before full enforcement was gradually attained—at the beginning of the twentieth century and thereafter—there had actually been an increase in the labor participation rate of children at the end of the nineteenth; in 1900 almost a fifth of youths ten to fifteen were enrolled in the labor force. It would be wrong to ascribe full credit for the subsequent reversal to legislative abolition of child labor. Rising incomes and the concomitant lesser need of children to work also played a role. However the cross-section analysis of a more recent period by Stigler which failed to find a significant effect of legislation may well understate its historical consequences in the industrial states, where the downward trend in enrollment rates reversed itself simultaneously with effective legal provisions [4, pp. 67–70].

A second observation, inherent in the very method of Table 2, is the much smaller opportunity cost of school attendance in rural areas. Not until 1900 did scholastic endeavors impinge upon the agricultural work year; the extent and timing of summer vacation was

more an economic requisite than a convenience to warm and weary students, and children were able to find direct employment within the household on an irregular basis. In industrial areas, where family enterprise was less prevalent, a job required regular participation and was less compatible with enrollment for the conventional school year. An English visitor in the 1880s remarked upon the much shorter rural school year as follows: "The absolute necessity for children over ten years of age to assist on the farm in the summer months has rendered it imperative to blend school and farm work in such a way that the parents may have assistance while the children's teaching is not sacrificed."

The 1900 data on education reflect this differential circumstance of agricultural areas equally well. A regression equation explaining the enrollment rates of states within the North Atlantic and North Central regions shows them to be unrelated to income per capita, but positively—and quite significantly statistically—related to the ratio of income originating from agriculture. Iowa, Nebraska, and Kansas, with enrollments as a proportion of children five to eighteen close to the 90 per cent mark, led the entire nation at that date. However when allowance is also made for average daily attendance and for the length of the school year, the agricultural-income and income-per-capita variables exchange roles; it is even more clearly the case when expenditures for schools are considered.[6]

---

[5] Note also that in Massachusetts until 1889, poverty of parent remained a valid reason for child employment rather than school attendance [1, p. 69].

---

[6] The relevant equations, with 20 observations each, are as follows:

$$En\ Rt = 68.5 - .0008\ Y/P + .255\ AgY/Y$$
$$\qquad\quad (.0062)\qquad (.052)\qquad\qquad R^2 = .60$$

$$Att.\ Rt. = 5.91 + .232\ Y/P - .066\ AgY/Y$$
$$\qquad\qquad (.127)\qquad (.106)\qquad\qquad R^2 = .17$$

$$Ex/pupil = 7.82 + .267\ Y/P - .069\ AgY/Y$$
$$\qquad\qquad (.053)\qquad (.044)\qquad\qquad R^2 = .68$$

where $En\ Rt$ is enrollment relative to population five to eighteen years of age; Y/P, income per capita; AgY/Y, the proportion of income emanating from agriculture; $Att.\ Rt.$, the actual days attended relative to population 5–18; and $Ex/pupil$, average expenditures per enrolled student.

The other regions were excluded in order to emphasize the positive relationship of enrollment to the proportion of farm income, followed by sign reversal for expenditures, in a set of states similar in terms of attitudes and educational history. The low enrollment rates in the South would have obscured this relationship while intensifying the negative rural effect upon expenditure and length of school year.

Table 3. Relative Expenditures for Education in the United States (Million Current Dollars)

Fiscal Years	Direct Expenditures (1)	Public Outlays (2)	Total Resource Costs (3)	Direct Expenditures Relative to GNP (4)	Resources Costs Relative to GNP (5)	Public Outlays Relative to Total Governmental Expenditures (6)	Public Outlays Relative to State and Local Expenditures (7)
1840	9.2			.006			
1850	16.2	7.6		.007			
1860	34.7	19.9	59.5	.008	.014	.13	.21
1870	95.4	61.7		.013		.10	.22
1880	106.4	81.5	180.7	.011	.018	.14	.26
1890	187.3	147.4		.015		.17	.26
1900	289.6	229.9	502.9	.017	.029	.16	.25[a]

[a] 1902.

SOURCES: Column 1 from column 2, Table 1. Column 3 is the sum of column 1 and line 9 of Table 2.

There is nothing inconsistent between this finding of little burden in rural areas and the poor state of their schools. Indeed the foregone earnings are so small precisely because the educational system was so limited. Farmers were presumably resistant to better and longer schools, even at identical income levels, due to their reluctance to bear the indirect cost of foregoing the product of their children. This was true even though the magnitude of the *potential* rural cost was appreciably smaller, given the ability to utilize child labor effectively during vacation periods and Saturdays. The attitudinal difference shows up convincingly in the disparity between urban and rural schools at the turn of the century. Within the North Central region, the average number of days attended per capita in cities in 1900 was 29.7, and in the rest of the area, 25.1. This margin is all the more striking since, as would be anticipated, rural areas had enrollment rates some 20 per cent higher. In terms of outlay per enrolled pupil, the contrast is a more substantial $22.69 to $12.46—a gap which even understates the total quality difference in the levels of urban and of rural education due to economies of scale implicit in the former.[7]

II

Table 3 now recapitulates educational expenditures from a relative viewpoint. What

[7] Inclusion of the South would exaggerate the urban-rural difference by a considerable margin.

it clearly demonstrates is the rapid—albeit apparently irregular—growth in the nineteenth century of investment in human capital as a proportion of national product. Less expected, perhaps, the rate of advance of direct expenditure has continued to the present without perceptible deceleration: the 1960 ratio of total costs to gross national product bears the same relationship to the 1900 value as that does to the 1840 ratio. If opportunity costs be included, the rate of growth has even markedly accelerated in the twentieth century.

At the same time—at least from 1880 on—education has not dramatically altered its relative command over governmental resources. Indeed, the recent proportion of total governmental expenditures allocated to education is almost identical to that which prevailed in 1900. This constancy, despite ever-rising absolute contributions, is the consequence of simultaneous expansion of other governmental functions. In the halcyon era of the Coolidge administration, educational outlays did rise to 20 per cent of total governmental expenditures, but the ensuing depression and widely expanded international commitments established a new and continued supremacy for the federal government. As state and local units declined in importance, it was inevitable education would do the same, since its support was virtually limited to these sources. Only as a result of ever-larger proportional contributions from state and local governments has education fared as well as it has: between 1860 and 1960 the share of education at this level has mounted from a fifth to well over a third. It is no

Table 4. European Educational Expenditures (Million Current Dollars)

	FRANCE		UNITED KINGDOM		GERMANY	
Fiscal Years	Expenditures	As Percentage of GDP	Expenditures	As Percentage of GNP	Expenditures	As Percentage of NNP
1860	13[a]	.4			24[b]	1.0
1880	41	.9	59	.9	69	1.6
1900	74	1.3	124	1.3	150	1.9

[a] *Circa* 1860.
[b] 1861–1862.

wonder that pressure upon these units has recently led to a belatedly expanded federal role.

Despite the gain in the percentage of gross national product allocated to education, the absolute level of less than 2 per cent in 1900 must be regarded as modest by present standards. In the latter 1950s, the mean percentage being spent by 56 countries ranging in per capita income from $57 to almost $2500 was 3.3, with only a small minority less than 2. The much greater current emphasis upon education is seen more clearly, however, by estimating nineteenth-century American expenditures on the assumption that the cross-sectional relationship prevailing in 1958 applied earlier as well. For the proportion of the population then five to nineteen years of age and at income-per-capita levels of the early period, the following expenditures (in millions of current dollars) are implied:[8]

1840	45.7
1860	130.4
1880	275.6
1900	546.0

The actual expenditures range from a fifth of those predicted in 1840 to half in 1900. Since the enrollment rates implied on a similar cross-sectional basis by the historical levels of income-per-capita and of occupational structure are less than those in fact attained in the United States, there can be no question that relative costs (and probably quality) of education have dramatically risen

from their previous levels. Lower-income countries, as they strive to compete in the present industrialized world, are thus forced to assume much greater burdens than the United States historically experienced.

Table 4 suggests that something not dissimilar was occurring even earlier. Germany, which along with France is in the lower per capita income rung, is seen to be spending a larger proportion of its income on education than is either the United States or the United Kingdom. France, in turn, ties with Great Britain. The reason for such displacement is to be found in the relatively small variance of expenditures per pupil. Expenditures relative to income can be thought of as the product of expenditures per pupil and pupils per capita, divided by income per capita. So long as countries spend similar sums per student and are equally motivated to provide education for the large mass of the population, the expenditure ratio will tend to move inversely with per capita income. In fact, at this time expenditures per pupil ranged from an estimated $12.79 in France to $16.78 in the United States, or over a substantially lesser range than did incomes per capita. The only reason the French expenditure ratio is not equal to the 1.7 per cent attained by the United States is the much smaller enrollment rate in France. Had the latter been equal to that of the United Kingdom, say, the French ratio would have increased to 1.6 per cent.[9]

---

[8] The basic regression equation from which these estimates were derived is based upon 56 national observations pertaining to 1958. Expenditures per capita were related to income per capita and to the proportion of the population five to nineteen years in the following way:

$$\ln \frac{Exp.}{P} = -6.392 + 1.211 \ln \frac{GNP}{P} + .281 \ln \frac{5\text{-}19}{P}$$
$$(.057) \qquad (.150)$$

$R^2 = .90$

---

[9] For convenience, the three components required to calculate the expenditure ratio in 1900 are as follows:

	Income Per Capita	Expenditure Per Pupil	Pupils Per Capita
France	$114	$12.79	.148
U.K.	239	16.40	.184
Germany	144	13.57	.200
U.S.	227	16.78	.225

Why expenditures per pupil should have this quality of invariance is more difficult to judge. In part the answer resides in the differential position of teachers in the income hierarchies of France and Germany relative to the United States. The average salary of teachers in the United States in the year 1896 was less than $300; in Prussia it was $377, with the additional perquisite of housing worth on average more than $60. As a multiple of average income, therefore, the American earned 1.3, the German approximately 3. The higher ratio of pupils to teachers in Germany helped to compensate for the differential, but insufficiently.

Such a higher salary was accompanied by the utilization of males as teachers even in the lowest grades. In the United States, of course, the story has been one of a progressive decline in the proportion of male teachers until they were less than a third of staff in 1900. The South had continued the longest to use men—a throwback to its earlier and more elitist educational structure. Yet it is well to emphasize that this substitution of women for men was of minor import compared to the relative level of salaries. At salaries paid in 1900, money could actually have been saved had the United States employed German instructional methods: 85 per cent male and many students per teacher. Or, to put it another way, the reduction in the United States salary bill in 1900 under actual conditions instead of those implied by the 1870 ratio of males to females is only 2 per cent. Within France and Germany a slightly wider salary differential for men and women teachers prevailed, but the force of this conclusion is not thereby diminished.

III

The United States, then, managed to educate a greater mass of its population in 1900 at levels of sacrifice neither markedly greater, nor less, than those of its industrial contemporaries. Its level of expenditure per pupil was the highest, but that was in some measure the consequence of its greater proportion of the population in expensive secondary and higher education. The philosophy of an educational ladder was more than social gospel. At the public elementary level alone, and for current expenditures, the variance is smaller than for total outlays. In 1900 the United States was expending $11.01, England, $10.30, France, $10.21, and Germany between $10.00 and $11.00.

The United States had accomplished this feat, moreover, without central governmental control—indeed with just the opposite. Whereas the late nineteenth century had witnessed the expansion of European public educational systems, typically this was accompanied by larger central grants and supervision. In England three fourths of the income of the primary schools in 1876 emanated from local sources, almost half of which was from private funds; by 1900 Parliamentary grants were making up more than 50 per cent of income and private fees had virtually disappeared. The French pattern was the same: in 1877 the central government made up only a quarter of revenue for public primary schools, in 1900 almost four fifths. The school-tax law in Prussia resulted in a similar tendency.

In the United States the possibility of national aid had come to the fore in conjunction with reconstruction in the aftermath of the Civil War. Any such plan had been rejected, postponing to the twentieth century access to the federal largess. Rather, the state and local units were required—principally by property taxes—to satisfy the growing demand for education. Two thirds of the burden fell upon local governmental units. Quite contrary to the principle that the locus of finance should be coterminous with the receipt of benefits, public education which had external economies beyond the local site was primarily supported there. Of special interest, state finance was significant only in the South, and there it provided neither the more ample funds nor the equalizing effect that might have been expected.

Local finance sufficed in the United States, although it could not be relied on elsewhere, in part because the consensus in favor of education had evolved gradually within American local communities themselves. Even the common-school revival, despite the impetus it generated in favor of state supervision and administration, did not fail to emphasize local participation. Under such circumstances, the educational commitment was a matter of course from parents to children rather than from community to schools. Whether or not the children migrated to carry the economic benefits with them, the responsibility for education was locally accepted and largely fulfilled.

As in most of the other realms of government in the United States in the nineteenth century, that responsibility manifested itself most clearly on the expenditure side, not on that of regulation. The increasing level of governmental contributions to education—which represented a higher proportion of revenues than in Europe—encouraged expansion of enrollment and increased quality of schools with a minimum of compulsion until the century's end. It was not, and is not, a paradigm of governmental intervention that can be relied on universally.

REFERENCES

1. Forest C. Ensign, *Compulsory School Attendance and Child Labor*, Iowa City, Athens Press, 1921.
2. Albert Fishlow, "The Common School Revival: Fact or Fancy?" Henry Rosovsky, ed., *Industralization in Two Systems: Essays in Honor of Alexander Gerschenkron*, New York, John Wiley and Sons, 1966, pp. 40–67.
3. Theodore W. Schultz, "Capital Formation by Education," *The Journal of Political Economy*, *68* (December, 1960), 571–583. [Reprinted above as essay 19.]
4. George J. Stigler, *Employment and Compensation in Education*, National Bureau of Economic Research Occasional Paper No. 33, New York, 1950.

21 CAPITAL FORMATION IN THE UNITED STATES DURING THE EARLY PERIOD OF INDUSTRIALIZATION: A REEXAMINATION OF THE ISSUES

Douglass C. North

I

It is frequently suggested that there are significant problems of capital formation during the early period of industrialization, and indeed economic historians have written a good deal about these difficulties. Whether we look at traditional writings on the subject, at the more recent theoretical

This is a revised and extended version of a paper published in *Second International Conference of Economic History, Aix-en-Provence, 1962*, Paris, Mouton & Co., 1965, pp. 643–656, and is reprinted by permission.

explanations by historians such as W. W. Rostow, or at economic analysis of under-developed areas, the role of capital formation in growth and industrialization has typically been looked upon as a central one.

Capital formation has been considered the critical problem for two different reasons: one, because the supply of savings was too small to promote sufficient capital formation for industrialization; or two, because the savings were in the hands of groups who for one reason or another would not put them into industrial economic activities. The implication in both cases is that while the rate of return on investment in manufacturing is high, it neither calls forth an increase in savings (the supply being inelastic to the interest rate) nor—in the second case—induces those who control the savings to invest in manufacturing enterprise.

This paper argues that the traditional problems that the economic historian has considered in connection with capital formation are too limited. It suggests a more pertinent range of questions relating to the problems of capital formation; and explores some empirical evidence with respect to the United States to indicate the relationship between one of these neglected aspects of capital formation and the course of American industrialization.

II

The traditional view of the problem has been that the supply of savings was too low. By this the economic historian presumably means that, all other things held constant, if the supply of savings was shifted to the right, and the rate of interest was thus lowered, there would be an acceleration in the rate of growth of manufacturing or indeed that manufacturing could initially have been undertaken or perhaps the Rostovian "take-off" would occur.[1] At the 1953 International

---

[1] Rostow (and many other economic historians and economists) identifies economic growth with industrialization, but this is not a necessary relationship as Denmark, New Zealand, and other countries have amply demonstrated. Since the theoretical and empirical evidence which shows there is no necessary identity is widely known, there is no need to cite it here. However since the traditional view of these problems has lumped them together, they are so considered in this section.

Economic Association Conference in Santa Marguerita, H. J. Habakkuk and Alex Cairncross both expressed doubts on the subject and buttressed these doubts with theory and evidence [9, pp. 149–170, 235–248]. More recently several case studies were presented at the 1960 International Economic Association Conference on the "take-off" which showed no such rapid acceleration in supplies of savings or in capital as a percentage of GNP during the period of industrialization [10]. Moreover the available quantitative evidence suggests that there are countries with rapid rates of economic growth and relatively low levels of capital formation, and countries with low rates of economic growth and high levels of capital formation—and vice-versa. In short there is no neat relationship between the level of capital formation and the pace of manufacturing development.

In the case of the United States there is specific evidence on the point. From 1808 to 1814 the conditions described above did occur—namely, the savings that had previously gone into shipping and the reexport trade were shifted into manufacturing as a result of embargo and war; and there ensued six years of rapid growth of manufacturing. With the end of the War of 1812 and the renewal of the import trade, most of this manufacturing went bankrupt and disappeared in the face of cheaper British imports. The critical element in this case was not the supply of capital. The firms that did manage to survive were large-scale, efficient ones, such as the Boston Associates at Waltham. While the size of the American market was probably a contributing factor it is at best only a partial or short-run explanation for the demise of American manufacturing in the period 1815–1819. As long as the U.S. market was of sufficient size to support one optimum-size firm in any given industry, there should be no long-run problems, and if foreign markets were open to U.S. manufacturers then even the size of the domestic market is not a limiting factor. This argument, however, must be modified by short-run market imperfections and institutional rigidities, and it is within this context that the size of the American market may have been an important factor in the period following the War of 1812.

The second traditional problem, inherited from the Marxists, is the notion that the class of savers—"merchant capitalists" in

this case—for one reason or another are unwilling to shift savings into manufacturing. This would suggest that in such countries there would be wide disparities between interest rates on funds going into mercantile activities and shipping and interest rates for funds in manufacturing. In the United States there is little evidence of such disparity in interest rates.[2] There is in fact clear and abundant evidence that this posed no particular problem. Not only did individual entrepreneurs who had been engaged in shipping and commerce shift their capital into manufacturing, such as the Boston Associates mentioned above, but there also evolved a group of financial intermediaries who were perfectly willing to put savings into manufacturing activities.[3] The lack of any significant disparity in interest rates suggests that such entrepreneurs and financial intermediaries were significant enough to make any "class prejudices" unimportant in the allocation of investment funds.

III

If these are not the problems of capital formation and industrialization, what exactly are they? A beginning to an answer can best be made clear by quoting from Simon Kuznets' study of "International Differences in Capital Formation and Financing" [11, p. 22]. Kuznets argues that the traditional definition of capital formation is far too narrow, and then goes on to say:

The measures used here and in many other statistical studies, which correspond to the narrower definition, present an incomplete and therefore somewhat misleading, picture of differences between developed and underdeveloped economies or between the early and later phases in the growth of developed economies. Not only capital formation, in its narrower sense, but also consumer expenditures, whose contribution to the increased productivity of the population varies as the consumption structure varies, are fundamental to the understanding of economic growth and its phases. Capital is what capital does: it raises the capacity for economic production. The minor share that capital formation as now measured constitutes of national product, particularly on a net basis, in both developed and underdeveloped countries is far from a true measure. It is hardly informative to say that net capital formation is, on the average, 10 to 15 per cent of national product in the leading industrial nations and 5 per cent or less in the underdeveloped ones. It would be more telling if we could say that the productivity-raising outlays in a developed country are about half of its national product (as they well may be) but only a few per cent in an underdeveloped country. Even more important, with the broader definition of capital we would have to examine carefully all newly produced resources and select, classify, and measure those that contribute in any way to greater productivity. We thus would get a better view of the conditions under which capital, in the narrower sense of the term, is most effectively utilized.

The dilemma of countries attempting to industrialize, both in the past and today, is not so much the deficiency in supply of savings as in the low yield on industrial capital investment. It is this low productivity of industrial capital that is the critical problem. One reason for the low productivity of capital is the efficiency and scale of organization. From Adam Smith through Allyn Young to (most recently) George Stigler, this has been considered an important determinant of growing productivity. As noted above, the size of the market may have been a factor in the failure of American industrialization in the period from 1816 to 1819. However while the size of the market may preclude industrialization, it is certainly not a sufficient argument in terms of the causes of industrialization.

Capital invested in manufacturing, even where a large potential market exists, may have a very low or even negative rate of return. An important limiting factor influencing the productivity of physical capital in manufacturing is the quantity and quality of other productive factors with which it is combined. Resource endowments are important, but for the development of manufacturing it is the complementarity between

---

[2] Professor Lance Davis in his careful study of early financial intermediaries [3, pp. 351–352] states:

All four firms did lend to industry, and the evidence seems to show no anti-industrial discrimination in the terms of the loans. In no case does there appear to have been any significant difference between the interest charged on industrial loans and that charged on nonindustrial grants; nor does there appear to have been any difference in the time periods of the loans or in the frequency of renewal. Only in the institutions' collateral requirements was there any significant difference. Industrial borrowers seem to have received more "loan on personal security" than did any other group of recipients, but this difference appears to have favored rather than discriminated against industrial borrowers.

[3] See [3, 4, and 5]. By 1839 most of the important types of financial intermediaries were already in existence in the United States.

human capital and physical capital which appears to be the most promising approach to the problem. While economic historians have long recognized that the inability of underdeveloped countries to employ modern technology efficiently was the result of lack of training, skills, and knowledge, this complementarity has not played a central role in the explanation of industrialization, nor have economic historians sought to explore the precise nature of the relationship.[4] While our knowledge of the returns on investment in human capital is still limited, it nevertheless appears to be the key to an understanding of one of the important underlying features of industrialization.

IV

The United States, which followed Great Britain in developing manufacturing, had available to it a large stock of knowledge, not only of pure science but of the way in which pure science was embodied in specific techniques. British machines and production methods had been devised in the light of British factor proportions (including natural resource endowments) and factor prices. Yet the United States, with different factor proportions and factor prices, had of necessity to modify the techniques to fit the special factor price problems which faced the American entrepreneur attempting to develop a manufacturing enterprise. This modification of productive techniques to the factor price relationships that existed in the United States required engineers, craftsmen, artisans, and mechanics. Substantial investment in human capital was necessary at this stage to modify the inherited techniques to the factor price requirements of another economy.[5]

The ability of Americans to adapt and modify English techniques to their own needs in the early period of American industrialization has received a good deal of attention both from contemporary observers and, in more recent times, from analysts of industrialization. It was the main object of investigation of an English commission which came to America in the 1850s.[6] Their investigations provide detailed descriptions of the way in which Americans modified and adapted British techniques to suit their own factor endowments. Case studies of American industry provide equally illuminating details of the ingenuity of American mechanics and craftsmen in adapting technology.[7] A recent study by H. J. Habakkuk comparing English and American technology in the nineteenth century brings together a good deal of this evidence and highlights the process in some detail [8].

What exactly were the differential factor prices in the United States as compared to England which led to the substantial

---

and wholesale and retail marketing facilities, but equally of the wide variety of professional services which are required. Physicists, chemists, engineers, lawyers, etc., all are necessary to the spread of manufacturing. Hirschman, Rostow, Chenery, and others have stressed the role of linkages in the growth of manufacturing. However it is one thing to note that certain kinds of manufacturing require extensive backward and forward linkages; it is quite another to explain why such induced investment should be located within a given economy. Backward linkages in the form of machinery, parts, machine tools, etc., can be imported; the forward linkages of finished goods can also be undertaken elsewhere. This has been the fate of many economies that built textile mills or railroads or lumber mills, only to find that the textile machinery, rails, railroad equipment, lumber-mill machinery, etc., were all imported rather than leading to expanding manufacturing activity at home. In some cases the failure to expand manufacturing at home via backward and forward linkages can be attributed to the relatively high price of its resource endowments. More often, however, it is lack of investment in human capital which—because of its complementarity with physical capital—results in the marginal productivity of physical capital in manufacturing being low.

[6] The results of this investigation were published in *The Report of the Committee on the Machinery of the United States of America* (Parliamentary Papers, 1854–1855), and in *New York Industrial Exhibition: Special Reports of Mr. George Wallis and Mr. Joseph Whitworth* (Parliamentary Papers, 1854), all republished in [13]. They are summarized in [1 and 12, p. 166].

[7] See particularly [7].

---

[4] It is the subject of extensive contemporary economic analysis. For a short summary statement see [14].

[5] While the focus of this paper is on the adaptation of technical knowledge from one economy to another during the initial period of industrialization, the sustained expansion of manufacturing equally requires a large investment in human capital. While the operatives in the factory itself may not be required to possess substantial skills, the spread of manufacturing with expansion in the size of the market leads to vertical disintegration and the development of a host of highly trained and skilled ancillary and complementary functions. I am thinking not only of the development of specialized capital-goods industries

modification of British techniques? Most important was the high cost of labor, particularly unskilled labor—hence the ubiquitous efforts by Americans to develop labor-saving machinery.[8] Whitworth and Wallis provide a careful description of the substitution of capital for labor (and contrast the techniques with those in use in England) in almost every field of manufacturing in America, and their detailed description provides precise documentation of the way in which the state of technical knowledge in various fields lent itself to such substitution.

Undoubtedly labor costs were the greatest factor differentials that existed between Britain and America. Certainly the price of capital, while higher in America, was not relatively as much higher as were American wages. Land, of course, was much cheaper in the United States, thereby reducing the cost of factory sites as compared to their English counterparts. In general, resource inputs were cheaper in America. Perhaps the most important single adaptation to U.S. factor proportions was in the source and transmission of power. Steam was the cheapest way of producing the power needed to run English machines. However in the United States, particularly in New England, the abundance of waterpower along the fall river line provided American mechanics and millwrights with the incentive to develop and improve on the efficiency of the waterwheel in order to make it an efficient substitute for steam as a source of power in the early American factory. The success of American mechanics in improving the efficiency of waterpower through better waterwheels and eventually turbines, and through the use of belting rather than gears, were important factors in reducing the cost of power relative to English competition. The highly efficient waterpower used in American mills was in effect the substitution of a natural resource for both capital and labor [8, pp. 32–33]. The success of American industrialization in the face of English competition thus rested on modifying techniques for the American scene, on developing processes in which both capital and resources were substituted for high-price labor.

What skills were required to successfully modify existing English technology? Technical progress at this time was more empirical than scientific. It depended more on the practicing mechanic, machinist, and millwright than the development of pure scientific knowledge. It was not the highly trained scientist with a great deal of formal education who was critical; it was the practicing mechanic-machinist, with some formal education but primarily a specialist in a variety of mechanical techniques which existed at the time. America in the early nineteenth century appears to have possessed an abundance of mechanics, machinists, millwrights, and carpenters with the requisite skill to undertake the transformation of British technology to suit American needs.[9] Whitworth and Wallis repeatedly ascribe technical adaptations to mechanics in a company's employment. As George S. Gibb [7, pp. 10–11] says:

The fact that Samuel Slater, in 1790, and Francis Lowell, in 1813, could find skilled native workmen to assist them is attributable to the training of many generations of farmer-mechanics in the workshops of colonial New England. The manufacturing enterprises which existed in the heart of America's eighteenth-century mercantile-agricultural economy were numerous and diversified, and the many skills of American craftsmen were full of portent for future industrial development. Varied and dextrous mechanical abilities were all but universal, and it is a fact of great significance that large segments of the population had long been accustomed to working with their hands. In organization the factories of the early nineteenth century were a distinct departure from the colonial workshops, but the Industrial Revolution in its infancy produced surprisingly few basic technical skills not already familiar to American mechanics. . . . There were few mechanical engineers and no industrial scientists, for the union of scientific theory with workbench skills was too new to have borne fruit. The competent mechanic at that time was the man who could hang a waterwheel and rig the shafting with that precise balance of forces which transferred clumsy wood and iron into harnessed power, and who could work a true plane surface with tools which he had made himself. The mechanic of 1813 was at once a carpenter, a millwright, and a toolmaker. Yet America, in 1813, had machine tools of a kind, and men who could use them to build intricate machines.

The widespread abundance of skilled craftsmen who were the important innovators of

Table 1. Occupation Distribution of Immigrants (Per Cent)

	Professional	Commercial	Skilled	Farmers	Servants	Laborers	Total
1820–1829	3.22	28.10	30.54	21.19	2.04	14.91	100.0
1830–1839	1.73	16.28	31.50	30.50	1.03	18.96	100.0
1840–1849	0.94	6.30	23.20	32.71	3.08	33.76	100.0
1850–1859	0.51	8.71	18.12	31.14	1.67	39.85	100.0

American industrial techniques is attested to not only in the literary evidence and in the numerous case studies of American industry, but it is reflected in the differential wage rates that apparently existed between England and America. While the money-wage of unskilled labor in America appears to have been one third to one half higher than in England, the money wage of skilled labor in America appears to have been only 20 per cent higher than that of their English counterparts. The weight of literary evidence suggests that this narrower differential for skilled craftsmen was not so much a function of demand but rather a function of differential supply between the two countries, and indeed this is the conclusion that Habakkuk himself comes to in his study of English and American technology.

V

Where did the skilled craftsmen come from who were the mainspring of these technological adaptations? Immigration was one important source. Contemporary accounts like those of Whitworth and Wallis and individual case studies attest to the important role that skilled immigrant craftsmen played in a number of industries.

Table 1 summarizes the occupational background by decade of immigrants and points up the fact that while professional and commercial occupations were relatively unimportant among immigrants, skilled laborers were an important percentage of immigrants, particularly in the decades through 1849. While immigrants, particularly those skilled immigrants, were an important supplement to American craftsmen and mechanics, it is still true that the basic source of our skilled labor was indigenous. It is not possible with our present state of knowledge to assign precise weights to the relative importance of formal education versus on-the-job training in this development of human capital in the United States in the first half of the nineteenth century. The implications of the previous sections are that the most important kinds of skills were those which came from "on-the-job training." Yet, quite clearly, formal education —particularly at the primary level—was an important adjunct in spreading these skills.

Contemporary observers ascribe a good deal of importance to the system of universal primary education that existed in America, and particularly in the Northeastern states, at this time. Whitworth and Wallis devote a good deal of attention to its significance both in the attitude and in the learning process of workers. New England entrepreneurs were self-conscious about the importance of primary education as an investment in improving the productivity of workers. The fragmentary evidence on formal education does suggest that Americans, particularly those in the Northeastern states, had a greater proportional investment in education than had other regions of the United States or other countries in the world. Table 2 presents a summary of this evidence.

Table 2. International Comparison of Relative School Population for 1850

Country	Ratio of Students to Total Population
New England	25.71
Denmark	21.73
U.S. (excluding slaves)	20.40
Sweden	17.85
Saxony	16.66
Prussia	16.12
Norway	14.28
Belgium	12.04
Great Britain (on the books)	11.76
Great Britain (in attendance March 3, 1851)	14.28
France	9.52
Austria	7.29
Holland	6.99
Ireland	6.89
Greece	5.55
Russia	2.00
Portugal	1.22

Table 3. Educational Level, Public Facilities, 1861

Region	Enrollment Rate (1)	Average Daily Attendance Rate (2)	Average Length of School (3)	Number of Days of School Per White Person 5–19[a] (4)
	(*Percentage*)		(*Days*)	
New England	62.8	74.9	135	63.5
Middle Atlantic	61.4	53.0	157	51.1
North Central	75.9	56.7	116	49.9
South	29.5	45.0	80	10.6
U.S. Total	57.4	56.2	124	40.3

[a] Column 1 times column 2 times column 3.

This data has been supplemented recently by a study of Albert Fishlow on education investment in nineteenth-century America which provides evidence of the rapid development of public educational facilities in the years before the Civil War [6]. While all regions in the U.S. increased such investment, the far higher levels of investment in the North and West as compared with the South are consistent with the whole pattern of economic development by region [12, chaps. X–XII]. The relevant data by Fishlow is summarized in the following table (Table 3).

In areas, such as the construction of canals and similar works, where skills requiring more formal education were essential—civil engineering, for example—the United States appears to have made an important beginning by the middle of the nineteenth century. From the graduates from the Army Corps of Engineers and from early civilian academies devoted to producing engineers we had, by the middle of the 1850s, developed a basic core of trained people in such important occupations.[10]

It is much harder to pinpoint the source of the widespread development of what were in effect on-the-job training skills which were so widespread in America—the mechanic, skilled millwright, skilled carpenter, who played such an important role. The arms industry and shipbuilding were two early and important sources of mechanical skills, and the important contributions made by early developments in the arms industry by Whitney, Colt, and Simeon North are well known.

Yet the origins of such skills are even more widely spread than these industries. They were evident in the agriculture of the early United States and in locally oriented flour milling, and sawmill industries that were scattered throughout American society. They suggest that an important part of the existence of these widespread skills was the fact that, with labor so scarce and the returns upon developing labor-saving devices in all of these activities so large, there was an important incentive to develop craftsmen's skills that led to the kind of "Yankee ingenuity" which appears to have been a characteristic of the American scene.

VI

The purpose of this paper has been to re-examine some of the issues involved in the study of industrialization. The arguments advanced are both limited and tentative, limited in the sense that the issues examined are purely the economic issues involved in growth and industrialization. No attention has been given to social structure and motivations in the broad range of noneconomic problems that underlie the efficiency of organization in economic societies. They are tentative because the empirical evidence advanced does no more than make clear that the United States had substantial investment in human capital during the period of industrialization, and the theoretical arguments only suggest an explanation of the low productivity of physical capital which may exist without the complementary existence of a large amount of human capital.

The main purpose of the essay has been

---

[10] Some fragmentary evidence on this point is available in [2]. Appendices A, B, and C, summarize the quantitative evidence.

to suggest that economic historians (as well as students of contemporary economic growth) would do well to reexamine the issues involved in industrialization, and they should begin by broadening the definition of capital. For the economic historian concerned with long-run changes in a society, a definition of capital which included all of the expenditures which were productivity-raising would undoubtedly be a more useful way of examining the problem. This would involve the economic historian in studies of measures to improve health, education, and a variety of other outlays as well.

This paper has focused specifically on one type of such outlays—namely, the investment in human capital—whether through formal education or on-the-job training. Its object has been to suggest that human capital is an essential prerequisite in adapting a technology from one economy to another when their factor prices and proportions are somewhat different. While the focus of this paper has been on the adaptability issue, this certainly does not exhaust the ways by which investment in human capital may turn out to be a critical factor in long-run growth and change.[11]

REFERENCES

1. D. L. Burn, "The Genesis of American Engineering Competition, 1850–1870," *Economic History*, Supplement to *The Economic Journal, 2* (January, 1931), 292–311.
2. Daniel H. Calhoun, *The American Civil Engineer, Origins and Conflict,* Cambridge, The Technology Press, 1960.

---

[11] I do not know of any studies that have been made of the changing demand for skills and knowledge during industrialization, but it does seem to me that it would be a rewarding piece of research. Clearly the kind of human capital that is most complementary with physical capital varies in development. The continuing complaint of underdeveloped areas that they have too many unemployed intellectuals and lawyers does not indicate that they have abundant human capital, but only that they have abundance of certain types.

3. Lance E. Davis, "United States Financial Intermediaries in the Early Nineteenth Century: Four Case Studies," Unpublished doctoral dissertation, The Johns Hopkins University, 1956.
4. Lance E. Davis, "Sources of Industrial Finance: The American Textile Industry, A Case Study," *Explorations in Entrepreneurial History, 9* (April, 1957), 189–203. [See below, essay 22.]
5. Lance E. Davis, "The New England Textile Mills and the Capital Markets: A Study of Industrial Borrowing, 1840–1860," *The Journal of Economic History, 20* (March, 1960), 1–30. [See below, essay 22.]
6. Albert Fishlow, "The Common School Revival: Fact or Fancy?" Henry Rosovsky, ed., *Industrialization in Two Systems: Essays in Honor of Alexander Gerschenkron,* New York, John Wiley and Sons, 1966, pp. 40–67.
7. George S. Gibb, *The Saco-Lowell Shops: Textile Machinery Building in New England 1813–1949,* Cambridge, Harvard University Press, 1950.
8. H. J. Habakkuk, *American and British Technology in the Nineteenth Century,* Cambridge, University Press, 1962.
9. International Economic Association, *Economic Progress,* Papers and Proceedings of a Round Table held by the International Economic Association, Louvain, Institute De Reserches Economiques and Sociales, 1955.
10. International Economic Association, *The Economics of the Take-Off into Sustained Growth,* Proceedings of a Conference held by the International Economic Association, New York, St. Martin's Press, 1963.
11. Simon Kuznets, "International Differences in Capital Formation and Financing," Universities-National Bureau Committee for Economic Research, *Capital Formation and Economic Growth,* Princeton, Princeton University Press, 1955, pp. 19–106.
12. Douglass C. North, *The Economic Growth of the United States, 1790–1860,* Englewood Cliffs, Prentice-Hall, 1961.
13. Nathan Rosenberg, ed., *The American System of Manufacture,* Edinburgh, Edinburgh University Press, 1969.
14. T. W. Schultz, "Investment in Human Capital," *The American Economic Review, 51* (March, 1961), 1–18.

VI THE MARKET FOR FUNDS

*I*n essay 22 Lance E. Davis examines the development of the market for funds in the United States between 1820 and 1930. He finds that during much of the period there were certain barriers to the flow of funds among regions and industries. These barriers resulted in geographic differentials in interest rates. Thus in 1880 the interest rate on farm mortgages in the Far West was 75 per cent greater than the corresponding interest rate in the Middle Atlantic region. Over time interest differentials, and presumably the barriers to the flow of funds, diminished. By 1930 the rate on mortgages in the East and West were nearly identical.

What were the impediments to the flow of funds during the nineteenth century? Were they artificial barriers created by the Eastern bankers who somehow managed to corner the market for funds? Davis provides little support for this stereotype. He suggests that it was the absence of Eastern financial institutions in the West, not their presence, which was responsible for the differentials. According to Davis a primary cause of the high Western rates was the high cost of processing loans in relatively small markets. These costs were inflated by the difficulty of obtaining information regarding the credit-worthiness of distant borrowers and the reliability of various securities. Not until the market for funds in Western communities became large enough to justify the establishment of local branches of Eastern commercial-paper houses, mortgage companies, and insurance companies, were such costs sharply diminished.

Allan Bogue's study of the money market of the prairie states also militates against the view that Western farmers were tortured on the financial rack of Eastern interests. Bogue cites data indicating that more than half the loans made in Illinois and Iowa during the nineteenth century were financed by local residents. The act of mortgaging was not in itself a sign of distress. Indeed, more than 83 per cent of the mortgages studied by Bogue were undertaken to purchase real estate or to improve it. Mortgages which might have been undertaken because of financial distress ranged between 3 and 14 per cent of the total. Nor were foreclosures as common as is believed. Of 2649 mortgages which were negotiated between 1852 and 1896 in three Iowa townships, only 84 (3.2 per cent) were foreclosed.

22 CAPITAL MOBILITY AND AMERICAN GROWTH

Lance E. Davis

It is necessary not only that capital be accumulated, but also that it be mobilized if an economy is to benefit from an increase in capital per person. The classical model of resource allocation assumes that within any economy capital is perfectly mobile. It implies, therefore, that once allowance is made for uncertainty and risk, returns on investment are equal in all industries in all regions. Such a model, while logically consistent, is not very useful for analyzing the process of economic growth. In the early stages of development, because the uncertainty discounts are high, capital is not very mobile. As a result, rates of return vary widely between industries and between regions; and growth in high-interest regions is retarded. Development, in part then, takes the form of a reduction in uncertainty discounts—a reduction that makes it possible for capital to move more freely between regions and industries.

In a Robinson Crusoe economy, where the saver is also the investor, capital mobilization presents no problem. The more complex the economy, however, the ,more difficult it is to transfer the command over resources gained by nonconsumption from the savers to those who wish to use these resources—that is, the investors. In the case of the United Kingdom each of several personal fortunes could have financed the entire Industrial Revolution. Despite these personal accumulations, the new industries were unable to acquire funds even at interest rates in excess of 20 per cent. At the same time the land-connected industries (agriculture, brewing, milling, and mining) were able to command large quantities of capital, although rates of return were near zero (and sometimes, perhaps, negative). In the case of the United States, the mobilization problem was even more complex. Not only did capital have to move from old to new industries, but mobilization frequently involved geographic movement as well. In general, most of the savings accrued in the developed areas (that is, in the Northeast), but the demand for capital moved steadily toward the West and South. At the same time as comparative advantage shifted, early accumulations in foreign trade and shipping had to be transferred into textiles and other light industry during the first half of the nineteenth century. In the second half, funds had to be mobilized for heavy industry; and in the present century petroleum, chemicals, and electronics have become great demanders of new capital.

That the uncertainty discounts and costs that led to immobility existed in 19th-century America is not surprising. The uncertainties attached to investments that cannot "be touched" in developing societies has been noted by economic historians writing about the Middle Ages in Europe and by economists about underdeveloped countries today. At the same time, in the absence of institutions designed to effect the transfer of funds, the investment costs faced by any saver attempting to channel his resources into an area or industry far removed from his immediate ken are quite high. The interposition of some financial market or intermediary between saver and investor tends to reduce both uncertainties and costs. Uncertainties are reduced by making the investments appear "more domestic" and costs fall both because of the existence of certain

indivisible investment costs and because of the external economics realized from more efficient market organization.

Likewise, although some financial institutions probably exist at almost any stage of economic development, shifts in the geographic or industrial composition of demand require considerable institutional adaptation —an adaptation that is more difficult if the economy is immature. Thus financial institutions tend to be wedded to particular locations and historic trade relations, and the managers of these institutions tend, in the early stages of development, to be as provincial as the savers on whose funds they are drawing.

This article attempts to examine the evidence of immobilities, both geographic and industrial, in the American economy and outlines the innovations that made capital market institutions more flexible and the educational process that increased the sophistication of the average saver.

I. GEOGRAPHIC BARRIERS

1. Capital to the West 1820–1920

In the early period, since the bulk of the nation's savings apparently accrued in the East, it was in the newly developing trans-Appalachian West that one found the most obvious effects of the barriers to capital mobility. Early in its history the West needed external capital to finance its transport system. In response to this demand, finance moved westward in the 1830s and 1850s; however, while some of the funds came from Eastern savers, the bulk were drawn from abroad [10, 11]. Significant barriers to domestic East-West capital flows existed, and firms unable to draw on the talents of the financial capitalists were largely forced to depend on local savings.

In the case of Western agriculture, the opening of the trans-Mississippi West coupled with a series of important technological developments in wheat production greatly increased the industry's demand for external finance. Threshers, first innovated in the West in the 1840s, were replaced in the 1850s and 1860s with more productive and much more capital-intensive machines, and by the Civil War reapers too were needed if a farm was to be profitable. Moreover as planter and shellers were developed, corn farming began to demand some investment in machinery. Local banks were unable to supply these additional requirements, and in the absence of normal alternatives, the farmers turned to the equipment manufacturers for credit. Since the manufacturers were also limited to local personal capital, this informal credit arrangement, while increasing intraregional mobility, did nothing to promote mobility between regions.

An examination of four of the West's most important manufacturing industries (milling, meat packing, oil refining, and agricultural machinery) indicates that the effects of imperfect capital mobility were not limited to agriculture. Although some short-term requirements were met from sources outside the region, local capital provided almost all the initial long-term finance; and most growth was financed through retained earnings. Moreover in those rare instances when outside capital did play an important role, it appears to have been almost entirely mobilized through personal contacts.[1]

In the case of meat packing, a movement from farm to factory revolutionized the industry in the mid '30s. Even after that date, despite some infusions of bank credit and short-term Eastern risk capital to finance inventories, most firms were organized on the basis of the proprietor's personal capital (or the pooled resources of two or three partners) and relied on their suppliers' willingness to defer payment to finance their inventories and upon retained earnings for growth. Although there was some increase in the local banks' contributions to short-term requirements, in essence this pattern of finance continued until the 1880s. At that time the changes wrought by the advent of refrigeration greatly increased the packers' demand for long-term external finance. The typical packer, without large personal resources or entry to the Eastern capital markets, found himself unable to innovate the new technology and, as a result, was frequently forced out of business. On the other hand, the few businessmen capable of

commanding finance were able to profit and expand.[2]

Between the end of the eighteenth century and the 1870s technology in flour-milling changed but little, and since the old technology offered no important economics of scale, average firm size remained small. Initial capital requirements seldom exceeded an amount that the miller himself could accumulate (although there are evidences of occasional loans from local farmers who expected to use the facilities), and growth depended largely upon ploughbacks. In the 1870s, however, the innovation of Hungarian reduction milling greatly increased minimum efficient mill size and, therefore, the industry's demand for external finance. Businessmen, however, found it extremely difficult to attract depersonalized capital (either from inside or outside the region), and well into the 1880s even the largest firms were still family enterprises.[3]

Meat packing attracted some short-term Eastern capital, and milling ultimately some British; but the agricultural machinery industry, although its large-scale capital requirements antedate both, appears to have remained almost entirely self-financed until the end of the century. The manufacture of plows and scythes had typically been carried on in small firms, but the development of mechanized reapers and threshers moved the industry out of the shop and into the factory.

---

[1] The evidence, in fact, suggests that in the cases of agricultural machinery, oil refining, and meat packing, industrial concentration can be traced in large part to differences in businessmen's ability to command capital through personal connections.

[2] Both the Swift and the Armour packing empires were based at least in part on mobilization talents of their owners. While most Western packers could find no outside sources of capital, Armour was able to utilize the financial resources of his brother's New York commercial house and Swift displayed a great ability to borrow from the commercial banks when others could not.

[3] In the 1880s the first outside capital began to flow into the Minneapolis mills, but even then it was British rather than American. Of the largest mills, Pillsbury had been purchased by British capital by the end of the '80s, but the Washburn mills remained a local enterprise until the formation of General Mills in the 1920s. Both of these concerns date from the 1870s. Because of the difficulties of mobilizing capital it was not unusual for a person of some wealth to build a mill and bring in a skilled operator as a partner. This latter transaction did little to depersonalize capital, as the experience of the Washburn mills (the nation's largest) indicates. W. D. Washburn built the original mills and brought in George Christian as an operating partner; however, several years later when the pair broke up it was Washburn who assumed operating control.

This move, however, was largely financed from personal investments and retained earnings. McCormick, the nation's largest producer of reapers, for example, brought together a series of partners to finance his Chicago factory and then used the firm's profits to buy them out. The J. I. Case Company (a major producer of threshers) was entirely self-financed. In neither case did depersonalized capital become important until much later. Case attracted some outside finance after the death of the founder in 1891, but McCormick remained a family enterprise until J. P. Morgan organized the International Harvester combine in 1902.

Like the meat-packing industry, the industrial structure of the oil refining industry was shaped in part by the immobilities of capital. Refining, based on the discoveries of "Colonel" Drake in the late '50s, remained an industry of small producers until the end of the next decade. In the early stage, firms tended to be financed by the personal accumulations of their owners, and occasionally when more capital was needed additional partners were enlisted. Rockefeller's first experience in oil refining, for example, was as a member of such a partnership. The '70s were marked by a series of new technological developments in refining; and, although the new technology greatly reduced costs, it also increased capital requirements.[4] As in meat packing, the new technology placed a great premium on a firm's ability to mobilize capital. Firms with access to outside finance were able to expand at the expense of those unable to afford the new technology, and Rockefeller, with his close ties to the Cleveland banking community, was able to take the first steps towards ultimate domination of the industry.[5]

[4] The new developments were concentrated in distilling and in techniques of integrating operations. Although quantitative data for the '70s is lacking, some indication of the increase in the demand for capital may be found in the industry's capitalization trends in the two succeeding decades. In the years from 1880 to 1899, although the number of firms declined by twenty per cent, the industry's capitalization almost tripled.

[5] When other firms were unable to adopt the new techniques because of lack of capital, Rockefeller with his carefully preserved banking connections was able to acquire sufficient loan finance to first build the most efficient firm in the Cleveland area and to then buy out many of his less efficient competitors. It was his Cleveland refineries that were the basis for Standard Oil.

2. Interregional Interest Rate Differentials, 1870–1914: The Short-Term Market

For the post-bellum decades it is possible to provide some quantitative short-term measure of the effect of those barriers to mobility. The major quantitative series for the analysis of short-term market have been derived from the annual reports of the Comptroller of the Currency.

Interregional interest differentials were a well-known phenomenon in the nineteenth century; and contemporaries generally assumed that they were the result of certain capital immobilities.[6] The term "disinclination of capital to migrate" was used to explain the phenomenon, and it was estimated that an interest differential of 2 per cent was necessary to overcome this barrier [2, p. 129].

Since it was 1913 before national banks were permitted to invest in mortgages, bank loans tended to be short-term; and the regional differentials in the rate of return tend to reflect differentials in the interest rate of short-term commercial paper. Figures 1 and 2 display net rates of return to national banks in the period 1869 to 1914.[7] The New

[6] It is, of course, true that other factors aside from uncertainty may have engendered (and probably did engender) a part of the differential. It is likely that in the early period Eastern lenders may have felt Western loans were more risky. In addition, since the average loan size in the West was smaller, these loans may have entailed a higher percentage of administrative costs. These reasons, on the other hand, cannot be used to explain away the entire differential. Since substantial differentials were also apparent in the net rates of return (after losses had been deducted) it must have become obvious that Western loans were not "all that much" riskier, but the differentials persist for some decades. Moreover, the differentials continued after the size differentials between Eastern and Western loans began to diminish.

[7] Region 0: New York City.
Region I: Maine, Vermont, New Hampshire, Massachusetts, Connecticut, and Rhode Island.
Region II: New York, New Jersey, Pennsylvania, Delaware, Maryland, and the District of Columbia.
Region III: Virginia, North Carolina, South Carolina, West Virginia, Georgia, Florida, Alabama, Mississippi, Louisiana, Texas, Arkansas, Kentucky, and Tennessee.
Region IV: Ohio, Indiana, Illinois, Michigan, Wisconsin, Minnesota, Iowa, and Missouri.
Region V: North Dakota, South Dakota, Nebraska, Kansas, Montana, Wyoming, Colorado, New Mexico, and Oklahoma.
Region VI: Washington, Oregon, California, Idaho, Utah, Nevada, and Arizona.

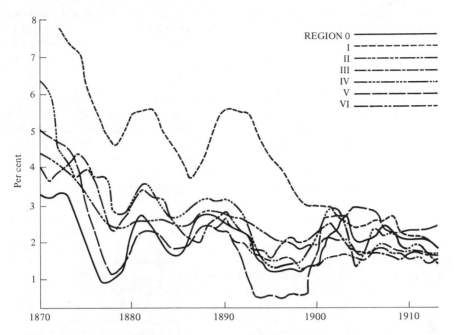

Figure 1. Three-Year Moving Average Net Returns, Reserve City Banks.

Figure 2. Three-Year Moving Average Net Returns, Non-Reserve City Banks.

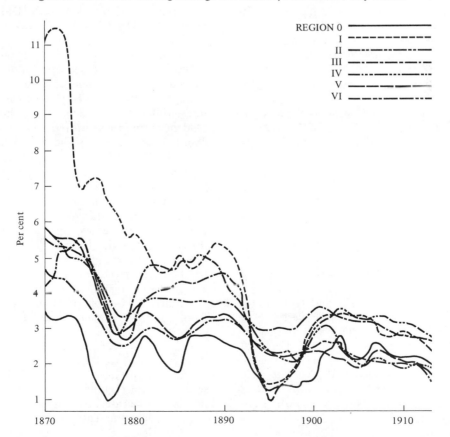

York City rate is displayed separately in each. Since it represents prevailing rates in the nation's financial center, it is a useful referent.

Both figures indicate that differentials were higher in the earlier years than they were in the later. This pattern suggests that there was a gradual movement toward a national short-term capital market during the period. Other evidence also appears to bear out this conclusion. The rates in the Eastern regions tended to close before those in the West and South. Moreover the differentials between banks in reserve cities tend to narrow before the differentials between the non-reserve-city banks.

The data show that, with the exception of the Pacific region, there appears to have been a marked decrease in the interest differentials between the reserve cities sometime in the late 1890's. In the early 1870s, with few exceptions, the New York City rate represented a lower boundary for the regional rates. In the latter years of that decade, however, the differentials between New York and Regions I and II largely disappeared. During the early 1890s the rate in Region IV tends to close on the Eastern rates; and, in the second half of that decade, the gap between rates in the East and those in Region IV narrows substantially. Although the differentials diminish between the Plains regions and those in the East, the rates in Region V remain above those in the East throughout the period. In the South the rates show much less of a tendency to close than in any other region. Thus, although the rates in Region III compare favorably in the 1870s with those in the East, by 1914 they are among the highest in the country.

These rates are, of course, weighted by total earning assets, and therefore they tend to be dominated by the rates prevailing in the largest cities in each region. An examination of unweighted rates indicates that the evolution toward a national market was more gradual.

The non-reserve-city rates display the same tendencies that were visible in the reserve city figures; however, in this case the rate of closure was much more gradual. In the late 1870s the rates in Region I and II come together, but they are still well above the New York rate. In fact, it is the beginning of the twentieth century before the differential between rates in these two regions and Region IV and those in New York City largely disappear. From that point on, however, it is difficult to select the New York rate from among the four.

Although the variance is much reduced, as late as 1914 the rates prevailing in the South, the Great Plains, and the Pacific Coast states are still substantially above those in the more eastern regions. With the non-reserve-city, as with the reserve-city banks, the South appears to be a case apart. In 1870 rates in Regions V and VI stood far above those prevailing in the East and South. However while Western rates were declining fairly rapidly, those in the South were moving much more slowly, and by 1914, rates in Region III appear more typical of the West than of the East.

The movements in the unweighted non-reserve-city rates follow the pattern set by the weighted series; but once again the trends are more gradual. Over-all, the picture seems clear. Between 1870 and 1914 a national short-term capital market gradually evolved. The movement started in the major Eastern cities and moved first to the large cities in the other regions. From that point the market grew to encompass those smaller city and country areas with the best banking facilities and finally those areas with the least-developed banking structures.

3. Interregional Interest Rate Differentials, 1870–1914: The Long-Term Market

The data on long-term interest rates are not as good as those from the "short-end" of the market. What evidence there is, however, strongly suggests that: (1) interregional interest differentials did exist, (2) there was a tendency for these differentials to decline over the period, and (3) the movement toward a national long-term capital market did not proceed as far or as fast as the movement in the short-term market.

The best data on long-term interest rates probably lie in the offices of the county recorders, where every mortgage was made a matter of public record. These recorded mortgage rates are not always reliable (particularly in the South and West), but they do provide a fair index of interregional differentials. The task of collecting these rates from every county (or even a sample of counties) would be, at best, heroic; however, the Census Bureau has surveyed records for the years 1880 to 1889. In addition, a study of farm mortgages in 1914–1915 provides some data on regional rates at the end of the period. These rates, as well as those for 1930, are reproduced in Table 1.

Table 1. Mortgage Interest Rates by Region

		ALL MORTGAGES[a]: REGION				
Year	I	II	III	IV	V	VI
1880	6.04	6.06	7.97	7.72	10.89	12.48
1881	5.90	5.80	7.96	7.39	11.28	11.40
1882	5.88	5.85	7.91	7.23	10.30	10.70
1883	5.87	5.83	7.87	7.25	9.94	10.77
1884	5.88	5.84	8.02	7.29	9.58	10.65
1885	5.83	5.79	8.08	7.31	10.09	10.88
1886	5.75	5.70	8.03	7.18	9.75	10.14
1887	5.69	5.69	7.86	7.10	9.57	9.49
1888	5.82	5.66	7.91	7.10	7.24	10.43
1889	5.78	5.66	7.80	6.90	9.00	9.95

		FARM MORTGAGES[b]: REGION				
Year	I	II	III	IV	V	VI
1880	6.03	6.11	8.02	7.81	10.51	11.94
1881	5.98	6.01	8.02	7.48	10.75	11.11
1882	5.93	5.90	7.93	7.34	9.65	10.52
1883	5.95	5.83	7.90	7.34	9.21	10.71
1884	5.95	5.79	8.05	7.40	9.03	10.10
1885	5.90	5.78	8.13	7.46	9.57	10.63
1886	5.86	5.76	2.02	7.32	9.60	9.84
1887	5.82	5.75	7.88	7.19	9.42	9.07
1888	5.88	5.70	7.90	7.22	9.09	10.19
1889	5.87	5.74	7.82	7.14	8.96	9.85
1914[a]	5.7	5.6	7.6	5.9	7.6	8.2
1914[b]	5.7	5.8	8.3	6.3	8.7	8.6
1930	6.1	6.0	6.8	5.9	6.5	6.9

[a] Without commission charge.
[b] With commission charge.

Table 1 indicates that marked regional differentials in mortgage rates existed during the 1880s. Over the period, rates averaged 5.9 per cent in Region I, 5.8 per cent in Region II, 7.9 per cent in Region III, 7.3 per cent in Region IV, 9.8 per cent in Region V, and 10.7 per cent in Region VI. (The farm mortgage rates displayed in the second half of the table show similar differentials.) Over the period, however, there appears to have been a movement toward greater equality. In 1880 the coefficient of variation for the six regional rates was 28 per cent (26 per cent for the farm mortgage rates), but by 1889 this figure had declined to 21 per cent (20 per cent for farm mortgages).

Although there appears to have been substantial movement toward a national market in the years before 1890, there is some question about the period 1890–1914. A comparison of the farm mortgage rates from the 1890 census with those from the Department of Agriculture survey of 1914–1915 suggests that progress toward a national market may not have been too great over the

period 1890–1914. The coefficient of variation for the 1914 figures is definitely less than that for the year 1880 (21 as compared with 26 per cent), but it is slightly higher than the figure for 1889. The two series are not, however, strictly comparable. Certainly the years after 1914 saw substantial progress. The next regional mortgage rates come from the 1930 census (the figures from the 1920 census do not include commission charges), and by that later date interregional differences have largely disappeared (the coefficient of variation is less than 2 per cent).

Additional evidence is found in the annual reports of the Comptroller of the Currency. Although earnings are not reported, the balance sheets of private banks, savings banks, and loan and trust companies are included. Since the loan and trust companies were almost all located in the East, they provide little interregional information. If, however, one is willing to accept two perhaps not-too-unreasonable assumptions, some interesting conclusions can be adduced from the balance sheets of the savings and private banks.

Let us assume that (1) if a banker is faced by two investment alternatives of equal risk, he will choose the one that yields the highest returns; and (2) the securities market for any bank is broader than the loan market for that same bank. Given these two assumptions it follows that a bank in a high interest area will tend to put a larger portion of its assets in loans (as opposed to securities), while a bank in a low-interest area will behave in the opposite manner. Thus the ratio of Loans/(Loans + Securities) is a fair index of the rate of interest on loans in any area.[8]

If each state year is taken as an observation, and if states are divided into regions and years into eras, the problem can then be formulated as an exercise in the analysis of variance where the rows are regions and the columns are time periods.[9] If there were no regional

---

[8] Legal restrictions on investment policy can affect portfolio composition, but since there were no restrictions on lending at home these legal restrictions would tend to increase the sensitivity of the ratios. Moreover, while state-to-state differences in legal regulation certainly did exist, these differences would tend to "wash out" between regions.

[9] Analysis of variance assumes that taken all together the observations are normally distributed and that they are homogeneous within each cell. In this case the normalcy assumption was not fulfilled with the raw data, but an arc sine transformation produced a distribution that met the two assumptions.

Table 2. Analysis of Variance of Loans/(Loans +
Securities) for Savings and Private Banks by Time
Period and Region of Location

Test No. 1
Savings Banks 1870–1914 Without Region V

	Degrees of Freedom	F Ratio	Significance Level
Years	7	7.46	.001
Regions	4	104.07	.001
Interaction	28	1.95	.001

Test No. 2
Savings Banks 1885–1914 All Regions

	Degrees of Freedom	F Ratio	Significance Level
Years	5	7.45	.001
Regions	5	80.33	.001
Interaction	25	1.27	.2

Test No. 3
Private Banks 1885–1914 Without Region I

	Degrees of Freedom	F Ratio	Significance Level
Years	7	3.74	.001
Regions	3	21.59	.001
Interaction	21	1.33	.2

differences in rates, there should be no significant row effects; if there were no variations
between time periods, there should be no
significant column effects; and if there were
no interactions between the interregional rate
differentials and the passage of time, the
interaction term should not be significant.

The results of three separate analyses of
variance tests are displayed in Table 2. In
the case of private banks, no banks in Region
I reported after 1890, and the analysis was
limited to the other five regions. Moreover
there were no reports from several regions
before 1885, and therefore the time period
was truncated to the period 1885–1914. In the
case of the savings banks, reports went back
into the 1870s for all regions except V, and
the first reports from institutions in that area
date from the quinquennium 1885–1889. As
a result, savings-bank test No. 1 covers the
time period 1870–1914 for all regions except
V; and test No. 2 includes all six regions for
the period 1885–1914.

These tests seem to substantiate the theses
advanced earlier. There is no question but
that there were significant differences between
the ratios in the various regions and various
time periods. Moreover it appears likely

that the differences arising from location may
have diminished over time. In every test the
F-ratio for both columns and rows was significant at the .001 level. The interaction term in
test No. 1 is also significant at the .001 level.
In tests No. 2 and 3, however, that same term
is significant at only the .2 level. At the same
time the exclusion of Region V from tests 2
and 3 causes an even further drop in the
significance of the interaction term. Moreover
the decrease in the interaction term between
test No. 1 and a test run on savings banks for
the period 1885–1914 without Region V is
significant at the .01 level. Thus the data
suggest that substantial progress toward a
national market was made in the period 1870–
1885 but that thereafter progress was slower.
It does not, however, indicate that there was
no progress after that date (the interaction
term is greater than one and is significant at
the .2 level), nor does it indicate that the
slowdown was a function of changing circumstances rather than merely of past progress (the more improvement has occurred
in the past, the less room there is for improvement in the future). These questions are still
open.

II. INDUSTRIAL BARRIERS

1. The East and South 1820–1920

Not only were there geographic barriers to
capital movement in the nineteenth century,
but there appear to have been industrial
barriers as well. Eastern savers were historically the nation's most sophisticated, but
even these savings were not easily mobilized.
The first two decades of the nineteenth
century saw a rapid decline in the profitability
of foreign trade, and a few years later the
Erie Canal triggered a similar fall in the
returns to Eastern agriculture. At first glance,
it appears that capital was quite mobile and
moved rapidly out of these declining industries and into more rewarding ventures.
A more careful examination of the evidence,
however, suggests that although the transfers
were fairly effortless, capital did not become
geographically mobile and to a large extent
was mobile between industries only when
the savers themselves moved with their
capital.

The cotton and woolen industries received
the bulk of the new capital. In the case of
cotton, the beneficiaries were all Eastern

firms; and despite the obvious locational advantages, no capital moved into the South. Moreover it appears there was also little personal divorcement in the capital transfer; a list of the officers of the new mills closely resembles a list of the successful merchants of a decade earlier.[10] A similar financial pattern is found in the history of the woolen industry. Original capital came in large measure from individuals who had accumulated savings in trade and agriculture, but these savers transferred themselves with their capital to the new industry. Again, this transfer implied little geographic mobility. As woolen manufacture began to move west towards its source of supply, the worsted mills (requiring heavy capital investment) remained concentrated in the East because capital was more plentiful in that area.

Outside of textiles capital was even less mobile. In the case of the boot and shoe industry, for example, the shift from shop to factory was financed almost entirely with internal funds and outside capital was not enlisted until late in the century. A similar inability to acquire impersonal finance marked the early history of the steel industry. Capital requirements in iron manufacture had been small and were usually met by the ironmaster himself with occasional (in the case of the largest enterprises) recourse to a few partners. The development of the Kelly and Bessemer processes created the possibility of economical steel production but also intensified the industry's need for external finance. The first Bessemer mill was finished only because the Pennsylvania Railroad (a prospective customer) was willing to advance $600,000 when the owner's personal finances were exhausted. Similarly (although they were not in the East) when Ward and Durgen began to build the first "Kelly" plant, financial demands greatly exceeded their personal accumulations, and it was only by appealing to other iron men, some in England and some in the United States, that they were able to acquire the necessary capital. Only gradually during the last decades of the nineteenth century were funds made available

to Eastern industry through "normal" channels.

If capital moved sluggishly within the East it moved almost not at all within the other "settled" region—the South. In many respects the South represents the most puzzling of the three regions. In the West mobilization of long-term capital was first achieved through the efforts of a few financial capitalists and by personal transfers from savers to capital-using firms. In the South even these crude methods were late developing. Much of the region's original accumulations had been in agriculture; but, despite declining returns in the "Old South" after the 1830s, capital did not flow into more lucrative activities. Some agricultural capital did move into the "New South" (Alabama, Mississippi, and east Texas) but usually only when it was accompanied by its owners. Moreover within the "Old South" there was practically no transfer from agriculture to industry. Despite locational advantages, textiles were unable to attract external finance; instead funds continued to be reinvested in agriculture. Not until well after the Civil War did the textile industry become firmly established in the South.

Although there were substantial locational advantages in the South, the shortage of finance in that area prevented major development until the 1870s. Even then it was impossible to raise local external capital, and the funds on which the industry grew came from the North (where people were more familiar with textile investment). As a result, throughout the entire period the Southern textile industry had to pay a premium price for their finance. Nor was this discrimination limited to stock and bond holders. Southern banks also discriminated against the new industry and textile firms had to appeal to Northern sources for even their short-term accommodations. The result was, of course, retarded growth. It was the second decade of the twentieth century before Southern textiles clearly dominated the American market: a domination they would almost certainly have achieved a hundred years earlier had capital been more mobile.

2. The New England Textile Industry Before 1860

The difficulties inherent in the mobilization of capital across even industrial borders is neatly illustrated by the case of the American textile industry. Although at first glance the

---

[10] An examination of the ownership of the large New England cotton textile mills indicates that the stockholders were almost all Massachusetts residents, and, although the firms' securities were listed on the Boston exchange, few shares were ever traded. Instead the firms depended almost entirely on personal subscription for both initial and additional finance.

industry appears to belie all questions of capital immobility, a closer examination shows that its entire history is closely bound up with the problem of immobile capital.

Without question the textile industry was the first of the American mass-producing industries, and the firms that produced those goods were among the giants of the world. Such firms required large blocks of capital, their balance sheets showed a large proportion of equity and loans, and the local stock exchange regularly quoted their shares. Altogether one could easily conclude that they must have been the recipient of large quantities of very mobile capital. In fact closer examination suggests that these firms managed to accumulate capital, but they never managed to mobilize it. If we look at the Massachusetts type of textile firms (these were the giants, after all), an analysis of the financial trends suggests that mobility was more apparent than real.

An examination of the records of nine "Massachusetts Type" firms suggests that the sources of capital utilized at any point in time depend, at least in part, upon two distinct factors—the historical date (reflecting the institutional environment and the willingness of investors to hold direct issues) and the age of the firm (reflecting the ability to generate finance internally). A multiple regression model with the proportion of assets financed by (1) equity (Y_1), (2) loans (Y_2), and (3) retained earnings (Y_3) chosen as the dependent variables and the year (X_1), firm age (X_2), and the quadratic terms: year^2 (X_1^2), age^2 (X_2^2) and year times age (X_1X_2), shows very clearly the problems of mobility and the hesitating steps achieved by that sector of the industry in overcoming them in the ante-bellum decades.[11] For the nine firms in the sample the regression equations are:[12]

$$Y_1 = 85.53 - .1149X_1 - \underline{.5372X_2}$$
$$+ .0001X_1^2 + \underline{0010X_2^2} + .0173X_1X_2$$

$$Y_2 = 10.98 - \underline{.6041X_1} - .1734X_2$$
$$+ \underline{.0274X_1^2} - .0267X_2^2 + \underline{\underline{.0322X_1X_2}}$$

$$Y_3 = 4.76 + .0712X_1 + 1.601X_2$$
$$+ .0016X_1^2 + \underline{\underline{.0491X_2^2}} - \underline{\underline{.0750X_1X_2}}$$

Throughout the period covered by the study (1827–1860) equity represented the most important source of capital. An examination of the regression curves shows, however, that the relative importance of this source declined both over the life of the firm and over historical time. Since the firms financed almost all of their original plant and equipment through the sales of equities, and since in general they did not increase their equity issues after the first few years of their existence, the declining importance of the equity contribution is not surprising. Among the firms in the sample, four sold no new equities after the fifth year of their life, and none sold new shares after the eleventh.

That the textile firms tended not to finance expansion through the sale of equity is obvious, the question of why is more difficult. Certainly in part it may reflect a desire by the present stockholders to prevent the dilution of their original equity. Moreover certain legal restrictions against issues below par may have contributed to the hesitation in the case of those firms not earning average profits. More important, however, is that fact that no ready market for the securities really existed. The issues themselves were very narrowly held. A study of eleven of the largest mills showed that the original holders of equity totalled only slightly over 500 people, and even as late as 1859 three quarters of the stock was still held by less than 750 persons. Moreover almost all of these people were concentrated in Massachusetts. Less than one half of one per cent of the original stockholders lived outside that state and even in 1859 this percentage had risen to only slightly above three. Occupationally the owners were concentrated in mercantile activities, and although there is some increase in female and trustee ownership toward the end of the period, this increase appears to reflect death and inheritance patterns rather than any widening of the market. In fact the chronicler of the Boston exchange warns his readers not to trust the published price quotations because "this class of securities . . . is almost exclusively in the hands of a few capitalists who have no desire to sell it when it is up, and

---

[11] The nine yield 175 firm-year observations. Since the 175 are obviously not independent, the relevant number of degrees of freedom is, no doubt, considerably smaller; however, there is good reason to believe that the number of independent observations is great enough to permit large sample tests to be used.

[12] The single underlined coefficients were significant at the 10 per cent level; those double-underlined were significant at the 1 per cent level.

can afford to hold it when it is down. It seldom finds its way onto the market...." In short, although it might appear that capital was mobilized through the sale of securities, the relevant area of mobilization was very small indeed, limited as it was to a relatively small group of Massachusetts merchants.

The effect of the development of the long-term credit market can be clearly seen in the regression relationship between loan capital and historical time. The year term is negative because of the serious repercussions of the depression of the 1840s that forced all firms to drastically reduce their borrowings. If those years are dropped, the year term becomes both positive and significant. Moreover, in both models the year^2 term is positive and significant: an apparent reflection of the entry of the nonbank intermediaries into the textile loan market in the years after 1845. The negative age coefficients are, however, more difficult to explain, but a separation of long- from short-term loans suggests at least one possibility. Such a separation produces negative age coefficients for short-term loans and positive for long. Perhaps, therefore, the decline in short-term credit reflects a reduction in demand as both internal finance and trade credit become more available, and the increase in long-term loans the greater borrowing power of established firms. While the textile firms themselves acquired even larger blocks of loan finance, their contribution to the general process of mobilization via the formal financial markets was not so marked. In the first place the firms themselves were forced into the informal markets for almost a quarter of their total loan finance, and although this proportion

declined somewhat over the ante-bellum decades, it was still significant in 1860. In the second place, the textile firms had better access to the formal markets than did most other manufacturing industries. This preferred entry may have helped educate the financial intermediaries to the desirability of industrial loans, but it also absorbed a large portion of the total available loan finance.

Compared to modern credit markets, one of the most interesting features of the ante-bellum market was the diversity of persons and institutions making significant contributions to the supply of credit (Table 3). Although, then as now, the commercial banks and the nonbank intermediaries were the dominant lenders, the textile firms also seemed willing to borrow from other manufacturing companies, mercantile wholesale houses, and any other institution or person showing a willingness to advance any amount of money. Throughout the two decades the activities of those "abnormal" lenders were very significant on the margin, and in some markets (particularly the very short-term) and in some periods, they actually came to dominate lending activities.

No New England industry maintained a better connection with the loan market than did the textile firms. The ability of the industry to maintain such close connections with the financial intermediaries can probably be attributed both to the dominant position of the textile industry in the Massachusetts economy and to the close personal relations that existed between that industry's stockholders and the managers of the financial enterprises. Whatever the cause, there can be no doubt that the textile industry did

Table 3. Twenty Years Summary of Relative Contributions of Eight Lender Groups to New Formal Loans by Length of Loan (Renewals and Trade Credit not Treated) (In Per Cent)

Lender	Demand and up to 30 Days	30 Days to Six Months	Six Months to One Year	One Year and Over	Total of 2385 Loans
Commercial	22.7	86.9	63.0	3.5	58.1
Savings banks	2.0	1.4	4.3	39.7	10.1
Trust companies	5.5	0.6	6.0	29.1	8.2
Insurance companies	1.2	1.7	1.7	1.5	0.9
Individuals	19.5	10.8	10.8	22.0	9.9
Mercantile houses	20.5	13.2	13.2	2.8	7.3
Manufacturing firms	26.2	1.0	1.0	0.6	4.9
Miscellaneous institutions	2.4	0.0	0.0	0.8	0.6
Total	100.0	100.0	100.0	100.0	100.0

receive the lion's share of the industrial loans made by these institutions. Take for example, the Provident Institution for Savings in the town of Boston, the largest savings bank in ante-bellum New England. Between 1839 and 1859 the Provident made 231 loans, exclusive of renewals, to 41 corporations in the textile industry, and only 13 loans to 5 industrial corporations not in the textile industry.

Despite these limitations the textile industry did help somewhat to mobilize loan capital within New England, although progress towards even a regional loan market was not complete by the time of the Civil War. Over time the proportion of nontextile industrial loans rose in the portfolios of both the Provident and the Massachusetts Hospital Life Insurance Company (the region's largest supplier of long-term loan finance). However, despite the gains within the Northeast, even textile capital was not very mobile across regional barriers, and in other regions the absence of close ties between the industry and both investors and financial intermediaries seriously retarded development.

III. SURMOUNTING GEOGRAPHIC BARRIERS

1. The Short-Term Market

The early periods of American development then were characterized by important barriers to capital flow both between regions and between industries. In part the process of development took the form of developing institutions that could surmount these barriers. On the one hand development took the form of the evolution of a series of financial intermediaries to stand between saver and investor and on the other of better formal markets to facilitate the process of direct investment.

In the case of the short-term market for funds, the local institutions were the commercial banks, but because of the legal environment and the difficulties in servicing distant loans these banks were not linked into a national financial network until the development of the commercial paper market.

In the United States there has always been a widely held view among lawmakers that local banks should serve the local communities. In the ante-bellum decades, a number of states actually passed laws prohibiting bank loans to persons living in other states. Despite these restrictions banks in low

interest areas began to seek more lucrative investment opportunities than those available at home; as a result, even before the Civil War the foundation for an active commercial-paper market in the East had been laid.

Since the market was centered in the large Eastern cities, it was the rates in these areas that were first affected; however, the market began to spread into the Midwest in the two decades after the end of the war. There are records of commercial paper dealers operating in Indianapolis in 1871. By 1880 commercial paper was being traded in Milwaukee, Chicago, and Minneapolis; and by the turn of the century nine or ten houses were operating in each of the latter two cities. The expansion of the market continued across the Plains and on to the Pacific Coast. By the early 1880s Kansas City had been integrated into the market; and by 1910 further growth had encompassed Wichita and Dallas. On the Pacific Coast broker's offices were opened in San Francisco, Seattle, and Los Angeles about the turn of the century.

"By 1913 it could be said that the commercial paper houses had branches or representatives 'in all large cities' in the United States," [9, pp. 39–40]. More important from the viewpoint of this study, in each case the timing of the expansion of the commercial paper market conforms fairly closely to the closing of the interregional rate differentials.

The profits earned by the commercial paper houses induced additional entry, and increased competition forced the brokers to extend the area of their operations in search of prime paper and good customers. The added competition began to infringe on long established monopolies. Among the first groups to feel the squeeze were the Western bankers who had been accustomed to high returns on their investments. In 1892 an Iowa banker said:

Until recently, Western bankers were able to maintain their loaning rates regardless of the depression of the eastern markets, but now there has arisen an element that wages constant war on the established rates. It is the festive note broker, who with his eastern capital, steps in to disturb the harmonious relations between banker and borrower, and just at the time there seems to be an opportunity to dispose of idle funds at a profitable rate, the banker is confronted with the alternative of cutting his rates or seeing his loans going to outside dealers.

Because of the increased activity in the commercial paper market, many small cities and towns were integrated into the national capital market; capital moved more easily across regional boundaries; and interest rates in the high-interest areas began to decline.

2. The Long-Term Market

The last third of the nineteenth century also saw some progress towards a national long-term market, but the evidence suggests that evolution slowed down during the last decade of the century. In the case of the long-term loan market no single institutional development was as important as the commercial paper house in the short-end, but both growth of life insurance companies and the development of mortgage banking appear to have made some contribution.

The period after the Civil War saw life insurance companies emerge as the nation's most important nonbank intermediaries. In the years from 1869–1914, the assets of the nation's life insurance companies increased more than twentyfold. This growth, as North has shown, is associated with the innovation of new types of life insurance policies (particularly industrial and tontine) [12]. These companies would not have played such an important role in the process of capital mobilization had it not been for the concomitant evolution of their investment policies. Within the companies, professional management developed, and one aspect of this development was a widening of investment horizons externally and, perhaps more important, the period was marked by a gradual easing of the legal regulations that had restricted the investment policy of many of the largest companies.[13]

Given professional management and an absence of legal restrictions, there were still substantial technical problems in handling distant investments. Therefore it might have taken longer for the insurance companies to become important forces in interregional mobilization had it not been for the parallel development of brokerage institutions designed to service their portfolios. The New York Life, for example, depended upon Vermilyea and Company to handle their securities account, and other firms appear to have employed similar agents. For mortgages, the mutuals frequently turned to western agents. A. F. Ward, for example, a Minneapolis mortgage broker and later an important Midwestern banker, acted as the resident mortgage agent for a number of insurance companies.

An examination of insurance companies located in various regions shows the impact of their developments in management and regulation. While large differentials are characteristic of the early years, they tend to decline over the period. For example a projection based on a linear regression through the mortgage rates earned by companies in the Middle Atlantic states and those in the Pacific region for the years 1878–1889 suggests that (if the trend had continued) the differentials would have disappeared in 1905 (as in fact they did). This result contrasts markedly with a parallel projection posed on regression through the mortgage census data for the years 1880–1889. In the latter case, rates would not have closed until 1921. Although these projections are very rough, they are quite suggestive. It does not appear unreasonable to conclude that the insurance companies, freed of their managerial and legal restrictions, were willing to move funds across regional boundaries before most private investors were willing to take this step. Moreover the data suggest that the companies were not large enough to arbitrage out the market.

For a short two-decade period in the 1870s and 1880s, the mortgage company played a

---

[13] See [14]. Insurance companies in Connecticut and Massachusetts, subject to less severe restrictions, did invest more widely than did firms with home offices in New York. Zartman has argued that it was changes in investment regulations that were most important in restricting the investment portfolios of the large insurance firms and that the period was marked by substantial reductions in legal limitations. As originally written, laws governing the investments of mutual life insurance companies tended to emphasize safety and to demand that funds be invested close to home. In the late 1860s only four states permitted investment in corporate securities; and most states had some restrictions on investment policy. During the last third of the century, however, many of these laws were altered to provide a wider range of legal investments. In New York, for example, the original law prohibited investments in mortgages anywhere out of the state. An 1868 amendment permitted insurance companies to invest in mortgages anywhere within fifty miles of New York; in 1875 the legal boundaries were extended to include every adjacent state; and in the 1880s the New York mutuals were granted the right to invest in mortgages anywhere. By 1905 only Georgia, Nebraska, Pennsylvania, and Texas retained laws prohibiting investment in out-of-state mortgages. Similarly, in 1905 California, Colorado, Utah, Connecticut, New Jersey, Pennsylvania, Illinois, and Wisconsin had all begun to permit some investment in corporate securities.

very significant role in the interregional mobilization of capital. At first the companies merely acted as middlemen. As long as they performed the brokerage function, they did little to reduce the uncertainty discounts of the Eastern investors, although, they did make Western investment easier. As competition increased, however, they began to guarantee the mortgages they sold; and from a guarantee it was an easy step to a general debenture issued against a portfolio of mortgages. The first mortgage companies were organized about 1870, but it was the middle 1880s before they began to issue bonds. At the height of their popularity (about 1890) there were at least 167 companies operating in the United States [8, p. 213].

The history of the mortgage company has yet to be written, but Allen Bogue has provided an excellent study of a single company (the J. B. Watkins Land Mortgage Company of Lawrence, Kansas) [1]. Moreover, examination of contemporary chronicles suggests that the Watkins firm was probably fairly typical of the larger mortgage companies. The firm was organized in 1870; began as a middleman but shifted into guaranteed mortgages and later into debentures; enjoyed twenty years of profitable existence; and went bankrupt in the early 1890s.

To succeed, it was necessary for Watkins to sell his mortgages (and later his bonds) quickly. To accomplish this end, he had by 1877 a branch office in New York City and sales agents in Buffalo, Albion, Batavia, Rochester, Syracuse, Rome, and Johnstown, New York; in Wilmington, Delaware; in Boston, Massachusetts; in Warner, New Hampshire; and in Ferrisburg, Vermont. In 1878, in search of still more investors, he opened a second branch in London, England.

In the early 1890s, in the face of agricultural depression, the J. B. Watkins Company, like most mortgage companies, collapsed. Many of those that managed to remain solvent turned to other lines of endeavor. The management of Wells Dicky, for example—one of the oldest and largest mortgage companies in the Upper Plains—withdrew entirely from the mortgage business and shifted the company's resources to other financial activities. The industry's collapse was in part a function of the tenuous financial structure on which it had been built; contributing factors were the narrow margin of profitability of farms west of the 98th meridian, the failure of Eastern investors to understand the nature of agriculture in this semiarid land, and of course the general price decline.

Although they operated for only a short period, the mortgage companies played a significant role in the movement of funds from the East into the Midwest. Moreover if progress toward a national long-term market did slow down after 1890, the failure of the mortgage companies may well have been a contributory factor.

3. Investor Education and Narrowing Interregional Differentials

The process of investor education was everywhere slow, but it proceeded more rapidly in some regions than others. In the East the original transfer from commerce and agriculture to textiles was a personal one and involved little education. The heirs of the original investors did, however, become acquainted with paper securities. The tempo of education increased as the Eastern saver began to buy the securities of railroad and canal companies and later (during the Civil War) the bonds of the federal government. Finally in the decades after the war, the sales campaign of the investment houses made stocks and bonds common words in the saver's vocabulary, and convinced even the most skeptical that a piece of paper could be as safe an investment as a house, farm, or factory.

Barring the early experiences with textiles, the Western investor's experience roughly paralleled the Easterner's. However because development came later in the West, the entire process was delayed several decades. Most frequently the Westerner's first contact with paper securities came from his investments in local transport projects; and although direct evidence is lacking, it appears logical to assume that his experience with these issues opened a wider range of depersonalized investments for him. Certainly by the early twentieth century the process had proceeded far enough to lead an important New York banker to say: "The whole great Mississippi Valley gives promise that in some day distant perhaps it will be another New England for investments. There is developing a bond market there which is of constant astonishment to eastern dealers."

The Washburn Flour Mills provide an interesting example of Western capital mobilization. When the original owners died, their heirs were anxious to sell and, in addition, the mills needed additional new capital for growth. However no outsiders were yet willing to invest. In 1898 an Eastern promoter, realizing the potential profits, attempted to bring in outside capital; but even at that late date he was unable to mobilize the necessary funds. Because of the firm's failure to acquire external finance through "normal" markets, growth was financed through the personal connections maintained by an officer (William Dunwoody) with the banking community. Ownership ultimately passed into the hands of the managers, but to finance the sale a two-and-a-half million dollar loan was negotiated through the Philadelphia commercial banks in 1914. For the first time "foreign" capital had been mobilized through normal channels. Finally, with the organization of General Mills in 1929, the company's stock was listed on a national exchange; and the process of mobilization completed.

In the South, however, saver education did not proceed as rapidly, as it had hardly begun. Although it is impossible to determine the exact causes of this delay, it almost certainly in part reflects the close ties that existed between land ownership and social position. Moreover since the area possessed a fine natural transportation network, there were few paper securities to act as educational vehicles.[14] Finally while federal bonds convinced many savers in the North and West of the safety of paper securities, the Southerner's experience with Confederate bonds could hardly have led him to the same conclusion.

As savers grew more sophisticated, better markets made it possible for them to place their funds in the areas with the greatest demand. Throughout much of the nineteenth century the formal securities markets had aided interregional mobilization of funds for the public sector and for the growing transportation industries. They had, however, made little direct contribution to manufacturing. By the end of the century, however, some changes were evident. In 1885 the New York Stock Exchange organized a department of unlisted securities, and this department became the route by which a number of distant manufacturing companies reached the "Big Board." More important, J. P. Morgan turned his attention to manufacturing and his success convinced many investors that paper investments in manufacturing were safe and profitable. International Harvester, for example, was a combine of Midwest firms. Most had been locally owned, but after the merger it was Eastern capital that poured in and released the local capital for other activities. Thereafter, imitation was easier. As investors became convinced of the profitability of paper securities, the number of brokerage houses increased. In 1900 no firm but Morgan (and perhaps Kuhn-Loeb) could successfully have marketed a major industrial issue, but by the 1920s several could and did. The increased competition reduced profits and increased capital mobility. Nor did the securities markets mobilize only Eastern capital. By the twentieth century the Old Northwest Territory had become a savings surplus area, and the securities markets began to mobilize these funds as well.

IV. CONCLUDING REMARKS

It appears, therefore, that the United States in the nineteenth century was marked by important barriers to interregional and interindustry capital mobility. Moreover that century was marked by a series of institutional innovations, designed on the one hand to speed the process of investor education and on the other to effect a series of intermediaries and markets, and together they speeded the flow of funds from industry to industry and region to region.

Still some interesting problems remain. First, why was the integration of the South into the financial network so slow? Second, is it possible to measure the economic cost of the capital immobilities? Third, what accounts for the types of institutions that emerge, and finally, what determines the timing of their emergence?[15]

[14] It has been argued that the existence of a natural transportation system may have actually retarded Southern development, and in this peculiar secondary sense at least the argument may have some validity. For a statement of the more usual argument see [13].

REFERENCES

1. Allan G. Bogue, *Money at Interest: The Farm Mortgage on the Middle Border*, Ithaca, Cornell University Press, 1955.

[15] [For greater detail on the topics covered in this essay see [3–7].—Editors' note.]

2. R. M. Breckenridge, "Discount Rates in the United States," *Political Science Quarterly*, *13* (March, 1898), 119–142.

3. Lance E. Davis, "Sources of Industrial Finance: The American Textile Industry, A Case Study," *Explorations in Entrepreneurial History*, *9* (April, 1957), 190–203.

4. Lance E. Davis, "Stock Ownership in the Early New England Textile Industry," *The Business History Review*, *32* (Summer, 1958), 204–222.

5. Lance E. Davis, "The New England Textile Mills and the Capital Markets: A Study of Industrial Borrowing, 1840–1960," *The Journal of Economic History*, *20* (March, 1960), 1–30.

6. Lance E. Davis, "Capital Immobilities and Finance Capitalism: A Study of Economic Evolution in the United States, 1820–1890," *Explorations in Entrepreneurial History*, Second Series, *1* (Fall, 1963), 88–105.

7. Lance E. Davis, "The Investment Market, 1870–1914: The Evolution of a National Market," *The Journal of Economic History, 25* (September, 1965), 355–393.

8. M. Frederiksen, "Mortgage Banking in America," *The Journal of Political Economy*, *2* (March, 1894), 203–234.

9. Albert Greef, *The Commercial Paper House in the United States*, Cambridge, Harvard University Press, 1938.

10. Leland Hamilton Jenks, *The Migration of British Capital to 1875*, New York, Alfred A. Knopf, 1927.

11. Reginald C. McGrane, *Foreign Bondholders and American State Debts*, New York, MacMillan, 1935.

12. Douglass North, "Capital Accumulation in Life Insurance between the Civil War and the Investigation of 1905," William Miller, ed. *Men in Business*, Cambridge, Harvard University Press, 1952, pp. 238–253.

13. Douglass C. North, *The Economic Growth of the United States, 1790–1860,* Englewood Cliffs, Prentice-Hall, 1961.

14. Lester Zartman, *Investment of Life Insurance Companies*, New York, H. Holt, 1906.

23 FINANCING THE PRAIRIE FARMER

Allan G. Bogue

The pioneer farmer of the 1830s in Illinois and Iowa was still settling in the timber or on the margins of the prairie adjacent to wooded lands. Close at hand were his fuel, his fencing materials, and the logs for a cabin or for the rough siding cut at a nearby sawmill. Although he might hire his rails split, or even buy them, the prairie pioneer of the 1830s could purchase them with his labor if need be. The range of farm machinery was still limited; a wagon, a couple of plows, a harrow, and the hand tools of axe, shovel, scythe, fork, and rake constituted the essential minimum. In addition the pioneer must have a pair of oxen with yoke and chains or a team of horses and their harness if he was to farm seriously. Three hundred dollars or less would purchase this minimum of equipment during the 1830s. For another $100 the settler could buy 80 acres of government land. A few cows or other stock might

Reprinted with omissions by permission from Allan G. Bogue, *From Prairie to Corn Belt: Farming on the Illinois and Iowa Prairies in the Nineteenth Century*, Chicago, University of Chicago Press, 1963, pp. 169–181.

cost an additional $100 to $150. The total investment was a modest one [3].

Forty years later the prairie pioneers were purchasing much of their fencing and usually constructed framed houses of sawed timbers and boards for their first dwelling. Their plows were more costly and they regarded a far wider range of additional equipment as indispensable. Mowers, hay rakes, reapers, corn planters, seeder or drill, and custom threshing had all become part of the farming patterns of the 1870s. Where the farmer of the 1830s often carried his water from stream or spring, the pioneer of the 1870s must ordinarily dig a well, on occasion hiring a professional well-digger to do the job. Although the pioneer of the 1870s in Iowa might be fortunate enough to obtain a farm from the 902,000 acres of land distributed under the homestead laws in northwestern Iowa, he was much more likely to pay several dollars an acre to speculator, railroad, or other large holder.

The Iowa Railroad Land Company estimated the cost of team and "outfit" to a small holder on the Northwestern Railroad Company lands in central and western Iowa as follows:

Team (oxen or horses)		$150 to $300
Wagon and yoke or harness		
	100	150
Two plows	35	50
Cultivator and harrow	20	45
Combination reaper and mower	200	252
Other tools	10	50
	$515	$847

The land company had set its prices at $3–$12 per acre, and only limited amounts were available at the lowest figure. Added, of course, to the costs of team, outfit, and land, were those for house, fencing, and well, plus the cost of other stock.

Undoubtedly the minimum investment necessary for farmmaking had increased considerably between the 1830s and the 1870s. Of course the new farmer of the 1870s, like his predecessor of the 1830s, might evade or defer his capital needs. He might work part time for others; he might farm as a tenant; he might borrow equipment or combine with a work ring to share equipment costs. He could, finally, purchase his land or equipment on credit, perhaps borrowing money from a third party to meet such expenditures, alternatives that bring us to the subject of farm credit.

Until 1820 the purchaser of government land could spread his payments over four years. So abused were the credit provisions of the land code that Congress approved the Revision Act of 1820, allowing cash sales only and a minimum price of $1.25 per acre. The implications of this congressional decision were far reaching. Now the pioneer farmer must depend solely on private enterprise for aid in meeting the cost of land. Hereafter the most urgent need of the Midwestern pioneer for credit would come in the weeks immediately prior to the federal land auctions. If he could qualify under the limited pre-emption laws of the 1830s or the general pre-emption act of 1841, the settler's claim was safe until the day of the land sale, provided, of course, that he had filed the required pre-emption declaration. But he must pay for his land before the day of the sale or see it go under the hammer.

Many of the settlers of Illinois and Iowa who purchased federal land could not qualify under the terms of the limited pre-emption laws of the 1830s, including as they did the provision that settlers must have been on their claims before a given date. Such men had to find their purchase money and hope as well that none appeared at the auction with more funds and an overpowering desire to buy improved claims. Historians have stressed that the squatters' club or claim association was designed to prevent greedy speculators from outbidding "actual settlers." They have written much less about its usefulness to the squatter who needed funds. Many of the speculators were just as willing to lend money to the squatters for the purchase of the claims as they were eager to buy land on their own account. The pressure of the claim clubs may well have induced capitalists to lend on more equitable terms than they otherwise would have been willing to do [2].

We cannot, unfortunately, discover the extent to which settlers in any area turned to the speculator for credit at the land sales. The working of the time-entry system has hidden many such loans. Under this system, the money lender purchased the land in his own name, giving the settler a bond for a deed that obligated the capitalist to deed all or a portion of the squatter's claim back to him if he paid the purchase price and substantial interest within six months or a year. Typically, the county records do not contain these bonds. Yet the system was at work at many land sales between 1830 and 1860, as the business records of land-speculators show. By comparing claim-club records and county records, we can also detect the time-entry system in operation. Shortly after the federal land sale a large purchaser of government land in Johnson County, Iowa—Morgan Reno, for instance—deeded a number of small tracts to members of the local claim club who had themselves failed to purchase at the auction. The county records, of course, fail to show the number of squatters who resorted to the capitalist and the time-entry system and who failed to pay out. They drifted elsewhere; their shattered dreams or miscalculations found no place in the recorder's indexes and registers. If some settlers turned in their need to capitalists or their agents in the land-office towns, there were many others who sought aid from parents or other relatives in the older states.

The period of cash sale and pre-emption included the lean years of the early 1820s and the hard times following 1837 and 1857. At such times the shortage of cash, so usual in the newly settled regions, was intensified by the general stringency throughout the country, and settlers paid rates of interest on entry loans that were high by any standard. Alfred Hebard wrote in his recollections of the government land sales at Burlington, "Parties were on hand with a plethora of specie—to loan, generally at a rate of about one hundred per cent, for a year—and many a man went home with a Title Bond of Doctor Barrett or some other party in his pocket in place of his certificate of purchase." *The Hawkeye and Iowa Patriot* of Burlington was more conservative than Hebard in estimating interest rates at the sales under way during October of 1839, reporting that speculators had been lending money to the squatters at rates of 20–28 per cent. A Fort Madison lawyer explained to an Eastern relative in 1840 that he could put money out on good security at rates ranging from 25 to 50 per cent. Territorial law in Iowa at that time allowed no contracts to specify a rate of more than 20 percent, but he suggested that all could be done legally if deeds of trust were used.

By the 1850s both Illinois and Iowa had adopted usury laws that set the maximum rate of interest at 10 per cent. The figure was unrealistic until at least the 1870s, and one must view interest tables based on the county mortgage registers with some skepticism as a result. Above the legal maximum stood the agent's commission, which might well be split with the lender, although state courts viewed such procedure as a patent evasion of the usury laws. Sometimes, no doubt, usurious rates were concealed by inflating the principal that notes and mortgages specified.

His saddlebags bulging with specie, land warrants or sound bank notes, the Eastern capitalist or his agent might appear before the land sales of the 1830s and 1840s in the land-office towns of Illinois and Iowa, prepared to lend to the settlers. His business ended, he would depart in a few weeks time, leaving a local attorney, perhaps, to oversee the loans and accept payment. At the same time local attorneys, real estate agents, and bankers managed to procure some funds from clients, relatives, or acquaintances in the older regions for similar use. By the 1850s the flow of such funds from the older states to the new Midwest was becoming more obvious, more widely disseminated, and much better organized than formerly.

From the late 1850s onward, more and more Eastern businessmen, professional folk, and prosperous farmers came to cherish the Midwestern farm mortgage as an investment. For some the mortgage business was a natural outgrowth of Western land speculation or investment in tax titles. To others the Western mortgage was simply a new but lucrative avenue of investment. Not only were individuals involved. Casting about for investments that combined safety with profit and sobriety with heady interest, the insurance companies turned eagerly to the farm mortgage of the Midwest. The laws of New York barred the insurance companies of that state from such investments until late in the century, but no such restrictions impeded the Connecticut Mutual, the Aetna, the Travelers, and other New England companies, or Midwest corporations like the Northwestern of Milwaukee.

As the farm-loan business grew, the local agents and would-be competitors strove vigorously to increase the flow of capital from the older states. Satisfied patrons of the loan agents told their friends of their formula for obtaining returns on their savings that were substantially above the current Eastern interest rates. If Stephen A. Foley, of Lincoln, Illinois, and John Weare, of Cedar Rapids, tapped the substantial coffers of the Davenport family, or Addison Goodell prospered from the investment of funds won originally in the thriving collar-and-cuff business of Troy, New York, there were many who built their lending business on the investments of professional folk, petty businessmen, and Eastern farmers who counted their savings by the hundreds of dollars rather than by the thousands. By the 1880s the desire of Eastern investors for Western farm mortgages amounted to a mild mania; in the exhilarating environment of the great plains, the dreams and greed of investor, agent, and borrower, fused in the great mortgage debacle of the late 1880s and 1890s [1, pp. 77–276]. This disaster had no parallel in Illinois or Iowa.

To the farmer, slightly bewildered by the speed with which his world was changing, the procedures of the loan agent may well have seemed an invasion of privacy. Well aware that investors would hold him responsible for foreclosures, the agent pried into the farmer's affairs. After such preliminaries, the agent, if satisfied, drafted the note and mortgage and informed the farmer that he had the money on hand or expected it as soon as the lender had received the mortgage papers.

The agent's eagerness to earn a commission on the loan might, of course, temper the quality of his investigation. Involved also in the negotiations was the bargaining power of the farmer. By 1870 at least, most county towns had several agents competing for the mortgage business. The farmer with good security and a fine personal reputation in the community might play them off against each other and win concessions on the interest rate, the amount of commission charged by the agent, or in the form and type of paper. Undoubtedly, there were efforts, at times, by local agents to set standard rates and terms and thwart the efforts of borrowers to encourage competition among them. Yet if the lenders of one town combined, they might find themselves undercut by the energetic agents of some nearby prairie center, as well as by petty lenders.

The mortgage study included in the 1890 census showed that in eight Illinois and Iowa counties, the percentages of mortgagees owning one to five mortgages varied in round figures from 38 to 70 per cent in Iowa and from 33 to 56 per cent in Illinois. Local lenders undoubtedly were heavily represented in this group. In the area studies of farm-mortgaging in Illinois and Iowa, we find that more than half of the funds loaned on farm security came from within the state concerned in most years of the nineteenth century. The West

generated much of the capital needed by its farmers. As many of the first generation of farmers left the land to retire to the county towns, they accepted mortgages for a portion of the sale price of their land. Local land-speculators, too, were willing to wait for their money, provided that the purchaser paid his interest. We can misunderstand the significance of these facts. Local loans often reflected land sales in which the seller was willing to wait for his money. Loans from Eastern sources more frequently represented fluid capital channeled into the Midwest and had, therefore, a sharper immediate impact upon the Western economy than did the local lending.

Some Western lending did involve the transfer of actual funds from lender to borrowers. Under the laws of both Illinois and Iowa, county officers loaned the school funds, derived from sale of the school-land sections, to local borrowers. At least one Iowa county used the proceeds from the sale of swamp lands in the same way. Substantial numbers of Illinois and Iowa farmers borrowed from the county funds in the 1850s and 1860s. When Croft Pilgrim, of Stark County, Illinois, wished to enlarge his farm in 1870, he arranged a loan from a widow who was living in Peoria. When Pilgrim's mother-in-law died several years later, her estate included several small mortgages. The professional and business people of the local villages and towns frequently lent their savings on land mortgages. Active and retired farmers who had been more than usually successful did the same.

Western banks seldom loaned on the security of agricultural land. The National Banking Act of 1863 with its amendments forbade national banks to hold real estate mortgages for any length of time, and the proprietors and officers of private and state-chartered banks were much more likely to serve as agents for nonresident capitalists than to lend bank funds on farm security. Such individuals or institutions, however, might have numbers of second mortgages on record, representing the commissions on first mortgage loans.

Few economic historians have studied farm-mortgage debt at the county and township level in Illinois and Iowa. Tentatively, we can say that the early farmers of the prairie triangle used the mortgage freely. The agricultural censuses of 1860, 1870, and 1880 give the names of 145 different farmers who were owner-operators in Hamilton Township of Hamilton County, Iowa. Of the group, thirty-nine failed to appear as a mortgagor on at least one indenture during the period 1853–1896. Twenty-three appeared in six or more mortgage transactions. In those communities settled from the 1840s onward, landowners usually encumbered from one third to one half of the agricultural land during the first generation of occupancy. Mortgaging proceeded most rapidly during the settling-in period and during years of prosperity. As the settlement period came to an end, the proportion of land under mortgage stabilized and in some cases dropped off. In communities where tenancy was most common, the percentage of land under mortgage was lower than in comparable communities elsewhere. Most loans were repayable at the end of five years or by installments over a short term of years. The long-term amortized loan was not common in this period. Nor should this be surprising. The tendency of interest rates in any particular community was ordinarily downward—not a condition which encouraged long-term financing.

Many factors affected the interest rate on farm loans in this period. The age of the community, estimates of soil fertility, transportation facilities, and the persistence and skill with which local businessmen sought outside capital were all involved. Of importance, also, was the competition of other Western communities for capital, the prevalent rates of return from other investments in older communities, and the stage of development of the financial channels along which Eastern capital flowed westward. Business conditions, generally, had their influence: in depression years the flow of capital westward greatly diminished.

Table 1 shows the interest rates recorded in the mortgages on agricultural land in three widely scattered Iowa townships between the early 1850s and 1896. In general the rates stayed close to the usury maximum during the 1850s, fell somewhat in the late 1860s and then rose again during the very late 1860s and the early 1870s. A pronounced break occurred during the late 1870s; thereafter, interest rates fell fairly steadily until 1896. The lower rates of the 1860s were in part attributable to the 8 per cent rate allowed on school-fund mortgages for a portion of this period, but private lenders, too, were filing some 8 and 9 per cent paper.

By modern standards the interest rates of

Table 1. Mean Mortgage Rate in Three Iowa Townships, 1852–1896

	WARREN TWP.		UNION TWP.		HAMILTON TWP.	
	Loans	Rate	Loans	Rate	Loans	Rate
1852	—	—	4	8.7	—	—
1853	1	10.0	6	13.5	1	10.0
1854	4	10.0	5	8.7	6	10.0
1855	2	10.0	8	8.0	—	—
1856	9	9.5	4	9.0	2	10.0
1857	8	9.3	15	9.5	11	10.0
1858	10	9.5	8	10.0	11	10.0
1859	12	10.0	7	10.0	11	10.0
1860	6	10.0	8	10.0	8	10.0
1861	9	10.0	4	10.0	6	9.3
1862	5	10.0	2	10.0	5	10.0
1863	14	9.2	4	10.0	2	10.0
1864	21	9.3	5	9.2	8	10.0
1865	20	9.3	6	10.0	9	8.8
1866	22	9.6	1	8.0	12	8.8
1867	39	9.5	7	8.9	8	7.3
1868	40	9.7	7	10.0	19	9.4
1869	32	9.9	4	9.3	16	8.7
1870	21	10.0	2	10.0	23	9.8
1871	37	9.9	3	10.0	13	9.3
1872	25	10.0	8	9.8	28	9.9
1873	26	9.9	12	9.8	23	9.9
1874	25	10.0	12	9.5	28	9.7
1875	34	10.0	13	10.0	53	9.9
1876	28	9.9	19	9.8	44	9.8
1877	30	9.8	29	9.9	22	9.9
1878	30	9.9	18	9.7	29	9.7
1879	20	9.6	29	9.8	25	9.0
1880	23	8.8	17	9.1	45	8.5
1881	17	8.3	23	8.8	42	8.5
1882	23	7.3	30	8.7	55	8.1
1883	15	6.8	25	8.9	48	7.7
1884	18	7.6	18	9.3	31	7.7
1885	20	7.7	18	9.3	34	7.8
1886	27	7.2	32	8.1	31	7.6
1887	17	7.0	34	8.9	45	7.5
1888	16	7.1	42	7.6	31	7.4
1889	18	7.1	19	9.2	17	7.3
1890	21	6.4	26	7.8	24	7.3
1891	14	6.7	19	6.9	42	7.2
1892	18	6.4	37	7.4	33	7.2
1893	16	6.1	22	7.8	43	7.1
1894	19	6.5	29	7.3	58	7.2
1895	18	7.0	41	7.2	57	7.1
1896	9	6.4	37	7.0	32	6.9

the 1850s appear high, and they would continue to be so until the mid-1890s. The county records do not reveal the actual market rate when it stood above the 10 per cent maximum that both Illinois and Iowa had set by the mid-1850s. Lenders simply inflated the principals specified in the notes to compensate for the 10 per cent rate, or, more usually, their agents extracted a more generous commission than usual and passed along a portion of it to the lender. Of six mortgage notes filed from Union Township in Davis County during 1853, the year of the 10 per cent usury law, two called for rates of 20 per cent and one for a rate of 12 per cent. Thereafter, lenders filed notes and mortgages that called for no more than 10 per cent. When John Weare, of Cedar Rapids, loaned the funds of John and Ira Davenport on Iowa farms during 1869 and 1870 at 10 per cent, however, he also deducted a 10 per cent commission and set half of it aside for the New Yorkers. When, as in some cases, these loans were only for a year, the borrowers were paying 20 per cent for their money.

Table 1 shows that there were definite differences between lending rates in the three Iowa Counties represented there. Comparison with rates in some Illinois communities would have shown still greater differences. In general, Illinois rates fell sooner than did those in Iowa. The arithmetic-mean rate for the decade of the 1880s in a township of Knox County, Illinois, for instance, was 7.1 per cent. In only one of the townships in Iowa had the rate fallen to this level by the end of the 1880s.

The farm has usually provided its operator with a home as well as a place of business. The foreclosure of a farm mortgage, therefore, has always held emotional implications for farm folk that are lacking in urban bankruptcies or business failures. If, on the one hand, a farm foreclosure was more than a business failure, farm foreclosure statistics on the other hand do not completely reveal the number of business failures by farmers. A few failing debtors always preferred to deed their property to the mortgagees on the best possible terms rather than to wait for formal proceedings. The foreclosure rate, as a result, does not include all of the operators who failed to clear their land of debt. Even so, it is probably the best single index of agricultural distress in the nineteenth century that we can find. Of 2649 mortgages negotiated in three Iowa townships between 1852 and 1896, 3.2 per cent ended in foreclosure proceedings. Table 2 shows the percentage of unsuccessful loans negotiated by five-year periods in these townships. Clearly the mortgagors of the years between 1865 and 1879 had the most difficulty in repaying their loans. Typically, foreclosure followed some years after the date of the original loans; in our three townships

Table 2. Foreclosure Proceedings in Three Iowa Townships

Years	Loans Negotiated	Foreclosures	Percentage
1852–1854	27	1	3.7
1855–1859	118	3	2.5
1860–1864	107	3	2.8
1865–1869	242	10	4.1
1870–1874	286	15	5.2
1875–1879	423	22	5.2
1880–1884	430	12	2.8
1885–1889	401	7	1.7
1890–1896	615	11	1.8
1852–1896	2649	84	3.2

the courts were most active in foreclosure cases between 1870 and 1884.

The suggestion that the very act of mortgaging was an indication of agricultural distress is, of course, quite erroneous. When George K. Holmes and John S. Lord prepared a special report on real estate mortgages for the census of 1890, they included a colorful catalogue of reasons for mortgaging, which ranged from alimony payments to the defense of wayward sons indicted for murder. The statistical record was more prosaic. More than 83 per cent of the mortgages in force in four Illinois counties represented expenditures for the purchase of real estate or its improvement. In four Iowa counties the percentage of mortgages filed for the same reasons ranged from 68 to 89 per cent. The categories of mortgages that could have included distress mortgages ranged in total from 3 to 14 per cent in the eight counties. More research on the reasons underlying mortgaging in earlier years is needed, but most mortgages reflected real estate purchases or other productive enterprises. Indeed it was characteristic of the credit system of the period that money was extremely difficult to obtain in periods of depression when borrowers might have sought credit to meet living expenses or personal debts.

County records give little indication of the amount of credit that farmers obtained on land contract; usually neither buyer nor seller felt compelled to record land contracts at the county seat. Although many large holders of unimproved lands sold on contract because these agreements could be canceled without court proceedings, the land-grant railroads and their land-company subsidiaries undoubtedly did the greatest amount of contract business.

The executive officers of the Illinois Central Railroad Company, for example, correctly realized in the 1850s that they must offer credit if they were to sell the lands of the road to farmers rapidly. Because the company had designated some of the lands in the grant for use in meeting specific obligations, credit terms varied somewhat on Illinois Central lands. On the so-called construction lands, the purchaser of the mid-1850s need pay down only two years of interest at 2 per cent on the cost price, commencing annual payments of one fifth of the principal, plus advance interest on the remainder at the beginning of the third year. For the unencumbered or free lands of the grant, the buyer must pay down 25 per cent of the cost in cash and retire the balance in one, two, and three years with interest at 6 per cent. The Illinois Central executives modified these credit terms later, but they established precedents in land disposal that all of the Midwest land-grants roads or their sales agencies followed [*4*, chaps. VIII and XII].

The courthouse vaults of the Corn Belt bulge with deed and mortgage indexes and registers containing information that will answer many questions about land tenure and credit. This is not true of chattel credit, however. State legislators saw little need to preserve a permanent record of chattel mortgages, concerned as these indentures were with security that was short lived and, on occasion, highly mobile. County recorders, therefore, have never been required to preserve a copy of chattel mortgages for more than a few years. I have found but one complete set of chattel books, covering an extended period of time in the nineteenth century, although more may, of course, exist. These records are in Lucas County, Iowa. Preliminary research in them shows that chattel mortgages most frequently served to protect the vendor of plows, wagons, and other farm machinery, as well as the seller of draft animals. Frequently, too, farm tenants bound themselves to pay rent to their landlords by mortgaging their growing crops. Interest rates on chattel mortgages were similar in trend to those on landed security. Typically, the chattel mortgage was the resort of the less well-to-do farmer. Local vendors seldom bothered to demand a mortgage from the farmer with abundant assets.

REFERENCES

1. Allan G. Bogue, *Money at Interest: The Farm Mortgage on the Middle Border*, Ithaca, Cornell University Press, 1955.
2. Allan G. Bogue, "The Iowa Claim Clubs: Symbol and Substance," *The Mississippi Valley Historical Review, 45* (September, 1958), 231–253.
3. Clarence H. Danhof, "Farm-Making Costs and the 'Safety Valve': 1850–1860," *The Journal of Political Economy, 49* (June, 1941), 317–359.
4. Paul Wallace Gates, *The Illinois Central and Its Colonization Work*, Cambridge, Harvard University Press, 1934.

VII SLAVERY AND THE CIVIL WAR

If any single essay can be identified as the study that launched the new economic history, it is "The Economics of Slavery in the Ante-Bellum South," by Alfred H. Conrad and John R. Meyer, presented below as essay 25. In that paper Conrad and Meyer systematically applied economic theory to the set of issues on which the century-long controversy regarding the economics of slavery has turned. In this connection they introduced a formal capital model, devised a demographic model of the slave population, and employed elements of production theory. They also searched the secondary literature to obtain reasonable estimates of the parameters and variables of their models.

Conrad and Meyer suggested that their essay represented a new departure both in substance and methodology. That characterization was widely accepted not only by those who agreed with their conclusions but also by those who did not. Certainly no prior study had so clearly identified the variables pertinent to the issue of the profitability of slavery. Nor had any previous study marshalled the available evidence bearing on the values of these variables so effectively. Their attempt to simulate the demographic behavior of the slave population was clearly an important new contribution to the historical debate. They also searched for evidence that would permit a decisive test of the efficiency of slave markets in the geographic allocation of labor.

Rather than ending the controversy regarding the economics of slavery, the work of Conrad and Meyer intensified it. However because of their study, the debate has been more sharply focused than before. Much of the research undertaken during the twelve years since the publication of their study has been devoted to improving the capital and demographic models employed by Conrad and Meyer or to refining their estimates of the values of crucial variables. As a consequence our understanding of the operation of the slave economy has been greatly increased. Not only do we have a clearer view of the operation of the purchase and rental markets for slaves, but we also have probed more deeply into the nexus between slavery and the development of the economy of the ante-bellum South.

Essay 26, by Yasukichi Yasuba, is one of the most important studies stimulated by the work of Conrad and Meyer. Yasuba pointed out that a rate of return calculated on the basis of the market price of slaves does not provide a decisive test of the economic viability of the slave system. He proposed an alternative test based on the difference between the cost of rearing a slave to maturity and the selling price of a mature slave. That difference is a "capitalized rent." Yasuba argued that a positive capitalized rent implies that slavery was economically viable. He also estimated the part of the slave price which represented capitalized rent over the period from 1821 through 1860. Yasuba found that the capitalized rent was positive and large at the beginning of the period and that it increased substantially as the period wore on. This implies that slavery was not only economically viable but that from the purely economic viewpoint it was actually becoming more deeply entrenched as the Civil War approached.

In essay 24 Robert W. Fogel and Stanley L. Engerman evaluate a number of the more important studies stimulated by the work of Conrad and Meyer. However essay 24 is less a review article than it is a preview of a book on *The Economics of American Negro Slavery* which Fogel and Engerman expect to complete by the end of 1971. Included in this paper are a test of the proposition that the market for cotton was on the verge of collapse on the eve of the Civil War; an index of the sanguinity of slaveholders with respect to the future of the slave system; an estimate of what the price of slaves would have been in 1890, if there hadn't been a Civil War; and a comparison between the rate of growth of per capita income in the South and in the rest of the nation over the period from 1840 to 1860.[1]

The widely held thesis that the Civil War had a far-reaching impact on the economic development of the nation has come under attack in recent years. Stanley Engerman surveys and evaluates this debate in essay 27. Engerman assembles data which bear on both the short-term and the long-term effects of the war. He finds little evidence to support either the proposition that the "war industries" in the North were immediately stimulated by government orders or the proposition that Northern victory accelerated the long-term rate of growth of the manufacturing sector.

---

[1] Since the basic draft of essay 24 was written during the second half of 1967, this paper does not reflect the research of Fogel and Engerman since that time. However their subsequent research has fortified rather than undermined the main conclusions of essay 24.

24 THE ECONOMICS OF SLAVERY

*Robert William Fogel and
Stanley L. Engerman*

This essay critically examines the long debate on the economics of American Negro slavery. The discussion is divided into three parts. Part I evaluates the positions of U. B. Phillips, Charles W. Ramsdell, and their followers. The Phillips-Ramsdell analysis, which dominated American historiography for half a century, holds not only that slavery stifled the economic growth of the ante-bellum South but also that slavery was unprofitable to investors and, hence, moribund. Part II deals with recent attacks on the Phillips-Ramsdell interpretation. Special attention is given to the studies by Alfred H. Conrad and John R. Meyer, Robert Evans, and Yasukichi Yasuba. In the course of this section we present an index of the sanguinity of slaveholders; estimate what the price of slaves would have been in 1890, if slavery had persisted;

We have benefited from the comments of a large number of historians and economists including Raymond C. Battalio, Thomas C. Cochran, Harry L. Coles, Robert Evans, Jr., John H. Kagel, H. Gregg Lewis, Chase C. Mooney, William N. Parker, Albert Rees, Kenneth M. Stampp, and George Stigler.

and present new data on the rate of growth of Southern per capita income between 1840 and 1860. Part III is a brief conclusion. There is also a mathematical appendix which derives the basic equations employed in the main body of the essay.[1]

Our main findings are as follows:

1. There is no evidence to support the contention that the market for cotton was on the verge of collapse when the Civil War began. Quite the contrary, during the half decade preceding the war, the demand for cotton expanded more rapidly than the supply of it.

2. The expected rate of return on an investment in slaves between 1830 and 1860 was high. It equaled or exceeded the average rates on alternative investment in industry.

3. The rise in the price of slaves is explained primarily by the rise in their productivity.

4. A large part of the price of eighteen-year-old slaves was a capitalized rent. The rental component in the price of slaves increased substantially between 1820 and 1860.

5. On the eve of the Civil War slaveholders were quite sanguine. They not only expected their social order to endure but foresaw an era of economic prosperity.

6. If slavery had persisted to 1890, it is probable that the real price of slaves would have exceeded the 1860 price by more than 60 per cent.

7. There is no evidence that slavery caused the economy of the ante-bellum South to stagnate. Between 1840 and 1860 Southern per capita income rose at least as rapidly as the national average.

I. THE PHILLIPS TRADITION

Discussion of the economic consequences of slavery has been dominated by the work of Ulrich B. Phillips.[2] A professor of history at Yale University, and for many years the doyen of those writing on the ante-bellum South, Phillips dealt with almost all the economic aspects of that era. His interpretation of the nature of slavery, first set forth

in an essay published in 1905, has persisted for more than half a century. Certain of its major features have been accepted not only by the followers of Phillips, but also by his critics.

According to Phillips slavery was necessarily a Southern institution. It did not gain strength in the North because the complexity of Northern agriculture precluded the successful employment of the "unintelligent Negro." The utilization of such labor was possible in the South for two reasons. First, the tasks required to raise cotton, tobacco, and rice were arduous but simple. Second, the plantation system provided the "strict guidance and supervision" required to make the African productive.

Still, said Phillips, if there had not been unusual conditions in the labor market, slavery would not have taken root even in the South. In his view the slave system was fostered by the "special prosperity" of the colonial era. "Hired labor was not to be had" in the prerevolutionary period because of the availability of free land. This circumstance by itself would not have sufficed to turn the South to men whose "inherited inaptitudes" were such that their labor was suited only to "special industries." However the "price of Africans in colonial times was so low that, when crops and prices were good, the labor of those imported repaid their original cost in a few years."

These propitious conditions came to an end, said Phillips, early in the nineteenth century. At the beginning of 1807 the congressional ban against the further importation of Africans was put into force. Within a decade the low and relatively steady slave prices of earlier years gave way to an era in which slave prices bounded upward far more rapidly than the price of cotton. To Phillips the ratio of slave to cotton prices was as crucial in evaluating the wisdom of an investment in slaves as the price-to-earnings ratio for evaluating the wisdom of an investment in corporate stocks. Although he recognized that "the slave trade involved questions of humanity and social organization," he argued that from a financial view, the market for slaves behaved like the stock and commodity markets. As in all such markets, said Phillips, there were "bull influences and bear influences, and occasional speculative campaigns. And when at times the supply was subjected to monopoly control, the prices tended to go wild."

---

[1] Equations with numbers prefixed by the letter A (as A.1, A.2, etc.) are listed in the Mathematical Appendix. Symbols used in the main body of the essay as well as those used in the appendix are defined in Appendix Table A.1.

[2] Unless otherwise identified, all paraphrasings and quotations of Phillips are from [25].

From 1815 on, Phillips continued, the market for slaves operated under the monopoly created when the importation of Africans was cut off. In Phillips' words:

1815 began the "ante-bellum" regime, in which the whole economy of the South was governed by the apparently capricious play of the compound monopoly of cotton and slave labor. The price of cotton was governed by the American output and its relation to the European demand. And the price of slaves was governed by the profits in cotton and the relation of the labor demand to the monopolized labor supply.

The consequence of the monopoly of labor was a steep rise in slave prices at the same time that the price of cotton was drifting downward. Between 1800 and 1860, said Phillips, the ratio of slave to cotton prices rose by over tenfold. The change in this ratio clearly indicated to Phillips that slaves were overvalued. Its rise could not be explained by a decline in the cost of maintaining slaves. Nor could it be explained by an increase in the productivity of slaves since, "in his capacity for work, a prime Negro in 1800 was worth nearly or quite as much as a similar slave in 1860." Proof of the last proposition was found in the annual rental charge or hire rate for slaves. Data gathered by Phillips showed little change in the hire rate between 1818 and 1860.

The rise in the ratio of slave to cotton prices, Phillips concluded, was primarily the consequence of speculation. The supply of slaves had been "cornered." Hence, "it was unavoidable that the price should be bid up to the point of overvaluation." This speculative pressure was reinforced by two other tendencies. First, there were economies of scale in cotton production. Thus plantation owners were constantly trying to increase the size of their slave force in order to reap the benefits of large-scale operation. Second, slaves were desired not only for productive purposes but also as symbols of social status and wealth. In other words slaves were not only a producer's good but also a consumer's good.

It should be stressed that Phillips never provided evidence that speculation, economies of scale, and conspicuous consumption were responsible for the rise in the slave-cotton price ratio. He merely asserted that these were the true explanatory factors. The only evidence he set forth pertained to the absolute and relative movement of slave prices and to the movement of the rental rate

of slaves. Phillips' contention that the rise in the slave-cotton ratio was a "wild flight" rested on three questionable assumptions—that the average pre-1815 profit from the employment of slaves was only moderate, that there was no increase over time in the average net earnings on a slave, and that the rate at which the net earnings from slaves were discounted remained constant over time.

Even more questionable is Phillips' contention that the rise in the slave-cotton price ratio was the result of a monopolistic control of the supply of slaves and of a "corner." Here Phillips was relying heavily on his analogy between the slave and the stock markets. For "wild flights" of stock prices were frequently explained by "corners." However a corner can exist only if an individual, or a group acting in unison, controls all or most of the supply of the asset in question. Yet such control never existed in the ante-bellum market for slaves. The millions of slaves were owned by tens of thousands of farms and households. No individual or group ever entered the market in control of more than a relatively small fraction of the supply. Phillips confused the concept of monopoly, which gives a seller control over the market price, with the existence of an inelastic and relatively fixed short-run supply. The ban on the African trade did not give a particular group of planters control over the price of slaves. Rather it made the short-run supply curve of slave labor inelastic and limited the rate at which the stock of slave labor could increase to the natural rate of increase of the domestic slave population.[3]

The preceding criticisms do not eliminate the possibility that slaves were overvalued (i.e., that the rate of return on the purchase price of slaves was below the rate on alternative investments). They do not even rule out the possibility that the rise in the slave-cotton price ratio was a wild speculative flight. They are an attack merely on Phillips' attempt to explain the cause of the alleged speculative flight. Moreover Phillips could be right in his contention that slaves were overvalued as a business investment, even if his thesis regarding speculation were wrong. For if slaves were held for dual motives—that is, if their owners viewed them simultaneously as producers' and consumers' goods—then one could find that the business income by

---

[3] The last point forms the basis of Yasuba's penetrating paper [42]. See essay 26, below.

itself was insufficient to justify the purchase price of slaves. In other words if slaves served this dual function, only part of their market price reflected their value as productive agents, the remainder of their price represented their value as items of conspicuous consumption.[4]

The issue of profitability can be resolved only by collecting the data required to compute the average rate of return that planters actually earned on their investment in slaves. More than a quarter of a century elapsed between the appearance of the Phillips' essay and the publication of profit estimates based on such data. During the 1930s studies appeared by several historians who culled the records and diaries of a number of the larger plantations for numerical information on business operations. While one of the most prominent of these scholars, Lewis C. Gray, reported that slavery was indeed a profitable business [16], most of the others [4, 10, 33, 40] found to the contrary. The majority held that a few planters earned as much as 6 per cent on their investment in slaves and that the most typical rate of profit was in the neighborhood of 2 or 3 per cent. Although later work proved that these low rates were erroneous—the consequence of accounting errors on the part of scholars unfamiliar with either economics or accounting—the studies of the 1930s have a considerable fillip to the thesis that slaves were overvalued.

The proposition that slavery was unprofitable to most planters suggests that the slave system was dying, or at least declining, due to its own contradictions. Phillips did not himself propound this thesis. It had been enunciated by earlier students of slavery. Some argued that slavery would collapse due to a decline in cotton prices brought about by overproduction. Others stressed the pressure of expanding slave population on land. George Tucker, for example, asserted that the slave system would disintegrate when the density of population went beyond 66 persons per square mile.[5]

The modern formulation of the thesis that Southern slavery had become moribund on the eve of the Civil War was set forth in a 1929 essay by Charles W. Ramsdell, a professor of history at the University of Texas.[6] Ramsdell argued that the viability of slavery depended on two conditions: (1) the existence of a large supply of productive, virgin land suitable for the growing of cotton, and (2) the maintenance of a high price for cotton. Ramsdell did not explain why he considered a large supply of virgin land a necessary condition for the continued viability of the slave system. Presumably he envisioned a decline in the marginal product of slave labor if the supply of slaves continued to expand while the quantity of land remained fixed. This interpretation is suggested by Ramsdell's assumption that slaves could only be employed profitably in the production of cotton or such other Southern agricultural staples as rice, sugar, and tobacco. However Ramsdell did not pursue this argument to its logical conclusion. His prediction of the imminent collapse of slavery was based not on the thesis of a land shortage but on the thesis that too much land was being allocated to the production of cotton.

Ramsdell argued that it was the rapid expansion of the cotton culture after 1858, and the subsequent decline in the price of cotton, that heralded the doom of slavery. To support his point he contrasted the last few years of the decade with conditions that prevailed at its start. Ramsdell noted that the fifties began with a high price for cotton and with a large supply of virgin land suitable for the production of cotton, the latter being located largely in Texas. Moreover, he continued, the production of cotton increased slowly between 1850 and 1857 and its price remained relatively stable, varying from about ten cents per pound to over thirteen cents. But 1858 began a period of rapid increase in cotton production and a simultaneous decline in price. Ramsdell stressed that the size of the cotton crop doubled between 1850 and 1860. About 70 per cent of the increase took place between 1857 and 1860.

What caused this sudden rise in output? It was due, said Ramsdell, "in part to the rapid building of railroads throughout the South toward the end of the decade, which brought new lands within the reach of markets and increased the cotton acreage; but part of the increase was due to the new fields in

---

[4] Economies of scale cannot explain a general overvaluation of slaves such as that envisioned by Phillips. If larger, more efficient plantations were bidding up the price of slaves, then while this price was too high for some planters, it was just right or too low for other planters.

[5] Cf. [16, p. 475].

---

[6] Unless otherwise identified all paraphrasings and quotations of Ramsdell are from [27].

Texas." To Ramsdell, prevailing circumstances clearly indicated that the future course of output was up, while that of prices was down. "Had not the war intervened," he continued, "there is every reason to believe that there would have been a continuous overproduction and very low prices throughout the sixties and seventies."

But what precisely was the "every reason" for Ramsdell's belief? It was merely his conviction that the virgin lands of Texas would have been brought into cotton production and that the increased output of cotton would have lead to a decline in its price. Yet even if one grants Ramsdell's proposition regarding the probable post-1860 expansion of the cotton crop, it does not necessarily follow that the price had to decline. What would have happened to the price of cotton depends on the circumstance under which the production of it expanded. If the allocation of new lands to cotton was the consequence of a rise in the world's demand for this fiber, the expansion of production could well have been associated with a rise in price. Ramsdell never probed issues such as this. He was convinced that the Texas lands created a threat to the existence of slavery from which there was no escape. "The replenishment of the soil" in the Old South would not have averted the impending catastrophe; it would merely have "resulted in the production of more cotton. . . . Prices of slaves must have dropped then, even in the Southwest; importation from the border states would have fallen off; thousands of slaves would have become not only unprofitable but a heavy burden, the market for them gone."

It is ironic that Ramsdell's position has been interpreted as one which argues that a shortage of land heralded the doom of slavery. That it was interpreted in this way is not difficult to explain. Ramsdell's forecast was embedded in an essay, entitled "The Natural Limits of Slavery Expansion," an essay which attempted to prove that slavery had reached a "natural frontier" in Texas and Missouri beyond which it could not expand. Yet, as we have seen, the economic mechanism which Ramsdell invoked to demonstrate the impending disintegration of the slave system was not a shortage of land, but the overproduction of cotton brought about by the allocation of too much land for that crop.

That Ramsdell's theory has been misnamed does not necessarily imply that it is wrong in its prediction of the impending dissolution of the slave system. At least one of the crucial assumptions of Ramsdell's argument seems sound. Available evidence does indeed suggest that large amounts of new land were devoted to cotton production. Interim findings of a large-scale statistical analysis of slave productivity in cotton production were recently reported by James D. Foust and Dale E. Swan.[7] Based on a random sample drawn from the manuscript schedules of the U.S. Census, the study finds that cotton output per worker in the principal cotton producing counties of seven states increased at an annual rate of 2.9 per cent between 1849 and 1859 [11, Table 1]. The rise in this index strongly suggests that other inputs required for cotton production increased more rapidly than labor. Data in the published census volumes support such a conclusion. Over the same period, improved land in use on the farms of these states increased at an annual rate of 4.0 per cent, while both the slave and total populations grew at only 3.0 per cent. Moreover it is likely that a "disproportionate" share of the new lands were allocated to cotton. The output of corn, the second most important crop of the seven states, grew more slowly (2.6 per cent) than both population and cotton (8.4 per cent), while the output of oats declined [37, pp. 130–131, 196–201]. Hence Ramsdell's hypothesis that much of the increase in the cotton crop is explained by a rapid increase in the amount of land devoted to it takes on considerable force.[8]

---

[7] Foust and Swan obtained their data from a sample of over 5000 farms drawn from the manuscript schedules of the 1850 and 1860 censuses. This sample was drawn and is being analyzed under the direction of Robert E. Gallman and William N. Parker.

[8] However it is unlikely that all of the increase in productivity was due to the rise in the land to labor ratio. The rate-of-growth transformation of equation A.2 is

$$\overset{*}{Q} - \overset{*}{L} = \overset{*}{A} + \alpha_2(\overset{*}{K} - \overset{*}{L}) + \alpha_3(\overset{*}{T} - \overset{*}{L})$$

The estimates of Conrad and Meyer suggest that $\alpha_2 = 0.04$ and $\alpha_3 = 0.31$. Substituting 2.9 for $\overset{*}{Q} - \overset{*}{L}$ and assuming that $\overset{*}{L}$ equaled the rate of growth of population (3.0 per cent), $\overset{*}{K}$ equaled the rate of growth indicated by the value of farm implements and machinery (5.1 per cent) [37, p. 197], and that $\overset{*}{A} = 0$, we may solve the equation for $\overset{*}{T}$. The computation yields a value of 15.1 per cent. This means that over the decade, the land used for cotton production would have increased 3.4 times. If we assume that it took two

But if Ramsdell was right on the land question, the decade of the 1850s was one in which land pressed on slaves rather than slaves on land. The increase in the land to labor ratio hypothecated by Ramsdell would have increased, not diminished, the marginal physical productivity of slaves. Other things being equal, this rise in the marginal physical product of slaves would have raised their value.[9]

Thus while Ramsdell has been interpreted as supporting and extending the Phillips' thesis—there is no doubt that this was his intention—Ramsdell's assumption that the land-labor ratio was increasing actually contains the seeds of the refutation of the proposition that slavery had become, or was about to become, unprofitable and moribund. All that remains to complete the task of turning Ramsdell's analysis against both him and Phillips is to show that he was wrong

acres to produce a 400 pound bale of cotton in 1850, there were 4,300,000 acres devoted to cotton production in the seven states (South Carolina, Georgia, Alabama, Mississippi, Louisiana, Arkansas, and Texas) in 1850, and there would have been 19,000,000 acres devoted to this crop in 1860. Thus the amount of new land devoted to cotton would have had to have exceeded the total quantity of land improved over the decade by some 60 per cent. The residual quantity of land is not enough to account for the observed production of corn, tobacco, wheat, and other crops in 1860. Hence it is probable that $\overset{*}{A}$ was positive. However the growth of the efficiency index may have been due primarily to an improvement in the quality of land employed in cotton production.

[9] See equation A.9. It is important to stress that any improvement in the physical productivity of slaves would have caused the price of slaves to increase, other things being equal. Since the Foust and Swan study provides evidence of such a rise in physical productivity, the main issue which remains is how much of the rise was due to an increase in the land to labor ratio.

While the Foust and Swan index is a reasonable proxy for the movement of slave productivity, it is not a definitive measure. Their study did not embrace the entire slave South but only a portion of it. Moreover they computed cotton production per slave rather than total product per slave. Hence the use of their index as a measure of the rate of growth of slave productivity involves the questionable assumption that the output of goods produced by slaves other than cotton grew at the same rate as cotton. Still, for reasons made clear below, it is unlikely that the correction of the error introduced by this assumption would alter the finding of a substantial rise in slave productivity.

in his interpretation of the available data on the movement of cotton prices.

Ramsdell held that the increased output of cotton during 1858–1860 reduced the price of that commodity, after nearly a decade of relatively high and stable prices, in such a way as to threaten the future of the slave system. Table 1 shows that this is a clear misinterpretation, of the course of cotton prices. Whether one looks at current or real prices, the price of cotton during 1858–1860

Table 1. The Price of Raw Cotton (In Cents Per Pound)

Year Ending August 31 (1)	Current Price (2)	Real Price (3)
1840	8.9	7.4
1841	9.5	8.6
1842	7.8	7.6
1843	7.2	7.8
1844	7.7	8.5
1845	5.6	5.8
1846	7.9	8.0
1847	11.2	10.8
1848	8.0	7.9
1849	7.6	7.8
1850	12.3	12.4
1851	12.1	12.2
1852	9.5	9.2
1853	11.0	9.8
1854	11.0	8.9
1855	10.4	8.0
1856	10.3	8.1
1857	13.5	10.4
1858	12.2	10.3
1859	12.1	10.8
1860	11.0	9.8
Three-Year Average		
1840–1842	8.7	7.9
1843–1845	6.8	7.4
1846–1848	9.0	8.9
1849–1851	10.7	10.8
1852–1854	10.5	9.3
1855–1857	11.4	8.8
1858–1860	11.8	10.3

SOURCES and NOTES: Column 1. The years given in this column are the commercial year. The crop harvested in 1839 was sold during the commercial year which ran from September 1, 1839, to August 31, 1840.

Column 2. [*39*, pp. 7–10].

Column 3. The deflator was constructed from the Warren-Pearson index [*36*, p. 115] with the base shifted to 1850. A commercial year index was constructed by taking a weighted average of the index numbers of the calendar years spanned by the commercial year. The weights were 0.333 and 0.667.

was not markedly below the price of earlier
years. Quite the contrary, the average real price
of 1858–1860 equalled or exceeded the average
of all but one of the other three-year periods
between 1840 and 1860 shown in Table 1.
Even the 1860 price, the lowest of the three
years singled out by Ramsdell, was high compared to previous experience. Only during
four of the eighteen years from 1840 through
1857 was the price of cotton higher than the
level of 1860. If the slave system was not in
mortal danger during the 1840s when the
price of cotton averaged a mere 7.9 cents per
pound, it was certainly not in danger during
1858–1860 when it averaged 10.3 cents—a
figure nearly 30 per cent in excess of the
average level of the forties.

Ramsdell anchored his argument on the
fact that the prices of 1858–1860 were below
the 1857 price. But as can easily be seen, the
1857 price was unusually high. Indeed if one
looks at the course of the real price of cotton
over the fifties, he observes a downward
movement of 35 per cent between 1850 and
1856. The downward trend was abruptly
reversed in 1857 when the price jumped by
28 per cent in one year. That price was well
above the twenty-one year average (from
1840–1860) of 9.2 cents per pound. In 1858
the price held fairly steady. It rose by 5 per
cent in 1859 and then declined by 9 per cent
in 1860. However the 1860 price was still
more than 10 per cent above the average of
the preceding twenty years.

Ramsdell went astray because he misinterpreted the significance of the leap in price
between 1856 and 1857 and the subsequent
decline in price between 1857 and 1860.
Ramsdell took note of the fact the downward price movement after 1857 was accompanied by a rise in cotton production. But
he failed to note, or to appreciate the significance of, the fact that the 1857 price was
18 per cent greater than the 1854 price even
though the crops and carry-over inventories
were of nearly identical sizes in these two
years (see Table 2).

The import of the last point is made clear
by Figure 1. Panel *a* of that diagram has a
single curve representing the American supply
of cotton in both 1854 and 1857. The curve
has zero elasticity since once the crop is
harvested, the supply cannot be increased.
The fact that only one curve is used to represent both years indicates that the supplies in
both years were of virtually identical amounts.
The demand curve for cotton in 1854 must

Table 2. The American Supply and the
Price of Raw Cotton: 1840–1860

Year Ending August 31 (1)	Supply (Thousands of Bales) (2)	Real Price (Cents Per Pound) (3)
1840	2135	7.4
1841	1660	8.6
1842	1742	7.6
1843	2464	7.8
1844	2187	8.5
1845	2649	5.8
1846	2260	8.0
1847	2026	10.8
1848	2775	7.9
1849	3303	7.8
1850	2672	12.4
1851	2732	12.2
1852	3478	9.2
1853	3838	9.8
1854	3454	8.9
1855	3383	8.0
1856	3994	8.1
1857	3501	10.4
1858	3645	10.3
1859	4605	10.8
1860	5769	9.8

SOURCES and NOTES: Column 1. The commercial year ran from September 1 to August 31.
Thus the crop of 1839 was sold during the
commercial year of 1840.

Column 2. [*39*, pp. 7, 8, 10]. The supply
comprises inventories carried over from the
previous commerical year plus the crop harvested for sale in the given commercial year.
The supply for the commercial year 1840 included the stock in inventory on August 31,
1839, plus the crop harvested in 1839. The
weight of the bales is 400 pounds.

Column 3. Table 1.

have intersected the supply curve at the
point which yielded a price of 8.9 cents per
pound. Similarly the demand curve of 1857
must have intersected the supply curve at a
point which yielded a price of 10.4 cents.
Thus as panel *a* indicates, the demand curve
must have shifted upward between 1854 and
1857. Panel *b* compares 1858 with 1859. It
shows that since both the price and the supply
increased, the demand for cotton must also
have increased.

By generalizing on the preceding analysis
it is possible to estimate the year to year
change in the demand for cotton over the
period from 1840 to 1860. The results of the
computation are presented in Table 3. The
annual rate of change depends on the value

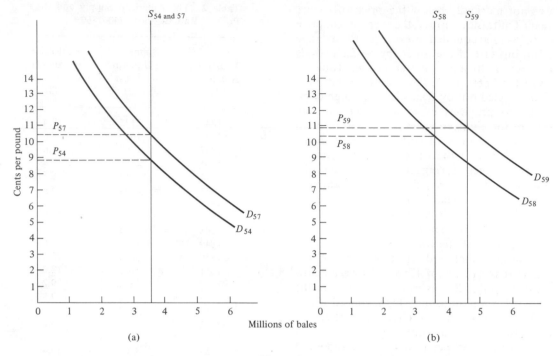

Figure 1

of the elasticity of demand (ε). Unfortunately this elasticity is not known; but it is unlikely that ε was below 0.5 or above 1.5. Hence three estimates of the change in demand are presented, one each for the upper and lower bound of the probable values of ε and one for $\varepsilon = 1.0$.[10] As Table 3 shows, the results are not very sensitive to the value of ε. The basic pattern is the same in all three cases. The year 1855 began a period of rapid increase in demand which lasted through 1860. Over this interval the cumulative increase in demand was probably between 89 and 131 per cent.

Several important implications emerge from Tables 1–3. Consideration of most of these points will be deferred to a later section of the essay. Here it is sufficient to emphasize that available evidence does not support the

notion of an overproduction of cotton on the eve of the Civil War. Quite the contrary, the sharp rise in output after 1857 was a lagged response to a substantial increase in demand. Despite the probable increase in the amount of land devoted to cotton during these years, and the substantial rise in the output of cotton that accompanied it, the supply of cotton did not increase rapidly enough to reduce the price to its earlier level. In 1860 the real price of cotton was still substantially above the average of the previous two decades.[11]

The discussion thus far has dealt with two aspects of the Phillips tradition—the profitability and the viability of slavery. The third,

---

[10] Gavin Wright recently fitted demand equations for cotton to time series data for the period 1827–1860. His results indicate that the elasticity of demand for U.S. raw cotton was between 0.41 and 1.32 in Great Britain and between 0.59 and 1.0 in the United States [41, p. 199]. In the case where the subsector demand curves are log-linear, the elasticity of total demand is a weighted average of the elasticities of the subsector curves, with the weights being the share of each market in total consumption. Thus Wright's findings put the bounds on the elasticity of the total demand curve at 0.45 and 1.25. See also [35].

[11] Essentially the same result is obtained if one looks at the data on the European market [39]. The British price of cotton rose by 40 per cent between 1855 and 1857 and then moved downward from 1857 to 1860. However the 1860 price was still 7 per cent above the 1855 price, although the European supply of cotton was 21 per cent greater in the later year than in the earlier one. Thus the demand for cotton increased by about 30 per cent over a five year period. Moreover in the subsequent commerical year ending in August, 1861, the British price of cotton rose by 42 per cent. This suggests that the pinch of the Civil War was felt almost immediately. In the commercial year ending in August, 1862, the British price of cotton was more than three times the 1860 price.

Table 3. Estimated Rate of Change in the Demand for Raw Cotton

Time Period	Percentage Change in Demand		
	$\varepsilon = 0.5$	$\varepsilon = 1.0$	$\varepsilon = 1.5$
1840–1841	−16.1	−9.6	−2.5
1841–1842	−1.4	−7.3	−12.8
1842–1843	39.6	37.7	35.9
1843–1844	−7.3	−3.2	1.1
1844–1845	0.0	−17.4	−31.8
1845–1846	0.1	17.6	38.1
1846–1847	4.1	21.0	40.6
1847–1848	17.1	0.3	–14.2
1848–1849	18.2	17.5	16.6
1849–1850	2.0	28.6	62.2
1850–1851	1.4	0.6	–0.3
1851–1852	10.5	−4.0	−16.7
1852–1853	13.9	17.6	21.3
1853–1854	–14.2	− 18.3	− 22.1
1854–1855	−7.2	−12.0	−16.6
1855–1856	18.8	19.6	20.3
1856–1857	0.7	12.5	27.5
1857–1858	3.9	3.4	2.8
1858–1859	29.0	32.2	35.3
1859–1860	19.3	13.6	8.1
1840–1845	9.8	− 2.7	− 13.9
1845–1850	47.5	115.7	215.4
1850–1855	1.7	− 18.3	− 34.4
1855–1860	88.7	108.9	131.2

The change in demand was computed from the data in Table 2 and the equation:

$$\overset{*}{D} = (1 + \overset{*}{P_c})^\varepsilon (1 + \overset{*}{S}) - 1$$

where

$\overset{*}{D}$ = the rate of change in demand
$\overset{*}{P_c}$ = the rate of change in the price of cotton
$\overset{*}{S}$ = the rate of change in supply
ε = the elasticity of the demand for raw cotton
The derivation of this equation is given in the mathematical appendix.

and perhaps the strongest, aspect of the Phillips interpretation, is concerned with the relationship between slavery and the pace of Southern economic development. Phillips argued that slavery stifled the economic development of the South. This contention was based on two propositions. The first was that the capitalization of labor created a shortage of capital that stifled the industrialization of the South. The earnings of Southern agriculture, he held, were being siphoned into the purchase of slaves rather than machines. The drain of Southern capital—especially the capital of the lower South—was brought about by interest payments to Northern creditors and by the purchase of slaves from the border states. Phillips' second proposition was that slavery reduced the mobility of labor, tending to fix it "rigidly in one line of employment."

Many scholars have followed Phillips in stressing the deleterious effects of slavery on Southern economic development. In so doing they have extended the list of ways in which slavery inhibited the region's progress. Guy S. Callender also believed that slavery inhibited Southern capital formation. His emphasis was not on a drain of capital out of the South, but on the "lack of [a] disposition to save." Callender did not doubt that the South had the ability to save. Indeed he held that the "enormous demand for cotton in the markets of the world, coupled with the natural advantages for its production in the South, was from an economic point of view precisely like the discovery of gold in California or Australia." It was slavery that prevented the South from exploiting its natural advantage. For "the social conditions which slavery fostered caused this [planter] class to expend that wealth in maintaining a luxurious and expensive style of living." As a consequence planters "furnished little capital for commercial enterprises either foreign or domestic, for starting manufacturing industries, for establishing banks and insurance companies, or for constructing canals and railroads" [2, p. 741].

Of the more recent attempts to explain the economic stagnation of the South, the most prominent is Eugene Genovese's thesis that slavery restricted the size of the Southern market for manufactured goods [13, pp. 157–179]. Genovese based his argument on the proposition that the slave system created a highly skewed income distribution; that is, it created a situation in which a small planter class received a disproportionately large share of the South's annual income and the rest of Southern society received a disproportionately small share. Genovese held that this type of income distribution led to a low level of demand for domestic manufactured goods. Planters preferred to purchase European commodities while slaves and low income whites lacked the purchasing power to support a large-scale industry. Genovese contrasted the Southern situation with that in the North and West. Agriculture in these regions was based on a large, relatively prosperous "middle class." It was this group which provided the market needed to support the big manufacturing enterprises of the era. Hence the explanation for the Southern failure to industrialize was that its small market could only support small-scale firms. But because they were small, Southern enterprises were unable to compete effectively with the factories of the North. As a consequence the South was condemned to be a rural, agricultural society dependent on outsiders for modern industrial goods.

Genovese also argued that the skewed income distribution reduced capital formation by depriving the poor whites and slaves of an income out of which they could save. At the same time rich planters were induced to engage in conspicuous consumption.

Still another explanation for Southern stagnation was recently put forward by Douglass C. North. He suggested that slavery limited the extent of Southern education and hence reduced the rate of human capital formation [23, pp. 133–134]. Unlike Phillips, who had earlier made a similar point, North considered the South wasteful of the potential of both white and Negro workers. Phillips had argued that slavery prevented the development of a skilled labor force by discouraging the non-planter whites, but he dismissed the possibility of improving the skills or intelligence of the Negro [26].

While the authors of the various attempts to establish a nexus between slavery and Southern stagnation frequently wrote as if they were in command of the evidence needed to confirm their theses, they never actually supplied such evidence. No one, for example, has ever demonstrated that rich planters as a class lacked a disposition to save. Nor has anyone shown that the expenditures of rich planters on personal consumption exhausted their income. Indeed it has never actually been shown that the South had a lower rate of growth than the rest of the nation in either total or per capita income.

We do not mean to suggest that these theories of Southern stagnation are sheer inventions. It is true that many planters lived lavishly; that some lacked the disposition to save; that some members of the population were extraordinarily rich while others were deeply impoverished; that the South lagged behind the North in the growth of its manufacturing industries; and that a smaller percentage of the population lived in cities below the Mason-Dixon line than above it. Yet all of these facts do not suffice to show that slavery hindered the growth of the Southern

economy or kept it from growing altogether. Not all economies have grown in the same way. It is possible that the ante-bellum South experienced a high and sustained rate of growth in per capita income even though it was more rural, more agricultural, and was characterized by a more unequal distribution of income than the rest of the nation.

II. THE REVISIONS

The attack on the arguments of Phillips, Ramsdell, and their followers began in the 1930s. It was spearheaded by Lewis Gray and Robert Russel [16, 28]. Although both believed that the economy of the ante-bellum South was stagnant when compared with the rest of the nation, they argued strongly for the profitability and viability of slavery. Gray's work is particularly important. It clearly set forth most of the general considerations related to the questions of profitability and viability elaborated in more recent discussions. Criticism of the Phillips tradition was continued in the early 1940s when Thomas P. Govan pointed to serious accounting errors on the part of earlier scholars who used plantation records to show that planters were unable to earn the average rate of return on an investment in slaves. Govan argued that the correction of these errors led to the conclusion that slavery was profitable [14]. The attack was renewed in the mid-1950s with the publication of Kenneth Stampp's wide-ranging study of the slave system. Like Govan, Stampp applied modern accounting techniques to plantation records in order to show that slavery was profitable. But unlike most of his predecessors Stampp also challenged several of the arguments used to buttress the proposition that slavery had caused the ante-bellum economy to stagnate [31].

The critique of the Phillips tradition took a new turn in 1958 with the publication of the seminal essay on "The Economics of Slavery in the Ante-Bellum South," by Alfred H. Conrad and John R. Meyer [3]. [See essay 25, below.] Their central innovation was the application of capital theory to the evaluation of the profitability of slaves. This path-breaking essay set off a new flurry of research which included such notable contributions as the paper by Yasukichi Yasuba. Shortly before the publication of the essay by Conrad and Meyer, Robert Evans, Jr., independently began work on his analysis of slavery [7].

As a consequence of the Conrad-Meyer study, and of the subsequent research which extended their findings, the Phillips interpretation has been toppled from the position of dominance which it held for half a century.

1. Profitability to the Planter

As noted on the preceding page, a series of studies published during the thirties attempted to assess the profitability of slavery through the examination of plantation records. Most of these investigations concluded that the return to an investment in slaves was quite low. Typical of such work is Charles Sackett Sydnor's *Slavery in Mississippi* [*33*]. Sydnor summarized his findings on the profitability of a representative plantation with fifty slaves as follows:

The chief source of income would be from cotton. Probably thirty of the fifty Negroes worked in the field. If these produced 5 3/4 bales each, there would be a total of 158 bales which, at ten cents a pound, would be worth $6320.00

The expenses of the plantation would be as follows: 50 Negroes at $600 each (in the late 'fifties the price was higher) represented an investment of $30,000. Calculating interest at 6 per cent, this amounted to $1800.00

At least an equal amount should be added for depreciation in slave property by accidents, deaths, old age, etc.   1800.00

As the average hand worked about twelve acres, 600 acres would be ample for pastures and woodland as well as fields. Allowing $10 per acre, the investment in land at 6 per cent interest involved a yearly carriage charge of   360.00

and it ordinarily depreciated at the rate of at least three per cent a year in value   180.00

Annual hire of an overseer, at least   300.00

Purchases from New Orleans or elsewhere of Negro clothing, miscellaneous plantation supplies, etc.   1000.00

Without including various miscellaneous expenditures, such as the purchase of corn and pork, of which few plantations produced enough, the total of the expenses and interest charges was   5440.00

Profit of the planter $ 880.00

If one divides the Sydnor's figure for the annual profit to the planter ($880) by his estimate of the investment ($30,000 for slaves and $6000 for land), the apparent rate of return is a mere 2.4 per cent.

The most obvious error in this procedure is, as Govan and Stampp pointed out, the subtraction from gross income of imputed interest charges for the capital value of the slaves and the land. The usual accounting procedure followed in computing a firm's profit is to deduct from gross income only operating and management expenses plus a charge for depreciation. In other words, the usual accounting procedure includes as a part of the definition of profit, the imputed interest which Sydnor allocated to his statement of expenses. Consequently to make the rate of return in Sydnor's case comparable to the profit rate of other enterprises, one must add to his profit figure of $880, the $1800 he imputed as interest on the investment in slaves and the $360 interest charge he imputed to land.[12]

Another error of the plantation studies pointed out by Govan and Stampp was the omission from plantation income of the gain derived from the reproduction of the slave labor force. As long as slave children could be sold or used on the plantation, this was an additional source of income. A capital gain was also to be derived from the increased value of existing slaves. The slaves held in the 1850s were usually purchased in earlier years at below their current market value. Still other errors were the exclusion of slave household services and slave land clearing and maintenance services, and the treatment of the personal expenditures of planters as costs rather than as a use of profits. Govan

---

[12] What Sydnor computed was "pure profit." Pure profit is the amount by which the profit of a firm exceeds the profit rate elsewhere in the economy. Hence a pure profit rate equal to or greater than zero indicates that an enterprise is profitable in the accounting sense of the term.

and Stampp argued that correcting the omissions and errors of earlier historians showed that their samples clearly demonstrated high rates of return to slave ownership in the antebellum period. Thus, for example, merely correcting Sydnor's error in deducting the imputed cost of capital raises the rate of return in his case from 2.4 per cent to a healthy 8.4 per cent.

The study of Conrad and Meyer marked a significant advance in the effort to deal with the issue of the profitability of slavery. Rather than confining themselves to the study of particular plantations whose representativeness was open to question, Conrad and Meyer decided to treat the purchase of a slave as a standard investment problem. "From the standpoint of the entrepreneur making an investment in slaves," they wrote, "the basic problems involved in determining profitability are analytically the same as those met in determining the returns from any other kind of capital investment." In posing the problem in this way, Conrad and Meyer were, of course, merely taking up one of Phillips' suggestions. For it was Phillips who originally stressed the similarity between the slave and stock markets. However while Phillips did not attempt to pass from his conceptualization of the problem to the measurement of the rate of return on an investment in slaves, Conrad and Meyer did.

Their instrument was a modified version of equation A.7, namely[13]

$$C = \frac{R_e + E_e}{i}\left[1 - \frac{1}{(1 + i)^n}\right] \qquad (1)$$

The symbols in this equation are defined as follows: C is the price of the slave plus the value of the average amount of land and equipment required by each slave, R_e is the expected annual net revenue derived from a slave, and E_e is the expected annual cost to the planter (rental value) of the land and equipment. The letter i represents the rate of return that planters earned on their investment in slaves and the associated land and equipment. It is determined by estimating the values of C, R_e, E_e, and n, and then solving equation 1 for i. The letter n repre-

sents the expected life of a slave at the time of his purchase.

Since male and female slaves performed somewhat different functions in slave society and generally sold at different prices, Conrad and Meyer argued that slaves of different sexes should be viewed as different types of capital assets. They viewed males as an asset used to produce agricultural staples. Females were employed not merely to produce staples but also to produce new slaves. Thus the price of a female turned in large measure on her capacity to produce offspring. But if males and females were different types of assets, it is possible that the average return on these assets differed. To test the possibility Conrad and Meyer estimated the return on slaves of each sex separately rather than attempting to determine the average return on slaves of both sexes.

The computation of the rate of return on males was the simpler case. The average capital cost per male slave (C) was taken to be equal to the average market price of a prime field hand plus the value of the average amount of land, animals, and equipment assigned to each field hand. Conrad and Meyer recognized considerable variation in the quality of the land on which slaves were employed. Hence they computed the capital cost per slave for each of four grades of land. The values of C thus derived ranged from $1350 to $1700, depending on the quality of the land on which the slave was employed.

Conrad and Meyer obtained a figure for the average annual net earnings on the slave, land, and equipment ($R_e + E_e$) by subtracting from their estimate of the gross earnings an allowance for the cost of maintaining slaves. The gross earnings of a typical prime field hand was taken to be equal to the average annual number of bales of cotton produced by such a slave multiplied by the farm price per bale. Since the number of bales produced by a slave varied with the quality of the land on which he worked, four estimates of gross earnings were obtained, corresponding to the four categories of land distinguished by Conrad and Meyer. From each of these estimates Conrad and Meyer deducted $20 per slave for the cost of maintenance and supervision. The resulting figures were the estimated values of ($R_e + E_e$) applicable to each grade of land.

The final estimate required for the calculation of the rate of return on male slaves was the average number of years between the

---

[13] Equation 1 reduces to equation A.7 since

$$P_s = C - \frac{E_e}{i}\left[1 - \frac{1}{(1+i)^n}\right] = \frac{R_e}{i}\left[1 - \frac{1}{(1+i)^n}\right]$$

purchase of a prime field hand and his death (*n*). Basing themselves on mortality tables for the 1850s, Conrad and Meyer put this figure at 30 years.

Applying their estimates to equation 1, Conrad and Meyer found that, on lands of intermediate quality, rates of return to an investment in male slaves varied between 4.5 and 8.0 per cent, depending on the prevailing farm price of cotton and the physical yield per hand. On soils of the poorest quality, such as those of upland pine country or the exhausted lands of the Eastern seaboard, the range of rates was merely 2.2 to 5.4 per cent. However in the "best lands of the new Southwest, the Mississippi alluvium and the better South Carolina and Alabama plantations," the range of rates ran as high as 10.0 to 13.0 per cent. Thus just as with modern-day investors in corporate securities, the profit experience of investors in slaves ranged from very poor to unusually good. On average investors in male slaves earned about 6 per cent of their capital, a rate which Conrad and Meyer found to be equal to average return that investors of the day were earning on railroad and corporate securities, commercial loans, and other comparable assets.

The computation of the rate of return on female slaves was considerably more complicated than the male case. Conrad and Meyer had to take account not only of the productivity of the female in the field, but of such additional matters as the productivity of her offspring between their birth and the time of their sale; maternity, nursing, and rearing costs; and the average number of offspring. Arguing that few females produced less than five or more than ten children, Conrad and Meyer computed upper and lower limits on the rate of return. It is important to note that their computation assumed that the tenth child would not be sold until thirty-eight years after the purchase of the female. It also assumed that the price of cotton during this period would persist at about the average of the forties and that the average price of prime slaves would persist at about the level which prevailed during 1845–1849.

Conrad and Meyer found that on land of about average quality, the lower and upper limits of the rate of return to an investment in female slaves were 7.1 and 8.1 per cent, respectively. Thus planters in the upper South who earned only 4 to 5 per cent on male slaves, still were able to achieve a return on their total operation equal to alternative opportunities. They did so by selling the offspring of females to planters in the West, thus earning rates of 7 to 8 per cent on the other half of their slave force. Proof of such trade was found not only in the descriptions of contemporaries, but also in the age structure of the slave population. The selling states had a significantly larger proportion of persons under 15 and over 50 while the buying states predominated in slaves of the prime working ages.

Conrad and Meyer presented their results as an estimate of the average rate of return actually earned on an investment in slaves during 1830–1860. This widely accepted interpretation of their result is wrong. For slaves purchased after 1835, in the case of males, and after 1827, in the case of females, would have been freed before the expiration of the earnings periods stipulated by Conrad and Meyer in their analysis. Nor can their computation be taken to be representative of slaves purchased before these dates. For the average price of slaves purchased before 1835 was considerably below the level assumed in the analysis.

What Conrad and Meyer did was to provide the answer to a question somewhat different than one usually presumed. That question is: "If investors during 1846–1850 believed that a prime slave would continue to be as productive as such slaves had been on average during the previous decade, and if they thought that the price of cotton as well as slave maintenance costs would also continue at the average level of the late forties, was the 1846–1850 price of a slave justified by business considerations alone?"[14] The computation of Conrad and Meyer answered this question in the affirmative for both male and female slaves. It showed that a person who purchased a prime slave during 1846–1850 at the prevailing market price could, if he based himself on recent experience, expect to earn about the same rate of return on his investment in slaves as was being earned on alternative long-term investment opportunities.

Although the Conrad and Meyer study does not tell us what planters actually earned

---

[14] As Yasuba and Evans pointed out, the price of slaves and the values of the other variables which Conrad and Meyer estimated in computing *i* from equation 1 pertain to the period 1846–1850 (Cf. Table 5, below).

from their investment in slaves, it does serve as an answer to the question originally posed by Phillips. Phillips had argued that the price of slaves after 1815 was unjustified by the income planters could obtain from employing slaves in the production of crops. Conrad and Meyer showed that for one of the post-1815 quinquennia, the price of slaves was fully justified by the value of the crops they produced. Consequently, at least for the quinquennium 1846–1850, Phillips' contention that the price of slaves was inflated by wild speculative flights, external economies, and conspicuous consumption is unwarranted.[15]

Unfortunately the study of Conrad and Meyer did not disclose whether the price of slaves was justified by normal business considerations in years other than 1846–1850. It remained for Robert Evans, Jr., to extend their analysis to the whole period from 1830 to 1860 [7]. However Evans' study was considerably more than a mere replica of the methods of his predecessors. There were several innovations in his analysis, the most important of which was his use of data on the annual rental or hire price of slaves as an estimate of the annual net earning from their employment. By so doing Evans managed to avoid many of the estimating problems which plagued Conrad and Meyer. Evans also improved upon their estimate of the average life expectancy of slaves.

The central equation Evans employed in his computation may be represented as follows:

$$P_{20} = \sum_{t=1}^{k} \frac{H\lambda_t}{(1+i)^t} + \frac{P_{20+k}\lambda_k}{(1+i)^k} \qquad (2)$$

where

P_{20} = the price of a prime slave at age 20

P_{20+k} = the price of prime slave at age $20 + k$

k = the number of years the investor held the slave

H = the average annual hire rate (yearly rental fee) for prime male slaves at the time the slave was purchased

λ_t = the probability that the slave would live through the year t (λ_k is the probability that the

---

[15] The Conrad and Meyer findings also indicate that the capital market worked well in the slave South.

slave would live through the age $20 + k$)

i = the internal rate of return which Evans sought to estimate

t = a subscript or exponent designating a year

As can be seen from a comparison with equation A.5, Evans' equation is the standard one for estimating the rate of return on a capital asset, modified to take account of the probability that the asset might be destroyed during a given year.

Like Conrad and Meyer, Evans computed the value of i on the assumption that the slave would be held for 30 years. However Evans allowed for the possibility that the slave would still be alive and able to work at the age of 50. He also computed the value of i on the assumption that slaves would be held for only 20 years. Since the result was virtually identical with the 30-year computation, Evans concluded that his findings were "not specific to the time period for which the slaves are held." Another of Evans' innovations was that he computed separate rates of returns for slaves in the upper and lower South. Finally Evans confined himself only to the consideration of the profitability of an investment in males.

The rates of return which Evans computed are presented in Table 4. Evans interpreted these figures as the average rates actually earned by investors in slaves. However this cannot be the proper interpretation of Table 4. For in his computation Evans assumed that the average hire rate prevailing in the year that a slave was purchased would continue throughout the period that the slave was held, although the average hire rate actually moved sharply upward between the first quinquennium of the thirties and the second quinquennium of the fifties (see Table

Table 4. Average Rate of Return on Slaves by Quinquennia, 1830–1860 (Per Cent)

Period	Upper South	Lower South
1830–1835	10.5	12.0
1836–1840	9.5	
1841–1845	14.3	18.5
1846–1850	12.6	17.0
1851–1855	13.8	12.0
1856–1860	9.5	10.3

SOURCE: [7, p. 217]

Table 5. Five-Year Averages of Hires and Weighted Prices of Slaves, 1830–1860

Period	UPPER SOUTH		LOWER SOUTH	
	Hire	Price	Hire	Price
1830–1835	$ 62	$ 521	$127	$ 948
1836–1840	106	957		
1841–1845	83	529	143	722
1846–1850	99	709	168	926
1851–1855	141.5	935	167	1240
1856–1860	142	1294	196.5	1658

SOURCE: [7, p. 216]

5). Evans also based his calculations on estimates which showed that in any given year a fifty-year-old slave was worth 52 per cent of the value of a twenty-year-old slave. But instead of applying these percentages to the prevailing prime price in the year during which the slave reached the age of fifty, Evans applied it to the price of the year in which the slave was originally purchased. Thus if a twenty-year-old slave was purchased in 1830 at $750, Evans assumed that he could be sold in 1860 at $390 (0.52 × $750). However since the 1860 price of prime slaves stood at $1800, the fifty-year-old slave could have been sold for $936 (0.52 × $1800), a price substantially in excess of that for which he was purchased. It is because Evans allowed for no change in the price of prime slaves between the date of purchase and the date of potential sale that he found the rate of return insensitive to the length of the period for which the slave was held. For quite clearly the rate of return on a slave actually purchased in 1850 and actually sold at the high prices prevailing in 1860 would have considerably exceeded the rate of return on a slave actually purchased in 1850, and actually confiscated without compensation in 1865.

As with Conrad and Meyer, Evans produced not a series of estimates of the rate of return actually earned by purchasers of slaves, but a reply to Phillips. Phillips had argued that the prevailing prices of slaves could not be justified by the prevailing hire rates; that is, Phillips believed that at prevailing hire rates, the prevailing prices of slaves were so high that a purchaser of slaves would be unable to earn a normal rate of return on his investment. Evans showed that the Phillips conjecture was false for every quinquennia from 1830 through 1860.

The findings of Conrad, Meyer, and Evans

constitute a serious, and probably irreparable, blow to the thesis that the price of slaves was largely attributable to conspicuous consumption. If conspicuous consumption had increased the market price of slaves over the level indicated by business considerations alone, the expected rate of return from an investment in slaves would have been below that earned on alternative investments. The computations of Conrad, Meyer, and Evans revealed no such profit deficit. Quite the contrary, their computations yielded average expected rates of return equal to, or in excess of, the averages which obtained in a variety of other (nonagricultural) enterprises.[16] These findings do not rule out the possibility that some planters were willing to pay a premium to buy slaves or that some planters held excessive numbers of slaves at prevailing prices. However they do show that the aggregate demand of this category of slave-owners was too limited to raise the market price of slaves above the level dictated by normal business standards; that is, the demand of those slaveowners who desired to hold slaves for conspicuous consumption was quite small relative to the total demand for slaves.

It should be remembered that the proponents of the thesis that slaves were held widely for reasons of conspicuous consumption never provided conclusive proof of their contention. The thesis did not appear to require a rigorous proof since the assumption that an investment in slaves was unprofitable made conspicuous consumption a plausible rationalization for the willingness of slave-owners to pay "excessive" prices. In this context it appeared to be sufficient merely to cite evidence which suggested that prestige attached to the ownership of slaves. However prestige attaches to the ownership of most assets of great value which bring high rates of return to their owners. To show that the ownership of slaves and prestige were positively correlated does not settle the issue of

[16] The average rate of return earned by nine leading New England textile firms over the period from 1844–1853 was 10.1 per cent [5, p. 201], or between 60 and 85 per cent of the rates shown in Table 4 for the comparable period, 1846–1855. Evans estimates that the average rate of return on the cost of construction earned by a group of twelve Southern railroads was 8.5 per cent for the decade 1850–1860, or between 60 and 90 per cent of the rates shown in Table 4 for the same period [7, pp. 207–208].

causality. Was the price of slaves high because the ownership of slaves brought prestige, or did the ownership of slaves bring prestige because their price was high? To distinguish between these alternatives one needs to know whether the expected return to slaves was below or above alternative rates. It was precisely on this point that exponents of the thesis of conspicuous consumption erred. The demonstration that an investment in slaves was highly profitable undermines the argument for conspicuous consumption, and with it, the attempt to portray slaveowners as a "precapitalist" or "acommercial" class which failed to respond to modern business incentives.

Perhaps the most formidable critique of the Conrad and Meyer finding is the one authored by Edward Saraydar [29, 30]. While Saraydar accepted the applicability of equation 1, he argued that faulty estimates of the values of $(R_e + E_e)$ and C led Conrad and Meyer to overestimate the average rate of return (i) to an investment in male slaves. Saraydar set out to correct these errors. He first cut the gross earnings of slaves by 15 per cent on the ground that the true average physical product of a prime field hand was not 3.75 bales but only 3.2 bales. With a raw cotton price of 8 cents per pound, this change would put the average gross earnings of a prime field hand at $102.40. From the last figure Saraydar subtracted $32 (instead of $20) to obtain $70.40 as his estimate of net earnings $(R_e + E_e)$. The last figure is only 70 per cent of the original estimate of $(R_e + E_e)$. Saraydar's upward adjustment of the average capital cost per slave was also substantial, amounting to $315 or 24 per cent of the figure allowed by Conrad and Meyer. The combined effect of the changes was the lowering of the rate of return on an investment in male slaves from about 6 per cent to a mere 1.5 per cent.

The crucial point in Saraydar's argument is his claim that Conrad and Meyer overestimated the physical productivity of slaves, for both his downward revision of gross slave earnings and his upward revision of the capital cost rest on this contention. Unlike Conrad and Meyer, who relied on the opinions of contemporary observers, Saraydar sought to estimate slave productivity from the published reports of the 1850 census. He proceeded by choosing a sample of counties for which he computed both the total cotton production and the total number

of slaves. Dividing the second figure into the first yielded the number of bales of cotton produced per slave. Arguing that half of the slave population was in the labor force, Saraydar multiplied bales per slave by two and took the resulting figure (3.2 bales) as his estimate of the output of cotton per prime male field hand.

However the output of cotton divided by the slave labor force yields an estimate not of product per prime male hand but of product per slave worker.[17] Since approximately half of the slave labor force was composed of women, who had a considerably lower average product than prime males, and since large parts of the labor force were children under 16 and persons over 50, it is evident that output per slave worker must be less than output per prime field hand. Thus while Saraydar was correct in recognizing that one could improve on the productivity estimates of Conrad and Meyer by making use of census data, his attempt to do so was marred by his failure to adjust for the fact that the average slave worker was considerably less productive than a prime field hand.

Two recent studies make it possible to carry forward the effort begun by Saraydar. The first, by Foust and Swan, strongly supports Saraydar's estimate of cotton output per slave worker [11]. Working with data drawn from the manuscript schedules of the census, Foust and Swan found that the output of cotton per slave in seven states during 1849 was 1.59 bales, a figure remarkably close to Saraydar's. Accepting 0.5 as the labor-force participation rate of slaves, Foust and Swan put the output per slave worker at 3.18 bales.

The second study, by Raymond Battalio and John Kagel, attempted to measure the productivity of average workers relative to the prime male field hand [1]. Basing themselves on material in the studies by U. B. Phillips and Lewis C. Gray, they argued that while the designation "prime field hand" was limited to males between the ages of 18 and 30, males remained "full hand" until they reached the age of 55. Males between 15 and 19 or between 55 and 60 were considered "three-quarter hand," while those from 10–14 and 60–65 were considered "one-quarter hands." Males under 10 or over 65 were assumed to be out of the labor force or

---

[17] This point was first made by Sutch [32].

at least not employed in field activities. On
the basis of evidence which showed that the
annual hire rate of females was about 50 per
cent of the figure for males, Battalio and
Kagel put the productivity of females of
all ages at 50 per cent of the productivity of
men of corresponding ages.

When these weights are applied to the
aggregate slave population of 1850, one finds
that a "full" field hand was 30 per cent more
productive than the "average" slave hand
implicitly defined by Saraydar, Foust, and
Swan.[18] If the productivity of prime hands
did not exceed those of full hands, one could
convert the Foust-Swan product per average
slave hand into product per prime field hand
by multiplying the latter by 1.3. Before carrying through this multiplication it is necessary
to correct three downward biases in the
Saraydar-Foust-Swan estimate of output per
average slave hand. First, their estimate is
based on "running bales" which in 1849
were 7 per cent heavier than the 400 pound
bales employed by Conrad and Meyer. In
the latter unit of measurement, the Saraydar-
Foust-Swan estimate of average slave product
is 3.4 bales. Second, Saraydar, Foust, and
Swan assumed that all slaves in the labor force
were employed in the field. Yet we know that
some slaves were house servants and some
were artisans and craftsmen. If 10 per cent
of the slave labor input of plantations had
been employed in nonfield activities then the
output of cotton per slave field-worker would
be 3.8 bales. Third, Saraydar, Foust, and
Swan assumed that cotton was the only
market crop produced in the Cotton Belt.
More specifically, they assumed that slaves
were able to produce only enough grain and
meat to feed the plantation or farms and that
no surplus was available for sale. However
the study by Battalio and Kagel revealed that
slaves produced a surplus of wheat and meat
per hand equal in value to one bale of cotton.
Consequently for the purpose of calculating
the gross revenue per slave field-worker, the
Battalio-Kagel study suggests that the previous figure of 3.8 bales should be increased

to at least 4.8 bales. If one then multiplies
the last figure by 1.3, he obtains 6.2 bales as
his estimate of average product per prime
field hand.

Of course this estimate of the average productivity of prime field hands is rough. The
proportion of labor input devoted to nonfield
tasks may well have exceeded 10 per cent.
On the other hand, the surplus food produced
on farms in the sample of South Carolina
farms studied by Battalio and Kagel may not
be typical of the entire South. Future statistical analysis of the data in the manuscript
census will undoubtedly yield more reliable
estimates. Yet there is reason to believe that
while future work will alter the components
of the estimate we have set forth, it will not
reduce the magnitude significantly. For the
application of the theory of factor prices to
the data on the annual hire rates of slaves
yields a similar estimate of the average productivity of prime field hands.

The data procured by Evans suggest that
most annual slave rentals were to the nonagricultural sector of the Southern economy.
The net value of the marginal product of
slaves withheld from the annual hire market
must have been equal to or greater than the
annual hire rate.[19] This relationship is
expressed by the inequality

$$H \le P_c \frac{\alpha_1 Q}{L_f} - M \qquad (3)$$

where

H = the annual net hire rate;
    $H = H_g - M$
P_c = the farm price of cotton
α_1 = the output elasticity of slave labor
    in cotton production
Q = the annual output of cotton
L_f = the number of equivalent full hands
M = the annual maintenance cost of
    slaves

It follows that the marginal physical product of prime male slaves retained in cotton

[18] The ratings of Battalio and Kagel imply that 67
per cent of the population was in the labor force.
However in full-hand equivalents, the labor force
participation rate is only 39 per cent. Since the
Saraydar-Foust-Swan estimate of the labor-force
participation rate is 50 per cent, it is necessary to
multiply their productivity figures by 50/39 (= 1.3) to
obtain output per equivalent full hand.

[19] This statement abstracts from the possibility that
risk to the well-being of slaves was higher when they
were rented out than when their masters employed
them. Hire contracts usually stipulated the obligations
of the lessee with respect to the maintenance and
general treatment of the slave, including the food,
clothing, and medical attention that was to be provided. Moreover, unlike inanimate objects, slaves
could report to their masters if they were abused.

production must have been equal to or greater than the sum of the annual hire rate and the maintenance cost of slaves divided by the price of cotton; i.e.,

$$\frac{\alpha_1 Q}{L_f} \geq \frac{H + M}{P_c} \qquad (4)$$

Moreover since α_1 is less than one, the average product of prime or full hands also must have exceeded $(H + M)/P_c$.

According to Evans the average annual hire rate of slaves over the quinquennium 1846–1850 was $168 in the lower South and $99 in the upper South. Conrad, Meyer, and Saraydar accept contemporary opinion that the average farm price of cotton was approximately equal to the New Orleans price per bale less $2.80. They also agree that the annual maintenance cost per prime hand was about $45.[20]

Since the average New Orleans price of cotton over the years 1846–1850 was $34.20 per bale, the foregoing considerations imply that the average product of prime field hands was at least 6.8 bales in the lower South and 4.6 bales in the upper South. One can convert these subregional estimates into a Southwide average by giving the figure for the lower South a weight of 0.57 and the figure for the upper South a weight of 0.43.[21] Consequently the annual hire rates imply that the average physical product of prime field hands probably exceeded 5.9 bales and thus confirm the previous conclusion that Conrad and Meyer underestimated the productivity of prime slaves.[22]

2. The Viability of Slavery and the Sanguinity of Slaveholders

Our discussion thus far has dealt with estimates of the rate of return based on both the prevailing market price of slaves and the current net revenue earned by owners of slaves. Until recently it was assumed that this rate was the crucial measure of the viability of the slave system. Yasukichi Yasuba [42] showed that the assumption was false.[23] Yasuba pointed out that slavery could be viable even though this rate of return was low and it could be moribund even if the rate were high. For if it became clear that the *future* earnings of slaves were going to rise, investors would bid the price of slaves up to a level that was appropriate to their expectations of *future* earnings. And if it became clear that slavery was moribund or declining, then even though current earnings were satisfactory, the price of slaves would fall because investors realized that the current earnings level could not be maintained. In this case the rate of return computed on the basis of current price and earnings would be too high. Phenomena such as those described by Yasuba are quite familiar to students of corporate finance. The ratio of current earnings to stock prices is frequently quite low for highly successful, rapidly growing firms (IBM and Xerox are well-known, recent examples) and quite high for declining firms.

Yasuba argued that two criteria were needed to establish viability. It had to be shown not merely that the rate of return (based on the current price and earnings) was equal to, or in excess of rates prevailing on alternative investments, but also that the current price of slaves equaled or exceeded the cost of producing slaves. The second criterion is needed to rule out the possibility that the high rate of return is the consequence of the historians' assumption that net earnings from slaves would continue at the observed level when in fact investors expected future earnings to decline to a level that would make slavery moribund. The first criterion is needed to show that the price of slaves was justified by the current earnings of slaves and thus rule out the possibility that the price was inflated by wild speculation.

Yasuba then proceeded to roughly calculate the cost of producing eighteen-year-old male slaves. He found that over the four decades from 1820 to 1860, the market price of such slaves was persistently in excess of

---

[20] The proper figure for maintenance cost in this case is the second option presented by Conrad and Meyer [3, p. 57].

[21] Estimated from the data in [11, Table 4] and the equation

$$\frac{Q}{L} = \sigma \frac{Q_u}{L_u} + (1 - \sigma) \frac{Q_l}{L_l}$$

where the subscripts designate the upper and lower South and σ is the weight to be applied to the upper South. It will be noted that σ is equal to L_u/L, to the share of the labor force engaged in cotton production that was employed in the upper South.

[22] Compare with the discussion by Sutch [32].

---

[23] The same point was made independently at later dates by Evans [7] and Sutch [32].

their reproduction cost by a substantial margin. During no quinquennia did the capitalized rent fall below 50 per cent of the market price. Moreover the general trend in the rent was, with the exception of the quinquennium of 1841–1845, sharply upward, rising from 50 to 99 per cent of the market price.

Yasuba's estimate of the level and trend of the capitalized rent is only intended to be a rough approximation. Yet as Yasuba argues, it is unlikely that the correction of any of the biases that may have crept into his estimates would alter his basic finding. One potential source of error is the assumption that the net income[24] from child labor increased with the ratio between the value of the cotton crop and the slave population. The possibility that this assumption introduces an upward bias can be eliminated by recomputing the rent series on the extreme assumption that breeders realized a zero net income from child labor. The capitalized rent derived on the basis of the new assumption is still positive throughout the forty-year period. It rises from $79 (11 per cent of the market price of a prime male) to $658 (41 per cent of the prime male price).

This modification probably produces a lower limit on the true rent component. The new series contains two strong downward biases. The first is introduced by the assumption of zero net income from child labor. The second arises from the fact that Yasuba estimated not the actual rental component of the slave price but the expected rent. What Yasuba computes for each quinquennium (for example, 1851–1855) is not the actual cost of raising a slave who became eighteen during the quinquennium. It is the cost a breeder would have incurred in raising a slave born during 1851–1855, if prevailing prices remained constant for eighteen years. Since the cost of rearing slaves increased over time, the gap between the 1851–1855 price of slaves and the *expected* rearing cost is less than the gap between the 1851–1855 price of slaves and the actual cost of rearing a slave who reached eighteen during 1851–1855.

Yasuba's finding also has an important implication for the issue of profitability. Both the study by Conrad and Meyer and

that by Evans estimated rates of return to investors who bought mature slaves in the open market. Since the market price contained a capitalized rent, and since it was breeders of slaves who captured the rent, the rate of return earned by purchasers of mature slaves would have been below that earned by planters who employed slaves bred on their own farms.[25] For to the extent that the market failed to anticipate the rise in slave productivity and prices, "insiders" received windfall gains not reflected in the computations of Conrad, Meyer, and Evans.

Yasuba's finding thus reinforces the previous conclusion regarding the profitability of slavery. It also provides convincing evidence that slavery was economically viable through the last four decades of the antebellum era. The rising capitalized rent indicates that, at least from an economic point of view, the slave system was becoming more entrenched as the ante-bellum era wore on. There is no evidence to support the proposition that slavery was moribund on the eve of the Civil War.[26]

What about the later decades of the nineteenth century? If there had not been a Civil War, and barring other political catastrophes, could the slave system have maintained its economic vigor? Yasuba's study provides no answer to this question. Other scholars have answered the question negatively. Earlier in this essay we considered Ramsdell's contention that slavery was moribund on the eve of the Civil War and his "prediction" that by the 1870s, in the absence of the war, the price of cotton would have declined to a point that was incompatible with the

---

[24] Yasuba defines net income as the income earned from child labor less capital costs incidental to work in the fields. His definition differs from the one presented above since he has not deducted maintenance costs.

[25] Essentially the same point was made implicitly by Sutch [32, p. 367].

[26] While Yasuba's findings rule out the possibility that slavery was threatened because profits earned on slaves were below those earned in alternative enterprises, they do not rule out the possibility that owners could have raised their profits by allowing slaves to purchase themselves and become free laborers. This possibility has been stressed by John E. Moes [3, pp. 99–107]. However, actual manumissions took place at a rate far less than the natural increase in the slave population. The slow rate of manumission may have reflected the fact that most owners could not have substantially increased earnings by permitting slaves to purchase their freedom. Or it may reflect the influence of various social and legal restrictions induced by racial prejudice. Unfortunately the data needed to discriminate between these alternatives do not appear to be available.

maintenance of the slave system. We argued that Ramsdell's prediction was unconvincing. It was based on a misreading of the course of cotton prices and on the false assumption that a *decline* in the labor to land ratio would, all other things being equal, depress the price of slaves.

There remains a second influential argument for the predication that slavery would have expired, within a decade or two after 1860, from its own disabilities. That is the contention that slavery would have been undermined by a *rise* in the labor to land ratio. To proponents of this view the rise in the labor-land ratio seemed assured because it was held that land suitable for the expansion of cotton production was limited, while the supply of slave labor would grow with the growth of the slave population. The thesis that slave economy was bound to be strangled by "natural limits" to the geographic expansion of the cotton culture was suggested but not developed in Ramsdell's essay. Nevertheless many scholars believe that the natural limits thesis is the principal basis for Ramsdell's contention that slavery was moribund. And others have advanced the same thesis independently.

One might be inclined to dismiss this argument out of hand. It appears to depend on the assumption that slaves could be used only in the production of cotton. Aside from implied calumny that slaves could not be taught other occupations, the assumption obviously exaggerates the identity between the cotton culture and slavery. According to DeBow, about 15 per cent of slaves worked in towns, and some of those living on plantations were employed as artisans of various sorts. Still, if DeBow was correct, between 55 and 60 per cent of slaves were involved in cotton production.[27] Although the cotton culture was not identical with slavery, it appears to have been the most important single occupation of slaves. Moreover the crude form of the "natural limits" thesis can be modified by arguing, not that all slaves had to be employed in the cotton culture, but that the proportion of slaves employed in cotton had to remain at about the ante-bellum level. The justification for limiting the flow of slaves into other areas of production need not imply a calumny against Negroes. It could be based on the argument that the slave system of labor organization was too rigid to permit the efficient involvement of a larger percentage of slaves in nonagricultural activity than had been achieved during the ante-bellum era. In any case there is a sufficiently large group of adherents to the natural limits thesis to warrant an objective test of it.

Equation A.9 makes such a test possible. This equation enables one to predict the rate of change in slave prices, given information on the rate of change in cotton prices ($\overset{*}{P}_{ce}$), the output of cotton ($\overset{*}{Q}_e$), the size of the labor force employed in cotton ($\overset{*}{L}_e$), the cost of slave maintenance ($\overset{*}{M}_e$) and the market rate of interest ($\overset{*}{i}$).[28] The values of all these variables for the post-Civil War era are known except the rate of growth of the slave labor force that would have been employed in cotton production and the cost of slave maintenance. However the unknown values are supplied by the natural limits thesis itself. Given the requirement that the proportion of the labor force devoted to cotton remain constant, and given the constancy in the labor-force participation rate, the rate of growth of slave labor devoted to cotton would have been equal to the rate of growth of the Negro population. Moreover the natural limits thesis implicitly accepts the constancy of the real living standard of slaves. Hence maintenance costs would have moved with the price level.

The results of the test are presented in Table 6. It shows that far from falling, the price of slaves would have risen at a rate of 1.29 per cent a year between 1860 and 1890. In other words prime hands in 1890 would have sold at 47 per cent more than they did in 1860. Since the price level declined between 1860 and 1890, the 1890 price of slaves in dollars of 1860 would have risen by over 66 per cent. This startling conclusion is explained by two factors. First, the annual hire rate of slaves (H_e) would have remained virtually unchanged in current dollars (or risen by 14 per cent in dollars of 1860). Second, the rate of return of capital invested in alternative occupations (i) dropped substantially. Indeed virtually all of the rise in the predicted price of slaves is attributable to the fact that the marginal value product of a slave would not have fallen off as it did on a unit of other capital goods.

---

[27] Cited in [7, p. 188].

[28] $\overset{*}{X}$ is a function of $\overset{*}{i}$.

Table 6. The Predicted Annual Rate of Change in the Purchase Price and Hire Rate of Prime Hands, 1860–1890

Variables and Weights		Values (Variables in Per Cent, Weights in Absolute Numbers)
1.	$\overset{*}{P}_{ce}$	0.15
2.	$\overset{*}{Q}_{e}$	1.67
3.	$\overset{*}{L}_{e}$	1.84
4.	$\overset{*}{M}_{e}$	−0.42
5.	$\overset{*}{i}$	−2.03
6.	$\overset{*}{X}$	−0.72
7.	$\overset{*}{P}_{s}$	1.29
8.	$\overset{*}{H}_{e}$	0.02
9.	ϕ_1	1.10
10.	ϕ_2	0.10

SOURCES and NOTES: Lines 1 and 2: [*39*, pp. 10–13]. Line 3: [*36*, p. 9]. Line 4: [*36*, p. 115]. Lines 5 and 6: The discount rate was assumed to move with the yield on long-term railroad bonds [*36*, p. 656]. Line 7: Computed from the data in this table and equation A.9. Line 8: $\overset{*}{H}_e$, the net hire rate, is equal to $\overset{*}{H}_{ge} - \overset{*}{M}_e$. $\overset{*}{H}_{ge}$ was computed from the data in this table and equation A.4. Lines 9 and 10: The base period net revenue was taken to be equal to the average hire rate in the lower South during 1856–1860 (see Table 5). The base period gross revenue was the net revenue plus $20.

The last observation brings us back to the constancy of the hire rate. This predicted constancy was completely unanticipated by the proponents of the natural limits thesis. It rests on two solid facts. The first is that the demand for American cotton grew a little more rapidly than the supply, down not only to 1890 but to World War I. Hence the price of cotton was higher in 1890 than in 1860. Second, the quantity of land devoted to cotton did not remain constant at the 1859 level. Quite the contrary, it grew at a rate (2.06 per cent per annum), which is in excess of that shown for the labor force.[29] In other words the assumption that the quantity of additional land available for use in cotton was almost exhausted by 1860 is false. The land devoted to cotton nearly doubled between 1860 and 1890; it more than doubled between 1890

[29] The 1859 acreage was obtained by dividing the 1879 yield per acre into the 1860 crop [*36*, p. 302]. This procedure probably leads to an understatement of the rate of growth of amount of land in cotton.

and 1925 [*36*, pp. 301–302]. The irony of the widespread acceptance of the "natural limits" hypothesis is that it was refuted by the man who is usually cited as its chief architect. For as noted above, Ramsdell's principal basis for predicting the demise of slavery was his belief that the land to labor ratio in cotton would grow rather than decline.

The analytical apparatus presented in the mathematical appendix to this chapter makes it possible to deal with another of the conundrums which have beset the debate on the economics of slavery. How much of the sharp rise in slave prices between 1830 and 1860 was due to the optimism of slaveholders? To answer this question we need to know whether slaveholders expected earnings from slaves to increase more rapidly than they actually did. The hire rate tells us the way in which *actual* earnings moved and equation A.11 permits us to deduce the way in which *expected* earnings moved. This equation states that if the discount rate is constant, the rate of change in the expected hire rate (expected net earnings) will be equal to the rate of change in the price of slaves.[30] Since available evidence indicates a high degree of stability in the yield on long-term government bonds during 1830–1860, the assumption of a constant discount rate seems warranted [*17*, pp. 304–305]. It follows that one can measure the change in the sanguinity of slaveholders by the change in the ratio of the *actual* slave price to the *actual* hire rate—in other words, by the change in the price-earnings ratio.

Indexes of the rate of change in the sanguinity of slaveholders are presented in columns 2 and 4 of Table 7. Several features of these indexes are noteworthy. First, slaveholders were not consistently sanguine. There were periods during which slaveholders were more optimistic than was justified by the movement of current earnings; but there also were periods during which their pessimism depressed slave prices more rapidly than earnings. Pessimism ruled the behavior of slaveholders in the upper South during the first quinquennium of the 1840s and the first quinquennium of the 1850s. Over 60 per cent of the precipitous fall in the average slave price which took place in the upper South between 1836–1840 and 1841–1845 was due

[30] For the purpose of constructing an index of sanguinity $\overset{*}{H}_e$ is to be interpreted as the certainty equivalent of the expected hire price. In this case the discount rate is net of a risk component.

Table 7. The Rate of Change in the Sanguinity of Slaveholders and its Effect on Slave Prices, 1830–1860

	UPPER SOUTH			LOWER SOUTH		
Period	Annual Rate of Change in Slave Prices $\overset{*}{P_s}$ (1)	Annual Rate of Change in Sanguinity $\overset{*}{I}$ (2)	$\dfrac{\overset{*}{I}}{\overset{*}{P_s}} \times 100$ (3)	Annual Rate of Change in Slave Prices $\overset{*}{P_s}$ (4)	Annual Rate of Change in Sanguinity $\overset{*}{I}$ (5)	$\dfrac{\overset{*}{I}}{\overset{*}{P_s}} \times 100$ (6)
1. 1830–1835 to 1836–1840	14.9	1.46	9.70	—	—	—
2. 1836–1840 to 1841–1845	−11.2	−6.75	60.2	—	—	—
3. 1841–1845 to 1846–1850	6.04	2.36	39.1	5.11	0.17	3.32
4. 1846–1850 to 1851–1855	5.70	−1.52	−28.2	6.01	6.16	102.
5. 1851–1855 to 1856–1860	3.42	3.42	100.	5.98	2.58	43.2
6. 1830–1835 to 1841–1845	0.15	−2.73	−1820.	−2.69	−3.83	14.2
7. 1836–1840 to 1846–1850	−2.95	−2.30	78.0	—	—	—
8. 1841–1845 to 1851–1855	5.91	0.37	6.18	5.56	3.94	70.9
9. 1846–1850 to 1856–1860	6.20	2.34	37.9	6.00	4.43	74.0
10. 1831–1835 to 1856–1860	3.64	0.37	8.8	2.26	0.49	21.6

SOURCES and NOTES:

Columns 1 and 4: Computed from the data in Table 5.

Columns 2 and 5: Computed from the data in Table 5 and the equation $\overset{*}{I} = \overset{*}{P_s} - \overset{*}{H}$.

Columns 3 and 6: A negative sign indicates that slave prices and hire rates were moving in the same direction but that the absolute change in slave prices was less than the absolute change in the hire rate. Thus the entry in col. 3, line 4 (−28.2) means that if not for pessimism the growth of slave prices would have been 28.2 per cent greater than it actually was. A negative entry in excess of 100 means that slave prices and hire rates were moving in the same direction but that the absolute change in slave prices was less than one half of the absolute change in hire rates. Thus the entry in col. 3, line 6 (−1820) means that if not for pessimism, the increase in slave prices would have been about 18 times larger than it actually was.

to the fact that slaveholders expected earnings to decline more rapidly than they actually did.[31] Second, for the whole period, expected earnings grew only slightly more rapidly than actual earnings. That the over-all rate of change in the sanguinity index is positive, is due largely to the buoyancy of expectations during the last half of the 1850s. Between 1830–1835 and 1851–1855, the sanguinity index declined slightly for both the upper and lower South. Third, expectations tended to be more volatile in the lower South than in the older area. Expectations in the newer region declined more rapidly during periods

---

[31] There is an important difference between the pessimism of 1841–1845 and that of 1851–1855. During the first period investors expected the low earnings of this quinquennia to decline further. During the second period they doubted that the high earnings of 1851–1855 could be maintained in future years.

The pessimism of investors during 1841–1845 explains a paradox in Evans' estimates of the rate of return to an investment in slaves. This paradox was pointed out by Thomas Govan: " But the results from this equation [presented above as equation 2] seem to me truly astonishing. From 1830 to 1835, a most prosperous period except for the winter of 1833–1834, the rate of return on capital invested in slaves is said to be 12% but in the period from 1841 to 1845, when operators of plantations, businesses, and factories were barely getting by, the rate of return is said to be 18.5%" [*15*, p. 246]. The paradox arose because

Govan accepted Evans' unwarranted claim that the computation revealed the actual rate of return earned by slaveowners. As we have pointed out, Evans' computation merely shows whether or not the current price of slaves was justified by their current earnings. For periods during which the price of slaves was below that justified by current earnings because investors were pessimistic about the future (as occurred during 1841–1845) Evans' computation will yield an inappropriately high rate of return. This is merely a way of stating that on the basis of the 1841–1845 earnings, the price of slaves was too low. Investors who took advantage of the prevailing pessimism by buying slaves at the depressed prices could hardly have avoided making a " killing." What Evans' computation revealed is the rate of return such purchasers could expect to earn if they bought slaves at the depressed price and if earnings continued at the 1841–1845 level during the years that followed.

of falling earnings and rose more rapidly during periods of rising earnings. Finally, slaveholders in neither region expected to see their peculiar institution abolished by an impending political catastrophe. During the decade of the fifties sanguinity was increasing quite rapidly, accounting for 40 per cent of the rise in slave prices in the upper South and 75 per cent of the rise in the lower South. Slaveholders not only expected their social order to endure but foresaw an era of prosperity.

That investors went through periods of pessimism and optimism should not be interpreted as supporting the claim that the price of slaves was determined by wild speculation. Pessimism and optimism were generally rooted in experience. The pessimism of the early 1840s was brought on by a decade of faltering demand during which the price of cotton dropped by nearly 70 per cent—to an all-time low of 5.6 cents per pound [*36*, pp. 123–124]. Similarly the optimism of the late 1850s reflected the booming demand for cotton which maintained the price of that commodity at quite a high level despite a record expansion in the cotton crop. Such behavior is characteristic of sober businessmen doing their best to perceive an uncertain future. It contradicts rather than supports the stereotype of the reckless speculator which has tended to dominate historical portraits.

We are now in a position to offer an explanation for the rise in slave prices between the first half of the 1830s and the last half of the 1850s that was so vexing to Phillips, Ramsdell, and their followers. The basis for the increase in slave prices was the rapid rise in the demand for cotton. Between 1830 and 1860 the demand for cotton shifted upward at an annual rate of 5.5 per cent. Since the supply of cotton increased just as rapidly, there was no rise in the price of cotton over these six quinquennia.[32] However the rapid rise in supply appears to have been accompanied by an increase in the land to labor ratio. This development, probably combined with an improvement in the quality of the land employed in cotton production, a rise in capital per worker, and improvements in methods of farming, raised the marginal physical product of slaves. The growth in the

marginal productivity of slaves was more rapid in the upper South (3.3 per cent per annum) than in the lower South (1.75 per cent).[33] Thus of the 3.6 per cent annual increase in slave prices in the older region, nine tenths is attributable to the rise in productivity, with sanguinity accounting for the rest. In the lower South optimism was a more important factor. But even here it was the increase in the marginal physical product of slaves that determined the course of their price, explaining eight tenths of the movement.

3. A Stagnant Economy?

Perhaps the most widely accepted proposition about the ante-bellum South is that slavery retarded the development of its economy and caused the South to stagnate economically. With few exceptions even those historians who have argued that slavery was both profitable and viable have accepted the view that slavery stifled the economic growth of the South. As noted in Part I the reasons advanced for the alleged stagnation of the South include the effect of slavery on income distribution and on the size of the market for manufactured goods. These factors are said to have reduced the rate of Southern capital formation, prevented the rise of a large-scale modern manufacturing industry, and led the South to specialize in the production of agricultural staples. Some historians have argued that specialization in cotton caused slavery rather than that slavery caused specialization. However proponents of both views have compared the ante-bellum South with the weak positions of various agricultural export producers in the world today, arguing that a shift away from agricultural specialization would have led to a more rapid rate of economic growth in the ante-bellum South.

At the outset it is necessary to stress that the views just summarized merge two separate propositions. The first is that slavery caused the Southern economy to stagnate. The second is that slavery retarded the growth of the Southern economy. These points are not

---

[32] Of course, as noted above, over shorter periods disparities between the rates of growth of demand and supply led to rather wide fluctuations in prices.

[33] A smaller rate of growth in productivity should not be misinterpreted to imply that slaves were less productive in the lower South. Quite the contrary, they were more productive in the new region both at the start and at the end of the period. However the relative edge of the new region declined over time.

identical, although they have usually been treated as if they were, because slavery could have retarded the development of the South even though the South actually experienced moderate, or even rapid, economic growth. We shall argue that available evidence contradicts the proposition that the ante-bellum economy was stagnant. Unfortunately the evidence needed to test the proposition that slavery retarded the economic growth of the South has not yet been compiled. While this point must remain moot for the present, we will also argue that several of the reasons advanced to demonstrate the retarding effects of slavery are of dubious validity.

It must be remembered that until recently no index of the over-all performance of the ante-bellum economy, such as regional income per capita, was available. Consequently those concerned with the issue of performance had to rely on proxies for this measure. Among the variables used as proxies were the relative share of the South in manufacturing output or employment and the extent of Southern urbanization. Since both the extent of urbanization and the share of the South in manufacturing were low, it was concluded that the over-all economic performance of the Southern economy was poor. However the justification for using these proxies is extremely dubious. The procedure assumes functional relationships between per capita income and the proxies, the validity of which have not been determined for recent time, let alone for the first half of the nineteenth century.

In any case it is no longer necessary to depend on such proxies, since the level and rate of growth of Southern per capita income can now be measured directly by applying Richard A. Easterlin's estimates of regional income to Robert A. Gallman's estimates of national income in 1840 and 1860.[34] The results of the computation are presented in

Table 8. This table gives two sets of estimates of the levels of regional and national per capita income. The first set records the per capita income of the total population; the second gives the per capita income of only the free population. These two sets of estimates differ because slaves were exploited in the sense that their owners expropriated the difference between the value of their marginal product and their maintenance cost[35] (i.e., the difference between what their wage would have been in a free market and what their wage actually was under slavery).[36]

Which of these sets of figures ought one to consider in judging the performance of the ante-bellum economy? The answer depends on the point that is at issue. The first set of figures treats slaves as consumers and implicitly assumes that their welfare was as important as that of free citizens. The second set implicitly treats slaves as "intermediate goods" used to produce the final products consumed by free persons—that is, it excludes the welfare of slaves as an ultimate objective of society. Hence an abolitionist would have measured the performance of the Southern economy by the first set of figures. A Southern politician, whose electorate was the slave-

---

[34] See [6; 12; 36, p. 13]. There were a number of revisions made in Easterlin's data in obtaining the estimates of Table 8. The most important of these was the estimation of income for Texas in 1840, so that Texas could be brought into the Southern region in both years (it was excluded from Easterlin's computations). To insure that this revision introduced no upward biases into the estimates of either the level or the rate of growth, Texas per capita income in 1840 was assumed equal to the 1860 level. The 1840 population was interpolated between the 1836 and 1846 estimates presented in Lewis W. Newton and Herbert P. Gambrell [22, p. 280]. Thus the regional breakdown in Table 8 differs from Easterlin's in including Texas in

the South, but accords with his placement of Delaware and Maryland in the Northeast. The Mountain and Pacific states were excluded from the national regional totals in both years.

Easterlin's estimates are the most detailed available for this period, but, of course, may not be perfectly accurate. Genovese, for example, has stressed the inferior quality of livestock in the South [13, pp. 106–123]. The importance of such biases awaits further study. However two points should be made. First, it is improbable that such a correction could reverse the finding that growth did occur in the slave economy. Second, while it is possible that such corrections would reduce the level of Southern income in 1860, they would not affect the growth rate if the same relative quality existed in 1840 and 1860.

[35] The "maintenance cost" per slave used in these calculations was $20 [see 16, p. 544]. It should be noted that while a higher maintenance cost would reduce the relative per capita income of free Southerners in 1860, it would raise the rate of growth of their income between 1840 and 1860. For example, if a $30 figure were used, the Southern per capita income would have been $144, compared to the North's $142, but the growth rate would have risen to 1.9 per cent, with that of the North remaining the same as in the previous calculation. Cf. Easterlin [6, p. 527].

[36] This statement is based on the assumptions that freedom would not have altered the distribution of labor among occupations and that the distribution of labor under slavery was efficient.

Table 8. Per Capita Income by Region, 1840 and 1860 (In 1860 Prices)

	TOTAL POPULATION		FREE POPULATION	
	1840	1860	1840	1860
National Average	$96	$128	$109	$144
North	109	141	110	142
Northeast	129	181	130	183
North Central	65	89	66	90
South	74	103	105	150
South Atlantic	66	84	96	124
East South Central	69	89	92	124
West South Central	151	184	238	274

SOURCE: See text and footnotes 34 and 35.

owning population, might have judged the performance of the economy by the second set of figures.

Table 8 shows that when slaves are treated as consumers, Southern per capita income in 1860 turns out to be $103. While this figure is 20 per cent below the national average, it should not be interpreted as indicating a low level of economic performance. Indeed this Southern figure exceeds the per capita income of the North Central states, which historians have viewed as being quite prosperous, by 15 per cent. Table 8 gives no support at all to those who have argued that the Southern economy was stagnating. Quite the contrary, between 1840 and 1860 the Southern economy grew at an average of 1.7 per cent, a figure that was not only in excess of the national rate (1.3 per cent) but which also exceeded the rate of growth of the North Central states. It is of interest to note that per capita income in each of the three subregions of the South increased more slowly than the national average. Nevertheless the South's over-all growth rate exceeded the national average because of a redistribution of Southern population from the old South to the new South, particularly to Texas and the other rich states of the West South Central subregion.[37]

[37] The relationship between the rate of growth of per capita income in the South and in its subregions is given by the following:
By definition

$$Y = \Sigma \pi_i Y_i; \quad i = 1,2,3 \qquad (A)$$

where

Y = Southern per capita income
Y_i = The per capita income of the ith subregion
π_i = The ith subregion's share of Southern population

The impression that the economy of the ante-bellum South was thriving is further accentuated by the second set of figures in Table 8. Treating slaves as "intermediate goods" raises the 1860 per capita income of the South to $150. Thus the average income of free Southerners exceeded the national average of all free persons. In this case the

It can be shown that the rate-of-growth transformation of equation A is

$$\overset{*}{Y} \approx \Sigma \psi_i (\overset{*}{\pi_i} + \overset{*}{Y_i}) \qquad i = 1,2,3 \qquad (B)$$

where ψ_i is the ith subregion's share of Southern income and the variables capped by an asterisk represent the annual rate of growth of the uncapped variables.

Substituting the following values for the variables in equation B—the ψ_i are the estimated regional shares for the midyear of the period—we obtain

	ψ_i	$\overset{*}{\pi_i}$	$\overset{*}{Y_i}$
South Atlantic	0.41	−0.8	1.2
East South Central	0.38	0.0	1.3
West South Central	0.21	3.8	1.0

Hence

$$\overset{*}{Y} \approx 0.41(-0.8 + 1.2) + 0.38(0.0 + 1.3)$$
$$+ 0.21(3.8 + 1.0)$$

or

$$\overset{*}{Y} \approx 1.67$$

Thus about 30 per cent of the annual growth in Southern per capita income was due to the redistribution of population among subregions and the balance to the growth of per capita income within the subregions.

Of course equation B can also be applied to the relationship between the North and its subregions or to the relationship between national and regional rates of growth.

relative advantage of the South over the West is even more striking. The average income of free Southerners exceeded that of free Westerners by nearly 70 per cent. Treating slaves as intermediate goods also gives a fillip to the Southern growth rate. It becomes 1.8 per cent, more than one third greater than the growth rate of the rest of the nation.

The difference between the level and the rate of growth of Southern "total" and "free" per capita incomes points up the substantial stake of the free population in the continuation of the slave system. The exploitation of slaves raised the per capita income of the free Southern population by 45 per cent and the annual rate of growth of their per capita income by about 8 per cent. Nor were slave owners the only ones who appear to have benefited from slavery. For if it is true, as is frequently asserted, that the existence of slavery retarded the rate of growth of the South's free labor force, then free wage workers also benefited from the existence of slavery. In this connection it is interesting to note that rate of increase in the average money wages of laborers between 1850 and 1860 was greater in the South than in the nation as a whole. Moreover the 1860 money wage of Southern farm laborers and domestics compared favorably with the national averages of these groups [*19*, pp. 539–542]. These considerations may have some bearing on why it was that the cause of the Confederacy enjoyed such strong support among free Southerners.

The preceding estimates of the growth rates actually attained under slavery cast a shadow on the thesis that slavery retarded the growth of the Southern economy. Since 1.7 per cent is quite a high growth rate, one that has been achieved over sustained periods only by a few nations, the retardation thesis now suggests that in the absence of slavery the progress of the ante-bellum South would have surpassed virtually all recorded experience. Still, since we do not yet possess data for the entire ante-bellum era, it is possible that the Southern performance during 1840–1860 was unusually good. The arguments put forward to buttress the retardation thesis ought to be considered on their merit.

The emphasis which Phillips placed upon lagging capital formation has made this the standard argument for Southern retardation. Yet virtually all of the attempts to demonstrate that slavery retarded physical capital formation are flawed. It is frequently suggested the investment in slaves absorbed funds which otherwise would have been spent on physical capital. However the crude version of this hypothesis is clearly wrong. The ban on the external slave trade halted the drain of funds outside of the South. After 1807 purchases of slaves only involved transfers of funds between persons within the South. Consequently the hypothesis must be based on more complicated arguments. For example John E. Moes [*21*] has argued that while expenditures on rearing children are considered consumption to parents in a free society, such expenditures are considered part of capital formation in a slave society. Then slave societies which have the same savings-income ratio as nonslave societies would devote less to nonhuman capital. On the other hand, it is not untenable to hold that rather than causing a drain of funds, slavery probably increased the ability of Southerners to procure loan funds from the North and England by providing a marketable asset which could be used for collateral. Moreover if the ratio of savings to income was higher the more unequally income was distributed, a slave society might devote more to all types of capital formation, despite the effect stressed by Moes. Unfortunately the data needed to discriminate among these, and other, conflicting alternatives are not currently available.

Underlying many of the arguments in support of the proposition that slavery retarded investment is the assumption that to the extent that slavery increased the inequality of the income distribution, it reduced the savings rate. This assumption is probably false. While we lack the data needed to determine whether spending propensities were higher in the South than in the North, or whether the South had more or richer upper-income families,[38] we do know that large consumption expenditures by the rich do not necessarily imply low savings. In 1928, for example, the per capita consumption of the top 1 per cent of income earners in the United States population was about $5200, while that of the remaining 99 per cent was under $600. Certainly this is a pronounced difference, and given normal human reactions this could (and did) lead to discussions of wasteful expenditures by the rich. Yet in this year

---

[38] The skewness of the distribution of income in the South remains very much an issue of debate. See [*24*, *20*].

the top 1 per cent had a savings-income ratio of 43.3 per cent, and accounted for over 100 per cent of estimated personal savings.[39] This suggests the possibility that the effects of large consumption expenditures on Southern capital formation may be overstated. That conspicuous consumption which did exist was probably carried on mainly by planters who were wealthy by the standards of the times. Their conspicuous consumption probably absorbed only part of their incomes, and their savings rates probably exceeded the national average. Indeed given what we now know about the relationship between income and savings, it is quite possible that savings in the South were higher than they would have been with a less skewed income distribution.

The argument that the skewed income distribution made the Southern market too small to support a large-scale, modern manufacturing industry is also open to question. The fact that planters purchased large quantities of clothing and shoes for slaves from Northern firms suggests the existence of a large market for manufactured goods on plantations. It can, indeed, be argued that the products ordered by planters were more standardized and amenable to mass production techniques than would have been the situation if slaves were themselves the source of demand. Given the small optimal size of manufacturing plants in 1860, it seems probable that the Southern market could have been large enough to support an internal manufacturing sector, if the South's comparative advantage had been manufacturing. Estimates presented by Genovese of cash expenditures per person in the South suggest that the region could have supported over fifty cotton textile plants and more than two hundred boot and shoe establishments of Massachusetts size.[40]

Manufacturing appears to be the only area in which the ante-bellum South lagged seriously in physical capital formation. This lag seems to have been due to the fact that the South's comparative advantage was in agriculture rather than to the lack of a disposition to save. The South did not falter in the financing of railroad construction. The region had 31 per cent of the nation's railroad mileage, with per capita mileage only slightly below the national average.[41] This network was financed predominately by indigenous capital. While the track to area ratio was lower in the South than in the rest of the nation, the Southern economy was favored by an unusually favorable system of navigable streams and rivers. Nor were planters lagging behind the rest of the nation in the application of machinery to farming. Expenditures on farming implements and machinery per improved acre were 25 per cent higher in the seven leading cotton states than they were for the nation as a whole [*37*, pp. 196–197].

On the other hand, there is no doubt that the South lagged badly in human capital formation. The deficiency of education in the South has been well documented. The education of slaves was prohibited by law, while that of the whites was certainly below the rest of the nation.[42] However the effect of the low level of education on the efficiency of production in the ante-bellum era is yet to be determined. While there is no doubt that education has been one of the important inputs of the productive process in recent years, it does not necessarily follow that education would have increased the efficiency of slaves in the production of agricultural staples. Consequently it might well be that

---

[39] [*18*, p. 236]. This is the boldest comparison, but more typical years of the 1920s can be used to demonstrate the same point. In 1925, for example, the ratio of consumption per capita of the upper 1 per cent to that of the rest of the population was 9:1; yet the upper income groups had a savings-income ratio of 42.9 per cent, and accounted for 51 per cent of personal savings.

[40] Genovese estimates 1860 cash expenditure in Mississippi at about $25 per person [*13*, p. 169]. If that figure is taken as typical of the entire South, cash expenditure would account for about one fourth of Southern per capita income in that year. Making the extreme assumption that outside the South all income

went into cash expenditures, while the Southern share was only one fourth, and that expenditures on boots and shoes and cotton textiles were proportional to all cash expenditures, we can use the value of output of those sectors to estimate total Southern cash expenditures on the specific goods. Total value of output and average output per Massachusetts plant are from [*38*, pp. xxi and xxiii]. In 1860 there were 217 cotton textile plants and 1354 boot and shoe establishments in Massachusetts. While the calculation is crude, the estimates are probably too low rather than too high.

[41] [*34*, p. 79]. Similarly Allen Fenichel shows that in 1838 (the only ante-bellum year for which data exist) the South had 38.2 per cent of the nation's total capacity of steam power in manufacturing [*8*].

[42] See [*9*].

although the failure to educate the Southern population retarded economic growth during the post-Civil War era, it had little effect on the growth rate during the period under question.

III. CONCLUSION

Much work remains to be done on the economics of slavery. The question of how the Southern economy would have developed in the absence of the slave system has not yet been attacked in a systematic way. Nevertheless the work of the past decade has substantially altered the old interpretation of the economics of the ante-bellum era. The slaveholders who ruled Southern society were not stubbornly clinging to a dying economic system which deprived them of profits, prevented their economy from growing, and depressed the income of free men as well as slaves. However heavy the yoke of slavery was for Negroes, it produced considerable prosperity for free men. Not only was the average income of free Southerners high, but it was growing more rapidly than the average income of all the other regions of the nation, including that of the relatively industrialized Northeast. If it was a sense of duty that prevented slaveowners from releasing their slaves, they were well rewarded for their nobility. The rate of return, calculated on the cost of rearing slaves, probably exceeded the rate that could have been earned in alternative investments. The threats that hovered over the slave system were political rather than economic. Although it was a moral and political anachronism, slavery was nevertheless a vigorous economic system on the eve of the Civil War. It was a political crisis, not an economic one, that destroyed the American system of slavery.

MATHEMATICAL APPENDIX

We assume that the slave-using sector of agriculture may be described by a Cobb-Douglas production function

$$Q = AL^{\alpha_1}K^{\alpha_2}T^{\alpha_3}; \quad \alpha_1 + \alpha_2 + \alpha_3 = 1 \quad \text{(A.1)}$$

The marginal product of labor is then

$$\frac{\partial Q}{\partial L} = \alpha_1 \frac{Q}{L} = \alpha_1 AK^{\alpha_2}T^{\alpha_3}L^{-(\alpha_2+\alpha_3)} \quad \text{(A.2)}$$

The Rental Market

Since agriculture was a competitive industry, the annual gross rental price of a slave was equal to the value of the marginal physical product of a slave. When the slave-sector production function is defined by equation A.1, the demand curve for slave hires (including the reservation demand of owners) is[43]

$$H_g = \alpha_1 P_c QL^{-1} \quad \text{(A.3)}$$

The rate of growth transformation of equation A.3 is

$$\overset{*}{H}_g = \overset{*}{P}_c + \overset{*}{Q} - \overset{*}{L} \quad \text{(A.4)}$$

The Purchase Market

In purchasing a prime field hand, a slaveholder was acquiring an asset with a long expected life. Consequently the price that an investor would be willing to pay for that asset is equal to the discounted present value of the income to be derived from it. Thus

$$P_s = \sum_{t=1}^{n} \frac{R_t}{(1+i)^t} + \frac{V}{(1+i)^n} \quad \text{(A.5)}$$

In the case of investors who held on to slaves until their death, equation A.5 reduces to

$$P_s = \sum_{t=1}^{n} \frac{R_t}{(1+i)^t} \quad \text{(A.6)}$$

If slaveholders based their purchase decisions on the assumption that the net revenue in future years would be equal to the average earned over some past period, equation A.6 could be written as

$$P_s = \frac{R_e}{i}\left[1 - \frac{1}{(1+i)^n}\right] \quad \text{(A.7)}$$

---

[43] The annual gross hire rate includes not only the payment to the owner of the slave, but also the annual cost of maintaining the slave. Rental contracts required the lessee to provide the slave with food, shelter, clothing, and medical care. The net hire rate (H) is equal to the gross hire rate (H_g) minus the cost of maintaining the slave (M).

The net revenue from a slave is equal to the difference between gross revenue and maintenance costs. Hence an alternative form of equation A.7 is

$$P_s = \frac{(-M_e + \alpha_1 P_{ce} Q_e L_e^{-1}) X}{i} \quad \text{(A.8)}$$

The rate of growth transformation of equation A.8 is

$$\overset{*}{P}_s = \phi_1(\overset{*}{P}_{ce} + \overset{*}{Q}_e - \overset{*}{L}_e) - \phi_2 \overset{*}{M}_e - \overset{*}{i} + \overset{*}{X} \quad \text{(A.9)}$$

which reduces to

$$\overset{*}{P}_s = \phi_1 \overset{*}{H}_{ge} - \phi_2 \overset{*}{M}_e - \overset{*}{i} + \overset{*}{X} \quad \text{(A.10)}$$

and

$$\overset{*}{P}_s = \overset{*}{H}_e - \overset{*}{i} + \overset{*}{X} \quad \text{(A.11)}$$

The Rate of Growth of the Demand for Cotton

If the demand for, and supply of, cotton are given by equations A.12 and A.13, respectively

$$Q = DP_c^{-\varepsilon} \quad \text{(A.12)}$$

$$Q = SP_c^{\gamma} \quad \text{(A.13)}$$

then in equilibrium, the price of cotton will be

$$P_c = \left(\frac{D}{S}\right)^{1/(\gamma+\varepsilon)} \quad \text{(A.14)}$$

If we let the end period value of these variables be indicated by primes, then the ratio of the end-period to the base-period price of cotton is

$$\frac{P_c'}{P_c} = \frac{\left(\dfrac{D'}{D}\right)^{1/(\gamma+\varepsilon)}}{\left(\dfrac{S'}{S}\right)^{1/(\gamma+\varepsilon)}} \quad \text{(A.15)}$$

or

$$(1 + \overset{*}{P}_c) = \frac{(1 + \overset{*}{D})^{1/(\gamma+\varepsilon)}}{(1 + \overset{*}{S})^{1/(\gamma+\varepsilon)}} \quad \text{(A.16)}$$

Solving the last equation for $\overset{*}{D}$ yields

$$\overset{*}{D} = (1 + \overset{*}{P}_c)^{\gamma+\varepsilon}(1 + \overset{*}{S}) - 1 \quad \text{(A.17)}$$

If the supply curve is absolutely inelastic, $\gamma = 0$ and A.17 becomes

$$\overset{*}{D} = (1 + \overset{*}{P}_c)^{\varepsilon}(1 + \overset{*}{S}) - 1 \quad \text{(A.18)}$$

Table A1. Definition of Symbols

Q	=	output of the slave-using production process
L	=	input of labor (number of slaves)
L_f	=	input of labor measured in equivalent full hands
K	=	input of capital
T	=	input of land
A	=	the efficiency index of the production function
α_j	=	the output elasticity of the inputs; $\Sigma \alpha_j = 1$
P_c	=	the price of cotton
H	=	annual net hire rate of a slave
H_g	=	annual gross hire rate of a slave
P_s	=	price of a slave
R	=	the annual net revenue derived from a slave
V	=	the value of the slave when the owner sells him
i	=	the rate of return or rate of discount
n	=	the expected number of years that a slave will be held
M	=	the annual maintenance cost of a slave
X	=	$1 - 1/(1 + i)^n$
ϕ_1	=	ratio of the gross revenue derived from slaves to the net revenue in the base period
ϕ_2	=	ratio of the maintenance cost of slaves to the net revenue in the base period
ε	=	the elasticity of the demand for cotton
γ	=	the elasticity of the supply of cotton
E	=	the annual rental value of the land and equipment used by slaves
D	=	the shift term of the demand curve for cotton
S	=	the shift term of the supply curve for cotton
Y	=	per capita income
π	=	a subregion's share of regional population
ψ	=	a subregion's share of regional income
C	=	the price of the slave and the land and equipment that he used
λ_t	=	the probability that a slave would live through year t
k	=	the number of years an investor held a slave
*	=	an asterisk over a variable indicates the rate of growth of that variable
e	=	use of the subscript e indicates the expected value of that variable
t	=	a subscript or exponent designating a year

REFERENCES

1. Raymond C. Battalio and John H. Kagel, "The Structure of Ante-Bellum Southern Agriculture: South Carolina, A Case Study," *Agricultural History*, *44* (January, 1970), 25–38.
2. Guy S. Callender, ed., *Economic History of the United States*, New York, A. M. Kelley, 1965.
3. Alfred H. Conrad and John R. Meyer, "The Economics of Slavery in the Ante-Bellum South," *The Journal of Political Economy*, *66* (April, 1958), 95–130; reprinted in their book, *The Economics of Slavery and Other Studies in Econometric History*, Chicago, Aldine, 1964, pp. 43–92. (Page references in the text are to the book.) [Reprinted below as essay 25.]
4. Charles S. Davis, *The Cotton Kingdom in Alabama*, Montgomery, Alabama State Department of Archives and History, 1939.
5. Lance E. Davis, "Sources of Industrial Finance: The American Textile Industry," *Explorations in Entrepreneurial History*, *9* (April, 1957), 190–203.
6. Richard A. Easterlin, "Regional Income Trends, 1840–1950," Seymour Harris, ed., *American Economic History*, New York, McGraw-Hill, 1961, pp. 525–547. [Reprinted above as essay 4.]
7. Robert Evans, Jr., "The Economics of American Negro Slavery," Universities-National Bureau Committee for Economic Research, *Aspects of Labor Economics*, Princeton, Princeton University Press, 1962, pp. 185–243.
8. Allen H. Fenichel, "Growth and Diffusion of Power in Manufacturing, 1838–1919," Conference on Research in Income and Wealth, *Output, Employment, and Productivity in the United States After 1800* (Studies in Income and Wealth, vol. 30), New York, Columbia University Press, 1966, pp. 443–478.
9. Albert Fishlow, "The Common School Revival: Fact or Fancy?" Henry Rosovsky, ed., *Industrialization in Two Systems: Essays in Honor of Alexander Gerschenkron*, New York, John Wiley and Sons, 1966, pp. 40–67.
10. Ralph Betts Flanders, *Plantation Slavery in Georgia,* Chapel Hill, University of North Carolina Press, 1933.
11. James D. Foust and Dale E. Swan, "Productivity of Ante-Bellum Slave Labor: A Micro Approach," *Agricultural History*, *44* (January, 1970), 39–62.
12. Robert E. Gallman, "Gross National Product in the United States, 1834–1909," Conference on Research in Income and Wealth, *Output, Employment, and Productivity in the United States After 1800* (Studies in Income and Wealth, vol. 30), New York, Columbia University Press, 1966, pp. 3–76.
13. Eugene D. Genovese, *The Political Economy of Slavery*, New York, Pantheon Books, 1965.
14. Thomas P. Govan, "Was Plantation Slavery Profitable?" *The Journal of Southern History*, *8* (November, 1942), 513–535.
15. Thomas P. Govan, "Comments" [to Robert Evans, Jr., "The Economics of American Negro Slavery"], Universities-National Bureau Committee for Economic Research, *Aspects of Labor Economics*, Princeton, Princeton University Press, 1962, pp. 243-246.
16. Lewis C. Gray, *History of Agriculture in the Southern United States to 1860*, Gloucester, Mass., Peter Smith, 1958.
17. Sidney Homer, *A History of Interest Rates*, New Brunswick, Rutgers University Press, 1963.
18. Robert J. Lampman, *The Share of Top Wealth-Holders in National Wealth, 1922–56*, Princeton, Princeton University Press, 1962.
19. Stanley Lebergott, *Manpower in Economic Growth*, New York, McGraw-Hill, 1964.
20. Fabian Linden, "Economic Democracy in the Slave South: An Appraisal of Some Recent Views," *The Journal of Negro History*, *31* (April, 1946), 140–190.
21. John E. Moes, "The Absorption of Capital in Slave Labor in the Ante-Bellum South and Economic Growth," *The American Journal of Economics and Sociology, 20*, (October, 1961), 535–541.
22. Lewis W. Newton and Herbert P. Gambrell, *A Social and Political History of Texas*, Dallas, Turner Co., 1935.
23. Douglass C. North, *The Economic Growth of the United States, 1790–1860*, Englewood Cliffs, Prentice-Hall, 1961.
24. Frank Lawrence Owsley, *Plain Folk of the Old South*, Baton Rouge, Louisiana State University Press, 1949.
25. Ulrich B. Phillips, "The Economic Cost of Slaveholding in the Cotton Belt," *Political Science Quarterly*, *20* (June, 1905), 257–275.
26. Ulrich B. Phillips, *American Negro Slavery*, Baton Rouge, Louisiana State University Press, 1966.
27. Charles W. Ramsdell, "The Natural Limits of Slavery Expansion," *The Mississippi Valley Historical Review*, *16* (September, 1929), 151–171.
28. Robert R. Russel, "The General Effects of Slavery Upon Southern Economic Progress,"

The Journal of Southern History, 4 (February, 1938), 34–54.

29. Edward Saraydar, "A Note on the Profitability of Ante-Bellum Slavery," *The Southern Economic Journal*, 30 (April, 1964), 325–332.

30. Edward Saraydar, "Reply" [to Richard Sutch, "The Profitability of Ante-Bellum Slavery—Revisited"], *The Southern Economic Journal*, 31 (April, 1965), 377–383.

31. Kenneth Stampp, *The Peculiar Institution: Slavery in the Ante-Bellum South*, New York, Alfred A. Knopf, 1956.

32. Richard Sutch, "The Profitability of Ante-Bellum Slavery—Revisited," *The Southern Economic Journal*, 31 (April, 1965), 365–377.

33. Charles Sackett Sydnor, *Slavery in Mississippi*, New York, Appleton-Century, 1933.

34. George Rogers Taylor, *The Transportation Revolution, 1815–1860*, New York, Holt, Rinehart and Winston, 1951.

35. Peter Temin, "The Causes of Cotton-Price Fluctuations in the 1830's," *The Review of Economics and Statistics*, 49 (November, 1967), 463–470.

36. U.S. Bureau of the Census, *Historical Statistics of the United States, Colonial Times to 1957*, Washington, D.C., 1961.

37. U.S. Bureau of the Census, Eighth Census (1860), *Preliminary Report,* Washington, D.C., 1862.

38. U.S. Bureau of the Census, Eighth Census (1860), *Manufacturing,* Washington, D.C., 1865.

39. James L. Watkins, *Production and Price of Cotton for One Hundred Years,* U.S. Dept. of Agriculture (Misc. Series, Bulletin No. 9), Washington, D.C., 1895.

40. Harold Woodman, "The Profitability of Slavery: A Historical Perennial," *The Journal of Southern History*, 29 (August, 1963), 303–325.

41. Gavin Wright, *The Economics of Cotton in the Ante-Bellum South,* Unpublished doctoral dissertation, Yale University, 1969.

42. Yasukichi Yasuba, "The Profitability and Viability of Plantation Slavery in the United States," *The Economic Studies Quarterly*, 12 (September, 1961), 60–67. [Reprinted below as essay 26.]

25 THE ECONOMICS OF SLAVERY IN THE ANTE-BELLUM SOUTH

Alfred H. Conrad and
John R. Meyer

I. OBJECTIVES AND METHODS

The outstanding economic characteristics of Southern agriculture before the Civil War were a high degree of specialization and virtually exclusive reliance on a slave labor force. The large-scale, commercial dependence upon slave labor was to distinguish the ante-bellum South not only from other regions in its own time but from all regions at all other times in American agricultural history. Because of this unique historical status, ante-bellum Southern agriculture has been a subject for special historical attention. Above all else, attention has been focused upon the proposition that, even without external

Reprinted with revisions by permission from *The Journal of Political Economy, 66* (April, 1958), 95–122.

intervention, slavery would have toppled of its own weight. This allegation has its source in the assertions of slave inefficiency to be found in the writings of men who lived with slavery: American or English liberals like G. M. Weston, H. R. Helper, or J. E. Cairnes and Southern slaveowners who, in a religious, self-righteous age, could find every motive for the protection of the slave system except that it was personally profitable. The argument is to be found most strongly stated in the work of later Southern historians, especially C. W. Ramsdell and U. B. Phillips, who take the position that the Civil War, far from being an irrepressible conflict, was an unnecessary blood bath. They argue that slavery had reached its natural limits and that it was cumbersome and inefficient and, probably within less than a generation, would have destroyed itself. To the question why emancipation was not resorted to, they reply that slavery was for the Southerners an important (and evidently expensive) duty, part of their "unending task of race discipline." On the other side, Lewis Gray and Kenneth Stampp have strongly contested this view, contending that Southern plantation agriculture was at least as remunerative an economic activity as most other business enterprises in the young republic.

The evidence employed in this debate has been provided by the few, usually fragmentary, accounting records that have come down to us from early plantation activities. The opposing parties have arranged and rearranged the data in accordance with various standard and sometimes imaginary accounting conventions. Indeed, the debate over the value of the different constituent pieces of information reconstructs in embryo much of the historical development of American accounting practices. For example, virtually all the accounting valuation problems have been discussed with relation to the slave question, including the role and meaning of depreciation, the nature and accountability of interest charges, and the validity of distinctions between profits and payments of managerial wages. But despite the fact that the problem is ostensibly one in economic history, no attempt has ever been made to measure the profitability of slavery according to the economic (as opposed to accounting) concept of profitability. This paper is an attempt to fill that void.

Specifically we shall attempt to measure the profitability of Southern slave operations in terms of modern capital theory. In doing so, we shall illustrate the ways in which economic theory might be used in ordering and organizing historical facts. An additional methodological point is also made evident by this exercise, namely, how the very simple statistical concepts of range and central tendency as applied to frequency distributions of data can be employed in interpreting or moderating inferences from historical facts [See 8].

In executing these tasks, we must ask first what is it we are talking about and, second, whether we can say anything that can be proved or disproved. For example, we must ask what the slave economy was. Was it cotton culture? Was it cotton and sugar and tobacco? Was it all the ante-bellum Southern agriculture? In answering we shall define slavery in terms of two production functions. One function relates inputs of Negro slaves (and the materials required to maintain the slaves) to the production of the Southern staple crops, particularly cotton. The second function describes the production of the intermediate good, slave labor—slave-breeding, to use an emotionally charged term which has colored, even determined, most of the historical conclusions about this problem.

What do we mean by "efficiency"? Essentially we shall mean a comparison of the return from the use of this form of capital—Negro slaves—with the returns being earned on other capital assets at the time. Thus we mean to consider whether the slave system was being dragged down of its own weight; whether the allocation of resources was impaired by the rigidity of capitalized labor supply; whether Southern capital was misused or indeed drawn away to the North; and, finally, whether slavery must inevitably have declined from an inability of the slave force to reproduce itself.

The hypothesis that slavery was an efficient, maintainable form of economic organization is not a new one, of course. Nor are we, by one hundred years at least, among the first to conclude that Negro slavery was profitable in the ante-bellum South. What we do feel to be novel, however, is our approach. Postulating that American Negro slavery was characterized by two production functions, we argue that an efficient system developed in which those regions best suited to the production of cotton (and the other important staples) specialized in agricultural production, while the less productive land continued to produce slaves, exporting the increase to the staple-crop areas. It is this structure that we are examining.

We propose to test the hypothesis by putting appropriate values on the variables in the production functions and computing the rate of return over cost, the stream of income over the lifetime of the slave. This rate of return, the marginal efficiency of slave capital, must, in turn, be shown to be at least equal to the rate of interest currently available in the American capital markets. It is further necessary to show that appropriate markets existed to make this regional specialization possible and that slavery did not necessarily imply the disappearance or misallocation of capital. Evidence on the ability of the slave force to maintain itself numerically will be had as a corollary result. For these purposes it is necessary to obtain data on slave prices and cotton prices, the average output of male field hands and field wenches, the life-expectancy of Negroes born in slavery, the cost of maintaining slaves during infancy and other nonproductive periods, and, finally, the net reproduction rate and the demographic composition of the slave population in the breeding and using areas.

Looked upon simply as a staple-commodity agriculture, the Southern system must appear to have been burdened—possibly even to have been on the verge of collapse— under the weight of areas of inefficient, unprofitable farming. We submit that this view is in error and that the error arises from the failure to recognize that an agricultural system dependent upon slavery can be defined operationally only in terms of the production function for both the final good —in our case, cotton—and the production function for the intermediate good—Negro slaves. Considered operationally, in terms of a neoclassical two-region, two-commodity trade system, it must be seen that a slave system produces labor as an intermediate good. The profitability of the system cannot be decided without considering the system's ability to produce chattel labor efficiently.

II. THE ECONOMIC RETURNS ON SLAVEHOLDING

From the standpoint of the entrepreneur making an investment in slaves, the basic problems involved in determining profitability are analytically the same as those met in determining the returns from any other kind of capital investment. The acquisition of a slave represented the tying-up of capital in what has appropriately been called a roundabout method of production. Like the purchase of any capital, a slave purchase was made in the anticipation of gaining higher returns than are available from less time-consuming or capital-using methods. This model is perhaps particularly applicable in the present case, because slave investments, like the forests or wine cellars of classic capital theory, produced a natural increase with the passage of time.

Investment returns are properly computed by using the capital-value formula, $y = x_t / (1 + r)^t$, where y is the cost of the investment, x_t is realized return t years hence, and r is the internal rate of return or what Keynes called the marginal efficiency of capital. When returns are realized over a number of years, the total earnings of the capital can be found by simple summation in this formula. The criterion for a profitable investment is that the marginal efficiency exceeds the interest rate (in the Keynesian terminology). From this statement of the problem, it is obvious that the following information is needed to determine the profitability of slaveholding from the slaveholder's point of view: (a) the longevity of slaves; (b) the costs of slaves and any necessary accompanying capital investments; (c) the interest rate; and (d) the annual returns from slave productive activities, defined to include both field labor and procreation. We shall consider each of these in turn and then put the pieces together to determine the approximate profitability of slave investments.

A. Longevity of Slaves

Slave longevity corresponds, of course, to the period for which a slave investment was made. We shall limit attention here to the purchase of twenty-year-old Negroes in the immediate pre-Civil War era and we shall deal only with the typical or median life-expectancy for this group. These limits greatly simplify the problem and still include the vast majority of relevant cases.

There is a scarcity of good longevity data for the period, but it is known that in 1850 Negroes lived just about as long as whites in the two states for which acceptable data are available. The available figures are given in Table 1.[1] There is doubt about the quality of these estimates because they show Negroes in New England expecting a longer life than whites. This is not the case today, nor was it the case in 1900, when the first good data became available. Also, Negroes appear in this table to have had a longer life-expectancy in 1850 than they had fifty years later. Although surprising, this may be perfectly correct. Negroes could have received better care under slavery, because the plantation owners had an economic interest in keeping Negroes alive. Furthermore the Negro in the period after emancipation generally lacked the means to participate equally in the new medical advances, in contrast to his position of roughly equal medical care in the period before 1860.

Life-expectation at birth does not tell us much, of course, about the expectation of a twenty-year-old man. Actually there are no data on Negro life-expectancy at different age levels in the prewar period except for some imperfect estimates made by Sydnor for Mississippi slaves. Using the average reported age at death of those over the age of twenty who died in 1850, he estimated a life-expectancy of twenty-two years for a twenty-year-old Mississippi slave. This figure is probably low for two reasons. First, the estimating procedure tells more about life-expectancy in the years preceding 1850 than after, unless we make the dubious assumption that there was no advance in medical and dietary knowledge around the middle of the century. Second, estimates from deaths reported at the end of ten-year intervals and averaged back over the decade would tend to underestimate life-spans at the younger ages. Doubts about the quality of the Sydnor data are borne out by consideration of the Massachusetts life expectancy of 40.1 years for twenty-year-old males, white and Negro, in 1850.[2] Looking back at the data in Table 1, there is no reason to expect twenty-year-old Massachusetts

Table 1. Expectation of Life at Birth in Years for White and Colored Males, United States, 1850

State	White	Colored
Massachusetts	38.3	39.75
Maryland	41.8	38.47
Louisiana	—	28.89

Negroes to have a lower life-expectancy than Massachusetts whites, though both clearly lived longer than Southern Negroes of the period. Taking all these factors into account, an estimate of thirty to thirty-five years of life-expectancy seems most plausible for twenty-year-old Negroes working as prime cotton hands on Southern plantations in the period 1830–1850, and a thirty-year life-expectancy will generally be used in the succeeding calculations.

B. The Cost of Capital Investment

The capital investment in plantation operations included investment both in slaves and in the land and equipment on which the slaves worked. The price of slaves fluctuated widely, being subject to the waves of speculation in cotton. Furthermore the price depended, among other things, upon the age, sex, disposition, degree of training, and condition of the slave. In order to hold these variables roughly constant, we shall confine our present analysis to eighteen twenty-year-old prime field hands and wenches. Some summary data on slave prices were compiled by U. B. Phillips on the basis of available market quotations, bills of transactions, and reports of sales in most of the important slave markets of Georgia. His estimates of the best averages for several years between 1828 and 1860 are presented in Table 2 [*10*, p. 267]. On the basis of these data it would appear that both the median and the mean price for prime field hands were in the range of from $900 to $950 in the period 1830–1850. Because of the substantial price increases in the last ante-bellum decade, these averages would run substantially higher for the entire slave period after 1830; specifically, about $1100–$1200. Since the prices of field wenches usually averaged about $100–$150 less than those of hands, they were probably in a range of $800–$850 in the years 1830–1850 and between $900 and $1100 for the entire period 1830–1860.

---

[1] In Table 1, the Maryland figures are for slaves only; the Louisiana data for slaves and free together.

[2] It is worth noting that there is general agreement that labor on the rice and sugar plantations was sufficiently more arduous to reduce Negro longevity in such locations. Therefore the Louisiana estimates are probably inordinately pessimistic, and the Maryland figures are better estimates of conditions prevailing on the cotton plantations. This, in turn, means that the thirty-to-thirty-five-year estimates used below are, if anything, a little conservative or too low.

Table 2. Estimated Average Slave Prices in Georgia, Selected Years, 1828–1860

Year	Average Price of Prime Field Hands
1828	$ 700
1835	900
1837	1300
1839	1000
1840	700
1844	600
1848	900
1851	1050
1853	1200
1859	1650
1860	1800

As for the nonslave capital, by far the most important was the investment in land. Since the land values varied widely, depending on the quality of the soil and the type of agriculture pursued, experimental control on our calculations requires that attention be confined to cotton culture. The range in cotton-land prices in the period 1830–1850 is fairly well bracketed by the $6 per acre paid for poor upland pine land in Alabama and the $35–$40 per acre paid for cleared Mississippi alluvium. Such a range even encompasses the costs of new lands in the Southwest. Although such land was obtained for nominal original cost, the usual costs of clearing, draining, and otherwise preparing it plus the transportation of slaves and supplies would amount to something in the range of $20–$30 per acre. There was also variation in the number of acres needed per hand. Counting garden land and woodlots, as well as productive fields, the usual number of acres per field hand was between 15 and 35, the exact figure depending primarily on the quality of the land. This meant an original land investment per hand of somewhere between $90 and $1400 with $180–$600 encompassing the vast majority of instances.

The price per acre was, of course, related to the durability of the land, which immediately introduces a further dimension into the capital cost problem. Cotton lands lasted between ten and forty years, depending upon original quality and fertilization. In the land-rich, labor-scarce economy of the nineteenth-century United States, fertilization was a rare practice. Furthermore planters clearly had the choice between operating less capital intensively on low-durability land or more capital intensively on high-durability land. For example, poor Alabama pine land might be expected to last ten years and require 30–35 acres per hand; this meant that $180–$210 had to be reinvested every ten years to utilize the slave force properly. Assuming thirty-year slave longevity and an 8 per cent interest rate, the present value of the land investment for one slave's lifetime was $302–$350 for an upland-pine operation. On the alluvium, by contrast, the land would typically outlast the slave in usefulness; assuming, though, that both lasted the same number of years and that 16 acres of cleared and 10 of uncleared land (at $10 per acre) were used per hand, a total land investment of $660 per hand is indicated. This difference in value of the land investment was presumably a function of different yields. At any rate the typical case was probably halfway between these two, involving a land investment of about $450 per hand.

Similar problems arise in estimating the investment in plows, gins, wagons, cabins, and miscellaneous implements. Such investments ran about $25 per hand in original outlay and had to be renewed every fifteen years. This gives a total present value in such items (again on the assumption of thirty-year slave longevity and 8 per cent interest) of about $33. A small investment was required in work horses and oxen, but in this case the stock was likely to be self-replenishing, reducing the costs to interest on the investment at most. Putting all these capital costs together indicates that $1400–$1450 was a fair approximation of the typical or average total investment per male slave in terms of present values. The range ran from $1250 to $1650.

C. Interest Rate

Determining the relevant rate of interest—the rate with which the cotton-slave returns must be compared—is perhaps empirically the easiest and conceptually the most difficult of the tasks in computing the economic returns on slave investments. While there is a relative abundance of data on interest rates in this period, none corresponds exactly to the desired rate. In a strict conceptual sense, the relevant rate of interest is that which plantation owners or other investors in Southern agriculture could have earned on their money in other pursuits if slavery had gone out of existence. This is difficult to arrive at on the basis of historical evidence, since it assumes circumstances contrary to the facts. The closest substitute would be earnings on other investments that were *least* dependent upon cotton and Southern agriculture. Given the importance of cotton in the American economy prior to the Civil War and the general interdependence of economic systems, even in so primitive an economy as that of the United States in the first half of the nineteenth century, it is difficult to find any conceptually correct figures.

However from many disparate sources it seems safe to estimate that a wholesale withdrawal of capital from slave operations in Southern agriculture would not have depressed marginal investment returns in the prewar United States economy much below 4.5–5 per cent. Similarly it seems safe to conclude that the withdrawn capital could not have expected to earn returns much in excess of 8 per cent. Between these high and low estimates, a return of 6 per cent seems the most probable and, therefore, appropriate for comparison in our model.

D. Annual Returns

The appropriate return figure to enter in the capital equation is the net return on current account, or the difference between gross sales and all out-of-pocket expenses. The expense deduction is limited to out-of-pocket expenses, because all the book charges that complicate the usual accounting procedures are taken into account in the process of constructing the capital cost estimate.

Estimates of plantation expenses have been taken primarily from three excellent, exhaustive records of the available material: J. L. Watkins' *The Cost of Cotton Production* [*13*], Lewis C. Gray's *History of Agriculture in the Southern United States to 1860* [*5*], and Kenneth Stampp's *The Peculiar Institution* [*12*]. A reasonably thorough check of these secondary sources against some primary sources and against one another for consistency indicates that these surveys have been reliably and accurately made. A digest of the estimates is present in Table 3. The total figure of $20–$21 annual out-of-pocket slave maintenance costs will be used in subsequent calculations. These costs are to be substracted from the annual gross return figures on slave activities.

For a male field hand the returns considered will be limited to the sales of products realized from his field labor; in the case of a female hand, an addition must be made for the returns realized on the labor and sale of her children. Because of these basic differences in the production functions for the two sexes, they will be treated separately.

For the male field hand, limited to the returns on his field labor, the gross proceeds will depend on the price of cotton and the quantity of his annual output. The output, in turn, will be crucially dependent on the quality of the land on which the slave was employed and, to a much lesser degree, upon the quality and amount of capital goods with which he was equipped. The figures in Table 4 illustrate the possible variation in productivity per hand. These estimates agree with frequent statements in contemporary journals that in the typical case a prime field hand could be expected to raise from 3.5 to 4 bales per year. The maximum seems to have been 7–8 bales on the best lands, and 2–3 bales was the minimum on the poorest land.

The relevant price of cotton for valuing these yields is the net price realized at the

Table 3. Typical Annual Out-of-Pocket Costs of Maintaining and Working Prime Field Hands on Southern Plantations in the Period 1840–1860

A.	Food and clothing	
	(1) Out-of-pocket costs where most food was produced on plantation and most clothing was hand-sewn	$ 2.50–$ 3.46
	(2) Cash costs if purchased	$25.00–$40.00
	(3) Out-of-pocket costs where some ready-made clothing and meat, fish, and other food "delicacies" were purchased	$ 7.00–$10.00
B.	Medical care	$ 1.50–$ 2.00
C.	Taxes	$ .39–$ 1.20
D.	Supervision	$ 5.00–$15.00
	Total, based on means of the estimates above and option 3 under A	$20.00–$21.00

Table 4. Reported Yields Per Prime Field Hand

Location	Year	Bales Per Hand
South Carolina coastal	1849	4-1/3
Mississippi (De Soto County)	1849	4
Unidentified	1844	7
Alabama (Cherokee County)	1855	4
Mississippi (Vicksburg area)	1855	8
New Southwest land	1850s	5
South Carolina upland	1852	3
Texas	1859	10
Arkansas River	1859	7

farm (in order that price and cost data be comparable). This means that export prices at the major ports must be adjusted downward by the amount of freight, insurance, storage, drayage, and factor's commission charges that were properly chargeable to the planter. Estimates by Gray and Watkins are fully compatible, and a marketing cost of from 0.7 to 0.8 cent per pound appears to be properly deductible from the export price in determining the price f.o.b. farm [5; 13, pp. 38, 39].

The export price itself fluctuated widely over the period. As can be seen from Table 5, New Orleans cotton prices averaged almost

Table 5. Weighted Yearly Average Prices of Short-Staple Cotton (Usually Louisiana or Mississippi Middling or Second Grade) at New Orleans for the Crop Years 1830–1860

Year	Price	Year	Price	Year	Price
1830	8.4	1840	9.1	1850	11.7
1831	9.0	1841	7.8	1851	7.4
1832	10.0	1842	5.7	1852	9.1
1833	11.2	1843	7.5	1853	8.8
1834	15.5	1844	5.5	1854	8.4
1835	15.2	1845	6.8	1855	9.1
1836	13.3	1846	9.9	1856	12.4
1837	9.0	1847	7.0	1857	11.2
1838	12.4	1848	5.8	1858	11.5
1839	7.9	1849	10.8	1859	10.8
				1860	11.1
Decade Average Price	11.2		7.6		11.2

Table 6. Realized Returns on Prime Field Hands Under Various Hypothesized Conditions

Case	Present Value of Capital Outlay Per Hand	Yield Per Hand (Bales)	Average Net Farm Price (Cents)	Approximate Internal Rate of Return (Per Cent)
1.	$1350–$1400	3-3/4	7	4.5
2.	$1350–$1400	3-3/4	8	5.2
3.	$1350–$1400	3-3/4	9	6.5
4.	$1600	4-1/2	7	5.0
5.	$1600	4-1/2	8	7.0
6.	$1600	4-1/2	9	8.0
7.	$1250–$1300	3	7	2.2
8.	$1250–$1300	3	8	3.9
9.	$1250–$1300	3	9	5.4
10.	$1700	7	7	10.0
11.	$1700	7	8	12.0
12.	$1700	7	9	13.0

50 per cent higher in the thirties and fifties than they did in the depressed forties. Even in the forties, however, the export price level was sufficient to insure an average net farm price of not much less than 6.5 cents. Since prices at any given port were usually equal to the Liverpool price minus ocean shipping rates, the New York and Mobile prices were generally somewhat higher. Taking all this into consideration, 7–8 cents seems a realistic and conservative estimate of the average realized farm price for the whole period.

Finally, the price, productivity, and capital cost estimates must be combined in order to compute the actual profitability of investments in male slave labor for cotton production. Capital costs must be included in the computations, since the present value of the capital outlay will depend, as was previously shown, upon the rate of return. In lieu of a single computation, several cases involving different capital outlays, yields per hand, and realized farm prices have been constructed; the results are given in Table 6.[3] Cases 1, 2, and 3 are the most typical; cases 4, 5, and 6 represent the situation on somewhat better land. These first six cases, with returns ranging between 4 1/2 and 8 per cent, encompass the majority of ante-bellum cotton plantation operations. Cases 7, 8, and 9 represent the minimum of profitability, or what might be expected on poor upland pine country or the worked-out lands of the Eastern seaboard. By contrast, cases 10, 11, and 12 show the upper range of profitability which was realized on the best lands of the new Southwest, the Mississippi alluvium, and the better South Carolina and Alabama plantations.[4]

---

[3] No allowance has been made in these computations for the expenses of maintaining slaves in their dotage. This does not appear to be a serious omission. Generally speaking, slaves were considered to be virtually fully productive in field labor until reaching their fifty-fifth year, which corresponds to the average life expectancy on the purchase of a twenty-year-old slave. Furthermore, the direct out-of-pocket costs of simply maintaining a slave were only $10–$15, figures considerably below productive value in field work. Given the possibility of specialized use of older labor in such occupations as gardening, nursery operations, and supervision, it seems doubtful if many slaves lived long enough to be economic drains on current account.

[4] A purist may ask how different returns can be realized in what is ostensibly the same type of economic activity in a relatively competitive industry. The question overlooks the fact that it took a much

The calculations in Table 6 represent an estimate of potential returns for the relatively simple production activities of prime field hands. With the female hand or prime field wench the situation becomes much more complex: in addition to her productivity, the productivity of her children and the returns realized on their sale must be considered. Similarly the extra cost of maintaining the children and the maternity and nursery costs associated with their birth must also be counted.

To make the calculations in this rather complex situation manageable, the following assumptions will be made:

1. Each prime field wench produced five to ten marketable children during her lifetime. (The computations for the ten-child or upper-limit case are shown in Table 7, while those for the lower limit of five children are shown in Table 8.) Furthermore we assume that successful pregnancies were spaced two years apart. It must be recognized that these figures represent assumptions more about what was achievable than about actual happenings. Slave infant mortality data are too poor to permit inferences about the latter.

2. The prime field wench was one half to two thirds as productive as a prime field hand when she was actually at work in the field. This estimate is based on the fact that when prime field hands and wenches were hired out, the hiring rate on the latter was usually one half to two thirds the hiring rate on the former. Thus it is assumed that the market hiring rate reflects the relative productivity of the two sexes. In addition, adjustments must be made for the time lost by the female during pregnancy and postnatal period. It is assumed here that three months' productive field time was lost for each successful pregnancy; the entire deduction has been made in the year in which the successful birth took place, despite the fact that it would probably be more realistic to assume that one month and a half was lost on each unsuccessful as well as each successful pregnancy. This allowance for "lost time" is probably too generous, since the only births that really cost any important productive field time were

---

larger initial outlay to attain productive situations like those in cases 10–12. This is all the more true since the capital outlay in these cases would be concentrated at the start of the undertaking, while in cases 7–9 some of the outlay would be delayed ten or fifteen years until the land wore out.

those occurring during the peak agricultural seasons, planting and picking times.

3. The wench's children began to be productive in field labor at age six, with the males becoming self-sustaining by age nine (that is, they then earned the adult maintenance charge of $20 per year), while females became self-sustaining by age thirteen. This can be represented by letting male productivity go up $5 every year between ages six and nine and letting female productivity increase by $2.50 for every year between the ages of six and thirteen. These rates are in keeping with the previously stated principle that females were roughly half as productive in field labor as males. After reaching a self-sustaining status at these ages, it is further assumed that their children's productivity continued to rise linearly until the children reached their full adult productivity at age eighteen; thus, male productivity is assumed to rise $10 per year between ages nine and eighteen and the female productivity $5 per year between ages thirteen and eighteen.

4. The typical wench had as many male as female children. For purposes of computation, the productivity, sales price, and other data for the two sexes have been averaged. For example, the final sales price of a typical child is assumed to be $875, halfway between the average price of $825 for prime field wenches and the average price of $925 for prime field hands.

5. Nursery costs were about $50 per successful pregnancy.

Using these assumptions, hypothetical annual returns for a typical prime field wench can be determined; such calculations are shown in Tables 7 and 8. In constructing these tables, it was assumed that the prime field wench and her children worked on land that returned 3.75 bales of cotton per year for every prime male hand employed; that is, the land is of approximately average fertility. Also, a 7.5-cent net farm price for cotton has been used. The first successful pregnancy has been assumed to occur in the second year after the prime field wench is purchased; further successful pregnancies occur at regular two-year intervals. The children were sold at age eighteen, and the annual maintenance cost per child was assessed at the rate of $10 per year for one–six-year-olds, $15 per year for seven–twelve-year-olds, and $20 per year, the full adult maintenance cost, for those age thirteen and over. The maternity costs have been included

in the annual charge for the children's upkeep; similarly, the $16 decline every other year for the first few years in the wench's own field returns represents the allowance for time lost because of pregnancy. Rates of returns were computed on the streams of net returns shown in the far right-hand columns of the tables on the assumption that the total investment in the prime field wench, land, and equipment amounts to $1200–$1300, figures which would appear to be very good averages. A rate of return of 8.1 per cent was thus obtained for the mother bearing ten children and a return of 7.1 per cent for the mother with five children.

These figures are, of course, somewhat higher than those calculated for the prime field hands. A proper working of the market mechanism would suggest that the attainable returns on the two sexes should be approximately equal. That is, the price differential between males and females should be such that the rate of return on the two types of investment turns out to be roughly equal in the typical or average case. The question therefore arises why a somewhat higher estimated return is given for the female.

Several answers can be made to this question. First, the difference between the estimated returns for the two sexes may arise because it probably took a somewhat higher return on the females to attract capital investment into that type of productive activity. Slave-breeding and slave-trading were not generally considered to be high or noble types of activity for a Southern gentleman. Indeed many plantation owners would stoop to all sorts of subterfuge to disguise the fact that they were engaging in any part of the slave trade or breeding operations. Second, the investment in the female was a longer-term affair; from Tables 7 and 8 it is apparent that the bulk of the returns on a female were realized twenty or more years after the investment was made, when the children had grown to marketable ages. To the extent that more distant developments are more uncertain, investments in female slaves could be expected to demand a higher return. Finally, the over-all average price of prime field wenches quoted from Phillips may be too low for proved "childbearers"; from contemporary comments, a female who had proved herself fertile was worth more than a female who had yet to bear her first child.

But these qualifications do not change the principal conclusion that slavery was

Table 7. Annual Returns on a Prime Field Wench Investment (Working on Land Which Yielded 3.75 Bales Per Prime Male Field Hand, Assuming a 7.5-Cent Net Farm Price for Cotton and Ten "Salable" Children Born to Every Wench)

Year from Purchase Date	Personal Field Returns	Child Field Returns	Child Sale Returns	Personal Upkeep	Child Upkeep	Net Returns
1	$ 56	$ —	$ —	$20	$ —	$ 36
2	40	—	—	20	50	− 30
3	56	—	—	20	10	26
4	40	—	—	20	60	− 40
5	56	—	—	20	20	16
6	40	—	—	20	70	− 50
7	56	—	—	20	30	6
8	40	3.75	—	20	80	− 56.25
9	56	7.50	—	20	45	− 1.50
10	40	15.00	—	20	95	− 50.00
11	56	22.50	—	20	60	− 1.50
12	40	37.50	—	20	110	− 52.50
13	56	52.50	—	20	75	13.50
14	40	75.00	—	20	130	− 35.00
15	56	97.50	—	20	95	47.50
16	40	127.50	—	20	150	− 2.50
17	56	157.50	—	20	115	78.50
18	40	195.00	—	20	165	55.00
19	56	232.50	—	20	130	134.30
20	40	195.00	875	20	170	920.00
21	56	232.50	—	20	130	138.50
22	56	195.00	875	20	120	986.00
23	56	232.50	—	20	120	148.50
24	56	195.00	875	20	110	996.00
25	56	232.50	—	20	110	158.00
26	56	195.00	875	20	100	1006.00
27	56	232.50	—	20	100	168.00
28	56	187.50	875	20	90	1008.50
29	56	225.00	—	20	90	171.00
30	56	180.00	875	20	80	1011.00
31	—	210.00	—	—	80	130.00
32	—	157.50	875	—	60	972.50
33	—	180.00	—	—	60	120.00
34	—	120.00	875	—	40	955.00
35	—	135.00	—	—	40	95.00
36	—	67.50	875	—	20	922.50
37	—	75.00	—	—	20	55.00
38	—	—	875	—	—	875.00

apparently about as remunerative as alternative employments to which slave capital might have been put. Large or excessive returns were clearly limited to a few fortunate planters, but apparently none suffered excessively either. This general sharing in the prosperity was more or less guaranteed, moreover, if proper market mechanisms existed so that slaves could be bred and reared on the poorest of land and then be sold to those owning the best. Slavery in the immediate ante-bellum years was, therefore, an economically viable institution in virtually all areas of the South as long as slaves could be expeditiously and economically transferred from one sector to another.

III. REPRODUCTION, ALLOCATION, AND SLAVE MARKETS

It thus remains to be determined whether an efficient supply mechanism—efficient in both its generative and its allocative functions—

Table 8. Annual Returns on a Prime Field Wench Investment (Working on Land Which Yielded 3.75 Bales Per Prime Male Field Hand, Assuming a 7.5–Cent Net Farm Price for Cotton and Five "Salable" Children Born to Every Wench)

Year from Purchase Date	Personal Field Returns	Child Field Returns	Child Sale Returns	Personal Upkeep	Child Upkeep	Net Returns
1	$ 56	$ —	$ —	$20	$ —	$ 36
2	40	—	—	20	50	− 30
3	56	—	—	20	10	26
4	40	—	—	20	60	− 40
5	56	—	—	20	20	16
6	40	—	—	20	70	− 50
7	56	—	—	20	30	6
8	40	3.75	—	20	80	− 56.25
9	56	7.50	—	20	45	− 1.50
10	40	15.00	—	20	95	− 50.00
11	56	22.50	—	20	60	− 1.50
12	56	37.50	—	20	60	13.50
13	56	52.50	—	20	65	23.50
14	56	75.00	—	20	65	46.00
15	56	97.50	—	20	75	58.50
16	56	127.50	—	20	75	88.50
17	56	157.50	—	20	85	108.50
18	56	191.25	—	20	85	142.25
19	56	225.00	—	20	90	171.00
20	56	180.00	875	20	75	1016.00
21	56	210.00	—	20	75	171.00
22	56	157.50	875	20	60	1008.50
23	56	180.00	—	20	60	156.00
24	56	120.00	875	20	40	991.00
25	56	135.00	—	20	40	131.00
26	56	67.50	875	20	20	958.50
27	56	75.00	—	20	20	91.00
28	56	—	875	20	—	911.00
29	56	—	—	20	—	36.00
30	56	—	—	20	—	36.00

existed in the ante-bellum South. That the slave force might reproduce itself was not sufficient; there must also have been a capital market capable of getting the labor to the areas where production was expanding if slavery was to be profitable. It will be useful to introduce the secondary propositions by stating several arguments which together form the orthodox opposition to the present hypothesis, the arguments follow in every case accompanied by a citation as a talisman against any possible charge that we are setting up straw men: (1) slaves are notoriously inefficient and unwilling workers [2, pp. 44–50; 9, pp. 100–110; 7, pp. 107–108]; (2) slave property, unlike wage labor, must be supported in the years before and after the slave is economically productive [11, pp. 174–175]; (3) slaveholding absorbed planta-

tion earnings [10]; (4) slave economies are constantly threatened by decline because they cannot in general maintain the number of slaves [7, pp. 111–113]; and (5) capitalization of the labor force inhibits the efficient allocation of labor [4, p. 71].

The first and second of these arguments are implicitly tested in the computation of the rate of return on slave capital. We are not concerned with efficiency per se, however that might be measured, or with the efficiency of slaves as opposed to free white laborers. The more sophisticated version of this efficiency argument—that slave ineptness forced the planters to use a particularly wasteful form of agriculture—is probably untestable because of the difficulties of identification when impetus or motives are being considered. It might be suggested as a partial answer, however, that extensive farming was not peculiarly a characteristic of slave agriculture or even of plantation cotton culture. It was common to all North American colonial agriculture and, as late as the end of the nineteenth century, was reputed to be characteristic of farming in the Northwest wheat lands. It is, generally, a salient feature of agriculture where labor is scarce relative to land. But insofar as slaves were inefficient, the inefficiency must be reflected in the returns computed in our model. Similarly, the costs of maintaining slaves in infancy and dotage are accounted for in our cost of production.

The third argument—that the South lost from the payment of interest and the constant enhancement of prices (and, therefore, overcapitalization of the labor force)—rests in part upon two misapprehensions, attributable to U. B. Phillips: (1) that capitalization involves a net loss through the payment of interest and (2) that slaves were, somehow, a fictitious form of wealth. We have already shown that slave capital earned returns at least equal to those earned by other contemporary forms of capital. For the overcapitalization part of the argument, it remains to be shown that slave prices did not run away from cotton values.

The last two of the assertions state the negative of our principal secondary hypothesis, which is that an efficient market system existed for the supply of slaves to the rapidly growing cotton industry of the Southwest from the exhausted land of the Old South. It will be shown below that the slave population, in all but the Louisiana sugar area, more than reproduced itself. It will be further shown that the border states were not depleted to provide for Western needs, but that only the natural increase was being exported. Finally, avoiding the emotion-wracked testimony of time, we will attempt to demonstrate the existence of regional specialization and an efficient market by comparing the demographic composition of the cotton and border states and by examining the price behavior in the market for Negro slaves.

A. Reproduction of the Slave Labor Force

The history of slavery is full of examples of slave economies which could not reproduce their population and collapsed because of a failure of supply. Frequently, as in the Roman case, the supply was dependent upon a steady flow of military prisoners. The Augustan peace and the stabilization of the borders of the empire are credited with the decline of Roman slavery for this reason. Similarly, the labor supply in the Caribbean sugar islands could be maintained only by importation. It is generally argued that slavery disappeared from Jamaica because of the inability of the slave population to reproduce itself once the slave trade had been closed and not because of abolition in 1834.

By contrast, the ante-bellum cotton-slave economy of the Southern states managed to maintain and allocate its labor supply by a system of regional specialization which produced slaves on the worn-out land of the Old South and the border states for export to the high yield cotton land of the Mississippi and Red River valleys. For the whole nation the Negro rate of increase in the six decades before the Civil War was only slightly below the rate for the white population; for most of the period, the slave rate was very much above that for free Negroes. In the South the disparity between Negro and white rates of increase is in favor of the Negro rate; considering the relative rates of immigration of whites and Negroes after the first decade of the nineteenth century, the discrepancy in natural increase is even more striking. The evidence in Table 9 does not admit of any doubt that the slave population was capable of producing a steady supply of labor for the plantation economy.

B. Slave Markets and Allocation

The more important issue, however, is whether or not the slave force could be allocated efficiently. The natural rate of increase was more than sufficient in the Old South to meet the needs of agriculture in the region, but in the West it was less than sufficient to meet the demands for increased cotton production. By direct export and by the migration of planters with their work forces, the Eastern areas supplied the needs of the Southwest. In every decade before the Civil War the increase of slaves in the cotton states was much above, and in the Atlantic and border states much below, the rate of increase for the whole slave population. Indeed, in the decades ending in 1840 and 1860 the net rate of population increase in the Old South was only slightly above the level sufficient to maintain the population at a constant level, 4.5 per cent and 7.1 per cent (see Table 10).

Table 9. Percentage Decennial Increase in White and Negro Population, 1790–1860

Decade Ending	TOTAL	WHITE	NEGRO		
			Total	Slave	Free
1800	35.1	35.8	32.3	28.1	82.2
1810	36.4	36.1	37.5	33.1	71.9
1820	33.1	34.2	28.6	29.1	25.3
1830	33.5	· 33.9	31.4	30.6	36.8
1840	32.7	34.7	23.4	23.8	20.9
1850	35.9	37.7	26.6	28.8	12.5
1860	35.6	37.7	22.1	23.4	12.3

Table 10. Percentage Rate of Population Increase, by Race, in the Cotton and Border States, 1790–1860

Decade Ending	COTTON STATES		BORDER STATES	
	White	Negro	White	Negro
1800	42.9	47.4	27.9	24.4
1810	37.5	61.3	23.5	23.4
1820	38.8	48.0	19.5	15.5
1830	40.0	46.8	19.0	14.0
1840	31.3	37.6	21.1	4.5
1850	34.1	35.6	34.5	11.0
1860	27.6	29.0	39.2	7.1

From 1790 to 1850 the increase of slaves in the Atlantic states was just 2 per cent per annum, while in the Gulf states (including Florida), Arkansas, and Tennessee the rate was 18 per cent per annum. A rough but probably conservative estimate of the export from the selling states between 1820 and 1860 is given by W. H. Collins. Taking the difference between the average natural increase and the actual rate in the selling states, Collins arrived at the following estimates:[5]

1820–1830	124,000
1830–1840	265,000
1840–1850	146,000
1850–1860	207,000

[5] [3, chap. iii] In the first decade the selling states include Virginia, Maryland, Delaware, North Carolina, Kentucky, and the District of Columbia; the buying states are assumed to be South Carolina, Georgia, Alabama, Mississippi, Tennessee, and Missouri. In 1830 Florida and in 1850 Texas were added to the buying group. Tennessee, Missouri, and North Carolina are very uncertain assignments, since these states were far from homogeneous slave-marketing areas; some parts imported, while other parts exported during the period. (Cf. [1, chap. xviii] for similar estimates, consistent with those given by Collins.)

Collins estimated that at least three fifths of the removals from the border states were due to emigration to the Southwest rather than to export. While this has little bearing upon the issue of allocative efficiency, it does have significance for the corollary assertion that the slaveowners of the border states, consciously or unconsciously, were engaged in a specialized breeding operation, producing chattel labor for the growing Southwest. In 1836 the *Virginia Times* estimated that "of the number of slaves exported [from Virginia], not more than one third have been sold, the others being carried by their masters, who have removed." Ruffin supposed that the annual sale in 1859 "already exceeded in number all the increase in slaves in Virginia by procreation." Bancroft goes beyond these estimates and states that "in the 'fifties, when the extreme prejudice against the interstate traders had abated and their inadequate supplies were eagerly purchased, fully 70 per cent of the slaves removed from the Atlantic and the border states to the Southwest were taken after purchase or with a view to sale, that is, were the objects of slave trading." Whatever the accuracy of these several estimates, which range from two fifths to four

Table 11. Slave Population by Age (Per Cent)

Age (Years)	1860			1850		
	Total	Selling States	Buying States	Total	Selling States	Buying States
Under 15	44.8	45.6	43.8	44.9	45.6	44.3
15–19	11.4	11.5	11.4	11.1	11.3	11.0
20–29	17.6	16.5	18.9	18.0	17.0	18.9
30–39	11.7	10.7	11.8	11.3	10.5	12.1
20–49	36.4	34.4	38.1	36.4	34.6	38.1
50 and over	7.5	8.5	6.7	7.5	8.5	6.6

fifths of total exports of slaves from the border and the Atlantic states, it is clear that sales of slaves provided an important capital gain for the exporting states. There is ample documentary evidence that planters in the Old South were aware of this, that some welcomed it and depended upon it, and that others were fearful of its effect upon the agriculture of the area and upon the tenability of slavery. Some spoke frankly about Virginia as a "breeding state," though the reply to such allegations was generally an indignant denial. Whether systematically bred or not, the natural increase of the slave force was an important, probably the most important, product of the more exhausted soil of the Old South.

The existence of such specialization is evident in the demographic composition of the cotton and breeding areas and in the price behavior in the markets for slaves. Table 11 demonstrates that the selling states contained, in 1850 and 1860, a greater proportion of children under fifteen and a substantially greater proportion of slaves above the age of fifty than did the buying states. While the disproportions are not great enough to characterize the selling states as a great nursery, the age composition is in the direction which our hypothesis would lead one to expect. The relationship between the prices of men and women in the slave market, when compared with the ratio of hiring rates for male and female field hands, gives an even stronger indication that the superior usefulness of females of breeding age was economically recognized. The relative hiring rates for men and women in 1860, shown in Table 12, can be taken as a measure of their relative values in the field.[6]

---

[6] The rates are quoted in [6, p. 90]. Three Virginia newspaper quotations give ratios ranging between 2 and 2.5, supporting these estimates. There is a possible

Table 12. Annual Hiring Rates for Male and Female Slaves (Including Rations and Clothing) by States, 1860

State	Men	Women	Ratio (Men:Women)
Virginia	$105	$ 46	2.28
North Carolina	110	49	2.25
South Carolina	103	55	1.87
Georgia	124	75	1.65
Florida	139	80	1.74
Alabama	138	89	1.55
Mississippi	166	100	1.66
Louisiana	171	120	1.43
Texas	166	109	1.52
Arkansas	170	108	1.57
Tennessee	121	63	1.92

To compare to these rates we have purchase prices of male and female slaves, in the same markets, in 1859 and 1860. The purchase prices should reflect the relative usefulness of the sexes for field work. More than this, however, if there is any additional value to slave women—for breeding purposes, presumably—there should be a premium in the form of a narrower price differential than is found in the hiring rates. The prices are shown in Table 13. Whenever possible, 1860 is used; wherever necessary, 1859. Table 13 includes age designations and, when available, a description of the grade or class represented in the average price. This evidence is a striking confirmation of the validity of the model. In every case the purchase-price differential is narrower than the hiring-rate differential. The price structure clearly reflects the added value

---

overestimate in these ratios, if they are to be used to infer relative usefulness in the field, since some allowance was probably made for time lost for delivery by pregnant females. No evidence has been found on this point, however.

Table 13. Selected Prices of Male and Female Slaves, 1859 and 1860

State (Year)	Age	Condition	Male Price	Female Price	Ratio
Virginia (1859)	17–20	Best	$1350–$1425	1275–1325	1.07
South Carolina	—	Prime	1325	—	1.03
	—	Wench	—	1283	
South Carolina (1859)	—	Field Hand	1555	—	.91
	—	Girl	—	1705	
Georgia	21	Best field hand	1900	—	.88
	17	(9 mo. inf.)	—	2150	
Georgia (1859)	—	Prime, young	1300	—	1.04
	—	Cotton hand houseservant	—	1250	
Alabama (1859)	19	—	1635	—	1.37
	18,18,8	—	—	1193	
Mississippi	—	No. 1 field hand	1625	1450	1.12
Texas	21,15	—	2015	1635	1.23
Texas (1859)	17,14	—	1527	1403	1.09

of females due to their ability to generate capital gains. It is especially interesting in this regard to note that the price ratios in Virginia and South Carolina, the two breeding states represented in the list, show practically no differential. This evidence clearly shows that the Old South recognized in the market the value of its function as the slave-breeding area for the cotton-raising West.

C. The "Overcapitalization" of the Labor Force

The aspect of slave economics that causes the most confusion and outright error is that which relates to the capitalization, and, in the ante-bellum Southern case, the presumed overcapitalization, of slave labor. Phillips speaks of an "irresistible tendency to overvalue and overcapitalize" and argues that slaveholding had an unlimited capacity for absorbing the planters' earnings through the continual payment of interest and the enhancement of prices. For the Cotton Belt this was presumably aggregated into a continuous public drain of wealth, first, to England and New England and, later, to the upper South [10, pp. 271 ff.]. Moreover a series of writers from Max Weber down to the most recent theorists of economic growth have argued that capitalization tends to rigidify the pattern of employment. "Free labor is necessary to make free transfers of labor possible. A production organization cannot be very flexible if it has to engage in the purchase or sale of slaves every time it changes its output" [4, p. 71]. But this is really a question of how good

the market is; no one, after all, claims that manufacturing is made suicidally inflexible by the fact that expanding sectors must buy the capitalized future earnings of machinery. There are three issues to be distinguished in this argument: first, the alleged tendency toward overcapitalization; second, the inflexibility of chattel labor and the difficulty of allocating it, geographically and industrially; and third, the loss of wealth.

First, was the Southerner his own victim in an endless speculative inflation of slave prices? The assertion of an irresistible tendency to overvalue and overcapitalize must mean that he was so trapped, if it means anything. Phillips answered the question by comparing the price of cotton with the price of prime field hands, year by year. He found, or believed he found, a permanent movement toward overcapitalization inherent in American slaveholding. But speculative overexpansion is capable of reversal; from the inflation of 1837 to the bottom of the depression of 1845, slave prices fell as sharply as cotton prices. If the rise from that lower turning point is a demonstration of speculative mania, it was a mania solidly based on the increase in the value of the crop per hand, owing to the concentration of production in more fertile areas, the greater efficiency of the American-born slaves, lowered transportation costs, and the development of new high yield varieties of cotton from the fourth decade of the century on. Finally, the choice of the initial period in Phillips' analysis exaggerates the decline in cotton prices relative to the price of slaves: at the turn of the century the

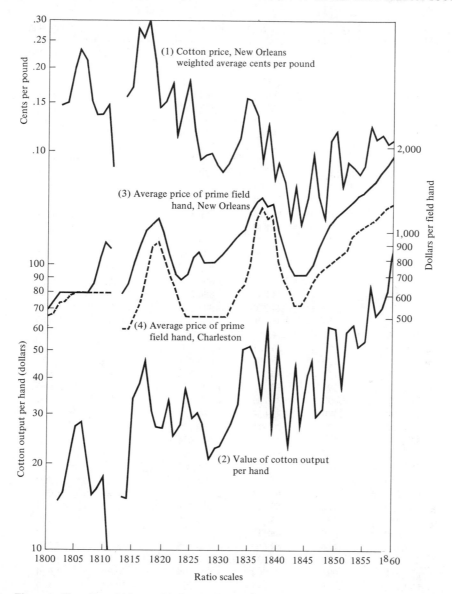

Figure 1. Slave Population and Prices and the Value of Cotton Production, 1802–1860.

demand for cotton was increasing rapidly, supporting remarkably high prices, while the unrestricted African slave trade kept domestic slave prices well below the level that might be expected in view of the level of profits. Table 14 and Figure 1 demonstrate the relationships among slave prices, cotton prices, and the value of cotton output per slave (of field work age, ten to fifty-four). Several things become clear in this comparison. To begin, the relationship between slave and cotton prices is significant for Phillips' purposes only if there is no increase in productivity. While he is struck by the fact that slave prices rise more rapidly than cotton prices in the long upswing starting in the

early 1840s, it is equally striking to observe that (New Orleans) slave prices rose about one and one-half times between the low point in 1843–1845 to 1860, while values of cotton production per hand rose more than three times from the low in 1842. Furthermore it would appear that slave prices fluctuate less than do cotton prices. This and the less clear-cut lag of the slave prices make it difficult to accept the image of unwary planters helplessly exposing themselves in a market dominated by speculators. It would make more sense to argue simply that the rising trend of slave prices coupled with a growing slave population is in and of itself a strong evidence of the profitability of slavery.

Table 14. Value of Cotton Production and Slave Population, 1802–1860, New Orleans Prices

Year	Crop (Thousands of Pounds)	Average Price (Cents Per Pound)	Value (Thousands)	No. of Slaves Aged 10–54 Years	Crop Value Per Slave	Price of Prime Field Hand	Crop Value Per Hand Per Dollar Slave Price
1802	55,000	0.147	$ 8,085	550,708	$ 14.68	$ 600	.02
1803	60,000	.150	9,000	568,932	15.82	600	.03
1804	65,000	.196	12,740	587,157	21.70	600	.04
1805	70,000	.233	16,310	605,381	26.94	600	.05
1806	80,000	.218	17,440	623,606	27.97	600	.05
1807	80,000	.164	13,120	641,831	20.44	600	.03
1808	75,000	.136	10,200	660,055	15.45	640	.02
1809	82,000	.136	11,152	678,280	16.44	780	.02
1810	85,000	.147	12,495	696,505	17.94	900	.02
1811	80,000	.089	7,120	717,376	9.93	860	.01
1813	75,000	.155	11,625	759,118	15.31	600	.03
1814	70,000	.169	11,830	779,989	15.17	650	.02
1815	100,000	.273	27,300	800,860	34.09	765	.05
1816	124,000	.254	31,496	821,731	38.33	880	.04
1817	130,000	.298	38,740	842,602	45.98	1,000	.05
1818	125,000	.215	26,875	863,473	31.12	1,050	.03
1819	167,000	.143	23,881	884,344	27.00	1,100	.03
1820	160,000	.152	24,320	905,215	26.88	970	.03
1821	180,000	.174	31,320	933,517	33.55	810	.04
1822	210,000	.115	24,150	961,818	25.11	700	.04
1823	185,000	.145	26,825	990,120	27.04	670	.04
1824	215,000	.179	38,485	1,018,421	37.99	700	.05
1825	255,000	.119	30,345	1,046,723	28.99	800	.04
1826	350,000	.093	32,550	1,075,024	30.28	840	.04
1827	316,900	.097	30,739	1,103,326	27.86	770	.04
1828	241,399	.098	23,657	1,131,627	20.91	770	.03
1829	296,812	.089	26,416	1,159,929	22.77	770	.03
1830	331,150	.084	27,817	1,208,034	23.03	810	.03
1831	354,247	.090	31,882	1,247,489	25.56	860	.03
1832	355,492	.100	35,549	1,275,061	27.88	900	.03
1833	374,653	.112	41,961	1,302,633	32.21	960	.03
1834	437,558	.155	67,821	1,330,206	50.99	1,000	.05
1835	460,338	.152	69,971	1,357,778	51.53	1,150	.05
1836	507,550	.133	67,504	1,385,350	46.79	1,250	.04
1837	539,669	.090	48,510	1,412,923	34.38	1,300	.03
1838	682,767	.124	84,663	1,440,495	58.77	1,220	.05
1839	501,708	.079	39,635	1,468,067	27.00	1,240	.02
1840	834,111	.091	75,904	1,507,779	50.34	1,020	.05
1841	644,172	.078	50,245	1,568,022	32.04	870	.04
1842	668,379	.057	38,098	1,611,269	23.65	750	.03
1843	972,960	.075	72,972	1,654,516	44.11	700	.06
1844	836,529	.055	46,009	1,697,762	27.10	700	.04
1845	993,719	.068	67,573	1,741,009	37.81	700	.06
1846	863,321	.099	85,469	1,784,256	47.90	750	.06
1847	766,599	.070	53,662	1,827,503	29.36	850	.04
1848	1,017,391	.058	59,009	1,870,750	31.54	950	.03
1849	1,249,985	.108	134,998	1,913,996	70.53	1,030	.07
1850	1,001,165	.117	117,136	1,979,059	59.19	1,100	.05
1851	1,021,048	.074	75,558	2,034,482	37.14	1,150	.03
1852	1,338,061	.091	121,764	2,080,554	58.53	1,200	.05
1853	1,496,302	.088	131,675	2,126,626	61.92	1,250	.05
1854	1,322,241	.084	111,068	2,172,698	51.12	1,310	.04
1855	1,294,463	.091	117,796	2,218,770	53.09	1,350	.04
1856	1,535,334	.124	190,381	2,264,843	84.06	1,420	.06
1857	1,373,619	.112	153,845	2,310,915	66.57	1,490	.05
1858	1,439,744	.115	165,571	2,356,988	70.25	1,580	.04
1859	1,796,455	.108	194,017	2,403,060	80.74	1,690	.05
1860	2,241,056	0.111	$248,757	2,460,648	$101.09	$1,800	.06

D. The Efficiency of Allocation

The second point relates to geographic allocation and, to a lesser extent, to the mobility of the slave labor force among crops. The slave prices in all regions move very closely with cotton prices and products per hand. It is clear, too, that the eastern prices move directly with the cotton-area slave prices, although in the last two decades the rate of increase of prices fell behind in the breeding area. If the market were extremely imperfect and the transfer between the breeding and consuming states inefficient, in contradiction to our hypothesis, then there should be much less evidence of regional arbitrage than is found here. In response to the western demand, Virginia and other eastern states shipped their natural increase to the cotton areas. Indeed, it is frequently argued that the transfer was too efficient and that the Old South was being continuously depressed by the high price of labor occasioned by western demand. Edmund Ruffin particularly took this position and argued that slave trade could not bring profits to Virginia but could result only in the paralysis of her industry. If true, this argument would be supported empirically by increasing real estate values on the western lands and decreasing values in the Atlantic and border states. That is, the chain of high cotton profits—high slave prices—increased cost of farming in the Old South should have depressed land prices in that area. Emigration, by reducing demand, should have meant more downward pressure. The only influence which operated in the direction of maintaining the value of land in the older states was the profit to be had from the increase and sale of slaves. Indeed, in 1850 and 1860 the value per acre of farm land and buildings in the border states was $7.18 and $12.33 and, in the Lower South for the same two census years, $4.99 and $8.54. Undoubtedly, the western cotton land earned a considerable rent in farming over the older land. It was this rent which maintained the flow of migration to the Cotton Belt. But that migration depended upon and supported the prosperity of the breeding states. It is not clear that slavery was able to continue only by skinning the topsoil and moving on, leaving exhausted land and low slave and land value in its wake. Quite the contrary, the evidence can plausibly be interpreted as indicating a unified, specialized economy in which the settlers on the naturally superior western lands (superior even before the deterioration of the older regions by single-crop cultivation of tobacco and cotton) were able to bid slave labor away from general farming and to make wholesale removal unnecessary, if indeed there had ever been such a necessity.

E. Slavery and Southern Economic Growth

Finally, there are two economic arguments about slavery and potential Southern growth to be considered. The assertion that slavery per se was inimical to economic growth rests in part upon the alleged inefficiency of slave labor in industrial pursuits and in part upon the loss of capital that might otherwise have gone into industrialization and diversification.

The inefficiency argument is not supported very securely. There were slaves employed in cotton factories throughout the South. Slaves were used in the coal mines and in the North Carolina lumbering operations. In the ironworks at Richmond and on the Cumberland River, slaves comprised a majority of the labor force. Southern railroads were largely built by Southern slaves. Crop diversification, or the failure to achieve diversification, appears to have been a problem of entrepreneurship rather than of the difficulties of training slaves. In the face of the demand for cotton and the profits to be had from specializing in this single crop, it is hardly difficult to explain the single-minded concentration of the planter.

In what ways was slavery allegedly responsible for the drain of capital from the South? The lack of diversification, to the extent of a failure even to provide basic supplies, made necessary the import of much food and virtually all manufactured articles from the North. But half of this assertion, the argument that laid the responsibility for the single-crop culture upon slavery, has been found questionable already.

The major avenues by which wealth is said to have been drained from the cotton states were the excessive use of credit (through dependence upon factors' services) and the "absorption" of the capital in slaves. The dependence upon advances was, in effect, a dependence upon the New York or London money market and was, therefore, an impediment to the accumulation of capital in the South. Good crop years bring the temptation to expand production; bad years do not bring any release from the factors. But resort to factoring is characteristic of speculative, commercial agriculture, whether or not the labor force is organized in slavery. It is also frequently argued that slavery gave Southern planters a taste for extravagant, wasteful display, causing the notorious lack of thrift and the relative lack of economic development, compared with that experienced in the North and West. This is doubtful inference, at best. Slavery did not make the Cavalier any more than slavery invented speculation in cotton. However, insofar as successful slave management required military posture and discipline, the Southerner's expensive image of himself as a *grand seigneur* was encouraged. It is beyond the scope of this paper to offer hypotheses about the reasons for the relative degrees of entrepreneurship in Charleston and Boston; in this context it is sufficient to state that slavery per se does not seem to have been responsible for the excessive reliance upon factoring and external sources of credit.

There remains only the absorption of capital in slaves to set the responsibility for lack of growth in the South upon the peculiar institution. Earnings that might have gone out of the South to bring in investment goods were fixed in the form of chattel labor. For the early years, during the external slave trade, there is some plausibility to this argument, though it is difficult to see how the capitalization of an income stream, excellent by contemporary standards, can be said to count as a loss of wealth. In the later years there was, except to the extent that Northern or English bankers drew off the interest, a redistribution of wealth only within the slave states: from the cotton lands back to the less profitable field agriculture of the older section. And to the extent that the old planting aristocracy used the profits to maintain the real or fancied magnificence of the preceding century, capital was absorbed. Slavery made this possible, so long as the natural increase could be shipped off. But, as Russel pointed out, slavery also made the profits in the cotton fields and the resultant demand for eastern hands. We are left with the conclusion that, except insofar as it made speculation in cotton possible on a grander scale than would otherwise have been the case and thereby weakened whatever pressure there might have been for diversification, capitalization of the labor force did not of itself operate against Southern development.

IV. CONCLUSION

In sum, it seems doubtful that the South was forced by bad statesmanship into an unnecessary war to protect a system which must soon have disappeared because it was economically unsound. This is a romantic hypothesis which will not stand against the facts.

On the basis of the computation of the returns to capital in our model of the antebellum Southern economy and the demonstration of the efficiency of the regional specialization, the following conclusions are offered.

1. Slavery was profitable to the whole South, the continuing demand for labor in the Cotton Belt insuring returns to the breeding operation on the less productive land in the seaboard and border states. The breeding returns were necessary, however, to make the plantation operations on the poorer lands as profitable as alternative contemporary economic activities in the United States. The failure of Southern agriculture on these poorer lands in the post-bellum period is probably attributable, in the main to the loss of these capital gains on breeding and not, as is so often suggested, to either the relative inefficiency of the tenant system that replaced the plantations or the soil damage resulting from war operations. These factors were unquestionably contributing elements to the difficulties of post-bellum Southern agriculture, but they were of relatively small quantitative importance compared with the elimination of slave-breeding returns.

2. There was nothing necessarily self-destructive about the profits of the slave economy. Neither the overcapitalization argument nor the assertion that slavery must have collapsed because the slaves would not reproduce themselves is tenable. Slave prices did not outpace productivity, and the regional slave price structure would imply a workable transfer mechanism rather than the contrary.

3. Continued expansion of slave territory was both possible and, to some extent, necessary. The maintenance of profits in the Old South depended upon the expansion, extensive or intensive, of slave agriculture into the Southwest. This is sufficient to explain the interest of the Old South in secession and does away with the necessity to fall back upon arguments of statesmanship or quixotism to explain the willingness to fight for the peculiar institution.

4. The available productive surplus from

slavery might have been used for economic development or, as in some totalitarian regimes of this century, for militarism. In spite of this good omen for development, Southern investment and industrialization lagged. It is hard to explain this except on the social ground that entrepreneurship could not take root in the South or on the economic ground that the South did not really own the system but merely operated it. Furthermore the American experience clearly suggests that slavery is not, from the strict economic standpoint, a deterrent to industrial development and that its elimination may take more than the workings of "inexorable economic forces." Although profitability cannot be offered as a sufficient guaranty of the continuity of Southern slavery, the converse argument that slavery must have destroyed itself can no longer rest upon allegations of unprofitability or upon assumptions about the impossibility of maintaining and allocating a slave labor force. To the extent, moreover, that profitability is a necessary condition for the continuation of a private business institution in a free-enterprise society, slavery was not untenable in the ante-bellum American South. Indeed, economic forces often may work toward the continuation of a slave system, so that the elimination of slavery may depend upon the adoption of harsh political measures. Certainly that was the American experience.

REFERENCES

1. Frederic Bancroft, *Slave Trading in the Old South*, Baltimore, J. H. Furst, 1931.

2. J. E. Cairnes, *The Slave Power,* New York, Follett Foster & Co., 1863.

3. W. H. Collins, *The Domestic Slave Trade of the Southern States,* New York, Broadway Publishing Co., 1904.

4. James S. Duesenberry, "Some Aspects of the Theory of Economic Development," *Explorations in Entrepreneurial History, 3* (December, 1950), 63–102.

5. Lewis C. Gray, *History of Agriculture in the Southern United States to 1860*, Washington, Carnegie Institution of Washington, 1933.

6. Matthew B. Hammond, *The Cotton Industry*, New York, American Economic Association Publications (New series, *I*), 1897.

7. W. Arthur Lewis, *The Theory of Economic Growth*, Homewood, Richard D. Irwin, 1955.

8. John R. Meyer and Alfred H. Conrad, "Economic Theory, Statistical Inference, and Economic History," *The Journal of Economic History, 17* (December, 1957), 524–544; reprinted in their book *The Economics of Slavery and other Studies in Econometric History*, Chicago, Aldine, 1964, pp. 3–30.

9. Frederick Law Olmstead, *The Cotton Kingdom,* New York, Mason Bros., 1861.

10. Ulrich B. Phillips, "The Economic Cost of Slaveholding in the Cotton Belt," *Political Science Quarterly, 20* (June, 1905), 257–275.

11. Ulrich B. Phillips, *Life and Labor in the Old South,* Boston, Little, Brown & Co., 1929.

12. Kenneth Stampp, *The Peculiar Institution*, New York, Alfred A. Knopf, 1956.

13. J. L. Watkins, *The Cost of Cotton Production,* U.S. Department of Agriculture, (Misc. Series, Bulletin No. 16), Washington, D.C., 1899.

26 THE PROFITABILITY AND VIABILITY OF PLANTATION SLAVERY IN THE UNITED STATES

Yasukichi Yasuba

Whether or not slavery in the ante-bellum South was profitable for planters has been the subject of dispute for a long time. Contemporary slave owners, economists, and politicians have offered evidence to support both sides of the argument. Some suggested that it was profitable to hold slaves because their physical inefficiency was more than compensated by their cheapness. Many others, however, insisted that slavery was an economic burden for planters and continued to exist only for noneconomic reasons. Later historians were also divided on this matter. Most influential among the pessimists was Ulrich B. Phillips who, upon examination of numerous testimonies by planters as

Reprinted by permission from *The Economic Studies Quarterly, 12* (September, 1961), 60–67.

well as the records of the prices of cotton and slaves, reached the conclusion that "by the close of the 'fifties it is fairly certain that no slaveholders but those few whose plantations lay in the most advantageous parts of the cotton and sugar districts and whose managerial ability was exceptionally great were earning anything beyond what would cover their maintenance and carrying charges" [7, pp. 391–392]. On the other hand, such writers as L. C. Gray, Thomas P. Govan, and Robert Worthington Smith, computing the rate of return directly from the plantation account books, found that slavery was profitable for planters [4, pp. 462–480; 3; 8].

Writers differed as to the meaning and interpretation of "profitability." Some were simply curious to know "whether planters of the Old South were making money from their operations" [3, p. 514]. Others went further and drew inferences concerning the economic viability of the system. A number of them reasoned that slavery was an economic burden for planters and it would eventually have toppled of its own weight without external intervention. They argued that Southerners defended their peculiar institution partly because they feared the social and political consequences which would ensue from emancipation and partly because they were blinded by the abolition agitation in the North [5, p. 275; 2, pp. 227–228, 231; 10, p. 202].

On the other hand some of those who found that slavery was profitable viewed their findings as disproving the hypothesis that slavery was not a viable institution. Two of the most recent studies along this line can be found in Stampp's *The Peculiar Institution* [9, pp. 383–418] and Conrad and Meyer's "The Economics of Slavery in the Ante-Bellum South [1]. In this paper, first, it will be pointed out that these two studies, like others before them, failed to define the concept of profitability correctly in relation to the question of viability of slavery. Then an appropriate measure of profitability will be suggested and, according to it, it will be concluded that slavery was an economically viable institution on the eve of the Civil War.

STAMPP: ACCOUNTANT'S CONCEPT OF PROFITABILITY

There is a slight, but conceptually important, difference between the profitability measure of Stampp and that of Conrad and Meyer. By profitability Stampp meant a rate of return on the original value of the investment in the plantation. In other words his initial question was, "allowing for the risks of a laissez-faire economy, did the average ante-bellum slaveholder, over the years, earn a reasonably satisfactory return from his investment?" [9, p. 390]. This is an accountant's concept, and as such it cannot be criticized. However when Stampp went on and reasoned that "during the last ante-bellum decade slavery was still justifying itself economically," [9, p. 408] he had crossed a line which he should not have crossed. For accountant's profitability is not necessarily identical with economic profitability, and economic viability depends solely on the latter.

To demonstrate the inadequacy of the accountant's concept in this respect, let us examine hypothetical cases of three planters who used land of the same quality and whose managerial abilities were identical. The first planter bought all his slaves in 1841, the second in 1845, and the third in 1849. The price of a prime field hand was highest in 1841 and lowest in 1845. If the rate of return in 1849 for the third planter was equal to what might be got from alternative investments, the rate of return for the first planter must have been less than adequate and that for the second planter more than adequate. Following Stampp's reasoning we have to say that, "if the slaveholder's economic self-interest alone were to be consulted, the institution should have been preserved" [9, p. 414] for the second and third planters, and it should have been abolished for the benefit of the first planter!

CONRAD AND MEYER: THE RATE OF RETURN ON COSTS INCLUSIVE OF RENT

Conrad and Meyer set out to test the hypothesis "that slavery in the South must have fallen before very long *because* it was unprofitable" [1, p. 443]. Naturally they tried to "measure the profitability of slavery according to the economic (as opposed to accounting) concept of profitability" [1, p. 96].

From scattered data for the period 1830–1860 they chose those values which seemed to show central tendencies for the life-expectancy and price of slaves, the costs of other capital investments, the market rate of interest, out-of-pocket costs, productivity, the price of cotton, and other relevant variables. Since there were definite upward trends in most variables, the method resulted, roughly speaking, in choosing average values for the period around 1845–1850. For this model, Conrad and Meyer computed the marginal efficiency of slave capital, *valuing slaves at the market price*.[1] The marginal efficiency turned out to be as high as in alternative investments, whereupon Conrad and Meyer rejected the above hypothesis.

The capital costs of slaves which are to be equated with the present value of the future stream of income in the equation of marginal efficiency of capital are determined by the nature of the problem at hand. If one is interested in the profitability of slave capital *in a particular industry*, say rice cultivation, in which only a fraction of the total slave population is used, the market price of a slave is the cost to be used in the calculation of profitability. A lower (than ordinary) rate of return based on the current price of slaves would then suggest the downfall of slave-using rice cultivation. Again, if one is interested in the profitability of slave capital *in a section* of the South, the Conrad and Meyer method would be meaningful for the same reason.

As a matter of fact, much of the confusion in the past seems to have stemmed from identifying the profitability of the slave system as a whole with the profitability of slave capital in certain regions or in certain uses. It was probably true that, in the 1850s, in such trades as canal and railway building, ditching, and tobacco processing, free workers were cheaper than slaves [5, p. 271; 6. p. 187]. It was also true that in the eastern and northern section of the South, the rate of return based on the current price of slaves was below the market rate of interest, or the rate of return from the alternative uses of capital [7, p. 391; 9, p. 411].[2] These facts were the omens of the decline of the use of slaves in these trades and sections, but they

had nothing to do with the future of slavery as a whole.

If one is interested in the viability of slavery as a whole, the costs which are to be equated with the present value of the future stream of income are not the price of slaves but the costs of reproduction of the capital, that is, the costs of rearing slaves. In the case of ordinary reproducible capital goods, a discrepancy between costs and price does not last long. For whenever the reproduction costs of a particular kind of capital good become smaller than its price, its supply will increase until the equality is restored. A movement in the opposite direction will take place when the costs are above the price. Ever since the prohibition of the slave trade, however, the supply of slaves was largely independent of their price [6, p. 174] and, hence, the discrepancy continued to exist. Indeed, as we shall see presently, towards the end of the period a large part of the price of slaves was capitalized rent. Conrad and Meyer computed their rate of return on the basis of costs inclusive of this rent. Thus what they actually proved was not the profitability of *the slave system* but rather the fact that the price of slaves did not show any significant over- or under-capitalization of annual net returns. A downward shift of the demand schedule for cotton may have taken place a few years earlier. Or an innovation in production method may have reduced the incidental costs some time before. Whatever changes had happened in the past in the marginal net revenue product must have been largely absorbed by the adjustment in the price of slaves. The internal rate of return based on the market value of slaves has always to remain more or less equal to the market rate of interest and thus cannot reveal anything even about the past performance of slavery, not to speak of the future.

A rate of return (on the market value of investment) lower than the market rate of interest is not impossible, if the rate of return is computed, as is done by Conrad and Meyer, from current statistics. For example, there may actually be a lag in the adjustments of the slave price behind the change in marginal net revenue product. In that case a lower rate of return would indicate a decline of slavery. On the other hand, the price of slaves, instead of lagging behind a past change, may anticipate a future change in marginal net revenue product and, if so, a lower rate of return would indicate a strengthening of the position of slavery. When there has been a

---

[1] It may be noted that Stampp's measure of profitability, when it is applied to newly acquired slaves, gives approximately the same results as that of Conrad and Meyer, although Stampp did not use the fancier formula for the marginal efficiency of capital. Therefore the criticism in this section applies also to Stampp.

[2] Of course if we compute the rate of return on the original costs of investment as Stampp did, it may turn out to have been "adequate" in the upper South, where most slaveowners bought their slaves when the prices were much lower. But this should not have prevented the slaveowners from liquidating their investment, if profitability on the market value of slaves was lower than the interest rate.

persistent long-run trend, the latter interpretation would seem to be a more convincing one. Still another possibility is that non-economic factors, for instance, prestige value attached to slaveholding, cause a lower rate of return to persist. If that is the case there is no reason to expect the downfall of slavery because of the lower rate of return.

THE CAPITALIZED RENT IN THE PRICE OF SLAVES IN THE ANTE-BELLUM SOUTH

Some writers, including Stampp and Conrad and Meyer, have suggested movements of the price of slaves as another measure of the position of slavery. Stampp, for example, noted that "in the final analysis, the high valuation of Negro labor during the 1850s was the best and most direct evidence of the continued profitability of slavery" [9. p. 414]. This argument is much more sensible than the one behind the use of the internal rate of return based on costs inclusive of rent; but it, too, has a serious defect in that it fails to take account of changes in the costs of rearing slaves. If the costs of rearing had increased by more than the price of slaves, it would hardly be justifiable to say that the profitability of slavery increased.

The correct statement to make is: If the portion of the price of slaves which represents capitalized rent was increasing, it is a sign of the increased profitability of slavery. To say that capitalized rent was positive is the same thing as to say that the rate of return based on the reproduction costs of slaves was above the market rate of interest, provided that noneconomic factors did not affect the determination of the price and there was no lag nor anticipation in capitalization. Conrad and Meyer showed that these conditions were satisfied in the ante-bellum South. Therefore to see if slavery in the ante-bellum South was viable, either the rate of return based on the reproduction costs of slaves or the amount of the capitalized rent in the market price of slaves may be examined. Here we chose to estimate the latter because it is simpler to compute.

As a starting point we shall compute capitalized rent for the model of plantation economy presented by Conrad and Meyer with two modifications. First, infant mortality should be introduced into the model. Although the available data may be poor, it seems better to use them than to neglect them. From four records of infant mortality cited by Stampp [9, p. 320], which include altogether some 300 live births, the ratios of the number of those who died within one year and of those who died between ages one and four to the number of survivors can be estimated. And then assuming that the first group died at the end of the first year and the second at the end of the third, expected gross costs for "breeding" an adult slave compounded at the interest rate of six per cent[3] and cumulated up to the nineteenth year, when the slave became a prime field hand, can be calculated. They are $728.[4]

Secondly, the incidental capital costs in employing slave children, which were neglected by Conrad and Meyer, should be taken into account. In order to avoid the difficulty arising from the difference between the total life of an asset and the length of the time during which it was used, we may assume that the slave owners rented land and capital goods for employing child labor. Rental is computed on an assumption that land and capital goods maintained the same efficiency throughout the lives, or alternatively, that a capital-mix which consists evenly of capital goods of all ages was rented. Annual rent for Alabama pine land which cost $195 and lasted ten years would be $26. Rent for Mississippi alluvium with a thirty-year life and costing $660 would be $48. Taking the arithmetic mean, we get $37. Rental of other capital goods would be $3, making the total incidental capital costs per adult slave per year $40.[5]

---

[3] Six per cent seems to be the appropriate discount rate for this period. Cf. [1, p. 103].

[4] The ratio, p_1, of the number of those who died within one year to the number of those who survived into adulthood was 0.396; and the ratio, p_2, of the number of those who died between ages one and four to the number of survivors was 0.156. The costs per death within one year, compounded up to the nineteenth year, c_1, were $188; the cumulated costs per slave who died between ages one and four, c_2, were $240; and, finally the cumulated costs per survivor, c_3, were $616. The gross costs for breeding an adult slave successfully were $p_1 c_1 + p_2 c_2 + c_3 = $728.

[5] [1, pp. 100–101]. Annual rent is computed in the following way: If x represents annual rent; c, the price of an asset; i, the market rate of interest; and n, the life of the asset, then

$$c = \sum_{t=1}^{n} \frac{x}{(1+i)^t}$$

$$\therefore x = \frac{i(1+i)^n}{(1+i)^{n-1}} \cdot c$$

According to Conrad and Meyer, slaves started to be productive at age six. The male slave's gross earning, starting from $5, went up $5 every year between ages six and nine, and $10 yearly after that until it reached the full adult productivity of $110 per year at age eighteen. The female slave's gross earning was half as much as that of male slaves [1, p. 107]. The average gross earning for male and female slaves was $3.75 at age six, $15 at age nine, and then went up $7.50 yearly until it reached $82.50 at age eighteen. Therefore cumulated gross earnings of a slave child averaged for male and female amounted to $637 in terms of the present value in the nineteenth year. If we assume that the ratio of the incidental capital costs to the gross earning was the same for all ages, the present value of the total incidental capital costs would be $309, so that the net value of pre-adult work was $328. Subtracting this amount from the gross rearing costs of $728, we get the average (male-female) net costs of rearing an adult slave of $400. The average price of male and female slaves at age eighteen was $875 [1, pp. 100, 108]. Therefore the part which capitalized rent represented in this price was $475.

The capitalized rent for a prime field hand and that for a prime field wench can be computed in the same manner for the Conrad and Meyer model. Deducting from the price of $925 the net rearing costs of $188, we obtain a capitalized rent for a prime field hand in the amount of $737. Similarly the capitalized rent for a prime field wench can be shown to have been $213 [1, pp. 107–108].

If we compute the rate of return on the net costs of rearing rather than on the price of slaves, it will be much higher than the market rate of interest. Therefore on the basis of the capitalized rent or the rate of return based on the rearing costs of slaves, there is no evidence that slavery would have collapsed for any economic reason.

THE TREND OF CAPITALIZED RENT, 1821–1860

Since Conrad and Meyer used averages over a period in which most variables showed upward trends, their model represented, roughly speaking, the period around 1845–1850. It may therefore be suspected that the capitalized rent computed above is significantly different from the figure for the end of the 1850s—some ten years later. Moreover

the capitalized rent, though it explains the increase in the slave labor force, does not tell whether or not the position of slavery was strengthened. Hoping to shed some light on these problems, we shall proceed to ascertain the trend of capitalized rent in the price of a prime field hand over a period of forty years prior to the Civil War.

Because of the lack of sufficient information, we have to make several auxiliary assumptions. First, we divide the period 1821–1860 into eight 5-year subperiods and assume that the Conrad and Meyer model represents subperiod 1846–1850. Secondly, we assume incidental capital costs to be proportionate to the gross earnings from cotton, which is determined by multiplying the 1846–1850 figures by the quinquennial average index of crop value per slave (with 1846–1850 as the base year). This index is computed from Table 17 in the Conrad and Meyer article.[6] The value of time lost by pregnancy is also multiplied by the index of crop value per slave.

Gross rearing costs other than the value of time lost by pregnancy are estimated on an assumption that it is proportionate to the cost of living index. For the latter G. R. Taylor's wholesale price index of commodities other than South Carolina export staples at Charleston is used [11, pp. 874, 876]. The index for 1818–1842 is linked with that for 1843–1861 by using the unweighted average of price relative of corn and wheat in Virginia for 1842 and 1843 [4, p. 1039]. Corn and flour are the most important items in Taylor's nonexport staples, each occupying 20 per cent of the total weight in the 1843–1861 series [11, p. 869].

The prices of slaves are taken from Table 17 in the Conrad and Meyer article. The arithmetic mean of the prices of a prime field hand for 1846–1850 is $936 as against the model price of $925. In order to adjust for the discrepancy, every value of the model is multiplied by 936/925. Thus for the period 1846–1850 the gross rearing costs were $737, the net income from child labor was $546, and the net rearing costs, therefore, were $191. Deducting this from the price of $936, we obtain a capitalized rent in the amount of $745.

Finally, it is assumed that there was no change in the long-term interest rate and in infant mortality over the whole period.

---

[6] [Table 14 of essay 25.–Editors' note.]

Capitalized rent is computed both in current and constant (1846–1850) dollars. Taylor's wholesale price index of all commodities at Charleston is used as a deflator. As above, the 1818–1842 index is linked to the 1843–1861 index by utilizing several commodity series. In addition to corn and wheat in Virginia, rice and cotton at Charleston [*11*, p. 870] and sugar at New Orleans [*4*, p. 1039] are taken into account. In the 1843–1861 series rice and cotton account for all of the export staples group, and sugar for 36 per cent of the imports group. The weight of each of three major groups, which Taylor failed to indicate in his article, is estimated from his index by solving a set of simultaneous equations. Thus, in linking, the following weights are used:

Corn	14.6
Wheat	14.5
Cotton	37.4
Rice	6.6
Sugar	26.9
	100.0

The result is shown in Table 1 and Figure 1. An upward trend is clear both in current values and in real values. As expected, fluctuations are somewhat damped in the real series, making the upward trend still easier to be seen.

CONCLUSION

Because of the uncertainties regarding the underlying evidence, the numerical values of the capitalized rent must be considered ten-

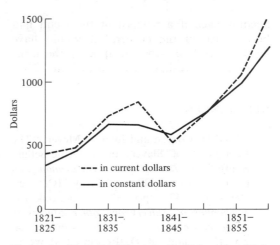

Figure 1. Capitalized Rent in the Price of a Male Slave, Age Eighteen.

tative. It is hoped that further inquiries into primary data may shed more light on the level and trend of the rent. It seems unlikely, however, that the upward trend will be reversed. Thus, in the ante-bellum South, slavery steadily strengthened its economic position. Extrapolation of the trend line is quite another problem and we admit that it would be hardly legitimate. In order to make a satisfactory forecast, we should need information about the probable changes in the factors which determine the level of the capitalized rent. At the present stage, therefore, only two things can be said in conclusion. First, the trend of the capitalized rent from 1821 to 1860 does not reveal any indication of an imminent downfall of slavery.

Table 1. Capitalized Rent in the Price of a Male Slave, Age Eighteen

	Average Price of a Slave (1)	Gross Rearing Costs (2)	Net Income from Child Labor (3)	Capitalized Rent in Current Dollars[a] (4)	All Commodity Price Index (1846–1850 =100) (5)	Capitalized Rent in Constant (1846–1850) Dollars[b] (6)
1821–1825	$736	$657	$349	$428	128	$334
1826–1830	792	614	286	464	105	442
1831–1835	974	671	431	734	113	650
1836–1840	1206	848	497	855	128	668
1841–1845	744	591	379	532	91	585
1846–1850	936	737	546	745	100	745
1851–1855	1252	807	600	1045	108	968
1856–1860	1596	938	922	1580	121	1306

[a] Column 1 minus column 2 plus column 3.
[b] Column 4 divided by column 5.

Second, even if a reversal of the trend had been "around the corner," it would have been difficult to wipe out quickly the large capitalized rent that existed in the late 1850s.

REFERENCES

1. Alfred H. Conrad and John R. Meyer, "The Economics of Slavery in the Ante-Bellum South," *The Journal of Political Economy, 66* (April, 1958), 95–130 and "Reply" (October, 1958), 442–443; reprinted in their book *The Economics of Slavery and other Studies in Econometric History*, Chicago, Aldine, 1964, pp. 43–92 and 98–99. [Reprinted above as essay 25.]
2. Ralph Betts Flanders, *Plantation Slavery in Georgia,* Chapel Hill, University of North Carolina Press, 1933.
3. Thomas P. Govan, "Was Plantation Slavery Profitable?" *The Journal of Southern History, 8* (November, 1942), 513–535.
4. Lewis C. Gray, *History of Agriculture in the Southern United States to 1860,* Washington, Carnegie Institute of Washington, 1933.
5. Ulrich B. Phillips, "The Economic Cost of Slaveholding in the Cotton Belt," *Political Science Quarterly, 20* (June, 1905), 257–275.
6. Ulrich B. Phillips, *Life and Labor in the Old South*, Boston, Little, Brown & Co., 1929.
7. Ulrich B. Phillips, *American Negro Slavery*, New York, Peter Smith, 1952.
8. Robert Worthington Smith, "Was Slavery Unprofitable in the Ante-Bellum South?" *Agricultural History, 20* (January, 1946), 62–64.
9. Kenneth N. Stampp, *The Peculiar Institution*, New York, Alfred A. Knopf, 1956.
10. Charles Sackett Sydnor, *Slavery in Mississippi,* New York, Appleton-Century, 1933.
11. George Rogers Taylor, "Wholesale Commodity Prices at Charleston, South Carolina, 1796–1861," *Journal of Economic and Business History, 4* (August, 1932), Supplement, 848–876.

27 THE ECONOMIC IMPACT OF THE CIVIL WAR

Stanley L. Engerman

During the past several years, the controversy concerning the political and economic impact of the Civil War has been reopened. The traditional interpretation, which is customarily associated with the names of Charles Beard and Louis Hacker, has come under heavy attack. On the political side, Robert Sharkey and Irwin Unger have questioned the proposition that the war was a political revolution which vested power in a northern business class which had been previously denied it. On the economic side, Robert Gallman's estimates of commodity production and national income have raised many questions about the propositions that the Civil War accelerated the course of economic growth and that the Civil War period itself was one of rapid economic expansion [*10, 11*]. Gallman's findings apparently helped to stimulate Thomas Cochran's notable essay, " Did the Civil War Retard Industrialization ? " [*3*].

Reprinted with revisions by permission from *Explorations in Entrepreneurial History*, Second Series, *3* (Spring/Summer, 1966), 176–199.

369

Despite these attacks, not all historians, political or economic, have modified their opinions. Quite the contrary, Cochran's critique of the Beard-Hacker thesis brought forth spirited counterattacks by Stephen Salsbury, Pershing Vartanian, and Harry Scheiber [*20, 25, 22*].

One of the major obstacles to the resolution of the debate is the extremely wide field over which the controversy has ranged. In this article I shall attempt to narrow the range of debate by defining the central issues in the controversy, analyzing some of the data used in the debate, and examining the conclusions drawn from these data. My emphasis will be on the economic rather than the political aspects of the problem. Political issues will be considered only to the extent that they bear upon the economic impact of the Civil War.

I. THE BEARD-HACKER THESIS

To Charles Beard and Louis Hacker, the Civil War was a great turning point in the political, social, and economic life of the nation. It was, in the words of the Beards, a "second American revolution" which ended in "the unquestioned establishment of a new power in the government, making vast changes in the arrangement of classes, in the accumulation and distribution of wealth, in the course of industrial development, and in the Constitution inherited from the Fathers" [*1*, vol. 2, p. 53]. Given this broad list of changes, it will be useful to mention specifically what are argued to be the key factors.

The main political shift stressed by Beard and Hacker is the presumed transfer of political power from the Southern agrarians to the Northern industrial capitalists. On attaining power these Northerners were supposed to have passed legislation which provided a framework for, if it was not the direct means of, their economic aggrandizement. These wartime measures as well as subsequent legislation, which presumably would not have become laws if the Southerners had still been in Congress, have been made the cause of the accelerated industrialization and growth in national income that was assumed to have occurred during the postwar era. In particular Hacker singles out the following wartime measures: the issuance of the greenbacks, the increase in tariffs, the institution of the National Banking System, the adoption of the Homestead Act, the grants of land and other subsidies to the transcontinental railroads, the passage of the Morrill Act, and the adoption of the contract labor laws [*14*, pp. 361–373]. These enactments, it is argued, not only led to increased profits for Northern industrialists but also benefited other groups who shared in the dividends of accelerated growth.

Perhaps the most important social change attributed to the war was the overthrow of Southern slavery. This theme was well established before the writings of Beard and Hacker. Three decades before the publication of *The Rise of American Civilization*, Carroll D. Wright made the creation of a free labor force in the South the central issue of the Civil War. Wright's theme was repeated and elaborated upon by Beard and Hacker. They argued that the Southern economy was stagnating in the ante-bellum era, and attributed this to the inefficiency of the slave system in the allocation of labor. Thus the war, and the end of slavery, provided the necessary conditions for subsequent industrialization and economic growth in the South.

Beyond this, Beard, Hacker, and their followers believed that the war had the "usual" stimulating effects of other wars. In analogy with the effects of World Wars I and II on the American economy, the years 1861–1865 are considered to have been a time of rapid economic expansion, with high levels of output and employment. Beard and Hacker, following Mitchell, argued that the inflation resulting from the issuance of greenbacks led to a fall in real wages and an increase in the share of income going to the rising class of industrialists [*18*]. War contracts meant large profits in the "war industries," while the combination of increased aggregate demand and the labor shortage arising from military needs led to rapid mechanization in industry. Significant changes in the techniques of production presumably took place in many industries, with boots and shoes, woolens, and men's clothing being particularly affected. The sales volume of agricultural implements was said to have risen markedly. Hacker also placed great emphasis on the shift within manufacturing to heavy industry in the postwar years—a shift which he believed was initiated by wartime demands. The wartime profits, the improvements in technology, and the shift toward heavy industry are all taken to be major explanatory variables in the accelerated growth of the postwar era.

Table 1. Commodity Output, by Region and Industrial Sector, 1860–1880 (1879 prices, millions of dollars)

	Non-South			South		
	Total	Agriculture	Manufacturing and Mining	Total	Agriculture	Manufacturing and Mining
1860	$1674	$ 853	$ 821	$710	$639	$ 71
1870	2337	1246	1091	534	477	57
1880	3876	1861	2015	838	738	100

NOTE: Tables 1 and 2 present regional breakdowns of Gallman's commodity output in agriculture, mining, and manufacturing for the respective years, in constant prices. These regional breakdowns are used for the purpose of estimating growth rates within regions and not for comparisons of the two regions at the same date. Since the ratio of labor force in commodity output to total labor force in the South was larger than in the non-South, such a comparison would provide too favorable a relative picture of the Southern economy. There is probably some overstatement of growth rates between 1860 and 1870 in both regions since the proportions of labor force in commodity output rose, but this does not affect the general conclusions. These commodity output estimates differ from Gallman's, because they exclude construction. They also differ from Easterlin's regional estimates, since the latter are adjusted to include non-commodity income. [See *10* and *4*].

II. LONG-TERM TRENDS, 1840–1900

It must be remembered that neither Beard nor Hacker had reliable statistical data upon which to base the arguments about the effects of the Civil War upon the rate and pattern of American economic development. While the scattered items upon which they leaned were consistent with their interpretations, they were often incomplete for the strong conclusions drawn. Fortunately, more complete and relevant data have become available in recent years.

The estimates of commodity output and national income prepared by Robert Gallman give a different view of economic growth before and after the Civil War than that conveyed by Beard and Hacker. Gallman's series indicate that the period between 1840 and 1860 was one of rapid expansion in total and per capita output, as well as one of pronounced change in the structure of economic activity. Total commodity output rose at an annual rate of 4.6 per cent between 1840 and 1860, and at an annual rate of 4.4 per cent between 1870 and 1900. Moreover, as measured by the absolute percentage point change in shares of output, the shift from agriculture to manufacturing was as rapid in the twenty years before the war as in the twenty years after it [*10*, pp. 16 and 26]. Thus the relative increase in the share of manufacturing in output was larger in the prewar than in the postwar period.

Even if one were to interpret the Beard-Hacker thesis as focusing only upon growth in the manufacturing sector, the data point

in a similar direction. Value added in manufacturing, which grew at an annual average of 7.8 per cent from 1840 to 1860, grew only at 6 per cent from 1870 to 1900 [*10*, p. 24]. It is true that the share (in current dollars) of value added in durable goods within manufacturing did rise from 42.7 per cent in 1860 to 48.6 per cent in 1870. However, this share fell back to 42.5 per cent in 1880, so that any wartime change apparently was not irreversible.

Hence it is clear that post-Civil War trends with respect to the shift toward manufacturing in the rate of growth in total commodity output, and the rate of growth in manufacturing output were not above the trends established in the prewar years.

However, the growth of total commodity output from 1860 to 1870 averaged only 2.0 per cent, the lowest rate during any decade in the nineteenth century. Similarly, the annual growth rate of manufacturing value added, 2.3 per cent, was also the lowest rate for any decade during the century.[1] Moreover, the manufacturing share in total commodity output rose only from 32 per cent to 33 per cent in the decade. That was due to the decline of Southern agriculture rather than to accelerated expansion in manufacturing (see Table 1). If we exclude the Confederacy, the relative

---

[1] The next lowest decade average rate of growth of commodity output in the nineteenth century was half-again as large; for manufacturing value added, it was twice as large [*10*, pp. 16 and 24]. Thus the rates of growth in the 1860s were uniquely low for the nineteenth century.

share of agriculture in total commodity output actually rose. Finally, the sharp decline in labor productivity in manufacturing from 1860 to 1870, 13 per cent, is a unique occurrence for the nineteenth century. Thus the new data show that while the Civil War decade marked a clear departure from the nineteenth-century trend, this departure is a direction opposite to that anticipated on the basis of the Beard-Hacker thesis.

Although the postwar years saw some return to prewar growth patterns, we should note that there was a slight decline in the rate of growth of commodity output. For this reason, perhaps, the Civil War decade can be regarded as a period bringing about retardation in American economic development. Even if one were to claim that the differential in growth rates was too small to be regarded as significant, the war may be considered to have retarded the economy in another way. The uniquely low rates of growth of commodity output during the war decade meant that the level of 1870 output was beneath the level expected on the basis of extrapolating the prewar trend. It is estimated that it was not until almost five years later that output reached the predicted 1870 level, and even if the rate of growth had not declined in the postwar period, this lag would have persisted. Thus the war decade saw a retardation in the growth of commodity output due both to a low rate of growth during the decade and to a decline in the rate of growth in the postwar era relative to that of the prewar years.

The growth in total commodity output can be separated into the growth in population and the growth in per capita output. When evaluating the aggregate behavior it is important to consider these components. The postwar rates of population growth were below those of the prewar period. Indeed, the Civil War decade marks the onset of a long period of decline in the rate of growth of population. Yet only a small part of this decline can be attributed to the direct and indirect effects of the war. Declines in the rate of growth of population have been associated with rising per capita income in most developed countries and follow from the fact that birth rates in these nations have fallen more rapidly than have death rates. In the United States the decline in the rate of growth continued almost uninterruptedly until the Second World War. Thus it appears that the impact of the war upon population

Table 2. Commodity Output Per Capita by Region, 1860–1880 (1879 prices)

	Non-South	South
1860	$ 74.8	$77.7
1870	81.5	47.6
1880	105.8	61.5

growth was overwhelmed by influences seemingly independent of the war.

Per capita output did grow more rapidly between 1870 and 1900 than it had in the two prewar decades—at an annual rate of 2.1 per cent as contrasted with the earlier 1.45 per cent. Suggestive as these figures may be, they do not necessarily support the Beard-Hacker thesis. The higher postwar rate may merely reflect a "catching-up" process induced by the decline in per capita commodity output during the Civil War decade. This possibility is suggested both by the fact that the immediate postwar years show the highest growth rates and the fact that the growth rate of per capita commodity output is the same between 1860 and 1900 and between 1840 and 1860. Not until almost 20 years after the war did per capita commodity output reach the level estimated by extrapolating the prewar trend, and it is at this time that the rate of growth returns to this earlier level.

This catching-up notion can be examined in more detail by looking at the regional trends in commodity output per capita (see Table 2).[2] The victorious North underwent little internal devastation and presumably benefited from wartime demands. However, the annual rate of growth per capita commodity output in the non-South from 1860 to 1870 was under 1 per cent, the lowest for any decade in the nineteenth century. While the annual growth rate between 1870 and 1880 was an unusually high 2.6 per cent, it was in part a catching-up phenomenon. The annual rate between 1860 and 1880, 1.75 per cent, was above the prewar level of 1.3 per cent. The non-Southern growth rate from 1880 to 1900 was equal to the national average, 1.9 per cent. Thus the data indicate that there was an increase in the rate of growth of per capita

---

[2] In subsequent paragraphs, comparisons will be made using data presented by Richard A. Easterlin [4]. Easterlin includes Oklahoma and Kentucky in the South, but this will not effect the conclusions drawn in this section.

income in the non-Southern states after the war, although (as shall be pointed out in the next paragraph) after 1870 they grew no more rapidly than did the Southern states. This increase, perhaps, is the key index favorable to the Beard-Hacker thesis.

It is in the South that the destructive effects of the war were most severely felt. Per capita commodity output declined by 39 per cent in the Civil War decade, and in 1880 was still 21 per cent below the 1860 level. Nevertheless, the growth rate of commodity output per capita in the 1870s, 2.6 per cent, was the same as that in the rest of the nation. From 1880 to 1900 Southern per capita income also grew at the national average, so that the negative impact of the war on the Southern growth rate appears to have been confined to the decade of the 1860s; but that impact was substantial. If Southern per capita income had grown in that decade at the same rate as it had during the prewar period, 1.6 per cent, it would have been almost twice the actual 1870 level. If the Civil War is to be considered a precondition for Southern economic growth, it was one which was exceedingly costly to the South as well as to the national economy.[3]

One important, indirect effect upon the subsequent growth attributed to the war was its effect upon the growth of capital stock, particularly industrial capital. It is argued that because of both wartime measures and postwar legislation, the share of national income going to the investing classes rose. More will be said about this question, but we do have sufficient data to compare both the growth of capital stock before and after the war and the pre- and postwar shares of capital goods in commodity output. The annual rate of increase of the total stock of fixed capital was higher from 1840 to 1860 (8.1 per cent) than from 1870 to 1900 (5.1 per cent), with the Civil War decade and that of the 1870s being periods of low growth. The stock of fixed capital in manufacturing did grow more rapidly in postwar years, at an annual rate of 6.8 per cent as contrasted with the prewar rate of 6.3 per cent, but the declining growth rates for other components reduced that of the total capital stock. The

share of capital goods in commodity output was higher in the postwar period, but we should note that Gallman's estimates show a rising trend in this ratio starting in 1840 [*12*]. Thus we need to account for the early upward movement, as well as the possible effects of the Civil War in explaining the increased share of output invested in the postwar period.

III. ECONOMIC EXPANSION DURING THE WAR YEARS

Gallman's series on commodity output and income in the nineteenth century contain no estimates in the 1860s. The discussion of the Civil War decade was based upon comparisons made between census years 1860 and 1870. Thus we cannot make inferences about the behavior of output in the Civil War years themselves. While such data as we now have for the war years may be weaker than the comprehensive estimates for 1860 and 1870, they suggest movements in the economy during the war, as distinguished from postwar developments. If the postwar part of the decade was a period of more rapid expansion than were the war years, the use of Gallman's data would suggest a more favorable picture of economic change during the war than is warranted, understating wartime declines and overstating increases.

The most frequently used production indexes for these years are those prepared by Edwin Frickey. His index of manufacturing output shows a much sharper rate of increase between 1866 and 1870 than during the war years. This is true not only for the total but also for both its durable and nondurable components. The index of overall industrial and commercial production also indicates a sharper rate of expansion in the postwar than in the wartime years [*8*, pp. 54, 64, and 127]. Similarly almost all the measures relating to agriculture cited by Rasmussen increased more rapidly from 1866 to 1870 than from 1861 to 1865 [*19*].

Other sources of data are New York and Massachusetts censuses for 1865. The Massachusetts census was for the year ending June 1, and the New York census was apparently for the same period. This means that wartime expansion is included, since the National Bureau of Economic Research places the Civil War peak in April, 1865 (the month the war ended). The behavior shown

---

[3] Indeed it was not until about twenty-five years after the start of the war that Southern per capita income returned to its 1860 level. It has become recognized that the ante-bellum South was not stagnating economically, so that the war was by no means a necessary condition for Southern growth [*4, 7*].

Table 3. Manufacturing Value Added and Employment, Massachusetts and New York, 1855–1870 (Value added in millions of dollars, 1879 prices; employment in thousands)

	Massachusetts		New York	
	Value Added	Employment	Value Added	Employment
1855	$117	224	$142	215
1860	127	224	173	230
1865	98	244	72	171
1870	145	279	221	352

by manufacturing output in these censuses makes reliance upon them hazardous for anything but suggestions. They should not be ignored, however, since they do represent the only comprehensive censuses of manufacturing output available for a Civil War year. The measured declines in 1865 were widespread, not concentrated in any one industry or region, and no statements of exceptional difficulty in data collection were made.

Manufacturing value added and employment in these states, at five-year intervals between 1855 and 1870, are shown in Table 3. (New York and Massachusetts together accounted for 33.3 per cent of manufacturing value added in 1860 and 31.7 per cent in 1870.)

While the patterns of change are not entirely consistent, and the postwar boom would have had to be unusually large, it is interesting that in both states declines in real output are shown not only between 1860 and 1865, but also between 1855 and 1865. While subject to more scrutiny, it appears at least that these two key manufacturing states did not have rapidly expanding manufacturing sectors during the war years.

As noted in the previous section, the Civil War decade did mark a rise in the share of capital goods in commodity output for the economy. In 1870 this ratio was at its nineteenth-century peak. However, the high share in this year may represent a catching-up to offset declines in the earlier part of the decade. This is suggested by the estimates of capital stock which Gallman and Howle have prepared on the basis of census data. The rate of growth of fixed capital fell from 8.5 per cent in the 1850s to 4.1 per cent in the 1860s [12]. Also suggestive in this regard is the residential building series prepared by Manuel Gottlieb. (Nonfarm residential buildings accounted for approximately 30 per cent of fixed capital in both terminal years of the decade.) Gottlieb's index shows a quantity of residential building in 1866–1870 about twice that of 1861–1865.

Similarly, Earle Ross, in his study of Iowa agriculture, stated that "the records indicate the great increase in machinery for the decade came in the years after the war," a conclusion also pointed to by the sales pattern of the McCormick company. Thus it is also doubtful that the war years were a period of investment boom.

The "War Industries"

It is crucial to note that the industries most frequently cited as affected by the Civil War do not fit into the category of war-related industries as that term is customarily used. Rather, they are consumer goods industries, or industries whose demand was derived from that for consumer products. This suggests that the techniques of war were pre-modern, and that any mechanization in heavy industries due to war demands was of minor importance in contrast with twentieth-century wars.

Indeed it has been shown that the consumption of iron attributable to small arms production during the war was only 1 per cent of total U.S. iron output between 1861 and 1865. The amount could have been used to lay about 650 miles of railroad track. The shortfall in mileage built during the war below the 1865–1860 level was 7 times that amount. Thus any expansion in iron output based upon arms production was more than offset by the effect of the war upon railroad construction.

Given the importance of consumer goods industries in war production, the relevant historical comparison becomes more difficult. If government demands merely replaced civilian demands for the same commodities, it is possible that no increase in demand over and above the probable nonwar situation occurred. Thus arguments based upon the magnitude of demand for these products may attribute too much to the effects of the war.

Because of the absence of consistent data

over the period, it is often difficult to discuss changes in rates of growth of output for specific consumer goods industries. However, some comparisons can be made on the basis of state and national census data. They suggest that the presumed effects of the war are often questionable, growth and technological change being rapid before the war in many industries.

The Massachusetts censuses for 1855 and 1865 provide some basis for discussing the changes in boots and shoes and textile production. Massachusetts accounted for about one half of the national output of boots and shoes, one third of the cotton textile output, and one fourth of the output of woolens in both 1860 and 1870.

Between 1855 and 1865 Massachusetts employment in the boot and shoe industry fell from 77,827 to 55,160, while output fell from 45 million pairs to 32 million. This decline has been attributed to the elimination of the Southern market, in which a standard low quality shoe was demanded for slaves, which was only partially offset by rising military demands. The absence of capital figures for 1855 precludes comparison of the degree of mechanization, but output per worker remained relatively constant over the decade. This was in a period when the ratio of male to female employment in the industry was increasing, presumably indicative of an improvement in the quality of the labor force.

The woolen industry did expand rapidly in the war period, possibly hitting a peak level of output in 1865 before declining to 1870. In Massachusetts, value added per worker rose 12 per cent between 1855 and 1865. However, this may not have been due to the introduction of new techniques. Yards worked per worker fell slightly, the increased dollar amount being attributable to a shift from the cheaper flannels to the more expensive cassimeres.

With the Massachusetts data we can examine another proposition about the effects of the war upon the textile industry. It is sometimes implied that the increased wartime output of woolens more than compensated for the decline in cottons and thus that total textile output increased. However, an index of value added for textiles (cottons, woolens, and worsteds) in Massachusetts declines 10 per cent from 1855 to 1865, with an employment decrease of 6 per cent. Moreover, based upon the changes in Massachusetts output, estimated U.S. textile output declined by about 30 per cent between 1860 and 1865.

Thus the growth in woolen textiles did not offset the decline in the production of cotton textiles.

The effect of the war upon the agricultural implement industry is one requiring more detailed study, since there is some ambiguity in the data currently available. The traditional interpretation argues that not only did the war create a labor shortage, but it also led to a considerable expansion of agricultural demand. In the latter regard, however, it is important to note that wheat and corn output had been growing rapidly before the war, and that foreign markets became important in the early years of the war. Indeed, in 1866 the Department of Agriculture was quite concerned with the shortfall in wheat output below an extrapolation based on growth in earlier years. Non-Southern wheat output declined in the last two years of the war, after peaking in 1863. While there was increased domestic consumption in the North, probably at least 50 per cent of the increase in non-Southern production in this period is to be attributed to foreign markets. Average annual corn output in the non-South in the years 1862–1865 was equal to the 1859 level, and then only because of a large harvest. For these crops, then, the war apparently did not lead to an acceleration in the rate of growth of output.

There also are some questions about the changes in reaper and mower sales in this period. Hutchinson noted that McCormick sales in 1862, 1863, and 1864 fell below the 1861 level. He then made the point in regard to an 1864 survey of agricultural implement manufacturers that "it is significant that very few of them increased their annual output since 1861" [15, p. 97n]. Hutchinson also pointed out that the unsold stock of reapers held by McCormick after the 1864 harvest was equal to 40 per cent of sales, and that in 1865 the implement manufacturers were attempting to cartelize. Reaper sales had been growing rapidly before the war and were higher after the war than during. Thus it is not clear that the war years were an abnormal boom period for the industry.

IV. PROFITS, INFLATION, AND GROWTH

One of the central parts of the traditional thesis concerns the effects of the wartime inflation upon income distribution. The general argument, presented most forcibly by Earl

Hamilton, is that in inflationary periods money wages lag behind prices, increasing the share of income going to profits. This shift to profits should lead to more rapid economic growth. In this section, I shall review the data used to demonstrate this point for the Civil War period and see what questions remain to be answered.

Real Wages and the Profit Share

There is little systematic evidence concerning income distribution for the war years. The main argument for the theory of an increase in the profit share is based upon what Mitchell called the residual claimant hypothesis. Since real wages apparently fell, and there was no marked rise in money interest rates or rents, the share going to the residual claimant— profits—must have risen. It is important to realize, however, that it is possible for real wages to fall without the profit share increasing. These are not mutually exclusive occurrences. Real wages can decline in proportion to total factor incomes, so that with unchanged employment the relative shares remain unchanged. However, the analysis is really more complex, since the relationship between changes in real wages and relative income shares would depend upon elasticities of substitution among factors of production in each industry, as well as effects arising from the shifting composition of output among industries. To argue directly from falling real wages to a shift to profits is not valid.

The decline in real wages, which appears firmly based statistically, does provide a major puzzle. This is particularly true since the traditional interpretation also argues that there was a labor shortage during the war, which encouraged mechanization. If this were true, the decline in real wages would be surprising (unless civilian output declined). Indeed, the Civil War pattern is markedly different from that of the two world wars of the twentieth century. In these wars, both periods of rapid inflation, real wages rose, as did the labor share in World War II.

There have been several attempts to explain the fall in real wages which do not imply an increase in the share of profits in income. David A. Wells, writing immediately after the war, argued that the quality of the labor force had deteriorated. Thus lower real wages could be based upon a decline in worker productivity. One possible source of deterioration, emphasized by Wells, is a shift in the sex composition of the manufacturing labor force.

The extent of this shift can be determined for New York and Massachusetts. The results are ambiguous. The ratio of male to total manufacturing workers in New York rose from 76.9 per cent to 81.5 per cent between 1860 and 1865, while in Massachusetts this ratio fell from 67.3 to 62.7 per cent. Moreover, changes in the age structure, as well as the importance of immigrants in the labor force, must also be determined in answering this question.

Another explanation is that of Kessel and Alchian [16]. They emphasize the role of the depreciating foreign-exchange rate and the wartime tax structure in reducing the output available to civilians. With the loss of cotton as a source of foreign exchange earnings, the price of foreign exchange to the U.S. rose, making imported goods more expensive. (Their measures show that money wages actually rose as rapidly as did the prices of the noninternationally traded goods which were included in the consumer price index.) They attribute "at least half" of the fall in real wages in 1864 to the fall in the terms of trade. The use of custom duties and excise taxes reduced measured real wages since they raised all prices and imposed a wedge between total output and the amount of goods available to civilians. Kessel and Alchian attributed "most of the fall in 1865 relative to 1860" to the "tax policy used to finance the war." These explanations, as that of Wells, suggest that total factor incomes fell, so that the fall in real wages provides no basis for arguing that profits increased during the wartime inflation.

Estimates of income by factor shares, prepared by Edward Budd, have recently become available [2]. Unfortunately, the series are for census years only, and therefore contain no direct evidence on the war period per se. However, the Beard-Hacker thesis can be interpreted as arguing for a long-run shift to profits, and the census-year data are relevant to this proposition. According to Budd, the share of wages in both total private income and in income originating in industry rose from 1860 to 1870—and indeed until 1890. While Budd does not give the distribution of property income among profits, rents, and interest, the main point is that the wage share rose relative to property income during and after the Civil War decade.

Growth Through Inflation

The preceding paragraphs argued that it is possible that no shift to profits occurred during the wartime inflation. There is another mechanism through which inflation can be argued to spur growth. Investor expectation of rising prices means that borrowing can occur at an effective real rate of interest lower than the nominal interest rate at the time of borrowing, thus encouraging investment.[4]

Expectations about the future rate of price change should be reflected in the money rate of interest. If the money rate did not rise during inflation it would imply either that investors did not expect the price rise to continue or that the anticipated real rate of interest had fallen. The few measures we have do indicate that interest rates did not rise in the expected manner during the war inflation. Bond yield data collected by Macauley show falling yields through late 1864, followed by a rise to 1866. (Mitchell's price index peaked in January 1865, but the gold premium reached its maximum in mid-1864.) Also, at a time when short-term commercial paper rates were rising (mid-1863 to late 1864), long-term bond yields were still declining.

Friedman and Schwartz have argued that foreign expectations of a subsequent fall in the price of gold led to the U.S. being a net capital importer after 1863. Foreigners were speculating the expected future fall of the price of gold in the U.S. by purchasing U.S. securities, and this explains, in part, the low level of interest rates in the period [9, pp. 66–76].

If these expectations were generally held by investors, this would tend to discourage investment during the war. This implication was clearly stated by Mitchell in another context. He noted the small number of business failures during the immediate postwar deflation and explained this as due to the lack of desire on the part of businessmen to borrow during the war in anticipation of a postwar fall in prices.

V. QUESTIONS ABOUT ECONOMIC LEGISLATION

Even if we were to assume that the economic legislation of the Civil War years would not have been passed (or would have been passed only after a long wait) in the absence of the war, the question of its impact upon economic growth remains to be examined. We have seen that there was a slight decline in the rate of

growth of total commodity output after the war. However, since it is possible to argue that without the legislation growth would have substantially retarded, it will be useful to see what can be said directly about the issue. Unfortunately, there are few economic analyses of the economic consequences of wartime laws. Such analysis is difficult, because one must consider not only the effects upon resource allocation and utilization but also possible effects via changing income distribution and rates of capital formation.

Existing studies suggest that the effects of the contract labor laws and the transcontinental railroad grants upon subsequent economic growth are small. In her careful book, Charlotte Erickson concluded that "contract labor was rare in America during the years after the Civil War." She demonstrated that the legislation became controversial, not because it led to any major inflow of labor but because it was periodically used to import skilled workers to break strikes [5, p. vii]. With respect to railroad grants, Robert Fogel has demonstrated that the Union Pacific yielded a social rate of return which made this investment justifiable. But this does not mean that it had a big effect upon the economy. The increase in national income made possible by the Union Pacific was only .01 of 1 per cent—much too small to bear the weight placed upon it by the Beard-Hacker thesis [6, chap. IV].

For other major pieces of economic legislation the effects upon growth remain to be determined. The impact of the tariff upon any one industry, let alone the entire economy, is still unknown. There is little to be found in the literature besides Taussig's agnosticism concerning possible benefits to either the specific industries or the economy [23]. Some presumption exists in favour of the conclusion that tariffs shifted the income distribution in favor of capital, but there is as yet no indication of the possible quantitative importance of this effect.

Similarly little is known about the effects of the National Banking System and the Homestead Act provisions on economic growth. Not much has been agreed upon concerning efficient financial arrangements for economic growth, and it is not clear that the war-induced act provided an improvement over existing arrangements or provided a better set of financial arrangements than other bills possible at the time. The National Banking System certainly did not lead to a period free of financial difficulties. Perhaps even less can

---

[4] This latter argument is based upon either asymmetry in the expectations of borrowers and lenders or some rigidity delaying interest rate adjustments.

be said about the effects of the Homestead Act. Despite the voluminous literature, we still do not know who obtained farm land, how successful they were, nor even the extent of the incentive provided by "free land." It is possible that the social implications of this act greatly exceeded its effects upon the rate of economic growth.

VI. POSTWAR INCOME REDISTRIBUTION

It has been argued that one of the mechanisms through which the rate of economic growth was spurred in the postwar period was income redistribution caused by the government debt. Krooss, for example, states [17, p. 473]:

In the postwar years, the interest and principal on the debt was paid by levying regressive taxes. Thus, the federal fiscal policy transferred money from consumers to savers, augmenting the amount available for investment and encouraging the expansion of industry.

The magnitude of such an effect can be estimated. We must know who held the bonds and the extent to which the tax system was regressive to establish redistribution of income. To determine the effects of income redistribution on growth we need information on the propensity to save at different income levels and the effect of increased capital formation upon the rate of economic growth.[5]

The sum of interest payments and debt retirement over the period 1866–1890 was slightly in excess of $3.8 billion, at an annual average of $153.2 million. The annual current dollar value of net national product for the decade centered in 1879 was $8.36 billion. Thus the total sum to be redistributed due to the debt was about 1.8 per cent of annual NNP.[6] If we assume that only the upper income groups received these funds, and that the entire tax was paid by lower income groups, this would be the maximum redistribution.

The effect of this redistribution of income upon the rate of capital formation will depend upon the savings-income ratio at different income levels. A plausible estimate of this difference, based upon Kuznets, is that the excess of the upper income group ratio over that of the lower income group was .40. Thus the redistribution would have increased the share of net capital formation in net national product by less than eight tenths of a percentage point. The effect of this increased capital formation upon the rate of growth of output can be estimated by the use of a familiar proposition of neoclassical economic analysis. The growth contribution of capital is equal to the product of the share of income going to capital and the rate of growth of the capital stock. Using Budd's estimate of the nonservice share as a measure of the share of capital in output, the increase in the growth rate resulting from the additional capital formation is about .09 of one percentage point—an amount less than one fortieth of the observed growth rate in the period. I conclude that any income redistribution due to government debt had a small impact on the rate of growth in the twenty-five years after the war.

VII. CONCLUSION

This review of some evidence relevant to the debate concerning the economic impact of the Civil War has not exhausted the possibilities. The effects of the war upon invention, upon the size of the government budget, and upon the nature and location of financial markets, for example, have been ignored. However it should be noted that a 1964 conference of economic historians concluded that "aside from commercial banking, the Civil War appears not to have started or created any significant new patterns of economic institutional change" [3, pp. 173–174].

While not always unambiguous in its implications, the evidence reviewed in this paper frequently runs counter to the Beard-Hacker thesis. Much work still remains on the analysis of the economic effects of the war but, at present, reservations regarding the traditional interpretation seem justified.

---

[5] The present analysis is concerned with the effects of payments made from lower income groups to higher income groups in each year. The possibilities of wealth effects or of previous declines in capital formation attributable to the purchase of bonds have been assumed away for simplicity. It is probable, therefore, that this analysis overstates the overall impact of any redistribution. Also assumed are constant returns to scale in production and disembodied technological change.

[6] Veterans' payments, usually considered to go to lower income groups, were rising during this period, and in the 1890s were 4 times payments to bondholders. Thus this analysis may not only overstate the effects during the period but also ignore offsets in later years.

REFERENCES

1. Charles A. Beard and Mary R. Beard, *The Rise of American Civilization*, New York, MacMillan, 1930.
2. Edward C. Budd, "Factor Shares, 1850–1910," Conference on Research in Income and Wealth, *Trends in the American Economy in the Nineteenth Century* (Studies in Income and Wealth, vol. 24), Princeton, Princeton University Press, 1960, pp. 365–398.
3. Thomas C. Cochran, "Did the Civil War Retard Industrialization?" *The Mississippi Valley Historical Review*, 48 (September, 1961), 191–210.
4. Richard A. Easterlin, "Regional Income Trends, 1840–1950," Seymour Harris, ed., *American Economic History*, New York, McGraw-Hill, 1961, pp. 525–547. [Reprinted above as essay 4.]
5. Charlotte Erickson, *American Industry and the European Immigrant 1860–1885*, Cambridge, Harvard University Press, 1957.
6. Robert William Fogel, *The Union Pacific Railroad: A Case in Premature Enterprise*, Baltimore, John Hopkins Press, 1960.
7. Robert W. Fogel and Stanley L. Engerman, "The Economics of Slavery," (printed above as essay 24).
8. Edwin Frickey, *Production in the United States: 1860–1914*, Cambridge, Harvard University Press, 1947.
9. Milton Friedman and Anna Jacobson Schwartz, *A Monetary History of the United States 1867–1960*, Princeton, Princeton University Press, 1963.
10. Robert E. Gallman, "Commodity Output, 1839–1899," Conference on Research in Income and Wealth, *Trends in the American Economy in the Nineteenth Century* (Studies in Income and Wealth, vol. 24), Princeton, Princeton University Press, 1960, pp. 13–71.
11. Robert E. Gallman, "Gross National Product in the United States, 1834–1909," Conference on Research in Income and Wealth, *Output, Employment, and Productivity in the United States After 1800* (Studies in Income and Wealth, vol. 30), New York, Columbia University Press, 1966, pp. 3–76.
12. Robert Gallman and Edward S. Howle, "Fixed Reproducible Capital in the United States, 1840–1900, Current Prices and Prices of 1860," (unpublished paper presented at the February 1965 meeting of the Purdue University Seminar on the Application of Economic Theory and Quantitative Techniques to problems of Economic History). [See essay 3, above.]
13. David T. Gilchrist and W. David Lewis, eds., *Economic Change in the Civil War Era*, Greenville, Del., Eleutherian Mills–Hagley Foundation, 1965.
14. Louis M. Hacker, *The Triumph of American Capitalism*, New York, Columbia University Press, 1940.
15. William T. Hutchinson, *Cyrus Hall McCormick: Harvest 1856–1884*, New York, Appleton-Century, 1935.
16. Reuben A. Kessel and Armen A. Alchian, "Real Wages in the North During the Civil War: Mitchell's Data Reinterpreted," *The Journal of Law and Economics*, 2 (October, 1959), 95–113. [Reprinted below as essay 34.]
17. Herman E. Krooss, *American Economic Development*, Second Edition, Englewood Cliffs, Prentice-Hall, 1966.
18. Wesley Clair Mitchell, *A History of the Greenbacks: With Special Reference to the Economic Consequences of their Issue: 1862–65*, Chicago, University of Chicago Press, 1903.
19. Wayne D. Rasmussen, "The Civil War: A Catalyst of Agricultural Revolution," *Agricultural History*, 39 (October, 1965), 187–195.
20. Stephen Salsbury, "The Effects of the Civil War on American Industrial Development," Ralph Andreano, ed., *The Economic Impact of the American Civil War*, Cambridge, Schenkman, 1962, pp. 161 168.
21. Robert Sharkey, *Money, Class, and Party: An Economic Study of the Civil War and Reconstruction*, Baltimore, Johns Hopkins Press, 1959.
22. Harry N, Scheiber. "Economic Change in the Civil War Era: An Analysis of Recent Studies," *Civil War History*, 11 (December, 1965), 396–411.
23. F. W. Taussig, *Some Aspects of the Tariff Question*, Cambridge, Harvard University Press, 1931.
24. Irwin Unger, *The Greenback Era: A Social and Political History of American Finance, 1865 1879*, Princeton, Princeton University Press, 1964.
25. Pershing Vartanian, "The Cochran Thesis: A Critique in Statistical Analysis," *The Journal of American History*, 51 (June, 1964), 77–89.

VIII IMMIGRATION, URBANIZATION, AND THE WESTWARD MOVEMENT

One of the most remarkable aspects of American economic development has been the mobility of its population. It has become customary to divide the process of population redistribution into three main categories. First there was the great international migration. Over the century which ended in 1920, a total of 34,000,000 immigrants arrived on American shores [3, p. 91]. Most of the immigrants were Europeans [4, p. 175]. Sixty per cent of all those who left European homelands turned to the United States [4, pp. 175, 185]. Second, there was the ceaseless westward movement. In 1790 Americans were huddled on the eastern rim of the continent. The geographic center of the population was on the eastern shore of the Chesapeake Bay. By 1960 the human center of gravity had moved 700 miles to the west and was located in Marion County, Illinois [3, p. 10]. Third, there was the shift from the countryside to the cities. When George Washington was sworn in as the first President of the United States, less than 6 per cent of his constituents lived in cities. The urban population did not surpass the rural population until Woodrow Wilson's administration. By the time that John F. Kennedy assumed office, 70 per cent of the population was urban [2, p. 14; 3, p. 29].

What were the factors which explain these movements? To what extent was population redistribution a response to economic forces? Which economic forces were most important? How did the shifts in population contribute to the growth of the economy? These are the questions examined by the authors of the essays in Part VIII.

Richard Easterlin (essay 28) and Simon Kuznets (essay 29) focus on the intercontinental migration. Easterlin attempts to disentangle "push" and "pull" factors in this movement. His examination of data on fourteen European nations over the period 1861–1910 indicates that the long-run tendency in the rate of emigration was a lagged response to the rate of each nation's population growth and to the level of per capita income. Easterlin suggests that countries which experienced high rates of natural increase in their population may have had difficulty in absorbing new additions to the labor force. Superimposed on the long-term tendency are cyclical variations in emigration which are closely related to variations in American business activity. That so many European nations had peaks in emigration rates which coincided with peaks in the growth of U.S. production, despite considerable variation in the peaks of their birth rate, suggests the existence of a significant "pull" effect in the intercontinental migration. Simon Kuznets examines the contribution of immigration to the growth of the American labor force. He estimates that if entry into the United States had ceased in 1870, the labor force in 1940 would only have attained about 70 per cent of its actual size.

Albert Fishlow (essay 30) and Robert Fogel (essay 31) are concerned with the role of railroads in the westward migration. Fishlow sets out to test the hypothesis, put forward by Joseph Schumpeter and others, that railroads were built ahead of population and demand. His test is based on the experience of the states of the Midwest in the years prior to 1860. Fishlow finds that railroads in this area were generally built in counties with relatively high population densities, not at random; that most railroads earned satisfactory profits from the beginning of their operation; that profit rates were not significantly correlated with the age of railroads; and that government subsidies to railroad construction were generally quite small. These findings lead him to reject the applicability of "construction ahead of demand" for the Midwest. Fishlow argues that railroads were nevertheless a potent force in promoting the westward movement because of what he terms "anticipatory settlement."

The Union Pacific Railroad was, according to Fogel, clearly a case in premature enterprise. Instead of defining prematurity on the basis of *ex post* experience, Fogel proposes an *ex ante* criterion: the probability that the road would fail as perceived by investors who were offered the opportunity to purchase Union Pacific bonds when the road was only half completed. In a chapter of his study not reprinted here, Fogel estimates that the market placed the probability of failure at more than 70 per cent [1, pp. 81–86]. This fear turned out to be misplaced. *Ex post*, the construction of the road was fully justified by its earnings. Fogel shows that over the decade following its completion, the private return on the cost of building the Union Pacific averaged 11.6 per cent and the social rate averaged 29.9 per cent. He then goes on to consider which of the various plans originally proposed for financing this premature enterprise would have been most efficient.

Jeffrey Williamson (essay 32) examines census data on the trend in urbanization in the Northeast during the ante-bellum era. He shows that the urbanization of this region accelerated after 1820, and reached peak rates during the decades of the forties and fifties. Williamson goes on to consider the inter-relationship between the growth of man-ufacturing and urbanization. He finds that manufacturing grew more through the "ur-banization" of industrial towns than through the "industrialization" of existing cities.

REFERENCES

1. Robert W. Fogel, *The Union Pacific Railroad: A Case in Premature Enterprise*, Baltimore, Johns Hopkins Press, 1960.
2. U.S. Bureau of the Census, *Historical Statistics of the United States, Colonial Times to 1957*, Washington, D.C., 1960.
3. U.S. Bureau of the Census, *Statistical Abstract of the United States*, 89th edition, Washington, D.C., 1968.
4. Walter F. Wilcox, ed., *International Migrations*, vol. I, New York, National Bureau of Economic Research, 1929.

28 INFLUENCES IN EUROPEAN OVERSEAS EMIGRATION BEFORE WORLD WAR I

Richard A. Easterlin

The focus of this paper is the unprecedented overseas emigration from Europe in the half century or more prior to World War I. From 1850 to 1914 over forty million persons left Europe, primarily for the New World. Since Europe's mean population during this period was less than 400 million persons, this implies a cumulative loss over six and a half decades equivalent to more than one tenth of the average population; with regard to labor force, a loss probably equivalent to more than one fourth.

All of the countries of Europe contributed to this movement, but the

Reprinted with revisions by permission from *Economic Development and Cultural Change, 9* (April, 1961), 331–351.

extent of participation varied widely. In view of the variety of possible factors affecting migration and the possibility of significant variation from one country to another in their relative influence, this is hardly surprising. Yet the fact that all of these countries were experiencing, though in varying degree, the impact of modern economic development raises the question whether it is possible to discern any regular influences, more or less systematically associated with economic development, which may account at least in part for the intercountry differences in behavior.

Clearly an adequate answer to this question calls for a much more extended investigation than can be undertaken within the scope of this paper. We have attempted, however, to assemble such data as were fairly readily accessible on emigration and two possible explanatory factors to see if any preliminary impressions emerge. Three aspects of the emigration movement are considered:

1. differences among countries in the secular level of emigration,
2. differences among countries in the long-term (primary) trend of emigration, and
3. the highly common long swings or "Kuznets cycles" in emigration.[1]

In seeking evidence of some regular influences responsible for the emigration patterns, we concentrate on two factors. The first is the rate of natural increase about twenty years prior to the emigration movement under study. The reasoning is that differences in natural increase rates result with a lag in differences in the rate of additions to the labor market. Relatively high additions to the labor market would be expected, other things remaining equal, to result in labor market slack (comparatively slower growth in wages, less secure employment, etc.) and to lead to relatively high emigration. Conversely, relatively small additions to the labor market would, by making for relative tightness, be expected to lead to relatively low emigration.

The rate of natural increase depends of course on both its birth and death rate components, and variation in both of these were

of significance during the period with which we are concerned. Even if all emigration were concentrated in a specific age group, say, 20–24 years, the lag one might expect between a change in natural increase due to a movement in the *death* rate and a change in emigration would vary according to the age-specific impact of the mortality change. Thus if the mortality decline were concentrated in the age group 0–4 one would expect a lag of twenty years; if in the age group 5–9, a lag of 15 years, and so on. At the extreme, if the mortality decline occurred only at very advanced ages, say over seventy years, when very few of the population were in the labor force, there would be no expected change in emigration as a result of the natural increase change. It is widely recognized, however, that the decline in mortality accompanying modern economic development occurred chiefly at the younger ages, most notably among infants, hence, the presumption that in general one might expect a lag of perhaps 20 years or so, whether or not the change in natural increase arose from fertility or mortality change. This problem could have been eliminated if, instead of taking natural increase as the independent variable, we used the rate of change in the working population of migratory age, particularly ages 20–29. Unfortunately such data are not readily available.

Our secondary explanatory variable is per capita income. The reasoning is that other things being equal the rate of emigration will vary inversely with the per capita income level. Of course if the per capita income figures related directly to the income situation of the persons of migratory age, then one would expect the observed differences to reflect the influences of differences in the rate of additions to the labor market and inclusion of our first variable would be unnecessary. But such is clearly not the case, since the per capita income figures include property as well as labor income and are averages over the whole population. Instead we take these figures as reflecting a complex of conditions associated with industrialization which govern the general level of economic opportunities available to workers in the economy. Thus our per capita income figures are taken as providing an indication of the general level of economic opportunities, while the natural increase rates provide a more direct reflection of the particular state of the labor market which young workers encounter. This, of course, is still some way from the ideal one

---

[1] The designation "Kuznets cycles" for the 15 to 20 year wave-like movements observable in so many economic series is suggested by O'Leary and Lewis in recognition of Kuznets' pioneering contributions to this subject [7].

might desire, the discounted value of the future income stream available to persons of migratory age.

It should be noted that we deal here with gross overseas emigration. No allowance is made for variation among countries in the ratio of net to gross or of continental to overseas emigration. The per capita income estimates are per head of the total population rather than per worker or per employed. Data for adjustment to the preferred conceptual basis were not readily available.

I. SCOPE AND SOURCES

1. Scope

The period covered by the analysis of secular levels and primary trends is 1861 through 1910. For the long swings analysis, a longer span, 1841 through 1920, is embraced, though data for some countries are not available throughout the entire period. Almost all of the principal European countries are included. The principal omissions are Ireland, which was clearly a unique case of economic catastrophe, and Spain and the Balkan countries, for which the time series were too short. However Spain was included in the long swings analysis as far as possible. Pre-World War I boundaries apply.

2. Sources

The primary source for the emigration and natural increase data is the compilation by the great Swedish demographer, Gustav Sundbärg. A later National Bureau of Economic Research migration study and Kuczynski's estimates of birth and death rates were used in some cases to piece out Sundbärg's series or secure greater chronological detail. Where the two latter works overlapped with Sundbärg's, the consistency of the estimates were uniformly very high. For the income figures, we used Michael Mulhall's estimates.

Clearly much more work can and should be done to identify the major deficiencies of both the demographic and income data. But it would be idle to suppose that complete answers to the questions of reliability can ever be obtained. At the same time, use of the figures for analytical purposes, such as that attempted here, itself provides some basis for evaluating the estimates. Our impression is that the results are encouraging, but this

of course is something the reader must judge for himself.

II. SECULAR LEVELS

Table 1 assembles the data regarding secular levels. For emigration the annual rates are averages of quinquennial estimates extending over the period 1861 through 1910; for natural increase, averages of decennial estimates for the decades from 1841 to 1890. The per capita income relatives in column 3 were obtained by averaging absolute income estimates for each country for 1870, 1880, 1890, and 1895, and expressing the result as a percentage of the figure for the United Kingdom.[2] The division of the countries into two groups is based not only on geographical location, but on the patterns of emigration and natural increase suggested by the data.

Turning first to column 1, one finds that among the Northern and Western (Group A) countries, annual rates of overseas emigration ranged from a secular low of 0.2 per thousand in France to a high of 6.6 per thousand in Norway. Among the Southern and Eastern (Group B) countries, the range was somewhat narrower, from 0.4 per thousand in Russia to 4.1 per thousand in Italy.

Were variations in secular emigration rates associated in a regular fashion with differences in secular natural increases rates, due allowance being made for a lag sufficient for the natural increase differences to translate themselves into differences in rates of addition to the labor market? If we consider first only the Group A countries, the similarity in rank order between columns 1 and 2 is striking. Norway had the highest rate of emigration and the highest rate of natural increase; France, in both instances, the lowest. And the progression as one moves from top to bottom is quite similar. With regard to magnitude the association is less consistent. This is most noticeable at the lower ends of the two columns, where accompanying a large increase in the rate of natural increase as one moves, say, from France to the Netherlands, there is a relatively small variation in the rate of emigration. This may be explained in part by the fact that we are dealing with a gross migration rate whose lower limit is

---

[2] [For sources and methods of computation see the article from which this selection is reprinted, Appendix, pp. 349–351.—Editors' note.]

Table 1. Secular Level of Intercontinental Emigration, Natural Increase, and Per Capita Income, by Country, Latter Half of Nineteenth Century

	Annual Average Rate of Intercontinental Emigration, 1861–1910	Annual Average Rate of Natural Increase, 1841–1890	Relative of Average Income Per Capita, 1870–1895, (UK = 100)
	(Per 1000 population)		
	(1)	(2)	(3)
A. *Northern and Western Countries*			
Norway	6.6	13.8	54
Great Britain	4.6	13.0	100
Sweden	4.0	11.5	57
Denmark	2.4	11.6	80
Finland	2.1	10.0	44
Germany	1.5	10.4	64
Netherlands	0.7	10.1	71
Belgium	0.3	8.4	72
France	0.2	2.5	76
B. *Southern and Eastern Countries*			
Italy	4.1	7.3	31
Portugal	3.8	8.5	29
Switzerland	1.7	6.9	58
Austria-Hungary	1.6	6.7	40
Russia	0.4	11.4	28

necessarily zero. If the rates were on a net basis (and allowance were made for intracontinental as well as overseas migration), the migration for France could and indeed would assume a negative value. In any event, this difference between the lower and upper natural increase ranges in the change in emigration per unit change in natural increase brings the measured correlation down somewhat, though it still remains significant $(r^2 = .59)$[3]. Experimentation with different periods for the lag suggests that the 20-year interval used here is better than a zero- or 10-year period (the only other ones for which a comparison could be made), though the improvement over the 10 year interval is slight and not statistically significant.

With regard to the Southern and Eastern countries, except for Russia, there is also some semblance of a positive association. In Italy and Portugal rates of emigration and of natural increase exceeded those in Switzerland and Austria-Hungary. However the differential in emigration rates associated with

a given difference in natural increase rates is perhaps somewhat larger for the Group B countries than what one would have expected on the basis of the figures for the countries in Group A. But a more noticeable contrast between the two groups is apparent if one compares the rates of emigration corresponding to given natural increase rates. This comparison suggests that at a given level of natural increase the emigration response was higher in the Southern and Eastern countries than in the Northern and Western. Because of these differences between the two groups of countries, the value of r^2, though still significant, drops to .40 when the figures in columns 1 and 2, excluding Russia, are correlated. If Russia is included r^2 drops to a barely significant .29.

The typically greater responsiveness of emigration at given natural increase levels in the Southern and Eastern countries suggests immediately the possible differential operation of per capita income levels, since the Group B countries are generally conceived to have been poorer during the period with which we are concerned. Mulhall's crude estimates (column 3) bear out the latter

---

[3] Throughout the paper, significance tests are at the .95 level.

Table 2. Rates of Emigration of European Countries, 1861–1910, Cross-Classified by Average Rate of Natural Increase, 1841–1890, and Relative of Average Income Per Capita, 1870–1895

Average Rate of Natural Increase 1841–1890 (Per 1000) population)	Relative of Average Income Per Capita (U.K. = 100), 1870–1895 (Per Cent)			
	20–39	40–59	60–79	80–100
13.0 +		Norway 6.6		Great Britain 4.6
11.0–12.9	Russia 0.4	Sweden 4.0		Denmark 2.4
9.0–10.9		Finland 2.1	Germany 1.5 Netherlands 0.7	
7.0–8.9	Italy 4.1 Portugal 3.8		Belgium 0.3	
5.0–6.9		Switzerland 1.7 Austria-Hungary 1.6		
< 5.0			France 0.2	

observation.[4] The simple correlation between emigration and per capita income is low or negligible, whether one considers all countries, all countries except Russia, or Group A alone. But when one takes account of income variations in association with differences in natural increase rates, some interesting relations emerge, though they are not strong enough to improve significantly the correlation.[5] In Table 2, the various countries have been classified on the basis of the figures in Table 1, according to relative income level and rate of natural increase, with the rate of emigration entered in the appropriate cell. Ignoring Russia for the moment, one finds a quite consistent pattern. Within each of the per capita income classes, emigration varies directly with natural increase, and within each of the natural increase classes, emigration varies inversely with per capita income.

In both cases there seems to be a suggestion of a curvilinear relationship. At a given income level, the emigration response to a given change in natural increase appears to be higher at the higher levels of natural increase. Correspondingly, in a given natural increase group the emigration response to a given income change appears to be greater at lower income levels. In general one gets the impression that among countries with relatively low levels of natural increase and high levels of per capita income, emigration does not vary much. But if natural increase is relatively high and/or per capita income exceptionally low, this makes for an exceptionally high emigration rate for the country.

Russia remains a puzzle, at least if one adopts the view that the figures here are consistent with the hypothesis that emigration was causally related to prior natural increase and current per capita income in the economy. Despite the fact that it had the lowest per capita income level and one of the highest

---

[4] Theoretically, of course, it is the income differential between country of origin and of destination that is relevant to the explanation of migration. However since one country of destination, the United States, was dominant for most of the emigration countries considered here, variations among the European countries in income differentials vis-à-vis the United States are due solely to variations in their absolute income levels; hence, the use of the latter here. A more refined analysis might attempt to take account of differences among the European countries in the distribution of emigrants by destination, but the crudity of the income figures hardly seems to warrant the attempt.

Mulhall's figures indicate that the United States

had a higher per capita income than every European country at every date except Great Britain in 1870 and 1880 [6]. It is hardly necessary to point out that an average income level in the country of destination lower than that in the country of origin is not inconsistent with migrants improving their particular earnings situation.

[5] The coefficient of determination for the multiple correlation of emigration rates with natural increase rates and per capita income for all countries except Russia is .54.

natural increase rates, the emigration rate for Russia is almost the lowest of all the countries considered. Various explanations suggest themselves, e.g., the availability of an extensive internal frontier which made internal migration a sizeable alternative to emigration; the persistence of legislative restrictions discouraging emigration; the disparate cultural background—the demographic patterns of the Slavic areas in other respects than emigration alone differ from the rest of Europe. Judging from the figures for the last two decades before 1910, it appears that the Balkan states would conform to the Russian emigration pattern. Clearly there is need, as indeed for all of the countries covered, for much more intensive study than is possible here.

III. PRIMARY TRENDS

From the mid-nineteenth to early twentieth century emigration rates in most European countries rose, but in varying degrees. The resulting change in the nationality composition of the migration stream has been associated with the spread of economic development across Europe. Thus, Kuznets observes that:

> The national origins of the European flow into the United States, in the succession from the British, to the German, to the Scandinavian, and then to the South and Southwestern European, reveal the progressive impact of the dislocation in Europe produced by changes in agriculture and by industrialization [3, pp. 45–46].

Changes in natural increase are sometimes cited as a specific element in the process. While we cannot pretend to more than cursory inquiry, it is of interest to see whether the data assembled here show any evidence of a systematic association between emigration and natural increase trends. We commence with a review of the trends themselves (Table 3).

Because the quinquennial emigration rates exhibit large swings of 15 to 20 years duration (see the section below), we have averaged the

Table 3. Primary Trend in Intercontinental Emigration and Natural Increase, by Country, Latter Half of Nineteenth Century

	ANNUAL AVERAGE RATE OF INTERCONTINENTAL EMIGRATION (Per 1000 Population)			ANNUAL AVERAGE RATE OF NATURAL INCREASE (Per 1000 Population)		
	1861–1880 (1)	1891–1910 (2)	Change, 1861–1880 to 1891–1910 (2) − (1) (3)	1841–1860 (4)	1871–1890 (5)	Change, 1841–1860 to 1871–1890 (5) − (4) (6)
A. *Northern and Western Countries*						
Norway	5.2	6.4	1.2	14.2	13.8	−0.4
Great Britain	3.6	5.0	1.4	12.0	13.6	1.6
Sweden	2.3	4.2	1.9	10.8	12.2	1.4
Denmark	1.6	2.6	1.0	11.0	12.7	1.7
Finland	0.6	4.0	3.4	9.6	14.4	4.8
Germany	1.6	0.8	−0.8	9.2	11.8	2.6
Netherlands	0.5	0.5	0	7.3	12.6	5.3
Belgium	0.2	0.4	0.2	7.0	9.7	2.7
France	0.2	0.2	0	3.2	1.8	−1.4
B. *Southern and Eastern Countries*						
Italy	0.8	7.8	7.0	6.2	8.7	2.5
Portugal	2.1	5.3	3.2	6.2	9.9	3.7
Switzerland	1.3	1.3	0	6.4	7.2	0.8
Austria-Hungary	0.2	3.1	2.9	5.1	7.5	2.4
Russia	neg.	0.8	0.8	8.1	14.2	6.1

figures for 1861–1880 and for 1891–1910 to secure a trend level estimate near the beginning and end of the fifty year period, and computed the change in trend level as a measure of the primary trend, columns 1 through 3. A similar procedure has been followed for natural increase rates with allowance for a twenty year lead over emigration, columns 4 through 6.

Comparison of the primary trend measures for the Northern and Western countries with those for the Southern and Eastern suggests a substantial difference. Only one of the Group A countries shows a primary trend figure in excess of 2.0, while three of the five Group B countries do. This, of course, is what one would have expected on the basis of prior knowledge about the shifting origins of American immigration. It should be noted, however, that in both groups of countries the trend is upward—of the fourteen countries in the analysis only Germany shows a downward trend. The growth in relative importance of the Southern and Eastern countries arises from the steeper slope of their trend, not from a general decline in emigration rates in the Northern and Western groups.

Do the differential trends in emigration rates reflect corresponding differentials in natural increase trends? There is perhaps some suggestion of this. Natural increase rates in the Group B countries tend to show a greater uptrend than those for Group A, as do the emigration rate trends. And the emigration trends for Finland and Switzerland, which initially appeared out of line with those for other countries in their respective groups, look more reasonable in the light of the trend in their natural increase rates. But there are also some important exceptions to the association between emigration and natural increase trends. Germany, the Netherlands, Belgium, and Russia show a substantial rise in the natural increase rate but little or no corresponding movement in emigration rate. If these countries are omitted the coefficient of determination between trends in emigration and natural increase rates is just significant at .39, but if they are included, it falls to a negligible value.

If the trends in emigration rates are compared with per capita income levels, significant inverse association is found. The coefficient of determination for all countries is .32, and if Russia is excluded, .45. On theoretical grounds there is little reason to suppose that

the *change* in the emigration rate of a country would be associated with its average income *level* during the period. But it is possible that differences in level were associated systematically with changes in other aspects of the economy which were responsible for the emigration trends. One possibility that comes to mind is the rate of change in per capita income. If low income countries had a small increase in real per capita income over the period, and coversely for high income countries, this might explain the observed correlation between emigration rates and income levels. Data on rates of growth are scarce; however, those available do not lend much support to this speculation. Of the group of seven countries, Great Britain which had the highest income level had one of the lowest growth rates, while Sweden with one of the lowest income levels had the highest growth rate.

If simultaneous account is taken of the trend in natural increase and per capita income level, no significant improvement over the correlations of emigration with per capita income alone results.

The findings of this brief primary trend analysis are inconclusive. While there is some suggestion that trends in emigration may have been related to those in natural increase, the relation is not pervasive enough to dominate the picture for the range of countries considered here. The emigration trends do show some association with per capita income levels, but more extended investigation is needed to determine whether this is accidental or can be reconciled with theoretical expectations through an implicit association between per capita income and some other variable(s) relevant to the explanation of trend movements.

IV. KUZNETS CYCLES

As has frequently been observed, overseas emigration from Europe was characterized by wide swings, whose magnitude dwarfs the shorter term fluctuations associated with the business cycle. Several writers have suggested that the swings were due in large part to earlier movements in natural increase or fertility [see, e.g., *8*, pp. 116–118]. In this view, a surge and then relapse in the rate of natural increase results some twenty years or so later in a corresponding surge and relapse in emigration. Kuznets, on the other hand,

Table 4. Summary of the Timing of Peaks and Troughs in Quinquennial Averages of Rate of Emigration, 1846–1920[a]

| | QUINQUENNIUM | | | | | | | | | | | | |
| | 19th CENTURY | | | | | | | | | | 20TH CENTURY | | |
	51–55	56–60	61–65	66–70	71–75	76–80	81–85	86–90	91–95	96–00	01–05	06–10	11–15
Total observations	13	14	14	14	15	15	15	15	15	15	15	1.5	15
Total peaks	7	1	0	6	7	0	5	5	2	0	8	3	4
Total troughs	1	3.5	6	0.5	1	12	0	0	1.5	10.5	0	1	0

[a] .5 indicates tie between specified quinquennia. In one case (1861–1865) there was two ties, so the total troughs are an integer.

reasons that the similarity among the European countries in timing of emigration swings suggests a common response to an external influence, and demonstrates that the timing of the emigration swings follow closely that of swings in economic conditions in the United States [*4*, pp. 31–36; *5*, pp. 26–34; *1*]. It is conceivable, however, that the various European countries were at the same time responding to a common swing in natural increase rates which they had experienced about two decades earlier. Hence we review the present data with the aim of testing this possibility.

Let us note first the evidence of Kuznets cycles in emigration. In preparing Table 4 the dates of peaks and troughs in the quinquennial averages of emigration rates have been marked off for each country. Table 4 makes it abundantly clear that the trend in emigration from the various countries was far from smooth. The duration of the fluctuations considerably exceeded that of "business cycles"; in most countries it was usually 15 or 20 years. In several of the countries with a particularly strong upward primary trend, notably Finland, Italy, and Austria-Hungary, the swings are less apparent. Elimination of the trend effect would very likely

bring the patterns for these countries more in line with those of the others.

As noted, a striking feature of the swings is the tendency toward fairly synchronous timing of the peaks and troughs in the various countries. Thus in 1846–1850, seven countries reached peaks in their emigration rates, but only one a trough. In the next decade, 1856–1865, ten countries showed troughs in emigration, and only one a peak. This tendency towards concurrence continues through the entire period.

The rates of natural increase, too, show fluctuations, though the duration is somewhat more variable, ranging typically from 10 to 20 years. (Table 5). There is some suggestion of similarity in timing among the various countries, though it is less pronounced than in the case of emigration. Particularly in the intervals, 1881–1890 and 1901–1905, the pattern is mixed.

Given then that there were highly synchronous swings in the rate of emigration from the various countries and, to a lesser extent, common swings in natural increase rates, did the former tend to follow with a fairly consistent lag the latter? This is the question to which Tables 6 and 7 are addressed. In the first column of Table 6 the

Table 5. Summary of the Timing of Peaks and Troughs in Quinquennial Averages of Rates of Natural Increase, 1841–1919[a]

| | QUINQUENNIUM | | | | | | | | | | | | | |
| | 19TH CENTURY | | | | | | | | | | | 20TH CENTURY | | |
	46–50	51–55	56–60	61–65	66–70	71–75	76–80	81–85	86–90	91–95	96–00	01–05	06–10	11–14
Total observations	8	8	8	8	9	13	14	14	14	14	14	14	14	14
Total peaks	0	1	4	4	0	1	6.5	2.5	4	0	7	4.5	4.5	1
Total troughs	6	2	1	2	5	1	1	4	0	7	1	4	1	0

[a] See notes to Table 4.

Table 6. Countries with Trough in Rate of Natural Increase in Specified Quinquennium Distributed According to Quinquennium of Trough(s) in Rate of Emigration 15 to 30 Years Later[a]

Number of Countries with Trough in Rate of Natural Increase in Specified Quinquennium		QUINQUENNIUM OF SUBSEQUENT TROUGH(S) IN RATE OF EMIGRATION										
		19TH CENTURY								20TH CENTURY		
Quinquennium	Number	61–65	66–70	71–75	76–80	81–85	86–90	91–95	96–00	01–05	06–10	11–15
1846–1850	6	3	0	1	5							
1851–1855	2		.5	0	2	0						
1856–1860	1			0	1	0	0					
1861–1865	2				2	0	0	0				
1866–1870	5					0	0	0	5			
1871–1875	1						0	.5	.5	0		
1876–1880	1							0	1	0	1	
1881–1885	4								2	0	0	0
1886–1890	3									0	0	0
1891–1895	7										1	0

[a] For any line the sum of emigration troughs may differ from the number of natural increase troughs because a given country may show more or less than one emigration trough in the subsequent 15 to 30 year period. See also the note to Table 4.

number of countries reaching a trough in natural increase rate in the specified quinquennium has been indicated (the entries in this column are the same as those in the last line of Table 5). Thus, we observe that in 1846–1850, six countries reached a trough in the rate of natural increase. The emigration rates for these six countries in the quinquennia falling 15 to 30 years later were then examined to determine whether any troughs occurred, and where this was the case, the number occurring was entered under the heading for the appropriate quinquennium. Thus the first line of Table 6 shows that of the six countries whose natural increase rates troughed in 1846–1850, three showed troughs in emigration rates 15 years later, one a trough 25 years later, and five a trough 30 years later. (The number of emigration troughs exceeds six because several countries showed two emigration troughs in the 15 to 30 year interval.) Table 7 presents similar data for the peaks in emigration and natural increase rates.

Table 7. Countries with Peak in Rate of Natural Increase in Specified Quinquennium Distributed According to Quinquennium of Peak(s) in Rate of Emigration 15 to 30 Years Later[a]

Number of Countries with Peak in Rate of Natural Increase in Specified Quinquennium		QUINQUENNIUM OF SUBSEQUENT PEAK(S) IN RATE OF EMIGRATION										
		19TH CENTURY								20TH CENTURY		
Quinquennium	Number	61–65	66–70	71–75	76–80	81–85	86–90	91–95	96–00	01–05	06–10	11–15
1846–1850	0	—	—	—	—							
1851–1855	1	1	0	0	1							
1856–1860	4		2	0	2	2						
1861–1865	4			0	2	2	0					
1866–1870	0				—	—	—	—				
1871–1875	1					1	0	0	1			
1876–1880	6.5						0	0	4	1		
1881–1885	2.5							0	1	1	1	
1886–1890	4								3	1	1	
1891–1895	0										—	—

[a] For any line the sum of emigration peaks may differ from the number of natural increase peaks because a given country may show more or less than one emigration peak in the subsequent 15 to 30 year period. See also the note to Table 4.

The two tables do not provide much encouragement for the hypothesis that Kuznets cycles in emigration resulted from prior swings in natural increase. The lags between turning points in emigration and natural increase vary from the lower limit of 15 to the upper of 30 years. If any lag is favored it is the 30 year one, but this implies that the typical age at migration was 30–34 years, which conflicts with evidence on the concentration in younger years. Of course one must not overlook the fact that the natural increase hypothesis does not require a consistent lag, because as noted earlier, the expected lag will vary if the impact of mortality decline varies among age groups over time. And clearly a fuller investigation would need to give more attention to magnitudes of movement. But so far as the present brief survey goes, there appears to be little support for the view of emigration swings as a lagged result of natural increase swings. This can be demonstrated in a different way if one reads the table starting with column rather than row headings as we have been doing. Consider, for example, in Table 6 the ten countries which show troughs in their emigration rates in 1876–1880. Half of these had troughs in natural increase rates in 1846–1850, but the natural increase troughs for the other half fell in quinquennia ranging from 1851–1855 through 1861–1865. And this pattern tends to characterize both tables. Countries tended to concur in the timing of their peaks and troughs in emigration rates, even though they differed with regard to their peaks and troughs in natural increase rates. Natural increase swings may, of course, have contributed to differences among countries in the *amplitude* of the emigration swings, and in certain countries may have played a part in affecting timing. But there seems to be little in the tables to support the view that a *general* influence among European countries giving rise to swings in emigration was a common swing in natural increase.

Thus we are led back to Kuznets' view that emigration in the several countries was responding to a common external force rather than similar internal conditions, in particular that associated with swings in economic conditions in the United States was a swing in the demand for labor which generated a common response among the European countries. Of course if movements in natural increase in the United States produced swings in additions to the labor force large enough

to supply the demand movements, there would have been little spillover demand for European labor. There were indeed long swings in natural increase in the United States, as Kuznets himself has shown, but a study of the evidence suggests that they were much too small to satisfy the labor demand swing [4].

In his analysis Kuznets shows for the period from 1870 on that swings in American immigration bore a close relationship to swings in the rate of growth of real per capita product [4; 5, pp. 26–34]. Further support is provided by a comparison of Abramovitz's long swings chronology for the United States with the timing of the peaks and troughs in the European emigration rates we are using here. In the first column of Table 8, below, the peaks are years which Abramovitz identifies as those preceding severe or protracted depressions or periods of relative stagnation, the troughs, as preceding sustained recovery from depression [1, p, 439]. In the second column we have listed the quinquennia in which emigration rates of the European countries tend to peak or trough. The high degree of agreement is immediately apparent. The impression that emigration did not reflect the relatively short swing from 1882 to 1892 is to some extent a statistical artifact, arising from our use of quinquennial averages for emigration. Data on annual immigration into the United States do show the imprint of this swing. However the amplitude of this swing in the United States was probably less than that of the others (indeed, Kuznets' smoothing technique, which is more drastic than Abramovitz's, eliminates this movement en-

Table 8. Long Swing Turning Points

	American Economy (1)	European Emigration Rates (2)
P	1853	1851–1855
T	1858	1856–1865
P	1873	1866–1875
T	1878	1876–1880
P	1882	1881–1890
T	1885	
P	1892	
T	1896	1896–1900
P	1907	1901–1915
T	1914	

tirely), and it seems likely that it would be less widely diffused in the European emigration figures than the others. The last peak in emigration, 1901–1915, stretches out longer than one might have expected from the movement in the American economy. A look at the data, however, shows that 11 of the 15 peaks occurring during this period fell in the first two quinquennia, 1901–1910.

There remains one final possibility to be investigated in considering the factors bearing on long swings in European emigration. Several studies have indicated that economic activity in the European countries also shows long swings. If these were common in timing and *inversely* related to those in the United States, then the view attributing dominant importance to swings in American demand would be weakened. However the available evidence, though fragmentary, does not indicate that this was typically the case. O'Leary and Lewis, on the basis of series referring primarily to industrial output and exports in France, Germany, Great Britain, and the United States lean toward the view that investment booms in the respective countries were fairly autonomous, and that there was no consistent pattern either of concurrent or offsetting swings [7]. Kuznets finds that comparison of the swings in rates of growth of total product in several countries does give some evidence of an internationally common chronology.

There seemed to be a tendency toward high rates of growth in product from the 1870s to the 1880s; toward low rates from the 1880s to the 1890s; toward high rates from the 1890s to the first decade of the twentieth century; and then toward low rates again in the World War I decade [*3*, p. 50].

Clearly, comprehensive study of the international diffusion of long swings is needed, but the material so far available shows little evidence of inversely related swings in American labor and European economic activity as a general occurrence, and to this extent is consistent with the view of swings in American labor demand as predominantly responsible for the common European immigration swings. So far as this brief analysis goes, therefore, it leads to a view with regard to Kuznets cycles consistent with Jerome's conclusion regarding the shorter term cyclical fluctuations in migration to the United States—that on the whole the movements were dominated by conditions in this country [*2*, esp. chap. 8].

V. IN CLOSING

The analysis presented here appears consistent with a view of European emigration prior to World War I of the following nature:

(1) Amidst the wide variety of influences affecting emigration patterns during this period several systematic forces were at work. Within the economies of the various countries certain factors, reflected here in our data on natural increase rates and per capita incomes, operated to establish the general level of emigration and, less obviously, the primary trend. The influence of these factors becomes more apparent as one takes longer term averages to eliminate the impact of shorter term forces, whether regular or not.

(2) Superimposed on the long period pattern were fluctuations of significant magnitude. Among the forces responsible for these, one element whose influence appears widely diffused is fluctuations in the growth of the demand for labor abroad, particularly in the primary destination country, the United States. This influence is apparent both in short-term business cycle fluctuations and the longer Kuznets cycles of 15 to 20 years duration.

Even if sound, this highly generalized view clearly requires much filling out in terms of specifics. Perhaps, however, it may provide a framework, based on the comparative experience of a number of nations, which might prove useful in further work.

REFERENCES

1. Moses Abramovitz, Statement in United States Congress, Joint Economic Committee, *Employment, Growth, and Price Levels, Hearings* (86th Congress, 1st Session), Part II, Washington, D.C., 1959, pp. 411–466.

2. Harry Jerome, *Migration and Business Cycles*, New York, National Bureau of Economic Research, 1926.

3. Simon Kuznets, "Toward a Theory of Economic Growth," Robert Lekachman, ed., *National Policy for Economic Welfare at Home and Abroad* (Columbia University Bicentennial Conference Series), New York, Doubleday, 1955, pp. 12–85. Reprinted in Simon Kuznets, *Economic Growth and Structure: Selected Essays,* New York, W. W. Norton, 1965, pp. 1–81.

4. Simon Kuznets, "Long Swings in the Growth of Population and in Related Economic Variables," *Proceedings of the American Philosophical Society, 102* (February, 1958), 25–52. Reprinted in Simon Kuznets, *Economic Growth and Structure: Selected Essays,* New York, W. W. Norton, 1965, pp. 328–378.

5. Simon Kuznets and Ernest Rubin, *Immigration and the Foreign Born,* National Bureau of Economic Research Occasional Paper No. 46, New York, 1954.

6. Michael G. Mulhall, *The Dictionary of Statistics,* London, Longmans, Green, 1903.

7. P. J. O'Leary and W. A. Lewis, "Secular Swings in Production and Trade," *Manchester School of Economic and Social Studies, 23* (May, 1955), 113–152.

8. Brinley Thomas, *Migration and Economic Growth,* Cambridge, University Press, 1954.

29 THE CONTRIBUTION OF IMMIGRATION TO THE GROWTH OF THE LABOR FORCE

Simon Kuznets

Through most of the period under review, migration in and out of the United States was relatively unrestricted; and the flows were quite substantial in both directions.[1] Data on emigration are scant prior to 1907, and it would

Reprinted by permission from " Long-Term Changes in the National Income of the United States of America Since 1870," International Association for Research in Income and Wealth, *Income and Wealth of the United States: Trends and Structure* (Income & Wealth, Series II), Cambridge, Bowes & Bowes, 1952, pp. 196–204.

---

[1] The movements which are most important here are those involved in a relatively permanent shift of residence, resulting in long-term addition to or withdrawal from the country's economically active population. Hence we are not concerned with tourists or visitors, but with the flows ordinarily designated "immigration" and "emigration."

Table 1. The Proportion of Foreign Born in Total Population and in the Labor Force, U.S.A., 1870-1940 (Population in Millions)

Year	Total Population (1)	Foreign Born (2)	Total Gainfully Occupied of Labor Force (3)	Foreign-Born Workers (4)	Percentage (2) to (1) (5)	Percentage (4) to (3) (6)	Percentage (4) to (2) (7)
1870	38.56	5.57	12.51	2.70	14.4	21.6	48.5
1880	50.16	6.68	17.39	3.49	13.3	20.1	52.2
1890	62.62	9.25	22.74	5.10	14.8	22.4	55.1
1900	75.99	10.34	29.07	5.74	13.6	19.7	55.5
1910	91.97	13.52	37.37	7.81	14.7	20.9	57.8
1920	105.71	13.92	42.43	7.75	13.2	18.3	55.7
1930	122.78	14.20	48.83	7.41	11.6	15.2	52.2
1940	131.67	11.59	52.79	5.80	8.8	11.0	50.0

take us too far afield to attempt to cover both the in- and outflow of migrants. For the present purpose it seems adequate to confine attention to the net result of the process, as it affected the resident population of the country. Since the flows across boundaries affected the native-born population of the United States but little, the net result of migration can be observed by gauging the relative importance of the foreign born in total population (Table 1).

The proportion of foreign born to total population stayed from 1870 to 1910, with minor fluctuations, at about one seventh—indicating that net immigration and mortality kept the growth of foreign born more or less at the same rate at which the native-born population grew. The break came after 1910: World War I sharply reduced the flow of immigrants, and immediately after the war legislative and administrative measures growing progressively more restrictive, reduced immigration to the United States to a minor fraction of what it had been in the decades preceding World War I. As a result, reduction of foreign born in the United States, primarily by mortality and only in small part by emigration, was not compensated by adequate immigration; and the share of foreign-born population in the total declined to 9 per cent by 1940 and should show a substantial further shrinkage in the 1950 Census data.

Because the immigrants were predominantly males, because by far the preponderant proportion of them (over 80 per cent) were over 14 or 15 and in the prime working ages, and because their participation in the labor force tended to be higher than that of the native population even for the same age and sex classes, the share of foreign born among the gainfully occupied was, throughout the period, markedly greater than their share in total population. Prior to 1910 the foreign born accounted on the average for somewhat over a fifth of the country's gainfully occupied, compared with only a seventh of total population. Even in 1940 the foreign born accounted for a ninth of the labor force, and only an eleventh of total population.

All the characteristics of immigrants (and emigrants) into the United States prior to the 1930s their responsiveness to short-term economic changes in the United States (the preponderance of the "pull" over the "push"), their sex and age characteristics, and their high labor force participation ratios —clearly indicate that this inflow of people was an economic response, an adjustment of population to this country's needs for it. Considering the magnitude and duration of this movement, it is difficult to exaggerate its importance as a factor in the economic growth of the United States. Since immigration brought in a large labor force, the cost of whose rearing and training was borne elsewhere, it clearly represented an enormous capital investment that dwarfed any capital inflows of the more orthodox type—a conclusion that stands with any reasonable estimate we can make of the money value of labor.

While the over-all volume of immigration responded to the short-, and sometimes longer-, term economic changes in this country—rather than to push in the countries of origin—distinguishing the latter reveals that the "push" exercised considerable influence on the *secular* changes in origin of American immigration. The shift from Great Britain and Ireland to Germany and the Scandinavian countries, and then to Italy and Eastern Europe, follows the trail of the Industrial Revolution in Europe. It at least suggests that immigration into the United States (and, at a far second remove, into other countries in the Western Hemisphere) provided a welcome alternative to population groups displaced by revolutionary changes in agriculture and industry, and thus facilitated in no small measure the course of industrialization in the European countries. This migration may thus be viewed as an adjustment of population to resources that affected a substantial part of the world, that in its magnitude and the extent to which it could adapt itself to purely economic needs has few parallels in history. Indeed it is matched only by the vast and free *internal* migration that occurred in the process of economic growth of such larger land-mass units as the United States and Russia.

This inflow of people may have been an even greater factor in the economic growth of the United States than is suggested by the percentages in Table 1. Many of the native born of this country at any given time are children of foreign born; and if no immigra-

tion had taken place, this country would have been deprived not only of the foreign born surviving at the time of record but also of the native-born children of immigrants.

Partly as a matter of curiosity we calculated the population and labor force of the United States on the assumption that starting in 1870 all foreign born are omitted, and net immigration is reduced to zero: (1) for the Census decade 1870–1880 the total net increase in native born was expressed as a ratio to the total population, including the foreign born in 1870; (2) this ratio was applied to native born in 1870 to yield an estimated net addition attributable to the native born alone; (3) the addition of the result under (2) to the native born of 1870 yielded a new figure for native born of 1880; (4) for the decade 1880–1890 we again applied the ratio of total increase in native born to total population (including foreign born in 1880) to the native born of 1880 secured in step (3) above, and calculated the increase in 1880–1890 attributable to the native born of 1880 (not actual but derived in step (3) on the basis of our assumption); and added this increase to the native born in step (3), to yield an estimate of native born in 1890. A repetition of the procedure for each Census decade gives us the figures in Table 2, column 2, with which the actually reported native born can be compared.

The effect of omitting the foreign born beginning with 1870 as progenitors of native

Table 2. Effects of Exclusion of Foreign Born on Total and Working Population, and Shares of Changes in Foreign Born in Changes in Total Population, U.S.A., 1870–1940

| Year | POPULATION (MILLIONS) | | GAINFULLY OCCUPIED (MILLIONS) | | PER CENT PROPORTION OF | |
	Total Native Born (1)	Same, Assuming No Foreign Born in 1870 or Later (2)	Total Native Born (3)	Same, Assuming No Foreign Born in 1870 or Later (4)	Change in Foreign-Born Pop. to Change in Total[a] (5)	Change in Foreign-Born Workers to Change in Total[b] (6)
1870	32.99	32.99	9.81	9.81		
1880	43.48	41.96	13.90		9.6	16.2
1890	53.37	50.23	17.64	15.95	20.6	30.1
1900	65.65	60.08	23.33	21.43	8.2	10.1
1910	78.46	70.17	29.56	24.31	19.9	24.9
1920	91.79	80.34	34.68	29.79	2.9	−1.2
1930	108.57	93.12	41.42	32.03	1.6	−5.3
1940	120.07	101.87	46.99	38.43	−29.4	−40.7

[a] Ratio of decadal changes in column 2, Table 1, to decadal changes in column 1, Table 1.
[b] Ratio of decadal changes in column 4, Table 1, to decadal changes in column 3, Table 1.

born reduces the latter to somewhat over 100 million in 1940, compared with an actual figure of 120 million. With no immigration the total population of the United States would have been not 132 but 102 million in 1940, or almost a quarter less.

Many American demographers have argued that less or no immigration might have slowed down, if not prevented, the decline in the birth rate and rate of natural increase of the native population. But this argument reduces itself largely to saying that, with no immigration, the economic rise of the native groups with the attendant industrialization and decline in the birth rate would not have been as great—which is but another way of attributing a large positive economic weight to the immigration stream. Since the procedure used here exaggerates the hypothetical additions to the native-born population by ascribing to the native born a rate of natural increase for total population, including the foreign born who because of their age structure and family rearing propensities tend to have a higher rate of natural increase than the native born, the purely demographic effects of omitting immigration and foreign born are probably not significantly exaggerated in column 2 of Table 2.

A similar calculation was made for the labor force, except that the changes were measured over a two-decade rather than a one-decade span, since it is more reasonable to assume that a labor force is produced in twenty rather than ten years. Here again, by attributing to the native-born population the propensities of total population including foreign born, we may have exaggerated the hypothetical rate of increase of the native-born labor force—and even more than in the case of total population because of the greater weight of foreign born in the labor force. Be that as it may, we arrive at a labor force of about 38.5 million in 1940, compared with the actual native-born labor force of 47 million, and the total labor force of almost 53 million.

Whatever specific criticism can be made of the calculations for columns 2 and 4, the conclusion suggested by them can scarcely be contended: without immigration between 1870 and 1930 the country's total population would have been not much greater than three quarters and its labor force about seven tenths of what they actually were in 1940. Nor is it likely that, with such substantially different magnitudes of population and labor

force, the economic growth of the country would have displayed the rate and structure that it actually did. The sheer difference in magnitudes, and particularly in the ratio of the labor force to total population (e.g., by 1940 the country would have had a labor force equal to its 1910 number of workers but a total population close to that in 1920), would have produced substantial changes in the structure of production and consumption.

The decline since 1910 in the contribution of immigration to the increase of the country's population and labor force has already been noted. But even before 1910 this contribution varied. Fluctuations in the shares of changes in the foreign born in the changes in total or in working population reflect this variation (columns 5 and 6). The shares are low in 1870–1880, rise markedly in 1880–1890, decline in 1890–1900, and rise again in 1900–1910. Obviously the processes whose net results are reflected in the successive totals of foreign born in this country were characterized by swings that must have differed from those in the native population, with respect to timing, amplitude, or both.

The explanation of these swings, as well as of the earlier emergence of negative entries for the labor force than in population in Table 2, columns 5 and 6, is provided by Table 3. We take gross immigration, an easily available series, as an index that adequately reflects swings in the rate of *net* immigration, since for the years when the latter can be calculated (i.e., when emigration data are available) the swings in it reproduce, with considerably wider amplitude, those in gross immigration. Variations in the last two columns of Table 2 are associated with larger than usual gross immigration in 1879–1888, smaller than usual in 1889–1898, and again a much augmented volume in 1899–1908. In other words, the long swings in the contribution of changes in foreign born to changes in total population or labor force are clearly due to long swings in the rate of gross (and presumably net) immigration.

The rates of change per quinquennium reveal these swings quite clearly (column 2), and the sequence suggested in our earlier discussion is pointed up (columns 3 and 4). Disregarding the decades after 1909–1918 as affected by legislation, we find the variations in the rate of change in gross immigration to be similar in timing, but of much wider amplitude, than the swings in rate of change in total population—suggesting quite strongly

Table 3. Rate of Change Per Decade in Gross Immigration and in Proportion of Males in the Latter, U.S.A., 1869–1948 (Annual Averages for Overlapping Decades)

Decade	Average Annual Gross Immigration (Thousands)	Pct. Change Per Quinquennium in (1)	Pct. Change Per Quinquennium, Total Pop.	Pct. Change Per Quinquennium, Flow of Goods to Consumers Per Capita	Pct. of Gross Immigration, Male	Change in (5),
	(1)	(2)	(3)	(4)	(5)	(6)
1. 1869–1878	292				61.5	
2. 1874–1883	369	26.4	12.2	29.2	62.6	1.1
3. 1879–1888	498	35.0	12.5	16.3	61.3	−1.3
4. 1884–1893	476	−4.4	11.5	3.6	61.3	0
5. 1889–1898	383	−19.5	10.5	4.2	60.7	−0.6
6. 1894–1903	410	7.0	9.5	14.3	63.8	3.1
7. 1899–1908	776	89.3	9.9	15.7	68.7	4.9
8. 1904–1913	972	25.3	10.2	10.1	68.0	−0.7
9. 1909–1918	696	−28.4	8.9	3.2	63.4	−4.6
10. 1914–1923	446	−35.9	7.5	6.9	57.8	−5.6
11. 1919–1928	416	−6.7	7.6	13.5	56.3	−1.5
12. 1924–1933	262	−37.0	6.8	4.0	50.3	−6.0
13. 1929–1938	90	−65.6	4.5	−1.2	42.9	−7.4
14. 1934–1943	48	−46.7	3.8	10.3	43.2	0.3
15. 1939–1948	75	56.2	5.4	17.4	39.9	−3.3

that the latter are, either synchronously or with a short lag, reflections of the former. But what is most interesting here is the relation between the fluctuations in the rate of change of flow of goods to consumers per capita and those in gross immigration. The two are quite similar, but the former precede the latter: the first peak in column 4 is in line 2, in column 2 in line 3; the first trough is in lines 4 and 5, respectively; the next peak in line 7 in both; the next trough in lines 9 and 10. Fluctuations in consumer goods (and the identically timed swings in net product) per capita seem to produce, with some lag, a pull on immigration, and are then reflected in swings in rates of growth in total population. It has already been suggested that the latter initiate, either synchronously or with a short lag, swings in the rate of change in residential and related construction; and therefore in total construction—with effects on the distribution of national product between consumer goods and capital formation. This sequence is here tied to the flow of migrants across the country's boundaries.

The ratio of males in total gross immigration (column 5) indicates the extent to which inflow of people was truly an economic response, and explains why the contribution of immigration to gainfully occupied began to

fall off before its contribution to total population. Except in the interval from 1934–1943 to 1939–1948 affected by the war, whenever the rate of change in gross immigration rose, the proportion of males tended to rise—with some lead in the former over the latter (columns 5 and 6). Thus the peaks and troughs in column 6 tend to coincide with or lead by half a decade the peaks and troughs in column 2, an observation true even of most decades affected by war and restrictive legislation. Since the male immigrants had by far the highest rate of participation in the labor force, this movement of the proportion of males is further support of the view that fluctuations in the rate of immigration were an economic response to varying opportunities for work in this country.

The proportion of males declined drastically after the 1904–1913 decade, since World War I and then restrictive legislation reduced the volume of immigration to a trickle. War, in general, impedes the movement of males more than that of females; and the restrictive legislation of this country, with its emphasis on family ties between already established residents and would-be migrants, also favored an easier movement of females. For this reason migration started at an earlier date to contribute less to the labor force than to total population. Finally, the drastic change in the sex ratio indicates an equally drastic change in the economic nature of immigration: instead of being a free and effective response to economic opportunities in this country, it has been transformed largely into a relief and personal adjustment process—which, however important for specific groups and individuals, cannot, in the nature of the case, approach the economic significance of the earlier process of free migration across boundaries.

30 THE DYNAMICS OF RAILROAD EXTENSION INTO THE WEST

Albert Fishlow

INTRODUCTION

The rapid pace of American railroad expansion in the 1850s has been noted often. No region was so transformed as the West. A few hundred miles of track, the remnant of the disappointed internal improvement schemes of the 1830s, emerged within ten years as a network whose extent surpassed even the most optimistic of those earlier dreams. By 1857 the Mississippi had been bridged and the railhead was on the verge of the Missouri. Iowa and

Reprinted and abridged by permission from Albert Fishlow, *American Railroads and the Transformation of the Ante-Bellum Economy,* Cambridge, Harvard University Press. 1965, pp. 163–204.

Wisconsin, achieving statehood just prior to the decade, were introduced to the wonders of steam locomotion bare years afterward. The much more densely settled state of Ohio was hardly provided with facilities before it was beset by excess capacity, all within the space of a single ten-year, exciting period.

The magnitude of these changes in the transportation sector was fully matched by changes in the other parts of the Western economy. Wheat and corn production expanded rapidly, the state of Illinois rising to leadership in both. The Old Northwest Territory, plus Iowa, accounted for something like 40 per cent of wheat production in 1850, half in 1860; the comparable proportion of corn output increased from 31 to 38 per cent. Agrarian prosperity was mirrored in land settlement and increasing land value. Urban settlements more than kept pace, particularly along the lakes. Most impressive of these new cities was Chicago, which almost quadrupled within the course of the decade, and about which a visiting Englishman could already write in 1866: "Chicago has grown to be the largest market in the world for corn, timber, and pork: the three great exports of North America."

This correlation between economic activity and transport improvement did not go unnoticed either by contemporaries or later analysts. A theoretical structure invoking lower transport costs can explain both the increasing agricultural supply area and the centralization of economic functions in urban nodes. The geographic extension of agriculture follows directly from the spatial displacement of the extensive margin. For industry, there is "the reallocation of the market area and the redistribution of industrial production in favor of the most efficient and the best situated firms." Another cause of concentration of industry is "the increased production and mass production economies caused by extending and enlarging the market area."

Such a logical relationship does not establish unequivocal causality, of course. If population migration had already extended the agricultural frontier, if urban agglomerations had already become prominent, transport improvement may have justified and reinforced such developments rather than initiated them. In 1808 Benjamin Latrobe rejected a primitive prototype of the railroad as a practical means of transport because it required much greater densities of population than then existed. Was the enthusiastic acceptance of the railroad in the 1850s the product of an already prospering economy and not its cause?

If one can establish the temporal precedence of railroad construction, the direction of the causal flow becomes unmistakable. Hence the crucial importance of the Schumpeterian notion of construction ahead of demand to his sweeping conclusion that "the Western and Middle Western parts . . . of the United States were, economically speaking, created by the railroad" [7, vol. I, p. 303]. Such a scheme, while it is consistent with my own notions of the place of railroad expansion in that development, is obviously much too simplified a version of the actual mechanism at work. After all, Ohio qualified for statehood only three years after the turn of the century, almost fifty years before railroads proliferated; more to the point, by the 1840s it ranked among the leading agricultural states. The first part of this chapter therefore subjects the assertion of railroad construction ahead of demand to careful scrutiny. What emerges is a more accurate statement of the dynamics of railroad construction in the West during the 1850s, and the perverse proposition that railroads were *not* constructed ahead of demand. This result does not entirely preclude railroad causality, however. Construction ahead of demand is inadequate because railroad promotion in already settled areas sparked anticipatory population movement to less settled areas. As a consequence, demand was already there when railroads were ultimately built farther west. In a larger sense, therefore, railroads *were* a leading factor. But first let us turn to the Schumpeterian formulation before elaborating upon this other explanation.

CONSTRUCTION AHEAD OF DEMAND

"As a rule," wrote an English investment counselor in the 1890s, "the American railroad came in advance of the settlers, and this contrasts with European custom. Apart from being impossible on account of our population density, the prospect of building a line through an unsettled country would be deemed an insane proceeding." Seventy years later, this characterization of American railroad development still has wide currency. Schumpeter's writings, of course, are responsible for much of its persistence. His dictum that many Midwestern railroad projects "meant building ahead of demand in the boldest acceptance of that phrase" can be neatly transformed into a theoretical case for the importance of the railroad [7, vol. I, p. 328]. Indirectly, too, Carter Goodrich's enlightening studies of the role of government in nineteenth-century American economic development have contributed to the vitality of this interpretation [5]. His work can be viewed as an explanation of the viability of such a developmental pattern of construction.

Indeed the sequence of zero population, railroads, and then economic development has become an implicit ideal type of construction ahead of demand. Unfortunately, despite such supposed eyewitness accounts, this specification (and implicit test) of the hypothesis is of little value. The real world bears no resemblance to this idyll: few areas of the country penetrated by railroad in the 1850s were frontier even in 1840, let alone without population altogether. A more general statement of the hypothesis, and less stringent tests, are necessary if the concept is not to be rejected out of hand.

Central to any redefinition must be the notion of an initial disequilibrium that is self-correcting over time not by adjustments along given demand and supply curves, but by induced shifts in the demand schedule. Thus when such projects are first planned or opened, the demand facing them is insufficient to justify them, as reflected by the lack of any profitable price that will clear the market. Over time, however, the sale of these essential services at prices less than full cost encourages income growth in the community so that the altered demand conditions merit the investment, and a profitable equilibrium is eventually attained. If the period involved is sufficiently long the present value of future returns may never exceed the cost of the project. In this instance no investment would have been forthcoming had a correct assessment of objective conditions been made; this is the domain of government subsidy or entrepreneurial error. A shorter period of transition introduces a second possibility. Rational investors, after allowance for the risk associated with estimation of expected rather than actual demand, would undertake this class of ventures.

Schumpeter himself tended to stress the first alternative when he asserted that "Middle Western and Western projects could not be expected to pay for themselves within a period such as most investors care to envisage" [7, vol. I, p. 328]. It is the one, of course, where the market allocates resources inefficiently from a social viewpoint—in the absence either of daring, and not always wise, entrepreneurs or external subsidy. The second set of the circumstances, while the private rate may still understate social priorities, will lead to less distortion since the projects will be undertaken in any event. But in both instances, whether ultimate financial success or no, it is the temporal precedence of supply under initially unfavorable conditions that sets the stage for the ultimate shifts in demand.

Three measures of construction ahead of demand emerge from this restatement of the concept. The first is *ex ante* and emphasizes investor anticipations concerning the configuration of demand facing the project. If the capital market absorbed the securities of Western railroads without a significant risk premium, this rules out widespread feeling that future returns were so far off that private investors could not participate profitably. Because of the unorganized capital markers of the period and the aggregative nature of our problem, this measure is not easily applied. A ready substitute, the prevalence of government aid, is. Subsidy is simply the limiting case in which the private market values prospects so dimly that funds are not available at any reasonable price. While it may miss intermediate graduations, "building ahead of demand in the boldest acceptance of that phrase" presumably will not be excluded.

But even if the project lures private investors because expectations of future profit are definite enough, construction ahead of demand cannot be ruled out. *Ex ante* measures all prove inadequate to the extent that realized operating experience differs from the anticipated. For an analysis of the investment decision they are central; but concern with actual effects requires reference to *ex post* indicators. Profits of the enterprise serve us well here. One of the implications of construction ahead of demand is that initial levels of demand are so low as to yield a less than profitable outcome. A second is that net earnings should increase over time as financial accounts register the supply induced shift of demand. Both implications are subject to test, although the variety of other factors changing over time requires considerable qualification of the second.

While positive and stable profits tend to

disprove the hypothesis, negative returns are more difficult to evaluate. They are compatible with a number of cases that one would not choose to label construction ahead of demand. For example, with a positive correlation between railroad construction and economic activity (generated from the side of supply of capital as well as the direct consequences of such building) some projects will reach fruition on the threshold of cyclical economic decline. The general reduction in demand causes such roads to fare badly; otherwise they might have done quite well. In no sense has construction ahead of demand in secular terms occurred. Profits must therefore be adjusted for cyclical variation if they are to be an accurate indicator. Or to take another relevant possibility: if railroads are manipulated as instruments of municipal competition and are unsuccessful, their financial statements as well as the laments of local businessmen will attest to this fact. Still a third factor contributed to poor operating results, namely mismanagement. One need only read the files of the *American Railroad Journal* at the end of the 1850s to appreciate how pervasive this factor was.

In all these instances, subsequent cyclical recovery, or change of management (or simply experience) may bring profitability. These cases conform to the typical temporal pattern of profit returns of roads constructed ahead of demand, although the circumstances are quite different. For certain purposes it makes no difference. In an aggregate model receiving its developmental impetus solely from the side of demand, the characteristic of investment without immediate output is what counts. But only in the pure case of construction ahead of demand, or development via excess social overhead capacity, is the investment primarily responsible for its ultimate fulfillment.

This asymmetry of the profits measure suggests the need of a third indicator. Population density, serving as a proxy for actual traffic demand, performs this function, but not alone. Some additional information is needed to determine when density is sufficient. To be sure, a population density of more than 90 persons to the square mile—the highest census classification — is obviously large enough to justify the construction of a railroad (but not necessarily many railroads). And at the other extreme, a frontier density of 2 to 6 persons per mile is a dubious source of demand; even geographically isolated mineral resources generated local agglomerations more substantial than this. But what of the intermediate range? Southern Michigan, for example, was largely populated with 18 to 45 persons to the square mile in 1850. The census described such regions as follows: "The third group—18 to 45 inhabitants to the square mile—almost universally indicates a highly successful agriculture." Yet Overton refers to the same area in 1846 as a "western wilderness," although no substantial change in population occurred between this date and 1850. He likewise speaks of John Murray Forbes as "fascinated by the prospect of sponsoring a railroad through the Michigan wilderness" [6, pp. 25, 27]. Most of the railroad construction of the 1850s took place exactly in areas of such intermediate and questionable densities.

This uncertainty can be resolved. If some railroads in an area of given population density earn satisfactory returns it is evidence that such a region can support railroads even if the recorded profits of other enterprises indicate otherwise. Some railroads in the East were unsuccessful, but the gains of others testify that the territory was not beyond the railroad frontier. Thus in conjunction with the record of *ex post* profits, population densities are a useful means of discriminating among doubtful cases of construction ahead of demand.

All three tests are utilized in the succeeding sections. Although each has its shortcomings individually, taken together they constitute a rigorous evaluation of the hypothesis. If roads earned profits from the start, did not show an upward trend in net earnings, were built through areas of previous and abundant settlement, and did not receive much government aid, virtually all would agree that construction ahead of demand had not taken place. That these were the typical characteristics of railroad development in the West in the 1850s is exactly what we shall argue. We begin with the relationship of settlement to construction.

THE PATTERN OF SEQUENTIAL CONSTRUCTION

One of the most striking features of Western railroad expansion in the 1850s is the regular progression of mileage added from more to less densely settled areas. Table 1 illustrates

Table 1. Railroad Mileage Added in Midwestern States, 1848–1860

Year	Ohio	Indiana	Illinois	Michigan	Wisconsin	Iowa
Up to 1848	275	86	55	244	0	0
1848	32	0	10	48	0	0
1849	16	0	5	27	0	0
1850	122	106	47	32	0	0
1851	333	152	45	36	20	0
1852	292	376	140	4	42	0
1853	500	379	390	0	18	0
1854	587	251	906	0	52	0
1855	385	226	462	86	156	68
1856	133	218	409	52	107	186
1857	129	123	74	46	291	90
1858	0	111	56	93	120	35
1859	174	60	103	83	78	154
1860	16	0	58	20	7	122
Up to 1861	2994	2088	2760	771	891	655

this tendency. By the end of 1852 Ohio already had one third of the total mileage it was to possess by the decade's end. Wisconsin and Iowa at the western extreme had virtually none; even Illinois had barely begun to manifest the railroad fever already gripping states farther east. Such regularity argues for deliberate rationality, with exploitation of opportunities as they became profitable, and postponement of projects in unpromising areas. If Western railroads were constructed ahead of demand, why not in some random fashion?

In any event, the very concentration of mileage in Ohio circumscribes the extent of construction ahead of demand. By the early years of the decade, as previously noted, Ohio already "is one of the most important members of that Union, both in wealth and in population, and exercises a degree of influence on our federal councils second only to the great states of New York and Pennsylvania," in the words of De Bow's *Encyclopedia*. It had begun a state-wide canal system in 1825 and completed it some ten years later; the consequences were rapid agricultural advance and population growth far before the 1850s. Railroads there were clearly not ahead of demand when they expanded rapidly.

Farther west, the 1850 population densities are sufficiently lower in states like Illinois, Iowa, and Wisconsin not to rule out the hypothesis. This is the theater in which such a process had to be staged, if anywhere. Yet even there the tendency previously described

in the large—that of sequential development of present opportunities—applies in the small as well. The first railroads in Illinois and Wisconsin were constructed in the rich tiers of counties lying astride the border between the states. The Galena and Chicago Railroad from Chicago, and the Milwaukee and Mississippi from its rival lake port, were both attempts to exploit the surpluses of the Rock River Valley, an area that already had contributed importantly to the large grain export of 1847 and 1848. Other roads in Illinois were built to counties beginning to feel the beneficial effects of the prior opening of the Illinois and Michigan Canal. Prominent among these were the Rock Island, and the Burlington line. This pattern of searching out the best opportunities first is quantified in Table 2.

Of the total number of miles of railroad built in Illinois by the end of 1853 more than 60 per cent were concentrated in the leading 11 wheat counties and the 8 largest corn growing counties, both as measured in 1850. This area was only one fourth of the total land area of the state, and the disproportion of railroad density is clearly due to the existing settlement and economic activity. Illinois railroads do not present a biased picture, as the additional evidence from the Wisconsin experience makes apparent. In that state the seven largest wheat producing counties plus Milwaukee, with but 10 per cent of the total area, contained one half of the state mileage at the end of 1860, and three fourths at the end of 1856.

Table 2. The Pattern of Railroad Construction in Illinois and Wisconsin, 1848–1860

| | ILLINOIS | | | WISCONSIN | |
Year	Entire State	11 Wheat Counties	8 Corn Counties	Entire State	7 Wheat Counties
1848	10	10	0	0	0
1849	5	0	0	0	0
1850	47	47	0	0	0
1851	45	36	0	20	20
1852	140	68	72	42	42
1853	390	94	60	18	18
1854	906	146	111	52	34
1855	462	23	21	156	100
1856	409	40	30	107	107
1857	74	0	0	291	75
1858	56	35	0	120	4
1859	103	41	15	78	38
1860	58	0	0	7	0

The less dramatic concentration in Illinois, indicating an earlier shift to construction in less developed areas in that state, is the product of two unusual circumstances. The Illinois Central, one of the two land-grant roads completed before 1860, went through the center of the prairie for this reason. Another cause of the divergence is found in the large number of east-west lines that bisected the state. These, numbering among them the Toledo, Wabash and Western; the Ohio and Mississippi; and the Terre Haute and Alton, were built to compete for the through service to the Mississippi River, not to develop local traffic. They were not supported by local interests, and were, on occasion, vehemently opposed; it was with much trouble that the Ohio and Mississippi, connecting St. Louis and Cincinnati, was finally able to secure an Illinois charter. Despite such distortions, the mileage built in counties which had attained importance *before* the railroad era was 31 per cent of the total against 25 per cent, the expected result if the spatial distribution were completely random.

By the time that the railroad reached into the prairie lands, moreover, that area was far from barren. The use of 1850 densities is misleading in this respect, since the mileage came much later. The migration westward, in full sway by 1852, inevitably led to the cheap and still unsold prairie land. The Illinois State Census of 1855 bears this out. Those prairie counties with smallest population in density in 1850 achieved a substantial increase in population by 1855; the number

of persons per square mile increased from four to nine and then to sixteen by 1860.

Between 1849 and 1856, 12 million acres of the public domain of 14 million acres still available in Illinois in 1849, most of it prairie land, had been sold. Some of the land fell into the hands of speculators of course, so total sales do not attest to settlement in the same proportion, but Gates estimates that about half did go to actual farmers [3, p. 109]. Thus by the time that many prairie railroads were finally completed, even if not in their earliest planning stage, not inconsiderable settlement and economic development had already occurred.

In the case of Iowa, the data confirm this more positively. Table 3 presents the population densities in the railroad counties of Iowa at various dates. The large increase in settlement occurred between 1850 and 1856, not later. Yet virtually no railroad mileage was built before 1856, as Table 1 shows, and it is therefore clear that the principal wave of settlement had markedly preceded the rail network in that state. The location of the Burlington and Missouri's land grant corroborates this conclusion. Although the land was bestowed in 1856, the railroad could not secure any east of Ottumwa, as far as the road reached before the Civil War and about 80 miles into the interior.

Table 3 makes another point: the existence of very much higher densities in the railroad counties than in the rest of the state. Such a circumstance is general and is the reason why state density data are of little value. For Iowa, Wisconsin, and Michigan, the 1860

Table 3. Population Densities in Railroad Counties in Iowa (Persons Per Square Mile)

	1850	1856	1860
Blackhawk	—	9.6	14.3
Buchanan	0.9	8.9	13.7
Cedar	6.8	16.5	22.4
Clinton	4.0	19.3	27.1
Delaware	3.0	14.1	17.4
Des Moines	31.1	—	47.2
Dubuque	18.0	43.0	51.9
Henry	20.1	35.6	43.1
Iowa	1.4	8.3	13.7
Jefferson	22.1	30.8	34.8
Johnson	7.2	23.4	28.4
Jones	5.2	15.1	23.1
Lee	36.8	51.3	57.0
Linn	7.6	20.4	26.3
Louisa	12.1	23.5	25.4
Muscatine	13.1	28.8	37.6
Scott	13.2	47.3	57.0
Van Buren	25.3	32.9	35.2
Wappello	19.6	30.7	33.6
Washington	8.8	19.6	25.1
State as a whole	3.5	9.3	12.2

statistics are 12.2, 14.2, and 13.0 persons per square mile. Coming as they do at the end of the period, these low densities clearly intimate construction ahead of demand in the previous decade. Yet the railroad areas in those states were much more densely populated; in Iowa, densities reached a level more than twice the state average, and a still larger multiple of those in counties without trackage.

This pronounced sequential pattern of Western railroad expansion suggests a rational exploitation of opportunity rather than the "insanity" imputed to American entrepreneurs. The absolute population densities, too, are quite respectable prior to railroad operation. The state censuses coming as they do at intermediate dates in the 1850s demonstrate this nicely. In themselves, these results cannot reject the hypothesis of building ahead of demand, however much doubt they cast upon it. It is still possible for the best of unprofitable opportunities to be taken up in order without altering the financial distastefulness of the totality. Because these American densities were unquestionably smaller than those exploited in Europe, and hence not obviously sufficient to support railroad transport, it still remains to be shown that different conditions of construction and operation could transform madness in a European context into profit maximization in the American West.

THE PROFIT EXPERIENCE

As a starting point, note how the pattern of railroad construction just described clearly suggests satisfactory results upon the early Western roads. Suppliers of capital would have soon become discouraged in the face of patently unfavorable operating results on those Western lines already completed early in the decade in the most settled areas. The Western railroad boom, in fact, continued strongly at least to the beginning of 1855. It was not the result of an absent capital constraint. In spite of the vast amounts of capital allocated to railroad construction, calm and detached judgment was not thrown to the winds. Many projected roads remained precisely in an inchoate stage: "If the elaborate railroad network planned for Illinois by different groups and individuals during the fifties had been constructed, all parts of the state would have been brought within 2 to 5 miles of railroad lines. The only obstacle which prevented the carrying out of these grand schemes was the lack of capital" [3, p. 85]. The capital market rationed resources, albeit imperfectly, between railroads and other enterprises. Hence the early roads could not all have been unprofitable.

These inferences are confirmed by direct evidence upon profits.[1] Some of the early lines were veritable bonanzas. The Galena,

---

[1] We should not place excessive weight upon dividends to shareholders as a measure of profits attained. Even when results were poor, many shareholders did receive interest payments during the construction period, and did obtain their equity at a discount, as when contractors received partial payment in stock. Moreover levered financial structure—large debt relative to equity—meant that residents along the right of way, most typically the source of equity finance, were able to capture the indirect, spatially fixed benefits such as increased land values for a smaller investment than otherwise. The emphasis upon swindling promoters and hapless farmers is somewhat misplaced accordingly. In Wisconsin the experience *was* unhappy, but only because the railroads were not built as promised. Once in operation, dividends to share capital understate the extent of the return to investors. The slightly smaller return to railroads in aggregate than the loan rate, implying in turn a return to equity less than that to the enterprise, must be interpreted in this light.

for example, paid a dividend of 10 per cent less than two years after opening and was a regular income producer throughout the period. Of the early Illinois lines in general, Gates writes, "these roads tapped the rich hinterland of Chicago and prospered at once" [*3*, p. 86]. It was more than Illinois produce which helped to make such lines as the Galena, the Rock Island, and the Burlington initial and continued successes. The rapidly increasing surpluses of Iowa and Wisconsin sent to a Chicago market contributed to their financial well-being also. The Michigan Central and Michigan Southern to the east benefited from a similar through traffic once they reached Chicago in 1852, as their profit statements vividly show.

Without such extraordinary opportunities as these, other lines did not flourish as conspicuously. Nonetheless the aggregate record tells a clear tale of success. Table 4 indicates the extent to which early returns on Western railroads bear out waiting demand. The returns of 5.6 and 7.2 per cent in 1849 and 1855–1856, respectively, do not compare unfavorably with profits earned in other sectors. As Conrad and Meyer state, "in contemporary chronicles it is obvious that Southerners and Northerners alike considered 6–8 per cent a reasonable rate of return and a reasonable asking price for loans." More to the point, perhaps, is the loan rate charged Western railroads themselves in the capital market. Seven per cent bonds with maturities of fifteen years and the like were negotiated in the early 1850s at 85–90 net, a discount that resulted in an effective rate of between 8 and 9 per cent. There seems to have been little variation until the tightness of 1854. Despite the veritable deluge of securities seeking placement, frequently of poorer quality than the earlier offerings, prices did not weaken.

Table 4. Net Earnings of Western Railroads (As a Percentage of Cost of Construction)

State	1849	1855–1856	1859
Ohio	7.5	6.4	3.7
Indiana	6.1	6.2	5.2
Michigan	4.2	10.2	4.6
Illinois	8.7	6.8	3.5
Wisconsin	—	12.5	3.1
Iowa	—	—	3.0
Total West	5.6	7.2	3.7

Eastern railroads earned only slightly more in 1849 than those in the West, 6.3 versus 5.6 per cent, and by 1855 the sign of the inequality was reversed: the 7.2 per cent of Western roads exceeded the 6.1 per cent of New England and Middle Atlantic mileage. To a large measure these results reflect the adaptation of Western railroads to lesser levels of gross receipts than those in the East. In 1855 Western traffic earnings came to about $4800 per mile against $7000 per mile for Eastern railroads. But relative to cost, the results are almost identical: 14 cents of receipts per dollar of cost in the West, 15 cents in the East.[2] Western railroads, hastily and cheaply built, were thus perfectly suited to the lower absolute demands found in the West.

Thus in private, not only social terms, railroads in the early 1850s were already beginning to justify their construction. Only subsequently, and in large measure owing to the panic of 1857, did they become financial burdens rather than blessings. Table 4 describes the transition: despite a more than 33 per cent increase in mileage between 1855–1856 and 1859, net earnings showed an $800,000 or 6 per cent, decline.

These aggregative data do not convey the entire complex developmnt of Western railroad fortunes. In particular, even by 1855–1856, declining profits had set in for many railroads in Ohio and Indiana. That is, contrary to the increase in earning capacity over time predicted by the notion of construction ahead of demand, one often finds actual deterioration.

However absolute decline in profits is not necessary to validate the contentions that returns upon roads in new areas were substantial in the first years of operation, and that there was no marked tendency toward increase over time. Newly opened roads in the farther West did in fact do better on the average than those in operation for a longer period of time in Ohio and Indiana. Thus in

---

[2] The lower Western gross receipts per mile are not evidence of construction ahead of demand. At such a level they were fully comparable to the gross revenues in the East at the end of the first decade of railroad operation there, and represented a much larger volume of physical output. To assert that Western levels in the 1850s are indicative of construction ahead of demand is to imply that Eastern railroad development in the 1830s was similarly premature. No one, to my knowledge, has argued that.

Table 5. Number of Railroads by Rate of Return and
Year of Completion, 1855–1856

	RATE OF RETURN		
Year of Completion	Less Than 5 Per Cent	5 to 10 Per Cent	Greater Than 10 Per Cent
Incomplete in 1856	5	1	1
1855	2	1	1
1854	3	5	1
1853	2	5	2
1852	2	2	5
1851	2	0	2
1850 or earlier	2	1	0

1855–1856 the aggregate return in Wisconsin was more than twice that in the already established states of Ohio and Indiana; Illinois ranks higher as well and would be substantially greater (10.8 per cent instead of 6.8 per cent) if not for the incomplete, land-grant Illinois Central, which was the exception of railroad development in the decade, not the rule.

In Table 5 we present the rate of return in 1855–1856 as a function of the age of the railroad. The rates are those of Table 4, with the dates of completion drawn from the Treasury Report of 1855 and Paxson's study of railroads in the Old Northwest. The hypothesis of independence between the rate of return and the age of the railroad cannot be rejected.[3] This does not necessarily disallow the notion of substantial supply induced shifts in demand over time. These may well have occurred although introduction of new facilities at a rapid rate prevented older roads from realizing the beneficial effects. But it then follows that the second, and large, wave of railroads did have demand waiting for them. The results do therefore bear upon the hypothesis. An even more telling *negative* relationship, which I almost would have expected, is denied as well. One reason why it does not appear is the cluster of railroads exhibiting extremely high returns in 1855–1856 and completed in 1852. A closer analysis

of four of these five railroads, however, indicates that their returns were high from their inception. This is the key point. Table 6 traces their path of profits over time. Although some upward trend is apparent for the Michigan Southern and the Terre Haute and Richmond, their initial yields are quite respectable from the start. Note, too, that the two incomplete roads earning 5 per cent or better, as shown in Table 5, were both in Wisconsin; railroad development at the geographic margin even for small sections of road was a paying proposition. Although not reflected either in Table 5 or in Table 6, because Iowa railroads do not appear in 1855 and by 1859 the panic had struck, early returns in that state conform to the same favorable pattern.

Despite the lack of a negative relationship, an element of overcommitment to railroads that were, and would continue to be, unprofitable did enter. Sometimes roads were built that were unneeded. Competition not only eroded monopoly profits but could be carried to excess as well.

By 1855 some of these unhappy consequences were quite apparent in Ohio, just assuming first place among the states in railroad mileage. There the aggregative profits of 6 per cent in 1855–1856 present a misleading aspect. Of the twenty reporting railroads, nine earned less than 5 per cent; three on the other hand were immensely profitable: the Cleveland, Painesville, and Ashtabula, the Cleveland and Toledo, both components of the lake shore route, and the Cleveland, Columbus, and Cincinnati. If these three be removed, the aggregate return in the state barely exceeds 4 per cent. These hard times did not descend owing to construction ahead of demand. They were the product of overextension of railroad mileage in a well-developed territory, an overextension dictated by a conjunction of technology, market structure, and local governmental subsidy.

As mileage initially increased in that state, attempts to arrange combinations, agreements, and formal liaisons began, going as far back as 1851. Given high fixed costs, profitability of railroads depended crucially upon the magnitude of receipts; if business was substantial, average costs could be reduced, and returns augmented. The incremental expenditure to subsidize potential allies was thus a rational move for each railroad taken in isolation. Hence the considerable support of Eastern trunk lines like

---

[3] A 2×2 contingency table was created by combining all railroads with returns over 5 per cent, excluding incomplete railroads, and dividing the years into two groups, one up to and including 1852, the other from 1853 on. χ^2 is then .027. For one degree of freedom $\chi^2_{.95} = 3.84$ and the hypothesis of independence is upheld by these data by a very decisive margin.

Table 6. Rate of Return Over Time, Selected Railroads (Per Cent)

Railroad	1852	1853	1854	1855
Michigan Southern	4.6	9.6	6.3	7.5
Michigan Central	7.4	6.6	7.2	8.2
Terre Haute and Richmond	5.4	7.9	10.6	12.2
Cleveland, Columbus & Cincinnati	13.2	—	12.6	15.9
Cleveland, Painesville & Ashtabula	—	—	—	—

the Pennsylvania and the Baltimore and Ohio given to favorite feeders through the state, such as the Pittsburgh, Fort Wayne and Chicago; the Steubenville and Indiana; the Central Ohio; and the Marietta and Cincinnati. Within the state, rivalries led the Little Miami to invest in the Springfield, Mt. Vernon, and Pittsburgh. The Cincinnati, Hamilton, and Dayton saw its defense in the promotion of the Hamilton and Eaton, and the Greenville and Miami. Others did likewise. What was rational for the individual road rebounded to the ultimate disadvantage of all as mileage, and competition, increased. Added to such railroad rivalry was commercial rivalry. Individual towns sought better access to market and encouraged additional construction by subsidy. When competitive construction flagged, the additional device of lower rates was not unfamiliar; such lower prices were promptly met, and, without substantial short-run market elasticity of demand, lower profits for all was the unfailing rule.

The distinction here between creation of excess capacity and construction ahead of demand does not depend upon the high level of population density alone, although that is sufficient evidence by itself. It is also true that the railroads in question continued to be unprofitable more than a decade later. The average rate of profit of ten Ohio railroads yielding low returns in 1855 was 2.5

per cent; in 1869 it was barely higher at 2.8 per cent and still less than half of the prevailing Ohio return. What was excess capacity earlier was not justified later. For Ohio railroads, at least, time was not necessarily a curative for entrepreneurial error.

Confounded with these competitive excesses is the cyclical decline on Western roads beginning even before the panic of 1857. Our aggregate data in Table 4 portray the situation from the side of net earnings over the interval 1855–1856 to 1859. To bring the annual pattern of gross receipts per mile of road into full focus, we present in Table 7 the continuous calendar year earnings of so-called "Chicago" railroads, representing almost half of Western revenues. Receipts per mile of road fell from a peak of more than $6000 in 1856 to a trough of little more than $4000 in 1859. The aggregate receipts of 1857 were not reached again until the railroad prosperity brought by the Civil War.

This reduction in revenues led to the inevitable series of defaults, receiverships, and reorganizations. In perspective, this first substantial crisis of the railroad age was relatively minor. In 1859 only 2500 miles were in receivership, or about 8 per cent of the total; the comparable statistic in 1877 and 1894 was 18 and 20 per cent, respectively. Nonetheless Western railroad fortunes were shattered. Security prices plummeted. Cole's index

Table 7. Gross Receipts, "Chicago Railroads"

Year	Gross Receipts (Thousands of Dollars)	Mileage Covered	Receipts Per Mile (Dollars)
1855	13,298	2,509	5,300
1856	17,343	2,782	6,200
1857	18,590	3,362	5,500
1858	15,197	3,504	4,300
1859	14,978	3,719	4,000
1860	17,690	3,728	4,700

of Western stock prices (1853=100) shows a decline from 90 in the spring of 1857 to less than 40 at the end of 1859. By contrast Southern railroad investment and receipts continued to increase until the end of the decade. Nor did New England roads feel the burden commensurately.

This discussion has indicated that early returns to the enterprises in the West were comparable to the returns to be earned in other sectors. Subsequently the aggregate return was driven downward by excess competition and by cyclical decline. Some Western roads, usually those that were profitable from the start, continued to prosper by reason of an erosion-proof monopoly of location. Ironically, it had been the example of these that led to the excess of competitive zeal and helped to reduce the global return. The later, and less satisfactory, experience clearly does not make a case for construction ahead of demand.

This analysis of the *ex post* profitability of Western roads does not yet complete the investigation. It is also of interest to determine to what extent these actual gains were foreseen by private investors. We have already hinted at the answer in the previous discussion. A closer examination of the magnitude of governmental aid will confirm the impression that railroad promoters found sufficient funds to pursue their objectives within the context of the market system.

THE PATTERN OF GOVERNMENTAL ASSISTANCE[4]

One of the usual concomitants of construction ahead of demand is reliance upon external subsidy. Without such aid there is little incentive to build where profits are expected to be far distant and uncertain at best. As a result of Carter Goodrich's recent painstaking efforts, the liberal extent of government participation in the development of the nineteenth-century transportation network has been well documented. Thus there exists a *prima facie* case for the feasibility, though not necessarily the occurrence, of premature construction.

Looked at more closely, however, the structure of aid in the 1850s clearly goes against

---

[4] [The analysis of this section has been omitted, and only the introduction and conclusion presented. For the detailed analysis see the book from which this selection is taken, pp. 189–196.—Editors' note.]

the hypothesis. All types of assistance, although usually treated identically for their developmental consequences, are not in reality the same. Whereas state and federal subsidies can easily serve as active incentives to initiate railroad construction, local aid is of a more passive character. It is offered subsequent to individual promotion and is often as much extorted by threat as voluntarily given. This difference in entrepreneurial content is reflected by the difference in the financial conditions surrounding the aid. Federal land grants were direct subsidies, state assistance primarily consisted of direct expenditure, but local aid was, as often as not, a loan ultimately to be repaid. Private profits had to loom somewhere on the horizon in the latter case. This distinction is not universally valid. Certain large cities could take the lead in the construction of railroads designed for trade diversion; and federal land grants could be allocated to roads already in process, like the Burlington. Yet, despite such exceptions, the identification of active aid with higher levels of governmental responsibility, and passive aid with the county and town levels, is a useful one.

Not only was governmental assistance in the West limited primarily to local funds, but these themselves were quite small. In Indiana sixteen counties and ten cities contributed less than $2,000,000; in Illinois, only $4,000,000. This amounted to less than 5 per cent of costs. As a proportion of total cost in Wisconsin, too, local aid amounted to less than 10 per cent.

This is not to assert that local investment was totally insignificant or that it was ever unwanted. Beyond a doubt the availability of such funds at an early stage of a project was an important asset when going to the capital market in search of further private funds. Local securities given in exchange for stock also were more marketable than the shares themselves. On the other side, however, it is true that the returns to municipalities from such local assistance, even if negligible financially, were often large. There were too many instances in which towns could be as easily avoided as traversed, and with eager competitors clamoring for relocation of the road, the chance could not be put to the test. Accordingly the social return from the investment was almost infinite in opportunity cost terms: in the absence of aid there would likely be only a mournful history of municipal decay and decline. Ironically, although the alternative of not securing the railroad was so baleful, the advantage of having it was limited because other localities all behaved in similar fashion. As a consequence none secured a relative advantage, and the global return was smaller than that to the individual participants. There can be no doubt that local aid contributed to the excess competition prevalent in Ohio by the mid-1850s; the communities of that state alone subscribed about as much as all those in Illinois, Indiana, and Wisconsin put together. The combination of local autonomy, economic decentralization, and rational decision-making led to a bias toward over-construction to be sure, but not ahead of demand.

The pattern of governmental aid in the West in the 1850s thus adds to the mounting evidence that railroads were not built ahead of demand. Assistance was predominantly local, and relative to total expenditures it was not a major factor. The experience is a sharp contrast to the earlier episode of state aid in the 1830s. More governmental funds were spent to build the thousand-odd miles of Western canals and two hundred miles of railroad in the 1830s and 1840s than was expended for the nine thousand miles of railroad between 1850 and 1860. Early in the latter decade Israel Andrews correctly sized up the fundamental difference in economic conditions that brought about that dramatic reversal:

> The numerous failures in the first efforts of the new States to construct works of internal improvement were not the result of accident, but a matter of necessity. The schemes were all premature.... The country had not been settled a length of time sufficient to designate the sites that were to become the great depots of trade, or the convenient routes for travel and business.... Both the old and the new system had its peculiar characteristics. The first proposed in the newly-settled states ... *anticipated* the wants of the country.... The works more recently commenced rest on a very different foundation. They were constructed, and are adapted, to supply wants which *actually* exist.

To which one can only give assent.

THE PROCESS OF ANTICIPATORY SETTLEMENT

To recognize the response of individual Western railroad projects to present profit opportunities is not completely to deny the causal influence of the railroad in that region's economic expansion in the 1850s. Even if they were not the exogenous force generating that development as suggested by Schumpeter, they obviously extended the range of profit opportunities once they were constructed. What was profitable previously at the higher transport rates became more so with lower charges, and, in addition, the railroad provided an efficient and rapid medium for personal movement. Thus subsequent development, although not initiated by the railroad, is partially explained by its endogenous, second-round effects. An analogy may clarify this point. An increased demand for steel, say, sets in motion demands for a whole host of other products and the larger production of these other industries generate still further demands. These additional demands, dependent on the internal characteristics of the industries involved, are important to the final result while not themselves the initiating cause of expansion.

It is unnecessary to concede this much. Although the first railroads built in the West in the 1850s were a response to existing economic opportunities, their effects transcended the areas they directly served. The larger, and more undeveloped, part of the West felt the repercussions too. Spatial fixity of rail service did not preclude personal mobility. Once the railroad reached Ohio, settlement in Illinois and Iowa became much more attractive than before. By the time railroads advanced farther west the population and economic development necessary to sustain them were already there—that is why those railroads were built when they were—so that individual, private projects were feasible. But the reason such settlement was waiting was the railroad itself, considered collectively. Hence the ramifications of early railroad construction exceeded the transport cost reduction it brought to the limited areas served. And although the favorable demand for American agricultural exports generated by the Irish famine is clearly one of the factors influencing the beginning of the boom, the continued westward migration from 1850 through 1853, in the face of unsatisfactory wheat prices and small international demands, testifies strongly to the influence of the railroad in the development of the decade.

This interpretation takes us far from a simple Schumpeterian world. Indeed, it almost turns that model on its head: instead of a heroic role for the railroad investor or even the state, the beneficiary of railroad construction displays the crucial attributes of foresight. The Western American farmer was different from his European counterpart or agrarians in underdeveloped countries today, and that difference consisted of a responsiveness to market forces and ubiquity of a profit motive.

The appreciation of land is central to all of this. The windfall gains accruing to individuals temporarily in advance of the main path of settlement might well outweigh the current incomes derived from production. Not only the future gains on land yet to be settled were relevant; past appreciation provided the wherewithal for further migration.

What the railroad brought, of course, was exactly higher land values, and much before its direct benefits mounted up. Speculative excesses insured that. It was the wise man who moved quickly and far. Examples of such anticipatory settlement before the railroad are legion.

The decision for anticipatory settlement apparently was well founded. The Bogues' data on profits of land speculators show the rate of return on Illinois prairie land abruptly increasing from 1855 through 1870 as improved transportation access and war inflation led to rapid rise of land values [1, p. 13]. The return noticeably starts upward prior to the war, suggesting that the construction of prairie railroads was making its influence felt. By contrast, earlier investments in land in the 1830s were premature (but not irrational), for the planned transport network of that decade never materialized.

Appreciation also had a negative aspect in encouraging anticipatory settlement. Some migrants, able to afford only a small sum for the purchase of land, were driven in the van of the railhead by necessity rather than choice. Paul Gates has generalized along these lines. Speculators created "poorly developed rural communities which meant thin farm development, promised little freight for prospective railroads, and made subsidies necessary if they were to be built in such areas" [4, p. 91].

Evidence of such speculation only confirms the opportunities for profit inherent in anticipatory settlement. But control over supply does not appear to have been carried as far as these statements imply. Had it, migration would have soon halted as land values rose exorbitantly and limited potential profits while at the same time excluding from the market those with little capital. Moreover

the settlement of the 1850s was pre-eminently an intensive one, leading to an extension of the productive, rather than the geographic, frontier. The four-state area of Indiana, Illinois, Wisconsin, and Iowa, all well within the geographic frontier, accounted for almost a quarter of the national population increase during the decade. The favorable operating results of railroads and the lack of significant governmental subsidies also make it doubtful that speculation drove settlers too far ahead of actual trackage.

Western railroad construction also exerted considerable influence on immigration. To be sure, other forces, the promise of free land for example, were operative, but the publicity surrounding railroad expansion surely must have attracted many to the profitable opportunities available in the West, in precisely the same way that internal migrants were. Indeed, there were direct encouragements. The trunk lines, in particular, ran special emigrant cars. From a comparison of foreign settlement in the Western states and the magnitude of emigrant traffic we can infer that almost all the foreign born reached the West by rail. As a consequence, Illinois and Wisconsin ranked second and third after New York in immigrant settlement during the period. That so many immigrants settled in the West immediately after arrival suggests their awareness of what railroad development meant for economic opportunity.

Brinley Thomas's opposing view that immigration was exogenous has little to support it [8]. His use of a mileage series as a proxy for total investment, when railroad investment, at any rate, clearly leads trackage, means that his timing is far from exact. Whereas his mileage series peaks in 1856, our new railroad investment series reaches its maximum in 1853–1854. For that matter, the 1880 census mileage added series peaks in 1854, had Thomas chosen that instead of Poor's Manual's version. Causality does not consist of simple temporal priority in any event. While the Irish immigration in the late 1840s was perhaps predominantly pushed (compare J. E. Cairnes' comment that "not far from one in every five of the multitudes who swarmed across the Atlantic had been driven by positive physical violence from his home"), the one million Germans who emigrated from primarily agricultural regions and came in especially large numbers in 1852, 1853, and 1854, could not have been unaware of the new opportunities for agriculture that were being created by railroad expansion. Expectation of future growth based upon the past accumulation and future increments of social overhead capital could easily have caused some lead of immigration ahead of actual economic growth without negating the influence of economic prospects. Pending further analysis, and more is needed, we should not be quick to overthrow the hypothesis advanced by Kuznets and others that the common response of many European countries suggests a single external cause, the state of the American economy [2]. Both through the expenditure effects discussed in Chapter III as well as the extension of profitable opportunities it brought to the West, the railroad was an important determinant of that economy in the 1850s.[5]

Thus far we have argued for a causal role for railroads in the population redistribution, internal and external, that occurred during the decade. In turn, that migration reacted upon railroad development in a significant way. Many Western projects earned satisfactory returns from the start only owing to the volume of passenger traffic. As late as the fiscal year 1856, when freight receipts for the country as a whole already exceeded passenger revenues by 20 per cent, in the West they were still equal. Net earnings at the same time were eminently satisfactory. Yet in 1859, with Western lines carrying considerably more freight than before, earnings were perilously low, both gross and net. The reason was the stagnation of the passenger traffic. Despite a more than 25 per cent increase in mileage over the intervening years, passenger receipts in 1859 exceeded those of 1856 by only 5 per cent; freight receipts were up by almost a third over the same interval.

The difficulties of Western railroads from 1857 on were thus a direct consequence of the break in the flow of migration westward, and not the result of a decline in freight shipments. As the report of the Indianapolis and Cincinnati Railroad sadly announced in 1858: "There will not be, as formerly, a tide of emigration to the West and North to swell our passenger receipts." When railroad prosperity began to return in late 1860 it was on an altered footing from the earlier profitable years and was built upon the firmer

base of growing commodity surpluses, not passengers. This transformation in turn mirrors the initial contribution of the railroad in influencing settlement and its subsequent redemption of the promise of lower cost transportation.

CONCLUSION

This chapter has analyzed the part played by the railroad in Western economic development in the 1850s. Theoretically one would clearly expect the addition of extensive rail facilities to increase the attractiveness of the West vis-à-vis other regions, and foreign countries too, and hence to affect both the regional allocation of resources and the total supply, the latter through immigration. A key issue, however, is whether such railroad influence was primarily exogenous or endogenous, whether railroads first set in motion the forces culminating in the economic development of the decade, or whether arising in response to profitable situations, they played a more passive role.

Those who have argued most strongly for railroad causality have typically relied upon some notion of construction ahead of demand. Accordingly this hypothesis became our starting point. It is fair to say, I believe, that the preponderance of evidence denies such a phenomenon before the Civil War.[6] Western railroad enterprises on the whole were initially successful, and some spectacularly so. By and large those that were not continued as poor investments long after and never generated self-fulfilling demand. No matter if we look to population densities, or to the structure of governmental subsidy, or to gross receipts, our impression must be that the expansion was rooted in rationality, not insanity. Even the excesses of construction and consequent rate competition are to be understood as the outcome of logical, and necessary, decisions by individual railroads (and municipalities).

Such results do not necessarily deny an important causal role to the railroad. Rather they seem to be consistent with an alternative linkage from the railroad construction of the

---

[5] [This reference is to the book from which this selection is taken—Editors' note.]

[6] A similar set of criteria casually applied to post-Civil War railroad construction in the states farther west suggest that this constituted a true episode of building before demand.

late 1840s and early 1850s to an on-going flow of westward migration that in turn led to continued railroad expansion. We have invoked a process of anticipatory settlement to explain both such a sequence and the vitality of private enterprise. Thus by the time railroads reached Iowa and Wisconsin, existing economic development justified their construction under private auspices, but only because of prior railroad development in Ohio. This newer interpretation may be amended by future research, but at the moment it seems to be a useful way of stating the dynamics of this western railroad expansion.

As far as first causes go, whether it was improved agricultural terms of trade, or lower English iron prices, or increased grain exports that set in motion the initial construction in Ohio, is not a very fruitful question. The process of economic development is too complex, and also too diversified, to permit of unequivocal prime movers. More relevant is the elaboration of mechanisms of diffusion of development, as we have tried to demonstrate here.

REFERENCES

1. Allan G. Bogue and Margaret Beattie Bogue, "'Profits' and the Frontier Land Speculator," *The Journal of Economic History, 17* (March, 1957), 1–24. [Reprinted above as essay 6.]
2. Richard A. Easterlin, "Influences in European Overseas Emigration before World War I," *Economic Development and Cultural Change, 9* (April, 1961), 331–351. [Reprinted above as essay 28.]
3. Paul W. Gates, *The Illinois Central and its Colonization Work,* Cambridge, Harvard University Press, 1934.
4. Paul W. Gates, *The Farmers Age: Agriculture 1815–1860,* New York, Holt, Rinehart and Winston, 1961.
5. Carter Goodrich, *Government Promotion of American Canals and Railroads, 1800–1890.* New York, Columbia University Press, 1959,
6. Richard C. Overton, *Burlington West,* Cambridge, Harvard University Press, 1941.
7. Joseph A. Schumpeter, *Business Cycles*, New York, McGraw-Hill, 1939.
8. Brinley Thomas, *Migration and Economic Growth*, Cambridge, University Press, 1954.

31 THE UNION PACIFIC RAILROAD: THE QUESTIONS OF PUBLIC POLICY

Robert William Fogel

Most contemporary accounts of the Union Pacific neglect the policy questions posed by government intervention in the building of the road. The slight is odd both because these questions were earnestly debated by Congress and the public for over 19 years and because the construction and subsequent operation of the road provide abundant data for testing the decisions finally reached by Congress. This curious treatment of the most massive enterprise sponsored by the American government during the nineteenth century appears to be due to an uncritical acceptance of the findings of the Wilson committee.

Reprinted with omissions by permission from Robert William Fogel, *The Union Pacific Railroad: A Case in Premature Enterprise*, Baltimore, Johns Hopkins Press, 1960, pp. 91–110.

The central thesis of the congressional in-quisitors was that the prostration of the Union Pacific was completely explained by the pernicious practices of the promoters. A "road built in accordance with the act of Congress," the inquisitors insisted, would have been a "strong," "solvent," "profit-able," "powerful" business institution. Thus, in accepting the findings of the Wilson com-mittee, historians have relied on the material that diverted attention from the policy deci-sions of Congress, that reduced the problems spawned by premature construction to a matter of personal morality.

However if the thesis that profiteering was the root cause of the prostration of the Union Pacific is rejected, if the enervation of the road was inherent in the Acts of 1862 and 1864, the questions of public economic policy blurred by the Wilson committee spring back into focus. First, should the Union Pacific Railroad have been built prematurely; that is, should the government have intervened to bring about the construction of a road that would not have been undertaken by un-aided private enterprise? Second, given the decision to intervene, what method of con-struction and financing would have been most efficient?

THE SOCIAL RATE OF RETURN

Properly conceived, the rate of return on the capital invested in the Union Pacific can be used as a basis for evaluating the economic wisdom of the government's decision to intervene in the building of a Pacific road. If the rate of return on the capital invested in the building of the Union Pacific was less than the market rate of return, then the con-gressional decision was, on economic grounds, clearly a blunder. On the other hand, a rate of return that equalled the market rate of return would not necessarily validate the action taken by Congress. It would indicate that the Union Pacific was only one of a number of equally profitable investments that could have been undertaken at the time. Under this circumstance government inter-vention would have added nothing to the economic development of the country; it would merely have substituted one particular enterprise for some other enterprise of equal importance. The name of economic develop-ment may be invoked only if it can be shown that the rate of return on the Union Pacific investment *exceeded* the market rate of return. Indeed the greater the margin by which the return on the capital so invested exceeded the market rate of return, the more confidence one would tend to have in the validity of the government decision to intervene.

It might be argued that profitability—the rate of return on an investment—is too narrow a criterion to be used for evaluating an investment decision when the objective is not private gain but national economic growth. Some of the most ardent proponents of a Pacific road strongly doubted its earning capacity. Senator Henry Wilson thought the idea that the Union Pacific would be able to earn enough to repay its debt to the govern-ment was "as visionary as anything that ever entered the brain of man." Nonetheless he was prepared to "sink $100,000,000 to build the road" that would open up the "central regions of this continent" and "connect the people of the Pacific and Atlantic." Senator Daniel Clark, who listed himself as a staunch supporter of a Pacific road, believed that "if the good God were to make the road for you, right through, you could not form a company in the country today that would run it without failure." And Representative James Campbell saw no contradiction be-tween his insistence that the project of a Pacific railroad would have to be "abandoned forever" unless it were heavily aided by the government and his prediction that the rail-road would do more toward extending com-merce and civilization over the continent "than any other enterprise of modern times." To the proponents of the Acts of 1862 and 1864, the Union Pacific was, then, an invest-ment that was of great *strategic* importance for the growth of the economy even though the company itself might earn less than the market rate of return on the capital required for its construction.

But what exactly is an investment that is unprofitable to the investing firm and yet is strategically important to the growth of the economy? From the point of view of a firm, an unprofitable investment is one which increases the value of the product of the firm by a sum which is less than would have been achieved, on the average, if the same amount of capital had been applied elsewhere. In other words, if only the investing firm is considered, the substitution of an unprofit-able investment for a profitable one is equiva-lent to a decrease in per capita national income. This implies that an investment which is unprofitable for the firm can be *strategically* important for the growth of the economy—for the increase in per capita income—only if it simultaneously serves to increase the productivity of labor and capital in firms other than the one in which the investment is made; that is, only if there are firms which benefit from the investment but which do not have to pay for these benefits. In such cases the receipts of the investing firm do not reflect the full social value of the investment. The existence of these unpaid benefits is a necessary condition for an investment to be unprofitable for a firm and still serve to increase per capita income. Thus investments which are privately unprofitable but which are strategically important for the growth of the economy involve not one but two rates of return—a private rate and a social rate. The private rate is based on the increase in the value of the product of the firm attributable to the given investment. The social rate is based on the increase in the value of the product of all firms attributable to the investment. Clearly it is on the basis of the social rate of return on the capital invested in the Union Pacific that the congressional decision to intervene must be evaluated.

The fact that the Union Pacific tottered on the brink of bankruptcy suggests that the road was an unprofitable venture. This suggestion might seem to be supported by an examination of the ratio of the net earnings to the book value of the Union Pacific for the decade 1870–1879. As shown in Table 1,

Table 1. The Rate of Return on the Book Value of the Union Pacific (In Current Dollars) (000 Omitted)

Year	Book Value of the Road (1)	Net Earnings (2)	Column 2 as a Per Cent of Column 1 (3)
1870	106,763	2,777	2.6
1871	112,397	3,921	3.5
1872	112,002	4,092	3.7
1873	111,621	5,223	4.7
1874	112,844	5,425	4.8
1875	115,768	6,452	5.6
1876	115,356	7,477	6.5
1877	115,019	7,152	6.2
1878	114,698	7,951	6.9
1879	114,187	7,726	6.8
Average rate of return on book value for the ten year period			5.1

Table 2. The Rate of Return on the Cash Expenditure on Construction (In Constant Dollars of 1869) (000 Omitted)

Year	Accumulated Expenditure on Construction (1)	Net Earnings Adjusted for Depreciation (2)	Column 2 as a Per Cent of Column 1 (3)
1870	53,060	2,240	4.2
1871	53,950	3,610	6.7
1872	54,830	3,670	6.7
1873	55,230	5,020	9.1
1874	55,490	5,490	9.9
1875	55,620	7,000	12.6
1876	55,630	8,760	15.7
1877	59,160	8,670	14.7
1878	59,160	10,530	17.8
1879	59,160	10,370	17.5
Average rate of return on construction expenditure for the ten year period			11.6

this ratio varied from a low of 2.6 per cent to a high of 6.9 per cent, the average for the entire decade being 5.1 per cent. And this over a span of years during which the average yield on the best grade of corporate bonds fluctuated between five and seven per cent. However Table 1 sheds little light on the economic wisdom of the congressional decision to build a Pacific road. The denominators of the ratios in column 3 include more than the cash expenditure on the construction of the Union Pacific. They also include the profit of the promoters and the discount on the company's bonds. Moreover Table 1 gives net earnings in current dollars. The period from 1870 to 1879 was one of sharply declining prices. Thus the real net earnings of the road were considerably greater than the figures of Table 1 indicate.

Table 2 corrects these and other errors. This table shows an annual ratio of real net earnings adjusted for depreciation to accumulated real cash expenditure on construction that varied between 4.2 and 17.5 per cent. The average for the decade was 11.6 per cent. These figures lead to a startling conclusion. The Union Pacific was premature by mistake! It was premature because private investors expected it to be unprofitable. But their expectations were based on an incorrect evaluation of the course of economic development. In actual fact the road was a highly profitable venture that should have been taken up by unaided private enterprise. Interestingly enough, only in the halls of

Congress did one find a sizable proportion of individuals who, like Senator James H. Lane of Kansas, stubbornly predicted that the completed Union Pacific would be "one of the great paying thoroughfares of the world." This fact might be taken as an indication that Congress perceived the true state of nature while private businessmen had failed to do so. The ability of Congress to have foreseen a large profit for the owners of the Union Pacific would, even in the absence of unpaid benefits, tend to justify the decision to intervene. Yet despite the appeal of the idea, there is no real evidence that the nation's political leaders possessed a superior vision. The optimism of Lane, and others, was probably more a matter of political expediency—rhetoric calculated to create a favorable atmosphere for the promotion of the road—than the expression of a personal conviction. At any rate, neither Lane, nor McDougall, nor Latham, nor several of the other optimists availed themselves of the opportunity to buy shares in this "great paying thoroughfare." Their names are not among the ones on the list of the original subscribers to the Union Pacific.

The case for government intervention rested on the conviction, held by businessmen and legislators alike, that the road would bring great social returns. The 11.6 per cent figure cited above is the average *private* return on the construction expenditure. It does not include the unpaid benefits of the road—the increase in national income brought about by the road but which failed to be reflected in the company's net earnings. While the conception of the social rate of return is clear, the calculation of it involves considerable practical difficulty. Given the necessary data, aggregate analysis would provide the most direct method of determining the social rate. If there had existed a nation which had been the twin of the United States in every respect except that it had not built the Union Pacific, the social rate of return on the investment could be determined by first finding the differences in annual national income between the two countries over the life of the investment, and then finding the rate of discount which made the present value of these annual income differences equal to the amount of the investment. However since the United States did not have such a national twin, this method of procedure is ruled out.

Alternative approaches involve the disaggregation of the increase in national income attributable to the Union Pacific. The net earnings of the road represent one part of the postulated increase in income. The rest is included under the heading of unpaid benefits. These unpaid benefits can be divided into four categories: (a) the increase in income, not reflected in the company's receipts, due to the opening up of lands in states through which the railroad passed; (b) the saving to private shippers in areas east of Omaha and west of Ogden City as a result of being able to utilize the Union Pacific for shipment to points beyond the territory traversed by the road at lower rates than would otherwise have prevailed; (c) the saving to the government as a result of being able to transport men, mail, and material at low railroad rates instead of high wagon and steamship rates; (d) the saving to producers outside the immediate territory of the Union Pacific as a result of a better division of labor made possible by the existence of the railroad. The sum of these unpaid benefits plus the net earnings of the road, then, would provide the desired estimate of the total increase in income attributable to the Union Pacific.

Unfortunately the data needed to determine the unpaid benefits falling into categories (b), (c), and (d) are not available. However it is possible to obtain an approximate estimate of the unpaid benefits of category (a)—the increase in national income, not reflected in the Union Pacific's receipts, brought about by the increase in the productivity of labor and capital when utilized on the lands opened up for commercial exploitation by the railroad. This figure plus the net earnings of the road would be less than the increase in national income attributable to the Union Pacific. Nonetheless it would convey some conception of the order of magnitude of the desired figure.

The basis for the estimate of the unpaid benefits of category (a) is the theory of rent. In 1880 the value of all lands on a strip approximately 40 miles on each side of the Union Pacific from Omaha to Ogden was about $158,500,000 (in dollars of 1869). This figure is the capitalization of the amount by which the value of the annual product produced by labor and capital on these lands exceeded the value of the product of the same amount of labor and capital working on marginal land. If the railroad had not existed, the overwhelming bulk of the lands surrounding the Union Pacific would have been unusable and the labor and capital employed

Table 3. Estimated Social Return on Construction Expenditure (In Constant Dollars of 1869) (000 Omitted)

Year	Accumulated Expenditure on Construction (1)	Net Earnings Adjusted for Depreciation (2)	Increase in National Income Due to Union Pacific But Not Reflected in Company's Earnings (3)	Sum of Columns 2 and 3 (4)	Column 4 as a Per Cent of Column 1 (5)
1870	53,060	2,240	5,860	8,100	15.3
1871	53,950	3,610	6,840	10,450	19.4
1872	54,830	3,670	7,810	11,480	20.9
1873	55,230	5,020	8,790	13,810	25.0
1874	55,490	5,490	9,770	15,260	27.5
1875	55,620	7,000	10,740	17,740	31.9
1876	55,630	8,760	11,720	20,480	36.8
1877	59,160	8,670	12,700	21,370	36.1
1878	59,160	10,530	13,670	24,200	40.9
1879	59,160	10,370	14,650	25,020	42.3
Average social rate of return for the ten year period					29.9

on them would have been employed elsewhere at either the intensive or extensive margins. Thus if in 1880 the railroad had been suddenly removed, the annual loss in income to society would have been the decapitalized fall in the value of the lands on the 80 mile strip. Put more positively, the increase in national income due to the Union Pacific, but not reflected in its receipts, is the decapitalized value of the amount by which the actual value of the lands on the 80 mile strip exceeded the value that would have obtained if there had been no railroad.

In 1860 the value of the lands in the 80 mile strip was about $4,370,000 (in dollars of 1869). This figure is the estimated value of the designated lands, given the labor and capital that existed in the United States in 1860. Since the quantity of labor and capital in the country increased during the decades that followed 1860, we would expect the value of the land in the 80 mile strip to have been somewhat higher than $4,370,000 in 1880 even if the Union Pacific had not been built. Between 1860 and 1880 the value of all farm lands in the United States increased by 32.9 per cent. Therefore it is reasonable to assume that even without the railroad, land values would have been 32.9 per cent higher than they were 20 years earlier. Hence the estimated value of the lands on the 80 mile strip in 1880 in the absence of the Union Pacific, given the labor and capital of 1880, is $5,800,000.

The approximate increase in the value of land due to the railroad, then, was

$152,700,000. If this figure is multiplied by a properly weighted average of the rates at which land rents in the relevant states were capitalized, the resulting figure—$15,630,000 —is an estimate of the increase in national income in 1880 due to the productivity of labor and capital on the lands made available by the Union Pacific but not reflected in the company's receipts.[1] Column 3 of Table 3 gives an estimate of this neglected increase in national income for the decade from 1870 through 1879. Adding these figures to the net earnings of the road, we find that the

---

[1] The preceding analysis involved two implicit assumptions that should be made explicit. First, it was assumed that the rate of population growth in the nation as a whole would not have been affected by the absence of the Union Pacific. Secondly, it was assumed that the absence of the Union Pacific would not have altered the rate of capital accumulation.

The justification for the first assumption lies in the fact that while the increase in income due to the opening up of the lands in the 80 mile strip is large relative to the investment in the Union Pacific, it is infinitesimal (in the neighborhood of 0.15 or one per cent) relative to national income in 1880. In view of this, it hardly seems likely that the absence of the railroad would have significantly altered any of the main variables upon which population growth is usually taken to depend.

Similarly, the amount of supramarginal land within the 80 mile strip was a small proportion of the total amount of supramarginal land in the country. Hence the absence of the Union Pacific would have had little influence on factor proportions—on which the rate of return to capital may be taken to depend—and therefore, on the rate of capital accumulation.

annual *social* rate of return on the capital expended on the construction of the road varied between 15.3 and 42.3 per cent. The average for the decade was 29.9 per cent. However 29.9 per cent is a minimum estimate of the social rate of return on the construction expenditure. The figure does not reflect the unpaid benefits of categories (b), (c), and (d), listed above. Clearly, then, from a social point of view the Union Pacific was a most profitable venture. There can be little doubt that the government was economically justified in intervening to build a road that would not have been built by unaided private enterprise.

THE EFFICIENCY OF THE ACTS OF 1862 AND 1864

While the extremely high social rate of return tends to confirm the government's decision to build a Pacific road, it does not imply that the particular method of construction and financing chosen by Congress was a good one. It is not possible to assess the economic efficacy of the construction scheme projected by Congress without first establishing a criterion of efficiency on the basis of which the relative merit of alternative construction schemes might be evaluated. The criterion to be used in this examination is the cost of the road to the firm. The most efficient method of intervention, then, would have been the method which made the cost of building the road to the firm a minimum.

If the Union Pacific had been a riskless enterprise, the cost of the road to the company would have been approximately the cash that was actually expended on construction—$57,028,272 through 1872. In this case the Union Pacific would not have been faced with "extra" charges for the service of the promoters or with premiums on borrowed money. However the Union Pacific was a highly risky enterprise. In the light of the risks attached to the building of the road, the promoters were, as we have seen, "entitled" to a construction profit of 11.1 million dollars. To the company, then, necessary construction expenditures included not only such items as the cost of materials, payments to the various subcontractors who did the actual work, legal and administrative expenses, etc., but also the "justifiable" profits of the promoters—the profit without which, under the Acts of 1862 and 1864, the indis-

pensable services of the promoters could not have been secured. Hence from the point of view of the firm, necessary construction expenditures were 68.1 million dollars.

Even this last figure does not give the full cost of the road to the company. For to the company, the cost of the road depended not only on the necessary construction expenditure but also on how much the company had to pay for the funds it needed to cover these expenditures. The cost of funds is usually given as the rate of interest. However it is also possible to measure the cost of funds by the present value of the interest and principal payments to which a borrower commits himself when he makes a loan. The present value approach poses the problem of the rate at which future interest and principal payments should be discounted. The solution to the problem is suggested by the fact that the cost of a loan to a borrower is always a conditional cost. The cost of a loan is, say, six per cent, or $60 per year on each $1000 advanced, *if, and only if,* the borrower fulfills his contractual obligation. However given the condition that the borrower will meet these obligations, the future payments are certain and the proper rate of discount is the market rate of interest. In other words, the *conditional* cost of funds to the Union Pacific was the present value of the payments it pledged to its suppliers of funds, discounted at the market rate of interest—6.02 per cent.

The money the Union Pacific needed to meet its construction charges was obtained in three ways. Approximately 11.0 million was secured through the company's sale of stock; 27.1 million dollars was provided by the government; the remaining 30.0 million dollars was procured through loans from private individuals or firms. Of the 30.0 million dollars, the Union Pacific acquired 23.7 million dollars by selling its first-mortgage bonds. But for every $871.57 the company received on this security it pledged to make future payments with a present value of $997.25. To the company, then, the cost of 23.7 million dollars was 27.1 million dollars. The remaining 6.3 million dollars needed by the road was obtained by selling income bonds. On this security the company committed itself to payments with a present value of $1106.35 for every $700.23 advanced, the cost of 6.3 million dollars being approximately 10.0 million dollars. If the premium the Union Pacific had to pay on the borrowed funds is added to the other construction charges, the cost of the road to the firm becomes 75.1 million dollars.[2]

During the course of the long debate on a Pacific road, both legislators and private citizens offered a host of schemes for government intervention, alternative to the one actually chosen by Congress. These proposals fall into three groups. The first group consists of proposals for "privately" owned roads, aided only by a government grant of land. The Gwin bill, one of the most prominent of these schemes, projected a grant of alternate sections of land for 40 miles on each side of the railroad. If this plan had been adopted, the Union Pacific would have received lands which were worth approximately $76,350,000 in 1880. This implies that if in 1869 investors had known the 1880 value of the lands, the most the railroad could have obtained on these lands would have been $40,100,000. Since the Union Pacific received one half of this amount of land under the Act of 1864, the most the additional land offered by the Gwin bill could have been worth was $20,050,000—about 7.1 million dollars less than the value of the bonds the Union Pacific received from the government under the Acts of 1862 and 1864. However this estimate of the value of these additional lands is much too favorable. When the Union Pacific mortgaged its lands in 1869, it received only 6.1 million dollars; and this on land which, in general, was more valuable than the additional lands of the Gwin bill, since it was located closer to the railroad. These considerations suggest that the railroad would not have received more than 6.1 million dollars in loans based on the additional lands —21.0 million dollars less than it received in government bonds. Even the Whitney bill, the most lavish of all the land-grant schemes, would not have closed the gap. Under the terms of the Whitney bill, the Union Pacific would have received additional lands of

[2] Under all of the plans considered in this chapter, the cost of the road to society would have been approximately the same—approximately 57.0 million dollars, the cash expenditure on construction. The cost of the road to the company is important for two reasons. First, it has a bearing on the post-construction financial stability of the firm. The greater the cost of the road to the company, the greater the bonded debt, and therefore, the fixed charges the completed Union Pacific had to carry. Secondly, it has a bearing on the question of equity—i.e., on the distribution of the social saving among individuals. See footnote 3 below.

41,360 square miles; yet the funds the road would have been able to raise on such a dukedom would still have been at least 14.9 million dollars less than the proceeds of the government bond issue. Moreover on the money borrowed on these lands, the road would have paid not six but over ten per cent in interest. Hence even the most lavish of the land-grant schemes was clearly inferior to—less efficient than—the one actually adopted by Congress.

The second group of alternatives consists of the type of proposal that held the center of the stage during the years from 1852 through 1860—the type of proposal embodied in the Douglas, Weller, Rusk, and McDougall bills. Like the purely land-grant schemes, all of these measures would have been less efficient than the plan under which the Union Pacific was actually constructed. In all of them the amount of government bond aid that would have fallen to the Union Pacific was less than half of the amount the Union Pacific actually received. Moreover these bills did not provide for the issuance of first-mortgage bonds so that the road would have had to raise the 23.7 million dollars brought in by the first-mortgage bonds on inferior securities. Finally, since most of these bills contained provisions for the eventual surrender of the road to the government, the risk to equity capital would have been even greater than the risk that obtained under the Acts of 1862 and 1864.

Of all the schemes that gained prominence during the long debate over a Pacific road, only three could have been more efficient than the one under which the Union Pacific was actually built. These three schemes constitute the final group of alternatives. The "Boston Plan," put forth by P. P. F. DeGrand, suggested the establishment of a corporation to which the government would have loaned $98,000,000 and private individuals would have subscribed $2,000,000. In return for its loan the government was to have received six per cent interest and half of the stock. If these amounts had been divided between the Central Pacific and the Union Pacific in proportion to the length of each road, the Union Pacific would have received 57.0 million dollars from the government and 1.2 million dollars from private subscriptions. In other words, under this scheme, the Union Pacific would have received all of the capital it needed for the construction of the road from the government at six per cent. For the private investors there would no longer have been a risk of inadequate funds (assuming they had the same information on construction costs that Durant and his associates had in 1863). Moreover for their investment of 1.2 million dollars, the private subscribers stood to gain 50 per cent of all of the net earnings of the road over the interest on the government loan. Under such provisions as these the cost of constructing the road would probably have been quite close to the cash expenditure on construction—$57,028,272.

The second potentially efficient plan proposed that a private firm build the road, but that the government guarantee the firm five or six per cent—i.e., approximately the prevailing market rate of return—on the cost of construction. This plan would have shifted all of the risk to the government. Hence the company would have had no trouble in obtaining all of the funds that it needed through the sale of stock. Indeed, if the firm had issued $57,000,000 of stock, the stock would have sold above par. For such stock would have been better than a government bond. The least the firm would have earned on its investment was the market rate of interest; and there was always the possibility that the road could have earned a great deal more.

The third plan called on the government to build the road itself. Since the government could have obtained all of the funds that it needed at the market rate of interest, the cost of the road to the firm would have been the cash expenditure on construction—$57,028,272.

Under all of the plans in the third group, the firm would have received all of the funds needed for construction at six per cent. Hence the fixed charges on the completed road would have been a minimum. The completed Union Pacific would have emerged as the "strong," "solvent," "powerful" business institution that the Wilson committee wanted it to be. However in each case this blissful state of events would have been due to the fact that the government intervened between the firm and the investing public, using the credit of the government to obtain funds from the public at six per cent and then supplying these funds to the firm at the same market rate of interest. In other words, the cost of construction would have been a minimum only because the government shifted the risk from private investors to itself. This type of intervention raises another

question of efficiency. Why should the government have been willing to provide funds to the firm at six per cent when the rate of return demanded by private investors was two, three, and four times as great? Would not a government advance at such low rates have represented a misallocation of capital? There were at least two good reasons for a government advance of funds at a rate well below the rate demanded by private suppliers of funds. First, in calculating the rate of return that they should demand on their money, private investors had to take into account the risk that the Union Pacific might fail because it could not obtain *all* of the funds needed to complete the road. If the government had built the road, or had supplied the funds needed to build the road, this risk would not have existed. Secondly, private investors evaluated the Union Pacific on the basis of the expected *private* earnings of the road. For the government the relevant consideration was the expected *social* earnings. Since the common contention of both government figures and private individuals was that a Pacific road would be socially profitable, the expected social earnings must have been at least equal to the market rate of return.

While all of the plans that make up the last group of proposals would have drastically reduced the cost of funds to the firm, they were not all equally feasible or equally desirable from the point of view of the government. Under the Boston plan the government was to supply 98 per cent of the money but it would have received considerably less than 98 per cent of the profit. The guaranteed profit plan also had an Achilles heel; it contained a tendency to waste. Since the company was guaranteed six per cent on the cost of the road, profit maximization might have acted as a spur to increasing rather than decreasing the cost of construction. These considerations suggest that from the point of view of the government, government construction might have been the most desirable means of obtaining a Pacific road. The great objection to a government enterprise arose from a distaste for the involvement of the government in business. However the government could have minimized this objection by selling the Union Pacific to private individuals shortly after the road was completed—say, in 1875 or 1876—at its capitalized value. If the last course of action had been followed, society would have reaped the same social gain that it did under the Acts of 1862 and 1864; but, in addition, the Union Pacific would have been a sound business institution and the government would have realized a tidy profit on the transaction.[3]

---

[3] This scheme would also have had important equity effects. If the road had been built by the government and then had been sold at its capitalized value, the profit that was reaped by the promoters and by those who bought Union Pacific bonds at a discount would have accrued to the government. This profit would have increased the income of the government, thus decreasing, *ceteris paribus*, the government's need for taxes. Hence the distribution of the social saving brought about by the road would have been wider in this case than was true under the Acts of 1862 and 1864.

32 URBANIZATION IN THE AMERICAN NORTHEAST, 1820–1870

Jeffrey G. Williamson

I. INTRODUCTION

No one has seriously challenged the familiar association either between levels of urban development and degrees of industrial maturity or between rates of change in these two indices. It has even become commonplace in macroeconomic growth theory to simplify the complexities of structural change into some variation of the urban-rural two-sector model, although in the real world shifts from commercial to industrial urban employment, let alone more complex inter-sectoral shifts, are of prime importance. Indeed, many of these growth models place great emphasis not upon changes in sector

This paper is a revision and extension of "Ante-Bellum Urbanization in the American Northeast," *The Journal of Economic History, 25* (December, 1965), 592–608, and is reprinted by permission.

productivity but upon resource shifts between low and high productivity employment, while in empirical studies urban and rural population data very often appear as explicit substitutes for sectoral employment. But given the paucity of macroeconomic data for the ante-bellum period, especially prior to 1839, one is left puzzled by our relative inattention to the wealth of population census data by residence. American economic history textbooks are stuffed with quantitative information on the number of cities, their spectacular growth, and the percentage of population urbanized, but these may not be the most effective uses of this great data pool. The plethora of urban histories and the abundant attention to urban rivalry may be useful complements but they are not very effective substitutes for quantitative analysis of overall American urbanization and experience with city size distribution. The very attention which the topic is currently receiving by economists, geographers, and historians suggests that much remains undone in the study of early American urbanization.

We can find important exceptions to this rule like any other. Not long ago Eric Lampard made a contribution to urban development literature which, in my opinion, should become a classic [2]. Moreover I suspect there has been little improvement on Weber's very modern statistical study (though written in 1899) with regard to rural-urban migrations, city size distribution, and aggregate urban growth [6]. Moving back even further, in 1846 Jesse Chickering processed huge amounts of population data on the dynamics of Massachusetts urban development [1]. Chickering examined hypotheses which are just as vital to the field of regional economics today: that industrialization disperses cities less evenly over space; that the process of urbanization is not shared equally throughout a developing state, but rather that rapid adolescent growth generates increasingly severe inequalities in urbanization levels between regions. The most recent break with traditional urban investigations by economic historians can be found in the interesting work of Smolensky and Ratajczak [4].

We cannot possibly cover in a paper of this length all of the many questions about the relationship between urbanization and economic growth which have been posed. The rest of this paper will report upon some aspects of an ongoing research project which has been statistically analyzing the relationship between economic growth and urbanization in the nineteenth century United States [5, 8]. The focus will be upon Northeast urbanization.

II. AGGREGATE URBAN DEVELOPMENT

Our first task is to define the urban unit. We have accepted the 1950 Census definition where urban population includes the aggregate of those townspeople residing in areas > 2500, U, and where the level of urbanization is simply the ratio of urban population to total population, P. One could endlessly debate whether a "city" of 2500 is indeed a legitimate urban unit but suffice it to say that the quantitative study itself suggests that the timing of American urbanization is quite insensitive to our urban definition. The major measurement problem arises with our choice of indices reflecting the *rate* at which urbanization occurs. We have settled on a relatively primitive measure: the incremental urbanization ratio, $\Delta(U/P)$. Since our first goal is to isolate changes in demographic structure, the incremental urban ratio is the most relevant statistic since it captures the share of the population transferred to a presumably more efficient use or productive location. The gains from such shifts and the potential importance of such structural change should be quite high in the early years of adolescent development. A very large reservoir of rural population exists with a correspondingly high potential for structural change. A mature economy is not able to generate dramatic rural-urban shifts in its later years since the benefits from redistribution have already been reaped in the past. However it should be made explicit that the incremental urban ratio imparts a bias in favor of those nations and regions embarking on industrial development from a high urban base: the index is a function of both the relative growth in the urban population and the initial urban ratio.

Most growth models appear to predict secular growth performance following some variant of the Gompertz or logistic curve. This seems all the more likely if we are interested only in trend of structural change in a simple two-sector model. The theoretical argument which predicts initial acceleration in urbanization rates is multifaceted but for the sake of brevity let us assume that agglomeration economies accruing in early growth stages coupled with a relatively elastic labor supply facing the urban economies are sufficient explanations. As development proceeds, the rate of acceleration in urbanization should reach a maximum from which it should thereafter decline while approaching the limiting urbanization ratio of 100 per cent: that is, agglomeration economies may still be operative in spite of the increasing size of cities but the labor supply curve facing the aggregate of urban areas becomes less elastic over time. First differences in urbanization are well defined. All of this suggests at least two very general hypotheses regarding American experience with urbanization:

(1) We anticipate that American regional experience with urbanization traced out sharp discontinuities as defined above. New England, the Middle Atlantic, and the Midwest should exhibit periods of accelerating urbanization typically compressed into short time periods ranging between three to four decades while the chronological order of their urban development should closely follow our general descriptions of American regional growth. Given the sequential nature of American development, we expect to find the envelope of these regions' experience to be somewhat different: the United States as a whole should trace out a more extended period of acceleration but the rate of urbanization at its peak should be less than that of *any* region at *its* respective peak.

(2) Beginning with modern development in the post Embargo era, the Northeast was faced with unique circumstances. Exogenous changes had created a set of regional comparative advantages in the 1820s and 1830s totally different from those prevailing in the 1790s and 1800s—a set of comparative advantages which favored manufactures tremendously. This was strengthened during the ante-bellum period by the settlement of empty western lands. This somewhat unique disequilibrium situation, coupled with scale effects (initial high urban ratios in 1820 built upon a commercial base), should have generated *higher* rates of urbanization in the settled portions of the Northeast. During their respective stages of urban acceleration, western New York and Pennsylvania, the Midwest, and the South must have undergone more gradual *endogenously* generated changes in comparative advantage favorable to urbanization. Changing relative factor prices and large scale manufacturing economies associated with increasing size of market must

have generated less remarkable increases in relative efficiency in manufactures. Thus we would predict rates of urban development to have been more dramatic in the Northeast, in general, and the settled Northeast in particular.

We begin by examining large Bureau of Census regions for the period 1790–1890 (Table 1). Each region in the United States which underwent modern sustained development in the nineteenth century traced out stages of urban stagnation, abrupt acceleration confined to three or four decades, then retardation from that maximum. The composite urban experience of the United States as a whole is the *only* exception to the rule. Her period of urban acceleration is at least five decades (reaching a maximum incremental urban ratio in the 1860s) or at most seven decades (reaching a maximum in the 1880s). If we choose the former date then it is certainly true that the incremental urban ratio did not decline from a maximum in the 1860s but at best fluctuated around that level for the rest of the century.[1] New England reaches a peak urbanization rate in the 1840s, the Middle Atlantic in the 1850s, and the Northeast also in the 1850s. All of these start their period of urban acceleration from the War of 1812 decade, and all reveal extremely mild rates of urbanization prior to that date. If we exclude the frontier from the Northeastern regions then experience with retardation is much more striking. Southern New England declines from a peak rate of urbanization much more dramatically than total New England. Similarly, when we exclude western

---

[1] We might note here that Lebergott's data on the sectoral distribution of the labor force imply a somewhat different historical pattern. The incremental nonagricultural labor force share is negative during the first decade of the nineteenth century. It then becomes increasingly positive, remaining at a high peak level in the 1830s, 1840s, and 1850s before undergoing sharp secular decline.

The figures for the incremental nonagricultural labor force share are:

1800–1810	−10.0%	1850–1860	−1.9%
1810–1820	4.9	1860–1870	0.4
1820–1830	8.2	1870–1880	1.2
1830–1840	7.5	1880–1890	8.6
1840–1850	8.3		

[*3*, Table A1, p. 510].

Table 1. Δ(U/P) by States and Regions, 1790–1890 (in Percentage)

	1790–1800	1800–1810	1810–1820	1820–1830	1830–1840	1840–1850	1850–1860	1860–1870	1870–1880	1880–1890
Maine	—	0.69	−0.26	0.28	4.69	5.69	3.08	4.40	1.58	5.50
New Hampshire	−0.42	3.29	−0.23	2.00	5.02	7.06	5.01	4.13	3.78	9.28
Vermont	—	—	—	—	—	—	0.03	4.97	3.10	5.19
Massachusetts	1.93	5.87	1.46	8.29	6.81	12.78	8.89	7.14	7.98	7.27
Rhode Island	1.74	2.60	−0.39	8.27	12.55	11.84	7.67	11.28	7.37	2.39
Connecticut	2.06	1.02	1.47	1.79	3.31	3.43	10.54	6.42	8.91	9.03
Western New York	—	—	3.18	1.70	1.77	4.44	5.03	8.17	4.19	9.95
Eastern New York	5.10	2.42	3.51	6.76	5.56	7.87	4.19	1.05	2.09	1.48
Eastern Pennsylvania	3.32	2.37	2.38	3.24	5.15	7.77	17.96	6.88	5.68	7.33
Western Pennsylvania	—	—	−2.77	1.05	1.62	4.08	1.92	7.66	5.14	6.78
New Jersey	—	—	2.52	3.03	4.88	7.01	15.10	10.10	10.69	8.20
New York	1.16	−2.35	−0.94	3.21	4.46	8.80	11.08	10.68	6.48	8.70
Pennsylvania	1.20	−1.46	0.19	2.27	2.58	5.70	7.23	6.49	4.36	7.00
Maryland	3.54	4.47	4.06	4.07	3.87	8.02	17.04	3.87	2.36	7.35
Northeast	1.17	1.62	0.11	3.15	4.37	8.00	9.22	8.55	6.51	8.17
Middle Atlantic	1.51	1.27	−0.18	2.95	3.85	7.41	9.88	8.87	5.93	7.84
New England	0.68	1.87	0.44	3.47	5.40	9.34	7.87	7.79	8.01	9.12
United States	0.94	1.19	−0.07	1.57	2.05	4.47	4.49	5.91	2.49	6.95
South	0.82	1.16	4.77	6.59	1.39	1.62	1.30	2.60	3.17	4.07
East North Central	—	—	2.84	1.28	1.37	5.18	5.01	7.56	5.88	1.04
South Atlantic	1.13	1.14	0.92	0.76	1.51	2.10	1.62	2.91	4.99	4.64
East South Central	—	—	0.17	0.76	0.57	2.11	1.68	2.88	−0.37	4.32
West South Central	—	—	−6.01	2.52	4.70	−8.31	−2.79	0.95	−0.73	2.56
Northeast[a]	2.05	2.32	1.47	4.36	5.65	8.76	8.68	6.02	6.31	6.39
Middle Atlantic[a]	3.61	2.67	2.52	4.99	5.56	7.84	9.56	4.52	5.11	4.65

[a] Excluding western New York and western Pennsylvania.

New York and Pennsylvania,[2] both the Middle Atlantic and the Northeast decline consistently and rapidly from peak urbanization rates in the 1850s. The East North Central traces out our expected pattern while the East South Central and the West South

Central, consistent with their nineteenth century economic performance, reveal either stability or erratic fluctuations in incremental urban ratios. The South Atlantic, of course, begins urban acceleration much later in the century. States within the Northeast, including the subsets within Pennsylvania and New York, also trace out first differences of Gompertz or logistic curves but with periods of acceleration compressed within two to four decades.

The timing of regional urbanization supports our conventional historical knowledge. With the exception of Vermont and the western frontiers of New York and Pennsylvania, each of the nine Northeastern states began an acceleration in urbanization rates with the 1820s. Western New York and Pennsylvania did not initiate their respective "urban take-offs" until the subsequent

[2] Our definition of eastern Pennsylvania encompasses those counties bordering on New Jersey, Delaware, and Maryland which had significant early settlement. These counties include all of those in the southeast quadrant with the outermost northern and western limit delineated by the following counties: Franklin, Perry, Snyder, Union, Northumberland, Schuykill, Lehigh, and Northampton. Eastern New York here includes Long Island and the immediate present-day New York City area; beyond that it contains all counties bordering on the Hudson River plus the following contiguous northern counties: Otsego, Schoharie, Montgomery, Schenectady, Fulton, Saratoga, Warren, and Washington.

decade, the 1830s. Maryland lagged behind still further (in spite of Baltimore's development but consistent with its position as a border state), not undergoing an acceleration until the 1840s. The East North Central lagged two decades behind the Northeast and began its dramatic urban growth in the 1840s as well. By this date Rhode Island had already completed her urban transformation, attaining a maximum incremental urban ratio in the 1830s. Massachusetts, Maine, New Hampshire, and eastern New York were not far behind since they reached a peak urbanization rate in the 1840s. Maryland, Connecticut, New Jersey, and eastern Pennsylvania terminated their urban acceleration in the 1850s. In the Civil War decade the frontier regions, in turn, terminated their transformations in urban structure: western Pennsylvania, western New York, and the Midwest all reached maximum incremental urban ratios in the 1860s. Only after the process had been completed elsewhere in the Northeast and Midwest did the backward rural regions timidly enter the stage. Tiny Vermont and the populous South play a repeat performance only after we are well into the second half of the nineteenth century.

Although New England had the shortest period of acceleration (three decades), it does not generally seem to be true that the settled Northeastern regions had less extended urban take-offs. It is apparent however that the older regions reached consistently higher maximum incremental urban ratios than frontier areas. At comparable stages of urban growth, southern New England, eastern New York, eastern Pennsylvania, New Jersey, and Maryland produced urbanization rates exceeding those of northern New England, western Pennsylvania, western New York and the Midwest. As predicted, it seems fairly clear that urbanization was more abrupt in the Northeast, in general, and the settled Northeast in particular.

III. SOME SPATIAL DIMENSIONS OF URBANIZATION

Economic historians have always expressed keen interest in spatial aspects of development, regional sources of growth, regional linkages, and the distribution of economic improvement. Most quantitative studies of American nineteenth-century history have revealed that regional divergence was typical of the first three quarters of that century.

We now have models which predict that early development is disequilibrating so that regional divergence in per capita income and output is associated with adolescent growth [7]. Does Northeastern experience support these generalizations? Is regional divergence more typical of periods of relatively rapid over-all structural change? We have hypothesized that state urban levels relative to the Northeastern average diverged during the period of very rapid urbanization (1820–1860) while convergence upon the Northeastern average would have been the case thereafter.

A brief examination of Table 2 should indicate the rather unique experience of the Northeast as the region underwent profound ante-bellum development. The ten decades from 1790 to 1890 are generally ones of *convergence*. The rural states (which are not

Table 2. Percentage Mean Deviation of Urban Ratios in the Northeast and New England, 1790–1890 (in Percentage)[a]

| | NORTHEAST | | NEW ENGLAND | |
Year	m.d.	Δm.d.	m.d.	Δm.d.
1790	76.8		91.6	
1800	70.6	−6.2	85.8	−5.8
1810	67.6	−3.0	86.6	+0.8
1820	66.0	−1.6	84.6	−2.0
1830	66.4	+0.4	86.6	+2.0
1840	58.7	−7.7	77.4	−9.2
1850	52.1	−6.6	66.8	−10.6
1860	43.1	−9.0	58.7	−8.1
1870	38.1	−5.0	53.7	−5.0
1880	37.6	−0.5	50.0	−3.7
1890	32.4	−5.2	42.7	−7.3

U_{it} = urban population of the ith state at census t

P_{it} = total population of the ith state at census t

$U_t = \sum_i U_{it}$

$P_t = \sum_i P_{it}$

u_{it} = the urban relative = $\dfrac{(U_{it})}{(P_{it})} \div \dfrac{(U_t)}{(P_t)}$

The unweighted mean deviation is

$$(m.d.)_t = \frac{\sum\limits_{i=1}^{n} |u_{it} - 1.00|}{n}$$

where n is the number of states.

[a] The mean deviation measures the average difference between the urbanization ratio of each state relative to the all-state ratio and one, which is the average of the state relative urbanization ratios. The higher is m.d., the greater the differences among the states.

necessarily equivalent to our "frontier" states) appear to have increased their urbanization levels far more rapidly than did the more developed and urbanized states. This result is mildly surprising given what else we know about regional divergence and imbalance in the early stages of dynamic growth.[3] Even more interesting is the variation around those declining trends in the mean deviation for New England and the Northeast. Those periods of most rapid urban development and structural change appear to be precisely those of most rapid rates of convergence. In the case of the Northeast, the three decades from 1800 to 1830 are ones of very low rates of convergence. The decades of most rapid urban growth, the 1830s through the 1860s, are ones of most *rapid* convergence. Indeed, the rate of convergence accelerates from the 1820s to the 1850s, where it reaches a peak: except for the interruption of the 1880s, the rate abates thereafter. The pattern for New England is generally the same. The period from 1810 to 1830 is actually one of stability in the degree of "inequality" in urban levels. The 1830s and 1840s are years of rapid urbanization and of most significant convergence in urbanization levels; thereafter the rate of convergence steadily declines again with the exception of the 1880s. The conclusion cannot be avoided: at least in terms of urbanization, rapid growth in the nineteenth-century Northeast consistently generated more rapid rates of convergence than periods of relatively slow urban growth. The opposite is the case for aggregate American experience. We are not prepared to state flatly that rapid growth was *not* a destabilizing force in Northeastern history. The evidence does suggest however that after the Embargo era the Northeast was never seriously plagued with problems of increasing regional imbalance, regional divergence, and "backwash" effects.

Urban ratios are at best only very crude measures of economic structure, but as noted above other evidence would appear to support the generalization that Northeastern states

found their economic structures becoming more and more similar throughout the period 1790–1890 with the most rapid rate of convergence centered on the decades of the 1830s, 1840s, 1850s, and 1860s. The next question is whether this convergence in levels of urban development was achieved while urban population was becoming more equally distributed throughout the region. Did urban population spread out from initial urban centers or did it become more heavily concentrated? If interstate migration were the only source of a state's urban population, one certainly would have to insist upon redistribution as the method by which convergence in urban levels took place. This assumption is clearly violated during our segment of history.

In his study of Massachusetts, Chickering identified 1830 as the beginning of a sharp break with the past. Referring to the period 1790–1830 Chickering observed that "the tendency [is towards] the centralization of the population near Boston" [*1*, p. 68] while from 1830–1850 he notes that "the tendency has been more and more in the population to locate themselves in the country towns, and to settle there in greater proportion than in the metropolis." Chickering appeals to the sharp decline in transportation costs during the 1830s to explain the reversal. What can we say about over-all Northeastern experience?

First, Table 3 suggests that throughout the nineteenth century urban population was far more unequally distributed than rural population. There are only two exceptions to the rule that $V_t^u > V_t^r$;[4] both of these appear in 1890. Second, although total population tended to concentrate over time, rural and urban population behaved in an inverse fashion. After the Embargo era, rural population became increasingly more unequally distributed in the Northeast while urban population diffused or became more equally distributed among Northeastern states. The 1820s initiate a reversal in the Northeast while for New England it is the decade of the 1830s. Spatial concentration of urban population was typically the case prior to those decades while diffusion away from the established centers is the case thereafter. The shift may be explained in part by sharply

---

[3] Similar data were computed for the United States aggregate but excluding the West North Central, Mountain, and Pacific regions. As predicted above, the periods from 1790 to 1820 and 1860 to 1890 are typically ones during which there is regional *convergence* in urbanization levels. The period of rapid American urbanization, 1820 to 1860, is one of regional *divergence*.

---

[4] V^u and V_t^r are the coefficients of variation of state urban and state rural population in year t. See the note to Table 3 for a definition of these coefficients.

Table 3. Measures of Relative Dispersion of Rural, Urban, and Total Population in the Northeast, 1790–1890

A. New England

	V_t^u	ΔV^u	V_t^r	ΔV^r	V_t^p	ΔV^p
1790	1.4012		.6097		.6501	
1800	1.3140	−.0872	.4928	−.1169	.5400	−.1101
1810	1.3904	.0764	.4127	−.0801	.4766	−.0634
1820	1.4017	.0113	.4050	−.0077	.4701	−.0065
1830	1.4278	.0261	.4053	.0003	.4767	.0066
1840	1.2978	−.1300	.4538	.0485	.5344	.0577
1850	1.2900	−.0078	.4564	.0026	.6008	.0664
1860	1.2815	−.0085	.4658	.0094	.6628	.0620
1870	1.2520	−.0295	.4678	.0020	.7572	.0944
1880	1.2700	.0180	.4659	−.0019	.7761	.0189
1890	1.2728	.0028	.4569	−.0090	.8555	.0794

B. Northeast (II): Six New England States, New Jersey, Eastern and Western New York, Eastern and Western Pennsylvania

1790	1.3211		.6148		.6566	
1800	1.3219	.0008	.4369	−.1779	.5051	−.1515
1810	1.2799	−.0420	.3949	−.0420	.4576	−.0475
1820	1.2918	−.0119	.4758	.0809	.4932	.0356
1830	1.2359	−.0559	.5788	.1030	.5672	.0740
1840	1.1355	−.1004	.6431	.0643	.6091	.0419
1850	1.0499	−.0856	.6640	.0209	.6259	.0168
1860	1.0119	−.0380	.6879	.0239	.6572	.0313
1870	.8975	−.1144	.7066	.0187	.6894	.0322
1880	.8590	−.0385	.7655	.0589	.6847	−.0047
1890	.8185	−.0405	.8263	.0608	.7070	.0223

C. Northeast (III): Excluding Western New York and Western Pennsylvania

1790	1.1163		.5027		.5412	
1800	1.1171	.0008	.4468	−.0559	.5043	−.0369
1810	1.1098	−.0073	.4330	−.0138	.5053	.0010
1820	1.1393	.0295	.4254	−.0076	.5113	.0060
1830	1.1377	−.0016	.4464	.0210	.5484	.0371
1840	1.0764	−.0613	.4888	.0424	.6021	.0537
1850	1.0425	−.0339	.5219	.0331	.6608	.0587
1860	1.0103	−.0322	.5975	.0756	.7407	.0799
1870	.9484	−.0619	.6675	.0700	.7965	.0558
1880	.9237	−.0247	.7401	.0726	.7924	−.0041
1890	.9032	−.0205	.8618	.1217	.8234	.0310

$$\text{NOTE: } V_t^p = \left[\frac{\sum_i (P_{it} - \overline{P}_t)^2}{n} \right]^{\frac{1}{2}} \Bigg/ \overline{P}_t$$

$$V_t^u = \left[\frac{\sum_i (U_{it} - \overline{U}_t)^2}{n} \right]^{\frac{1}{2}} \Bigg/ \overline{U}_t$$

$$V_t^r = \left[\frac{\sum_i (R_{it} - \overline{R}_t)^2}{n} \right]^{\frac{1}{2}} \Bigg/ \overline{R}_t$$

where P = total population, U = urban population, R = rural population, the "bar" refers to the all state mean, and n is the number of states.

V_t^p, V_t^u, and V_t^r are the coefficients of variation for the respective population groups. The coefficient of variation provides a measure of the dispersion of the states around the all-state average. The higher the coefficient of variation, the greater the differences among the states.

declining internal transportation costs; it also may be explained by the changing impetus of urbanization from a foreign trade-commercial bias to a domestic manufacturing bias. Third, the rate of urbanization in the Northeast and the rate of spatial diffusion of urban population were closely allied. The period of maximum ΔV^u, or maximum rate of urban population diffusion, was generally from 1840 to 1870: for New England, the decade 1830–1840 was a peak ΔV^u; for Northeast (II), 1860–1870 and 1830–1840 in that order; for Northeast (III), 1860–1870 and 1830–1840.[5] It would appear that rapid structural change and urbanization was consistent with diffusion of urban population and urban development spread most vigorously throughout the Northeastern states during such periods of dramatic change. Fourth, Northeastern experience with concentration can be separated into two quite distinctive periods. The first three or four decades after 1790 generally were ones of urban concentration and rural diffusion. Thus for New England V_t^r declined sharply from .6097 in 1790 to .4053 in 1830 reflecting the extensive agricultural settlement of northern New England. At the same time, if anything, urban population became more concentrated in the three Southern states, especially Massachusetts, since V_t^u increased from 1.4012 in 1790 to 1.4278 in 1830. Industrialization sharply reversed this pattern. Between 1830 and 1890, V_t^u declined from 1.4278 to 1.2728 while V_t^r rose from .4053 to .4569. Thus urbanization and industrialization tended to be diffused among the New England states while agricultural employment became more and more concentrated. This secular pattern is consistent with the notion that natural resources are relatively immobile. Nevertheless this evidence is not consistent with twentieth century evidence for the American economy as a whole. The decades between 1920 and 1950 are ones of *greater* convergence in regional economic structure and income per capita than in any past secular period. This is also a period of *declining* rates of spatial redistribution of various countrywide aggregates. In Northeastern history, the period of most rapid convergence in state economic structure (level of urbanization) is also one of maximum redistribution of urban population.

IV. COMMERCIAL AND INDUSTRIAL SOURCES OF URBAN GROWTH

It has been suggested by many historians that pre-Civil War urban development had a predominantly commercial rather than an industrial flavor. Lampard begins his description of the period 1840–1860 with appropriate caution:

> It would be misleading to suggest that this explosion of American cities was due entirely to the growth of urban manufactures. It was much more the outcome of a continental development carried out with railroads: colonialism on a continental scale [2, p. 119].

Lampard appeals to city census data and concludes that the economic structure of the fifteen "great cities" in 1860 reveals the relative insignificance of manufacturing in all but a few cases.[6] The reference to "insignificance" is based on the proportion of manufacturing employment to total urban *population*. Lampard then goes on to note that:

> Nevertheless, there were already several sizeable urban-industrial concentrations, mainly in the Northeastern manufacturing area, with populations ranging from 19,000 to 50,000, such as Lowell with 36 per cent in manufactures and Lynn with 45 per cent. These were the true forerunners of American coketowns [2, p. 120].

Admittedly, Lampard was concerned with over-all American experience while our interest is with the Northeast. Nevertheless, using the same census data, treated somewhat differently, we reach much stronger conclusions.

Table 4 presents evidence which summarizes the average economic structure of fifty American cities all with populations in 1860 exceeding 10,000 and all except seven with populations exceeding 20,000. The 1870 data are available directly from the Ninth Census while the 1860 data is in part derived from 1870 characteristics: urban manufacturing employment is reported by city in the 1860 Census but total employment is not, and to overcome this we have applied the 1870 city labor participation rates to the 1860 city population data.

We might first note the general *similarity* in the economic structure of cities between 1860, 1870, and 1950. Especially for those in

---

[5] The rate of diffusion is a maximum when the decline in the coefficient of variation is largest.

[6] It is also true that the "fifteen great cities" of 1860 were less industrially oriented than cities of smaller size.

Table 4. Regional Summary on the Manufacturing Employment Share in the Labor Force
for 50 American Cities (in Percentage)

| | PERCENTAGE | | CHANGE | RELATIVE TO NATIONAL AVERAGE | |
	1860	1870	1860–1870	1860	1870
A. (Excluding Washington, D.C.)					
New England	43.0	49.2	6.2	135.6	120.3
Middle Atlantic[a]	35.2	44.1	8.9	111.0	107.8
West	22.3	35.1	12.8	70.3	85.8
South	16.1	27.0	10.9	50.8	66.0
United States	31.7	40.9	9.2	100.0	100.0
B. (Excluding Washington, D.C., Boston, New York, Philadelphia, Baltimore, New Orleans)					
New England	52.6	55.9	3.3	170.8	137.3
Middle Atlantic[a]	32.0	45.2	13.2	103.9	111.1
West	22.3	35.1	12.8	72.4	86.2
South	21.4	28.6	7.2	69.5	70.3
United States	30.8	40.7	9.9	100.0	100.0

[a] Middle Atlantic here includes Maryland and Delaware.

the Northeastern tier of states, *but also those in the Midwest* (*1870*), the ratio of manufacturing employment to total employment indicates that these cities had either an equal or greater manufacturing orientation in 1870 than in 1950. For Jersey City the figures are respectively 21.3, 35.2, and 32.8 per cent; for Newark, 73.5, 60.8, and 38.8 per cent; for New Haven, 54.0, 35.4, and 35.4 per cent; for Rochester, 39.6, 49.3, and 44.3 per cent and so on. Even relative to their industrial maturity in 1950, and even allowing for a considerable lack of employment data comparability over time, by 1860 most of the cities in the Northeast and many in the Midwest fully qualified as industrial-urban complexes if judged *only* by these broad occupational characteristics. (We are not concerned here with firm size, capital intensity, or technological efficiency. To be more explicit, city size is not our interest here nor is sectoral productivity: only the sectoral distribution of economic activity is at issue.)

Secondly, we might note the relationship between urban industrial maturity and the timing of regional urbanization. One would reasonably predict that in 1860 those regions of earliest urban take-off would also contain the most industrially oriented city economies. Is the manufacturing employment share in the labor force, M/L, significantly higher in those regional economies which lead in the process of American urban development?

New England, the first to generate and complete an urban transformation, has an average M/L among its twelve important urban centers of 43.0 per cent in 1860. The Middle Atlantic, which lags behind New England growth, has an average M/L of 35.2 per cent, while by 1870 its cities were fully as industrialized as New England's in 1860. The West and the South, lagging urban development still further, have even lower M/L shares; 22.3 and 16.1 per cent, respectively. The narrative runs much the same if we exclude the great seaboard cities from the sample. Excluding the *atypical* cities of Boston, New York, Philadelphia, Baltimore, and New Orleans, the figures are 52.6 per cent for New England, 32.0 per cent for the Middle Atlantic, 22.3 per cent for the West, and 21.4 per cent for the South.

The regional ordering of urban-industrial structure is the same for 1870 but the relative change in industrial orientation of American cities differs between regions. Those regions whose peak rates of urban transformation lie closest to the Civil War decade are also those which undergo the most significant increases in the manufacturing employment share. New England had the lowest Δ(M/L) since her urban-industrial transformation had already been completed long before 1870. The Middle Atlantic had the next lowest index. The Midwest had the highest. The South shared some of this continuing urban employment shift into manufacturing but at a rate considerably below the industrializing Midwest—hardly a surprising result.

The comparative experience of the Northeast with industrialization-urbanization can be more effectively described by using an alternative technique. If we again only consider urban areas equal to or exceeding 10,000 we can define the following terms:

M^U = manufacturing employment at census year t in urban areas

L^U = total labor force at census t in urban areas

P_t^U = total urban population at census year t

The increase in total urban manufacturing employment during the Civil War decade can be written simply as

$$\Delta M^U = \left(\frac{M^U}{L^U}\right)_{70} \cdot \left(\frac{L^U}{P^U}\right)_{70} \cdot P_{70}^U$$

$$- \left(\frac{M^U}{L^U}\right)_{60} \cdot \left(\frac{L^U}{P^U}\right)_{60} \cdot P_{60}^U$$

Let us make the not unreasonable assumption that the urban labor participation rate remains unchanged in the aggregate over time. Then it follows that

$$\Delta M^U = \left[\left(\frac{M^U}{L^U}\right)_{70} \cdot P_{70}^U - \left(\frac{M^U}{L^U}\right)_{60} \cdot P_{60}^U\right]$$
$$\cdot \overline{\left(\frac{L^U}{P^U}\right)}$$

$$= \left\{\left[\left(\frac{M^U}{L^U}\right)_{60} + \Delta\left(\frac{M^U}{L^U}\right)\right] \cdot \left[P_{60}^U\right.\right.$$
$$+ \Delta P^U\Big] - \left(\frac{M^U}{L^U}\right)_{60} \cdot P_{60}^U\Big\} \cdot \overline{\left(\frac{L^U}{P^U}\right)}$$

$$= \left[\Delta P^U \cdot \left(\frac{M^U}{L^U}\right)_{60} + \Delta\left(\frac{M^U}{L^U}\right) \cdot P_{60}^U\right.$$

$$\left. + \Delta P^U \cdot \Delta\left(\frac{M^U}{L^U}\right)\right] \cdot \overline{\left(\frac{L^U}{P^U}\right)}$$

The increase in urban manufacturing employment can thus be written as the sum of (1) increased urban population, with the same ratio of manufacturing employment to labor force, (2) an increased ratio of manufacturing employment to labor force with an unchanged urban population, and (3) some combination

of these two effects, always holding the aggregate labor participation rate constant.

Let us put the importance of these cities into some perspective. In 1870 New England manufacturing employment represented by our sample of twelve cities accounted for almost 10 per cent of total U.S. manufacturing employment while for 16 per cent of the manufacturing employment of all the fifty cities represented in Table 4. The figures for the Northeast are 39 and 66 per cent, respectively. The entire set of 50 cities in 1870 represented 58 per cent of American manufacturing employment. The residual, 42 per cent, is therefore mainly manufacturing employment in cities less than 10,000 and, to a far lesser extent, rural manufacturing. Although they are ignored here, those smaller cities are being examined more intensively in our present research. (It appears that at least in the Northeast these smaller cities may have been more manufacturing oriented than their larger sisters.[7])

The comparison between Northeastern experience in the middle of the nineteenth century and the experience elsewhere in the U.S. is quite striking. As a region which had already industrialized, most of the Northeastern increments in manufacturing employment (1860–1870) can be explained by increased urban population (53.4 per cent) while only 35.2 per cent can be attributed to the "industrialization" of existing urban population. In the rest of the United States, where industrialization was less mature and urban development had been more conditioned by commercial forces, the relative contribution of these components is more evenly divided. Increased urban population

---

[7] These are as yet only rough approximations but we have computed indices of manufacturing orientation (the share of manufacturing employment in total urban employment) of Northeastern cities by size class (1860) for those greater than 10,000.

	10,000–24,999	25,000–49,999	50,000–99,999	100,000
New England	44.6%	34.8%	56.9%	26.5%
Middle Atlantic	30.2	36.7	40.9	30.1
Northeast	36.9	35.6	45.3	29.4

With the significant exception of New England cities between 10,000 and 24,999 in size, the relative importance of manufacturing increases with city size up to the 50,000–99,999 range, while the "great cities," of course, are definitely commercially oriented.

accounted for 38.3 per cent of the increments in manufacturing employment, industrialization of existing urban population accounted for 37.3 per cent, and the combination of effects for 24.4 per cent. New England experience during the decade would appear to clinch the case: increased urban population accounted for 65.6 per cent of that region's increase in M^U, increased ratio of manufacturing employment to labor force for 24.4 per cent, and the combination of effects for 9.7 per cent. With the exception of Vermont, each Northeastern state underwent impressive increases in the importance of manufacturing employment relative to total nonagricultural employment during those four decades. The largest increase by far occurs in the 1840s. The 1850s are followed by a steady decline in the relative importance of manufacturing as a share in nonagricultural employment. This, of course, is consistent with the now common observation that mature development generates an increasingly important tertiary sector.

REFERENCES

1. Jesse Chickering, *A Statistical View of the Population of Massachusetts from 1765 to 1840*, Boston. Charles C. Little and James Brown, 1846.

2. Eric Lampard, "The History of Cities in the Economically Advanced Areas," *Economic Development and Cultural Change, 3* (January, 1955), 81–136.

3. Stanley Lebergott, *Manpower in Economic Growth*, New York, McGraw-Hill, 1964.

4. Eugene Smolensky and Donald Ratajczak, "The Conception of Cities," *Explorations in Entrepreneurial History,* Second Series, *2* (Winter, 1965), 90–131.

5. Joseph A. Swanson and Jeffrey G. Williamson, "Firm Location and Optimal City Size in American History," L. S. Schnore, ed., *The New Urban History: Quantitive Studies at the Frontier,* forthcoming.

6. Adna Ferrin Weber, *The Growth of Cities in the Nineteenth Century,* New York, The Macmillan Company, 1899.

7. Jeffrey G. Williamson, "Regional Inequality and the Process of National Development: A Description of the Patterns," *Economic Development and Cultural Change, 13* (July, 1965), Supplement.

8. Jeffrey G. Williamson and Joseph A. Swanson, "The Growth of Cities in the American Northeast, 1820–1870," *Explorations in Entrepreneurial History*, Second Series, *4* (Fall, 1966), Supplement.

IX THE EFFECTS OF MONETARY AND FISCAL POLICY

The government's monetary and fiscal policies have a profound effect on output, employment, and prices. Dramatic changes in these economic variables will, of course, have far-reaching political and social repercussions. It is not surprising, then, that some of the most passionate historical controversies turn on the possible consequences of monetary and fiscal policies. Among the most frequently debated issues are the repercussions of Jackson's war with the Second Bank of the United States, the effect of the monetary policies pursued by the federal government during the Civil War on the distribution of income, the causes and consequences of the post-Civil War deflation, and the role of New Deal fiscal policies in the recovery from the Great Depression of the 1930s.

The essays in Part IX suggest that many historians have seriously misconstrued the economic and social, if not the political, repercussions of some of the most frequently discussed fiscal and monetary policies. In essay 33 Hugh Rockoff cites evidence which contradicts the widely held view that Andrew Jackson's policies, particularly his war against the Second Bank of the United States, were responsible for the rapid inflation of the middle 1830s and for the recession that followed it. Reuben Kessel and Armen Alchian (essay 34) throw into doubt the contention that the Civil War inflation brought about a redistribution of income from workers to capitalists. That presumed redistribution has been made a foundation for the view that the Civil War greatly spurred industrialization. The successful return to the gold standard is re-evaluated by James Kindahl (essay 35) in an analysis which casts new light upon the agitation over greenbacks and bimetallism in the post-Civil War era. In essay 36 E. Cary Brown contradicts both those historians who hailed the fiscal policies of the New Deal as a great success and those who condemned them as a failure. Brown holds that fiscal policy was never really attempted under the New Deal.

I. MONETARY AND FISCAL POLICY

Monetary policy refers to the actions of the government which affect the quantity of money in the economy. In discussing the effects of changes in the money supply we need not be directly concerned with the motives for government action or inaction. We are interested in the effects of the changing money supply upon the level of output and of prices, regardless of the factors which motivated these changes.

In defining fiscal policy, however, the question of motive has been considered important. Fiscal policy is generally restricted to those changes in the government budgetary level of expenditures, taxes, and transfer payments which are undertaken with the objective of influencing the over-all level of prices and output. The effects of government expenditures and taxes upon the allocation of resources and the distribution of income are generally considered separately from the purely aggregate effects upon national income and the price level.

It is often true that the same action will have both a monetary and a fiscal aspect. There are basically five different ways in which the government can finance expenditures. These are: taxation, sale of public assets (as land in the 19th century), sale of public debt (internally and externally), printing of money, and forced draft (as in the military services). Budgetary deficits—the excess of expenditures and transfer payments above taxes and revenues from the sale of public assets—can be financed either by creation of public debt or by the printing of money. When deficits do occur they have both fiscal and monetary effects. In the first three selections of Part IX, emphasis is upon monetary effects. In essay 36, the discussion is limited to the fiscal effects of budgetary changes.

Economists have developed rather complex analytical models with which to analyze the effects of monetary and fiscal measures upon the economy.[1] These models show how levels of output, of employment, and of prices may

---

[1] For presentation of these models at an undergraduate level, the reader should consult a textbook in Macroeconomics or National Income Analysis, such as [1, 3].

We shall not present the general model. It will be familiar to those who know the basic Keynesian model including a monetary sector. In the introduction we shall present only truncations of the general model which are useful for understanding the included essays.

The economics of monetary and fiscal policies has recently become a major area of controversy within the economics profession. However this debate is germane only to essay 36, as will be discussed below. For the others there is general agreement that concentration on monetary aspects is appropriate.

be affected by changes in the money supply and the level of government taxes and expenditures. The extent of these effects depends upon the empirical magnitudes of certain key parameters and on the degree of flexibility of prices (and wages). It is particularly important in analyzing the effects of monetary and fiscal policies upon the economy to determine whether prices are free to vary in either direction. An increase in the level of national income measured in money terms could mean a changed level of real output, a changed level of prices, or both. In general, the longer the period under observation, the more flexible are prices. Moreover when the resources of an economy are fully employed, an increase in the level of money income means an increase in the level of prices rather than in the level of real income. In essays 33, 34, and 35, existing conditions in the economy justify the assumption that prices were flexible. Essay 36 proceeds on the assumption that the level of prices was rigid.

II. MONETARY POLICY

This section will discuss three related topics dealing with monetary policy as a background to essays 33, 34, and 35. These are: the monetary standard and international exchange rates, the determination of the domestic money supply, and the equation of exchange (or quantity theory of money).

A. The Monetary Standard and International Exchange Rates

The question of the monetary standard—whether it is to be gold or silver monometallism, bimetallism, or pure fiat—has been among the most heated politico-economic questions. While much of the political debate about the properties of metals has been rather nonsensical, the choice of the standard is important because of the constraints that standard imposes on the money supply and hence on the domestic economy. If the United States and other countries are on, say, a gold standard, in which each domestic money is defined in terms of gold and each country is committed to maintain convertibility between gold and other domestic money, the monetary authorities are unable to arbitrarily fix the quantity of money.

With each national money defined in gold it is easy to compute the fixed rate of exchange between currencies. Since each country is committed to maintaining these fixed rates, it may be necessary for monetary authorities to pursue actions aimed at foreign exchange stability which would not be taken if the domestic economy alone was considered. Certain relationships must exist between relative price levels and interest rates for fixed exchange rates to be maintained. The adoption of fixed exchange rates, via the acceptance of the gold standard, reduces the discretionary authority of monetary policy-makers and means that the domestic money supply will be influenced by the events in foreign countries.

The United States has generally been on some form of metallic standard. At first both gold and silver were standards; since the Civil War era gold alone has been the effective standard. While the commitment of the government and of the banking sector to maintain convertibility into specie was frequently waived for short intervals at times of war and financial panic, the years 1861–1879 were the only extended period during which convertibility was suspended.[2] Prior to 1933 government payments of specie could be initiated by both American citizens and foreigners, and there was an internal drain as well as an external drain of specie. Since 1933 government payments in gold have been restricted to foreigners. With the exception of the period from the Civil War to resumption the United States has therefore had fixed exchange rates vis-à-vis its important trading partners. However between 1861 and 1879 the exchange rate was flexible, which means the price of foreign currencies in terms of dollars was free to vary.

---

[2] In this period gold dollars (fixed in terms of metallic content) were circulating alongside greenback dollars. However greenbacks were not convertible at par. The price of gold dollars in terms of greenback dollars varied with economic and political conditions. The value of a gold dollar was greater than that of a greenback dollar, the excess being the premium on gold. Britain maintained the gold standard, so that gold dollars could be used as foreign exchange. The foreign exchange rate was calculated as the product of the (constant) price of pounds in terms of gold and the (varying) price of gold in terms of greenbacks. A positive premium on gold meant an increase in the price of pounds in terms of greenback dollars—an adverse change in the foreign exchange rate of the United States.

Foreign exchange rates, when flexible, vary with the demand for and supply of the different national monies. The exchange rate between the United States and Britain (the price of pounds in terms of dollars) is set by the American demand to obtain pounds in exchange for dollars and the British demand to obtain dollars in exchange for pounds. American citizens will demand pounds in order to import British goods and services and to purchase British assets (capital exports from the U.S.). The demand for dollars is based upon British desire to purchase U.S. goods and services, and to acquire American assets (a capital import for the U.S.). An increase in the American demand for pounds would increase the number of dollars paid for a pound, while an increased British demand for dollars would reduce the number of dollars paid for a pound. In the former case the dollar has depreciated, in the latter it has appreciated.

Ignoring capital flows, there is a relationship between changes in the exchange rate and in the prices of trading partners which will be anticipated as long as the underlying determinants of supply and demand for traded goods have not changed. The purchasing-power-parity theory states that the exchange rate between two countries tends to vary with their relative internal price levels. In equation 1, $\overset{*}{X}$ is the rate of change of the

$$\overset{*}{X} = \overset{*}{P}_{US} - \overset{*}{P}_{GB} \qquad (1)$$

number of dollars paid per pound, $\overset{*}{P}_{US}$, the rate of change of the United States price level, and $\overset{*}{P}_{GB}$, the rate of change of the British price level. This equation states that if the U.S. price level doubled relative to the British price level, the number of dollars paid per pound would also double. Under these circumstances the purchase of a British good costs twice as many dollars as previously, but the ratio between the number of U.S. dollars paid for a domestic good and that paid for British goods would be unchanged. Under the assumptions of equation 1, the condition for maintaining an unchanged exchange rate is equality in the rates of change in the price levels of each country (i.e., maintenance of the relative price level). When there are capital flows, the condition for a constant exchange rate is modified. If there was a capital inflow into the United States, repre-

senting an increased demand for dollars, U.S. prices would have to rise more rapidly than British prices in order to keep the exchange rate constant. Conversely capital outflows from the U.S. and constancy in the exchange rate would require that U.S. prices increase less rapidly than British prices. Since the purchasing-power-parity theory holds only when the underlying demand and supply relationships for traded goods are stable, caution must be exercised in empirical applications. Nevertheless the purchasing-power-parity theory is useful in understanding the relationship between internal price levels and the foreign exchange rate.

When the exchange rate is fixed, the adjustment to changing conditions by alterations in the foreign exchange rate is precluded. Then movements of specie will substitute for movements in exchange rates.[3] An increased American demand for pounds would lead to a flow of specie from the U.S. to Britain. An increased British demand for U.S. goods or assets would raise the demand for dollars and hence lead to a flow of specie from Britain to the United States. How large a specie flow is necessary to restore domestic equilibrium depends on the effect of the specie flow on the domestic money supply and thus on the level of prices and/or real output. If a country wishes to avoid, say, an outflow of specie it is necessary to reduce the demand for foreign currency by restricting the domestic money supply, thus holding down domestic prices and/or real income relative to those of other nations. If policies to avoid specie movements do not work satisfactorily, it may either be necessary to suspend specie payments for a period of time or else to redefine the metallic content of money.[4] In 1839 and 1861 (as well as several other times) the U.S. took the former course in the presence of undesired specie outflows; in 1933, by devaluation, the latter. Since the purchasing-power-parity theory gives the conditions for maintenance of fixed exchange rates, it

---

[3] Some minor discrepancy from the calculated exchange rate par may exist, due to costs of shipping and insuring specie, without generating specie movements. These costs fix the gold points, the prices of foreign exchange at which specie inflows and outflows will occur.

[4] Devaluation is a reduction in the metallic weight of specie, raising the price of foreign currencies in terms of domestic money. Revaluation is an increase in the metallic weight.

gives the conditions for the successful resumption of the fixed exchange rate, as in
1879.

B. Determination of the Money Supply[5]

The money supply is defined as the total of
bank liabilities plus currency held by the
nonbank public. In equation 2, M is the
money supply, C the currency held by the
public, and D the bank liabilities held by the

$$M = C + D \qquad (2)$$

public. Three agents are involved in the
determination of the domestic money supply.
They are: government (including the central
bank), banks, and the households and business firms in the economy. In discussing the
monetary expansion equation we shall first
assume constant various behavior parameters,
the explanation of whose changes form an
important part of historical analysis. This
will make clear the relationships among the
three agents in the determination of the
quantity of money.

The government will affect, if not determine, the quantity of high-powered money
(H) in the economy. High-powered money
includes specie and government fiat issues,
and is held by the nonbank public as currency (C) and by banks as reserves (R)
(equation 3). When held by banks, high-
powered money provides the base for a
multiple expansion of bank liabilities. While

$$H = C + R \qquad (3)$$

the proportions of the total high-powered
money held by banks and the public vary,
affecting the size of the money supply, neither
sector can determine the quantity of high-
powered money in the economy. The quantity is affected by government issues of fiat
money and, in conjunction with the conditions of international trade and capital flows,
by the commitment to a metallic standard.
Prior to the Civil War the major form of
high-powered money was specie, and therefore the quantity of high-powered money
depended upon international factors. While
in the Civil War and afterwards the government issued various forms of fiat money

(greenbacks, national banknotes, Federal
Reserve System liabilities, etc.) which served
as high-powered money, the commitment to
a gold standard did mean some long-run
constraint upon the domestic money supply
and high-powered money issues which would
not have existed in the absence of the monetary standard.

For the study of some questions, we may
assume, further, that the banks and public
are indifferent concerning the form of high-
powered money they hold, be it specie or
government fiat. Of course, this would not
be a useful assumption for the study of
problems such as the periodic financial crisis.
Indeed the problems discussed in essays 33
and 34 are cases in which economic disturbances arose because specie was preferred to
other forms of money.

The banking sector holds high-powered
money as reserves against which it creates
liabilities to be held by the public. At earlier
times these liabilities took the form of both
bank deposits and bank notes. Despite the
frequent nineteenth-century confusions on
this point, the particular form which these
liabilities took was irrelevant for most economic matters. In more recent times the sole
bank liability has been deposits. If the banks
held 100 per cent reserves against their
liabilities, either because of legal requirements or their own volition, then no multiple
expansion of the money supply would occur. If
fractional reserves against liabilities are permitted, then the banking system can create
liabilities which are a multiple of the amount
of high-powered money held as reserves.
The reserve ratio (r in equation 4) may be

$$R = rD \qquad (4)$$

that fixed by legal requirements or it may be
set at a profit-maximizing level by the banks.
It will vary with the probability of being
called upon to convert bank liabilities into
high-powered money. The stereotyped "wildcat bank" was one with a low ratio of reserves
to deposits, but as Rockoff shows in essay 33,
low reserve ratios may be found in conservative banks. In creating liabilities by lending
to the public, banks can bring about a redistribution of purchasing power. These
"forced savings" brought about by the
banking sector have been a cause of great
controversy concerning banks and their regulation, though it has been argued that "forced
savings" have promoted a more rapid rate

---

[5] This formulation follows that in [2, chaps. 1 and
2]. See also [4, Appendix B].

of growth than would otherwise have occurred.

The third agent, the nonbank public, holds
money in the forms of both currency (high-
powered money) and bank liabilities. The
determination of the fraction of its money
to be held in the form of currency (c in
equation 5) is affected by the ease and convenience of holding these alternative forms

$$C = cM \qquad (5)$$

and by expectations concerning the ability
of the banking sector to convert its liabilities
into high-powered money. The greater the
confidence in the ability of the banking sector
to maintain convertibility, the lower the ratio
of high-powered money to money held by
the public.

Holding r and c constant, equations 2–5
can be solved to express the money supply
in terms of the three determinants, as shown

$$M = \frac{1}{c + r - cr} \cdot H \qquad (6)$$

in equation 6. By simple algebraic manipula-
tion one can obtain equation 7.[6] Equation 7

$$\overset{*}{M} = \overset{*}{H} + \frac{M}{H}(1-r)\left[-\frac{dc}{dt}\right]$$

$$+ \frac{M}{H}(1-c)\left[-\frac{dr}{dt}\right] \qquad (7)$$

makes it possible to predict the independent
effects of changes in the three determinants
(H, r, and c) upon the money supply.[7]
Equation 7 can also be used to measure the
contribution, *ex post*, of changes in each to
the behavior of the money supply without
any attribution of cause-and-effect, as both
equations 6 and 7 are identities. The measurement of contributions in this sense does not
concern itself with determining an initial
cause, though it can be helpful in showing
where to look for the underlying causes of
changes in the money supply, and thus in
the levels of prices and of output.

———————
[6] Equation 7 was obtained from equation 6 by
taking natural logarithms and differentiating with
respect to time. See [2, p. 17].

[7] However changes in c often lead to changes in r,
and vice versa, so that it may not be possible to treat
these two determinants separately in many cases.

C. The Equation of Exchange

The equation of exchange is an identity which
holds true at each moment of time. With the
introduction of assumptions as to the determinants of the behavior of certain of the
variables it can be translated into a more
familiar variant, the quantity theory of money.
We will not be concerned here with the
theoretical controversies as to whether the
quantity theory of money should be regarded
as a theory of the determination of the price
level or of the demand for money, nor
whether either variant provides a good explanation (prediction) of economic events at
all times. Although tautological, the equation
of exchange nevertheless provides a useful
framework within which to sort out economic
relationships and hence aids in the explanation of changes in prices and income.

Economic transactions can be looked at
as an exchange of money for output. The
value of money income can be expressed
either as the total value of goods and services produced (GNP) or as the sum of
annual monetary turnover (the money supply
times income velocity). This identity leads to
the formulation in equation 8, with M the
money supply, V income velocity (the number

$$MV = PY \qquad (8)$$

of times each unit of money turns over in
the purchase of national income), P the price
level, and Y real national income. The rate-
of-change formulation, equation 9, states that
the rate of change of the money supply plus

$$\overset{*}{M} + \overset{*}{V} = \overset{*}{P} + \overset{*}{Y} \qquad (9)$$

that of velocity is equal to the rate of change
of the price level plus that of real national
income. Using equation 9 we can partition
changes in money national income into
changes in the money supply and changes in
velocity.

For analysis it is useful to introduce information concerning the extent to which
changes in the terms of the equation of
exchange are exogenously or endogenously
related to other variables. The most basic
assumption is that, to a considerable extent,
the explanation for changes in M can be
considered independent of changes in veloc-
icity, real income, or prices, and that exogenous changes in M will lead to variations

in these other terms.[8] While the existence of
an international monetary standard with
fixed exchange rates means that changes in
the demand and supply of traded commodities and in capital movements will lead to
movements in specie, and although changes
in bank reserve ratios and the public's currency ratio may be attributable to seemingly
independent movements in output and prices,
much evidence suggests that it is often
plausible and useful to regard changes in the
money supply as an exogenous, rather than as
an endogenous, force in the explanation of
economic changes.

If velocity does not change ($\overset{*}{V} = 0$), or
more generally, if $\overset{*}{V}$ is predictable from the
values of other variables (and not equal to
$-\overset{*}{M}$), changes in the money supply lead to
changes in the level of money income. This
means changes in the level of prices, the level
of real output, or both, depending upon the
availability of unutilized resources and the
degree of price flexibility. Since it seems
appropriate for longer-term analysis, particularly in the nineteenth century, to consider
prices sufficiently flexible to provide for full
employment of resources, this would imply
$\overset{*}{Y}$, the rate of growth of real output, is independent of changes in the other variables
of the equation-of-exchange. Therefore any
excess of $\overset{*}{M}$ plus $\overset{*}{V}$ above $\overset{*}{Y}$ will lead to price
increase, while a short-fall implies a price
decrease (equation 10). Within short periods

$$\overset{*}{P} = \overset{*}{M} + \overset{*}{V} - \overset{*}{Y} \qquad (10)$$

when the level of real national income cannot
be varied the behavior of prices depends only
upon $\overset{*}{M}$ and $\overset{*}{V}$. If velocity is also constant
($\overset{*}{V} = 0$), then the price level will change proportionately with the (exogenous) change in
the money supply (equation 11).

$$\overset{*}{P} = \overset{*}{M} \qquad (11)$$

D. Historical Studies of the Effects of Monetary Policy

1. THE BANK WAR (ESSAY 33)

The main issue of concern to Rockoff is the
effect of Jacksonian policies, particularly the

severing of the government's connection with
the Second Bank of the United States after
1832, upon the behavior of the price level
in the 1830s. Following work by Macesich
and Temin, he uses equation 7 to test the
customary view that the Jackson victory led
to a sharp increase in the money supply by
encouraging "wildcat banking."[9] He concludes that the increased money supply cannot be explained by "wildcat banking" since
the banking system's reserve ratio actually
rose after 1831. Rather the increased money
supply was due to an expansion of high-
powered money via specie inflow. The ending
of the inflation in 1837 and the sharp deflation after 1839 are attributed to the reduction in the money supply generated by an
increased desire for specie by the public and
the banks, rather than marked specie outflows.

The specie inflows from Mexico and Britain
are explained by exogenous capital movements, which not only directly increased the
U.S. money supply but, as implied by the
purchasing-power-parity theory, permitted
price increases to occur without any offsetting
drain. Another important permissive factor
in the U.S. inflation was the increased British
price level. Britain also contributed to the
post-1839 price decline by pursuing policies
designed to prevent further specie outflows
from that nation.

Rockoff goes on to analyze the effect that
the Bank of the United States could have
had upon other banks. He presents a model
of a bank's determination of its reserve ratio
to suggest how this ratio was influenced by
the existence and demise of the Bank of the
United States. However, since developments
in the international sector had such far-
reaching effects on the U.S. economy, much
of the force has been removed from arguments which place the blame for the price
inflation and deflation of the 1830s upon the
political and economic policies of the
Jacksonians.

2. THE CIVIL WAR INFLATION (ESSAY 34)

During the Civil War the great increase of
government expenditure forced the Northern
states to suspend payment in specie. This led
to a sharp inflation in which the price level
increased more rapidly than money wages.
From this decline in real wages there has

---

[8] For justification and use of this approach in the
study of American monetary history see [2] and [4].

[9] For a discussion of earlier work see [5, chap. 1].

been inferred a redistribution of income away from workers to capitalists. In essay 34 Kessel and Alchian find other explanations for the decline in real wages; explanations which do not imply a redistribution of income towards profits.[10]

Kessel and Alchian suggest that the increased prices in the Civil War years may have resulted in a decline in real personal income per capita rather than redistribution adverse to wage-earners. In their discussion they rely heavily on the purchasing-power-parity theory, using it to predict expected changes in the level of foreign exchange rates. With specie payments suspended the U.S. had flexible exchange rates vis-à-vis the rest-of-the-world. Thus the domestic price of gold was determined by the foreign exchange rate since other countries remained on the gold standard. In other words the gold premium measured the increased dollar price of foreign exchange.[11]

Three explanations of the decline in real wages are provided. First is the adverse movement in the foreign exchange rate (the gold premium), relative to the internal prices of the United States. By using equation 1 to predict what the foreign exchange rate would have been if all U.S. prices had moved proportionately, and showing a sharper than expected rise in the price of foreign exchange, Kessel and Alchian demonstrate a decline in the U.S. terms-of-trade.[12] They attribute this decline mainly to the cessation of cotton exports from the South. Equation 1 also enters into the second explanation, the inappropriate choice of 1860 as a base year for making real wage comparisons. Kessel and Alchian argue that an abnormal foreign trade situation resulted in unusually favorable terms-of-trade, so that real wages were higher than could be maintained normally. The third reason for declining real wages was the increases in prices resulting from increased

excise taxation and import duties. Since the incidence of these taxes is not known, however, their effect on the distribution of income is also unknown. For these reasons Kessel and Alchian, while not denying that further study might indicate income redistribution, argue that the measured decline in real wages need not have shifted income towards profit-earners. Rather it was consistent with a general decline in measured income within the private sector.

Kessel and Alchian point out that a major burden of wartime inflation fell upon those individuals who held their wealth in the form of money balances prior to the price increases. The price increases, resulting from the increased money supply, meant these individuals now held nominal balances with less purchasing power than before the inflation. It is they who suffered from the unanticipated inflation brought about by the government's attempt to draw resources away from the private sector. Thus the authors' statement that the greater the reliance upon inflation to finance the cost of the war, the less the burden of the war measures upon wage-earners follows from the plausible assumption that workers held a relatively low share of money balances.

3. THE RESUMPTION OF SPECIE, 1879 (ESSAY 35)

After the Civil War there was not an immediate return to a metallic standard. There was a decade of political agitation before passage of the Resumption Act in 1875 provided for a return to specie at the ante-bellum metallic content (and thus exchange rate) by 1879. James Kindahl analyzes the conditions which made resumption possible in 1879, and specifies the decisions of the government which made this policy successful. He uses this analysis to discuss whether resumption could have been successfully accomplished before that date, answering that question in the negative. He also refutes the contention that the success of resumption was the fortuitous result of a wheat export boom.

Kindahl describes the conditions necessary for resumption, using the purchasing-power-parity theory of equation 1. To successfully re-establish the prewar foreign exchange rate, the U.S. price level had to return to the same relative position vis-à-vis other nations which had existed before suspension. Under this

---

[10] For a more detailed discussion of these issues see above, pp. 369–379. As stated in their concluding section Kessel and Alchian do not deny the possibility of income redistribution. They intend only to point out that exclusive concern with the monetary inflation does not provide a basis for the claims made by Mitchell and many subsequent writers.

[11] See footnote 2, above.

[12] The terms-of-trade is the ratio of export prices to import prices. An adverse change in the terms-of-trade means the ratio has fallen—imports have become more expensive relative to exports.

condition the premium on gold would have been zero. Because the U.S. was importing capital from abroad, and because of changes in the conditions affecting the supply of and demand for traded goods, it was not necessary for the relative price levels to return exactly to the ante-bellum ratios. Nevertheless the appropriate ratio still required a sharp drop in U.S. prices from their Civil War high, and a sufficient decline was not achieved till 1879. By using equation 10 Kindahl shows the arithmetic of this price decline. Both $\overset{*}{V}$ and $\overset{*}{M}$ were positive, so that the fall in the price level is the result of the very rapid growth of real output in the 1870s. The specific role of the government was the rather passive one of not generating a more rapid growth of the money supply (high-powered money fell sharply between the end of the War and 1867, and then remained relatively unchanged to 1879), rather than any policy of forced monetary contraction. The accumulation of the gold reserve, necessary for maintaining the specie standard after resumption, actually made the accomplishment of resumption more difficult by increasing the demand for gold, and therefore the gold premium. The key to the successful resumption was the rapid growth of output, which in conjunction with the slowly growing money supply, brought about the necessary decline in the U.S. price level.

III. FISCAL POLICY

A. The Basic Model

Only the simplest model of income determination is necessary to understand the mechanics of fiscal policy as analyzed in essay 36. The model assumes unemployed resources and rigid prices, with changes in the money supply affecting neither real output nor prices. While its appropriateness for the study of the 1930s has been the subject of disagreement, this model remains a widely accepted and useful framework within which to discuss the adequacy of fiscal policy.[13]

---

[13] For an alternative version of the monetary (and fiscal) history of this period see [2, chaps. 7, 8, and 9]. Friedman and Schwartz argue that monetary policy could have been utilized in the 1930s to promote expansion, so that Brown cannot ignore monetary effects of fiscal policies. If correct, Brown has overstated the expansionary effects of fiscal measures.

Within the closed economy there are three sources of aggregate demand for final output (Y)—consumption by households (C), investment by business firms (I), and government expenditures (G). Since we are assuming a constant price level the equation expressing national income as a sum of final demands (equation 12) need not distinguish between

$$Y = C + I + G \qquad (12)$$

real and money values. Consumption is determined by the income of consumers after the payment of a lump-sum tax (T) to the government.[14] This relationship, the consumption function, is shown in equation 13. The

$$C = b + a\,(Y - T) \qquad (13)$$

constant, b, is the amount spent upon consumption at zero income, and a, is the marginal propensity to consume, describing the effect of increments to disposable income upon consumption expenditures. Empirical studies indicate that a is greater than zero but less than one. In this model it is assumed that investment (I), government expenditures (G), and tax collections (T) are set exogenously, independent of the other variables in the system, and that once determined they are not affected by the level of income.

Since consumption varies with the level of income, while investment, government expenditures, and taxation do not, by substituting equation 13 into equation 12 the equilibrium level of national income can be expressed in terms of the exogenous components (equation 14).[15] The expression $1/(1 - a)$ is called the

$$Y = \frac{1}{(1 - a)}\,[b + \bar{I} + \bar{G} - a\bar{T}] \qquad (14)$$

multiplier. It shows the cumulative effect of exogenous expenditures which arises from their initial effect upon consumption, thus further changing income and, in turn, consumption in successive rounds until this effect disappears. The greater is a (the more consumers spend out of each additional dollar of income) the larger is the multiplier. The expression $a\bar{T}$ indicates that taxes do not reduce consumption by their full amount,

---

[14] Transfer payments by government are considered negative taxes.

[15] A bar placed over a variable means that it is set exogenously.

but by an amount varying with the marginal propensity to consume. Tax changes influence aggregate demand only to the extent that consumption spending is affected.

The net contribution of the government to aggregate demand is $\bar{G} - a\bar{T}$. Government expenditures increase the demand for final output. Taxes, by reducing private disposable income, reduce the consumption demand for output. Even if the budget were balanced ($\bar{G} = \bar{T}$), there would be a net fiscal contribution to aggregate demand. The net income attributable to governmental budgetary policy is the product of the aggregate demand contribution, $\bar{G} - a\bar{T}$, and the multiplier. Both terms vary with the magnitude of the marginal propensity to consume.

While, even at this level of abstraction, we may regard the government as fixing the level of expenditures, the treatment of the tax side is too simple. In most cases what the government sets is the rate of taxation to be applied to income. Tax receipts vary with the level of income achieved. The same tax rate and government expenditures can provide different measured fiscal contributions, depending upon the level of other exogenous components and thus national income. Similarly, the multiplier in this case is more complex, since part of any change in income affects tax collections rather than disposable income.

Because of the sensitivity of tax collections to the level of income, use of the actual budget expenditures and receipts provides a poor basis for comparison of the government's fiscal policy in different years. If, for example, investment falls and income declines, the budget deficit can increase at constant tax rates and even with increased tax rates. To avoid considering these deficits created by income declines as fiscal contributions to aggregate demand, the concept of a full-employment budget is used. This full-employment budget measures what the government's fiscal contribution would have been if the economy had achieved full-employment. This concept, devised by Brown, has been widely adopted, becoming a central part of the analysis of the President's Council of Economic Advisers during the 1960s.

B. Fiscal Policy in the 1930s (Essay 36)

E. Cary Brown's path-breaking article presents a detailed judgment of the effects of fiscal policy during the New Deal. The analysis is based upon the concept of a full-employment budget. The tax rate, t, was estimated from tax schedules and multiplied by the estimated level of full-employment income, Y^F, in determining full-employment tax collections.[16] With estimates of the marginal propensity to consume and the level of government expenditures the potential fiscal contribution at full-employment can be measured. The full-employment contribution to aggregate demand is $G - atY^F$. Since G, Y^F, and t were increasing, Brown then contrasts the fiscal policies in different years by comparing the ratios of the fiscal contribution to the full-employment level of income. For Brown's measure of the expansionary effects of fiscal policy to be the same in different years, the fiscal contribution must rise at the same rate as full-employment income. Any increase in expenditures or decrease in taxation which increases the fiscal contribution might still be considered contractionary if it was at a rate below that in the full-employment level of income.

Brown indicates that in only two years during the 1930s was fiscal policy markedly more expansionary than it was in 1929. This is based upon considering the budgets of federal, state, and local governments in measuring the fiscal contribution. The federal government's fiscal policy was expansionary throughout the 1930s, but did not make a sufficient contribution to offset the marked contractionary pressure coming from state and local governments. Brown concludes that fiscal policy on any major scale was not a feature of the New Deal; the Roosevelt administration followed conservative fiscal practices. The failure of fiscal policy to promote recovery in the 1930s was "not because it did not work, but because it was not tried." Although federal expenditures had increased, the expansionary effect was reduced by the increased tax rates legislated at all levels of government. The importance of these tax increases has been obscured because the decline in national income due to the reduction in investment spending meant tax collections increased much less than did the tax rates.

---

[16] Brown regards some taxes as fixed and others as variable. Thus his measure of fiscal contribution is not that in the text, but $\bar{G} - (a\bar{T} + atY^F)$. The tax rate is assumed constant at all levels of income.

REFERENCES

1. Gardner Ackley, *Macroeconomic Theory*, New York, Macmillan, 1961.
2. Phillip Cagan, *Determinants and Effects of Changes in the Stock of Money, 1875–1960*, New York, Columbia University Press, 1965.
3. Thomas F. Dernburg and Duncan M. McDougall, *Macro-economics,* 3rd ed., New York, McGraw-Hill, 1968.
4. Milton Friedman and Anna Jacobson Schwartz, *A Monetary History of The United States, 1867–1960*, Princeton, Princeton University Press, 1963.
5. Peter Temin, *The Jacksonian Economy*, New York, W. W. Norton, 1969.

33 MONEY, PRICES, AND BANKS IN THE JACKSONIAN ERA

Hugh Rockoff

I did not join in putting down the Bank of the United States to put up a wilderness of local banks. I did not join in putting down the currency of a national bank, to put up a national paper currency of a thousand local banks. I did not strike Caesar to make Anthony Master of Rome.

Thomas Benton (1837)

In the past few years scholars have continued the debate over Andrew Jackson's economic policies. The purpose of this essay is to highlight those points which have now been firmly established and to clarify certain issues that have not yet been adequately considered. The first section of the paper provides a brief history of the debate. The second section presents the

The author is indebted to Charles Dryden, Ian Hirst, and Richard Zecher for helpful criticisms.

crucial data on prices and the money supply. The third and fourth sections attempt to develop the most plausible interpretations of this data. The fifth section contains some concluding remarks.

I. THE CONTROVERSY

The economic fluctuations which historians have tried to explain can be set forth quite briefly. An inflation developed in the early 1830s, after almost two decades of falling prices. Prices rose moderately from the first quarter of 1830 to the fourth quarter of 1833. This inflation was interrupted by a mild contraction in 1834. Commodity prices then raced upward for the next two years. In addition, the prices of slaves, urban real estate, and other assets reflected the boom psychology. Sales of government land increased enormously, and state governments authorized bond issues for internal improvements in unprecedented amounts. The inflation came to an end with the crisis of 1837; prices fell and banks were forced to suspend convertibility. There was a recovery in 1838, but another crisis occurred the following year. This time prices did not recover after the crisis; instead the country underwent one of the most severe deflations in its history.[1]

The interpretation of these events as caused by government policies grew out of the controversies of the period. A direct causal relation was posited between the policies of the Jackson administration and the economic fluctuations. In particular, Jackson's attack on the Second Bank of the United States, the Bank War, was cited as the ultimate cause of the contraction of 1834 and the inflation of 1835 and 1836. The Bank of the United States, the only commercial bank chartered by the federal government, had prospered in the 1820s under its third president, Nicholas Biddle. But Jackson, who became President in 1828, was hostile to the Bank. In an effort to head off Jackson's campaign, Biddle attempted to have the Bank rechartered in 1832, four years before the original charter was to expire. The recharter bill passed Congress, but was vetoed by Jackson. About one year later the Treasury, on Jackson's order, removed its deposits from the Bank and placed them in "pet" state banks. Anticipat-

ing this move, Biddle undertook a policy of reducing the current liabilities of the Bank. Contemporary commentators and recent scholars such as Meerman have been in agreement that Biddle's policy produced the contraction of 1834 [8]. The only controversy concerns whether Biddle's contraction was pressed farther than economically necessary to protect the Bank, in order to force Jackson into restoring the deposits.

As illustrated by the remark of Benton quoted above, contemporaries believed that the acceleration of the inflation came about because Jackson's attack on the Bank had deprived it of the power to hold the state banks in check, thus permitting a rapid expansion in the supply of banknotes. A subsidiary explanation was the "speculative mania" that gripped the nation. These explanations have survived, more or less in their original forms, in the literature of political and social historians.[2]

In August of 1836 Jackson issued the Specie Circular which ordered federal land agents to accept only specie. When a panic developed in 1837, Jackson's critics were quick to blame the circular. By and large political historians have agreed that by subjecting certain banks to heavy demands for specie, the circular precipitated the crisis. This situation was presumably aggravated by the movement of funds under the Distribution Act, which allocated the federal surplus among the states. Others have argued that while the crises did not result from the latter Jacksonian measures, they were the inevitable result of the preceding boom which they thought had resulted from earlier Jacksonian policies. At times the latter explanation seems to rely as much on faith in divine retribution as on economic analysis. Jackson's opponents continued to blame Jacksonian policies for the deflation of the early 1840s. But more recently historians have followed Van Buren who, in his Presidential address, attributed the deflation to the excesses of the preceding period, caused of course by the "speculative mania" rather than by Jacksonian policies, and to the depression in the foreign trade sector.

Conspicuously absent in these explanations is an understanding of the relationship that existed among prices, the supply of specie, and conditions in the international capital

---

[1] For the wholesale price index which provided the basis of this paragraph see [*13*, p. 158].

[2] There is an excellent summary of the views of political and social historians in [*17*, chap. 1].

market. This deficiency was rectified after sufficient time had elapsed for scholars to approach the issues with less partisan motives. Perhaps the most influential writer to integrate international and domestic factors was the economist, sociologist, and historian, William Graham Sumner [*14, 15*]. Sumner argued that the weakening of the Bank of the United States was of secondary importance in causing the inflation of 1835 and 1836. In his words, the primary factor was:

the great and really irrational importance which was attached by Europeans to the extinguishment of the debt of the United States, and their exaggerated willingness on that account to lend their capital in America [*14*, p. 258].

Sumner also rejected the notion that the Specie Circular was crucial in producing the crisis of 1837. Instead he emphasized two international factors—the curtailment of credit by the Bank of England as the English boom came to an end, and the concomitant fall in the price of cotton [*14*, pp. 266–268]. Sumner's interpretation of the deflation of the early 1840s was in the same vein, stressing international forces.

While recent analyses by economic historians have modified and extended earlier interpretations, the same basic conflict concerning the role of government policies has been repeated. The interpretation in terms of federal policies has been developed by Bray Hammond and Fritz Redlich [*5, 11*]. Both argue that the Bank of the United States was an early central bank. It possessed, in their view, the power to regulate the money supply and alter the course of business. Moreover they assert that, at least during its heyday, the Bank used its power wisely [*5*, pp. 300–306; *11*, pp. 110–145]. Implicit in this analysis is the idea that even if Jackson's attack on the Bank was not the direct cause of the inflation, it prevented the Bank from taking effective offsetting actions in response to changing economic conditions. While the issues raised by Hammond and Redlich are interesting as well as highly controversial, the remainder of this paper will focus on the work of those economic historians who have sought to deepen the "Sumnerian" interpretation with the use of available statistical data and economic theory.

Various aspects of this interpretation have been worked out by Smith and Cole [*13*], Smith [*12*], Macesich [*6*], North [*10*], Timberlake [*18, 19*], Williamson [*20*], and Temin [*16, 17*]. This interpretation stresses the importance of the British price level and the Anglo-American capital flow for the understanding of American price behavior in this period. During the 1830s the English price level rose, while British capital exports were redirected to the United States. This meant, with fixed exchange rates, that the American price level consistent with equilibrium in the balance of payments was now higher than it had been. In the early 1840s, on the other hand, international conditions required that there be an American deflation in order to produce balance of payments equilibrium.

Peter Temin, whose recent book represents an important contribution to the debate, accepts the proposition that the Anglo-American capital flow permitted the American inflation [*17*]. The effect of movements in the British price level is not stressed. But he argues that the way in which the stock of money was changed was different from that usually imagined and that this difference is crucial in understanding the economics of the period. In the textbook model of adjustment under the gold standard, the attempt to transfer capital drives the exchange rate to the specie import point and gold flows from the transferor to the transferee. Temin shows that the major sources of the specie increase were increased silver imports from Mexico and decreased silver exports to the Orient, rather than a movement of gold from Britain to the United States. He argues further that had there been any substantial drain of specie from Britain, the Bank of England would have raised the discount rate. This action would have cut the entire inflationary process short, since the Anglo-American capital flow was sensitive to British interest rates. His strongest evidence for this assertion is the banking crisis of 1837 which seems to have been a consequence of the Bank of England raising her discount rate in response to a loss of reserves [*17*, pp. 87–88].

It is obvious from the foregoing survey that nearly all of the participants in the debate have used a quantity theory framework for analyzing the Jacksonian inflation (and subsequent deflation). We shall not challenge this procedure. It is a simple hypothesis and seems consistent with the evidence. The debate has centered on which particular components of the money stock have changed and for what reasons. This is the subject of the next section.

II. THE DATA ON THE SUPPLY OF MONEY AND PRICES

In this section we use the procedure developed by the Chicago School of monetary theorists to decompose changes in the stock of money into changes produced by three proximate determinants.[3] This procedure is based on the identity shown in equation 1. M is the

$$M \equiv \frac{S}{\frac{C}{M} + \frac{R}{D} - \left(\frac{C}{M}\right)\left(\frac{R}{D}\right)} \tag{1}$$

stock of money, S the stock of specie, D the amount of bank notes and deposits held by

[3] This procedure is described by Friedman and Schwartz [3, pp. 794–95]. Equation 1 is actually a simple algebraic transformation of the Friedman-Schwartz equation which has been employed by Philip Cagan [1, chaps. 1 and 2]. See [6] for an application of this method to the late Jacksonian period.

the public, R the specie held by banks, and C the specie held by the public. The underlying idea is that each of the proximate determinants is controlled by a different set of economic agents—S is set by the conditions of international trade, R/D by the banking system, and C/M by the nonbank public. Table 1 which is taken from Temin [17, pp. 71, 159], gives the value of each determinant annually between 1820 and 1845. The yearly percentage change that would be produced in the money supply by a given change in one of the determinants, holding other determinants constant, is then calculated by dividing the initial money supply into that money supply computed from equation 1 with the new value of the determinant inserted, and dividing by the number of years in the period. Table 2 gives the results of this calculation for certain segments of the Jacksonian period.

Three important conclusions emerge from Table 2. First, the assumption that changes in the supply of money were associated with

Table 1. Prices and the Stock of Money, and Its Three Determinants, 1820–1845

Year (1)	Prices (2)	Money ($ Millions) (3)	Specie ($ Millions) (4)	Reserve Ratio (%) (5)	Currency Ratio (%) (6)
1820	114	85	41	32	24
1821	106	96	39	30	16
1822	109	81	32	21	23
1823	101	88	31	25	15
1824	98	88	32	27	13
1825	108	106	29	19	10
1826	95	108	32	20	12
1827	92	101	32	20	14
1828	89	114	31	18	11
1829	89	105	33	22	12
1830	85	114	32	23	6
1831	89	155	30	15	5
1832	91	150	31	16	5
1833	95	168	41	18	8
1834	90	172	51	27	4
1835	108	246	65	18	10
1836	122	276	73	16	13
1837	111	232	88	20	23
1838	106	240	87	23	18
1839	115	215	83	20	23
1840	87	186	80	25	24
1841	87	174	80	23	30
1842	74	158	90	33	35
1843	71	194	100	35	26
1844	74	214	96	27	24
1845	77	241	97	23	23

SOURCES: Column 2 [13, p. 158]. Columns 3–6 [17, pp. 71, 159].

Table 2. The Contribution of the Three Determinants Compared with Changes in the Stock of Money and Prices, 1820–1843[a]

Variable	Annual Rates of Change (%)			
	Mild Deflation 1820–1829 (1)	Inflation 1829–1839 (2)	Deflation 1839–1843 (3)	Intense Inflation 1833–1836 (4)
Prices	−2.8	2.6	−12.1	8.3
Money	2.3	7.2	−2.6	16.5
Specie	−2.4	9.2	4.7	19.2
Reserve ratio	1.9	.6	−6.6	2.7
Currency ratio	2.0	−2.4	−1.5	−5.1
Interaction of ratios[b]	.8	−.2	.6	−.5
	Fraction of the Change in the Stock of Money Produced by Each of the Determinants			
Specie	−1.04	1.28	−1.81	1.16
Reserve ratio	.83	.08	2.53	.16
Currency ratio	.87	−.33	.58	−.31
Interaction of ratios	.35	−.03	−.23	−.03

[a] The picture of each subperiod will alter somewhat depending on the particular dates chosen, but the general conclusions drawn in the text will not be affected.

[b] The interaction term arises because the contribution of each ratio depends on the values of the other ratio and these change within the periods. In addition, because of rounding the components in each column may not add to the appropriate totals.

SOURCE: Computed from Table 1. See text.

changes in the price level seems justified. However a simple proportional relation between money and prices did not occur. Apparently the demand for money was growing rapidly throughout the period, with growth more rapid at its end than at the beginning. Second, increases in the stock of specie account for most of the growth of the money stock in the inflationary period (columns 2 and 4). This means that even though most of the increase in the stock of money *consisted* of bank money, because banks created several dollars in deposits and notes for each dollar of specie held in reserves, the ratio of specie in reserve to bank liabilities created remained roughly constant. Thus the belief that the inflation developed when state banks took advantage of the demise of the Bank of the United States by decreasing their reserve ratios is incorrect. Third, the decline in the stock of money in the deflationary period (column 3) was produced primarily by an increase in the bank reserve ratio, which offset a continued growth in the stock of specie.

III. THE SOURCES OF THE INCREASE IN SPECIE

Changes in the stock of specie in the 1820s and early 1830s can be explained by the difference between imports of specie from Mexico and exports to the Orient (mainly China). This is illustrated in Figure 1. The dotted line cumulates the difference between imports from Mexico and exports to the Orient beginning in 1825 and ending in 1839. In the mid-1830s this line diverges from the solid line which cumulates total net imports of specie. This divergence was produced primarily by three autonomous specie inflows. These were: an influx from Britain in 1834, associated with the high interest rates prevailing in the United States during the crisis of 1834; an influx from France in 1836, resulting from an indemnity payment, and a second influx from Britain in 1838.[4] This last

---

[4] The influxes from Britain were $6 million in 1834 and $10 million in 1838. The French indemnity amounted to $4 million [17, p. 81].

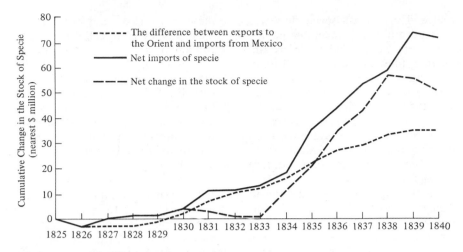

^{a}If all the data were available, net imports of specie and net changes in the stock of specie
(which are set equal in 1829 when the later series begins) would be almost identical since
American production of the precious metals was limited. The reasons for the large discrepancies shown in the chart are unknown.

SOURCES: Mexican imports less exports to the Orient, and net specie imports [17, p. 81].
Net changes in the stock of specie, Table 1.

Figure 1. Sources of Changes in the Stock of Specie, 1825–1839.^{a}

influx was caused by a combination of high interest rates in the United States and low interest rates in Britain. The behavior of the Bank of England was crucial. It lowered its discount rate in February of 1838 and later that year purchased securities in the United States. Since the reasons for the changes that took place in the inflow from Mexico and outflow to the Orient are more complex we shall have to examine them in greater detail.

For many years prior to the mid-1820s the United States had been making large shipments of silver to China in order to cover purchases of tea and silk. In the 1820s two developments occurred which made it possible for the United States to radically alter the nature of its trade with China. First, American-owned balances in London were increasing as Britain shifted her capital exports towards the United States. Second, China's demand for opium, most of which was supplied by British India, was increasing rapidly. China's traditional trade surpluses were disappearing. Under these circumstances it made sense for Americans to draw bills on London and use these to purchase goods in China. The Americans were saved the inconvenience of using specie and the Chinese accepted the bills readily because they could be used to purchase opium [4, pp. 161–165;

17, pp. 80–82]. In 1825 Biddle introduced long dated bills drawn on London, which were called China or India bills, and they soon displaced specie in the China trade [2, p. 112]. Some idea of how rapidly this occurred can be gained from an examination of Table 3. In effect, America, through this roundabout way, was allowed to take part of her capital imports from Britain in the

Table 3. Imports of Specie and Bills into Canton by Americans, 1820–1833

Year	Specie (Millions of Dollars)	Bills on London (Millions of Dollars)
1820	6.3	
1821	3.0	
1822	5.1	
1823	6.3	
1824	4.1	
1825	6.5	
1826	5.7	
1827	1.8	.4
1828	2.6	.3
1829	.7	.7
1830	1.1	.4
1831	.2	1.2
1832	2.4	.7
1833	.7	4.8

SOURCE: [4, p. 219].

form of specie. This indirect specie flow was permitted because it offset an increased net specie inflow from China, and therefore did not require an outflow of specie from Britain.

The most important source of specie flow in the 1830s was Mexico. If conditions in Mexico and the rest of the world had remained stable while the inflation proceeded in the United States there would have been a diminution in the flow of Mexican silver to the United States. Since the silver content of the United States dollar remained fixed, the increased price level meant a decline in the purchasing power of Mexican silver. Instead the Mexican flow was greatest in those years in which the American inflation was most intense. It therefore appears that there was some change in the supply conditions of Mexican silver.

Temin, who brought this problem to light, has suggested that there may have been an increase in the productivity of the Mexican mines [17, p. 80]. One difficulty with this argument is that although we might expect the posited supply shift to have been permanent, there was a decline in the import of silver in the late 1830s. An astute contemporary observer, the editor of *Niles Register*, thought that the silver imports resulted from a capital flow in search of a safe haven from political uncertainty.[5] But this is not the whole explanation because Mexico's silver exports were also being used to purchase additional commodity imports. What was probably the most important factor in producing this extraordinary Mexican silver flow was a rapid rate of inflation within Mexico.

During the years in which Santa Anna was in power, the Mexican government took to financing its deficits with copper coins worth more than twice their weight in unminted copper. The profit attracted counterfeiters who added substantially to the government issues. Inevitably, while the American purchasing power of silver fell in absolute terms it rose relative to its purchasing power in Mexico. Gold and silver, we are told, were used abroad in such amounts that they almost disappeared from domestic circulation. The situation became so serious that in first months of 1837 the minting of copper was forbidden and a national bank was authorized for the purpose of reducing the number of copper coins outstanding by allowing people to exchange them for bonds. But apparently

these measures did not work, and the government was forced to call down the value of the copper coins. This reform occurred on March 8, 1837 [7, p. 76; 9, pp. 14–17]. This was the same month in which the panic of 1837 began with the failure of a bank in New Orleans, the traditional entrepôt for Mexican silver. Temin has suggested that the Opium War was more closely connected with the Jacksonian inflation than the Bank War [17, p. 82]. We could take the same logic further and substitute Santa Anna for Andrew Jackson as the villain of the piece.

In addition to the pattern of specie movements from Mexico and to China the fundamental role of British capital exports and rising British prices should not be forgotten. In the absence of these two forces the American inflation (generated by the sources discussed above) would have led to a balance of payments deficit, and a drain of the new specie to some other country.

IV. THE BANK RESERVE RATIO

The Myth of Wildcat Banking

The romantic image of the wildcat bank—a bank whose notes were redeemable at a point so far from human habitation that it was frequented only by wildcats—has done much to strengthen the notion that it was the restraint exercised by the Bank of the United States that prevented an inflationary issue of paper money. We do not wish to argue that these stories have no basis in fact. But we do wish to show that both economic theory and the empirical evidence suggest that the quantitative impact of wildcatting was probably negligible.

A profit-maximizing bank would regulate its note issue so that the marginal returns from any issue of notes were equal to the present value of the costs of issuing the note and administering the increased circulation. If we assume that the banks issue all notes at the same time, the marginal returns, as determined by the assets which could be purchased from an additional note, will reflect the declining market value on all notes as the size of the issue increases. Thus the equilibrium condition for a bank will be

$$P + N \left(\frac{dP}{dN}\right) = \frac{dR}{dN} + C \qquad (2)$$

---

[5] In the issue for February 21, 1835, p. 428.

P is the market value (the value receivers place upon the bank note) of a bank note of given face value in the purchase of an asset; $N(dP/dN)$ is the decline in market value of notes which a bank suffers on its circulation as it issues more notes; dR/dN are the additional noninterest bearing reserves (generally specie) it holds; and *C* is the discounted present value of all other costs of issue. The usual model of a wildcat bank assumes that *P* is always the face value of the bank note, that dR/dN can be zero because no one will brave the wildcats in order to redeem their notes, and that *C* (primarily the costs of printing notes) is negligible. From these assumptions it follows that there is no effective economic limit on the circulation of a wildcat bank.

However this analysis overlooks the fact that bank notes did not always circulate at their par value. A one-dollar bank note, for example, might be worth only 95 cents in gold. A note was essentially a noninterest bearing convertible bond. Its price depended on people's attitudes towards the condition of the bank, including its reserve ratio, and the physical costs of redemption. If the bank attempted to expand its circulation without increasing its reserves, people would probably consider this to increase the chance of bankruptcy and would discount the bank's notes. This would lower their attractiveness to potential borrowers who would now pay a lower price to borrow a given face value of notes from the bank. However when noteholders attempted to redeem their notes at face values the bank would be forced to absorb a loss. This loss could be foisted upon the public only by the bank's going out of business. The bank could have maintained

the price of its notes and limited the risks of bankruptcy by increasing its reserves as it increased its circulation. But as the bank widened the area in which its notes circulated it would find its marginal reserve needs increasing because people living in areas distant from the bank would be less receptive to its notes than would people living in its immediate vicinity. Thus profit considerations, summarized in part by equation 2, would determine the size of a bank's note issue, its reserve ratio, and since it had monopoly power over its own issues, the specie price of its notes. If the public was suspicious of banks with low reserves then "unsound" banking would not generally pay.

As Temin shows, the evidence strongly contradicts the view that wildcat banking was widespread. Table 4 indicates that reserves were higher in the frontier regions, which are usually thought of as the loci of wildcatting, than in the settled regions. The pattern revealed in Table 4 may have been due largely to differences in state banking laws, but economic factors undoubtedly played a role. A lengthy discussion of these factors is beyond the scope of the present paper. But it will be useful, for the purpose of underscoring the profit-maximizing approach to the wildcat bank sketched above, to indicate briefly several interpretations of Table 4 based on economic variables. First, interest rates were higher in the frontier regions, which would tend to produce lower reserve ratios. But the cost of obtaining reserves on short notice on the frontier was greater. Where the density of banks was greater, there could be some economizing on reserves. Second, Western bankers faced a portfolio diversification problem that Eastern bankers

Table 4. The Regional Pattern of Reserve Ratios[a]

Year	New England	Middle Atlantic	Southeast	Southwest	Northwest
1834	,06	.22	.24	.13	.46
1835	.07	.16	.21	.15	.28
1836	.07	.14	.18	.14	.30
1837	.09	.19	.24	.13	.32

[a] Regions: New England: Me., N.H., Vt., Mass., R.I., Conn.
Middle Atlantic: N.Y., Pa., N.J., Del., Md., D.C.
Southeast: Va., N.C., S.C., Ga., Fla.
Southwest: La., Ark., Ala., Miss., Tenn., Ky.
Northwest: Wisc., Mich., Ill., Ind., O., Mo.

SOURCE: [*17*, p. 75].

did not. In the West nearly all loans were secured directly or indirectly by the agricultural products of the region. Hence the Western banker could not spread his risks and might be forced on that account to hold more reserves. Finally, the fear of wildcat banking might have led to frequent and massed withdrawals in the West, forcing bankers in those regions to hold greater reserves to maintain the face value of their notes.

With a few exceptions the relative regional patterns shown in Table 4 were stable. The major exceptions, decreases in the reserve ratios in the Middle Atlantic, Southeast, and Northwest regions between 1834 and 1835, may simply reflect a return to normal banking behavior after the contraction of 1834. In the light of traditional argument, the relatively low reserve ratios of the New England banks, a bastion of conservative banking practice, and the general increase in reserve ratios between 1835 and 1837 are unexpected. These findings suggest that the interpretation of bank behavior in the ante-bellum period is often more complex than the emphasis on so-called wildcatting implies.

The Effect of the Bank of the United States on the Bank Reserve Ratio

The Bank of the United States could influence the reserve ratios of state banks directly through its policy of redeeming state bank notes as well as by its own issue policy. Attention is often drawn to the Bank's policy of rapidly redeeming notes of state banks. This forced the state banks to hold more reserves than if the Bank of the United States was willing to hold a large inventory of state bank notes. But this policy was apparently not varied over time, nor is there any reason to think that it would have been abandoned when the Bank of the United States lost its federal charter.

More important, because of the relative size of the Bank of the United States, was the effect upon the money supply arising from the Bank's own issue policy. If it was conservative issuing notes, state banks would be forced to go along or risk consistently unfavorable clearing balances. Conversely, if it increased its circulation state banks could do likewise without fear of losing specie because they could answer any presentation of notes for redemption by presenting Bank of the United States notes in return. The

Bank's power to control the money supply through its issue policy was substantial because its own notes were close substitutes for specie reserves and because of the dominating position of the Bank of the United States in the economy. It was not unusual for the Bank to be holding more than a quarter of the total reserves within the banking system.

Recognition of this state of affairs has led some historians to suppose that the change in the relative importance of the state banks vis-à-vis the Bank of the United States produced by the transfer of federal deposits could have caused a substantial change in the money supply and thus the price level. It is assumed, by those who hold this position, that the reserve ratio of the state banks was well below the reserve ratio of the Bank of the United States so that a shift of the government's funds to the state banks would put specie in the hands of bankers who were more willing to use it in creating money. This argument is another manifestation of the belief in the importance of wildcat banking.

We can test this hypothesis by making use of equation 3:[6]

$$\frac{dM}{M} = \frac{g}{S}\left(\frac{R_1}{D_1} - \frac{R_2}{D_2}\right) \qquad (3)$$

where the new symbols are g, the government deposits transferred to the state banks,

---

[6] Equation 3 can be derived from equation 1 as follows:

$$M \equiv \frac{S}{\dfrac{C}{M} + \dfrac{R}{D} - \left(\dfrac{C}{M}\right)\left(\dfrac{R}{D}\right)} \qquad \text{(text equation 1.)} \quad (6.1)$$

This can be rewritten as

$$M \equiv \frac{S}{c + r - cr} \qquad (6.2)$$

where $c = \dfrac{C}{M}$ and $r = \dfrac{R}{D}$

Differentiating totally we have

$$\frac{dM}{M} = \frac{dS}{S} - \frac{c(1-r)}{c(1-r)+r} \cdot \frac{dc}{c}$$
$$- \frac{r(1-c)}{r(1-c)+c} \cdot \frac{dr}{r} \qquad (6.3)$$

By assumption $dS/S = dc/c = 0$. Hence (6.3) reduces to

R_1/D_1, the reserve ratio of the Bank of the United States, and R_2/D_2, the aggregate reserve ratio of the state banks. In January of 1832, immediately preceding the removal of the deposits, g was \$12,600,000, S was \$30,000,000, R_1/D_1 was .17, and R_2/D_2 was .14. Thus the effect of the transfer of all of the government's deposits would have been to increase the stock of money about 1.3 per cent.[7] This calculation indicates that the relocation of government deposits could

$$\frac{dM}{M} = -\frac{r(1-c)}{r(1-c)+c} \cdot \frac{dr}{r} \qquad (6.4)$$

Moreover,

$$r = \phi r_1 + (1-\phi)r_2 \qquad (6.5)$$

where ϕ is the proportion of bank money held in the Bank of the United States, and r_1 and r_2 are the reserve ratios of the Bank of the United States and the rest of the system respectively. Differentiating totally and holding r_1 and r_2 constant we obtain

$$\frac{dr}{r} = \frac{\phi r_1}{r}\frac{d\phi}{\phi} - \frac{\phi r_2}{r}\frac{d\phi}{\phi} \qquad (6.6)$$

We assume that the percentage change in ϕ is equal to $-g/D_1$, where g is the amount of federal deposits and D_1 is the initial total of deposits in the Bank of the United States. Thus (6.6) reduces to

$$\frac{dr}{r} = \frac{g}{R}[r_2 - r_1] \qquad (6.7)$$

Substituting (6.7) into (6.4) we have (3)

$$\frac{dM}{M} = \frac{g}{S}[r_1 - r_2]$$

which is the desired equation.

The intuitive meaning of equation 3 is that the shift in deposits ultimately frees $gr_1 - gr_2$ in reserves, which has the same effect on the money supply as an equal increment to the stock of specie.

[7] The hypothetical nature of this calculation should be emphasized. It merely describes the change in the equilibrium stock of money. The reserve ratios of the banks and the currency ratios of the public are held constant, and it is assumed that the reserve ratios apply to government deposits, all of which are transferred. The calculation does not describe the path the money supply will follow in reaching the new equilibrium. In point of fact, government deposits in 1832 exceeded the amount of specie in the Bank of the United States. If all the deposits had been removed at once and if the recipient banks had demanded immediate payment in specie, the Bank of the United States would have been forced out of business. Instead, the deposits were shifted over a period of time and the Bank was able to raise sufficient specie by contracting its liabilities. The sources for the values used were: g, [2, p. 503]; S, r_1, and r_2, [17, pp. 38, 71, and 186].

not have played a significant role in the inflation in the absence of further changes in the lending practices of banks.

Moreover the potential benefits to the community from the Bank of the United States should not necessarily be identified with greater state bank reserve ratios, which would be implied by the identification of central banking with a conservative issue policy. The existence of the Bank of the United States (or of any large bank, such as the Suffolk Bank of Boston) might inspire public confidence in the banking system and so permit bankers to operate with fewer reserves. The reduction in the ratio of specie to money would be a benefit to the nation because it took real resources to produce specie reserves. Thus Table 4 could be reinterpreted as showing the efficiency with which reserves were used in different sections of the country. Banks in New England, perhaps as a result of the Suffolk Bank system, appear the most efficient. This suggests that the absence of the Bank of the United States may have been most important, not in the inflationary years 1833–1836, but rather in the great deflation of the 1840s. As shown in Table 2, the deflation was in great measure produced by an increase in the reserve ratio of the banking system. The increase in this ratio seems to have been the result of frequent bank runs. In other words, there was a significant decline in public confidence in the banking system. But to what extent this decline in public confidence was due to the Bank War, as opposed to such factors as the outright failure of the Bank of the United States after it had received a charter from Pennsylvania, or the failure of state banks that had invested heavily in state bonds, or those that had been opened during the boom is difficult to judge. To the extent that the equilibrium stock of money was determined by the conditions of international trade, the increase in the bank reserve ratio substituted for a decline in the specie stock, while the total money stock would be the same. The increased importance of specie imposed real costs upon the economy which could have been avoided if people had maintained confidence in the banking system.

V. CONCLUSION

The foregoing essay has presented the rather clear outline of the monetary history of the

Jacksonian Era that has emerged from recent research. To summarize, the inflation was produced by an increase in the stock of specie. The sources of this increase were specie imports from Mexico heightened by a contemporaneous inflation in that country, episodic influxes from Britain and France, and, on the other side of the ledger, the ending of what had been a continuous drain of specie to the Orient. More fundamentally, the inflation was produced by British capital exports and high British prices that permitted the U.S. to run a large balance of payments deficit without losing specie. The evidence is so strong that the belief that the inflation was caused by an increase in the amount of paper money relative to the amount of specie seems to have been definitely vanquished. The deflation of the early 1840s was brought about by a decline in the public's confidence in the banking system and the response of bankers to a less favorable climate. The stock of specie was actually increasing throughout this period.

The most intriguing set of questions raised by this portrait concern the relationship that existed between monetary and real phenomena. In a world of flexible and perfectly anticipated prices the Jacksonian price cycle would have had few consequences for employment, output, and the distribution of wealth. Very little is known about how closely the Jacksonian economy approached this ideal. Further research on this issue would prove to be most rewarding.

REFERENCES

1. Phillip Cagan, *Determinants and Effects of Changes in the Stock of Money, 1875–1960,* New York, Columbia University Press, 1965.
2. Ralph C. H. Catterall, *The Second Bank of the United States,* Chicago, University of Chicago Press, 1902.
3. Milton Friedman and Anna Jacobson Schwartz, *A Monetary History of the United States, 1867–1960,* Princeton, Princeton University Press, 1963.
4. Michael Greenberg, *British Trade and the Opening of China, 1800–1842,* Cambridge, University Press, 1951.
5. Bray Hammond, *Banks and Politics in America,* Princeton, Princeton University Press, 1957.
6. George Macesich, "Sources of Monetary Disturbances in the U.S., 1834–1845," *The Journal of Economic History,* 20 (September, 1960), 407–434.
7. Walter Flavius McCaleb, *The Public Finances of Mexico,* New York, Harper & Brothers, 1921.
8. Jacob Meerman, "The Climax of the Bank War: Biddle's Contraction 1833–1834," *The Journal of Political Economy,* 71 (August, 1963), 378–388.
9. Ministerio de Hacienda y Crédito Público, Mexico, *Memoria de las Casas de Moneda 1849,* Mexico, 1849.
10. Douglass C. North, *The Economic Growth of the United States 1790–1860,* Englewood Cliffs, Prentice-Hall, 1961.
11. Fritz Redlich, *The Molding of American Banking: Men and Ideas,* New York, Hafner Publishing Co., 1951.
12. Walter Buckingham Smith, *Economic Aspects of the Second Bank of the United States,* Cambridge, Harvard University Press, 1953.
13. Walter Buckingham Smith and Arthur Harrison Cole, *Fluctuations in American Business, 1790–1860,* Cambridge, Harvard University Press, 1935.
14. William Graham Sumner, *A History of Banking in the United States,* New York, The Journal of Commerce and Commercial Bulletin, 1896.
15. William Graham Sumner, *Andrew Jackson,* Boston, Houghton Mifflin, 1924.
16. Peter Temin, "The Economic Consequences of the Bank War," *The Journal of Political Economy,* 76 (March/April, 1968), 257–274.
17. Peter Temin, *The Jacksonian Economy,* New York, W. W. Norton. 1969.
18. Richard H. Timberlake, Jr., "The Specie Circular and the Distribution of the Surplus," *The Journal of Political Economy, 68* (April, 1960), 109–117.
19. Richard H. Timberlake, Jr., "The Specie Standard and Central Banking in the United States Before 1860," *The Journal of Economic History,* 21 (September, 1961), 318–341.
20. Jeffrey G. Williamson, "International Trade and United States Economic Development: 1827–1843," *The Journal of Economic History, 21* (September, 1961), 372–383.

34 REAL WAGES IN THE NORTH DURING THE CIVIL WAR: MITCHELL'S DATA REINTERPRETED

Reuben A. Kessel and
Armen A. Alchian

The hypothesis that inflation causes real wages to decline has won wide acceptance among economists. Probably the strongest piece of empirical evidence that has been mustered in its support is the data on wages and prices contained in Mitchell's famous study of inflation in the North during the Civil War. It is the thesis of this essay that there exists an alternative explanation that Mitchell failed to consider which constitutes a more satisfactory explanation of the phenomena he observed. The purpose of this essay is to present this alternative explanation.

Reprinted with the omission of most footnotes and the appendix by permission from *The Journal of Law and Economics, 2* (October, 1959), 95–113.

In his study of inflation in the North during the Civil War, Mitchell, after examining the evidence for the period, concluded:

> All of the statistical evidence that has been presented in the preceding pages supports unequivocally the common theory that persons whose incomes are derived from wages suffer seriously from a depreciation of the currency. The confirmation seems particularly striking when the conditions other than monetary affecting the labor market are taken into consideration. American workingmen are intelligent and keenly alive to their interests [3, pp. 347–348].

The evidence that led Mitchell to this conclusion consists primarily of the time series of real wages shown in Table 1.

Mitchell also arrived at the conclusion that "real profits were unusually large during the Civil War, therefore, but large because real wages, rent, and interest were low," with virtually no direct evidence on real returns to profit receivers. In reaching this conclusion that real profits increased because real wages and real returns to rent and interest receivers declined, Mitchell postulated, and this is not explicit, that the rate of return to all agents of production taken jointly was constant between 1860 and 1865 [3, chaps. 6 and 7].

The price index for Mitchell's real-wage calculations is based on the median observation of ninety wholesale prices, using 1860 as a base. Observations (January, April, July, and October) were recorded for every year studied. The observations for the wage index are weighted. Mitchell, in his chapter on prices, argues that a wholesale price index ought to be satisfactory for detecting the effect of the issuance of greenbacks upon prices, but he revealed some reservations about the suitability of this index for cost-of-living calculations. Despite these reservations, Mitchell used this wholesale-price index for measuring real wages.

The representativeness of the ninety com-

Table 1. Average Change in Real Wages of Over 5000 Wage-Earners

Date	Index of Real Wages	Date	Index of Real Wages
Jan., 1860	100	Jan., 1863	89
July, 1860	100	July, 1863	86
Jan., 1861	102	Jan., 1864	81
July, 1861	104	July, 1864	71
Jan., 1862	102	Jan., 1865	67
July, 1862	101	July, 1865	97

Table 2. Consumers' Prices, Money Wages, and Real Wages

Year	Prices	Wages	Real Wages
1860	100	100	100
1861	104	99	95
1862	117	104	89
1863	140	119	85
1864	170	142	83
1865	179	155	87

modities in Mitchell's wholesale-price index of wage goods (or, for that matter, prices generally) is highly questionable. His index, like most wholesale-price indexes, contains no rent component. Internationally traded goods are strongly represented, and this, as will be developed, gives the index a strong upward bias for most of the time period with which Mitchell was concerned. (Almost two thirds of the commodities that could be unambiguously classified as either domestic or international were found to be international.) Furthermore many of the commodities in the index—opium, copper, linseed oil, soda ash, quinine, oxide of zinc, sulfuric acid, turpentine, rubber, copperas, lead, tin plate, and alum—should be regarded as of little direct significance for measuring prices of wage goods.

Yet it is easy to make too much of the fact that Mitchell employed a wholesale-price index as a deflator. In his subsequent work on the Civil War, Mitchell computed a consumer's price index for this same period with an independent set of data [4]. These data (reproduced as part of Table 2) also reveal a substantial fall in real wages, although neither as large a fall as observed when the wholesale price index is used nor as sharp a recovery in 1865. They buttress Mitchell's conclusion that real wages fell during the Civil War. Incidentally, this later study seems to have shaken Mitchell's earlier confidence in the alertness of American workmen to their interests; and he observes in this later work:

> In the '60s and, though in somewhat less degree, in the '70s, the labor market of the United States was one in which individual bargaining prevailed. Now the individual laborer is a poor bargainer. He is ignorant of the possibilities of his situation, exposed to the competition of others with the same disabilities, more anxious to sell than the employer to buy. Moreover, custom in the form of rooted ideas about what is a "fair wage" has a peculiarly tenacious hold upon the

minds of both parties in the labor market, weakening the wage-earner's aggression and strengthening the employer's resistance [4, pp. 275–276].

Mitchell readily accepted the hypothesis that inflation accounted for the observed fall in real wages, with substantially no consideration of conditions other than monetary, despite his protestation to the contrary.[1] Because of his failure to consider conditions other than monetary (i.e., "real forces"), Mitchell accepted an explanation of his observations that is inconsistent with the way economists explain changes in price ratios in markets other than labor. He rejected a standard explanation with a wide range of applicability in favor of an *ad hoc* explanation, without first showing the inapplicability of the standard explanation. It is the thesis of this paper that, if Mitchell had considered nonmonetary conditions more extensively, he would not have regarded his observations as unequivocally supporting the hypothesis that the observed fall was attributable to inflation. Indeed there are grounds for inferring that the inflation resulting from the issuance of greenbacks led to a higher level of real wages than Mitchell would have observed in the absence of inflation.

Mitchell's real-wage data and the observed fall in real rates of return to other agents of production can be explained as a consequence of three nonmonetary phenomena. These phenomena can be regarded as "real" forces, in the sense that the implications of their existence for real wages can be analyzed by the theory of relative prices as distinguished from monetary theory. These three forces are (1) the outbreak of warfare between the North and the South, which curtailed, if it did not eliminate, previous trading relationships; (2) the special economic characteristics of the base year, 1860; and (3) the tax system used to divert resources from the community to the government. All three of these phenomena operated jointly and independently of inflation to drive up the prices of goods and services relative to wages and other factor incomes generally during the Civil War. The remainder of this paper is concerned with the economic implications of these events.

---

[1] The factors other than monetary that Mitchell considered are: (1) the withdrawal of one seventh of the labor force for war services; (2) more fully employed workers during the war than before the war started; and (3) a decline in the average quality of the labor force [3, pp. 348, 350, and 383, respectively].

I. THE OUTBREAK OF WARFARE

The outbreak of the Civil War almost completely destroyed the triangular trade relationship between the North, the South, and England. Before the war the North had an export surplus on current account in its trade with the South and a deficit with England, while the South had a surplus with England. Hostilities and the ensuing blockade forced all three parties into what must be presumed inferior trade relations with a consequent loss in real income for all. In particular, the North was left with inferior markets for its exports and inferior sources for many commodities, such as cotton and turpentine formerly imported from the South. Similarly, the South had to find new markets for its cotton and new sources for the manufactured goods and foodstuffs previously obtained from the North.

An examination of the relevant trade statistics leads to the conclusion that the outbreak of hostilities presented the North with what would be regarded, by modern standards, as an incredibly difficult balance-of-payments problem. Before the war, roughly two thirds of all exports of goods and services for the entire country consisted of cotton. This source of foreign exchange was, for all practical purposes, completely lost to the South and hence to the North. Moreover Southern sources of cotton were in part replaced by imports of cotton from abroad. This implies that not only did the North lose much of its power to earn foreign exchange at the prewar exchange rate but also that its foreign-exchange "requirements" increased because foreign cotton in part replaced Southern cotton.

During the early years of the war the loss of foreign-exchange earnings resulting from decreased cotton exports were partly offset by extraordinarily large Northern wheat crops at a time when crops were short elsewhere in the world. Consequently, exports of wheat, particularly to England, increased sharply. Wheat exports, as compared with prewar, increased by a factor of between four and five during the fiscal years 1861, 1862, and 1863. Nevertheless, total wheat exports in each year represented less than one fourth of the decline in the yearly value of cotton exports caused by the Northern blockade. Consequently, one would expect enormous deficits on current account for this reason and large exports of gold as a result.

The difficulties of the North with respect to its trade balance on current account were aggravated by capital flights during the early part of the war. Before the war the United States was normally a net importer of capital. This source of foreign exchange was lost during the early years of the war, and, in addition, many foreign investors converted their American securities into gold. Net interest payments to foreigners declined by one third between 1860 and the wartime low point (1863). In part, these capital movements out of the country were offset by the sale of American-owned ships abroad. Nevertheless for the early years of the war, international capital movements intensified the North's balance-of-payments problems.

The problem of reconciling the reduction in the North's ability to pay for imports with its desires for imports was resolved by a measure undertaken to achieve quite another purpose. The suspension of specie payments was the consequence of the incompatibility between the issuance of greenbacks and the maintenance of convertibility of notes into gold at prewar exchange rates. As a result, the North abandoned the gold standard at the end of 1861. Gold became a commodity that was freely bought and sold without the government's taking a position in the gold market. Consequently, gold was released from some of its monetary functions, and the hoarding which had begun as a result of gold's under-valuation at the old exchange rate was reversed.

Abandonment of the gold standard, while the major trading countries of the world remained on this standard, made the price of foreign exchange a function of the price of gold, or, to use the language of the times, the premium on gold. Inconvertible fiat money, referred to popularly as "greenbacks" and officially as "United States notes," were issued as a means of war finance and became the currency of the times (except in California and Oregon). As a result the price of gold as measured in greenbacks determined the the cost of foreign exchange. The free-exchange rate eliminated the development of foreign-exchange "shortages," and the magnitude of the foreign-exchange problem of the North was largely unrecognized both then and now.

After the abandonment of the gold standard, the price of gold rose relative to prices generally. This change in the real cost of gold (i.e., the increase in the cost of gold as measured by the exchange value of gold for goods and services generally) is crucial for sustaining two related propositions: (1) that Mitchell's wholesale-price index overstated the rise in prices because of the strong representation of internationally traded goods in the index, and (2) that nonmonetary forces played a role in reducing real wages as measured by Mitchell.

A rise in the price of gold relative to prices generally implies that the real costs of imports rose. Or, to put the matter another way, the amount of a typical export the North exchanged for a pound of pepper increased. This is equivalent to saying that the terms of trade turned against the North. However inflation should not cause the terms of trade to change. Inflation, according to purchasing-power-parity theory, causes the money cost of foreign exchange to rise as the price level of domestic goods and services within a country rises relative to comparable price levels abroad. Consequently, the domestic prices of imports should increase *pari passu* with the general price level as a result of inflation.[2] Any increase in the domestic price of imports beyond what is implied by purchasing-power-parity theory reflects the operation of nonmonetary forces. Changes in the prices of domestic goods vis-à-vis corresponding foreign price levels reflect the increase in the greenback cost of gold attributable to inflation. The rise in the price of gold beyond that attributable to the inflation is to be ascribed to nonmonetary or "real" forces.

As a practical matter, foreign price levels can in this instance be represented by English prices, since most of American foreign trade was with England. Therefore the ratio of United States to English domestic prices can be used as an indicator of how much the exchange rate (i.e., the price of gold) should have risen as a result of the issuance of greenbacks. And the difference between the rise in the price of gold predicted by purchasing-power-parity and the actual price of gold is imputable to noninflationary forces.

---

[2] During an inflation that was generally anticipated, i.e., one in which the nominal stock of money fell and velocity rose, and the interest rate reflected the future course of prices, there are reasons for expecting the exchange rate to increase more than the price level. The evidence presented by Mitchell on the behavior of interest rates during the Civil War suggests this inflation was largely unanticipated. See [3, pp. 367–368].

Table 3. Exchange Rates Implied by Purchasing Power Parity Compared with Actual Exchange Rates and Real Wages.

Year	Actual Exchange (1)	Real Wages (2)	England Consumers Price Index (Wood) (3)	England Wholesale Prices, Sauerbeck Index (4)	U.S. Consumers Price Index (Hoover) (5)	(5)÷(3) (6)	(5)÷(4) (7)	(5)÷(3)[a] (8)	(5)÷(3)[b] (9)	(5)÷(4)[b] (10)
1860	Parity	100	100	100	100	100	100	100	100	100
1861	Parity	98	103	99	101	98	102	98	97	99
1862	113	91	100	102	114	114	112	107	107	104
1863	145	85	96	104	140	146	135	128	126	119
1864	203	80	96	106	177	184	167	163	152	142
1865	157	88	96	102	176	183	172	167	157	153

[a] Imports are excluded from the Hoover index.
[b] Internationally traded goods are excluded from the Hoover index.

Fortunately at that time English prices and price ratios were relatively stable. Therefore it is of little consequence whether a wholesale or a consumers' price index is used. This is borne out by calculations of purchasing-power-parity based on the Wood (consumers') and Sauerbeck (wholesale) price indexes. If there had been less stability, then the Wood index would be better. It is strongly weighted by rents and includes marketing costs in bringing goods from the wholesale to the retail level. Both classes of services are

unambiguously noninternational. The results of these calculations are summarized in Table 3. For the United States the consumers' price index computed by Ethel Hoover with the Weeks data is used in preference to Mitchell's consumers' price index. It is decomposed to show the relative price movements of imports, international goods, and domestic goods. (See Fig. 1.)

The greatest discrepancy between purchasing-power-parity exchange rates and actual exchange rates occurred in 1864 when real

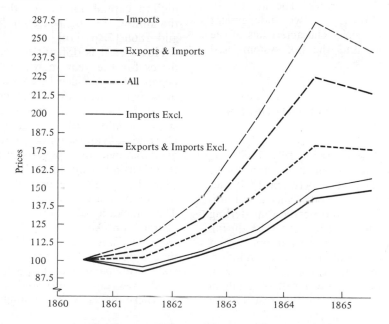

Figure 1. Hoover's Consumer Price Index Decomposed into Imports, Imports Plus Exports, All Except Imports, and All Except Imports and Exports.

wages were at their lowest. (See Table 3.) And this was the time when grumbling about the cost of living was loudest:

> There was indeed much grumbling over high prices, especially toward the end of the period, which must not be mistaken for direct dissatisfaction with government exactions. The spirit was most pronounced when the premium on gold was highest, in the summer of 1864, and when, consequently, the war was coming home to the people every day through high prices [*1*, p. 136].

Similarly, the second largest discrepancy occurred in 1863, when the fall in real wages ranked second in severity. And, of course, the differences between purchasing-power-parity and actual exchange rates are in the right direction. The exclusions of internationally traded goods from the Hoover index suggest that a rise in the prices of internationally traded goods, imports in particular, which was not compensated for by a decline in other prices accounted for most of the observed fall in real wages during these two years. This is precisely what would be expected if one argued that adverse movements in trade terms lowered real incomes.

Mitchell's observations, however, are far from fully explained. In 1865 real wages were lower than they were in 1860, although, with the given premium on gold, purchasing-power-parity theory implies that they should have been roughly identical. Similarly, the prices of imports should have been lower in 1865 in order to reflect the absence of a discrepancy between purchasing-power-parity and actual exchange rates. The answer to these problems turns on two independent phenomena, the special characteristics of the base year, 1860, and the tax system used for financing the war.

II. THE BASE YEAR FOR MITCHELL'S CALCULATIONS

The fiscal year that started in July, 1860, was a very remarkable one in many respects. It was the only such year between 1850 and 1877 that the United States was a net importer of gold. Mitchell observed that sterling was selling at a discount in New York during part of this year, which is what one would expect if gold were being imported. An inflow of gold, for a country on a gold standard, can be rationalized as the result of a fall in internal prices relative to the rest of the

world. This implies an increase in exports and a fall in imports. An alternative to this explanation was used by Mitchell. He argued that the inflow of gold was a consequence of a depression at home which reduced the flow of imports with little effect on exports. Part of Mitchell's explanation of this depression was the failure of Southerners to pay Northern creditors, which caused some business failures and a worsening in general business conditions.

Neither of these interpretations of events can be justified by the movements of the well-known price indexes of the time or by data reflecting the international trade of the time. The deficit on current account for fiscal 1860–1861 increased by a factor of three over the previous year. Moreover the widening of the trade gap on current account is primarily, although not wholly, attributable to a decline in reported exports. Clearly, part of the reason these gold imports are not explained by either of these hypotheses is that the trade data are internally consistent only if one assumes that there was an extraordinarily large inflow of capital during this year. Simon and Graham both estimate international capital movements from the balance-of-payment statistics for the time. For fiscal 1860–1861 Graham simply has an unexplained excess of debits over credits of about $80 million, which represents about one third of total credits [*2*, p. 231]. Simon obtained capital flows as a residual after estimating gold flows and trade of all kinds on current account. His estimate of a $100 million capital inflow for the year exceeds the inflow for the peacetime years of 1865 and 1866 [*5*, p. 116].

However it is difficult to accept such estimates for the year in which the Civil War began. This year can be characterized as one in which it was widely recognized that the country was at the brink of war. This circumstance would hardly appeal to English and Continental investors. A rereading of the available evidence suggests, if anything, that there was a net outflow of capital during this year. Fiscal 1861 ended about two and a half months after the firing on Fort Sumter. The blockade of Southern ports was proclaimed on April 19, 1861. Southern states were seceding from the Union during the preceding winter. With the secession of these states, in particular Louisiana, reports of what was going into and coming out of Southern ports were no longer reported to

Washington. As a result, Southern exports, which, for all practical purposes may be regarded as cotton, were grossly understated in the Commerce and Navigation publications issued by the government in Washington. These official trade statistics report exports of about $40 million of cotton. Yet available evidence suggests that about $190 million of cotton were in fact exported. Since cotton is harvested in the fall, there was plenty of time to ship the cotton crop of 1860 before the blockade of 1861. Hunt reported that cotton exports in physical terms for 1861 had declined only 20 per cent from the previous year. When price differences are taken into account, there was almost no fall in value. This interpretation is supported by data reflecting imports and stocks of cotton in England, which at the time was receiving over 80 per cent of her cotton from the United States. These cotton exports, combined with an increase in the exports of grain of about $40 million, resulting from our abundant crops and unusually small crops abroad, explain the bulk of the gold inflow. It is true that imports into Northern ports decreased somewhat during this fiscal year, but this decrease may have been more than offset by unreported increases in imports into Southern ports. Some imports that normally were shipped into the North were instead shipped directly to the South. And the South probably imported larger quantities than usual in anticipation of hostilities and the blockade.

The calendar year 1860 is labeled by Thorp as "Prosperity; Recession," with the "slackening" coming late in the year. This recession continued into the fall of the following year and gave way to a rapid revival of business activity. The recession in 1861 was associated with a large number of business failures resulting from the unwillingness of Southerners to remit to Northern creditors. Thorp also characterizes 1860 as a foreign-trade boom year. Given the high world prices for wheat that prevailed at this time, this evidence, considered in conjunction with the extraordinary gold inflows, implies that 1860 was a year when the terms of trade were relatively favorable for the country. This favorable development is by and large attributable to the extraordinary output and prices of wheat that occurred and should not normally be expected to recur. Consequently, real wages as measured by Mitchell, particularly with respect to imports, were abnormally high

during *this year*. These considerations suggest that the real-wage level measured by Mitchell in 1860 was higher than the level that normally could be sustained.

III. THE TAX SYSTEM USED TO FINANCE THE CIVIL WAR

Three means of war finance, important because of their implications for real wages during the Civil War, are the use of excises, import duties, and the tax on money imposed by inflation. Excises and import duties grew in importance during the war years with extension of coverage and increases in rates. In 1861 the Morrill tariff (under consideration in the House of Representatives before the war) was enacted. This tariff increased the cost of many imports, particularly iron and wool. While this tariff was announced as a revenue measure, the heaviest duties were imposed on commodities produced in the United States, and revenue was in part sacrificed for protection.

In 1862 a comprehensive system of excise taxation was enacted. Specific taxes were imposed on the production of iron, steel, coal oil, paper, leather, and several other goods. A general ad valorem tax was imposed on manufacturing output. Import duties were also increased. In 1864 all these taxes were once more increased and enlarged in scope.

Every ton of pig-iron produced was charged two dollars; every ton of railroad iron three dollars; sugar paid two cents a pound; salt, six cents a hundred weight. The general tax on all manufactures was five per cent. But this tax was repeated on almost every article in different stages of production. Raw cotton, for instance was taxed two cents a pound; as cloth it again paid five cents.

Wells observed that, under the impact of these turnover taxes, "the government actually levied and collected from eight to fifteen and in some instances as much as twenty per cent on every finished product." The average rate on dutiable commodities, which had been 37 per cent under the act of 1862, became 47 per cent under that of 1864. Indeed import duties became so high in 1864 that collections from this source decreased relative to the preceding year as a result of smuggling. The 5 per cent tax on manufacturing imposed in 1864 was increased to 6 per cent in 1865. Needless to say, as a result of the imposition of these taxes, revenues from

Table 4. Receipts from Custom Duties and Internal Revenue (In Millions of Dollars and as a Percentage of All Receipts)

	1861	1862	1863	1864	1865
Customs	$39.6 (61.4%)	$49.1 (10.1%)	$69.1 (9.8%)	$102.3 (10.9%)	$84.9 (7.1%)
Internal Revenue	0	0	$37.6 (5.3%)	$109.7 (11.7%)	$209.5 (17.5%)

customs and internal revenue increased enormously over their prewar level.[3] (See Table 4.)

It is evident that these excises and import duties diverted resources from consumers to the government and raised the price of all goods and services relative to factor incomes. These excises were to a great extent turnover taxes and as such became imbedded in the prices observed by Mitchell in the latter years of the war. As a consequence, taxation operated to widen whatever divergence existed between the value of final output and the sum of the payments to the cooperating agents of production. This means that some of the fall in real wages Mitchell observed resulted from custom duties and excises and would have taken place whether or not inflation occurred during the Civil War.

As a result of the extensive use of turnover taxes, real wages as measured by Mitchell ought to have fallen, even if the foreign-exchange rate were equal to the rate implied by purchasing-power-parity. Consequently, the level of real wages observed in 1865 ought to be below that of 1860, by an amount greater than the differential attributable to the abnormally high real wages in 1860. This comprehensive system of excise taxation taxed imports much more heavily than it taxed goods produced in the United States, and imports as a class were therefore forced up in price relative to domestically produced goods and services. The fall in real wages attributable to taxation should be concentrated upon internationally traded goods, and this appears to be the case. Or this is why, at the end of the war, the prices of imports were high relative to domestic goods, despite equality between the exchange rate implied by purchasing-power-parity and the actual rate.

The inflation associated with the Civil War in the North was caused by a government-imposed tax on cash balances. Through the exchange of greenbacks for real resources, the government progressively reduced the real value of a unit of currency, and the rising prices that resulted imposed economic losses upon money holders. But if inflation had not occurred, and if real expenditures by the government had not been reduced, then alternative taxes would have had to be employed. If the inflation tax on cash balances were replaced by a tax on income or wealth, then Mitchell's real-wage measurements would be unaffected. On the other hand, if the alternative tax were higher tariffs or turnover taxes, then a greater fall than Mitchell measured is implied. If turnover taxes or higher tariffs are regarded as the alternatives to taxing through inflation, the Civil War inflation kept the real wages measured by Mitchell from falling more than they in fact did. Therefore a rationale exists for a conclusion that is the converse of Mitchell's—were it not for the inflation, he would have found that real wages would have fallen more than they did.

IV. CONCLUSION

The analysis contained in this paper constitutes an alternative explanation that is better than Mitchell's interpretation of these data in at least two senses: (1) It explains why the fall in real wages was greater with respect to internationally traded goods than it was with respect to domestic goods. The wage-lag hypothesis implies that there ought to be no difference between the fall in real wages with respect to the two classes of goods. Consequently the interpretation of events presented

---

[3] Total receipts include the issuance of greenbacks. It must be remembered that not all internal revenue came from excises. A general income tax was imposed in 1862 and was raised in 1864 to 5 per cent on moderate incomes and 10 per cent on incomes of more than $10,000. About 20 per cent of all internal revenue receipts were from income taxes in 1864 and about 15 per cent in 1865.

here constitutes, at least in this respect, a fuller explanation of Mitchell's observations. (2) The interpretation presented in this paper is consistent with the analysis used by economists to explain similar changes in price relationships in markets other than labor. And, in general, the hypothesis which explains a wider range of phenomena is to be preferred.

However a word of caution is in order. It is possible that the destruction of prewar trading relationships, the rise in the premium on gold relative to prices, and the excises and import duties could have so affected factor incomes that the returns to labor did not decrease *pari passu* with the fall in the sum of all factor incomes. All the preceding analysis has assumed that what happened to real factor incomes also happened to real wages. The analysis presented here has not included the effects of the change in the composition of the final output of the economy on the real demand for labor. Nor have we considered the impact of the mobilization of manpower for the armed forces, the influx of new migrants into the United States during the concluding years of the war, or the damage to Northern resources imposed by Southern armed forces, upon the supply of labor. A more complete analysis might still find that there was some lag of wages behind prices to be explained by monetary forces. Alternatively, it might reinforce the argument presented here, or indicate that both explanations have a role to play in interpreting Mitchell's data. However, in the absence of such a demonstration, and in view of the preceding evidence, it appears that Mitchell's conclusion—that "all of the statistical evidence that has been presented in the preceding pages supports unequivocally the common theory that persons whose incomes are derived from wages suffer seriously from a depreciation of the currency"—cannot be sustained [3, p. 347].

In summary, the fall in real wages observed by Mitchell can be explained by the kind of analysis appropriate to the analysis of changing price relationships in other markets. An ad hoc theory is unnecessary. This fall in real wages can be rationalized as a consequence of the extraordinary level of real wages in the base year 1860, the rise in the price of foreign exchange relative to domestic prices and wages, and the tax system used to finance the war. Most of the fall in 1865 relative to 1860 is attributable to the tax policy used to finance the war. The extraordinary characteristics of the 1860 base ought to be assigned minor responsibility. In the year 1864 the fall in real wages was greatest, and so, too, was the discrepancy between purchasing-power-parity exchange rates and the actual rate. This analysis suggests that at least half of the fall in that year was attributable to the relative rise in the foreign exchange rate and that taxes and the properties of the 1860 base account for the remainder.

REFERENCES

1. Emerson D. Fite, *Social and Industrial Conditions in the North During the Civil War*, New York, Peter Smith, 1930.
2. Frank D. Graham, "International Trade under Depreciated Paper: The United States, 1862–79," *The Quarterly Journal of Economics*, 36 (February, 1922), 222–273.
3. Wesley C. Mitchell, *A History of the Greenbacks: With Special Reference to the Economic Consequences of Their Issue: 1862–65*, Chicago, University of Chicago Press, 1903.
4. Wesley C. Mitchell, *Gold, Prices, and Wages Under the Greenback Standard*, Berkeley, University of California Press, 1908.
5. Matthew Simon, "The United States Balance of Payments, 1861–1900," Conference on Research in Income and Wealth, *Trends in the American Economy in the Nineteenth Century* (Studies in Income and Wealth, vol. 24), Princeton, Princeton University Press, 1960. pp. 629–711.

35

ECONOMIC FACTORS IN SPECIE RESUMPTION: THE UNITED STATES, 1865-1879

James K. Kindahl

The "greenback" period in the United States (1862–1879) has attracted the interest of a number of historians and economists at various times. Although several competent studies have considered many political and economic aspects of the period, there seems to be no general agreement on the reasons why resumption of specie payments was successful in 1879 and whether it could have been successful before that date.

During the Civil War the government had issued a sizable quantity of

Reprinted with omissions by permission from *The Journal of Political Economy, 59* (February, 1961) 30–48.

legal-tender notes (the "greenbacks"). Since gold dollars sold at a premium over greenback dollars, and since resumption at the prewar parity obviously could not be successful until the equilibrium level of the premium fell to zero, attention has not unnaturally centered on the premium on gold. The rather common references to "activities of speculators" and "lack of public confidence in the greenback" neglect the fundamental economic forces determining the level of premium. Like many popular explanations, however, they contain a germ of truth and, indeed, may be very useful in explaining short-term variations in the premium. These explanations are virtually powerless to explain the fall in the premium from its peak (as an annual average) of 102 in 1865 to zero by the end of 1878. The purpose of this paper is to provide an explanation for this phenomenon.

At the outset it should be noted that specie payments on the greenbacks could have been instituted at any time at *some* parity without difficulty. Since, at the time, no serious thought was ever given to devaluation as a method of achieving convertibility, the term "resumption" will be used here in its conventional meaning, the institution of specie payments on the greenbacks at the prewar level.

I. THE ORIGIN OF THE GREENBACKS

In 1860 the money supply of the United States was composed of gold and silver coins, copper pennies, and the notes and deposits of state-chartered and unincorporated banks. All non-gold money was in principle convertible into gold coin. No paper currency was issued by the federal government.

During the early part of the Civil War the Secretary of the Treasury found it difficult to sell enough government securities to the public on the terms specified by Congress to meet the increased expenditures arising out of the war. In August, 1861, Salmon P. Chase, the Secretary of the Treasury, completed arrangements whereby a syndicate of banks in Boston, New York, and Philadelphia would purchase $50 million worth of government bonds with specie immediately and would have options to buy two more issues of $50 million each in October and December of 1861. Soon after the first installment of bonds was issued to the banks, a controversy arose between Chase and the bankers of the

syndicate. Chase ordered that gold coin in payment for the bonds be deposited immediately in the subtreasury. The bankers requested that the money be kept on deposit, credited to the government, until needed; this, they said, would provide needed protection of the specie reserves of the banks. Chase insisted, nevertheless, on immediate payment. The banks reluctantly complied and replenished their reserves by a successful resale of the bonds to the public. The banks took the second installment of bonds in October and again resold the bonds to the public. The banks accepted the third installment of bonds in November, a month ahead of schedule. The market price of government securities dropped sharply in December, 1861, before the banks had sold the third installment of bonds. The banks were unwilling to sell the bonds at the lower price, and so did not replenish their reserves in that manner. A general fear of suspension led to a withdrawal of gold from the New York City banks by individuals and by the banks of the interior. The New York banks thereupon suspended specie payments on December 30. Soon after, the other banks in the country suspended specie payments also, and the government refused specie payments on its own Treasury demand notes, which had been in circulation since August, 1861.

In December, 1861, Secretary Chase proposed to Congress the establishment of a national banking system, the members of which could issue notes on the basis of government bonds. On February 25, 1862, the Act resulting from this request was passed. It provided for the issue of not more than $150 million in legal-tender United States notes (greenbacks); the outstanding Treasury demand notes were to be counted as greenbacks. The Act made no mention of the national banking system recommended by Chase. The Act, which later became known as the First Legal Tender Act, was followed by two additional authorizations for issues of legal-tender notes. By 1864 a total of $450 million in legal-tender notes had been authorized.

Various kinds of government currency, other than United States notes, were issued during the Civil War. By the middle of 1862 the value of the silver in the subsidiary silver coins totaling one dollar in face value was more than one dollar in currency. Subsidiary silver rapidly disappeared from circulation. This caused considerable difficulty in ordinary commerce, since the smallest denomination of greenbacks authorized by law was five dollars. Congress attempted to remedy this situation by authorizing, in July, 1862, the use of postage stamps as currency; later, special nongummed stamps were issued for this purpose. In October, 1863, a different series of government notes, the "fractional currency," was issued in small denominations to replace the "postage-stamp currency."

Still another kind of legal-tender currency was issued during the Civil War. Interest-bearing notes of the Treasury, with one-, two-, and three-year maturities, were issued and given legal-tender properties by an act of Congress. As short-term interest-bearing notes they would ordinarily be considered as "near-monies," but, by act of Congress, they were money! According to Mitchell, several issues of non-legal-tender short-term government securities also circulated as money. In addition, a series of Treasury demand notes was issued in 1862; most were retired by the end of 1863.

The national banking system was begun during the Civil War under laws passed by Congress in 1863 and 1864. Another class of banks was thus introduced into the country. The notes of national banks were secured by government bonds deposited in the Treasury; the deposits of national banks, on the other hand, had no more security than did the deposits of nonnational banks, except insofar as reserve requirements of national banks were generally higher than those of nonnational banks.

Thus, whereas prior to the Civil War the money supply of the United States had been composed of specie and the notes and deposits of state and private banks, by the end of the war it was composed of the notes and deposits of national banks as well as state and private banks, plus a variety of government currency. Specie, on the other hand, was no longer a freely circulating part of the money supply, except on the West Coast, where gold was the monetary standard throughout the greenback period.

As soon as specie payments were suspended at the end of 1861, a premium on gold arose; that is, the price of a gold dollar in terms of bank deposits or Treasury demand notes rose above a dollar. When the greenbacks were issued, ordinary bank deposits were automatically convertible into greenbacks, since the greenbacks were legal tender for all private debts; the gold premium was customarily quoted in terms of greenbacks.

II. THE PREMIUM ON GOLD

The meaning of the premium on gold which prevailed until 1879 can be seen from a description of the process of foreign exchange at the time. When an American importer wanted to buy foreign exchange, he first bought gold (or gold certificates) with his greenback dollars and then took his gold to a foreign-exchange dealer, from whom he bought foreign exchange. The price of foreign exchange was invariably quoted in terms of gold dollars. There was thus no market in which foreign exchange was bought and sold in terms of American currency, and hence there were no price quotations for foreign exchange in terms of American currency.

Thus the product of two prices determined the price of foreign exchange to an American buyer; the price of foreign exchange in gold multiplied by the price of gold in greenbacks was the effective foreign exchange rate. Price fluctuations in the market in which gold dollars and foreign-exchange funds were exchanged were very small, however, compared with the price fluctuations in the market in which gold and paper dollars were exchanged. Price fluctuations in the former market were limited by the specie flow points, just as if the country had been on a gold standard. The highest quotation for bankers' short-term bills on London in the period 1867–1880 was \$4.95 in gold (par = \$4.8665) in January, 1867; the highest quotation recorded thereafter was \$4.94 in 1871. Apparently the gold export point was no more than 7 cents in gold above the par ratio. Since the gold export and import points are approximately symmetrical around the par ratio, price fluctuations in this market could not have been more than 14 cents in gold, or 3 per cent of the lowest possible quotation. Fluctuations in this market, then, had relatively little effect on the price of foreign exchange that was approximately the price of gold in currency. Hence the price of gold can validly be analyzed as a flexible foreign-exchange rate.

During the entire period of suspension, gold was sold on a free exchange; the Gold Exchange of New York was organized like a stock exchange, complete with margin trading. Thus a free market in what was effectively foreign exchange was in active operation. Good statistics on the daily price of gold in currency from this market are available for analysis.

The level of a flexible exchange rate is

determined by the relevant supply and demand schedules for foreign exchange. During the greenback period, changes in the price level in the United States relative to foreign price levels were of a substantial order of magnitude. These changes in relative price levels probably were the major influences causing shifts in the supply and demand curves for foreign exchange. Hence the well-known "purchasing-power-parity" theory of foreign-exchange rates, made famous by Gustav Cassel, should provide a good approximation to the observed data. The purchasing-power-parity theory states that, if two countries whose foreign-exchange markets are in equilibrium experience nonproportionate changes in their general price levels, then, *ceteris paribus*, the foreign-exchange rate between the two countries must move in the same manner. For example, if American price levels double under a system of effectively free exchange rates while foreign prices remain constant, then the price of foreign exchange in terms of American currency must also double, *ceteris paribus*. Thus the theory implies that the exchange rate will move in such a way that the terms of trade in real goods between the United States and the rest of the world will not change in spite of the fact that the internal value of the American monetary unit has changed.

Price levels can be measured only by index numbers. The most reliable price index numbers for this period are wholesale price indexes. Mitchell's wholesale price index is used in this study as an indicator of American price levels. Sauerbeck's English price index is used in this study as an indicator of world price levels, since England was on a gold standard.

The calculation of the purchasing-power-parity ratios is shown in Table 1. Column 5 of Table 1 shows the ratio of the American wholesale price index to the product of the English wholesale price index and the price of gold in greenbacks. This "adjusted price ratio" is an index of relative prices in the United States and England, adjusted for changes in the exchange rate. In effect it is an index of the relative prices of American and English goods, as seen by an American. If the indexes were perfect measures of relative prices, and if changes in nominal relative prices were the only factors influencing the exchange rate, the adjusted price ratio would be a constant over time. In fact the ratio is

not constant; however it remained fairly stable over the period 1865–1891 and showed no consistent trend over time. Between 1866 and 1891 the ratio remained between 1.01 and 1.27; in the preresumption period, 1866–1878, the ratio varied between 1.04 and 1.24. During the war years, 1862–1865, the ratio was considerably lower owing to the unsettled conditions created by the war. The closeness of these extremes in the postwar period compared with the movements in the American price level, together with the absence of a discernible trend in the ratios over time, indicates that much of the variation in the exchange rates can be explained by general price-level movements.[1] The similarity of the limits for both the pre- and post-resumption periods substantiates the assertion that the price of a gold dollar prior to resumption was determined by basic economic forces in international trade and was not influenced by the fact of inconvertibility as such.

A necessary condition for successful resumption was that the premium on gold be zero, that is, that the price of gold be $1.00 in currency. If the premium on gold be zero, the adjusted price ratio (col. 5, Table 1) is the same as the unadjusted price ratio (col. 3, Table 1). Hence the limits of 1.01 and 1.27 bracket, approximately, the value or range of values to which the unadjusted price ratios had to fall in order that resumption be successful. These limits can be narrowed further by taking into account international capital movements, which are an additional factor affecting the exchange rate.

According to Taussig and Graham, the effect of international borrowing by (say) the United States under a system of flexible exchange rates is to lower the price of foreign currency in terms of American currency, because of the increase in foreign demand for American currency to transfer the loan. This will be true if the demand schedule for American currency by foreigners shifts upward relative to the American demand for foreign exchange. This will not necessarily occur; for example, all the proceeds of the loan may be spent in the lending country, so

---

[1] The Spearman-rank-correlation coefficient between the purchasing-power-parity ratio and the price of gold (that is, between cols. 3 and 4 of Table 1) is .85 for the period 1862–1878 and .91 for the peacetime years 1867–1878. These coefficients are both significant at the .01 level.

Table 1. Purchasing-Power-Parity Ratios and International Capital Movements, 1862–1891[a]

Year	U.S. Price Index (1)	English Price Index (2)	U.S. Price/ English Price (3)	Price of Gold (4)	Adjusted Price Ratio[b] (5)	International Capital Movements (Millions of Gold Dollars)[c] (6)
1862	98	97	1.010	1.016	0.99	− 1.1
1863	118	95	1.242	1.371	0.91	+ 12.6
1864	148	95	1.557	1.562	1.00	+110.6
1865	200	97	2.061	2.019	1.02	+ 68.7
1866	172	99	1.737	1.404	1.24	+ 94.4
1867	172	100	1.720	1.414	1.22	+145.6
1868	158	100	1.580	1.400	1.13	+ 72.7
1869	158	99	1.595	1.375	1.16	+169.2
1870	149	97	1.536	1.233	1.24	+ 99.4
1871	133	98	1.357	1.127	1.20	+100.9
1872	134	104	1.288	1.120	1.15	+242.8
1873	134	107	1.252	1.147	1.09	+182.9
1874	130	105	1.238	1.120	1.10	+ 82.2
1875	128	100	1.280	1.127	1.13	+ 86.9
1876	118	95	1.242	1.140	1.09	+ 1.8
1877	110	96	1.145	1.079	1.06	− 57.3
1878	99	93	1.064	1.025	1.04	−162.9
1879	89	88	1.011	1.000	1.01	−160.2
1880	99	89	1.112	1.000	1.11	+ 29.4
1881	106	88	1.204	1.000	1.20	− 40.8
1882	108	86	1.255	1.000	1.25	+109.5
1883	100	85	1.176	1.000	1.18	+ 51.1
1884	94	81	1.160	1.000	1.16	+105.3
1885	89	76	1.171	1.000	1.17	+ 32.9
1886	89	73	1.219	1.000	1.22	+135.9
1887	85	70	1.214	1.000	1.21	+230.2
1888	90	71	1.267	1.000	1.27	+285.0
1889	85	72	1.180	1.000	1.18	+201.6
1890	82	71	1.154	1.000	1.15	+192.6
1891	87	72	1.208	1.000	1.21	+134.5

[a] Fiscal years ending June 30.
[b] Ratio of U.S. price to English price (col. 3), divided by price of gold (col. 4).
[c] Value of net capital imports (+) or net capital exports (−).

the foreign-exchange market may not be affected by the loan. These are exceptional cases, though; generally, a correspondence between international borrowing and changes in the exchange rates is to be expected.

The observed movements in the adjusted price ratios during the period 1866–1891 give some indication of the effects of international capital movements. If conditions were such that international borrowing tended to lower the exchange rates in terms of American currency, then the observed adjusted price ratios should have been relatively high during periods of net capital inflows and relatively

low during periods of net capital outflows. The observed adjusted price ratios (col. 5, Table 1) lie between 1.09 and 1.27 in every year except for 1877, 1878, and 1879. The United States was a net importer of capital in every year from 1866 through 1891 except for the years 1876–1879 and 1881. The largest capital outflows occurred in 1877, 1878, and 1879. The large capital outflows thus correspond in time with the relatively low adjusted price ratios. The highest values of the adjusted price ratios occur in 1866, 1867, 1870, 1871, 1881, 1886–1888, and 1891; except for 1881 these were all years of substantial net import of capital by the United States. The reverse is not the case, however; some years of large inflows of capital have moderate adjusted price ratios (1868, 1869, 1872–1876, and 1884). The data on capital movements do not distinguish between accommodating short-term capital movements, which would not have influenced the exchange rate in the manner described above, and other types of capital movements. It may be that the composition of the capital account changed in the years that do not conform to expectation. In any case, the data suggest that there was a relation between the adjusted price ratios and international capital movements, as Taussig and Graham asserted.[2]

This analysis suggests that the limits of the equilibrium adjusted price ratio in the absence of capital movements are something like 1.08–1.18, that a larger figure corresponds to capital inflows and a lower figure to capital outflows. How far did American price levels, relative to foreign price levels, have to fall in order that successful resumption could take place? The answer clearly depends upon the capital movements to be expected after resumption. If the United States were to export capital, the American price level would have to fall to something less than 8 per cent above the English price level, where both price levels are measured by index numbers on the base 1860 = 100. If no capital movements were to take place, the American price level could be about 8–18 per cent above the English price level. In fact the United States was an importer of capital after resumption, and a price level about 20 per cent higher than the English price level was maintained. These figures, of course, are only approximations to the correct orders of magnitude.

Apparently resumption would not have been successful much before 1879 if it had been attempted without additional preparation. The import of capital characteristic of the immediate post-Civil War period ceased for a time after the end of the fiscal year 1875. In fiscal 1875 the ratio of American to English prices was 1.28; by the analysis given above, American prices were still too high, relative to English prices, for resumption to be suc-

cessful. In the fiscal year 1876 the price ratio was 1.24, but capital movements were almost neutral that year; the price ratio was still too high to allow resumption, given the state of international capital movements. In fiscal 1877 and 1878 the price ratios were 1.14 and 1.06, respectively. Had there been imports of capital in these years, resumption probably would have been successful; but these were years of large capital outflows. In 1879 the price ratio was 1.01. The year 1879 was one of large capital outflows, but the price ratio had fallen to a level substantially below the level estimated as the lower bound of the equilibrium ratio in the absence of international capital movements. Thus the evidence suggests that resumption took place in the first year in which it would have been successful.[3]

It has been said that large grain exports in the calendar years 1879 and 1880, following crop failures in Europe, were an important factor in the success of resumption and that the United States might have had to abandon the gold standard late in 1879 or in 1880 had this fortuitous circumstance not occurred. The analysis here indicates that the underlying conditions for successful resumption were met during fiscal 1879 and that no further help was necessary. During the fiscal years 1880 and 1881 (which included the grain exports from the harvests of 1879 and 1880) the adjusted price ratio rose to 1.11 and 1.20, respectively, from the low point of 1.01 in 1879. Capital was imported in moderate amounts in 1880, and exported in 1881. This suggests that the grain exports in fiscal 1880 and 1881 were not a crucial factor in maintaining specie payments; rather, they were a factor which allowed American prices to rise, relative to English prices, more than would have happened otherwise.

III. THE PRICE LEVEL

A necessary condition for successful resumption of specie payments after the close of the Civil War was a fall in the American price

---

[2] The Spearman-rank-correlation coefficient between the adjusted price ratios and the international capital movements is .53 for the period 1867–1891, and .60 for the preresumption period 1867–1878. The former coefficient is significant at the .01 level, the latter at the .05 level.

[3] This does not imply that there was no way in which resumption could have taken place prior to 1879. Had the government adopted a policy which forced deflation at a faster rate than actually occurred, resumption could have taken place earlier. The discussion here is intended to show that the conditions for successful resumption were not met prior to 1879.

level relative to foreign price levels. Mitchell's median wholesale price index fell from a peak of 216 (1860 = 100) in January, 1865, to a trough of 84 in April, 1879. The lowest point reached before resumption was 90 in July, 1878. Thus wholesale prices fell by 58 per cent from January, 1865, to July, 1878, and by 61 per cent from January, 1865, to April, 1879. This deflation made possible the successful resumption of 1879.

The well-known identity $MV = PY$ or $P = MV/Y$, where P is the price level, M is the quantity of money, Y is real income, and V is the income velocity of money, is useful for investigating price-level movements.[4] Independent measures of all variables of this equation cannot be obtained, of course. Income velocity is measured here as the ratio of money income to the quantity of money. Obviously a fall in the price level must be accompanied by a fall in the quantity of money, a fall in income velocity, a rise in real income, or some combination of these.

Simon Kuznets has constructed annual estimates of net national product, in current dollars and in 1929 dollars, beginning with 1869. These estimates, together with the implicit price indexes, are given in Table 2. Because of the paucity of data for constructing these estimates, their reliability is open to question; however, they are the only annual estimates of any measure of national income available.

The money supply, as defined in this study, is composed of currency and silver coins outside the Treasury; notes and deposits of nonmutual banks, minus float, interbank deposits, and vault cash; and gold coin and gold deposits valued at the market price. Deposits of capital-stock savings banks are included in the money supply because most of these banks were, in effect, commercial banks, distinguished from an ordinary commercial bank only by the inclusion of the word "savings" in the bank title.

Kuznets' estimates of national product are on a calendar-year basis; the appropriate estimate of the quantity of money to use in estimating income velocity is, therefore, a year average. Data for estimating the average yearly

---

[4] As used in this study, the identity is merely a truism which is useful as a method of organizing the analysis. It contributes nothing new and hence makes no implicit or explicit assumptions about the truth or falsity of any version of the "quantity theory of money," with which this equation is often identified.

Table 2. Net National Product, 1868–1882 (Millions of Dollars)

Year	Net National Product (Current Dollars) (1)	Net National Product (1929 Dollars) (2)	Implicit Price Index[a] (3)
1869	5,822	7,358	79.1
1870	5,486	7,276	75.4
1871	5,742	7,307	78.6
1872	6,935	9,587	72.3
1873	7,018	9,959	70.5
1874	6,880	9,977	69.0
1875	6,763	10,158	66.6
1876	6,983	11,041	63.2
1877	7,351	12,022	61.1
1878	7,349	12,915	56.9
1879	7,888	14,517	54.3
1880	9,978	16,824	59.3
1881	9,835	16,947	58.0
1882	10,791	18,105	59.6

[a] Column 1 divided by column 2.

supply of money are not available. Figures on the amount of government currency and specie outside the Treasury are available only for June 30 of each year; figures on nonnational bank deposits and notes are available only for average deposits in January prior to 1873; data are also available for the averages of the six-month periods ending May 31 for the years 1874–1881 and also for the average deposits for the six-month periods ending November 30 for 1875–1881 and for June 30 after 1881. Figures on national bank deposits and note issues are available for the four or five national bank call dates through the year.

This heterogeneity of the data makes it impossible to estimate the yearly average of the money supply. As a substitute, estimates of the stock of money at midyear dates (June 30) are used here (Table 3). These estimates were made by taking the national bank call dates nearest June 30 as a basis for the national bank data and by taking a linear interpolation of the nonnational bank data to estimate nonnational bank notes and deposits as of June 30. Figures on government currency and specie outside the Treasury refer to June 30 of each year, so no adjustment is necessary for those figures.

The proper treatment of gold coins as part of the money supply is not clearcut. Since gold coin stood at a premium over currency, the stock of gold coin must either be excluded completely from the money supply or

Table 3. Money Supply in the Hands of the Public[a] (Millions of Dollars)

Year	National Bank Deposits (1)	Non-National Bank Deposits (2)	National Bank Notes (3)	Non-National Bank Notes (4)	Government Currency Outside Treasury (5)	Vault Cash, National Banks (6)	Vault Cash, Non-National Banks (7)	Vault Cash, Mutual Savings Banks (8)	Gold Coin Outside Treasury (Nominal Value) (9)	Excess of Market Value over Nominal Value of Gold Coin (10)	Silver Dollars and Certificates (11)	Money Supply in the Hands of the Public[a] (12)
1867	411	279	284	16	474	206	34	7	67	26	—	1311
1868	452	298	292	3	390	156	36	7	55	30	—	1320
1869	413	324	286	2	350	113	40	8	65	24	—	1304
1870	448	379	282	2	366	144	47	9	85	10	—	1373
1871	488	491	304	2	384	163	60	11	61	8	—	1504
1872	518	565	322	1	388	166	68	11	73	10	—	1632
1873	538	551	332	1	392	179	66	13	66	10	—	1632
1874	550	560	333	1	414	199	66	15	66	7	—	1650
1875	591	596	325	1	398	181	71	14	50	8	—	1703
1876	560	595	306	1	377	166	71	14	68	8	—	1663
1877	570	564	289	—	387	165	71	13	75	4	—	1640
1878	528	511	299	—	382	155	69	12	73	1	1	1557
1879	557	525	313	—	364	152	75	12	90	—	8	1619
1880	703	643	330	—	377	199	89	12	198	—	26	1976
1881	880	776	341	—	375	219	96	12	282	—	68	2396
1882	894	893	341	—	372	209	97	12	320	—	87	2590

[a] The money supply in the hands of the public (column 12) is defined as the sum of columns 1–5 and 9–11, less the sum of columns 6–8. Individual figures may not add to the totals because of rounding.

included at its market value. Gold was the monetary standard on the West Coast throughout the greenback period, although the greenback dollar was the standard in the rest of the country. At least part of the gold coin in the country was held for foreign-exchange purposes, since gold was equivalent to foreign exchange. The special gold-coin deposits held in the New York banks were probably held mostly for this purpose. After resumption took place, the deposits held for purposes of foreign exchange were indistinguishable from other deposits. In order that the estimates of the money supply for the years prior to resumption be comparable to the estimates for the years after resumption, gold must be included in the money supply at its market value.

The estimated quantity of money increased in each year from 1869 through 1875. Obviously the fall in the price level in those years was not caused by a fall in the money supply. Kuznets' implicit price index fell by 16 per cent from 1869 to 1875. This occurred as the money supply rose by 31 per cent, income velocity fell by 11 per cent, and real national product rose by 38 per cent. Between 1875 and 1878, Kuznets' price index fell by 15 per cent; it occurred as the money supply fell by 9 per cent, real income rose by 27 per cent, and velocity rose by 19 per cent. For the period 1869–1878 as a whole, Kuznets' price index fell by 28 per cent as the money supply rose by 19 per cent, velocity rose by 6 per cent, and real income rose by 75 per cent.

The generally lower price level in 1878 (just before resumption) relative to 1869 was the factor which permitted resumption in 1879. By the analysis of the preceding section, resumption could not have been successful in 1869 because the price level was too far above foreign prices. The money supply in 1878 was substantially higher than it was in 1869; measured income velocity was slightly higher in 1878 than in 1869. The data thus indicate that the lower price level of 1878, compared with 1869, was maintained only because of the rise in real output over the period. Had real output remained constant over the period, prices would have been higher in 1878 than in 1869, *ceteris paribus*. The growth in real output was an important factor in the deflation in both the subperiods 1869–1875 and

1875–1878. From 1869 to 1875 the fall in velocity, together with the rise in real income, more than offset the rise in the money supply during those years. From 1875 through 1878 a rise in real income combined with a fall in the money supply more than offset a rise in velocity.

Income velocity is computed as the ratio of net national product (in current dollars) to the money supply. Errors in the estimates of national product or the money supply will give rise to corresponding errors in income velocity. For purposes of the analysis here, the absolute level of income velocity is immaterial; only changes in the level are relevant. So long as the money stock is not considerably underestimated—or national product is not considerably overestimated—for the later years of the period in question *relative to* the earlier years, the conclusions remain substantially unaltered.

The figures given in Table 4 show, if anything, an increase in velocity over the period. Thus average velocity for 1869–1871 was 4.08, whereas average velocity for 1876–1878 was 4.46. Had national product been overstated by 9 per cent—or the money supply understated by 9 per cent—in the latter period relative to the former, velocity would have been the same in the two periods. In this case the increase in velocity would not have worked *against* the growth of real income

as a deflationary pressure; none of the fall in prices could be attributed to a fall in velocity or to a fall in the money supply, however. It seems reasonable, then, to attribute at least the major portion of the fall in prices to the rise in real output, despite any doubt as to the accuracy of the estimates.

The earliest date for which figures on national product are available is 1869. No estimates of the money supply are available for the years prior to 1867; hence, a quantitative analysis of the deflation from 1865 to 1869 is impossible. However some important factors which tended to exert a depressing effect on the price level can be identified.

1. As soon as any area of the Confederacy was conquered by the Union armies, its Confederate currency ceased to be the official money of that area. Any value the Confederate currency retained depended upon the possibility of sending it to an unconquered area of the Confederacy or on the possibility of a Confederate victory in the war. After the Union victory both of these props under the Confederate currency were destroyed, and the currency became worthless. All banks of the South were ruined during the war, so that all money in the South in the immediate postwar period came from the stock of currency formerly held in the North only. The result was a drain of currency into the South from the North and a consequent downward pressure on the price level in the North.

2. At the conclusion of the war, the Secretary of the Treasury began a policy of contraction of the greenback circulation. This downward pressure on the stock of money came at a time when the greenbacks were flowing into the South. Some measure of the amount of this contraction (which ceased in 1867) is afforded by Table 5. Although the announced policy of the government was to contract the circulation of greenbacks (United States notes), the percentage decline in the amount of "other government currency" outstanding (col. 4, Table 5) was considerably greater than that of the greenbacks. The issues of legal-tender interest-bearing notes included in "other government currency" were redeemable at fixed dates between 1864 and 1868 and ceased to pay interest after maturity. Once they came into the Treasury, they were retired. This fall in the amount of government currency outstanding was a depressing influence on the price level, since it reduced the quantity of high-powered money outstanding.

Table 4. Income Velocity, 1869–1882

Year	Net National Product (Millions of Current Dollars) (1)	Money Supply (Millions) (2)	Income Velocity[a] (3)
1869	5,822	1,304	4.46
1870	5,486	1,373	4.00
1871	5,742	1,504	3.82
1872	6,935	1,632	4.25
1873	7,018	1,632	4.30
1874	6,880	1,650	4.17
1875	6,763	1,703	3.97
1876	6,983	1,663	4.20
1877	7,351	1,640	4.48
1878	7,349	1,557	4.72
1879	7,888	1,619	4.87
1880	9,978	1,976	5.05
1881	9,835	2,396	4.10
1882	10,791	2,590	4.17

[a] Column 1 divided by column 2.

Table 5. Government Currency Outside the Treasury, 1864–1869 (Thousands of Dollars)

Fiscal Year	Legal Tenders (1)	Fractional Currency (2)	Subsidiary Silver (3)	Other U.S. Currency (4)	Total (5)
1864	415,116	19,133	9,375	169,252	612,876
1865	378,917	21,729	8,713	236,567	645,876
1866	327,792	24,687	8,241	162,739	523,459
1867	319,438	26,306	7,082	123,727	476,553
1868	328,572	28,999	6,520	28,859	392,950
1869	314,767	30,442	5,695	3,343	354,241

3. The cessation of issue of new government currency at the end of the Civil War had the effect of stopping the inflation, or at least of slowing its rate of growth. This fall in the rate of rise of prices may well have caused a sufficient change in expectations of future price movements to cause a drop in velocity of some significance, thus exerting a depressing influence on the price level.[5]

4. Although there are no estimates of national product for years prior to 1869, there is reason to believe that real national product was increasing significantly in the years from 1865 to 1869. Several indexes of production for these years are given in Table 6; all show substantial rates of growth for these years.

A traditional explanation of the success of resumption is that the country was "allowed to grow up to the currency" after the Civil War. If "the currency" is interpreted to mean the total money supply, there is much truth to this explanation.

IV. GOVERNMENT POLICY AND RESUMPTION

In the latter part of 1865 Hugh McCulloch, then Secretary of the Treasury, began a policy of contraction of the greenbacks by retiring them as part of the surplus revenue which existed at the time. In December of that year the House of Representatives passed a resolution expressing approval of the contraction as a necessary condition for resumption. This resolution, of course, did not have the force

of law and provided no mechanism for substantial withdrawal of the greenbacks. In April, 1866, Congress withdrew part of its support by passing a bill, which became law, limiting the contraction of the greenbacks to not more than $10 million in the succeeding six months and to not more than $4 million in any month thereafter. In February, 1868, the policy of contraction was halted completely when Congress prohibited the retirement and cancellation of any more greenbacks. In 1865, $400 million worth of greenbacks were outstanding; about $44 million of these were retired between 1865 and 1868.

No positive governmental action to facilitate resumption was taken for almost a decade after 1868. The short-lived contraction policy was a step in the direction of early resumption, but it was much too small an operation to accomplish this objective.

In March, 1869, the "Public Credit Act" became law. This act pledged that the principal of the government bonds would be paid in coin, unless the issuing law expressly provided otherwise, and stated that the "faith of the United States" was pledged "to make provision at the earliest practicable period for the redemption of the United States notes in coin." No mechanism was set up for this

Table 6. Indexes of Physical Production, 1865–1869[a]

Year	Agricultural Production	Manufacturing Production	Mining Production
1865	64	60	51
1866	70	74	60
1867	76	77	61
1868	80	81	65
1869	84	88	67

[a] Base: average annual production, 1866–1880 = 100.

---

[5] The effect of the cessation of the inflation was to lower the cost of holding money so that more should have been demanded; that is, velocity should have fallen.

latter purpose, no date was specified, and no individual was charged with the responsibility for achieving this objective. Nothing was done in the ensuing years, as a result of this act, to facilitate resumption.

The immediate postwar policy of contraction of greenback circulation was reversed completely just after the Panic of 1873. Tax receipts fell off after the panic, at a time when the cash reserves of the Treasury were low. To meet the expenses of the government, the Treasury reissued about $26 million of the greenbacks that had been retired under the contraction policy of 1865–1868. In June, 1874, Congress raised the required amount of the greenback issue to $382 million. This made the notes paid out in 1873–1874 part of the permanent stock of greenbacks.

The Resumption Act, which became law in January, 1875, was the authority under which resumption was finally accomplished. This law required that the Treasury redeem greenbacks in specie on demand, on and after January 1, 1879, but it set up no definite mechanism by which specie payments were to be maintained. The provisions of the act for this purpose were confined to authorizing the Secretary of the Treasury to use any surplus revenue to build up a redemption fund and to issue bonds for this purpose. The other sections of the act provided no aid to resumption; among them were orders that subsidiary silver be substituted for fractional currency, that the seigniorage fee on coining gold be abolished, and that the limitations on the total amount of national bank notes which could be issued be abolished. Another section of the act provided that greenbacks were to be retired in the amount of 80 per cent of new national bank-note issue until the outstanding greenbacks were reduced to $300 million. The act did not specify what was to be done with the remaining greenbacks after resumption. That question was not settled until May, 1878, when another act prohibited any further withdrawal of greenbacks and required that any greenbacks received by the Treasury be paid out again.

In 1877 John Sherman, Secretary of the Treasury, began to accumulate a gold reserve for redemption of the greenbacks. Through a combination of sales of bonds and retention of surplus revenue, over $133 million in gold coin, earmarked for a redemption fund, had been accumulated by January 1, 1879, the date fixed for resumption.[6] No direct action was taken to correct the fundamental barrier to resumption, the price level.

A gold reserve was essential for successful resumption in order that day-to-day variations in specie flows could be accommodated. In this matter government policy made a substantial contribution to the success of resumption. However no positive government policy of deflation was pursued through the entire period 1865–1879, except for the short-lived contraction policy of 1865–1868. Indeed, later policy tended more in the opposite direction; contraction of the greenback circulation was first prohibited, then some new issues were made. The net effects of government policy, so far as greenbacks are concerned, is perhaps best illustrated by the following statistics: the value of greenbacks outside the Treasury was $328 million on June 30, 1866, and $320 million on June 30, 1878.

A policy of deflation could have taken the form of restrictions on private creation of money, that is, restrictions on bank-note issue and on deposit-creation privileges. State bank notes were practically taxed out of existence by the 10 per cent tax imposed in 1866. The purpose of this tax, though, was to induce state banks to become national banks, and the privilege of note issue was extended to national banks. Before 1875 there was an effective limit on the total amount of notes outstanding, for the maximum aggregate circulation of national banks was fixed by law, as was the maximum amount of Treasury currency outstanding. In this somewhat negative manner, some limit on the amount of money in circulation was fixed, for in the long run the ratio of currency to deposits was determined by the desires of the public. The government also refrained from the issue

---

[6] The build-up of the gold reserve made the apparent conditions for resumption more difficult to attain. The increased demand for gold by the Treasury required that the United States achieve a larger favorable balance of trade to maintain the larger inflow of gold; that is, the Treasury demand for gold flows made the premium on gold higher than it otherwise would have been. As soon as the Treasury demand for a *stock* of gold was equal to the stock of gold in the Treasury, the Treasury's *flow* demand for gold was zero at the going price, and the effect of the Treasury's purchases on the premium disappeared. The Treasury's accumulation of gold, then, did not make the long-run conditions for resumption more difficult to attain; it merely made these conditions harder to attain during the time the build-up was actually taking place.

of new government currency, except for the one case already noted. Since the government's note issues provided reserves for bank expansion, this policy helped to keep the banks from expanding further.

The government policy of refraining from expanding the money supply was a negative policy, strictly speaking, but it was a note-worthy accomplishment. Failure of the government to take expansionary measures in the monetary sphere during a period of deflation is tantamount, in its effect, to the pursuit of deflationary measures during a period of price stability. The inflationist movement is ample evidence that this fact was understood at the time.

36 FISCAL POLICY IN THE THIRTIES: A REAPPRAISAL

E. Cary Brown

The question of how effectively fiscal policy promoted recovery in the thirties has agitated a good fraction of the profession at one time or another. The advent of the Second World War shifted attention away from this question, and the insight and improvements gained from the major developments in national income measurement and analysis have not been properly reapplied to this highly interesting period. Some recent studies have been made of the dynamic aspects of fiscal policy in the 1937 recession. But I would like to reexamine the direct annual static effects of fiscal policy on demand in the thirties, ignoring specific timing problems.

Some measure of the contribution of fiscal policy to effective demand will be needed for this purpose. Early work in this field developed the concept of

Reprinted with omissions by permission from *The American Economic Review, 46* (December, 1956), 857–879.

net-income-creating expenditures of government—a major forward step towards a more careful measurement of the direct effects of fiscal policy. But, important as was this early concept, it has a number of weaknesses in measuring the impact of fiscal policy on total demand. A reformulation is made in Section I. The findings from the application of this revised concept are set forth in Section II.

I. CONCEPT OF FISCAL CONTRIBUTION TO EFFECTIVE DEMAND

Governmental financial activities make many and varied contributions to demand for goods and services. Government expenditures directly increase demand for output; taxes decrease private demand for it. Monetary activities—open market and similar lending-borrowing actions, and changes in reserve requirements—can also affect rates of private demand. These initial shifts in demand in turn lead to induced changes in private spending. The resulting multiplied effects on income depend among other things on the relationship of governmental taxing and spending to national incomes. Finally governmental financial activities can give rise to variations in private demand through substitution effects induced by changes in relative prices or in expectations, and these may either contract or expand private demand still further. It is impossible to include all of these effects in a measure of fiscal contribution to total demand. Some narrowing is necessary.

1. The concept we will use excludes monetary activities entirely to the extent this is feasible, by omitting all governmental as well as private lending and borrowing activities. Earlier studies included some of these activities and excluded others.

2. Modern income analysis distinguishes between the way in which government purchases, taxes, and transfers, respectively affect demand, whereas the older studies lumped them all together. The income effects of taxes and transfers are now understood to result from changes in disposable income and profits. In assuming that taxes and government purchases affect total demand equally without regard to sign, the older studies either assumed a private marginal propensity to spend of unity, or made no adjustment for the portion of taxes or transfers coming out of saving. In our concept this obvious correction will be made.

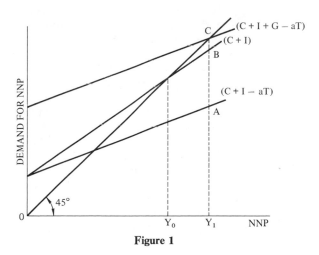

Figure 1

3. The initial effect of fiscal policy on total demand for goods and services at any particular income level depends on tax-transfer yields and purchases of goods and services. These amounts in turn result from a movement along given tax-transfer and expenditure schedules (automatic policies) and shifts in such schedules through legislation or other governmental action (discretionary policies). The initial effect on total demand (the multiplicand) can be converted into an induced change in income by applying the proper multiplier.

These concepts are illustrated in Figure 1. The middle schedule $(C + I)$ relates the amount of private demand for output to various levels of income. The lower schedule $(C + I - aT)$ represents the previous schedule less the reduction in private demand from the net tax yield (taxes less transfer payments). The vertical distance between these schedules $(AB$ at $OY_1)$ represents the reduction in private demand (aT) resulting from the tax-transfer schedule (T). To this schedule showing the reduced private demand is added government purchases $(AC$ at $OY_1)$, assumed to be autonomous. The difference between this highest schedule $(C + I + G - aT)$ and the initial one $(C + I)$ represents the amount by which the government has shifted the total demand schedule $(BC$ at $OY_1)$ through fiscal action—the combined effect of spending and taxing. This initial shift in demand has given rise to induced changes in income and demand for output and a new equilibrium OY_1 is the only one consistent with the new aggregate demand schedule. In Figure 1, OY_1 is greater than OY_0, the equilibrium consistent with the aggregate demand schedule $(C + I)$, but it need not necessarily be.

It is clearly a matter of convenience whether we measure the total effects of the government budget on income (OY_1 less OY_0 in Figure 1) or the effects of the government budget in shifting the demand schedule (BC at OY_1 in Figure 1). If we want the effect on equilibrium output, however, we must estimate not only the shift in the demand schedules attributable to the budget, but must also know how private demand schedules behave with changes in income. While our knowledge of the initial effects of taxes (and transfers) on demand could certainly be improved on, it is in a considerably less precarious state than quantitative notions of the multiplier. The former depends essentially on the relationship of spending to disposable income and profits, while the latter depends in addition on the relationship of disposable income and profits to national product or income. If we limit our study, then, to the multiplicand—the vertical shift in aggregate demand—we can avoid this latter problem.

4. The size of the vertical shift in the demand schedule, however, depends on the income level at which it is measured. It is usually assumed that government purchases are autonomous, and we follow that assumption here. But taxes and transfers vary with income. Assuming for simplicity that the marginal propensity to spend (a) is constant, Figure 2 shows the shift in the demand schedule attributable to fiscal policy. The G schedule represents autonomous government purchases. The aT schedule represents the relationship to income of the demand-reducing effects of taxes less transfers. The net direct effect on demand is represented by the distance between the two schedules. It is positive, or expansionary, for income levels below OY_1, and negative, or deflationary, above income level OY_1.

An important test of fiscal policy is whether it was more or less expansive or more or less contractive from one year to another at some

Figure 2

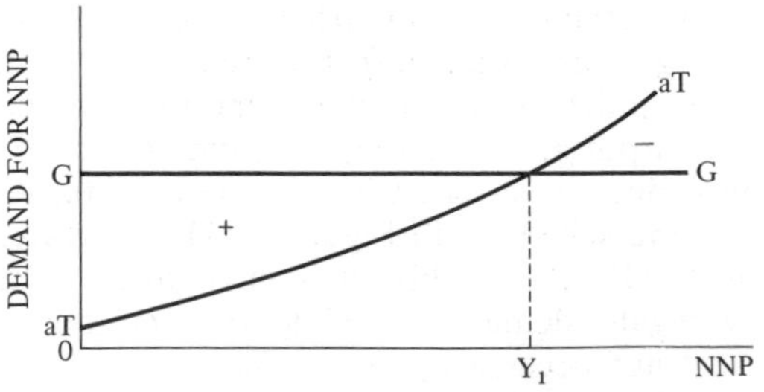

particular level of income. But if the shift in the demand schedule attributable to fiscal policy is to be measured consistently from one level of income rather than from the variable incomes actually observed, which shall it be? For purposes of policy, that of "full employment" seems the most relevant income level. Our test then becomes whether total full-employment demand is enhanced or reduced by fiscal activity.

5. In this study we have treated government expenditures (both purchases and transfers) as autonomous. Taxes have been roughly adjusted to full-employment levels by separating them into two categories—"fixed" and "variable." The "fixed" taxes are assumed to be autonomous and the variable to increase proportionately with income. Various assumed and constant marginal propensities to spend out of transfers and taxes have been used. These problems are discussed further in Appendix A.[1] Considerable refinements could be made in these crude procedures, and we hope they will be undertaken. However a fairly wide range of assumptions have been tried in these computations, and it is doubtful that refinements would upset any of the major findings.

6. A still further adjustment is necessary to appraise the significance of fiscal policy in relative terms. Since the economy was growing throughout the thirties, a given effect on demand in real dollars in 1929 would have less relative impact in later years. We have interpolated between 1929 and 1942 to estimate the full-employment level of income for successive years in this period and have found a growth rate of slightly more than 3 per cent per year since 1929. All real dollar shifts in demand have then been expressed as percentages of full-employment income. A constant fiscal contribution to total demand means that the shift in the aggregate demand schedule that we attribute to fiscal policy is a constant per cent of full-employment income. In absolute terms it is an amount growing at about 3 per cent per year.

II. SUMMARY OF FINDINGS

The results of the statistical manipulations discussed in Section I are presented in Table 1.

[1] [Both Appendix A and Appendix B have been omitted. See the original article, pp. 869–879.—Editors' note.]

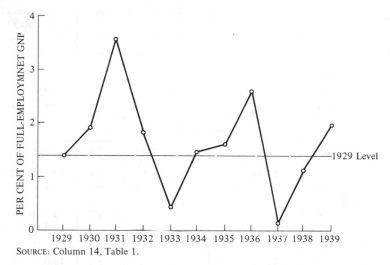

Figure 3. Effect of Fiscal Policy on Full-Employment Demand (all Governments).

The general reader's attention is directed to column 14 for the main findings of the study. Statistical qualifications are considered in more detail in Appendix A, and a sample computation can be found for 1933 in Appendix B.[2]

Subject to all the limitations of analysis and procedure discussed previously and in Appendix A, certain broad findings seem to stand out:

1. The direct effects on aggregate full-employment demand of the fiscal policy undertaken by all three levels of government

was clearly relatively stronger in the thirties than in 1929 in only two years—1931 and 1936—with 1931 markedly higher than 1936. (Table 1, column 14, and Figure 3.) These were years in which large payments were made under the veterans' adjusted compensation programs—programs passed by Congress over the vigorous opposition of both the Hoover and Roosevelt administrations.

If they were eliminated, 1931 would remain clearly above 1929, but 1936 would fall below it. In three other years—1930, 1932, and 1939—the expansionary effect of fiscal policy was somewhat higher than in 1929, while in 1934 and 1935 it was virtually the same. In two years—1933 and 1937—fiscal policy was

---

[2] [See footnote 1.—Editors' note.]

Figure 4. Effect of Fiscal Policy on Full-Employment Demand (Federal, State, and Local Governments).

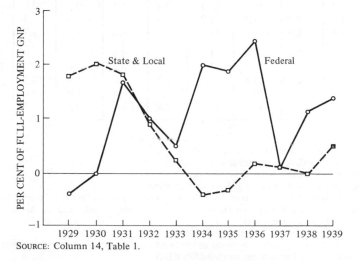

SOURCE: Column 14, Table 1.

Table 1. Effect of Fiscal Policy on Aggregate Demand Schedule (Money Figures in Billions)

Calendar Year	G in Current Prices (1)	T in Current Prices (2)	Actual G/P_g (3)	Actual T/P_p (4)	F.E. T/P_p (5)	Initial Shift in Full-Employment Demand When $a =$			Adjustment for Divergence between Cost of Public and Private Goods	When $b =$		
						.7 (6)	.8 (7)	.9 (8)	G/P_p (9)	.6 (10)	.8 (11)	1.0 (12)
All Governments												
1929	$ 8.5	$ 9.5	$13.6	$12.4	$12.4	$ 4.9	$ 3.7	$ 2.4	$11.0	−$1.6	−$2.1	−$2.6
1930	9.2	8.9	15.1	11.9	13.0	6.0	4.7	3.4	12.3	−1.7	−2.2	−2.8
1931	9.2	6.4	15.9	9.4	11.0	8.2	7.1	6.0	13.5	−1.4	−1.9	−2.4
1932	8.1	6.4	15.1	10.5	13.7	5.5	4.1	2.8	13.3	−1.1	−1.4	−1.8
1933	8.0	6.7	14.9	11.6	16.6	3.3	1.6	0.0	13.8	−0.7	−0.9	−1.1
1934	9.8	7.4	17.2	12.4	17.5	5.0	3.2	1.4	16.4	−0.5	−0.6	−0.8
1935	10.0	8.0	17.4	13.0	17.3	5.3	3.6	1.8	16.3	−0.7	−0.9	−1.1
1936	11.8	8.9	20.3	14.3	18.3	7.5	5.7	3.8	19.0	−0.8	−1.0	−1.3
1937	11.7	12.2	19.7	19.0	23.2	3.5	1.1	−1.2	18.3	−0.8	−1.1	−1.4
1938	12.8	11.3	22.1	17.9	23.3	5.8	3.5	1.1	20.2	−1.1	−1.5	−1.9
1939	13.3	11.2	22.8	18.0	22.5	7.0	4.8	2.5	21.4	−0.8	−1.1	−1.4
Federal												
1929	1.4	2.6	2.5	3.4	3.4	0.1	−0.2	−0.6	1.8	−0.4	−0.6	−0.7
1930	1.5	1.8	2.9	2.4	3.0	0.8	0.5	0.2	2.0	−0.5	−0.7	−0.9
1931	1.8	−0.3	3.4	−0.4	0.3	3.2	3.2	3.1	2.6	−0.5	−0.6	−0.8
1932	1.6	0.1	3.2	0.2	1.5	2.1	2.0	1.8	2.6	−0.4	−0.5	−0.6
1933	2.5	1.2	5.2	2.1	4.7	1.9	1.4	1.0	4.3	−0.5	−0.7	−0.9
1934	4.6	1.8	8.4	3.0	5.6	4.5	3.9	3.4	7.7	−0.4	−0.6	−0.7
1935	4.6	2.1	8.3	3.4	5.5	4.4	3.9	3.3	7.5	−0.5	−0.6	−0.8
1936	5.4	2.0	9.3	3.2	5.4	5.5	5.0	4.4	8.7	−0.4	−0.5	−0.6
1937	5.1	4.9	8.8	7.6	10.2	1.7	0.6	−0.4	8.0	−0.5	−0.6	−0.8
1938	5.9	3.9	10.6	6.1	9.4	4.0	3.1	2.1	9.3	−0.8	−1.0	−1.3
1939	5.8	3.6	10.2	5.8	8.5	4.2	3.4	2.5	9.3	−0.5	−0.7	−0.9
State and Local												
1929	7.1	6.9	11.0	9.0	9.0	4.7	3.8	2.9	9.2	−1.1	−1.4	−1.8
1930	7.7	7.1	12.3	9.5	10.0	5.3	4.3	3.3	10.3	−1.2	−1.6	−2.0
1931	7.4	6.7	12.5	9.8	10.8	4.9	3.9	2.8	10.9	−1.0	−1.3	−1.6
1932	6.5	6.2	11.9	10.2	12.2	3.4	2.1	0.9	10.7	−0.7	−1.0	−1.2
1933	5.5	5.5	9.7	9.5	11.9	1.4	0.2	−1.0	9.5	−0.1	−0.2	−0.2
1934	5.2	5.6	8.9	9.4	11.9	0.6	−0.6	−1.8	8.7	−0.1	−0.2	−0.2
1935	5.4	5.9	9.0	9.6	11.8	0.7	−0.4	−1.6	8.8	−0.1	−0.2	−0.2
1936	6.4	6.9	11.0	11.1	12.9	2.0	0.7	−0.6	10.3	−0.4	−0.6	−0.7
1937	6.6	7.3	10.8	11.4	13.0	1.7	0.4	−0.9	10.3	−0.3	−0.4	−0.5
1938	6.9	7.4	11.5	11.7	13.9	1.8	0.4	−1.0	10.9	−0.4	−0.5	−0.6
1939	7.5	7.6	12.6	12.2	14.0	2.8	1.4	0.0	12.1	−0.3	−0.4	−0.5

Column	Description
1	Government purchases in current prices
2	Taxes less transfers in current prices
3	Actual government purchases in 1947 prices
4	Actual taxes less transfers in 1947 consumer prices
5	Full-employment taxes less transfers in 1947 consumer prices (Columns 20 plus 22)
6–8	Initial shift in full-employment demand (Column 3 minus 5 multiplied by the assumed marginal propensity to spend disposable income [a])
9	Actual government purchases in 1947 consumer prices
10–12	Adjustment for divergence between government and consumer prices (Column 9 minus 3 multiplied by the assumed marginal propensity to spend GNP [b])

| NET SHIFT IN DEMAND AS PER CENT OF F.E. GNP | | | | | Real GNP | | REAL TAXES—T/P_p | | | GRANTS-IN-AID | | | |
| When $b = .6$ and $a =$ | | | When $a = .9$ and $b =$ | | | | Fixed | Variable | | G | G/P_g | T | T/P_p |
.7 (13)	.8 (14)	.9 (15)	.8 (16)	1.0 (17)	Actual (18)	F.E. (19)	(20)	Actual (21)	Full Employment (22)	(23)	(24)	(25)	(26)
All Governments													
2.2%	1.4%	0.5%	0.2%	−0.1%	$149.3	$149.3							
2.8	1.9	1.1	0.8	0.4	135.2	154.0							
4.3	3.6	2.9	2.6	2.3	126.6	148.0							
2.7	1.8	1.0	0.9	0.6	107.6	163.9							
1.5	0.5	−0.4	−0.5	−0.7	103.7	169.1							
2.6	1.5	9.5	0.5	0.3	113.4	174.4							
2.6	1.6	0.6	0.5	0.4	127.8	179.9							
3.6	2.6	1.6	1.5	1.3	142.5	185.6							
1.4	0.2	−1.0	−1.2	−1.3	153.5	191.5							
2.4	1.2	0.0	−0.2	−0.4	145.9	197.5							
3.0	2.0	0.8	0.7	0.5	157.5	203.7							
Federal													
−0.2	−0.4	−0.7	−0.8	−0.9			$−1.5	$4.9	$4.9	$0.1	$0.2	$0.0	$0.0
0.2	0.0	−0.2	−0.3	−0.5			−1.5	3.9	4.5	0.1	0.2	0.0	0.0
1.7	1.7	1.6	1.6	1.4			−3.2	2.8	3.5	0.3	0.5	0.0	0.0
1.0	1.0	0.9	0.8	0.7			−2.3	2.5	3.8	0.1	0.2	0.0	0.0
0.8	0.5	0.3	0.2	0.1			−2.1	4.2	6.8	0.5	0.9	0.0	0.0
2.4	2.0	1.7	1.6	1.5			−2.0	4.9	7.6	1.6	2.7	0.0	0.0
2.2	1.9	1.6	1.5	1.4			−1.9	5.3	7.4	1.7	2.9	0.0	0.0
2.7	2.5	2.2	2.1	2.0			−4.3	7.4	9.7	0.6	1.0	0.1	0.2
0.6	0.1	−0.5	−0.5	−0.6			−2.6	10.2	12.8	0.6	1.0	0.2	0.3
1.6	1.2	0.7	0.6	0.4			−3.3	9.4	12.7	0.6	1.0	0.2	0.3
1.8	1.4	1.0	0.9	0.8			−3.5	9.3	12.0	0.7	1.2	0.3	0.5
State and Local													
2.4	1.8	1.2	1.0	0.7			5.6	3.4	3.4				
2.7	2.0	1.4	1.1	0.8			5.9	3.6	4.1				
2.5	1.8	1.1	0.9	0.8			6.0	3.8	4.8				
1.6	0.9	0.1	−0.1	−0.2			6.2	4.0	6.0				
0.8	0.1	−0.7	−0.7	−0.7			5.3	4.1	6.6				
0.3	−0.4	−1.1	−1.1	−1.1			4.8	4.6	7.1				
0.3	−0.3	−0.9	−1.0	−1.0			4.6	5.1	7.2				
0.9	0.2	−0.5	−0.6	−0.7			5.3	5.3	7.6				
0.7	0.1	−0.6	−0.7	−0.7			5.3	6.2	7.7				
0.7	0.0	−0.7	−0.8	−0.8			5.3	6.4	8.6				
1.2	0.5	−0.1	−0.2	−0.2			5.5	6.7	8.5				

Column	Description
13–17	Net shift in demand at full employment, expressed as a per cent of full-employment GNP (Combinations of columns 6 through 8 and 10 through 12 divided by column 19)
18	Actual gross national product in 1947 prices
19	Full-employment gross national product in 1947 prices ($GNP_t = \$149.3 \cdot e^{.0315\,(t-1929)}$ developed by interpolation between 1929 and 1942)
20	Fixed taxes (primarily property) in 1947 consumer prices
21	Actual variable taxes (primarily income, commodity, and sales) in 1947 consumer prices (Column 4 minus 20)
22	Full-employment variable taxes in 1947 consumer prices (Column 21 multiplied by quotient of 19 divided by 18)
23	Grants-in-aid (made by the federal government to state and local governments) for purchases in current prices
24	Grants-in-aid for purchases in 1947 prices
25	Grants-in-aid for transfers in current prices
26	Grants-in-aid for transfers in 1947 consumer prices

markedly less expansionary than in 1929, and in 1938 slightly less so.

The trend of the direct effects of fiscal policy on aggregate full-employment demand is definitely downward throughout the thirties. For recovery to have been achieved in this period, private demand would have had to be higher out of a given private disposable income than it was in 1929. Fiscal policy, then, seems to have been an unsuccessful recovery device in the thirties—not because it did not work, but because it was not tried. While differing in many details, this finding bears out Hansen's conclusions reached in 1941: "Despite the fairly good showing made in the recovery up to 1937, the fact is that neither before nor since has the administration pursued a really positive expansionist program. . . . For the most part, the federal government engaged in a salvaging program and not in a program of positive expansion" [1, p. 84]. It is in sharp contrast to Smithies' view: "My main conclusion on government policy from the experience of the thirties is that fiscal policy did prove to be an effective and indeed the only effective means to recovery" [2, p. 26].

2. The federal government's fiscal action was more expansionary throughout the thirties than it was in 1929 (Table 1, column 14, and Figure 4). In 1929, its fiscal action resulted in a substantial net drag on total demand. But this changed sharply in 1931 to an expansionary effect (although here again the vetoed veterans' adjusted compensation should be borne in mind). Expansion continued throughout the period except for the sharp drop in 1937, which represented a shift in demand

of over 2 1/2 per cent of GNP in one year. It was followed by expansionary activity on a fairly large scale, but not of sufficient size to approach that of 1934–1936.

3. State and local governments' fiscal policy was expansionary through 1933, but decreasingly so (Table 1, column 14, and Figure 4). By 1934 it had fallen clearly below 1929 and remained in an almost neutral position throughout the rest of the period. The federal government's policies were little more than adequate in most years of the thirties to offset these contractive effects of state and local governments. Indeed if we take the seven years from 1933 on, in only two was the federal share significantly more than enough to offset state and local shrinkages.

4. The primary failure of fiscal policy to be expansive in this period is attributable to the sharp increase in tax structures enacted at all levels of government. Total government purchases of goods and services expanded virtually every year, with federal expansion especially marked in 1933 and 1934 (Table 1, columns 1 and 3, and Figure 5). But full-employment tax yields more than kept pace. Our rough estimates show that in 1929, a year of full employment, all governments combined had a deficit (federal surplus and state and local deficit), while 1933 to 1939, except for 1936, were years of surplus or approximate balance at full employment.

The changes made in the tax structure in this period were marked, but their quantitative impact has been masked by the sharp fall in total income and tax yields. The federal Revenue Act of 1932 virtually doubled full-employment tax yields and essentially set the

Figure 5. Governmental Purchases and Taxes (at Full Employment).

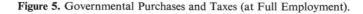

Source: Columns 3 and 5, Table 1.

tax structure for the entire period up to the Second World War. Since the highly deflationary impact of this tax law has not been fully appreciated, some of its major provisions are briefly noted here.

The Revenue Act of 1932 pushed up rates virtually across the board, but notably on the lower- and middle-income groups. The scope of the act was clearly the equivalent of major wartime enactments. Personal income tax exemptions were slashed, the normal-tax as well as surtax rates were sharply raised, and the earned-income credit equal to 25 per cent of taxes on low incomes was repealed. Less drastic changes were made in the corporate income tax, but its rate was raised slightly and a $3000 exemption eliminated. Estate tax rates were pushed up, exemptions sharply reduced, and a gift tax was provided. Congress toyed with a manufacturers' sales tax, but finally rejected it in favor of a broad new list of excise taxes and substantially higher rates for the old ones. While some of these excises were later repealed, most remained throughout the decade. Somewhat later in the thirties, processing taxes made further temporary inroads on demand, and the social security taxes began in 1937 to exert a pronounced effect.

State and local government were also active in new revenue legislation throughout this period. The major changes were to find the state governments moving heavily into general sales and excise taxation, personal and corporate income taxes, and the gasoline tax.

In brief, then, it took the massive expenditures forced on the nation by the Second World War to realize the full potentialities of fiscal policy. Until then, the record fails to show its effective use as a recovery measure. Indeed the general expansionary policy seems stronger in the early part than in the later part of the decade.

REFERENCES

1. Alvin H. Hansen, *Fiscal Policy and Business Cycles,* New York, W. W. Norton, 1941.
2. Arthur Smithies, "The American Economy in the Thirties," *The American Economic Review, 36* (May, 1946), 11–27.

INDEX

71 72 73 74 7 6 5 4 3 2 1